**SUSTAINABL**
**CRIMINAL JUST**

*Sustainable Development, Inte* provides a serious and timely p criminal law can protect the in leading academics and internatic and practices of international crin their elaboration, interpretation, a the potential and limitations of inte basic foundations of sustainable de in penalising serious forms of econc indirect linkages that have develop mechanisms of criminal accountabil the scope of international criminal ju this book provides a unique and urger global justice and sustainability.

Sébastien Jodoin is a PhD Candidate, at the Yale School of Forestry & Envirc nance, Environment, and Markets Initia with the Centre for International Sustai Justice Project, which seeks the recognit forms of economic, social, and environn international law. Jodoin previously workec Justice, Amnesty International Canada, and Tribunals for Rwanda and the former Yugc Public Scholar Award from the Yale Graduate research 'that engages and betters the world a

Marie-Claire Cordonier Segger is an internati field of sustainable development. She is Head Development Law Organisation (IDLO), an in tered in Rome, Italy, with a unique mandate for the IDLO, she provides legal advice and techn implementation of international treaties on sustai Americas, Africa, and Asia Pacific and to the Unit serves, pro bono, as Councillor of the World Futu national Law Association's Committee on Sustain Director of the Centre for International Sustainabl ated Fellow in the Lauterpacht Centre for Internat and Visiting Professor in the University of Chile Fac than 80 papers and 14 books on sustainable developm and is co-editor of the Cambridge University Press se Sustainable Development. She holds a DPhil (Oxo (McGill), and BA Hons (Carl).

## TREATY IMPLEMENTATION FOR SUSTAINABLE DEVELOPMENT

Over the past three decades, a series of international treaties have entered into force to address pressing global concerns of social and economic development and environmental protection. On climate change, biodiversity and biosafety, desertification, agriculture and seeds, and trade and investment liberalisation, new regimes have been established to implement global commitments related to sustainable development, many with nearly universal membership. Successful domestic implementation of these international treaty regimes is one of the most significant challenges facing international law today. Although much has been written on the content and form of treaty law, there is relatively little that examines the transition from international legal theory and treaty texts to domestic regulation and practice.

This series of books addresses this need and provides a serious contribution to ongoing global debates by conducting a detailed analysis of how myriad new treaty regimes that cover the future's most pressing concerns can be made to work in practice.

*Series Editors:*

Marie-Claire Cordonier Segger

Markus Wilheim Gehring

*Volumes in the Series:*

*Legal Aspects of Implementing the Cartagena Protocol on Biosafety*
edited by Marie-Claire Cordonier Segger, Frederic Perron-Welch, and Christine Frison (2013)

*Sustainable Development, International Criminal Justice, and Treaty Implementation*
edited by Sébastien Jodoin and Marie-Claire Cordonier Segger (2013)

# Sustainable Development, International Criminal Justice, and Treaty Implementation

Edited by

**SÉBASTIEN JODOIN**

Yale School of Forestry & Environmental Studies
Centre for International Sustainable Development Law

**MARIE-CLAIRE CORDONIER SEGGER**

International Development Law Organization
Lauterpacht Centre for International Law
Centre for International Sustainable Development Law

CAMBRIDGE
UNIVERSITY PRESS

CAMBRIDGE UNIVERSITY PRESS
Cambridge, New York, Melbourne, Madrid, Cape Town,
Singapore, São Paulo, Delhi, Mexico City

Cambridge University Press
32 Avenue of the Americas, New York, NY 10013-2473, USA

www.cambridge.org
Information on this title: www.cambridge.org/9781107032934



First published 2013

Printed in the United States of America

*A catalog record for this publication is available from the British Library.*

*Library of Congress Cataloging in Publication Data*

Sustainable development, international criminal justice, and treaty implementation / Sébastien Jodoin, Yale University, School of Forestry & Environmental Studies, Marie-Claire Cordonier Segger Centre for International Sustainable Development Law, editors.
pages cm
Includes index.
ISBN 978-1-107-03293-4 (hardback)
1. Sustainable development – Law and legislation. 2. International criminal law. 3. Environmental law, International. I. Jodoin, Sébastien, 1982– editor of compilation. II. Cordonier Segger, Marie-Claire, 1973– editor of compilation.
K3585.S865 2013
344.04′6–dc23 2012051701

ISBN 978-1-107-03293-4 Hardback

# Contents

# List of Editors, Contributors, and Editorial Assistants

## EDITORS

**Marie-Claire Cordonier Segger** is a leading international jurist in the field of sustainable economic development. She serves as Head of Economic Law for the International Development Law Organization, spearheading legal programs on climate finance and green economy, natural resources governance, and sustainable trade and investment. Pro bono, she is also a Councillor of the World Future Council, a Visiting Professor for the University of Chile, an Affiliated Fellow at the Lauterpacht Centre for International Law at Cambridge University, Senior Director of the Centre for International Sustainable Development Law (CISDL), Rapporteur of the Sustainable Resources Governance Committee of the International Law Association, and Co-Lead of the World Bank's Environment and Natural Resources Law Thematic Working Group, among other roles. She has authored or edited 14 books, including *Sustainable Development Law* (OUP 2004), *Sustainable Development in World Trade Law* (Kluwer 2005), and *Sustainable Development in World Investment Law* (Kluwer 2010); and more than 80 papers in five languages. She holds a BA Hons, degrees in common and civil law from McGill University where she held Millennium and Wainwright Scholarships, a master's degree from Yale University where she held a Teaching Fellowship; and a doctorate in international law from Oxford University, where she held Chevening and SSHRC awards.

**Sébastien Jodoin** is a PhD Candidate, Trudeau Scholar, and SSHRC Doctoral Fellow at the Yale School of Forestry & Environmental Studies and a member of the Governance, Environment, and Markets Initiative at Yale. He also serves as a Lead Counsel with the Centre for International Sustainable Development Law and directs the One Justice Project, which seeks the recognition, investigation, and prosecution of serious forms of economic, social, and environmental harm as crimes under domestic and international law. Jodoin previously worked with the Canadian

Centre for International Justice, Amnesty International Canada, and the United Nations International Criminal Tribunals for Rwanda and the former Yugoslavia. He holds graduate degrees in law, international law, and international relations from McGill University, the London School of Economics, and the University of Cambridge and has been called to the bar in Ontario. Sébastien has received numerous awards and honours, including the 2012 Public Scholar Award from the Yale Graduate School of Arts & Sciences, a John Humphrey Fellowship in Human Rights from the Canadian Council on International Law, and a Public Interest Law Articling Fellowship from the Law Foundation of Ontario.

## CONTRIBUTORS

**Rt. Hon. Sir Dennis C. M. Byron** is the President of the Caribbean Court of Justice. He also serves as President of the Commonwealth Judicial Education Institute and is a former President of the United Nations International Criminal Tribunal for Rwanda and a former Chief Justice of the Eastern Caribbean Supreme Court. In 2000, Justice Byron was knighted by Queen Elizabeth II and was appointed a member of Her Majesty's Most Honourable Privy Council. In 2004, he was appointed as an Honorary Bencher of the Honourable Society of the Inner Temple.

**Riane Eisler** is President of the Center for Partnership Studies, keynotes conferences worldwide, consults for governments and businesses, and pioneered the extension of human rights to 'women's rights' and 'children's rights'. Her books have been translated into 30 languages and include *The Real Wealth of Nations*, offering a new conceptual framework for economics, and *The Chalice and the Blade*, a new reading of our past and present, and the possibilities for our future.

**Matthew Gillett** is a Legal Officer in the Office of Prosecutor of the UN International Criminal Tribunal for the former Yugoslavia. He previously worked in the Trial Chambers in the United Nations International Criminal Tribunal for the former Yugoslavia and in the Office of the Prosecutor at the International Criminal Court.

**Dr. Maja Göpel** is a political economist with a focus on institutionalism that combines theory and practice in her engagement for fair and sustainable societies. Since November 2006, Maja has worked with the World Future Council, first as Campaign Manager for Climate and Energy issues and now as Director of Future Justice. Maja holds a Ph.D. in Global Political Economy in the field of World Trade and has studied at the universities of Siegen, Sevilla, Fribourg, Hamburg, York (Toronto), and Kassel.

**Alexandra R. Harrington** is a Visiting Assistant Professor of Law at Albany Law School and a D.C.L. candidate at the McGill University Faculty of Law. She is also an Associate Fellow at the Centre for International Sustainable Development Law.

**Jarrod Hebpurn** is a candidate for a DPhil in international law at the University of Oxford and a Legal Research Fellow with the Centre for International Sustainable Development Law. He has experience in the Competition group of the Australian corporate law firm Mallesons Stephen Jaques. He holds an LLB from the University of Melbourne and BCL and MPhil degrees from the University of Oxford.

**Prof. Fannie Lafontaine** is a Professor in the Law Faculty of Laval University and the Director of the International Criminal and Humanitarian Law Clinic. She previously worked inter alia at the United Nations (OHCHR) and at the International Commission of Inquiry on Darfur. She has published mainly in the fields of international criminal law, Canadian criminal law, and international and Canadian human rights law; she is the author of the book *Prosecuting Genocide, Crimes against Humanity and War Crimes in Canadian Courts* (Carswell 2012).

**Prof. Lisa J. Laplante** is a human rights lawyer who worked with the Peruvian Truth and Reconciliation Commission. She is a Visiting Law Professor at Marquette University and a project director with Praxis: An Institute for Social Justice. She has worked with Human Rights First, Human Rights Watch, the International Institute of Human Rights in Costa Rica, and the Center for International Justice and Law in Costa Rica. She holds a BA from Brown University, an MEd from the University of Massachusetts at Amherst, and a JD from New York University School of Law, where she was a Root-Tildern-Kern Public Interest Scholar.

**Prof. Frédéric Mégret** is an Associate Professor of Law at the McGill University Faculty of Law, where he serves as the Canada Research Chair on the Law of Human Rights and Legal Pluralism and the Director of the McGill Clinic for the Sierra Leone Special Court. He has worked for the International Committee of the Red Cross, assisted the defence counsel of one of the accused before the UN International Criminal Tribunal for Rwanda, and was a member of the French delegation at the Rome conference that created the International Criminal Court. Professor Mégret has also advised the Liberian government on the design of a human rights vetting procedure for its armed forces.

**Salim A. Nakhjavani** is Assistant Co-Prosecutor at the Extraordinary Chambers in the Courts of Cambodia and Senior Lecturer at the Faculty of Law of the University of Cape Town, South Africa, where he conducts research and teaches international criminal law and public international law.

**Dr. Roger O'Keefe** is a Senior Lecturer in Law and the Deputy Director of the Lauterpacht Centre for International Law at the University of Cambridge, as well as a Fellow of Magdalene College, Cambridge. He has published and lectured widely on international criminal law and on the international legal protection of cultural property. His book, *The Protection of Cultural Property in Armed Conflict* (Cambridge University Press 2006), has recently been reissued in paperback.

**Ken Roberts** is a Canadian lawyer called to the bar of Ontario. He has worked at the United Nations International Criminal Tribunal for the former Yugoslavia since 1998, where he has held positions including Deputy Registrar and Senior Legal Officer in Chambers. He has published a number of articles in the area of international criminal law and is Chairperson of the Board of Directors of the NGO International Criminal Law Services Foundation.

**Pubudu Sachithanandan** is an Associate Trial Attorney in the Office of the Prosecutor of the International Criminal Court, where he has worked since 2003. Previously, he worked as a research assistant at the University of Heidelberg and the University of Colombo. He holds an LLB and an LLM in public international law from the University of London and an MSt in international human rights from the University of Oxford.

**Prof. Charles Séguin** is an Assistant Professor in environmental economics at the Université du Québec in Montréal. He holds a PhD in natural resource economics from the University of California, Berkeley, and holds degrees in economics from McGill University and Queen's University.

**Prof. Gerry Simpson** holds a Chair of Law at the University of Melbourne Law School and is a Professor of Public International Law at the London School of Economics and Political Science. He is the author of *Great Powers and Outlaw States* (awarded the American Society of International Law's annual prize for Preeminent Contribution to Creative Legal Scholarship) and the recently published *Law, War and Crime: War Crimes Trials and the Reinvention of International Law*.

**Alain-Guy Tachou-Sipowo** is a candidate for an LLD in international law at Laval University in Québec; a contributor to the Institute of Security Studies of Pretoria, South Africa; and a research and teaching assistant to the Peace and Security Program of the Institut Québécois des Hautes Études Internationales.

## EDITORIAL ASSISTANTS

**Hannah Cochrane** currently serves as Legal and Research adviser to the New Zealand Immigration and Protection Tribunal. She previously interned with the International Federation for Human Rights and the International Criminal Tribunal for Rwanda and holds a J.D. from Pace University School of Law.

**Geraint Edwards** is currently Head of Policy at an EU legal affairs company in Brussels. Previously he was *Maitre de Langues* at the Law Faculty of the University of Angers in France, teaching English and European law.

**Katherine Lofts** currently serves as a Legal Officer with the One Justice Project and as an Associate Fellow with the Centre for International Sustainable Development

Law. She holds a BCL and LLB as well as an MA in English literature from McGill University.

**Megan McKee** holds a JD from the University of Pittsburgh School of Law and a BA from McGill University. She is currently a senior editor and editorial board member at JURIST Legal News & Research.

**Nathalie Senst** is a lawyer in Toronto. She holds an LLB from the University of Ottawa. Through her passion for human rights and development, she has lived and worked in both Cambodia and Tanzania.

# Foreword

*Rt. Hon. Sir Dennis C. M. Byron*

The challenges facing the world are immense and unprecedented. If overuse in recent years has rendered this statement hackneyed, its urgency cannot be overstated. As the global population continues to expand, the planet's ecosystems teeter on the brink of irreversible collapse. Meanwhile, millions of people continue to live in dire poverty, struggling to meet their basic needs despite expanded economic activity that has greatly increased the wealth and material well-being of some segments of the population.

It is not only the scale of the challenges facing us that is unprecedented; it is also their increasing interconnectedness. From the current crisis in the global financial system to the devastating effects of climate change, the interrelated nature of the factors determining sustainable development is undeniable. Sadly, the diagnostic posed by the Brundtland Commission on Environment and Development is as accurate today as it was 25 years ago when it was first posed, because the world continues to face a series of interlocking global crises in the fields of environment, development, and energy that are 'rapidly closing the options for future generations'.[1]

In this context, it is clear that the challenge of achieving sustainable development raises fundamental questions of justice on a global scale. How can we ensure that the fruits of development are shared equitably, while also sustaining the ecosystems on which all life depends? What should be our response to individuals, corporations, or governments that seriously infringe on the human rights of others, destroy the basic conditions that make development possible, or carry out gross environmental destruction? What responsibilities do current generations have toward generations to come? Such questions touch on different conceptions of justice – distributive, retributive, and restorative.

[1] Brundtland Commission, *Our Common Future: Report of the World Commission on Environment and Development* (2007), 8.

The connection to distributive justice is clear. Many of the earth's resources are finite, and those that are not are being taxed to the limit. Experts predict a future increasingly marred by resource conflicts, and the gap between the rich and the poor continues to grow. The question of how to achieve a fair and socially just allocation of resources, both among and between generations, is thus one of the most pressing of our time.

But it is increasingly evident that we must also consider aspects of retributive and restorative justice to address the challenges posed by sustainable development. The last hundred years have seen the rise of international criminal law in the wake of the Second World War – from the Nuremburg and Tokyo tribunals, to the international tribunals for the former Yugoslavia, Rwanda, Sierra Leone, and Cambodia and the International Criminal Court. Nevertheless, the tools of international criminal law have remained underdeveloped and undertheorised with respect to their connection to development, and sustainability, and social justice. And yet it can be argued that serious violations of economic, social, and cultural rights and environmental destruction on a large scale often spring from the intentional acts of individuals, rather than from systemic causes alone, and these behaviours may be morally reprehensible enough for individual criminal liability to attach to their perpetrators. Individual criminal liability therefore holds tremendous potential to strengthen the rule of law by ensuring compliance with the global norms and fundamental rights that underpin it. After all, as propounded in a famous dictum of the International Military Tribunal in Nuremberg, international crimes are 'committed by men, not by abstract entities, and only by punishing individuals who commit such crimes can the provisions of international law be enforced'.

A restorative conception of justice may also provide important insights for the field of sustainable development. International criminal processes aimed at truth, reconciliation, and accountability in the wake of crimes and conflicts may support the conditions for sustainable development in the future, and the concepts underpinning sustainable development may, in turn, inform the practice of international criminal tribunals. Indeed, although the contributions of international courts and tribunals to global justice cannot be underestimated, the future of international criminal justice necessarily lies at the domestic level through the effective prosecution of international crimes, strengthened legal systems, and enhanced opportunities for the rule of law and justice.

Bringing together these different conceptions of justice in the service of sustainable development is vital to mounting a robust response to the challenges we face. This book offers exciting perspectives on this integration, providing wide-ranging analyses of the intersections between sustainable development and international criminal justice by leading scholars and practitioners in these fields. As such, it makes an important contribution towards developing a conceptual basis to underpin future thinking in this domain. It interrogates the boundaries of criminalisation as a means to tackle the challenges of sustainable development and explores future directions to end impunity for egregious acts and conduct that are so crucial in securing a sustainable and just future for all. The contributions in this book also offer original reflections on the linkages between the objectives and means of achieving sustainable development and the pursuit of international criminal justice. These reflections probe the limitations of international law's fragmented response to the complex and interrelated problems that bedevil us at the intersections of criminality, sustainability, and development.

In his opening argument at the International Military Tribunal in Nuremberg, Justice Jackson, Counsel for the United States, declared as follows:

> The privilege of opening the first trial in history for crimes against the peace of the world imposes a grave responsibility. It is a responsibility that the wrongs which we seek to condemn and punish have been so calculated, so malignant, and so devastating, that civilization cannot tolerate their being ignored, because it cannot survive their being repeated.[2]

By exploring the fundamental linkages between international criminal justice and sustainable development, this book offers powerful insights into a broader range of wrongs that we should seek to address, as well as a broader range of means for restoring peace to the world. I am hopeful that some of the ideas presented in this book will be taken up by others for the benefit of present and future generations.

[2] "Opening Statement before the International Military Tribunal," Trial of the Major War Criminals before the International Military Tribunal (Nuremberg: IMT, 1947), 98.

# Acknowledgments

The World Future Council and the Centre for International Sustainable Development Law provided significant support for the production of this volume, and the assistance of both institutions is gratefully acknowledged. We are particularly grateful to Jakob von Uexkell, Justice Christopher Weeramantry, and Dr. Maja Göpel who, in the World Future Council's project on future justice and on crimes against future generations, were enthusiastic supporters of the research that has been included in this volume and the many related initiatives, meetings, and reports that have accompanied it over the last four years.

We must also thank many former judges and colleagues at the International Criminal Tribunals for the former Yugoslavia and Rwanda, who were very supportive of this research. We are pleased that a few of them were able to contribute chapters to this volume.

We dedicate this book to our spouses, Sebastien's loving and supportive wife, Sarah, who endured quite a few lonely evenings and weekends in The Hague, Arusha, Cambridge, Ottawa, and New Haven so that he could work on this book; and Marie-Claire's brilliant and kind husband, Markus, whose companionship and patience have proven beyond measure over the years.

Sébastien Jodoin
Marie-Claire Cordonier Segger

# Table of Abbreviations

| | |
|---|---|
| CISDL | Centre for International Sustainable Development Law |
| ECCC | Extraordinary Chambers in the Courts of Cambodia |
| ECHR | European Court of Human Rights |
| ICC | International Criminal Court |
| ICCPR | International Covenant on Civil and Political Rights |
| ICESCR | International Covenant on Economic, Social and Cultural Rights |
| ICJ | International Commission of Jurists |
| ICJ | International Court of Justice |
| ICL | International Criminal Law |
| ICTR | International Criminal Tribunal for Rwanda |
| ICTY | International Criminal Tribunal for the former Yugoslavia |
| IGOs | Intergovernmental Organizations |
| IHL | International Humanitarian Law |
| ILA | International Law Association |
| IMT | International Military Tribunal |
| IPCC | Intergovernmental Panel on Climate Change |
| JCE | Joint Criminal Enterprise |
| JPOI | Johannesburg Plan of Implementation |
| MEA | Multilateral Environmental Agreements |
| NGOs | Non-governmental Organizations |
| OAS | Organization of American States |
| OECD | Organization for Economic Co-operation and Development |
| SCSL | Special Court for Sierra Leone |
| SPSC | Special Panel for Serious Crimes in East Timor |
| STL | Special Tribunal for Lebanon |
| TRC | Truth and Reconciliation Commission |
| UNCBD | United Nations Convention on Biological Diversity |
| UNCCD | United Nations Convention to Combat Desertification |

| | |
|---|---|
| UNCED | United Nations Conference on Environment and Development |
| UNDP | United Nations Development Programme |
| UNEP | United Nations Environment Programme |
| UNESCO | United Nations Educational, Scientific and Cultural Organization |
| UNFCCC | United Nations Framework Convention on Climate Change |
| UNGA | United Nations General Assembly |
| UNSC | United Nations Security Council |
| WFC | World Future Council |
| WHO | World Health Organization |
| WSSD | World Summit on Sustainable Development |

# PART I

# Accountability and Sustainability in International Justice

# 1

# Introduction

## *The Sustainability of International Criminal Justice*

*Sébastien Jodoin and Marie-Claire Cordonier Segger*

### 1. INTRODUCTION

The spring of 1992 featured moments of both hope and horror that captured the world's attention and led to transformative developments in international law.

Hope was inspired by the Earth Summit held in Rio de Janeiro in June 1992, launching a new era of cooperation to both protect the environment and eradicate poverty for the benefit of present and future generations.[1] Since its recognition in the *Rio Declaration on Environment and Development*, the concept of sustainable development and its corollaries such as the principles of intergenerational equity, precaution, and common but differentiated responsibilities have been incorporated into hundreds of international economic, environment, and development-related treaties and instruments. In the next 20 years, the international community would seek, with varying, sometimes underwhelming results, to strengthen and integrate the economic, environmental, and social pillars of sustainable development in laws and policies at the national, regional, and international levels.[2]

The world reacted with horror to the brutal campaign of ethnic violence and cleansing led by Serb forces in that same spring of 1992, during the early stages of the Bosnian war. These acts shocked the global conscience and galvanised momentum toward to the creation by the UN Security Council of the International Criminal Tribunal for the former Yugoslavia (ICTY) in the following year.[3] Although this ad hoc tribunal was established to try the perpetrators of international crimes committed during the wars of the former Yugoslavia, its significance has extended far beyond this particular context. Along with a similar tribunal established for the Rwandan

[1] *Rio Declaration on Environment and Development*, Annex 1 in *Report of the United Nations Conference on Environment and Development* (3–14 June 1992), UN Doc. A/CONF.151/26 (1999).

[2] See generally M. C. Cordonier Segger & A. Khalfan, *Sustainable Development Law: Principles, Practices & Prospects* (2004).

[3] P. Hazan, *La justice face à la guerre: de Nuremberg à La Haye* (2000), ch. 2.

genocide one year later, the ICTY would revitalise the field of international criminal law and provide important political, institutional, and legal precedents for the establishment in 2002 of a permanent International Criminal Court (ICC).[4] As a result, an established set of rules and mechanisms could emerge at both national and international levels for holding individuals criminally accountable for breaches of fundamental rules of international law.[5]

Twenty years later, efforts aimed at buttressing the role of sustainability and accountability in international law remain dynamic and influential, if not always entirely successful. At the United Nations Conference on Sustainable Development held in Rio de Janeiro in June 2012, states adopted a nonbinding programme for policy change and implementation, focusing on effectuating a transition toward a green economy and confirming institutional reforms to make sustainable development more achievable.[6] Without denying the gains achieved at this conference, it is clear that the ambitions of current commitments for global sustainability fall far short of addressing the scale of economic, environmental, and social challenges currently confronting the world.

Meanwhile, the ICC entered its second decade of existence in July 2012, with 118 state parties, a new prosecutor from the African continent, and 15 cases in seven situations.[7] Other ad hoc and hybrid international criminal tribunals are coming to the end of their mandates, having tried hundreds of individuals involved in a wide variety of conflicts ranging from the genocide in Cambodia to the wars of the former Yugoslavia.[8] As a result of the expense and complexity of international tribunals, some of the energies in this field have been shifting away from the international context to focus on national-level investigations and prosecutions and are becoming increasingly entrenched in a renewed global agenda supporting peace building, the rule of law, and legal empowerment.[9] Nonetheless, the potential for political instability and violent conflict in numerous regions around the world, most notably in the Middle East and North Africa, and for ongoing conflicts in fractured regions such as the Democratic Republic of the Congo suggests that the demand and momentum for international criminal justice in some form are unlikely to decrease any time soon.

4 Rome Statute of the International Criminal Court, United Nations Diplomatic Conference of Plenipotentiaries on the Establishment of an International Criminal Court, UN Doc. A/CONF.183/9, (1998) Arts. 15 and 17–19.

5 See generally A. Cassese, *International Criminal Law* (2008).

6 United Nations Conference on Sustainable Development, 'The Future We Want', 22 June 2012, UN Doc, A/CONF.216/L.1.

7 S. Ford, 'The ICC Turns Ten: A Look at its Development', JURIST – Forum, July 6, 2012, http://jurist.org/forum/2012/07/stuart-ford-icc-ten.php.

8 For an overview of recent and future developments in the field of international criminal law, see C. Stahn and L. van den Herik, eds., *Future Perspectives on International Criminal Justice* (2009).

9 See M. Bergsmo, *Complementarity and the Challenges of Equality and Empowerment* (2011).

These milestones and the significant body of international law and practice that they represent have led to numerous academic and political stock-taking exercises over the last two years.[10] This volume does not duplicate this work, but rather focuses on providing a unique and timely perspective on international law and policy on sustainable development and international criminal justice – considering in theory and practice both the contribution of criminal law to the realisation of more sustainable development, and the potential of sustainable development law to prevent conditions driving criminal behaviour. Drawing on the practice and experience of a wide variety of international criminal tribunals and processes, the chapters in this book examine existing and prospective legal practices that bear on how the fields of sustainable development and international criminal law can contribute to one another's elaboration, interpretation, and implementation.

In what follows, we provide an introductory overview of the key themes addressed in this volume and the arguments developed in particular chapters. Part I situates this work within broader debates on the potential and the limitations of international criminalisation as a means for protecting and securing the basic foundations of sustainable development, while also noting the potential of sustainable development law to improve conditions of life and livelihoods that offer alternatives to criminal behaviour. Part II discusses how existing international crimes penalise or fail to penalise serious forms of economic, social, environmental, and cultural harm. Part III focuses on the indirect linkages that have developed between the principles and practices of sustainable development and various mechanisms of international criminal justice. Finally, Part IV addresses future directions in the interpenetration of these two fields and the integration of different forms of justice.

## 2. SUSTAINABILITY AND ACCOUNTABILITY IN INTERNATIONAL LAW

During the last several decades, the relative success of international courts and tribunals in investigating and prosecuting international crimes and in contributing to complex processes of truth, reconciliation, and accountability in states recovering from the damaging and fracturing effects of conflict has been one of the most remarkable achievements in the field of international law. Not only has the field of international criminal law contributed to the development of international humanitarian law and international human rights law but it has also established the principle that individuals *can and should* be held accountable for the most serious violations of international law – what the *Rome Statute* of the ICC defines as 'grave crimes that

[10] Indeed, both the Review Conference of the Rome Statute of the International Criminal Court held in Kampala, Uganda, in June 2010 and the aforementioned United Nations Conference on Sustainable Development held in Rio de Janeiro in June 2012 actively facilitated stock-taking exercises by policy makers and academic experts alike.

threaten the peace, security and well-being of the world' and 'atrocities that deeply shock the conscience of humanity'.[11]

This powerful recognition and application of the principle of individual criminal liability have sparked real enthusiasm for further criminalisation of activities covered by many areas of international law, with all of the contradictions and complications that this may imply.[12] The field of sustainable development has not been inimical to the siren song of criminalisation. Although (or perhaps because) the current global architecture for sustainable development lacks a set of effective compliance and redress mechanisms, policy makers, scholars, and activists have considered or proposed initiatives aimed at developing new regimes and forms of liability for serious forms of environmental harm[13] (and to a lesser extent, economic and social harm as well),[14] whether at the level of states, corporations, or individuals. Against this background, the chapters in Part I of the book discuss the opportunities and challenges of recognising serious forms of economic, social, or environmental harm as international crimes and their implications for the fields of international criminal justice and sustainable development.

Chapter 2, 'Criminal Justice, Sustainable Development, and International Law', by Marie-Claire Cordonier Segger sets the stage by briefly outlining the contours of international law on sustainable development and its relationship to international criminal law. This chapter opens with an explanation of the concept of sustainable development, demonstrating how international understanding of its meaning has evolved over time and characterising sustainable development as a global objective – a purpose of many international treaties that is supported by several key legal principles such as precaution and public participation. Then, the chapter briefly explores how severe degradation of the natural resources, social, and ecological systems upon which people depend for survival may make criminal behaviour more likely and more difficult to prevent. As such, the chapter also briefly discusses how international treaties on sustainable development and the principles of international law on

11 Rome Statute, preamble.

12 See F. Mégret, 'Three Dangers for the International Criminal Court: A Consensual Look at a Consensual Project', (2001) XII *Finnish Yearbook of International Law* 193.

13 See, e.g., S. D. Murphy, 'Does the World Need a New International Environmental Court?', (2000) 32(2) *George Washington Journal of International Law & Economics* 325; M. A. Drumbl, 'International Human Rights, International Humanitarian Law, and Environmental Security: Can the International Criminal Court Bridge the Gaps?', (2000) 5(2) *ILSA Journal of International & Comparative Law* 363; B.- S. Cho, 'Emergence of an International Environmental Criminal Law?', (2000) 19(1) *UCLA Journal of Environmental Law and Policy* 11; T. Weinstein, 'Prosecuting Attacks that Destroy the Environment: Environmental Crimes or Humanitarian Atrocities?', (2005) 17 *Georgetown International Environmental Law Review* 697; D. Zaelke, D. Kaniaru, and E. Krucíkova (eds.), *Making Law Work – Environmental Compliance & Sustainable Development* (2005); P. Utting and J. Clapp (eds.), *Corporate Accountability and Sustainable Development* (2008); P. Higgins, *Eradicating Ecocide: Laws and Governance to Stop the Destruction of the Planet* (2010).

14 See, *e.g.*, S. I. Skogly, 'Crimes against Humanity – Revisited: Is There a Role for Economic and Social Rights?', (2001) 5(1) *International Journal of Human Rights* 58; J. G. Stewart, *Corporate War Crimes. Prosecuting the Pillage of Natural Resources* (2010).

sustainable development can and do themselves contribute to achieving the further important goals of a world with less crime. Finally, the chapter turns to a consideration of how international criminal law, particularly the Rome Statute, can and does support sustainable development.

Chapter 3, 'Crime, Structure, Harm', by Gerry Simpson considers proposals to criminalise new forms of serious harm in international law in light of international criminal law's successes and failures in expanding its scope of application and providing justice for existing crimes. At its best, he argues, the recognition of economic, social, cultural and ecological crimes would be founded on a sophisticated appreciation of the manifold processes 'that constitute the shadow global political economy'. This appreciation might, Simpson maintains, lead 'international criminal law to move in the direction of structural causes of mass atrocity or threats to international peace and security that result from economic and environmental choices rather than more obvious forms of violence'. Yet Simpson also identifies the challenges of applying international criminal law to forms of economic, social, cultural, or environmental harm. Such forms of harm are not easily or frequently reducible to the actions, and therefore responsibility, of identifiable individuals. They may also distract attention from other 'remediable structural and everyday cruelties'. In fact, either of these criticisms could be made of existing international crimes such as genocide and crimes against humanity, which straddle an uneasy line between individual and collectivist forms of guilt. In these ways, Simpson shows us that projects aimed at criminalising new forms of serious harm must, whatever their merits, grapple with both the potential and the serious contentions of our current system for international criminal justice.

Chapter 4, 'The Case for a General International Crime against the Environment', by Frédéric Mégret reviews the merits of criminalising one particular form of harm that falls within the ambit of sustainable development, namely environmental crime. Mégret examines, in turn, the arguments in favour of criminalisation (viewed in relation to other forms of regulation and remedies), those in favour of criminalisation *at the international level* (as opposed to the domestic level), and those that support both criminalisation and its internationalisation. Mégret builds a convincing case in all three respects, one that emphasises the deterrent potential and social value of recognising environmental crimes, the functional and normative advantages of providing for their repression at the international level, and the progressive recognition of environmental harm as a serious violation of international obligations and interests. Mégret thus argues that grave forms of environmental harm may be as deserving of the status of international crime as other serious breaches of international law because of their transnational character – they are 'global crimes *par excellence* because they are ubiquitous in their materialization and potentially absolute and irreversible in their impact'. Mégret closes his chapter with a forward-looking description of what might be some of the core features of a future international crime against the environment, including the need to ensure that its elements provide a focus on conduct that is deserving of criminalisation at the international level.

The chapters in Part I of the book thus underscore the potential as well as the challenges of extending the scope of international criminal law to encompass serious forms of economic, environmental, social, and cultural harm. Part I suggests that, although we should not see international criminalisation as a panacea for addressing acts and conduct that strike at the very foundation of sustainable development, we should also recognise that this view is equally true of the traditional domains that have fallen within the scope of international criminal law. Whether one seeks to prevent and punish war crimes, environmental crimes, or even crimes against future generations, it must be recognised that the field of international criminal justice comes with its inherent strengths and weaknesses and its own history and character.

## 3. SUSTAINABLE DEVELOPMENT AND INTERNATIONAL CRIMES

To be sure, the criminalisation of new forms of harm is consistent with the development of international criminal law, which can be seen as the successive extension of the principle of individual criminal accountability to a constantly expanding list of serious violations of international law – piracy and war crimes to begin with; followed by crimes against humanity, aggression, and genocide in the postwar era; later extending to the other crimes of apartheid and torture; and potentially expanding to offences such as terrorism in the near term. What is more, the ad hoc international criminal tribunals have – not without some controversy – consistently expanded the scope of application of existing international crimes to cover a growing variety of acts and conduct, victims, and contexts.[15]

Whether through new interpretations of existing international criminal law or through the creation of new international crimes, the principle of individual criminal liability may come to apply to conduct that falls within the scope of sustainable development. The chapters in Part II of the book include detailed analyses of how existing international criminal law applies or could apply to sanction conduct that destroys the basic underlying conditions of sustainable development, including severe environmental damage, violations of social and economic rights, violations of international rules governing cultural heritage, and other large-scale threats to present and future generations.

Chapter 5, 'Environmental Damages and International Criminal Law', by Matthew Gillett examines how international criminal law has dealt or can deal with damages to the natural environment. As Gillett shows, there are a number of existing international crimes that directly address the issue of environmental harm through ecocentric or anthropocentric approaches. Gillett examines the war crime of causing long-term and severe damage to the environment and a few other provisions

[15] See G. Mettraux, *International Crimes and the ad hoc Tribunals* (2005).

in international humanitarian law – especially those laws relating to arms controls – to see whether they could form a basis for prosecution under international criminal law. There are also existing international crimes, including other war crimes, crimes against humanity, and genocide, that indirectly address environmental harm. Despite these promising options for prosecuting environmental harm, Gillett points out that international and national authorities have consistently failed to prosecute cases involving environmental destruction, contributing to a sense of impunity for these acts and conduct and leaving an important jurisprudential void. Through a review of existing international crimes and their application to historical examples of environmental damage, Gillett provides further context for understanding the role that international criminal law can play in preventing and punishing severe damages caused to the environment, as a pillar of sustainable development. Gillett concludes that, in addition to enforcement and application of existing crimes, a new crime covering environmental damage in peacetime may be required to ensure that the environment truly benefits from the protection of international criminal justice.

Chapter 6, 'Violations of Social and Economic Rights and International Crimes', by Salim Nakhjavani considers the possibility that such violations might be addressed, directly or indirectly, through international criminal justice. Nakhjavani situates his chapter within a broader discussion of the relationship between international criminal law and the field of international human rights law as a whole. One common way of conceptualising the relationship between these two fields is to focus on their commitment to the protection of common legal interests that 'uphold the oneness and wholeness of *humanity*, in its individual and collective dimensions'. The challenge remains that a straightforward pairing between human rights violations and international crimes is often not possible, especially in the case of socioeconomic rights. Although a number of existing international crimes, especially crimes against humanity, could be used to punish serious violations of social and economic rights, international criminal lawyers and judges have not taken advantage of these opportunities. Nakhjavani argues that a more fruitful view of this relationship would 'conceive of core international crimes and the suite of international human rights instruments, including those protecting socioeconomic rights, as co-evolving species within a complex adaptive system'. The greatest potential for co-evolution lies in the crime against humanity of persecution in light of the interpretative importance accorded to human rights by the Rome Statute. According to Nakhjavani, the sporadic use of international human rights law to inform the interpretation and application of international crimes may eventually catalyse new legal approaches that effectively protect economic and social rights through international criminal law.

Chapter 7, 'Cultural Heritage and International Criminal Law', by Roger O'Keefe addresses the protection of cultural heritage in international criminal law. O'Keefe reviews numerous statutory provisions and the extensive case law of various international criminal tribunals – including cases as early as those of the International

Military Tribunal at Nuremberg – to analyse the many ways in which existing war crimes and crimes against humanity afford protections to places and objects of cultural significance and the sentencing practices that have developed for these crimes. O'Keefe also discusses the rejection of the notion of 'cultural genocide' as an international legal concept. In so doing, O'Keefe provides perhaps the strongest set of examples of the use of international criminal law to protect an issue area of concern to sustainable development, demonstrating the role that international criminal prosecutions can play in protecting interests that have intergenerational and nonmaterial significance.

Chapter 8, 'The Crime of Aggression and Threats to the Future', by Alexandra Harrington examines the links between the crime of aggression and new threats to the future, with a specific focus on environmental and socioeconomic harms. Harrington begins by reviewing the history and nature of the crime of aggression, which is recognised as one of the four core crimes of international law, but that has not been prosecuted since the Second World War. Harrington then discusses various examples of environmental and socioeconomic harms, including climate change and the phenomenon of disappearing states, and whether they could rise to the level of seriousness captured by the crime of aggression. Looking at the various elements of the definition of this crime adopted at the Kampala Review Conference of the ICC in June 2010, Harrington highlights the challenges, especially in terms of *mens rea* requirements, of expanding the meaning of aggression to cover large-scale threats to the future that fall short of the traditional use of international force. Although drawing the line between which of these threats should or should not count as aggression is a complex enterprise, Harrington points out that the negotiations that eventually led to the definition of the crime of aggression were similarly tortuous.

By demonstrating how forms of economic, social, and environmental harm may already amount, whether directly or indirectly, to existing international crimes, the chapters in Part II highlight the many political and legal gaps that must be addressed before concerns relating to sustainable development may be fully woven into the scope of application of international criminal law. These chapters also suggest that the complexity of creating and applying economic, social, economic, and cultural crimes can actually be seen as contiguous with the definition and prosecution of other international crimes that are no less useful or potent for all their convolutions.

## 4. SUSTAINABLE DEVELOPMENT AND THE MECHANISMS OF INTERNATIONAL CRIMINAL JUSTICE

Although existing international crimes may not fully or adequately capture acts and conduct that directly bear on the economic, social, and environmental pillars of sustainable development, a number of indirect linkages exist between the fields of international criminal justice and international law and policy on sustainable development. Scholars and policy makers have long recognised the roles of transitional justice[16] and peace building[17] in development; however, the notion that the mechanisms and process of international criminal justice may themselves contribute to the realisation of more sustainable development is relatively novel.

Of course, to the extent that international criminal processes provide some measure of reconciliation, truth, accountability, and deterrence in the aftermath of conflicts,[18] they may address some of the underlying conditions that support human development in the long term. Of greater interest perhaps are the opportunities for using sustainable development principles and practices to inform the creation and application of international legal responses to international crimes. These linkages represent an important and underexplored area of international law and policy that is the focus of the chapters in Part III.

Chapter 9, 'Intergenerational Equity and Rights in International Criminal Law', by Jarrod Hepburn discusses the principle of intergenerational equity and the concept of the rights of future generations in international criminal law. After reviewing how intergenerational equity is featured in international law and policy on sustainable development, Hepburn turns to its role in international criminal justice. Given its objectives of addressing the lasting consequences of international crimes and conflicts, Hepburn avers that intergenerational equity and rights may be seen as being at the heart of the international criminal justice system. To begin with, international criminal law pursues a broad range of objectives beyond the prosecution of international crimes, including 'the development of a historical record of a conflict, support for peace and reconciliation of fractured societies, prevention of international crimes not only through deterrence but also through public memorialisation, capacity building in domestic judicial systems, and a sense of closure for victims'. In addition, a number of international crimes, most notably the crime of genocide, are specifically directed towards the protection of future generations. In all of these ways, Hepburn suggests that, although international criminal justice focuses on the crimes of the past, it has much to contribute to the protection of future generations.

16 See, *e.g.*, P. de Grieff and R. Duthie (eds.), *Transitional Justice and Development – Making Connections* (2009); R. Duthie, 'Toward a Development-Sensitive Approach to Transitional Justice', (2008) 2(3) *International Journal of Transitional Justice* 292.

17 See, e.g., Nicole Ball and Tammy Halevy, *Making Peace Work: The Role of the International Development Community* (1996); M. Brenk and H. van de Veen, 'Development: No Development without Peace, No Peace without Development', in Paul van Tongeren et al. (eds.), *People Building Peace, Successful Stories of Civil Society* (2005).

18 See, e.g., Richard J. Goldstone, 'Justice as a Tool for Peace-Making: Truth Commissions and International Criminal Tribunals', (1996) 28(3) *New York University Journal of International Law and Politics* 485; Payam Akhavan, 'Beyond Impunity: Can International Criminal Justice Prevent Future Atrocities?', (2001) 95(1) *American Journal of International Law* 7; International Center for Transitional Justice, and Human Rights at the University of California (Berkeley), *Forgotten Voices: A Population-Based Survey on Attitudes about Peace and Justice in Northern Uganda* (2005); International Center for Transitional Justice, and Human Rights at the University of California (Berkeley), *A Voice for Victims* (2005).

Chapter 10, 'Corporate Liability and Complicity in International Crimes', by Ken Roberts explores the different modes of liability in international criminal law that could be applied to hold the officers of corporations accountable for their involvement in the commission of international crimes. Roberts begins by explaining how the role and impacts of transnational corporations in developing countries, especially in the extraction of natural resources in conflict-affected or fragile states, have called attention to the complicity and responsibility of businesses in serious violations of international law. Roberts assesses, in turn, whether the three principal modes of liability in international criminal law – aiding and abetting, joint criminal enterprise, and superior responsibility – could be used to hold corporate officers accountable for international crimes. Roberts demonstrates that each of these modes of liability could be used to capture acts and conduct committed by corporate officers in relation to international crimes. He concludes therefore that international criminal law provides a promising framework for instilling some measure of accountability in the operations of transnational corporations.

Chapter 11, 'The Contribution of International Criminal Justice to Sustainable Peace and Development', by Fannie Lafontaine and Alain-Guy Tachou Sipowo provides a thorough review of the record of international criminal justice in contributing to peace-building and postconflict development and its potential for doing so. Lafontaine and Sipowo begin by examining the role that international criminal justice has played in promoting and building the rule of law at the international level by addressing threats or breaches of international peace and security in specific conflicts, as well as contributing to the development of the fields of international criminal law and international humanitarian law more broadly. Lafontaine and Sipowo then turn to discuss how a variety of processes of international criminal law in a variety of postconflict situations (in particular, the Balkans, Rwanda, Sierra Leone, Uganda, Cambodia, and Latin America) have strengthened the rule of law in domestic legal systems through the proactive practice of complementarity, judicial capacity building, and practices of restorative justice. On the whole, they argue that the success of international criminal justice in building peace and fostering development depends on whether or not its practices and processes are aligned with and complemented by other postconflict initiatives aimed at strengthening the rule of law, protecting human security, and promoting peace and reconciliation.

Chapter 12, 'Reparations for Victims and Sustainable Development', by Pubudu Sachithanandan provides an overview of the regimes for providing reparations to victims of international crimes and discusses how they could be used to promote sustainable development. Sachithanandan offers a comprehensive review of the different types of reparations (symbolic, monetary, and process-based) and the various mechanisms through which they may be provided, including truth commissions, expert commissions, trust funds, and national courts. To be sure, the author notes, reparations are first and foremost meant to act as a concrete recognition of the suffering of victims of international crimes. Yet, to be effective in addressing the long-term and collective consequences of international crimes, reparations must improve the living conditions of victims and contribute to the sustainable development of their communities. In discussing the complex relationship between reparations and processes of postconflict recovery and development, Sachithanandan highlights the key issues that must be addressed to find the appropriate means for the pursuit of sustainable development through reparations. They include issues relating to financing, the identity and selection of victims and beneficiaries, the scope of reparations, gender justice, and the challenges of accountability and implementation. Although the practice of reparations in international criminal justice is still in its relative infancy, Sachithanandan shows that there is much scope for innovation that may lead to sustainable, empowering, and equitable outcomes for victims and affected communities.

The chapters in Part III provide important reflections on the indirect linkages that exist between international criminal justice and sustainable development. Interestingly, all of the authors emphasise the need for international criminal justice to be implemented in a manner that complements, rather than replaces, other legal and nonlegal initiatives and processes that address international crimes and their consequences. This emphasis suggests that, although it is useful to further develop the linkages between international criminal justice and sustainable development, it must be done in a way that respects their respective areas of responsibility and avoids needless duplication and agenda overload.

## 5. MAKING INTERNATIONAL CRIMINAL JUSTICE MORE SUSTAINABLE

Throughout this volume, it becomes apparent that the fields of international criminal justice and sustainable development have much to gain from further interaction with one another, whether through the interpretation or creation of international law or through more collaborative institutional practices on the ground. At the same time, the authors in this volume recognise that much work remains for this relationship to deliver on its full potential. The chapters in Part IV offer some concluding thoughts on the future of this relationship, with a view to laying out a future research and policy agenda for how the field of international criminal law can engage with the global objective of sustainable development.

Chapter 13, 'Sustainable Development, Conflicts, and International Crimes,' by Charles Séguin considers how sustainable development can play a role in preventing the commission of international crimes by addressing the factors conducive to the very emergence of conflicts and the commission of crimes. As Séguin explains, various aspects of unsustainable development, such as economic inequality and underdevelopment, resource scarcity, and natural resource predation, may play critical roles in the emergence of armed conflicts and the commission of international crimes. In laying out a future agenda for the prevention of international crimes,

Séguin reviews how several key principles of international law on sustainable development, including those related to the eradication of poverty, good governance, and the sustainable and equitable management of natural resources, can play key roles in preventing conflicts and crimes.

Chapter 14, 'Transitional Justice and Peace Building for the Future: Diagnosing and Addressing the Socioeconomic Roots of Violence through a Human Rights and Intergenerational Framework', by Lisa Laplante goes beyond a discussion of international criminal justice alone to discuss how the broader field of transitional justice should be responsive to concerns related to social and economic justice, sustainable development, and intergenerational justice. Laplante focuses on domestic processes of transitional justice in Latin America and the challenge of putting an end to cycles of violence fuelled by socioeconomic grievances. She argues that mechanisms such as truth commissions should expand their mandates to include a legal framework that diagnoses the deep-rooted social and economic conditions that cause poverty, exclusion, and inequality and how they can be addressed through the promotion of sustainable development. As summed up by Laplante, 'assuring sustainable development offers the surest means of protecting the rights of future generations and ensuring that they do not suffer the same tragic fate of their predecessors'.

Chapter 15, 'Protecting the Majority of Humanity: Towards an Integrated Approach to Crimes against Present and Future Generations', by Riane Eisler explores the potential use of international criminal law to protect what she identifies as the majority of humanity (i.e. women and children). According to Eisler, international criminal law should be used to punish and repress serious violations of the Convention on the Elimination of All Forms of Discrimination against Women, the Convention on the Rights of the Child, and the Declaration on the Elimination of Violence against Women. Although they take place in the so-called private sphere, away from the usual, transnational concerns of international criminal justice, Eisler makes the case that various forms of violence against women and children are deserving of the status of international crimes. In particular, Eisler argues that international criminal law could be used to protect women and children by reinterpreting various crimes against humanity and by including 'gender' and 'childhood' as criteria for the application of the crimes of genocide.

Chapter 16, 'The Responsibility to Prevent: Early Warning Systems to Protect Future Generations', by Maja Göpel discusses the use of early warning systems in the prevention of international crimes. She explains that early warning systems identify the factors and conditions that make it more likely that individuals will commit international crimes. Such systems have most notably been developed in relation to genocide and could be further developed to cover crimes against humanity as part of a global responsibility to prevent serious human rights violations. Göpel goes further, arguing that an early warning model can be designed to identify those laws and policies that contribute to the escalation of situations that have an already unsustainable imprint. She suggests how one such early warning system based on the principles of sustainable development can be used to track the evolution of patterns of unsustainable development into international crimes, including apartheid and small arms trading.

Chapter 17, 'Conclusion: Protecting the Rights of Future Generations through Existing and New International Criminal Law', by Sébastien Jodoin concludes this volume by examining how existing and new international criminal law can be used to protect the rights of future generations. Like a number of other authors in this book, Jodoin argues that a number of existing international crimes could be used to prosecute conduct detrimental to future generations. Doing so would require certain innovations in the application of crimes against humanity and genocide that expand the *actus reus* of these crimes to cover the types of human rights violations that are the focus of crimes committed against future generations. The greatest impediments to the use of these crimes are their narrow scopes of application that restrict their application to situations involving mass violence or mass violations of fundamental human rights, which target present generations. Jodoin thus argues that it is imperative that new international crimes be recognised through innovative legal developments to ensure that serious violations of international economic, social, and cultural rights and international environmental law be prohibited in a more complete manner than under existing international criminal law. Jodoin briefly discusses a proposed new category of crime, 'crime against future generations', which seeks to fill many of the gaps identified by other authors in this volume. He demonstrates how this category of crime builds upon a number of principles and developments in international law and policy on sustainable development, environment, human rights, and international crime. Returning to some of the debates on the potential and drawbacks of international criminalisation for sustainability, Jodoin also offers some thoughts on the feasibility of recognition of this crime through a new international convention, and its utility in strengthening existing legal frameworks as well as eventually changing human culture and behaviour.

## 6. CONCLUSION

By recognising that international crimes 'threaten the peace, security and well-being of the world' and that their international repression served the interests of both 'present and future generations', the preamble to the Rome Statute of the ICC highlights the fundamental role played by international criminal justice in providing the basic conditions for global sustainable development, such as peace, accountability, and the rule of law. Indeed, there is little doubt that genocide, crimes against humanity, and other international crimes are completely incompatible with the pursuit of sustainable development and undermine the economic, social, and environmental pillars that make it possible.[19]

[19] See, in this regard, R. Mani, *Beyond Retribution: Seeking Justice in the Shadows of War* (2002) (proposing that building peace requires the incorporation of the legal, rectifying, and distributive dimensions of justice).

Yet, this book suggests that the contributions that international criminal law may make to sustainable development go beyond the prevention and repression of international crimes and conflicts. Whether through the novel creation and application of its crimes or innovations in the implementation and coordination of its mechanisms, the field of international criminal justice has much to gain from further engaging with the principles and practice of international law on sustainable development.

Ultimately, the relationship between international criminal justice and sustainable development is an interesting and promising one because of the complementary nature of these two fields. Given the relative weakness of its enforcement mechanisms, international law and policy on sustainable development would likely benefit from the extension of the principle and practice of individual criminal liability to its core areas of concern. Likewise, the effectiveness of international criminal justice would be significantly enhanced if its various mechanisms and institutions were aligned with and informed by some of the holistic and long-term thinking that pervades the field of sustainable development.

Of course, conceiving of linkages between these legal frameworks in such mutually supportive terms also reveals a basic tension between the straightforward potency of models of human agency and their corollary assumption of moral responsibility that is characteristic of criminal justice, and the structural focus of the complex conceptual models that inform the notion of sustainability. Rather than privileging one of these perspectives over the other, this book proposes that both are needed and that a promising future for international law would lie in developing innovative practices for accommodating different forms of justice – criminal, social, sustainable, and transitional – as part of concerted efforts to secure peace, security, and well-being in the broadest sense possible.

# 2

# International Law, Criminal Justice, and Sustainable Development

*Marie-Claire Cordonier Segger*

## 1. INTRODUCTION

Many economic development decisions have environmental and social impacts, and the concept of 'sustainable development' has gained great currency in international debates. Through two UN Conferences, a special session of the UN General Assembly, and a World Summit, sustainable development has been recognized as an important global policy goal and has become the subject and purpose of many international treaties.[1] Disputes on sustainable development matters have also been argued before many prominent international tribunals.[2] In the 1992 United Nations Conference on Environment and Development (UNCED),[3] the 1997 United Nations General Assembly (UNGA) Special Session on Sustainable Development,[4] the 2002 World Summit on Sustainable Development,[5] and the 2012 United Nations Conference on Sustainable Development,[6] as well as through a series of recent international, regional, and bilateral environmental, economic, and development agreements,[7] states have made sweeping commitments to sustainable development.

1 M. C. Cordonier Segger, and A. Khalfan, *Sustainable Development Law* (2004).

2 M. C. Cordonier Segger, C. J. Weeramantry, and Y. Saito, eds, *Sustainable Development Principles in the Decisions of International Courts and Tribunals* (2013).

3 Agenda 21, UN Doc. A/CONF.151/26 (1992), and the Rio Declaration on Environment and Development, UN Doc. A/CONF.151/26 (vol. I) (1992).

4 UN Doc. A/RES/S-19/2 (1997).

5 Johannesburg Declaration on Sustainable Development, UN Doc. A/CONF.199/20 (2002).

6 *The Future We Want*, UN Doc. A/RES/66/288 (2012).

7 See, e.g., the 2000 Cartagena Protocol on Biosafety to the Convention on Biological Diversity; the 2010 Nagoya-Kuala Lumpur Supplementary Protocol on Liability and Redress to the Cartagena Protocol on Biosafety; the 2010 Nagoya Protocol on Access to Genetic Resources and Fair and Equitable Sharing of Benefits Arising from the Utilisation to the Convention on Biological Diversity; and the 2001 Stockholm Convention on Persistent Organic Pollutants.

Warmest thanks to Audrey Mockle, CISDL Legal Researcher, and Katherine Lofts, CISDL Associate Fellow, for their excellent legal research, editing assistance, and substantive insights.

Yet, questions remain as to the contours of international law on sustainable development and how international law can foster, rather than frustrate, sustainable development. Of relevance to this volume, it remains to be better understood how international law on sustainable development can contribute to the realisation of criminal justice and also how international criminal law contributes to sustainable development. To address these questions, this chapter briefly outlines the contours of international law on sustainable development; it then considers how international criminal law can contribute to sustainable development and, conversely, how international treaties and principles for sustainable development seek to address conditions of lawlessness in which international crime becomes more likely. This chapter first explains the concept of sustainable development, demonstrating how international understanding of its meaning has evolved over time and characterizing sustainable development as a global objective – as a purpose of many international treaties that is supported by several key legal principles, such as precaution, intergenerational and intragenerational equity, and public participation. Then, the chapter argues that the severe degradation of natural resources, leading to the loss of social and ecological systems upon which people depend for survival, may make criminal behaviour both more likely and more difficult to prevent. As such, the chapter also briefly discusses how international treaties and the principles of international law on sustainable development may contribute to the achievement of a world with less crime. Finally, the chapter turns to a consideration of how international criminal law, particularly the Rome Statute, may support sustainable development. While recognising the rudimentary nature of current Rome Statute provisions to prevent the destruction of natural resources and to promote more sustainable development, the chapter briefly speculates that, in the future, these provisions might be expanded to include the recognition that deliberate acts that remove all possibility of sustainable development – compromising the very livelihoods and survival of future generations – could be considered internationally criminal.

## 2. MAKING DEVELOPMENT 'SUSTAINABLE'?

Sustainable development refers to state efforts to achieve progress (development) in a way that can be maintained over the long term ('sustainable'). The preamble to the 1986 *Declaration on the Right to Development* defines development as

> a comprehensive, economic, social and cultural process which aims at the constant improvement and well-being of the entire population and of all individuals on the basis of their active, free and meaningful participation in development and in the fair distribution of the benefits resulting therefrom.[8]

[8] UNGA Res 4/128 (4 December 1986) UN Doc A/Res/41/128/.

Development has come to be described as an iterative process that seeks to improve human conditions and find viable livelihoods for peoples in developing countries. In UNGA debates, many states have argued for a 'right to development'.[9]

Concerns about the sustainability of development patterns have gained currency and are influencing the positions of many countries.[10] Scientists are worried that if populations continue to increase and all human beings adopt the extraction, production, consumption, and pollution patterns common in most developed countries, humanity will quickly exceed the carrying capacity of the world's resources.[11] In short, there is a concern that current models of economic development are unsustainable, that they cannot be maintained, and that their benefits will not last over time. However, even though current development models may indeed be unsustainable, states are sovereign over their own natural resources and have been unwilling to accept too many international limits to the exploitation of these resources.[12] Given that developed countries achieved their present standard of living through exploitation of resources, developing countries have been understandably reluctant to refrain from adopting the same patterns. This problem led to a stalemate between developed and developing countries on issues of environment and development, one that was bridged by the concept of sustainable development. Essentially, it was agreed that countries would continue to develop their economies, but in a way that integrates environmental protection and social justice so that the benefits can last over the long term. In short, a more sustainable development.

In global policy debates, the concept of sustainable development was recognized relatively quickly. In 1972, the United Nations convened an international Conference on the Human Environment (UNCHE), which resulted in the *Stockholm Declaration on the Human Environment*,[13] the creation of the United Nations Environment

9 'Declaration on the Establishment of a New International Economic Order', UNGA Res 3201 (S-VI) (1 May 1974) UN Doc A/Res/3201(S-VI); see also 'Declaration on the Right to Development', UNGA Res 41/128 (4 December 1986) UN Doc A/Res/41/128.

10 See, e.g., Report of the United Nations Conference on Sustainable Development, UN Doc. A/CONF. 216/16 (2012); Report of the World Summit on Sustainable Development, UN Doc. A/CONF.199/20* (2002); UN General Assembly, Draft Decision on Open Working Group of the General Assembly on Sustainable Development, UN Doc. A/67/.L.48/Rev.1.

11 See, e.g., M. Wackernagel and W. E. Rees, *Our Ecological Footprint: Reducing Human Impact on the Earth* (1996); Millennium Ecosystem Assessment, *Ecosystems and Human Well-Being: Scenarios, Vol. II* (2005); and J. Rockström et al., 'Planetary Boundaries: Exploring the Safe Operating Space for Humanity', (2009) 14 *Ecology and Society* 32.

12 See, e.g., N. Schrijver, *Sovereignty over Natural Resources: Balancing Rights and Duties* (1997).

13 'Stockholm Declaration', UN Conference on the Human Environment (16 June 1972) UN Doc A/Conf 48/14/Rev. 1, 11 ILM 1461 (1972); for discussion, see, e.g., G. D. Meyers and S. C. Muller, 'The Ethical Implications, Political Ramifications and Practical Limitations of Adopting Sustainable Development as National and International Policy', (1996) 4 *Buffalo Environmental Law Journal* 1; see A. Geisinger, 'Sustainable Development and the Domination of Nature: Spreading the Seed of the Western Ideology of Nature', (1999) 27 *British Columbia Environmental Affairs Law Review* 43.

Programme (UNEP), and increased impetus to agree on certain multilateral environmental agreements (MEAs) such as the 1973 *Convention on International Trade in Endangered Species* (CITES).[14] The Stockholm Declaration recognises, in Principle 14, the need to reconcile conflicts 'between the needs of development and the need to protect and improve the environment'. However, key elements of the declaration also highlighted deep divides between developed and developing countries on a global environmental protection agenda.[15]

In 1983, responding to increasingly heated debates between developed and developing countries, the UN General Assembly established the World Commission on the Environment and Development (WCED), mandating it '[t]o propose long-term environmental strategies for achieving sustainable development to the year 2000 and beyond'.[16] In response, in 1987, the WCED, chaired by Prime Minister Gro Harlem Brundtland of Norway, delivered its report, *Our Common Future*,[17] to the UNGA. The most generally accepted definition of sustainable development is found in the Brundtland Report, where it is defined as 'development that meets the needs of the present without compromising the ability of future generations to meet their own needs'.[18] In Resolution 42/187, 'Report of the World Commission on Environment and Development', the UN member states noted the need for 'a reorientation of national and international policies towards sustainable development patterns' and emphasised 'the need for a new approach to economic growth, as an essential prerequisite for eradication of poverty and for enhancing the resource base on which present and future generations depend'.

In 1992, in response to the Brundtland Report, the UN convened a global conference in Rio de Janeiro – the United Nations Conference on Environment and Development (UNCED, or the Rio 'Earth Summit').[19] The 1992 Earth Summit contributed to global understanding of the concept of sustainable development, and led to several specific outcomes. These included the 1992 *Rio Declaration*, a short consensus declaration agreed by the heads of state assembled in Rio; the 1992 *Agenda 21*, which is annexed to the declaration and contains an extensive global action plan on specific environment and development issues; and three international treaties signed by a record number of countries: the 1992 *United Nations Framework Convention on Climate Change*,[20] the 1992 *United Nations Convention on Biological*

[14] Convention on International Trade in Endangered Species of Wild Fauna and Flora (adopted 3 March 1973, entered into force 1 July 1975) 993 U.N.T.S 243, 12 I.L.M. 1085.

[15] Stockholm Declaration, *supra* note 13, at 11, 23.

[16] 'Process of Preparation of the Environmental Perspective to the Year 2000 and Beyond, Meeting no. 102', UNGA Res. 38/161 (19 December 1983) UN Doc A/RES/38/161.

[17] World Commission on Environment and Development, *Our Common Future* (1987), ix.

[18] *Ibid.*, at 43.

[19] A. Kiss and D. Shelton, *International Environmental Law* (1994), 67.

[20] United Nations Framework Convention on Climate Change (opened for signature 4 June 1992, entered into force 21 March 1994) 1771 UNTS 107, 31 ILM 849.

*Diversity*,[21] and the 1994 *United Nations Convention to Combat Desertification*.[22] The 1992 Rio Declaration,[23] a short document of 27 principles, affirms the focus on human development that is central to the concept of sustainable development and lays out a series of 'principles' that can help achieve sustainable development. Agenda 21, which was negotiated by the states engaged in the UNCED process, complements the Rio Declaration by providing an 800-page 'blueprint' for sustainable development. This 'blueprint' had two purposes. First, it contained plans to halt and reverse the effects of environmental degradation, and second, it sought to promote sustainable development in all countries.[24] To meet these goals, Agenda 21 noted the need for international action to codify and develop 'international law on sustainable development'.[25] However, most of the details on sustainable development goals and standards, as well as commitments meant to achieve this objective, remained to be worked out through the three treaties signed at the UNCED and the new institutions recommended at the conference. The global treaties signed at the UNCED became one of the principal arenas in which new standards, rules, and regimes helped clarify the content of a commitment to sustainable development. Yet, there was very little mention of international crime in Agenda 21, simply glancing references to compatibility with international obligations,[26] the eradication of corruption,[27] and the removal of sources of distortion in trade and investment.[28]

Two important follow-up mechanisms were recommended by the Brundtland Report and Agenda 21: a Global Environment Facility (GEF), hosted by the World Bank, the UNEP, and the UNDP (as implementing agencies), and a United Nations Commission for Sustainable Development (UNCSD) that first convened on 25 November 1992.[29] Meeting on a yearly basis since then, the UNCSD has reviewed implementation of the Agenda 21 blueprint at national, regional, and international

[21] United Nations Convention on Biological Diversity (opened for signature 5 June 1992, entered into force 29 December 1) 1760 UNTS 79, 143; 31 ILM 1004.

[22] United Nations Convention to Combat Desertification in those Countries Experiencing Serious Drought and/or Desertification, Particularly in Africa (opened for signature 14 October 1994, entered into force 16 December 1996) 1954 UNTS 3, 33 ILM 1328.

[23] 'Rio Declaration on Environment and Development (Annex 2)', Report of the UN Conference on Environment and Development Vol. I (13 June 1992) UN Doc A/CONF.151/26 (Vol. I), (1992) 31 ILM 874; 'Agenda 21 (Annex 2)', in Report of the UN Conference on Environment and Development Vol. I (13 June 1992) UN Doc A/CONF.151/26 (Vol. I).

[24] N. A. Robinson, ed., 'Agenda 21: Earth's Action Plan', IUCN Environmental Policy & Law Paper No. 27 (1993).

[25] See in particular, *Agenda 21, supra* note 3 at paras 39.1–39.10.

[26] 'Agenda 21 (Annex 2)', in Report of the UN Conference on Environment and Development Vol. I (13 June 1992) UN Doc A/CONF.151/26 (Vol. I), at Art 2.22(c).

[27] *Ibid.*, at Arts 2.33 and 2.38(b).

[28] *Ibid.*, at Art 2.35.

[29] M McCoy & P McCully, *The Road From Rio: An NGO Action Guide to Environment and Development* (1993) at 45; Robinson, *supra* note 24, at 655.

levels.[30] The UNCSD mandate is broad,[31] but it has not touched a great deal on matters of criminal law. In 1997, a Special Session of the UN General Assembly, the 'Earth Summit+5', was held in New York to review progress toward the objectives set in Rio. The resulting declaration, the *Programme of Further Action to Implement Agenda 21*, called on governments, international organizations, and major groups to renew their commitment to sustainable development and emphasised that economic development, social development, and environmental protection are three interdependent and mutually reinforcing 'pillars' of sustainable development.[32] It also noted, in terms of international law, that progress has been made implementing UNCED commitments through a variety of international legal instruments,[33] emphasising that implementation of and compliance with commitments made under international treaties and other instruments on sustainable development remain a priority.[34] Again, however, UN General Assembly sessions have not specifically focused on criminal law or the role that international courts and tribunals may play in resolving sustainable development disputes.

In 2002, the World Summit on Sustainable Development (WSSD) brought together an estimated 45,000 participants in Johannesburg, South Africa. The United Nations objectives for the summit were to review the achievements of the 1992 UN Conference on Environment and Development (UNCED) and reinvigorate the global commitment to sustainable development.[35] States focused on how best to *implement* sustainable development in a context of globalisation and renewed their commitments to international development assistance. Outcomes included the 2002 *Johannesburg Declaration* and the *Johannesburg Plan of Implementation*. The Johannesburg Declaration provides a political commitment to sustainable development from heads of state.[36] The 2002 Johannesburg Plan of Implementation (JPOI) was designed as a framework for action to implement the commitments originally agreed at UNCED and to address a few additional challenges that had arisen since 1992. It is more streamlined than Agenda 21, with 11 chapters covering poverty eradication, consumption and production, the natural resource base, health, small island developing states (SIDS), Africa, other regional initiatives, means of implementation, and the

[30] *Ibid.*

[31] See 'Establishment of the Commission on Sustainable Development', UNESC Res 1993/207 (12 February 1993) UN Doc E/1993/207; 'Institutional Arrangements to Follow up the United Nations Conference on Environment and Development', UNGA Res 47/191 (29 January 1993) UN Doc A/RES/47/191 [3]–[5], Mccoy & Mccully, *supra* note 29 at 45.

[32] 'Programme for the Further Implementation of Agenda 21', UNGA Res S-19/2 (19 September 1997) UN Doc A/Res/S-19/2.

[33] *Ibid.*, at Art. 14.

[34] *Ibid.*, at Art. 110.

[35] In December 2000, the UN General Assembly decided to convene a 10-year review of progress since UNCED (A/RES/55/199). See 'Ten-Year Review of Progress Achieved in the Implementation of the Outcome of the United Nations Conference on Environment and Development', UNGA Res 55/199 (20 December 2000) UN Doc A/RES/55/199.

[36] Johannesburg Declaration, *supra* note 5.

institutional framework for sustainable development (governance). The JPOI contains more than 30 specific time-bound targets for action (including reaffirmations of targets agreed in the *Millennium Development Goals* and other instruments).[37] It focuses attention on priorities identified by the UN secretary-general in the areas of water and sanitation, energy, health, agriculture, and biodiversity (the so-called WEHAB issues).

Although the 2002 JPOI does not highlight international law or international criminal justice, heads of state did agree that a firm commitment ought to be made to the 'ideals of the United Nations, the principles of international law and those enshrined in the Charter of the United Nations, as well as to strengthening the United Nations system and other multilateral institutions and promoting the improvement of their operations'.[38] Specific reference was made to the prevention of child labour,[39] international terrorism,[40] and corruption.[41]

In contrast to the 1992 Rio Earth Summit, the 2002 Johannesburg WSSD was not a forum for the adoption of new treaties on sustainable development; many regional and multilateral treaties to encourage sustainable development of different resources had been negotiated over the intervening decade.[42] Indeed, the JPOI

37 The other significant commitments from the meeting include using and producing chemicals in ways that do not harm human health and the environment, reducing biodiversity loss by 2010, restoring fisheries to their maximum sustainable yields by 2015, establishing a representative network of marine protected areas by 2012, improving developing countries' access to environmentally sound alternatives to ozone-depleting chemicals by 2010, and undertaking initiatives by 2004 to implement the Global Programme of Action for the Protection of the Marine Environment from Land Based Sources.

38 *Report of the World Summit on Sustainable Development*, WWSDOR, 2002, UN Doc A/CONF.199/20, at Art. 142.

39 *Ibid.*, at Art. 12.

40 *Ibid.*, at Art. 115.

41 *Ibid.*, at Arts. 140(e) and 142.

42 *Convention on the Protection and Use of Transboundary Watercourses and International Lakes*, 17 March 1992, 1396 UNTS 269; *Convention on the Transboundary Effects of Industrial Accidents*, 17 March 1992, 2015 UNTS 457; *Convention on the Protection of the Marine Environment of the Baltic Sea Area*, 9 April 1992, 1772 UNTS 218 [*Helsinki Convention*]; *Convention on the Protection of the Black Sea against Pollution*, 21 April 1992, *Law of the Sea Bulletin* No 22 (January 1993), p 31; *United Nations Framework Convention on Climate Change*, 9 May 1992, 1771 UNTS 107; *Convention on Biological Diversity*, 5 June 1992, 1760 UNTS 79; *Convention for the Protection of the Marine Environment of the North-East Atlantic*, 22 September 1992, 2354 UNTS No 1-42279; *Agreement for the Implementation of the Provisions of the United Nations Convention on the Law of the Sea of 10 December 1982 Relating to the Conservation and Management of Straddling Fish Stocks and Highly Migratory Fish Stocks*, 4 August 1995, 2167 UNTS 3; *United Nations Convention to Combat Desertification in Those Countries Experiencing Serious Drought and/or Desertification, Particularly in Africa*, 14 October 1994, 1954 UNTS 31; *Convention to Ban the Importation into Forum Island Countries of Hazardous and Radioactive Wastes and to Control the Transboundary Movement and Management of Hazardous Wastes within the South Pacific Region*, 16 September 1995, [2001] ATS 17 [Waigani Convention]; *International Convention on Liability and Compensation for Damage in Connection with the Carriage of Hazardous and Noxious Substances by Sea*, 3 May 1996, [1996] PITSE 9; *Protocol to Amend the International Convention on Civil Liability for Oil Pollution Damage*, 30 May 1996, 973 UNTS 3; *Kyoto Protocol to the United Nations Framework Convention on Climate Change*, 11 December 1997, 2303 UNTS 148; *Convention on Access to Information, Public Participation in Decision-Making and Access*

highlights more than 60 existing economic, environmental, and social instruments playing a role in achieving sustainable development and mentions more than 200 others.[43] The 2002 JPOI also strengthens international recognition of certain key principles of international law on sustainable development, including the principles of common but differentiated responsibility, precaution, openness, transparency, and public participation;[44] it emphasises international instruments and techniques to put these principles into practice. At the insistence of the South African and other governments, the summit also shifted the focus of sustainable development towards a more integrated social agenda, one that balances the environmental, social, and economic pillars of sustainable development and focuses on strategies to address poverty eradication, sanitation, and health, not just environmental protection and development.

The 2012 UN Conference on Sustainable Development (UNCSD) sought to highlight the shift from planning to implementation, from state-centred strategies to participation, and from isolated, territorial decision making to integration. It also sought broad policy agreement on several key themes, including how to achieve a global 'green economy' and how to better implement sustainable development through improved governance systems. It was moderately successful. The 2012 Rio Declaration, titled *The Future We Want*, provides a diverse agenda and is accompanied by partnership actions valued at US$211 billion to be taken by states, international organizations, civil society, and others.[45] Although *The Future We Want* does not explicitly refer to criminal law or criminal justice, it clearly recognises the importance of the rule of law, the contributions of judicial and other institutions, and the need for accountability and innovative legal measures. Further, the *Rio+20 Declaration on Justice, Governance and Law for Environmental Sustainability* emphasises the importance of accessible and impartial dispute resolution mechanisms in achieving the objectives of sustainable development.[46]

*to Justice in Environmental Matters*, 25 June 1998, 2161 UNTS 447 [*Aarhus Convention*]; *Rotterdam Convention on the Prior Informed Consent Procedure for Certain Hazardous Chemicals and Pesticides in International Trade*, 10 September 1998, 2244 UNTS 337; *Cartagena Protocol on Biosafety to the Convention on Biological Diversity*, 29 January 2000, 2226 UNTS 208; *2000 Protocol on Preparedness, Response and Co-operation to Pollution Incidents by Hazardous and Noxious Substances*, 14 March 2000, [2007] ATS 41; *European Agreement concerning the International Carriage of Dangerous Goods by Inland Waterways (ADN)*, 26 May 2000, ECE/TRANS/220 1; *Stockholm Convention on Persistent Organic Pollutants*, 22 May 2001, 2256 UNTS 119.

43 Cordonier Segger and Khalfan, *supra* note 1.

44 M. C. Cordonier Segger et al., 'Prospects for Principles of International Sustainable Development Law after the WSSD: Common but Differentiated Responsibilities, Precaution and Participation', (2003) 12 (1) *Review of European Community and International Environmental Law* 54.

45 *The Future We Want*, *supra* note 6; 'Partnership for Sustainable Communities,' http://futurewewant.org/2012/partnership-for-sustainable-communities/.

46 World Congress on Justice, Governance and Law for Environmental Sustainability, *Rio+20 Declaration on Justice, Governance and Law for Environmental Sustainability* (2012), www.unep.org/rio20/Portals/24180/Rio20_Declaration_on_Justice_Gov_n_Law_4_Env_Sustainability.pdf (accessed 24 January 2012).

In sum, over the past 30 years there has been an extensive policy-making process related to sustainable development, engaging nearly all member states of the United Nations. The United Nations sought a bridge between developed and developing countries to resolve serious problems of environmental degradation and the lack of social and economic development. The concept of sustainable development provided that bridge. However, states neither agreed on one single accepted definition nor on criteria for sustainable development applicable to issue areas. Rather, they focused on developing greater global consensus on how to achieve sustainable development in different spheres of law and policy – signing and ratifying international treaties where necessary – leading to the emergence of international law on sustainable development. However, the policy debates guiding this international law on sustainable development have, to this day, not yet fully engaged with or incorporated the field of international criminal law. Much remains to be done.

## 3. SUSTAINABLE DEVELOPMENT IN INTERNATIONAL LAW: RECONCEPTUALISING THE DEBATE

The most accepted short description of sustainable development continues to be the one given in the Brundtland Report and subsequently adopted by the UN General Assembly: 'meeting the needs of the present without compromising the ability of future generations to meet their own needs'. This vague statement has not been particularly helpful in determining the exact parameters of an international treaty commitment to sustainable development or the precise normative content of sustainable development in international law.

However, one international accord does provide an agreed definition of sustainable development: the 2002 *Convention for Cooperation in the Protection and Sustainable Development of the Marine and Coastal Environment of the Northeast Pacific*. At Article 3(1)(a), states agree that

> sustainable development means the process of progressive change in the quality of life of human beings, which places them as the centre and primary subjects of development, by means of economic growth with social equity and transformation of production methods and consumption patterns, sustained by the ecological balance and life support systems of the region. This process implies respect for regional, national and local ethnic and cultural diversity, and full public participation, peaceful coexistence in harmony with nature, without prejudice to and ensuring the quality of life of future generations.[47]

This definition emphasises certain aspects of the concept of sustainable development that have been recognised by states in the global policy-making process. First, it

[47] Convention for Cooperation in the Protection and Sustainable Development of the Marine and Coastal Environment of the Northeast Pacific (18 February 2002), http://dinrac.nowpap.org/3-sea-north-west-pacific-convt.htm (accessed 1 January 2008).

focuses on sustainable development as human-centred, in that it involves finding new ways to improve the quality of life for people. Second, it focuses on the need to reconcile and integrate environmental protection and social development with economic development. Third, it notes that development that is sustainable should be able to last over the long term, though the environmental limits of ecosystems and resources are dynamic and the relevant time horizon depends on the resource and ecosystem in question. However, given the limited membership in this convention, this statement is scarcely a universally recognised or agreed definition, nor does it make clear the normative consequences of the commitment.

In the global summits and other processes summarised earlier, there have been repeated calls for better law and policy to integrate complementary objectives of environmental protection and socioeconomic development. For these calls to take best effect, it is important to understand the legal status of existing commitments to sustainable development. How can we characterise a commitment to sustainable development in international law? At least three views currently provide different pictures of the status of sustainable development in international law, each with different normative consequences.

First, some states and nongovernmental organizations have argued that sustainable development is a new customary principle of international law, one that is in the process of being established as binding upon all but a few persistently objecting states.[48] If sustainable development were a principle of international law (recognised in treaty and emerging as customary law), it seems most likely that its fundamentally normative character would be a requirement for the integration of environment and socioeconomic development, in which states take environmental protection into account in the development process, and vice versa.[49] A slightly more optimistic view would be that, in building on this commitment to the integration of environment, social, and economic priorities in the development process, states are also beginning to recognise a right to promote sustainable development, implying a related duty not to interfere unduly with each others' efforts to do so.[50] To support this contention, there is clearly a great deal of general state practice, and the weight of *opinio juris* appears to support the proposal that *certain* states engage in the promotion of sustainable development because they feel bound by a principle of sustainable development. However, there is a lingering lack of clarity as to whether *most* states undertake such a commitment due to a sense of legal obligation or simply due to a common commitment to a noble political goal. Essentially, it is not clear that a principle of sustainable development has emerged in international customary law as yet.

48 D. Hunter, D. Zaelke, and J. Salzman, *International Environmental Law and Policy* (2001); Kiss and Shelton, *supra* note 19; Philippe Sands, *Principles of International Environmental Law* (2003).

49 See, e.g., *Case Concerning Pulp Mills on the River Uruguay* (Argentina v. Uruguay) ICJ Judgement of 20 April 2010, at paras. 175 and 177 [Pulp Mills].

50 *Ibid.*

Second, others note that international law on sustainable development has mainly emerged in international treaties and accords.[51] Sustainable development is a common purpose of many states when they sign international environmental, economic, and other treaties. In some cases, such as recent treaties related to energy, desertification, or food and agriculture, it might even be seen as a primary objective of the international agreements.[52] Viewed in this light, sustainable development is a purpose of many hard law or binding treaties rather than a single customary principle in itself. In the context of many multilateral and bilateral treaties, states have committed themselves to a policy objective of sustainable development. Sustainable development was once a marginalised 'second objective' of many environmental and economic treaties, but it is gaining prominence as these regimes develop and evolve. Several social and human rights treaties, inasmuch as they address development issues, are also incorporating a sustainable development objective. As the object and purpose of international treaty law, sustainable development will be taken into account and will shape the interpretation of the treaty rules and beyond.

Third, even if sustainable development were mainly an objective rather than a principle of international law, its invocation by states may still engage a certain interstitial normativity, helping push or pull other principles into play and encouraging states to use certain legal or institutional mechanisms to secure progress towards sustainable development as a policy objective.[53] Sustainable development, as presently applied in treaty negotiations or dispute settlements, has been described by Vaughan Lowe as a 'meta-principle', one that acts 'upon other legal rules and principles – a legal concept exercising a kind of interstitial normativity, pushing and pulling the boundaries of true primary norms when they threaten to overlap or conflict with each other'.[54] From this viewpoint, the substantive aspect of the 'interstitial norm' is the requirement that economic development decision making take social and environmental concerns into account (and vice versa). All three sets of priorities need to be reflected in the substantive outcomes of a given dispute or conflict, even when doing so means extra costs for the proponent of a project,[55] and there must be respect for a right to continue a development project once these issues have been taken into consideration.[56]

51 Cordonier Segger and Khalfan, *supra* note 1.

52 *Ibid*. See also H. G. Ruse-Khan, 'A Real Partnership for Development? Sustainable Development as Treaty Objective in European Economic Partnership Agreements and Beyond', (2010) 13(1) *Journal of International Economic Law* 139–80.

53 V. Lowe, 'Sustainable Development and Unsustainable Arguments', in A. Boyle and D. Freestone (eds.), *International Law and Sustainable Development: Past Achievements and Future Challenges* (1999), 27; he references further, A. D'Amato, 'Agora: What Obligation Does Our Generation Owe to the Next? An Approach to Global Environmental Responsibility', (1990) 84 AJIL 190.

54 Lowe, *supra* note 54, at 31.

55 See Arbitration regarding the Iron Rhine ('Ijzeren Rijn') Railway between The Kingdom of Belgium and the Kingdom of the Netherlands, Award of 24 May 2005, *UNRIAA* XXVII 35.

56 See Pulp Mills, *supra* note 50.

Taking this interstitial character into account, evocation of the sustainable development 'policy objective' might therefore imply further normative consequences. In particular, although the question of sustainable development itself as a customary legal norm or an object/purpose of treaty law may not yet be resolved, it is clear that there exists a growing body of international law on sustainable development. As such, 'international law on sustainable development' today can also be used to describe a 'group of congruent norms',[57] a corpus of international legal principles and treaties that aim to promote sustainable development, often in the areas of intersection between international economic law, international environmental law, and international human rights law. Certain procedural and substantive norms and instruments, which help balance or integrate these fields, form part of this body of international law and play a role in its implementation.

In its interstitial character, sustainable development may push or pull states to use and apply certain international mechanisms and practices, guiding the future development and implementation of this body of international law. When states adopt sustainable development as a policy objective, this can bring further international legal norms into play to realise this interstitial purpose. As Lowe observes, there is 'an immense gravitational pull exerted by concepts such as sustainable development, regardless of their standing as rules or principles of *lex lata*. That is plain when they are used by judges as modifiers; but it is also true when they are used in the same way by states as they negotiate (either with other states, or within their own governmental apparatus) on ways of reconciling conflicting principles'.[58] Just as the prohibition on armed attack serves to maintain world peace, and a prohibition on trade in endangered species serves to conserve nature, so might a prohibition on exhaustion of a transboundary natural resource without good faith consultation with affected states serve to promote sustainable development.

Certain principles that aim to contribute to and achieve sustainable development *as an objective* may come to be used so often, and to be accepted so generally, that they do indeed gain recognition as customary international rules themselves, binding on all states that have not persistently objected.[59] The ILA *Declaration*

57 Lowe, *supra* note 54, at 26.

58 *Ibid.*, at 35.

59 In the 1972 Stockholm Declaration, the 1987 Brundtland Commission's Legal Experts Group on Principles of International Law for the Protection of the Environment and Sustainable Development, the 1992 Rio Declaration, the 2002 World Summit on Sustainable Development Johannesburg Plan of Implementation, several international experts reports, and other processes, states and legal scholars have sought to identify principles of international law related to sustainable development. In 2002, the International Law Association's Committee on the Legal Aspects of Sustainable Development released its New Delhi ILA *Declaration on Principles of International Law Relating to Sustainable Development* as a Resolution of the 70th Conference of the International Law Association in New Delhi India, 2–6 April 2002. See 'ILA New Delhi Declaration of Principles of International Law Relating to Sustainable Development', (2002) 2 *International Environmental Agreements* 209; N. Schrijver and F. Weiss, 'Editorial Introduction', (2002) 2 *International Environmental Agreements* 105; see also International Law Association, *Report of the Expert Group on Identification of Principles of*

*on Principles of International Law Relating to Sustainable Development* thus notes that 'sustainable development is now widely accepted as a global objective and that the concept has been amply recognized in various international and national legal instruments, including treaty law and jurisprudence at international and national levels'. It outlines seven principles of international law on sustainable development.[60]

Given the comprehensive and balanced decade of study and analysis conducted by the ILA committee and the relative normative clarity of its findings, the 2002 New Delhi Declaration provides the most current benchmark of the important principles of international law on sustainable development.[61] First, it recognises a duty of states to ensure the sustainable use of natural resources whereby states have sovereign rights over their natural resources, and a duty not to cause (or allow) undue damage to the environment of other states in the use of these resources. Second, it recognises a principle of equity and the eradication of poverty. Third, it recognises a principle of common but differentiated obligations. Fourth, it recognises a principle of the precautionary approach to human health, natural resources, and ecosystems. Fifth, it underlines the principle of public participation and access to information and justice. Sixth, the ILA New Delhi Declaration posits a principle of good governance. Seventh, and perhaps most telling, it recognises a principle of integration and interrelationship, in particular in relation to human rights and social, economic. and environmental objectives. This last may indeed be simply another more accurate name for the norm discussed earlier as a 'principle of sustainable development'.

As such, several rather functional principles guide the main international treaties on sustainable development and are gaining recognition by states. This list is not exhaustive, and not all principles have yet been recognised as binding rules of customary international law. In some cases, they might never be. However, they are increasingly being made operational in binding international treaties, forming part of international law and policy in the field of sustainable development.

In summary, it is not clear that sustainable development has yet been accepted as a binding customary norm in international law. However, as noted by Boyle and Freestone, '[e]ven if there is no legal obligation to develop sustainably, there

*International Law for Sustainable Development* (1995); International Law Association, *Report of the Sixty-Second Conference* (1987) 1–11, 409–87.

60 N. Schrijver and F. Weiss, *International Law and Sustainable Development: Principles and Practice* (2004), 1–152, 699–706; Cordonier Segger and Khalfan, *supra* note 1, at 95– 191; D. French, *International Law and Policy of Sustainable Development* (2005); See also 7 CISDL Legal Working Papers detailing the meaning, scope, and existing status in international law of each proposed ILA New Delhi Declaration Principle, www.cisdl.org/projects001.html.

61 M. C. Cordonier Segger, 'Significant Developments in Sustainable Development Law and Governance: A Proposal', (2004) 28 *Natural Resources Forum* 61; Cordonier Segger et al., *supra* note 45, at 54.

may nevertheless be, through incremental development, law "in the field of sustainable development"'.[62] A growing body of international treaty law on sustainable development is being implemented by states, and when they commit to sustainable development in a treaty or international legal process, their commitment is not legally meaningless. It involves an obligation to seek a balance between sometimes conflicting economic, environmental, and social priorities in the development process, in the interests of future generations. The balance can be achieved through procedures and substantive obligations that differ depending on the treaty instrument and the area of law and policy that is regulated. Furthermore, the normative consequences of a commitment to sustainable development may not be the same as a straightforward prohibition or prescription. However, if one adopts a more complex view of international law as part of a series of interactional regimes, a legal commitment to sustainable development has interstitial meaning and normative force both in international treaties and in soft law co-operation arrangements. This interstitial normative character may well encourage states to adopt and implement sustainable-development-related principles and measures, both inside existing treaty regimes and even beyond.

## 4. CONTRIBUTION OF INTERNATIONAL LAW ON SUSTAINABLE DEVELOPMENT TO THE REDUCTION OF CRIME

The characterisation of sustainable development as an objective of international treaties has a direct bearing on the rest of this chapter, which focuses on how international law on sustainable development can contribute to criminal justice and, in the end, perhaps even to a world with less crime. It is beyond the scope of this chapter to fully develop these arguments; indeed many other chapters in this book provide interesting insights on this question. Here, it is perhaps enough to suggest that, although further research is still needed, it is possible that severe degradation of the natural resources, leading to the loss of the social and ecological systems upon which people depend for survival, may make criminal behaviour both more likely and more difficult to prevent. In certain contexts, at least, the existence of international treaties on sustainable development and the principles of international law on sustainable development may contribute to co-operation between states aimed at reducing such circumstances. This may, in turn, support the work of those who strive for a world with less crime. By way of illustration, three examples are briefly discussed.

First, the UN Framework Convention on Climate Change was established in 1992 to prevent dangerous anthropogenic interference with the levels of greenhouse

[62] A. Boyle and D. Freestone (eds.), *International Law and Sustainable Development: Past Achievements and Future Challenges* (1999), at 17, citing P. Sands, 'International Law in the Field of Sustainable Development'.

gases (GHGs) in the atmosphere. As mentioned earlier, the UNFCCC commits to sustainable development as both an objective and a right, and it operationalises this commitment in the provisions encouraging renewable energy technologies and establishing a clean development mechanism, among other measures. Parties to the UNFCCC commit to the adoption of domestic policies and measures to mitigate climate change by limiting anthropogenic emissions of GHGs and protecting GHG sinks and reservoirs.[63] Additionally, parties routinely publish national inventories of anthropogenic emissions and promote the development and diffusion of technologies that reduce or prevent GHG emissions.[64] They also commit to the sustainable management of GHG sinks and reservoirs and to the adoption of strategies for adapting to the impacts of climate change, such as the development of plans for coastal management, water resources, agriculture, and the protection of areas affected by drought and floods.[65] The UNFCCC also sets out differentiated duties for developed country parties and establishes a Conference of the Parties (COP) for the purpose of regularly reviewing the implementation of the UNFCCC and its related instruments. As part of the first COP in 1998, the Kyoto Protocol to the UNFCCC was drafted; parties to it committed to set reductions in GHG emissions.[66]

Although the prevention of crime is not directly incorporated into the provisions of the UNFCCC or the Kyoto Protocol, their objectives and mechanisms indirectly reduce the potential for severe conditions that might drive people to crime. By negatively affecting access to and the quality of natural resources vital to human well-being, climate change undermines security and reduces social control and state capacity, thereby increasing the risk of crime, societal crisis, and violent conflict.[67] To better understand these linkages, without entering into fallacies of causation, further research is needed, likely combining observations from legal, geography and ecology, economics, human security, and other disciplines. For present purposes, it is enough to simply observe that the UNFCCC and its regime seek to address a very pressing global challenge that, if ignored, could lead to very difficult conditions for many deeply threatened coastal and other regions of the world, with attendant consequences in terms of human suffering and potentially increases in crime.

Second, the UN Convention to Combat Desertification and Drought, Especially in Africa was agreed in 1994 to encourage states to develop co-operative action

63 UNFCC, *supra* note 20, at Art 4.1(f).

64 *Ibid.*, at Art. 4.1(b)(c)(g)(h).

65 *Ibid.*, at Art. 4.1(d)(e).

66 *Kyoto Protocol* , *supra* note 43.

67 J. Barnett and W. N. Adger, 'Climate Change, Human Security and Violent Conflict', (2007) 26 *Political Geography* 639; R. Agnew, 'Dire Forecast: A Theoretical Model of the Impact of Climate Change on Crime', (2012) 16 *Theoretical Criminology* 1; C. Raleigh and H. Urdal, 'Climate Change, Environmental Degradation and Armed Conflict' (2007) 26 *Political Geography* 674; A. Y. Chan, 'Mitigating Pollution May Help Prevent Violent Conflicts', (2012) 102 *Current Science* 960, at 960.

plans to prevent and address desertification and drought, including through the restoration of degraded areas. As mentioned earlier, the UNCCD commits to sustainable development as an objective and a principle; it operationalises this commitment through the adoption of integrated social, environmental, and economic development approaches that are intended to 'contribute to the achievement of sustainable development' in particular areas and, through the adoption of integrated regional and national strategies that focus on 'sustainable management of land and water resources', lead to 'improved living conditions'. Parties to the UNCCD create National Action Programs (NAP) intended as long-term strategies to prevent desertification and drought.[68] Included among the measures undertaken in NAPs are early warning systems, mechanisms for assisting environmentally displaced persons, drought contingency plans, food security systems, alternative livelihood projects, and the development of sustainable irrigation programs for crops and livestock.[69] Furthermore, parties agree to collaborate in the areas of information collection, research and development, adaptation of technology, capacity building, and education.[70] The UNCCD also commits parties to make every effort to ensure the availability of adequate financial resources for NAPs, particularly for African and other developing countries.[71] The UNCCD establishes a Conference of the Parties that oversees and regularly reviews its implementation.[72] Additionally, Regional Implementation Annexes delineate specific commitments, planning frameworks, and financial mechanisms for different regions.[73]

Though it makes no explicit reference to the prevention of crime, the UNCCD directs parties to pay special attention to the socioeconomic factors contributing to the desertification process.[74] Desertification leads to a vicious cycle of ecological degradation, decreased food production, and widespread poverty that causes mass displacement and conflict,[75] which in turn increase the incidence of criminal activity.[76] Additionally, the UNCCD suggests that NAPs ought to include measures aimed at the eradication of poverty, at capacity building, and at the strengthening of institutional and legal frameworks, among others.[77] Further analysis of the linkages

68 UNCCD, *supra* note 22.

69 *Ibid.*, at Art. 10(3).

70 *Ibid.*, at Arts. 16–19.

71 *Ibid.*, at Arts. 20–21.

72 *Ibid.*, at Art. 22.

73 *Ibid.*, at Annex I–V.

74 *Ibid.*, at Art. 5(c).

75 A. Rechkemmer, 'Societal Impacts of Desertification: Migration and Environmental Refugees?', in H. G. Brauch et al. (eds.), *Facing Global Environmental Change: Environmental, Human, Energy, Food, Health and Water Security Concepts* (2009), 151, at 154.

76 A. A. G. Babiker, 'Urbanization and Desertification in the Sudan with Special Reference to Khartoum', (1982) 6 *GeoJournal* 69, at 70; Rechkemmer, *supra* note 76, 151 at 154; A. A. Yousef and A. El-Monem Hegazi, 'Security Impacts of Desertification in Egypt', in W. G. Kepner et al. (eds.), *Desertification in the Mediterranean Region: A Security Issue* (2006), 187, at 199.

77 UNCCD, *supra* note 22, at Art. 9(4).

between desertification and crime is necessary, likely combining observations from many disciplines. At this point, there is preliminary evidence suggesting that the UNCCD and its regime address a very pressing global challenge that, if left without remedy, could lead to very difficult conditions for many already vulnerable and marginalized populations, with attendant consequences in terms of human suffering and potentially increases in crime.

Third, several regional fisheries conventions, under the UN Convention on Law of the Seas and its Agreement on Straddling Fish Stocks, have been signed to encourage states to develop co-operative action plans to prevent and address the unsustainable exploitation of key fish stocks upon which many fishing communities depend for their livelihoods. Several of these treaties commit to sustainable development of particular fisheries as an objective and establish mechanisms for scientific co-operation and binding regimes to jointly manage the resources, preventing their collapse. For example, the *Agreement on Fisheries between the European Economic Community and the Kingdom of Norway*[78] is based on a common desire of both parties to 'ensure the conservation and rational management of fish stocks of the waters adjacent to their coasts'.[79] To that end, the agreement holds that each party will determine the total allowable catch for particular stocks and allotments for each other's fishing vessels, according to a mutually satisfactory balance.[80] Furthermore, each party commits to establish measures deemed to be required for the conservation, rational management, and regulation of fisheries while taking into account the need not to jeopardise the possibilities for fishing allowed to vessels of the other party.[81]

Agreements of this kind constitute an effective measure to curb the illegal, unreported, and unregulated (IUU) fishing that frustrates efforts to achieve long-term sustainability in fisheries.[82] IUU fishing activity has ties to organized national and international crime and is now considered by some to be an environmental crime itself.[83] In recent years, Somali pirates have attempted to justify their criminal activity by arguing that they act to protect their coastline from illegitimate fishing by

78 *Agreement on Fisheries between the European Economic Community and the Kingdom of Norway*, 29 August 1980, Official Journal L 226, 29/08/1980 P. 0048-0050.

79 *Ibid.*

80 *Ibid.*, at Art. 2(1)(a)(b).

81 *Ibid.*, at Art. 2(2).

82 K. L. Cochrane and D. J. Doulman, 'The Rising Tide of Fisheries Instruments and the Struggle to Keep Afloat', (2005) 360 *Philosophical Transactions: Biological Sciences* 77, at 83; E. J. Molenaar, 'Participation, Allocation and Unregulated Fishing: The Practice of Regional Fisheries Management Organisations' (2003) 18 *International Journal of Maritime and Coastal Law* 458, at 480; C.-C. Schmidt, 'Economic Drivers of Illegal, Unreported and Unregulated (IUU) Fishing', (2005) 20 *International Journal of Maritime and Coastal Law* 479, at 494.

83 Cochrane and Doulman, *supra* note 83, at 83, D. J. Agnew & C. T. Barnes, 'Economic Aspects and Drivers of IUU Fishing: Building a Framework', in Organization for Economic Co-operation and Development (ed.), *Fish Piracy: Combating Illegal, Unreported and Unregulated Fishing* (2004), 169, at 195.

foreigners.[84] The increase of transnational criminal activity at sea calls for a strengthening of existing regional agreements and the enactment of new ones.[85] In this field, preliminary surveys of legal scholarship and practice do suggest that the transboundary management of natural resources such as fisheries is key for sustainable development; in addition, unsustainable management can lead to very difficult conditions for many precarious and vulnerable communities, with attendant consequences for livelihoods and potential increases in criminal activity, such as illegal fishing or piracy.

This chapter does not argue that sustainable development laws are directly preventing crime in the world today. After all, it is not even clear whether criminal laws deter the commission of crimes in all circumstances.[86] However, by preventing extreme degradation of natural resources due to pressing global challenges such as climate change, desertification, or the collapse of fishing stocks, which can have a disproportionate impact upon marginalised groups with little to lose, international treaties on sustainable development may contribute to human security, reducing the potential for conditions in which crime is perhaps more likely.

## 5. CONTRIBUTION OF INTERNATIONAL CRIMINAL LAW TO SUSTAINABLE DEVELOPMENT

Last, it is important also to consider how international criminal law, particularly the Rome Statute, may support sustainable development. Current Rome Statute provisions to prevent the destruction of natural resources and promote more sustainable development may be somewhat rudimentary.[87] For example, the definition of war crimes includes provisions relating to 'widespread, long-term and severe damage to the natural environment',[88] the right of a state's citizens to benefit from the exploitation of natural resources and any resulting national development,[89] and the right to food and water;[90] however, these provisions only apply in situations of international

84 C. Bueger, J. Stockbruegger, and S. Werthes, 'Pirates, Fishermen and Peacebuilding: Options for a Sustainable Counter-Piracy Strategy in Somalia', (2011) 32 *Contemporary Security Policy* 356, at 375; L. M. Diaz and B. H. Dubner, 'On the Evolution of the Law of International Sea Piracy: How Property Trumped Human Rights, the Environment and the Sovereign Rights of States in the Areas of the Creation and Enforcement of Jurisdiction', (2009) 13 *Barry Law Review* 175, at 177; N. Ford, 'The Calm before the Storm', (2012) *The Middle East* 42, at 42.

85 R. Warner, 'Joining Forces to Combat Crime in the Maritime Domain: Cooperative Maritime Surveillance and Enforcement in the South Pacific Region', (2008) 8 *New Zealand Armed Forces Law Review* 1, at 6.

86 See, e.g., R. Paternoster, 'How Much Do We Really Know about Criminal Deterrence?', (2010) 100 *Journal of Criminal Law & Criminology* 765; D. M. Kennedy, *Deterrence and Crime Prevention: Reconsidering the Prospect of Sanction* (2008).

87 For other discussions of the Rome Statute and sustainable development within this volume, see, e.g., Chapters 3, 6, 7, 8, 9, 15, and 17.

88 Rome Statute of the International Criminal Court, UN Doc. A/CONF. 183/9, at Art. 8(2)(b)(iv).

89 *Ibid.*, at Art. 8(2)(b)(xvi).

90 *Ibid.*, at Art. 8(2)(v)(xxv).

armed conflict. Similarly, the definition of crimes against humanity encompasses the right to health and safety through its provision against forced labour and forced prostitution,[91] but only when committed as part of a widespread or systematic attack directed against a civilian population.

Of course, the narrow focus of these crimes and their limited scope of application are far from what is required to secure the pillars of sustainable development.[92] In the future, these provisions might be expanded to include the recognition that deliberate acts that remove all possibility of sustainable development, compromising the very livelihoods and survival of future generations, could be considered internationally criminal. Indeed, as Sébastien Jodoin in Chapter 17 and Jarrod Hepburn in Chapter 9 suggest, 'crimes against future generations' could be recognised as an extension of other preexisting crimes in the international arena. To this end, amendments to the Rome Statute of the ICC may be proposed by any state party and may be adopted by a two-thirds majority.[93] These matters are discussed in greater detail elsewhere in this volume.

## 6. CONCLUSION

A great deal of progress has been made in recent years, though more is needed. Turning to the future, states and others have increasingly begun to focus on the implementation of the objective of sustainable development in different contexts, including in domestic and international criminal law. In this way, international law on sustainable development is defining new rights and duties among states. The challenge for future legal scholarship – and action – will be to implement this global commitment in the interest of a common future.

[91] *Ibid.*, at Art. 7(1)(c)(g).

[92] See S. Jodoin & Y. Saito, 'Crimes against Future Generations: Harnessing the Potential of Individual Criminal Accountability for Global Sustainability', 2012 7(2) *McGill International Journal of Sustainable Development Law & Policy* 115–55.

[93] Rome Statute, *supra* note 89, at Arts. 121 and 122.

# 3

# Crime, Structure, Harm

*Gerry Simpson*

## 1. INTRODUCTION: AN ORIGIN AND SOME FUTURES

Upon leaving the National Portrait Gallery in Trafalgar Square from its side entrance, visitors might find themselves facing, among the remembered masters of imperial glory, a statue of a nurse. Her name is Edith Cavell, and her execution by the Germans, in October 1915, caused a sensation. After her trial in which she was convicted of charges of having aided the escape of Allied soldiers from Belgium, her execution prompted outrage in the British press and became a lightning rod for anti-German sentiment. UK Prime Minister David Lloyd George promised war crimes trials for the defeated Germans, and the Treaty of Versailles included a provision calling for the trial of the Kaiser for crimes against the sanctity of nations (Article 227).[1] No such trial came to pass, of course. Instead, the Kaiser spent the remainder of his life in exile in the Netherlands. Meanwhile, the Treaty of Versailles became associated with collective punishment through intensely punitive reparations of a whole state, Germany, and war crimes trials were held not before the international criminal court anticipated in Article 227, but before the German Supreme Court in Leipzig.[2] This episode has long been characterised as a failure of institution building,

[1] Following Cavell's execution, Alfred Zimmerman, the German secretary for foreign affairs, elaborated what might be the first feminist theory of international law. He said: 'No criminal code in the world – least of all the laws of war – makes such a distinction [between men and women]; man and woman are equal before the law, and only the degree of guilt makes a difference in the sentence for the crime and its consequences.' For Zimmerman, women, unequal virtually everywhere, could at least be equally executed. Zimmerman went on to lose the war for Germany with his famous Zimmerman Telegram thought to be responsible for bringing the United States into the conflict. Treaty of Versailles Arts. 228–30 at www.yale.edu/lawweb/avalon/imt/partxiv.htm. See, too, C. Bassiouni, 'From Versailles to Rwanda in Seventy-Five Years: The Need to Establish a Permanent International Criminal Court', 1997 (Spring) 10 *Harvard Human Rights Journal* 11–62.

[2] These trials are regarded as a failure. See G. Bass, *Stay the Hand of Vengeance: The Politics of War Crimes Tribunals* (2000); C. Mullins, *The Leipzig Trials: An Account of the War Criminals' Trials and a Study of German Mentality* (1921); J. F. Willis, *Prologue to Nuremberg: The Politics and Diplomacy of Punishing War Criminals of the First World War* (1982). The reparations included in the war guilt

political nerve, and moral responsibility; however, it marks the moment when the international political order began to imagine itself embracing a system of criminal justice in which individuals could be held responsible for breaches of foundational social norms.[3] This haphazard and still-reversible development has solidified into an institutional apparatus designed to hold international malefactors to account for crimes against humanity, war crimes, genocide, and, perhaps eventually, the crime of aggression.

There are three possible futures for this apparently impressive programme and for the field of international criminal law more generally. Each of these futures would have obvious implications for the possible amalgamation of unsustainable development and international crime. In the first, the field goes into an abrupt recession. One way to understand this outcome is to recognise that the whole field of international criminal justice seems deformed by a combination of novelty and ubiquity: There is a huge amount of it about, but not much of it has been about for long. Therefore, international criminal lawyers combine rank immaturity (a sense of making it up as we go long) with imperial overconfidence (the sense that we are taking over international law or have become indispensable to peace building and war making). But this overconfidence masks a sense of insecurity about the place and position of the discipline. Although international criminal justice seems to be at the top of its game – post *ex post factoism*, pre-inertia – this atmosphere of precariousness pervades the whole discipline. It is as if 'they' might take it all away from us or lose interest in justice or return to politics or state responsibility or peace or pragmatism. Reading the memoirists, for example – Telford Taylor, Louise Arbour, Richard Goldstone – one gets a sense of this fragility.

Goldstone's account of his professional life adopts these twin tones of confidence and insecurity. On the one hand, he views international criminal justice as the main

clause have been largely discredited: 'Germany democracy is thus annihilated at the very moment when the German people was about to build it up after a severe struggle – annihilated by the very person who throughout the war never tired of maintaining that they sought to bring democracy to us. Germany is no longer a people and a state, but becomes a mere trade concern placed by its creditors in the hands of a receiver': T. Paulin, *Invasion Handbook* (2002).

3 The first international criminals or, in the provocative phrase, 'enemies of mankind', were, of course, not war criminals or aggressive heads of state but pirates. Piracy is regularly invoked as the first international crime or the first offence to give rise to universal jurisdiction or the precursor to contemporary offences against the dignity of humankind. See, e.g., J. Kaufman in *Filartiga* v. *Pena-Irala*, 630 F.2d. 876 (2d Cir. 1980) at 890. The origins of this development are acknowledged throughout the jurisprudence of war crimes. The war criminal, like the pirate, is characterised as an enemy of humankind – '*hostis humanis generis*' – operating outside the bounds of law and outside the jurisdiction of national law (e.g. *Eichmann*). He or she is engaged in *a form* of killing or plundering that is unacceptable. War criminals thus became the successors to pirates (see a critical discussion in E. Kontorovich, 'The Piracy Analogy: Modern Universal Jurisdiction's Hollow Foundation', (2004) 45(1) *Harvard Journal of International Law* 183–237. Pirates threatened international society because the particular form of violence they indulged in was a departure from legitimate violence. This, in turn, gave rise to a new class subject to universal jurisdiction (e.g. Geneva Convention IV, Article 149). For a fuller discussion see G. Simpson, *Law, War and Crime* (2007).

game in public international law.[4] He says elsewhere that, without international tribunals, international law would be rendered a bit pointless.[5] This assessment is astonishingly dismissive and casual. The implication is that everyone from Suarez to Oppenheim has been, more or less, wasting his or her time and that criminalisation (what Judith Shklar memorably called 'tribunality') somehow completes the project of international law or gives it some much-needed teeth.[6] From this perspective, other areas of international law are just preparing the ground for a full-blown criminalisation of the different harms that they prohibit.

On the other hand, Goldstone seems afflicted by the possibility that international criminal justice might be undermined or damaged by the usual cast of unenlightened politicians, petty UN bureaucrats, and spineless states. Certainly, the completion strategies intended to result in the eventual closure of the ICTY and ICTR, the glacial progress of prosecutions and trials at the ICC, the internal tensions at the ECCC in Cambodia, and local retrenchments in Spain, Belgium, and, perhaps, the United Kingdom suggest a field coming to the end of its glory years (1993–2010). Could it be that international criminal lawyers will look back at this period rather as they used to gaze nostalgically on the Nuremberg and Tokyo War Crimes Trials?

A second future would involve the consolidation of the regime, with the ICC replacing ad hoc and hybrid tribunals and supplementing continuing developments within nation-states. There is something to this optimism. The Rome Statute incorporates, after all, an inbuilt ad hoc mechanism by which the Security Council can refer a situation to the prosecutor for investigation. The Security Council Darfur referral under Resolution 1593 is the first and only example of this mechanism, but it led directly to the Bashir indictment. The referral of the Sudan to the ICC, then, can be reframed as the creation of a new ad hoc mechanism. Equally, self-referrals from the Democratic Republic of Congo, Uganda, and the Central African Republic under 13(1) of the Rome Statute resemble in their formation the hybrid tribunals in Sierra Leone and Cambodia, with states engaging – sometimes co-operatively, sometimes reluctantly – with international institutions (the ICC, the UN Secretary-General) to bring perpetrators to trial. In addition, the ICC has already prompted (indeed, required) states to enact domestic legislation giving domestic courts wider jurisdiction over alleged war criminals. In the case of British soldiers accused of torturing and murdering Baha Mousa in southern Iraq, one of the soldiers, Corporal Payne, was charged with having committed a war crime 'contrary to Section 51(1) of the *International Criminal Court Act 2001* namely inhumane treatment . . . as defined by Article 8(2)(a)(ii) of Schedule 8 [a schedule containing the Rome Statute]'.[7] Two

4 R. Goldstone, *For Humanity: Reflections of a War Crimes Investigator* (2000).

5 Global Governance public discussion, The Brahimi Panels: The Goldstone Report and the Peace Process, Speech Delivered at the LSE, London, 8 March 2010.

6 J. Shklar, *Legalism* (1964) passim.

7 Charge Sheet, *R* v. *Payne* (commencing 7 September 2006) ('Trial Hearing'), available at http://www.army.mod.uk/apa/courts_martial_trials/payne_and_others/_charge_sheet.htm, accessed at 14 Aug 2007.

other soldiers, Fallon and Crowcroft, also were charged with war crimes defined in the Rome Statute. These cases transformed the Mousa killing from a matter of internal military discipline into a potential war crime, to be set beside other suspected breaches of the Rome Statute[8] by Thomas Lubanga (in the Democratic Republic of Congo), Joseph Kony (in Uganda), and high-ranking government officials and Janjaweed militia leaders (in Sudan).[9] So, while non-ICC assertions of universal jurisdiction may become less frequent, implementing statutes will perhaps take their place.

These first two futures concern acts associated with war or political repression. A third possible future for international criminal law might feature instead a radical expansion in the types of acts encompassed by 'retributive legalism'. In 2009, I received an email from a former student who was involved in efforts to establish an International Criminal Climate Court. A meeting to discuss the court was to take place at the House of Lords, NGOs had been mobilised and the decade-young International Criminal Court was to be the model. At around the same time, James Hansen was calling for the criminalisation of large-scale polluters: a war crimes-style tribunal for the climate changers.[10] When I put this idea to people at dinner parties or at conferences, the response was invariably the same. The visceral thrill of punishing Big Oil or holding the owners of four-wheel-drive behemoths indirectly responsible (complicity in climate change perhaps?) for 'environmental crime' gave way to a sense that the problem of $CO_2$ emissions or ozone depletion implicates so many people as to make criminalisation vulgar, unjust, and implausible.[11]

Yet, the history of international criminal law is a history of unrealistic and revolutionary ideas and schemes transformed into living institutions. The plan for a permanent international criminal court proposed in the interwar period gave rise to a treaty signed by only one state (India); by the end of the 20th century a statute for a permanent international criminal court had been adopted by the international community, and a few years later the requisite 60 states had ratified the treaty, thereby bringing the court into being. The idea of holding states responsible for atrocities committed against their own citizens would have seemed outlandish at the end of the 19th century; 'sovereignty was never having to say sorry'. Before Nuremberg, international law just was not interested in a state's internal policies towards its own citizenry. Malcolm Bull, the political theorist, summed it up recently when he wrote:

[8] Rome Statute of the International Criminal Court, opened for signature 17 July 1998, 2187 UNTS 3 (entered into force 1 July 2002).

[9] *Prosecutor* v. *Lubanga*, ICC-01/04–01/06 (2006); *Prosecutor* v. *Kony* ICC-02/04–01/05 (2005); *Prosecutor* v. *Harun and Kushayb* ICC-02/05–01/07 (2007).

[10] J. Hansen, 'Global Warming Twenty Years Later: Tipping Points Near' (2008). Speaking as a private citizen (23 June 2008) at the National Press Club and at a Briefing to the House Select Committee on Energy Independence & Global Warming at http://www.columbia.edu/~jeh1/2008/TwentyYearsLater_20080623.pdf.

[11] The same can be said of other collective failures to prevent significant harms such as AIDS or extreme poverty that are also frequently characterised as criminal.

'States don't really mind their citizens dying (provided they don't all do it at once): they just don't like anyone else to kill them.'[12] Or, as Hitler put it, brutally, 'Who remembers the Armenians?' But here again, what seemed impossible in the 19th century – the outlawing of war (states went to war by right; they were, as Nietzsche argued, 'cold-hearted monsters'; what did we expect?) – had become a 20th-century norm.

The move towards economic, social, cultural, and ecological crimes accords also with a tendency in legal scholarship to push further into the global context of war, crime, and peace. There is an increasing sense that understandings of criminalisation will be limited without an appreciation of the processes that constitute the shadow global political economy or the distribution of life chances and wealth in the global polity. A typical recent development in this direction has been to think about the crisis in Darfur as a consequence of petro-politics or the Balkan Wars as the result of IMF stringencies imposed in the dying days of the Tito regime. This broader understanding seems to offer a promising rebuke to the acontextual, thin tribunality of international criminal justice enthusiasts who see people killing each other unnecessarily and decide that someone must be made an example of.[13] All of this might lead to a sense that international criminal law ought to move in the direction of addressing structural causes of mass atrocity or threats to international peace and security that result from economic and environmental choices, rather than more obvious forms of violence.

It is likely, then, that proposals to criminalise new forms of serious harm will seem less eccentric as time progresses. It is likely also that their initial appeal will be tempered by the realisation that criminal law has its limits when it comes to producing either large-scale social and economic transformation or, even more ambitiously, justice.

## 2. FROM EXCEPTION TO NORM: A BRIEF HISTORY

At the beginning of the Great War, the idea of war crimes trials would have been regarded with bemusement – another cranky notion associated with late Victorian pacifism. By the end of the war, and greatly aided by the execution of Nurse Cavell,

[12] B. Malcolm, 'States Don't Really Mind Their Citizens Dying (Provided They Don't All Do It at Once): They Just Don't Like Anyone Else to Kill Them', *London Review of Books*, December 2004, 3–6.

[13] The problem with pushing up and out (utterly commendable as it seems – no one has ever lost points by calling for a more nuanced, contextual approach) is that we, as international criminal justice types, do not really know how the global political economies (official or extracurricular) actually operate. And if we did, we do not know what difference it might make to our work. So it seems important to know what produces the DRC (colonialism, voodoo economics, consumerism), but acquiring that knowledge might not help us in our work or might make us abandon this work altogether in favour of trying to persuade Western consumers to stop buying mobile phones and driving round the corner for fish and chips.

war trials had become a subject of respectable policy. Lloyd George and his senior cabinet officials favoured such trials: The punishment of gross wrongdoing through some form of individual responsibility seemed unobjectionable. The Kaiser had invaded several European countries, his troops had committed various outrages, and he had plunged Europe into a four-year-long catastrophe. At the Imperial War Cabinet, Lloyd George used a language of opprobrium that has become a familiar rhetorical tool for those seeking to justify the project of international criminal law.

However, there was opposition to war crimes trials both within the Imperial War Cabinet and at the Versailles Peace Conference itself. Billy Hughes, the Australian prime minister at the time, resisted this move to retribution. In particular, he wondered whether 'treason against mankind' could be a crime. Was not aggression, for example, just something that states *did*? Criminalising the Kaiser was a bit like criminalising history. Should not Moses and Alexander the Great be placed on trial, too, asked Hughes?[14] This historical relativism was found, too, at the Commission on the Responsibilities of the Authors of the War convened by the Versailles Peace Conference.[15] Tasked with determining the applicability to the defeated Central Powers of crimes against humanity, war crimes, and the crime of aggression, the commission agonised over the appropriateness of law in confronting mass atrocity and interstate war. In relation to the criminalisation of war, the majority at the commission stated,

> [A]ny inquiry into the authorship of war must, to be exhaustive, extend over events that have happened during many years in different European countries, and must raise many difficult and complex problems which may be more fitfully investigated by historians and statesmen than by a tribunal appropriate to the trial of offenders against the laws and customs of war.[16]

A powerful American dissent was even more forthright about the problems inherent in criminalising structural harms.[17] There are important lessons here for those who wish to create new international crimes.

A quarter of a century later, at the Tokyo War Crimes Trial, the same concerns were raised by the Indian judge, Justice Pal, in a now famous dissent. Like the delegates to the Versailles commission, Pal was worried that the causes of war were not particularly prone to legal resolution. As Judith Shklar put it, in discussing Pal: '[T]he historic causes of the war simply defy legal judgement.'[18] Pal argued that wars, unlike acts of murder but like most momentous political decisions and collective social or economic activity, do not fit readily into a legal matrix. It is not at all clear, according to Pal, what or who is responsible for a particular act of war: Is it due

[14] Bass, *supra* note 2, at ch. 3.

[15] 'Commission on the Responsibility of the Authors of the War and on Enforcement of Penalties', (1920) 14(1) *American Journal of International Law* 95, at 154.

[16] 'Commission on the Responsibility of the Authors of the War and on Enforcement of Penalties', (1920) 14(1) *American Journal of International Law* 95, at 118–19.

[17] *Ibid.*, at 127–51.

[18] Shklar, *supra* note 6.

to an economic depression? An alienated underclass? The scarcity of some prized good such as land or oil? Even if one was to identify a specific socioeconomic or political cause, then attributing individual criminal responsibility remained highly problematic. Quincy Wright, writing in 1925, argued that wars were more akin to diseases: 'In so far as wars cannot be attributed to acts of responsible beings, it is nonsense to call them illegal.'[19] So Pal took the view that the whole effort to define aggression and attribute responsibility for it was misguided and ahistorical.

In the end a proposal for a war crimes trial did make it into the Treaty of Versailles, but no international trials took place until 25 years later when the Allies convened major war crimes trials at Nuremberg and Tokyo and various zonal trials in postwar Germany. The idea from the beginning was to punish evil and prevent it from recurring. 'Never again' became the slogan. And after a recess from 1948 to 1993 when there were only domestic trials – in Lyon, in Jerusalem, in Frankfurt, in Tel Aviv – international criminal law became an intensely active institutional field. By the end of the 20th century, there were at least five forms of international or 'internationalised' criminal jurisdiction: a permanent international criminal court created in Rome in 1998 (e.g., *Prosecutor* v. *Lubanga*), two ad hoc tribunals (e.g., *Prosecutor* v. *Milosevic*, *Prosecutor* v. *Kambanda*), a bunch of hybrid tribunals from Freetown to Phnom Penh to Lebanon (e.g., *Prosecutor* v. *Taylor*, the 'Duch' trial, Security Council Resolution 1757 [2007]), domestic courts exercising local jurisdiction (e.g., *R.* v. *Payne*), and the same courts exercising forms of extraterritorial, piracy-like, jurisdiction over foreigners (e.g., *Pinochet*). Exception (at Versailles) had become, almost exactly 80 years later, norm (at Rome). Even in civil courts, war crimes, crimes against humanity, genocide, and torture are regularly litigated at the domestic (*Kadic* v. *Karadzic* and *Titan Corporation* in the United States, *Jones* v. *Saudi Arabia* in the UK) and international (*Bosnia* v. *Serbia*) levels. There are currently two cases before the International Court of Justice that are centrally concerned with international criminal law matters. In one (*Belgium* v. *Senegal*), a state is being sued for not pursuing a torturer zealously enough and, in another (*Germany* v. *Italy*), for overzealousness in pursuing retribution for war crimes. In some ways, then, and though the spectres of Pal, Hughes, Wright, and others may well haunt this project, the field – energetic, hybrid, diverse, and increasingly concerned with the repression of corporate or structural harm through doctrines of complicity or criminal enterprise – is ripe for a move into economic, social, cultural, and environmental crimes.

## 3. CRIME AND SUSTAINABLE DEVELOPMENT

The fields of economic, social, and cultural rights and of environmental law as well seem ready for an injection of retributive energy. Preventing humanitarian or ecological disasters is at least as large a challenge as achieving nuclear disarmament

[19] Q. Wright, 'The Outlawry of War', (1925) 19(1) *American Journal of International Law* 76, at 76.

or outlawing war. But there are several obstacles to achieving any sort of solution at the level of interstate co-operation.

The proposal that international criminal law be used to punish environmental harms illustrates these obstacles. First, in the absence of transparent and enforceable standards, there is a serious risk that some states will free-ride. In other words, they will enjoy the long-term environmental benefit of green practices and will continue to reap the economic benefits of pursuing environmentally unfriendly and still cheaper economic policies. Unilateral compliance with international standards in the absence of uniform compliance might have adverse economic consequences for individual states without changing planetary prospects at all. Second, global environmental degradation has asymmetrical effects on states. In the climate change context, most states will suffer as a result of the planet heating up, but some will suffer more than others. The projected average increase in temperatures (2.5 per cent by 2150) is just that: an average. Some regions will boil, whereas others will experience only a mild rise in temperatures; indeed, there may well be a small number of states and groups that benefit from the increasing temperatures (wine growers in Sussex, summer tourism in Norway). Still others may experience a cooling effect (I have heard this predicted for my home country, Scotland, which is cold enough as it is but that may lose the warming effects of the Gulf Stream as it begins to absorb melting ice caps from the Arctic). The problem here is that some states may not think it in their interests to conclude any sort of agreement on climate change *at all*. Third, and this is a problem for those who would criminalise global environmental harm, there is the deeply troubling problem of historical responsibility. Should the challenge of global warming be met by those who caused it, or by those who will experience it? This question goes to the heart of one of the perceived flaws of the Kyoto Protocol; namely, that it failed to impose any obligations on developing world states. That decision seemed fair at the time. After all, the developing world was not thought to be responsible for global warming, and of course, it was still *developing*. Yet, the strategic imperative to reach agreement may work against the moral imperative to allocate blame or responsibility or to establish criminal sanctions. One way to reach agreement is to buy the co-operation of Russia (this happened at Kyoto) and the United States. But this sort of strategic behaviour may also seem remarkably unjust (why should the rich villains be compensated by the poor victims?). Finally, there is the whole problem of sovereignty. The fact is that states do not *have to* sign up to anything. It is a basic principle of international law that states are bound to observe and respect only those norms or rules to which they have consented.

In the face of all these obstacles, combining sustainable development and international criminal law may seem both imperative and quixotic. It seems imperative because, in the absence of agreement within society, the temptation to punish deviants will always arise. The criminal law, here, can be viewed as a shortcut to achieving important social goals. Why wait for the resisters, flat-earthers, and polluters to consent to collective action of some sort when the criminal law can be applied against them? And why rely on a treaty body to monitor and manage compliance with international economic, social, and cultural rights when this body identifies serious violations of these rights but can do very little to actively prevent or punish them? Jonathan Charney wrote some time ago, in an influential essay entitled 'Universal International Law', that the time had come to abandon international law's reliance on the consent of all sovereign states in establishing binding legal norms. Instead, in the light of the serious problems facing humanity, norms could be created in the absence of agreement and applied to delinquent states. International criminal law extends this theory by applying it to individual violators of international norms.[20] Given the problems associated with ordinary consensual international law, there may be some purchase in thinking about 'authoritarian international law'. After all, as the High Level Panel warned: 'Most attempts to create governance structures to tackle the problems of global environmental degradation have not effectively addressed climate change, deforestation and desertification.'[21] Meanwhile, as the Committee on Economic, Social and Cultural Rights has stated,

> in effect, despite the rhetoric, violations of civil and political rights continue to be treated as though they were far more serious, and more patently intolerable, than massive and direct denials of economic, social and cultural rights.[22]

As others in this volume discuss, international criminal law already has had the occasional encounter with other areas of international law. Indeed, it can be viewed as part of international law's enforcement machinery. One way, then, to promote a new relationship between sustainable development and crime is to intensify and extend the use of an existing body of norms.

For instance, in terms of environmental harm, the links exist already in classical international law, international humanitarian law, and international criminal law itself. International lawyers earlier proposed the criminalisation of serious environmental degradation in a decidedly odd and ultimately unsuccessful initiative by the International Law Commission (ILC). In its 1996 Draft Articles on State Responsibility, the ILC proposed that a distinction be drawn between state delicts ('ordinary' breaches of international law) and state 'crimes' (breaches of norms of fundamental importance to the international community).[23] There is, of course, a conceptual puzzle here. The distinction between delict (or tort) and crime depends usually on the presence of some public authority (the state or sovereign in national legal systems) capable of bringing a criminal prosecution. No such sovereign exists in international law; there are sovereigns, but no Leviathan capable of instituting a

[20] J. Charney, 'Universal International Law', (1993) 87(4) *American Journal of International Law* 529–51.

[21] *High Level Panel Report*, para. 54.

[22] CESCR, Statement to the World Conference on Human Rights, UN Doc. E/1993/22, para. 5.

[23] ILC Draft Articles on State Responsibility (1996) at http://untreaty.un.org/ilc/texts/instruments/english/commentaries/9_6_1996.pdf.

system of criminal law. As Luis Moreno-Ocampo, the chief prosecutor at the ICC, has said of the Rome Statute, it is a 'criminal justice system without a state'.[24] The ILC's answer to this was to propose that certain offences (crimes) be subject to a particular form of interstate action. For example, states committing crimes would be subject to far more intrusive remedies, countermeasures would be available to all states (as opposed to only those with a 'legal interest'), and reparative action would not be restricted, for example, by the need to ensure that the offending state retain its 'dignity' (Articles 51–53). The list of 'crimes' enumerated in Article 19 of this document was unremarkable (war crimes, crimes against humanity, aggression), but for the inclusion of long-term and severe environmental destruction. This, of course, is an example of a state crime and not the individual criminal responsibility with which international criminal law is commonly concerned. To this extent it perhaps belongs to the familiar interstate regime already tasked with regulating environmental law and found in international legal landmarks from the Trail Smelter judgement to the 1973 Stockholm Declaration to the Rio Framework Convention in 1992. Nevertheless, and despite its deletion from the 2001 articles finally adopted by the ILC, it remains a provocative idea.

Of course there are at least two other places where we find a coupling of international criminal law and environmental destruction. Additional Protocol I to the Geneva Conventions, for example, prohibits

> the use of methods or means of warfare which are intended or may be expected to cause such damage to the natural environment and thereby to prejudice the health and survival of the population (Article 55).

And in the Genocide Convention, it is a crime to 'deliberately inflict on the group conditions of life calculated to bring about its physical destruction in whole or in part'.[25]

To put things perhaps rather dramatically, we have reached a juncture in human history where the Geneva and Genocide Conventions could begin to have universal applicability. In other words, we now live in a global political economy in which there is the widespread use of 'methods and means of production which . . . may be expected to cause such damage to the natural environment and thereby to prejudice the health and survival of the [global] population'. Or, to deploy the language of the Genocide Convention, the infliction of conditions of life calculated to bring about our collective physical destruction is becoming ubiquitous. In light of all this, expanding the scope of international criminal justice to encompass economic,

[24] L. Moreno-Ocampo, 'The Tenth Anniversary of the ICC and Challenges for the Future: Implementing the Law', Speech Delivered at the LSE, London, 8 October 2008.

[25] The ILC's Draft Code on Crimes against the Peace and Security of Mankind (1996) also contains provisions attaching individual criminal responsibility to environmental crimes. See T. McCormack and G. Simpson, 'The ILC's Draft Code on Crimes against the Peace and Security of Mankind', (1994) 5(1) *Criminal Law Forum* 1–55.

social, cultural, and environmental crimes seems to be a promising response to our troubles.

Others will speak of the problems of intergenerational equity (Hepburn in Chapter 9) or the detailed application of international criminal law doctrine to encompass economic, social, cultural or environmental damage (see Part II of this book); without wishing to preempt later chapters (especially Chapter 4 by Mégret), let me end by examining briefly two possible problems associated with the project to criminalise new forms of damage.

The first is the problem (already adverted to) of identifying those responsible for massive violations of economic, social, or cultural rights or environmental degradation.[26] This is a general problem with mass crime in modern societies. As Arendt remarked, the modern state is merely

> the latest and most formidable form of . . . dominion: bureaucracy or the rule of an intricate system of bureaus in which no men, neither one nor the best, neither the few nor the many, can be held responsible.[27]

Yet, international criminal law's core instruments are concerned to advertise the centrality of individualised justice just as the key commentaries are keen to enumerate its virtues. The statutes of the ICTY, ICTR, and ICC follow the Nuremberg Principles by placing individual accountability on centre stage. The charter of the International Military Tribunal (IMT) gives it (in Article 6) jurisdiction over 'persons' who acting as 'individuals' commit any of the listed crimes. The ICTY Statute states, at Article 7(1), 'A person who planned, instigated, ordered, committed [. . . a crime . . . ] shall be individually responsible for the crime'. Article 6 makes clear that this jurisdiction is to be found over 'natural persons', not abstract entities. The Rome Statute, too, refers to its jurisdiction over natural persons and individual responsibility (Article 25).

The law of war crimes, then, seems to mark a switch from the abstractions of the general field of public international law (the 'abstract entities' referred to by the IMT at Nuremberg) to the flesh and blood corporeality of human culpability. This is also a turn from structure to agency. The central idea behind individualised liability is that a defendant ought not to be punished for acts perpetrated by other individuals. Collective responsibility, as Cassese puts it, is 'no longer acceptable'.[28] These doctrinal efforts promise simplicity (it is no longer necessary to explain the reasons why crimes are committed – 'motive', as the court in *Jelisic* noted, is not relevant to questions of intent), parsimony (the question of guilt is pared down to an investigation of one person's mental state and capacity), and depoliticisation

[26] The following four paragraphs are drawn from my book, *Law, War and Crime* (2007).
[27] H. Arendt, 'Reflections on Violence', *New York Review of Books*, February 1969, 38.
[28] A. Cassese, *International Criminal Law* (2003), 137.

(the central questions become narrowly psychological rather than expansively political).[29]

These doctrinal projects are frequently undone by the insight that the very acts criminalised under international law are those least susceptible to individualised justice. International criminal law's core offences are crimes against humanity, serious violations of the laws of war (war crimes), genocide, and aggression – as reflected in the IMT Charter at Nuremberg and in the crimes included under Article 5 of the Rome Statute. In each of these cases, the paradigm crimes are, what Jose Alvarez called, 'crimes of state' (i.e. crimes arising from organisational choices or collective tendencies).[30] This characterisation as crimes of state is likely to be even truer of economic, social, cultural, and environmental crimes where the diffusion of responsibility is more pronounced and the difficulty in identifying particular malefactors greater.

When Stettinius met Eden and Molotov in San Francisco in the middle of 1945, the Americans had already formulated their plan to criminalise a whole stratum of German society:

> We proposed to put on trial the Nazi organizations themselves rather than the individuals and convict them all of criminal conspiracy to control the world. . . . Once having provided the organisation to be guilty, each person who had joined the organisation voluntarily would ipso facto be guilty of a war crime.[31]

The mass criminality outlined and envisaged in these plans, as well as in the core ideas of conspiracy and criminal organisation, of course departed from Western standards of individual guilt and personal responsibility at the very moment of international law's apparent and much trumpeted transformation from a body of law exclusively concerned with state responsibility to one in which individual humans and not abstract entities would be judged by the ideals of the international legal order.

At its inception, international criminal law was revealed as a composite of collective and individual notions of responsibility, and this carries over to the trials in The Hague where there developed a number of successor doctrines to those elaborated in the 1940s. The ICTY, for example, has developed a doctrine of 'joint criminal enterprise' (a phrase not even found in its statute). The ICTY utilised this doctrine in convicting Dusko Tadic, when it conceded that many crimes committed in war, rather than being individual acts of wrongdoing, 'constitute a manifestation of the collective criminality'.[32] Joint criminal enterprise is attractive to war crimes courts

29 *Prosecutor* v. *Jelisic* IT-95-10, (Appeals Chamber), 5 July 2001, at para. 49.

30 J. Alvarez, 'Crimes of States/Crimes of Hate: Lessons from Rwanda', (1999) 24 *Yale Journal of International Law* 365.

31 M. Marrus, *Nuremberg War Crimes Trials: A Documentary History* (1997), 35.

32 *Prosecutor* v. *Tadic*, Appeal Judgement, Case No. IT-94-1-A para. 191, 15 July 1999, available at www.unhcr.org/refworld/docid/40277f504.html.

because it is sensitive to the reality of organised crime during periods of armed struggle. More controversially, however, courts use this doctrine to avoid the responsibility of determining who actually killed or tortured in specific cases. It is sufficient that the court is able to show that the accused was involved in the system of criminality and had some knowledge of its ultimate criminal purpose; it has not always been necessary for the accused to have shared in that criminal purpose. Doctrines such as complicity and command responsibility are other ways in which courts reach beyond direct perpetration to capture organisational or system criminality. And international criminal law has a history of criminalising whole organisations (e.g. Articles 9–11 of the IMT Charter) though this form of guilt by association has not been utilised in the field since then. Most officials and theorists now accept Lord Holt's dictum that 'a corporation is not indictable, but the particular members of it are'.[33]

It is probable that initial efforts to criminalise economic, social, cultural, and environmental damage will be required to adopt collectivist doctrines such as command responsibility, joint criminal enterprise (JCE), or complicity to prosecute individuals who are deemed to have some personal responsibility for massive violations of the rights to health, water, food, or housing or for severe pollution. In cases where crimes are produced by a 'complex network of connivances' these doctrines are likely to be highly attractive to prosecutors.[34]

But there is the obvious danger of criminalising political behaviour and, as well the corollary of this, the politicisation of criminal law.[35] In any event, doctrines such as JCE have been criticised on the basis that they depart from the fundamental principle that guilt is a matter of individual psychopathology combined with acts or behaviour. With economic, social, cultural, and ecological crimes, the dispersion of culpability, the continuing legality of so much structural behaviour, the sheer ubiquity of the 'offence', and the difficulties in teasing individual responsibility from collective action are likely to be particularly acute.

Holding individuals (or corporations) responsible for such international crimes is likely to be problematic, but there is a prior question: why criminalise at all? As I have said elsewhere, the recent enthusiasm on the part of international lawyers for international criminal courts is a little bewildering. Richard Goldstone takes this enthusiasm to its extreme and manages to consign international law's history into the dustbin when he says, 'It seems to me that if you don't have international tribunals, you might as well not have international law'.[36] This spasm of criminalisation reflects general trends in criminal justice. Andrew Ashworth has argued that 'what we see increasingly is the tendency to assume that the only satisfactory way to

33 Quoted in A. Eser, 'Criminality of Organisations', in A. Nollkaemper and H. van der Wilt (eds.), *System Criminality in International Law* (2009), 222.

34 A. Gattini, 'A Historical Perspective', in A. Nollkaemper and H. van der Wilt, *System Criminality in International Law* (2009), 121.

35 See *Milosevic*, Rule 98b *bis*. Decision at para. 288ff.

36 R. Block, 'First, Catch You; R War Criminal', *The Independent*, 30 April 1995. www.independent.co.uk/news/business/first-catch-you-r-war-criminal-1617609.html.

respond to some sort of anti-social conduct is to create a new criminal offence'.[37] At the same time, however, international lawyers are embracing retribution in an era when commentators and practitioners working in, say, criminology or penology have seriously problematised the whole idea of prison-based criminal law. International criminal lawyers may have hitched themselves to a dead horse.

All of this makes the rise and fall of international criminal justice a decidedly mixed blessing for international lawyers and ought to give human rights and environmental lawyers pause before embarking on this course of action. The very structure of the international system too, may be an argument against applying criminal law to new international harms. Alberto Toscano describes Danilo Zolo's *Victor's Justice: From Nuremberg to Baghdad* (2006) as an argument against international criminal law on the basis that the norms and machinery associated with this project instrumentalise the needs and imperatives of the hegemons. In relation to aggression, Toscano quotes Justice Pal: 'Only lost wars are international crimes.'[38] Would expanding the scope of international criminal law to encompass new forms of harm avoid the same instrumentalisation?

Wedding crime to sustainable development may be a dramatic approach to creating international impact, and the combination of sustainable justice and international criminal law could still be a fruitful one, provided the reservations explored earlier are taken seriously. But with justice perpetually not quite present and with so many children dying on our watch, and given this generation's disastrous commitment to neurotic, suicidal, and conspicuous overconsumption in the face of extreme poverty on the one hand and ecological catastrophe on the other, this is not the moment to permit solemn self-satisfaction as we contemplate our efforts to eradicate the most obvious examples of wrongdoing.[39] Instead, we require attentiveness and conscientiousness to the personal vanities, structural failures, and human failings that contribute so greatly to moral and material catastrophe. It may be right, despite the reservations expressed in this chapter, to pursue war criminals or new types of international criminals and to prosecute them in humanity's courts. But we are disbarred from getting too much pleasure out of this task while remediable structural and everyday cruelties persist.

[37] Ashworth, 'Introduction', in A. Snare (ed.), *Beware of Punishment* (1995), iii. On the other hand, international criminal law remains embryonic when contrasted with the typical Western legal order. At the moment, the risks of overcriminalisation remain small (I thank Rob Cryer for this insight).

[38] A. Toscano, 'Sovereign Impunity', (2008) 50 *New Left Review* 128, 130.

[39] On the relationship between patterns of consumption in the West and ecological degradation, see Rio Declaration, Principle Eight, 31 ILM (1992) 874.

# 4

# The Case for a General International Crime against the Environment

*Frédéric Mégret*

## 1. INTRODUCTION

Two decades ago, Ethan Nadelmann anticipated that one area

> in which global prohibition regimes almost certainly will play an increasingly prominent role is in efforts to protect newly endangered species, to reduce pollution of the seas and the skies, and to conserve forests and other dimensions of the earth's natural resources.[1]

Indeed, in 1995, UN member states were urged to 'consider acknowledging the most serious forms of environmental crimes in an international convention'.[2] Suggestions have been made since to create a general offence of environmental degradation,[3] ecocide,[4] or geocide[5] and even of criminalising harm done to future generations.[6] Academic suggestions for criminalisation of particular environmental harms keep emerging at regular intervals.[7]

[1] E Nadelmann, 'Global Prohibition Regimes: The Evolution of Norms in International Society', (1990) 44 *International Organization* 479, at 523.

[2] The Role of Criminal Law in the Protection of the Environment, ECOSOC Res 1994/15, (25 July 1994). Ann., Recommendations Concerning the Role of Criminal Law in Protecting the Environment, para. (k).

[3] T. Howland, 'Chernobyl and Acid Deposition: An Analysis of the Failure of European Cooperation to Protect the Shared Environment', (1987) 2 *Temple International and Comparative Law Journal* 36, at 35. Also N. Belaidi, *La Lutte Contre les Atteintes Globales a l'Environnement: Vers un Ordre Public Ecologique?* (2008) (speaking of a 'délit general d'atteinte à l'environnement').

[4] M.A. Gray, 'The International Crime of Ecocide,' (1995) 26 *California Western International Law Journal* 215; C.H. Lytton, 'Environmental Human Rights: Emerging Trends in International Law and Ecocide', (2000) 13 *Environmental Claims Journal* 73.

[5] L. Berat, 'Defending the Right to a Healthy Environment: Toward a Crime of Geocide in International Law', (1993) 11 *Boston University International Law Journal* 327.

[6] See, e.g., World Future Council, *Crimes against Future Generations* at www.worldfuturecouncil.org/fj_crimes.html.

[7] L. M. Pinzon, 'Criminalization of the Transboundary Movement of Hazardous Waste and the Effect on Corporations', (1994) 7 *DePaul Business Law Journal* 173; D. Torrens, 'Protection of the Marine

Yet to this day, these calls have largely remained dead letter. Small evolutions are, of course, noticeable. There are a few notable international offences that seek to protect the environment from severe forms of degradation. For example, Protocol I to the Geneva Conventions includes a 'prohibition of the use of methods of warfare which are intended or may be expected to cause (widespread, long-term, and severe) damage to the natural environment'.[8] In the contemporary circumstances of international humanitarian law, such a prohibition probably entails international criminal responsibility. More than international offences *stricto sensu*, there is a degree of international mandating of criminal sanctions for the violation of certain environmental norms ('indirect' criminal law).[9] The International Convention for the Prevention of Pollution from Ships (Marpol treaty)[10] and the Convention on the Prevention of Marine Pollution[11] (and a range of regional treaties) deal with ocean pollution. CITES has some criminal implementation provisions,[12] as does the Basel Convention on the Control of Transboundary Movements of Hazardous Wastes and their Disposal.[13] The Council of Europe has adopted a convention on the protection of the environment through criminal law,[14] and the EU has also adopted a similarly worded directive.[15] Some animal protection[16] and some ocean[17] protection treaties include penal provisions. The United Nations also, at one point, devoted attention to the role of criminal law in protecting the environment, mostly in the context of fighting organised crime.[18] A recommendation was made that

> [n]ational and supranational authorities should be provided with a wide array of measures, remedies and sanctions, within their constitutional and legal frameworks

Environment in International Law: Toward an Effective Regime of the Law of the Sea', (1993) 19 *Queen's Law Journal* 613.

8 Protocol I, Art. 55.

9 I have argued elsewhere that this internationally mandated domestic criminal law is legitimately considered part of international criminal law and that there is no clear criterion to fundamentally distinguish it from the supranational criminal law that is deemed partly worthy of prosecution by international criminal tribunals. Crimes in the first category may one day move to the second, and crimes in the second are always partly reliant on the mechanisms of the first. See F. Mégret, 'International Criminal Law', in J. Beard and A. Mitchell (eds.), *International Law in Principle* (2009).

10 *International Convention for the Prevention of Pollution from Ships* (MARPOL 73/78).

11 *Convention on the Prevention of Marine Pollution by Dumping of Wastes and Other Matter* (1972).

12 See *Convention on International Trade in Endangered Species of Wild Fauna and Flora* (1975).

13 See *Basel Convention on the Control of Transboundary Movements of Hazardous Wastes and their Disposal* (1992).

14 *Convention on the Protection of the Environment through Criminal Law*, ETS No. 172 (1998).

15 Directive 2008/99/EC of 19 November 2008 on protection of the environment through criminal law.

16 For example the *Convention for the Regulation of Whaling* (Sept. 24, 1931).

17 For example, the *International Convention for the Prevention of Pollution of the Sea by Oil* (May 12, 1954).

18 Ad Hoc Expert Group on More Effective Forms of International Cooperation against Transnational Crime, including Environmental Crime (7–10 December 1993).

> and consistent with the fundamental principles of criminal law, in order to ensure compliance with environmental protection laws.[19]

These efforts, nonetheless, remain episodic and quite limited in scope. The Protocol I prohibition, the only true instance of a supranational offence against the environment, is ultimately less concerned with protecting the environment as such than it is, fundamentally, with regulating war. The more dynamic efforts to mandate states to resort to criminal sanctions to buttress their environmental protection clearly all originate in the context of systems of regional association and integration. They are mainly seen only in one region, Europe, and even there efforts remain limited (the Council of Europe Convention has not yet entered into force). UN efforts have never amounted to much, and the Convention against Transnational Organized Crime eventually entirely omitted any reference to the environment.[20] None of these initiatives, moreover, really attempt to deal with global environmental threats as such.

The question of what is, or should be, criminalised internationally is a more complex one than it first seems. Any argument intent on suggesting criminalisation as a response to international woes must address two questions: why criminalise at all, and why criminalise *internationally*? It is not enough to suggest that the international community has an interest in certain behaviour not occurring: clearly there are many things in which the international community is interested that it does not and most probably does not feel it could address through criminal enforcement.

In fact, international criminalisation could be seen to be, in essence, *doubly subsidiary*. First, criminalising the environment is subsidiary to the search for alternate means to deal with a given issue. Domestically, civil and administrative law would be the obvious options, although of course not exclusive ones. Even if more adjudicative solutions are recommended, it is hardly evident that criminal ones would be preferred. Internationally, interstate adjudication remains, of course, a possibility and one that has been increasingly explored.[21] Transnationally, civil suits are also available to make environmental claims; the Alien Torts Claim Act in the United States is an example.[22] Moreover, international human rights law and its attendant

[19] The Role of Criminal Law in the Protection of the Environment, ECOSOC Res 1994/15, (25 July 1994).

[20] The convention makes no mention of the environment. In comparison, trafficking in persons, smuggling of migrants, and illicit manufacturing and trafficking in firearms were all considered to be relevant global issues for the purposes of the convention.

[21] ICJ, Case Concerning the Gabčíkovo – Nagymaros dam, Judgement of 25 September 1997.

[22] N. L. Bridgeman, 'Human Rights Litigation under the ATCA as a Proxy for Environmental Claims', (2003) 6 *Yale Human Rights and Development Law Journal* 1; H. M. Osofsky, 'Environmental Human Rights under the Alien Tort Statute: Redress for Indigenous Victims of Multinational Corporations', (1996) 20 *Suffolk Transnational Law Review* 335; A. Bernstein, 'Conjoining International Human Rights Law with Enterprise Liability for Accidents', (2000) 40 *Washburn Law Journal* 385.

machinery are increasingly touted as likely routes to enforce some environmental norms.[23]

Second, international criminalisation is necessarily subsidiary to domestic forms of criminal law. Here the main interest lies in respecting *autant que faire se peut* sovereignty, and not unduly or precociously internationalising issues that could just as well be treated domestically, on the basis of a broad complementarity principle. The sovereignty argument is particularly sensitive when it comes to the criminal law, given its close association with the core of domestic public order.

A number of arguments can nonetheless overcome the traditional objections to international criminalisation, both in respect to criminalisation itself (Section 2) and to internationalisation specifically (Section 3). The two are closely related, because the argument is as much about whether one should 'criminalise' certain international behaviour as it is about whether one should 'internationalise' that repression. In fact, some sources point simultaneously to the need to both criminalise and internationalise (Section 4). The chapter finishes with a concise description of what might be some of the core features of a future international crime against the environment (Section 5).

## 2. ARGUMENTS FOR CRIMINALISATION

### 2.1. *Criminological Arguments*

Over the past decade, significant work has laid the theoretical bases for a criminology of environmental protection (or 'green' or 'conservation' criminology).[24] Domestically, it is generally understood that at a certain level civil and administrative remedies lack both the element of stigmatisation and deterrence needed to deal with fundamentally transgressive behaviour.[25] Although this notion has taken time to take hold in the environmental field because of its close association with administrative law, it is now quite widely recognised in many jurisdictions. The criminal law serves as an enforcer of certain norms that would otherwise not exert sufficient pull in terms of values or interest to constrain the actions of all actors. The record of criminal prosecutions for pollution has in fact been presented as good, having a

23 See for example A. E. Dehan, 'An International Environmental Court: Should There Be One,' (1992) 3 *Touro Journal of Transnational Law* 31; A. E. Boyle and M. R. Anderson, *Human Rights Approaches to Environmental Protection* (1998); P. E. Taylor, 'From Environmental to Ecological Human Rights: A New Dynamic in International Law', (1997) 10 *Georgetown International Environmental Law* 309.

24 C. Gibbs et al., 'Introducing Conservation Criminology: Towards Interdisciplinary Scholarship on Environmental Crimes and Risks', (2010) 50 *British Journal of Criminology* 124.

25 For a summary of critiques of 'soft' approaches to global environmental protections, see R. McLaughlin, 'Improving Compliance: Making Non-State International Actors Responsible for Environmental Crimes', (2000) 11 *Colorado Journal of International Environmental Law and Policy* 377, at 378. In the case of civil remedies, there is the constant worry that economic actors may simply internalise the risk of having to pay damages and see environmental responsibility as simply a cost of doing business.

'very substantial effect' in terms of deterrence and reinforcing systemically other areas of compliance.[26] At a certain level, the argument for criminalisation of violations of fundamental environmental rules is a variant of the general idea that some criminal element is required to make good on the promise of all significantly prohibitionist regimes.

International criminal law remedies, moreover, unlike for example the contribution that may be expected from the ICJ or international human rights bodies, target individuals. There may have been an age when the environment would mostly be harmed by the acts of states, and softer environmental regulatory approaches still seem to have very much the needs of precarious interstate coordination in mind. But if the reasoning that 'international crimes are committed by individuals, not abstract 'entities' were ever true, it would be true of environmental degradation. In that respect, international criminal law is arguably ideally suited to repressing crimes that are primarily committed by non-state actors,[27] especially if states come to see themselves as the guarantors of a certain global public interest against the encroachments of, for example, corporations.

Deterrent justifications of criminal punishment when it comes to environmental crimes may be even stronger than with other areas of international criminal law. One of the criticisms of arguments that ascribe deterrent value to international criminal law is that most 'atrocity' or 'conflict' related crimes are committed in the heat of political passions or in something akin to the 'fog of war'. This makes the traditional deterrent conceit of rational calculators deciding not to commit a crime rather than face a sanction a slightly improbable one. Many attacks on the environment, conversely, may be decided in a (relatively) very cold-blooded, deliberate way on the basis of perceived benefits and costs. Criminalisation might thus seem to be, all other things being equal, optimal in this particular context.[28]

### 2.2. *Criminal Law Arguments*

Although the emergence of an international criminal law of the environment is hardly a foregone conclusion, and much discussion needs to go into the particulars of what should be criminalised and how (see Section 4), there seems to be a dearth of arguments that fundamentally militate strongly against criminalisation. International

[26] S. Smith, 'Changing Corporate Environmental Behaviour: Criminal Prosecutions as a Tool of Environmental Policy', in R. Eckersley (ed.), *Markets, the State, and the Environment: Towards Integration* (1995).

[27] At least in such cases, no added ambiguity or overlap arises with mechanisms of state responsibility as it does when international criminal tribunals exercise jurisdiction over what might be called 'sovereign nonstate actors' (e.g. heads of state). R. Maison and C. Leben, *La Responsibilite individuelle pour Crime d'État en Droit International Public* (2004).

[28] Although it should be noted that, criminologically, this more deliberate nature of environmental offences is much discussed. D. B. Spence, 'The Shadow of the Rational Polluter: Rethinking the Role of Rational Actor Models in Environmental Law', (2001) 89 *California Law Review* 917.

environmental law already, by and large, distinguishes between licit and illicit uses of the environment, and there is no reason to think that it could not do the same thing with international crimes.

One argument that is sometimes heard in relation to the environment is that principles of environmental law may be quite vague and broad, because they are designed for interstate relations and responsibility rather than the exacting demands of criminal justice. International environmental law typically relies heavily upon both customary international and soft law instruments. This reliance may raise legitimate concerns about respect for the legality principle and the idea of *nullum crimen sine lege*. More generally, and on the basis of domestic experience, any drive to criminalise may raise fears of overcriminalisation and excessive prosecutorial discretion.[29] However, the vague character of international environmental law is only a problem to the extent that the passage to more international criminal practices is not accompanied by a refinement of what actually is punishable within environmental law. The argument was also made in the 1990s that the Geneva Conventions or the Genocide Convention were not international criminal law instruments and would pose insurmountable problems for the purpose of assessing guilt. Although perhaps not without difficulty, these claims have broadly been addressed. In addition, much of existing international criminal law once relied on broad standards as contained, for example, in the chapeaux of international offences, and these standards have in due course been successfully explicated and illustrated. At most, the indeterminacy of international criminal law is a function of its youth.

Finally, arguments that environmental violations are less grave than existing international crimes are highly subjective and constructed. Some environmental violations are clearly less grave than some major instances of core crimes, but some could have consequences that are or could be very similar if not worse. Moreover, the fact that environmental offences are relatively less grave than some international crimes is hardly a justification for not recognising them internationally. International law has already steadily moved to criminalise or to require states to criminalise offences that are less grave than genocide or crimes against humanity (torture, corruption, terrorism, drug trafficking, etc.). Therefore, international environmental offences might be the equivalent of domestic regulatory offences: less grave, but offences nonetheless.

### 2.3. *Environmental Arguments*

International environmental lawyers have at times made a strong case for co-operative, 'consensual' types of regulation.[30] Some have even suggested that reliance

[29] C. J. Babbitt, D. C. Cory, and B. L. Kruchek, 'Discretion and the Criminalization of Environmental Law', (2004) 15 *Duke Environmental Law & Policy Forum* 1.

[30] J. Brunnee and S. J. Toope, 'Environmental Security and Freshwater Resources: Ecosystem Regime Building', (1997) 91 *American Journal of International Law* 26, at 203; D. Bodansky, 'International Law

on criminal law to enforce environmental prohibitions may 'do more harm than good by alienating and polarizing member states'.[31] But this assertion seems to be based on a misunderstanding that criminal law methods would replace alternative means of dealing with the environment or that they would apply to all violations of international environmental law as opposed to only the worst ones. At least when it comes to the more deliberately hostile and harmful damage done to the environment, presumably even apologists for consensual norms will agree that something more is needed than a regime of incentives. There is, moreover, plenty of space internationally for a diversity of regulatory approaches to such a complex problem as global environmental damage.[32] In fact, the enforcement of international environmental law may remain, above all, an issue of noncriminal remedies, even as criminal law gains a role in 'backing' more ordinary environmental constraints. Apart from its role in ensuring greater compliance, criminal law signals certain social values as particularly worthy of respect; as such it can only reinforce the general perception of the environment as a prized externality that deserves to be protected adequately.

### 2.4. *Normative Arguments*

In addition to arguments in favor of criminalisation that draw on these more general considerations, attention should also be paid to the dynamics of international criminal law and to what must be a search for normative and moral consistency. If international criminal law already represses acts 'causing widespread, long-term and severe damage to the environment' in armed conflict, then it will be increasingly difficult to argue that it should only criminalise such attacks in the context of warfare and why they should not be equally reprehensible in peacetime.[33] The notion of crimes against humanity, for example, has been thoroughly separated from that of armed conflict. It should be the consequences of the damage that matter, in ultimate analysis, not the particular context within which the acts occur. In this respect, although clearly armed conflict has traditionally served as a conduit for the introduction of criminal notions into international law, it arguably only did so as part of its

and the Design of a Climate Change Regime', in U. Luterbacher and D. F. Sprinz (ed.), *International Relations and Global Climate Change* (1996).

[31] G. W. Downs, K. W. Danish, and P. N. Barsoom, 'Transformational Model of International Regime Design: The Triumph of Hope or Experience', (1999) 38 *Columbia Journal of Transnational Law* 465, at 483.

[32] This is also evident in the development of other international legal regimes. For example, the emergence of an international offence of genocide has not done away with a variety of international efforts to prevent, detect, and fight genocide.

[33] See Chapter 6. Also see M. Wattad, 'The Rome Statute & Captain Planet: What Lies between Crime against Humanity and the Natural Environment', (2009) 19 *Fordham Environmental Law Review* 266, at 268 and 281–82. Indeed, from a moral point of view one might almost be a little more understanding towards attacks on the environment launched in the thick of battle, albeit on the basis of a deeply flawed logic from a humanitarian point of view, than towards attacks that do not have this excuse and are launched from the comfort of normalcy.

salience in the grammar of statehood. It should be noted that the devastation sown by some human activities under the cover of 'peace' is often far greater than that caused in 'war'. The international community in the long term should criminalise, to the same degree, behaviour that is of equal gravity in terms of its consequences.

## 3. ARGUMENTS FOR INTERNATIONALISATION

### 3.1. *Functional Arguments*

A laissez-faire position might emphasise that states will sooner or later criminalise and prosecute behaviour that is antithetical to their interests and that it is not for the international community to step in as long as there is a reasonable prospect of them doing so. At a certain level, the international community already, very indirectly, benefits from the punishment of a range of environmental crimes in domestic legal systems.

However, this is where the study of both international law and international environmental protection precisely cautions against entrusting the state with too much responsibility. Internationalisation of repression is perhaps, first and foremost, presented as a functional necessity, given the lack of incentives for states to promulgate their own criminal legislation to protect the environment or their lack of willingness to enforce it. As Ethan Nadelmann puts it,

> the most important inducement to the creation of international prohibition regimes is the inadequacy of unilateral and bilateral law enforcement measures in the face of criminal activities that transcend national borders.[34]

Left to their own devices, there is a very real risk that states will either fail to criminalise offences or will criminalise according to terms that do not adequately do justice to the gravity of the offences involved. Even when they have criminalized those offences, they may not actively seek to enforce their own laws.[35]

Moreover, even if states do criminalise independently, the existence of differing environmental legislations may still create incentives for environmental 'dumping'. The often straddling, even global, nature of many environmental crimes multiplies the risks of competing jurisdictions, of double jeopardy, and of one state's exercise of jurisdiction frustrating the protection of the public order of another. It can also lead to the waste of prosecutorial resources. This trend is already evident in some federal states where overlapping prosecutions create significant tensions.[36] The creation of common international environmental offences would at least have the merit

[34] Nadelmann, *supra* note 1, at 481.

[35] M. Grandbois, 'Le Droit penal de l'Environnement: Une Garantie d'Impunité?', (1988) 21(1) *Criminologie* 57.

[36] J. F. Cooney, 'Multi-Jurisdictional and Successive Prosecution of Environmental Crimes: The Case for a Consistent Approach', (2006) *Journal of Criminal Law and Criminology* 435.

of reinforcing cross-border judicial co-operation and raising the likelihood of such procedures as extradition. The absence of appropriate supranational environmental offences may also create conditions for assertions of 'creeping' domestic jurisdiction, whereby states extend their territorial or protective capacity to prosecute. For example, the U.S. Oil Pollution Act criminalises pollution in the high seas in a way that is not normally contemplated by the United Nations Convention on the Law of the Sea (UNCLOS) (which the United States has not signed).[37] There is clearly a delicate tension between the need to protect the marine environment and the principle of freedom of the seas.

Difficulties in enforcing international environmental law are notoriously linked to problems of co-ordination among egotistic actors, prisoners' dilemmas, and the tragedy of the commons.[38] States may all have an interest, all other things being equal, in certain attacks against the environment being prohibited and punished. The effective repression of environmental harms that affect all, no doubt, creates a beneficial externality. But, apart from the fact that they may not see what is in their best interests in the long term (because of imperfect information, for example), states also have a short-term interest in not being the ones that take on the responsibility of repression. This is not only because of the immediate costs of carrying out prosecutions but also more generally because serious criminal legislation is likely to have substantial political and economic costs. For example, the threat of criminal sanctions might deter the state or companies operating or incorporated within it from participating in certain economically worthwhile activities, particularly in a context where some states will most likely not consider themselves bound by the international criminal legislation and will reap the benefits of not having to abide by the rules in a context where others do (a classic free-rider problem).[39]

Whether one believes the best way out of the dilemmas raised by the global commons is through privatisation[40] or some form of collectivisation of the commons,[41] a higher degree of institutionalisation and centralised control has long been touted as

37 S. J. Darmody, 'The Oil Pollution Act's Criminal Penalties: On a Collision Course with the Law of the Sea', (1993) 21 *Boston College Environmental Affairs Law Review* 89.

38 The term was first popularised by Garrett Hardin in the 1960s. See G. Hardin, 'The Tragedy of the Commons', (2009) 1 *Journal of Natural Resources Policy Research* 243.

39 Note that the problem of free-riding is less crucial when it comes to the forms of political violence in such crimes as genocide or crimes against humanity. States that become parties to the Rome Statute can be seen as essentially protecting themselves both against others and against themselves. Although others, including non parties, may also benefit, they do not really 'pay' for a service with others then free riding on a positive externality. In fact, the argument in the United States might typically be something to the effect that the state parties to the ICC, having thus relatively bound their hands in relation to the use of force, then benefit from the positive externality of other states (i.e. the United States) not being so bound. In the case of a credible global environmental regime, it would be quite crucial to obtain universal participation, lest some states unduly benefit from the efforts undertaken by others.

40 T. L. Anderson and J. B. Grewell, 'Property Rights Solutions for the Global Commons: Bottom-Up or Top-Down?', (1999) 10 *Duke Environmental Law & Policy Forum*.

41 P. M. Wijkman, 'Managing the Global Commons', (1982) 36 *International Organization* 511.

a way out of such dilemmas. Of course, institutionalisation and centralisation must be realistic possibilities, and the fears of some environmentalists about reliance on criminal law solutions may simply be linked to skepticism about the possibility of establishing a reliable system of international criminal sanction in the first place. An international criminal system only in name – one inciting some actors to rely upon its promise, yet unable to deliver – is the worst possible outcome, worse even than one in which states, entertaining no hope as to the promise of the supranational, may at least act as decentralised de facto guardians of some environmental interests. However, even as the tragedy of the commons makes it unlikely that a regime of international environmental criminal law will be set up, such a system may nonetheless be one of the only means for alleviating state concerns about the pitfalls of horizontal co-operation, such as free-riding.

### 3.2. *Inherent Arguments*

In addition to purely functional arguments about the (continued) inadequacy of domestic means, part of the claim to the legitimacy of international criminal law has certainly flowed from a perception that it was dealing with problems that were 'inherently' international. Typically, the argument is that there is something involved that is too serious or important to the international community to be entirely delegated to states and domestic law – even if domestic systems might conceivably be up to the task.[42] This is still a high threshold to meet, and states will only internationalise on a perceived needs basis, but it is important to acknowledge that there are also symbolic factors at work.

Different types of arguments have typically been made in favor of internationalisation of the criminal law (or 'penalisation' of public international law) based on what one might loosely term 'titles' or at least 'claims' to jurisdiction. Some of these claims seem least partly applicable in the case of environmental harm. First, international criminal law has been developed to deal with transnational phenomena that affect certain fundamental international values. Trafficking offences (persons, drugs, works of art, protected species) come to mind. This could also be a prominent basis for criminalisation of international environmental harms, such as transboundary pollution or the extra-territorial activities of multinational corporations.[43] A second category of international criminal law deals mostly with 'interstate' relations and offences that affect the proper functioning of the international system. Aggression is the emblematic crime, and clearly there are some harms to the environment that some states might direct against others. A third category of international offences

42 A. Cassese, 'Reflections of International Criminal Justice', (1998) 61 *Modern Law Review* 6.

43 Some early treaties protecting the environment specifically emphasised the transboundary character of pollution and traffic (e.g. Basel Convention on the Control of Transboundary Movements of Hazardous Wastes).

focuses more on harm caused to human beings, typically atrocities and mass violations of their rights. Emblematic offences in this category include genocide, crimes against humanity, and war crimes. Apart from the fact that attacks against the environment might be a way to commit some of the latter crimes, it is quite clear that massive environmental harm will very often have an impact on populations. In short, it is not inconceivable that attacks against the environment could fall under all three of these traditional bases for criminalising certain types of behaviour internationally (a bit like piracy in earlier days).

However, none of these traditional grounds for criminalising internationally necessarily captures the full dimension of offences against the environment: many grave attacks on the environment may not strictly have a cross-border nature or at least not one that is easy to pin down; the predominantly public view that characterises both interstate crimes (aggression) or 'human rights' crimes (crimes against humanity) has traditionally had difficulty accommodating a nonstate paradigm, even as many environmental harms will be committed by nonstate actors (i.e. corporations). Moreover, all of these grounds may have quite an anthropocentric inclination,[44] which raises dilemmas for international environmental protection.

In short, the gravest crimes against the environment, especially those that affect the global environment, are neither strictly transnational nor interstate nor cosmopolitan. Rather, they should arguably be seen as part of a new category of 'global' crimes. There are two ways one can understand a crime as being 'global'. The first is that such a crime provokes a sort of 'global' condemnation; that, to use the classical expression, it 'shocks the conscience of mankind'. There is a case that certain harms done to the environment – for example, massive oil spills – have had the 'shocking of mankind' quality that has become a hallmark of international crimes. Yet the problem may be precisely that world public opinion is not particularly shocked by all grave environmental harms (and there are many that have much graver consequences than even major oil spills, yet fail to evoke a similar level of indignation). At any rate, there has always been something slightly circular about such claims: attacks on the environment, no more than any number of other types of internationally harmful acts, naturally 'shock the conscience of mankind'. This is a socially constructed notion: such attacks will be 'shocking' by the time the international community decides they are and has created offences that reflect this level of stigma – hence, the feeling of *petitio principii*.

In this respect, a second and perhaps more promising way of understanding the global character of certain crimes is in the more concrete sense of 'having a global impact'. Major environmental crimes could be an example of a new category of

[44] This is evident, for example, in the requirement in the ILC's Draft Code of Crimes against the Peace and Security of Mankind that methods or means of warfare that cause harm to the environment must do so in a way that 'gravely prejudice(s) the health or survival of the population'. UN Doc. A/CN.4/472 (1996).

international crimes that pose a threat to the continued existence of global communal life (and thus incorporate all the earlier mentioned dimensions, even as they transcend them). Imagine, for example, that someone were to attempt to destroy the Amazon rainforest entirely, with huge consequences to the global environment. Domestically, this might fall under a whole range of offences, but they would be radically insufficient to express our sense of outrage. The offence might not be particularly directed against any of the states where the Amazon is located (for example, they might even consent to or be involved in it); it would not be a crime against humanity in the sense that is generally understood in that it would not systematically target a civilian population or represent a generalised or systematic attack as such, nor might it even incorporate any specific nefarious intention towards human beings; it might be transborder, but not in the way that, for example, trafficking offences are understood to be cross-border *stricto sensu*; rather it would be, literally, 'borderless'.

Instead, what would make this a crime of considerable proportions is the impact it would have on the conditions of global life for humanity. Grave crimes against the environment are global crimes *par excellence* because they are ubiquitous in their materialisation and potentially absolute and irreversible in their impact. In some ways, such global crimes would be the characteristic crimes of a world operating under conditions of globalisation.

### 3.3. *Consistency Arguments*

Finally, several arguments show that this evolution towards a new type of 'global' offence against the environment is consistent with trends observable historically and in both international criminal and international environmental law.

First, there are notable historical antecedents to crimes being considered international on the basis of their global reach. One could probably make the argument that what was wrong about piracy was not simply that it may have affected state relations, 'shocked the conscience of mankind', and disrupted trade but also that it threatened a fundamental global interest in the high seas being a common public good, free for all to navigate and use. Inflicting grave harm on the environment might be construed as the modern-day equivalent of piracy, either because it actually occurs on the high seas[45] or because, even as it occurs concretely on the territory of a particular state, its impact is global. One might also build on a notion that briefly appeared much later, in the process leading to Nuremberg, that of 'non-localisability'. In 1943, in the Moscow Declaration, the Allies stipulated that although most war criminals should be returned to the country where they committed their crimes, offences that 'have no particular geographical location' should be punished internationally. This

45 S. P. Menefeee, 'The Case of the Castle John, or Greenbeard the Pirate: Environmentalism, Piracy and the Development of International Law', (1993) 24 *California Western International Law Journal* 1.

character of being beyond reach and/or ubiquitous has thus presided in some of the most significant developments in international criminal law and could do so again.

Second, some parts of international criminal law seem already to be evidence of a new 'global' approach, even though they are typically not the most publicised aspects. For example, consider the United Nations Convention against Transnational Organized Crime: although it does not go as far as to describe the various crimes it creates as 'international crimes', it certainly mandates states to criminalise a whole range of offences that can be said to fundamentally run counter to global communal life (corruption, bribery, money laundering, human trafficking, etc.). All of these are arguably traceable to a global interest in not allowing certain forms of exploitation, oppression, or violence to stand in the way of a minimally functioning domestic-international order. The same is true when it comes to offences involving the Internet, for which issues of jurisdiction become increasingly complex and blurred. After a while, it may become meaningless to put much emphasis on where a crime was committed and where it produced its consequences if it was committed simultaneously in several locations and has an impact that is, by nature, global. In this context the domestic and the international are increasingly conceptualised as a continuum, rather than being dichotomous.

Third, international environmental law's broad evolution has clearly been in the direction of tackling threats to the environment as global much more than as international, cosmopolitan, or transnational issues. The argument might be that a number of phenomena analyzed domestically do not by themselves suffice to constitute a crime and that it is only by seeing them in their aggregate dimension that one can assess their full significance. Environmental problems being of an inherently global nature, the argument goes, so should their regulation. In turn, it seems to make sense that international environmental criminal law should ultimately follow the preferred route of its underlying prescriptions (international environmental law), rather than, for example, international criminal law's logic.[46]

## 4. ARGUMENTS FOR INTERNATIONAL CRIMINALISATION

Finally, a set of arguments simultaneously militate for criminalisation and internationalisation of environmental harm and thus are examined together. Both

[46] In that respect, international criminal law is less a substantive, purposive project than a technique that is put to use by various other projects, whether it be protecting states, humanity, or transnational relations. Of course, in the process, international criminal law ends up being modified in its technique and operation by its encounters with several objects of regulation: for example, the need to repress piracy leads to the invention of universal jurisdiction; the need to repress crimes committed by state leaders leads to the emergence of international criminal tribunals, changes in the laws of immunity, and the evolution of modes of command responsibility. Sometimes, the end product – a particular version of international criminal law – ends up being confused with the project itself, even though international criminal law is only ever really a technique in the service of a project that necessarily lies beyond it.

internationalisation and criminalisation, in this context, reflect a global 'upgrading' of the values that could be protected by an international environmental offence. The legal evidence that certain fundamental harms to the environment are ripe for the intervention of international criminal law is abundant and springs from various sources. It is not inconsequential that a great many states now criminalise harms to the environment domestically and that generally domestic environmental regulation in the twentieth century has been characterised as a form of 'top-down' global institutionalisation.[47] This characterisation reflects an implicit adherence to both criminal and global models of environmental regulation. Although the idea that domestic criminalisation leads to a 'general principle of law recognised by civilised nations' that would necessarily bind the international community to do the same[48] attempts too much,[49] there is no doubt that in practice it reinforces the legitimacy of international criminalisation.

More generally, efforts towards greater criminalisation could draw on an increasingly strong association between the global environment and both domestic and international *ordre public*.[50] The protection of the environment, in particular, has been linked saliently to other fundamental values of the international system. First, there is the recognition by such bodies as the Security Council, that attacks on the environment have consequences in terms of international peace and security.[51] Second, there is the recognition that the environment is tied to the protection of human life and some basic human values.[52] In that respect, the strong association that is made with human rights – one of the great engines of international criminal law's growth – is among the most promising, even if one may fault it for being excessively anthropocentric. Third, there is the recognition that protection of the environment is key to development and that, conversely, a damaged environment is closely correlated with poverty.[53] To the extent that criminalisation of grave attacks on the environment does not fall hostage to its association with these values, then it will emerge stronger. Indeed, at a certain level, the integrality of the environment to the basic condition of human life on earth would seem

47 D. Frank, A. Hironaka, and E. Schofer, 'The Nation-State and the Natural Environment over the Twentieth Century', (2000) 65 *American Sociological Review* 96.

48 S. McCaffrey, 'Crimes against the Environment', in M. C. Bassiouni (ed.), *International Criminal Law* (1986), 556.

49 R. Provost, 'International Criminal Environmental Law', in I. Brownlie, G. S. Goodwin-Gill, and S. Talmon (eds.), *The Reality of International Law: Essays in Honour of Ian Brownlie* (1999), 451.

50 It is mostly francophone doctrine that has emphasised this point. See the very complete Belaïdi, *supra* note 3. Also M. Boutelet and J. C. Fritz, *Towards an Ecological Public Order* (2005).

51 L.A. Malone, 'Green Helmets: A Conceptual Framework for Security Council Authority in Environmental Emergencies', (1995) 17 *Michigan Journal of International Law* 515; N. Schrijver, 'International Organization for Environmental Security', (1989) 20 *Security Dialogue* 115.

52 S. C. Aminzadeh, 'A Moral Imperative: The Human Rights Implications of Climate Change', (2006) 30 *Hastings International & Comparative Law Review* 231.

53 See Agenda 21 (1992); Rio Declaration on the Environment (1992).

sufficiently important to justify that it one day will constitute the heart of world public order.

The increasing *erga omnes* nature of environmental obligations is also a good indicator that international criminalisation is not too remote. Historically and analytically, there has certainly been a strong association between discussion and recognition of *erga omnes* status and criminalisation. Although analytically distinct, both can be said to emerge from the materialisation of a strong communal interest. A norm could be *erga omnes* in the sense that any state could invoke its breach, and yet it not separately constitute a crime; however, few crimes will not simultaneously incarnate *erga omnes* obligations. The *erga omnes* character of environmental obligations is buttressed by many treaty formulations, soft law, and litigation, which points to the fundamentally shared nature of the environment. The global climate, for example, has been recognised as 'the common concern of mankind'.[54] Judge Weeramantry has spoken in no uncertain terms of the characteristically *erga omnes* nature of obligations whose violation involves 'environmental damage of a far-reaching and irreversible nature'.[55]

Increasingly, moreover, the environment has, at least rhetorically, been presented as a value whose encroachment constitutes a violation of an international criminal character. The draft Articles on State Responsibility, for example, once included a notion of 'international crimes' of the state, which included 'a serious breach of an international obligation of essential importance for the safeguarding and preservation of the human environment, such as those prohibiting massive pollution of the atmosphere or of the seas'.[56] Roberto Ago, the rapporteur, insisted that it was

> undeniable that the obligations flowing from these rules are intended to safeguard interests so vital to the international community that a serious breach of those obligations cannot fail to be seen by all members of the community as an internationally wrongful act of a particularly serious character, as an 'international crime'.[57]

The ILC's Draft Code of Crimes against the Peace and Security of Mankind also included provisions relating to willful and severe damage to the environment.[58] Criminalisation, in this context, manifests the perception of an increasingly collective interest, even if such strong formulations have come and gone.

54 UN GA 43/53 (1988).
55 ICJ, Separate Opinion of Vice-President Weeramantry, Gabčíkovo-Nagymaros Project (Hungary/Slovakia), 25/09/1997, p. 114.
56 Draft Arts. on State Responsibility art. 19(3) (2001).
57 Report ILC, 28th session, vol. III, p. 109.
58 Draft Code of Crimes against the Peace and Security of Mankind Art. 20(g) (1996).

## 5. CONTOURS OF AN INTERNATIONAL OFFENCE AGAINST THE ENVIRONMENT

### 5.1. *Structure*

What might an international criminal offence against the environment look like? The need for some central offence or codification of existing offences that synthesise what the international community considers to be the most threatening has already been felt. Drafting techniques that have been used with some success to define genocide, crimes against humanity, war crimes, aggression, terrorism, or trafficking offences could be used in the context of the environment. These techniques typically involve use of a chapeau to contextualise and broadly define the nature of the offence. In the case of an international offence against the environment, that chapeau might mention any generalised or systematic attack (or harm inflicted to, if one wants to soften the purposiveness of an attack) on the environment (drawing inspiration from crimes against humanity in highlighting a broad target) that is intended or may be expected to cause widespread, long-term, severe, or irreversible damage to the environment (drawing inspiration from Protocol I but adding the notion of irreversibility and making the characterisations of the damage alternative, rather than cumulative). To avoid the pitfalls of the 1991 ILC's Draft Code of offences, which was faulted for being too vague as a result of being only a chapeau, a list of offences would follow that could draw on existing international environmental treaties that set out clear penal prohibitions (Basel, CITES, Marpol). That list could be rearranged with the evolution of time.

### 5.2. *Nature of Harm*

Criminal offences are defined on the basis of real or potentially serious harm, and an international crime against the environment should presumably introduce a threshold to qualify certain harms as indictable. The diffuse and long-term impact of environmental damage raises some difficulties. If too narrow a view is taken of environmental damage – requiring, for example, that harm has already occurred and affected a population – then many cases of significant harm to the environment may not come to be seen as offences. Conversely, if too broad a view is taken of environmental damage, then a risk of overcriminalisation arises, as persons become liable for very distant and possibly unforeseeable harm. There will certainly be cases where the damage is neither diffuse nor indirect, and international criminal law might well choose to target those as a matter of priority. However, domestic legislation may already take these cases quite into account. International law, conversely, may be particularly apt at detecting long-term harm potential, particularly the sort that might affect future generations.

Whatever the view one takes on the fundamental issue of whether the environment should be protected in itself or to the extent that it acts as a support system for human beings, there is no doubt that the need to correlate environmental harm to actual harm to populations adds a very significant, substantive, and evidentiary hurdle that would hinder the prosecution of environmental crimes. The precautionary principle and the diffuse, long-term, and aggregate impact of environmental harm suggest, on the contrary, that certain attacks on the environment that are clearly in violation of international environmental law should be punished without the need to prove that they have already provoked harm to identifiable populations. In this context, it may be possible to construct a broad international offence of 'endangerment' on the model of those that already exist domestically.[59] The endangerment could be merely theoretical in that the prosecution would not have to prove that it actually endangered anyone; in other words, it would be assumed that the violation of environmental prohibitions is by itself a form of endangerment. This would, of course, not exclude prosecutions for offences where the harm has actually occurred.

### 5.3. Mens Rea

The issue of *mens rea* will be key to the creation of any international offence against the environment. At the very least, harm that is willingly committed against the environment should be criminalised. A knowledge *mens rea* coupled with indifference or wilful blindness would also seem to be sufficient for the purposes of international criminalisation. Morally, knowledge and indifference are functionally equivalent to intention. From an environmental point of view, this sort of subjective recklessness is likely to be much more present than intention, certainly more so than with other existing international crimes.[60]

The more contentious question is whether an objective fault (i.e. negligence) might suffice to establish international criminal responsibility for grave harm to the environment. It is worth noting that some form of negligence may be a sufficient basis of criminal liability internationally, although this remains very much the exception rather than the rule. Under the case law of the ad hoc tribunals, for example, culpability of the military superior might result from a failure to properly monitor subordinates. That is akin to negligence in cases where the superior 'should have known' that they were committing certain crimes. It is true that such an extension of international criminal liability has been resisted by liberal criminal lawyers who view it as dangerously in tension with principles of fairness to the accused.[61] Yet

[59] Indeed, international humanitarian law under Protocol I already envisages the long-term character of harm to the environment as one of its defining characteristics. Arts. 35 and 55 of Protocol I speaks of 'widespread, long-term, and severe damage to the natural environment'.

[60] Recklessness, for example, is incompatible with the very notion of genocide and may also be with that of crimes against humanity.

[61] D. Robinson, 'The Identity Crisis of International Criminal Law', (2008) 21 *Leiden Journal of International Law* 925.

the issue seems less whether there should be criminal liability for negligence at all than what crime such a *mens rea* should lead to (e.g. genocide as such or a specific offence of dereliction of duty). The doctrinal discomfort raised by the implications of such notions as 'genocide by negligence' is that it inaccurately portrays what is at stake. This will be less of a concern with offences specifically crafted to reflect the relatively lesser gravity of strict liability offences. Moreover, the fact that international environmental law has made so much of the precautionary principle would seem to be conducive to a greater recognition of liability by negligence.[62]

## 6. CONCLUSION

This chapter has suggested that strong arguments exist both for the criminalisation and the international criminalisation of grave harm to the environment. It has further outlined what might be some key features of an emerging international offence against the environment that is not simply the result of haphazard international environmental developments, but is the product of a criminological, penal, international, and normative synthesis. In this conclusion, I turn to a few more concrete issues about what might be the future shape of an international criminal law of the environment.

If certain harms to the environment become international crimes, what sort of international crimes would they be? The distinction between crimes whose domestic enactment is mandated by international law and crimes of international law is tenuous, and there is no reason in principle why crimes in one category could not become part of the other. The emphasis has, until now, mostly been on requiring states to criminalise certain harms.[63] The 'upgrading' to more centrally administered forms of international criminal law merely reflects evolving attitudes as to what is 'truly grave' and whether there is a specific need for international enforcement resources. In fact, there is a strong argument that the gravest crimes against the global commons are not primarily domestic, but instead are international crimes whose prosecution may simply be outsourced to domestic courts.

The 'type of international crime' issue is closely tied up with the problem of enforcement. If the international community feels that a particular type of international crime can be repressed domestically, then it will tend to go for an 'indirect enforcement' model, one that puts emphasis on repression by states. Conversely, if states persistently fail to comply with their *aut dedere aut judicare* obligations, international criminal lawyers will feel validated in exploring more ambitious alternative options.

[62] McLaughlin, *supra* note 25, at 392.

[63] This was the approach initially favored by the AIDP. See XIIe Congrès International de Droit Pénal, Resolutions on the Protection of the Environment through Penal Law (Sept. 1979), 50 *Revue international de droit pénal* 231 (1980). It is also the approach currently chosen by the EU. See Directive 2008/99/EC of 19 November 2008 on protection of the environment through criminal law.

The possibility of universal jurisdiction and of making certain environmental crimes the object of international or supranational jurisdiction might be anticipated. The bases for universal jurisdiction would be similar to those that should make some behaviour internationally criminal in the first place: that they affect the whole of the international community, so that each state has an interest in repressing them even if they were not committed in its territory or by its nationals. There have long been suggestions that certain attacks on the environment occurring on the high seas should be treated as the functional, modern equivalent of piracy.[64] Here, universal jurisdiction might extend to offences committed within the jurisdiction of states (as with war crimes or torture) to the extent that the global environment thoroughly deconstructs the notion of territory. Current litigation in the field of international human rights is increasingly making the case that victims thousands of miles away from the polluters can legitimately sue states transnationally for global harm to the environment.[65]

In some ways, the arguments for universal jurisdiction are even stronger normatively for environmental crimes than for other crimes that are traditionally seen to justify it. For example, although torture clearly 'shocks the conscience of mankind', the actual impact of a single act of torture on a state and population thousands of miles from where torture is committed will be limited; its impact on the entire international community may be even more theoretical. Conversely, the impact of grave environmental damage in one country on other countries may well be very significant and concrete. The exercise of universal jurisdiction in such a case would thus merge both protective jurisdiction and a form of *dédoublement fonctionnel* on behalf of the global community.

Calls have also been heard for grave harm to the environment to fall under some sort of supranational jurisdiction,[66] even under the ICC itself.[67] These arguments are also fundamentally the same as those for universal jurisdiction, except for the obvious institutional (what court?) and political (who would support it?) implications. Prosecuting certain environmental offences before an international criminal jurisdiction may prove necessary when states decide to provide significant jurisdictional 'cover' to offenders and universal jurisdiction is either unavailable or not particularly appropriate. It would more generally send a signal about the reprehensibility of the

64 J.C. Klotz, 'Are Ocean Polluters Subject to Universal Jurisdiction – Canada Breaks the Ice', (1972) 6 *International Lawyer* 706.

65 J. T. Roberts, 'Globalizing Environmental Justice', in R. D. Sandler and P. C. Pezzullo (eds.), *Environmental Justice and Environmentalism: The Social Justice Challenge to the Environmental Movement* (2007), 285.

66 K. F. McCallion and H. R. Sharma, 'Environmental Justice without Borders: The Need for an International Court of the Environment to Protect Fundamental Environmental Rights', (1999) 32 *George Washington Journal of International Law and Economics* 351.

67 McLaughlin, *supra* note 25; P. Sharp, 'Prospects for Environmental Liability in the International Criminal Court', (1999) 18 *Virginia Environmental Law Journal* 217.

behaviour involved and the willingness of the international community to stand as one against it. As with international criminal tribunals' prosecution of 'core crimes', there is a central constitutive message in the idea that the international community is not simply 'complementary' to domestic prosecutions, but has an actual interest in standing in for itself as 'more than the sum of its parts'.

**PART II**

# Sustainable Development and International Crimes

# 5

# Environmental Damage and International Criminal Law

*Matthew Gillett*

## 1. INTRODUCTION

During the First Gulf War in 1991, Saddam Hussein ordered the remnants of the retreating Iraqi army to burn over 600 Kuwaiti oil wells.[1] The ensuing fires burned a million tons of oil, producing over 50,000 tons of sulphur dioxide, a huge amount of carbon dioxide, and over 100,000 tons of sooty smoke. Atmospheric pollution spread as far away as the Himalayas.[2] Although the plumes of thick black smoke did not produce the predicted grave health implications for human beings, lasting environmental damage was caused by oil leaking from damaged wells into surface pools. Soot flurries falling onto these oil pools combined with sand and gravel to form a layer of 'tarcrete' covering almost five percent of Kuwait's land area.[3] The fallout constitutes an ongoing threat to the fragile desert ecosystems of the region.[4]

Although the Iraqi Special Tribunal eventually tried Hussein for some of the atrocities committed at his behest, he never faced justice for his shocking attacks on the environment. His impunity for serious environmental destruction of an international nature is unsurprising. Although various prohibitions of international

[1] I. Peterson, 'The Natural Environment in Times of Armed Conflict: A Concern for International War Crimes Law?', (2009) 22 *Leiden Journal of International Law* 325, at 342; M. Schmitt, 'Green War: An Assessment of the Environmental Law of International Armed Conflict', (1997) 22 *Yale Journal of International Law* 1, at 15, 19, 75.

[2] S. Earle, 'Persian Gulf Pollution: Assessing the Damage One Year Later,' *National Geographic*, February 1992, 122, cited in Schmitt, *supra* note 1, at 19. See also Neil Popovic, 'Humanitarian Law, Protection of the Environment, and Human Rights', (1995) 8 *Georgetown International Environmental Law Review* 67, at 70.

[3] Five per cent of Kuwait's total land (approximately 17,800 square kilometres) is approximately 850 square kilometres.

[4] See R. Block, 'Kuwaiti Oil Wells', in A. Dworkin et al. (eds.), *Crimes of War 2.0: What the Public Should Know* (2007).

All views expressed herein are those of the author and do not represent those of the Office of the Prosecutor of the International Criminal Tribunal for the former Yugoslavia or the United Nations.

criminal law extend to environmental destruction either directly or indirectly, no individual has ever been convicted under them for environmental crimes.[5] The lack of successful prosecutions for environmental destruction is a collective failing of the international community.

The international community's inaction in the face of serious environmental damage also results in a jurisprudential vacuum. In the absence of judicial guidance on the prosecution of environmental damage in specific cases, the analyses contained in this book sit at the frontier of the study of international criminal law. This chapter presents an analysis of the provisions and principles of international criminal law that provide a basis for future prosecutions for environmental damage. Being forward looking, the assessments contained herein attempt to match normative aspirations with the practical steps necessary to apply the existing provisions and principles. It explains two key theoretical perspectives that underlie the prohibitions – anthropocentrism and ecocentrism – as well as the benefits and drawbacks of each approach. Where possible, historic examples of environmental damage are provided to show the issues likely to arise in connection with the prosecution of similar acts in the future. A recurring theme emerging from the analysis is the unexploited potential of international criminal law to end the impunity of those responsible for massive environmental destruction.

## 2. ANTHROPOCENTRIC AND ECOCENTRIC APPROACHES TO INTERNATIONAL CRIMINAL LAW

Environmental damage during armed conflict is not a new phenomenon. For example, the Book of Kings in the Old Testament of the Bible recounts how, during the ninth century BCE, the Israelites engaged in tactics of altering the local environment in an attack against the Moabites.[6] Likewise, prohibitions of environmental damage have a long pedigree. Restrictions on harming the natural environment were set out in the Old Testament.[7] Moreover, Muhammad's companion, the first caliph Abu Bakr, is said to have instructed his Muslim army to avoid burning or harming trees in the seventh century CE.[8]

[5] T. Weinstein, 'Prosecuting Attacks that Destroy the Environment: Environmental Crimes or Humanitarian Atrocities?', (2005) 17 *Georgetown International Environmental Law Review* 697, at 698.

[6] See Bible, Revised Standard Version, Old Testament ('Bible RSV'), 2 Kings 3:24–25 ('[T]he Israelites rose and attacked the Moabites.... And they overthrew the cities, and on every good piece of land every man threw a stone until it was covered; they stopped every spring of water, and felled all the good trees till only its stones were left in Kir-har'eseth, and the slingers surrounded and conquered it.') See also G. A. Smith, *The Book of Deuteronomy* (1918), 249.

[7] Bible RSV, Deuteronomy 20:19 ('If you besiege a town for a long time, making war against it in order to take it, you must not destroy its trees by wielding an axe against them. Although you may take food from them, you must not cut them down. Are trees in the field human beings that they should come under siege from you?')

[8] See Y. Aboul-Enein and S. Zuhur, *Islamic Rulings on Warfare* (2004), 22 ('Stop, O people, that I may give you ten rules for your guidance in the battlefield. Do not commit treachery or deviate from the

Despite these early developments, international laws and prosecutions against environmental damage have been slow to arrive.[9] A significant cause of this tardiness is the predominantly anthropocentric conception of international law applicable to armed conflict.[10] The environment has traditionally been viewed through an anthropocentric lens and characterised as an exploitable resource existing for the benefit of humankind. In addition, during times of armed conflict, the environment is usually relegated in significance behind military and political values.[11] As a result of this approach, there are few provisions of international criminal law directly protecting the environment against serious damage.

In recent years, it has become clear that the environment cannot sustain the damage caused to it during armed conflicts. Although there is a general consensus amongst states and other actors in the field of international criminal law that humankind's detrimental impact on the environment must be curbed, the theoretical underpinnings for this ecologically protective accord are less united.[12] On the one hand, many commentators adhere to the essentially utilitarian anthropocentric approach, valuing the environment to the extent it is able to serve the interests of humankind.[13] On the other hand, an emerging view ascribes the environment an intrinsic value, irrespective of whether human beings suffer as a result of its destruction.[14] This latter view is termed the ecocentric approach. Adherents to the ecocentric approach seek not only the application of international criminal law to environmental damage per se but also the development of new prohibitions criminalising damage to the environment, during and outside of a state of armed conflict.[15]

right path. You must not mutilate dead bodies. Neither kill a child, nor a woman, nor an aged man. Bring no harm to the trees, nor burn them with fire, especially those which are fruitful. Slay not any of the enemy's flock, save for your food. You are likely to pass by people who have devoted their lives to monastic services; leave them alone.')

9 See Section 5, *infra*.

10 See Schmitt, *supra* note 1, at 6, 56, 62.

11 M. Drumbl, 'Waging War against the World: The Need to Move from War Crimes to Environmental Crimes', (1998) 22 *Fordham International Law Journal* 122, at 123. The early international law publicist Hugo Grotius recognised the harm of taking a purely anthropocentric approach. He stated that 'if trees could speak, they would cry out that since they are not the cause of war it is wrong for them to bear its penalties'. Hugo Grotius, *On the Law of War and Peace* (1646) (F. W. Kelsey trans., 1995) at 747 cited in J. Cohan, 'Modes of Warfare and Evolving Standards of Environmental Protection under the International Law of War', (2003) 15 *Florida Journal of International Law* 481, at 500.

12 The split between the anthropocentric and ecocentric views resulted in the inclusion of two separate provisions addressing 'widespread, long-term, and severe' environmental damage in Additional Protocol I, Art. 55 from an anthropocentric view and Art. 35(3) from an ecocentric view, as discussed in more detail later; Schmitt, *supra* note 1, at 69–70.

13 See, e.g., Brigadier-General J. Garrett III, US Army, 'The Army and the Environment: Environmental Considerations during Army Operations', in R. Grunawalt, J. King, and R. McClain (eds.), *Protection of the Environment during Armed Conflict* (1996), Vol. 69 at 42, 45–46.

14 See, e.g., E. Jensen, 'The International Law of Environmental Warfare: Active and Passive Damage during Armed Conflict', (2005) 38 *Vanderbilt Journal of Transnational Law* 145.

15 See Section 6, *infra*.

Even where international criminal law does directly address environmental damage, it is relatively conservative. Only the most serious harm to the environment is designated as criminal. Debates in the international criminal law literature tend to focus on intentional and extraordinary destruction of the natural environment, such as the burning of the oil wells in Iraq[16] or the use of chemical agents to defoliate the Vietnamese forests in the 1970s.[17] Contrastingly, traditional ecological perspectives see many other types of human activity as potentially criminal because of the massive damage they cause to the environment. Examples include large-scale commercial fishing with fishnets, clearing wilderness for property development, and the construction of extensive motorway systems.[18] In this respect, ecological perspectives about the impact of societal activities on the environment seek to apply international criminal law beyond its current reach. Nonetheless, they are instructive for the future development of international criminal law.

Contrary to international criminal law, domestic criminal law prohibitions against environmental damage tend to be ecocentrically oriented: they criminalise damage to the environment per se, without being necessary to show harm to human beings or human interests. Although various domestic systems differ in their specific approaches to regulating environmental damage, a common feature is the existence of an environmental protection authority, specifically charged with enforcing the law protecting the environment and prosecuting offenders.[19] Breaches of environmental law in domestic systems are usually sanctioned by monetary fines, but are also increasingly regulated through custodial sentences.[20] Core values underlying and incorporated in domestic environmental legal instruments include the precautionary principle, intergenerational and intragenerational equity, and the protection of biodiversity.[21] These progressive values should be incorporated into international criminal law where appropriate, as discussed herein. Nonetheless, environmental crime is often perpetrated through international operations with effects in multiple countries. In this light, the limits of domestic law as a tool for combatting such transnational harm are self-evident and support the need to

16 Peterson, *supra* note 1, at 342; Schmitt, *supra* note 1, at 19, 75; Weinstein, *supra* note 5, at 708 (all discussing whether the burning of the oil wells in Iraq qualified as a war crime under the existing provisions of international law).

17 Peterson, *supra* note 1, at 331–32; A. Schwabach, 'Environmental Damage Resulting from the NATO Military Action against Yugoslavia', (2000) 25 *Columbia Journal of Environmental Law* 117, at 126 (all discussing operations carried out by the U.S. Army during the Vietnam War and international criminal law).

18 See R. White, *Crimes against Nature: Environmental Criminology and Ecological Justice* (2008), 11.

19 *Ibid.*, at 184.

20 See, e.g., 'West Virginia Health and Safety Official Sentenced to Prison', U. S. Environmental Protection Agency Press Release, 26 October 2009; *R* v. *Walters*, [1993] 1 NZLR 533 (New Zealand Court of Appeal); L. Westra, *Ecoviolence and the Law: Supranational Normative Foundations of Ecocrime* (2004), 231.

21 White, *supra* note 18, at 185.

develop effective sanctions under international criminal law against environmental damage.[22]

## 3. PROHIBITIONS OF ENVIRONMENTAL DAMAGE IN INTERNATIONAL CRIMINAL LAW

### 3.1. *Ecocentric Prohibitions*

Serious damage to the environment is criminalised in a number of provisions and principles of international criminal law. Two provisions of international criminal law are specifically ecocentric. Article 8(2)(b)(iv) (second limb) of the Rome Statute of the ICC and Article 35(3) of Additional Protocol I both prohibit causing widespread, long-term, and severe damage to the natural environment.[23] In addition to these provisions of international criminal law, ecocentric prohibitions are established in the Convention on the Prohibition of Environmental Modification Techniques[24] and under customary international law,[25] as described in Rules 43–45 of the International Committee of the Red Cross study on customary international humanitarian law.[26]

#### 3.1.1. Article 8(2)(b)(iv) of the Rome Statute of the International Criminal Court

A specific provision on 'widespread, long-term and severe damage' to the environment was first included in draft versions of the Rome Statute at the suggestion of New Zealand and Switzerland.[27] The formulation ultimately included in the Rome Statute, Article 8(2)(b)(iv), prohibits

> [i]ntentionally launching an attack in the knowledge that such attack will cause incidental loss of life or injury to civilians or damage to civilian objects or *widespread, long-term and severe damage to the natural environment* which would be clearly excessive in relation to the concrete and direct overall military advantage anticipated. (emphasis added)

22 *Ibid.*, at 193.

23 These two provisions differ in significant respects, as explained herein.

24 1977 Convention on the Prohibition of Military or Any Other Hostile Use of Environmental Modification Techniques, 31 UST 333, TIAS No 9614 ('ENMOD').

25 Customary international law can be described as evidence of a general practice accepted as law amongst the actors in public international law; see 1945 Statute of the International Court of Justice art. 38, 59 Stat. 1031; It consists of state practice and *opinio juris*, the latter of which refers to the 'subjective' or 'psychological' acceptance of a sense of legal obligation.

26 J. Henckaerts and L. Doswald-Beck (eds.), *Customary International Humanitarian Law* (2005) ('ICRC Rules').

27 Working Paper submitted by the Delegations of New Zealand and Switzerland, UN Preparatory Committee on the Establishment of an International Criminal Court, A/AC.249/1997/WG.1/DP.2 (1997), at 3.

The second limb of this provision, causing an attack that would result in widespread, long-term, and severe environmental damage, is ecocentric. The reach of Article 8(2)(b)(iv) is limited, because the provision only applies to international armed conflict. Many scholars find this limitation of Article 8(2)(b)(iv) to international armed conflict illogical and troubling.[28] Furthermore, its reach may be limited by the chapeau statement of Article 8, which notes that the court has 'jurisdiction in respect of war crimes in particular when committed as part of a plan or policy or as part of a large-scale commission of such crimes'. These qualifications have the potential to exclude many human-caused environmental disasters from the ambit of Article 8(2)(b)(iv).

Article 8(2)(b)(iv) requires that an 'attack' be launched. The attack does not have to be directed against the environment per se. It is sufficient that the attack is launched with the knowledge that it will cause damage of sufficient gravity to the environment. An example of an 'attack' is the American defoliation campaign during the Vietnam War – 'Operation Ranch Hand'.[29] During this operation, the U.S. Army sprayed more than 200 million gallons of herbicides, including the infamous Agent Orange, on the forests of Vietnam and Laos and cleared lands with large 'Roman plows' in an effort to remove the forest cover being used effectively by the Viet Cong and North Vietnamese army.[30] Encompassing many individual strikes, this overarching campaign would qualify as an attack.[31]

The most authoritative interpretation of the term 'natural environment' is that of the International Law Commission (ILC), which states that

> the words 'natural environment' should be taken broadly to cover the environment of the human race and where the human race develops, as well as areas the preservation of which is of fundamental importance in protecting the environment. These words therefore cover the seas, the atmosphere, climate, forests, and other plant cover, fauna, flora and other biological elements.[32]

[28] See, e.g., Dr. M. Wattad, 'The Rome Statute & Captain Planet: What Lies Between 'Crimes against Humanity' and the 'Natural Environment'?', (2009) 19 *Fordham Environmental Law Review* 265, 268; Drumbl, *supra* note 11, at 136. See also *Prosecutor v. Dusko Tadic*, Decision on the Defence Motion for Interlocutory Appeal on Jurisdiction, Case No.IT-94-1-A, App.Ch., 2 October 1995 ('Tadic Jurisdiction Decision'), para. 97.

[29] See A. Schwabach, 'Ecocide and Genocide in Iraq: International Law, the Marsh Arabs, and Environmental Damage in Non-International Conflict', (2004) 15 *Colorado Journal of International Environmental Law and Policy* 1, at 7; T. Schofield, 'The Environment as an Ideological Weapon: A Proposal to Criminalize Environmental Terrorism', (1999) 26 *Boston College Environmental Affairs Law Review* 619, at 635–6; Schmitt, *supra* note 1, at 9–10.

[30] See Schwabach, *supra* note 17, at 126.

[31] But see Peterson, *supra* note 1, at 336, 338, 342.

[32] International Law Commission, *Draft Code of Crimes against the Peace and Security of Mankind* (1991) 43(2) *Yearbook of the International Law Commission* 94, at 107, para. 4, cited in Peterson, at 328–29. See also Schmitt, *supra* note 1, at 5.

The term 'natural environment' also refers to the usability of the environment. Thus rendering the environment unusable – for example, through the dispersal of anti-personnel landmines throughout an area – would qualify under Article 8(2)(b)(iv).[33] The 'natural environment' is not limited to that part of the environment belonging to or under the control of an opposing party, but also covers damage to a party's own territory.[34] Tactics such as the Dutch version of 'scorched earth' in the 17th century, in which it destroyed dikes to flood its own lowlands and stall the advance of its enemies, would qualify as attacks on the natural environment.[35]

The core of Article 8(2)(b)(iv) is constituted by three terms – widespread, long-term, and severe. These three terms are conjunctive in Article 8(2)(b)(iv): they must all be met for criminal responsibility to arise.[36] The threshold for widespread, long-term, and severe damage is high. Typical battlefield damage is not likely to reach the threshold.[37] In light of the serious and ongoing damage caused by Saddam Hussein's intentional burning of over 600 Kuwaiti oil wells during the First Gulf War, as described earlier, the Article 8(2)(b)(iv) criteria would appear to be met. Nevertheless, some commentators consider that this malicious act would not reach the threshold, despite the serious and lasting damage it caused.[38] The continued debates in the literature about the legal characterisation of Hussein's burning of the oil wells demonstrate the difficulty of satisfying the terms of widespread, long-term, and severe.[39] However, the parties agreeing to the terms of the Rome Statute made it clear that the instrument was intended to end impunity for crimes of grave concern to the international community.[40] In accordance with the Vienna Convention on the Law of Treaties, the terms of the Rome Statute must be interpreted in light of its object and purpose.[41] Given the various interpretations of the terms 'widespread', 'long-term', and 'severe' in international law, as discussed herein, those interpretations consistent with the Rome Statute's purpose of ending impunity for grave crimes, including sufficiently serious damage to the environment, should be

33 See Schmitt, *supra* note 1, at 5 (referring to the term 'natural environment' in Art. 35(3) of Additional Protocol I).

34 Peterson, *supra* note 1, at 328.

35 See Schmitt, *supra* note 1, at 7.

36 But see Popovic, *supra* note 2, at 77 ('environmental damage that meets any one of the three elements is more than the international community should tolerate, even in times of war').

37 See *travaux préparatoires* to Art. 35(3) of Additional Protocol I CDDH/215/Rev.1, para. 27, in 15 Official Records of the Diplomatic Conference on the Reaffirmation and Development of International Humanitarian Law Applicable in Armed Conflict, Geneva 1974–77, at 268–9 (1978), cited in Cohan, *supra* note 11, at 503; see also Peterson, *supra* note 1, at 336.

38 See, e.g., Peterson, *supra* note 1, at 342; Schmitt, *supra* note 1, at 19, 75.

39 See Peterson, *supra* note 1, at 343.

40 1998 Rome Statute of the International Criminal Court Preamble, 2187 UNTS 90 ('Affirming that the most serious crimes of concern to the international community as a whole must not go unpunished... Determined to put an end to impunity for the perpetrators of these crimes and thus to contribute to the prevention of such crimes').

41 1969 Vienna Convention on the Law of Treaties, 1155 UNTS 331, Art. 31(1).

preferred.[42] These terms should not be interpreted so strictly as to prevent serious environmental destruction from ever being prosecuted.

The term 'widespread' refers to the required geographical scope of the environmental damage. The specific threshold in terms of square kilometres remains undefined. The Environmental Modification Convention (ENMOD) defines 'widespread' as several hundred square kilometres.[43] Other minimum requirements suggested by commentators rise to thousands of square kilometres.[44] However, imposing a high minimum threshold for 'widespread' is inappropriate in light of the massive variation in the geographic size of state parties to the Rome Statute, which include the world's second largest country in terms of size – Canada (nearly 10,000,000 square kilometres) – alongside minute countries such as Liechtenstein (160 square kilometres) and the Cook Islands (240 square kilometres). These small countries are unlikely to have intended a definition of 'widespread' that would exclude the destruction of their entire natural habitat from consideration.

One possibility is a relative standard, defining 'widespread' according to the size of the territory within which the damage occurs, and leaving it to the ICC judiciary to apply this standard in particular cases.[45] According to this approach, 100 square kilometres of environmental destruction in Liechtenstein may be considered sufficiently widespread, even if the destruction of 100 square kilometres of environmental damage in Nunavut were not considered to reach the widespread threshold. Accordingly, for the purposes of Article 8(2)(b)(iv) the determination of a single absolute standard of 'widespread' may not be possible.

The notion 'long-term' refers to the temporal duration of the environmental damage. As with the term 'widespread', the specific minimum duration of 'long-term' remains undefined. The parties to ENMOD agreed that 'long-lasting' in Article 1 refers to a period of several months or a season.[46] However, the 'long-term' duration required in Articles 35(3) and 55 of Additional Protocol I has been interpreted to mean a period of decades.[47] Because the most serious aspects of the damage caused by Saddam Hussein's lighting of the Kuwaiti oil wells lasted a shorter time than expected, many commentators considered this to fall short of the long-term requirement of Additional Protocol I.[48] Nonetheless, in light of the need to ensure that the Rome Statute is effective in punishing the commission of serious damage to the environment, an overly restrictive interpretation of 'long-term' should

[42] The principle of *nullem crimen sine lege* must also be borne in mind.

[43] Understanding I of the Conference of the Committee of Disarmament ('ENMOD Memorandum of Understanding'), reprinted in A. Roberts & R. Guelff eds., *Documents on the Law of War* (1989).

[44] Peterson, *supra* note 1, at 331–32.

[45] But see Peterson, *supra* note 1, at 331.

[46] See ENMOD Memorandum of Understanding, *supra* note 43.

[47] Schmitt, *supra* note 1, at 71, 107.

[48] See, e.g., Y. Dinstein, *The Conduct of Hostilities under the Law of International Armed Conflict* (2004), 194, cited *in* Peterson, *supra* note 1, at 342.

be avoided. Instead, 'long-term' should be interpreted in line with the understanding of the state parties to ENMOD.

The term 'severe' refers to the intensity of the damage caused to the environment independent of its geographic ambit or temporal duration. Severe environmental damage denotes damage going beyond typical battlefield destruction, as discussed earlier. Examples of environmental destruction that have been described as sufficiently severe include the 'dam-buster' raids during the Second World War. These raids destroyed the Mohne and Eder dams in an effort to cut off water from the Ruhr industrial complex. They resulted in the death of more than 1,300 civilians and cut off drinking water and energy to four million Germans.[49] In other guidance, most commentators agree that Saddam Hussein's environmental destruction committed during the First Gulf War was sufficiently severe.[50]

The plain terms of Article 8(2)(b)(iv) make it clear that knowledge of the expected environmental damage satisfies the *mens rea* element. The fact that the primary motive behind the attack was a military one will not absolve an accused.[51] However, even proving this indirect intent will be difficult. For example, if high winds fanned flames arising from an attack, thereby leading to far greater damage than caused by the initial impact of the attack, would this be attributable to an accused? Even more complex questions of causation would likely arise in relation to damage such as that resulting from the release of chemicals into the environment.[52]

In the First Gulf War, Saddam Hussein warned that he would destroy the Kuwaiti oil wells if the coalition forced the Iraqi army out of Kuwait.[53] Despite this malice aforethought, prosecuting Hussein under Article 8(2)(b)(iv) would have been complicated (in a hypothetical scenario where Article 8(2)(b)(iv) was in operation in 1991). It might have been difficult to prove that he was aware of the extent of possible environmental damage.[54] This shows why the terms of Article 8(2)(b)(iv) should not be interpreted too strictly. For each increase in the thresholds of the damage elements (widespread, long-term, severe), the difficulty of proving that an accused had the requisite knowledge increases exponentially.[55]

One means of addressing potential problems relating to *mens rea* is educating military decision makers about the environmental consequences of military actions and related prohibitions of international law. The International Committee of the

49 See Schmitt, *supra* note 1, at 8.

50 See, e.g., Peterson, *supra* note 1, at 342; Schmitt, *supra* note 1, at 19, 75.

51 See also International Criminal Court, Elements of Crimes, UN Doc. PCNICC/2000/1/Add.2 (2000), at 20 ('ICC Element of Crimes').

52 See, e.g., Peterson, *supra* note 1, at 335 (questioning whether Art. 8(2)(b)(iv) would apply if the damage were reversible).

53 See quote at start of chapter.

54 Weinstein, *supra* note 5, at 705.

55 See generally J. Lawrence and K. Heller, 'The First Ecocentric Environmental War Crime: The Limits of Article 8(2)(b)(iv) of the Rome Statute', (2007) 20 *Georgetown International Environmental Law Review* 61, at 79–85.

Red Cross (ICRC) has started this important work through the publication and distribution of the *Guidelines for Military Manuals and Instructions on the Protection of the Environment in Times of Armed Conflict*.[56]

The final clause of Article 8(2)(b)(iv) – 'would be clearly excessive in relation to the concrete and direct overall military advantage anticipated' – introduces a balancing test into the evaluation of environmental damage caused by armed conflict. The balancing test distinguishes Article 8(2)(b)(iv) from genocide and crimes against humanity, which are absolutely forbidden irrespective of any anticipated military advantage.[57] Because of this clause, Article 8(2)(b)(iv) cannot be seen as purely ecocentric. Even if the harm it seeks to prevent (damage to the environment) is ecocentric, it allows the prohibition to be overridden where military interests require it.

The ICC Elements of Crimes state that the 'military advantage anticipated' is assessed from the perspective of the perpetrator on the basis of the information available to him or her at the time of launching the attack.[58] However, it is unclear whether the 'clearly excessive' element is assessed from the perpetrator's subjective viewpoint or from an objective viewpoint. The Elements of Crimes state that the perpetrator must make the 'value judgement' inherent in the provision, which supports the subjective approach. However, the following sentence of the Elements of Crimes requires that '[a]n evaluation of that value judgement must be based on the requisite information available to the perpetrator at the time'.[59] This qualification implies that an assessment of the perpetrator's value judgement is required, which supports the objective approach.

However, these apparently conflicting sentences can be reconciled. In accordance with the first sentence, the court should satisfy itself as to whether the perpetrator carried out the value judgement. If the perpetrator concluded that the environmental damage was not justified by the military objective, then liability would arise. Conversely, if the perpetrator considered that the environmental damage was justified, then the court would carry out the 'evaluation' of the perpetrator's assessment, as referred to in the Elements of Crimes. A finding that the perpetrator's evaluation was a reasonable one would result in an acquittal. However, a patently unreasonable assessment by the perpetrator would not be grounds to escape liability.

The problem with taking a purely subjective approach is that every military commander or political leader accused under Article 8(2)(b)(iv) will claim that they considered the environmental damage to be justified. This occurred in the Second World War prosecution of the German General Lothar Rendulic for excessive damage caused by his scorched-earth tactics.[60] Given the complications and vagaries of

[56] ICRC, 'Guidelines for Military Manuals and Instructions on the Protection of the Environment in Times of Armed Conflict' (1996) 311 *International Review of the Red Cross* 230, www.icrc.org/web/eng/siteeng0.nsf/html/57JN38 (last accessed 16 October 2009).

[57] See Drumbl, *supra* note 11, at 135.

[58] ICC Elements of Crimes, *supra* note 51, at fn. 36. See also Weinstein, *supra* note 5, at 708, fn. 95.

[59] *Ibid.*, fn. 37.

[60] See Section 4.1, *infra*.

measuring environmental harm, as well as the commitment of military commanders and political leaders to their military objectives,[61] it will be very difficult to prove that they did not believe the environmental damage was justified, no matter how unreasonable their assessment.

In any event, the balancing of environmental damage against military imperatives will be difficult to carry out.[62] For example, the dropping of atomic bombs on Nagasaki and Hiroshima during the Second World War caused massive and predictable environmental damage.[63] There is no doubt that these attacks would satisfy the widespread, long-term, and severe requirements of Article 8(2)(b)(iv). However, there is also no doubt that the attacks entailed a huge military advantage. Debates have raged ever since as to whether the damage was excessive in relation to the military advantage gained. Thus, even the clearest cases of environmental damage may be difficult to assess under the balancing test.

### 3.1.2. Article 35(3) of Additional Protocol I to the Geneva Conventions

Article 35(3) of Additional Protocol I to the Geneva Conventions is the predecessor to Article 8(2)(b)(iv) of the Rome Statute. It remains in force to this day and is important to discuss because it is not restricted by all the limits that apply in the context of the International Criminal Court. Article 35(3) states: 'It is prohibited to employ methods or means of warfare which are intended, or may be expected, to cause widespread, long-term and severe damage to the natural environment.'

Where the widespread, long-term, and severe damage criteria are met, the provision sets out an absolute prohibition. It does not contain a diluting 'military necessity' or 'proportionality' balancing test. Instead, it protects the environment per se.[64] Some parties consider the ecocentric and absolute nature of Article 35(3) problematic. Upon review of the provision, the Joint Chiefs of Staff of the U.S. Armed Forces considered the lack of any balancing test 'militarily unacceptable'.[65] The United States, France, and the United Kingdom are all persistent objectors to Article 35(3), particularly in relation to nuclear weapons.[66]

As in Article 8(2)(b)(iv) of the Rome Statute, the terms 'widespread, long-term and severe' in Article 35(3) are conjunctive. These terms have already been assessed, as has the definition of 'natural environment'.[67] Article 35(3) has not yet provided

61 See, e.g., Garrett, *supra* note 13, at 45–46 ('environmental considerations should not obstruct the application of the principles of war during armed conflict').

62 Cohan, *supra* note 11, at 494.

63 See Schmitt, *supra* note 1, at 8.

64 Y. Sandoz et al. (eds.), Commentary to Additional Protocols of 8 June 1977 to the Geneva Conventions of 12 August 1949 (1987), para. 1441 ('ICRC Commentary').

65 Cohan, *supra* note 11, at 505.

66 J. Marsh, '*Lex Lata* or *Lex Ferenda*? Rule 45 of the ICRC Study on Customary International Humanitarian Law', (2008) 198 *Military Law Review* 116, at 118.

67 See Section 3.1.1 *infra*.

the basis for any successful prosecutions under international criminal law. However, the assessment carried out by a committee from the Office of the Prosecutor of the ICTY of the applicability of Article 35(3) to the NATO actions during its bombing campaign against the Federal Republic of Yugoslavia (FRY) in 1999 provides some guidance.[68]

The committee found that the conditions for the application of Article 35(3) 'are extremely stringent and their scope and contents imprecise'.[69] It stated that Articles 35(3) and 55 'only cover very significant damage', and 'it is thought that the notion of "long-term" damage in Additional Protocol I would need to be measured in years rather than months'.[70] The committee found that the NATO bombing campaign did cause damage to the environment, but that the damage did not reach the threshold required by Additional Protocol I.[71] Although the committee's report confirms that the threshold of environmental damage required for Article 35(3) is high, it adds little detail to the analysis of the elements of Article 35(3). This further highlights the need for judicial consideration of the terms 'widespread,' 'long-term', and 'severe'.

### 3.1.3. Convention on the Prohibition of Environmental Modification Techniques (ENMOD)

ENMOD was created in the wake of the Vietnam War. It is designed to address the long history of using environmental modification techniques as a means of war.[72] It prohibits state parties from using hostile environmental modification techniques that have 'widespread, long-term or severe effects as the means of destruction, damage or injury to another state party'.[73] Unlike Article 8(2)(b)(iv) and Article 35(3), the terms of the ENMOD prohibition are not conjunctive. Furthermore, it prospectively prohibits activities that are not currently feasible due to technological constraints.[74] Consequently, ENMOD provides broad coverage against damage that is either widespread or long-term or severe (or any combination thereof).

However, ENMOD is only of indirect relevance to international criminal law. It does not impose individual criminal responsibility for breaches of its terms.[75]

68 See Office of the Prosecutor Press Release, Prosecutor's Report on the NATO Bombing Campaign PR/P.I.S./510-e (2000); Final Report to the Prosecutor by the Committee Established to Review the NATO Bombing Campaign against the Federal Republic of Yugoslavia ('Final Report on NATO'), www.icty.org/sid/7846 (last accessed 4 October 2009). Views on the final recommendations of the report are mixed. See, e.g., P. Benvenuti, 'The ICTY Prosecutor and the Review of the NATO Bombing Campaign against the Federal Republic of Yugoslavia', (2001) 12 EJIL 503.

69 Final Report on NATO, *supra* note 68, para. 15.

70 *Ibid.*, at para. 15.

71 *Ibid.*, at paras. 14, 17.

72 Weinstein, *supra* note 5, at 700.

73 ENMOD, *supra* note 24, at Art. 1.

74 Jensen, *supra* note 14, at 154.

75 Cohan, *supra* note 11, at 524.

Instead, its enforcement is post hoc and political in nature.[76] Accordingly, ENMOD is primarily useful as an interpretive aid for other provisions and principles that do entail individual criminal responsibility.

### 3.1.4. Customary International Law

Customary international law features a number of principles that protect the environment. For example, the obligation on states not to use their territory to harm the territory and natural environment of other states is well established in customary international law.[77] Although untested to date, the theoretical possibility of carrying out prosecutions under customary international law for serious environmental damage is significant. Customary international law prohibitions could provide the foundation for prosecutions in internationalised tribunals[78] or in domestic courts on the basis of universal jurisdiction.[79] The following principles of customary international law could potentially provide a basis for the prosecution of individuals for serious damage to the environment.

In its landmark study on customary international humanitarian law, the ICRC concluded that its Rule 45 forms part of the corpus of customary international law: 'The use of methods or means of warfare that are intended, or may be expected, to cause widespread, long-term and severe damage to the natural environment is prohibited. Destruction of the natural environment may not be used as a weapon.'[80]

The first sentence of Rule 45 reflects Article 35(3) of Additional Protocol I, which has also been incorporated into Article 8(2)(b)(iv). The fact that 110 states have ratified the Rome Statute further confirms the customary status of the rule.[81] Rule 45 does not contain the additional balancing test that the state parties chose to add into Article 8(2)(b)(iv) of the Rome Statute.

The ICRC study found that Rule 45 'arguably' applies to non-international armed conflict.[82] In this respect, Rule 45 presents an alternative way of overcoming one of the most serious limitations inherent in Article 8(2)(b)(iv) – the

[76] Weinstein, *supra* note 5, at 701.

[77] See Legality of the Threat or Use of Nuclear Weapons, 1996 I.C.J. (Advisory Opinion) (General List 95), Para. 29, 35 I.L.M. 809, para. 1343 ('Nuclear Weapons Case'); Jensen, *supra* note 14, at 161; Schwabach, *supra* note 29, at 16; Schmitt, *supra* note 56, at 271.

[78] For example, at the ICTY, prosecutions for crimes established in customary international law are permissible where the prohibition satisfies the four so-called Tadicconditions. Tadic Jurisdiction Decision, *supra* note 28, at para. 94. See also Final Report on Nato, *supra* note 68, at para. 15.

[79] For an in-depth discussion of universal jurisdiction and its application in domestic legal systems, see L. Reydams, *Universal Jurisdiction: International and Municipal Legal Perspectives* (2005).

[80] ICRC Rules, *supra* note 26, at 151.

[81] But see J. Bellinger and W. Haynes, 'A US Government Response to the International Committee of the Red Cross Study Customary International Humanitarian Law', (2007) 89 *International Review of the Red Cross* 443, cited in Marsh, *supra* note 66, at 129, 132.

[82] Marsh, *supra* note 66, at 156–57.

restriction to international armed conflict. However, Rule 45 is not unlimited in application: the ICRC has acknowledged that it does not apply to nuclear weapons.[83]

The ICRC study also discussed other principles of customary international law that impose prohibitions on damaging the environment.[84] In Rule 43 it clarifies that the international humanitarian law principles of distinction, military necessity, and proportionality apply to attacks against the natural environment resulting from military operations.

The destruction of the environment during hostilities in the absence of any military objective is criminal, just as the destruction of civilian objects is criminal.[85] However, for such damage to constitute a crime under international criminal law, it must be sufficiently serious to be of concern to the international community as a whole.[86] Similarly, breaches of the principles of necessity (destruction of the environment through the unnecessary or wanton application of force) and proportionality (destruction of the environment disproportionate to the expected military advantage) would also have to be sufficiently serious for international criminal law to apply.

A breach of the principle of necessity, namely the unnecessary or wanton application of force, constitutes an international crime.[87] The International Military Tribunal at Nuremberg found that breaching the principle of necessity constitutes a violation of international law:

> [Military necessity] does not permit the killing of innocent inhabitants for purposes of revenge or the satisfaction of a lust to kill. The destruction of property to be lawful must be imperatively demanded by the necessities of war. Destruction as an end in itself is a violation of international law. There must be some reasonable

83 J. Henckaerts, 'Customary International Humanitarian Law: A Response to US Comments', (2007) 89 *International Review of the Red Cross* 473, at 482. Note that many treaties contain prohibitions against the use of nuclear weapons on specific vulnerable areas of the world; for example the 1959 Antarctic Treaty; 1963 Treaty Banning Nuclear Weapon Tests in the Atmosphere; 1967 Treaty for the Prohibition of Nuclear Weapons in Latin America (Treaty of Tlatelolco); 1971 Treaty on the Prohibition of the Emplacement of Nuclear Weapons and Other Weapons of Mass Destruction on the Sea-Bed and the Ocean Floor and in the Subsoil Thereof; cited in Popovic, *supra* note 2, at 82–83.

84 Marsh 2008, *supra* note 66, at 133.

85 ICRC Rules, *supra* note 26, at rule 43.

86 See, e.g., 1993 Statute of the International Criminal Tribunal for former Yugoslavia Art. 1, 32 ILM 1192 ('ICTY Statute'); Tadic Jurisdiction Decision, *supra* note 28, at para. 94; Rome Statute, *supra* note 40, at Preamble, Art. 1, Art. 8(1); 2002 Statute of the Special Court for Sierra Leone Art. 1, 2178 UNTS 138.

87 See ICRC Commentary, *supra* note 64, at para. 1395. See also Nuclear Weapons Case, *supra* note 77, at 31; St Petersburg Declaration Renouncing the Use, in Time of War, of Explosive Projectiles under 400 Grammes Weight, 1868, *Laws of Armed Conflicts* 101; 'Instructions for the Government of the United States in the Field by Order of the Secretary of War,' 24 April 1863 (also known as the Lieber Code); Jensen, *supra* note 14, at 156; Schmitt, *supra* note 1, at 52, 106; Schmitt, *supra* note 56, at 271, 294.

connection between the destruction of property and the overcoming of the enemy forces.[88]

Fifty years later, the Appeals Chamber of the ICTY reaffirmed this prohibition.[89]

Despite its central role in international humanitarian law, the principle of necessity lacks precision. The question arises whether it could constitute a basis per se for a criminal prosecution for damage to the environment. At no point in Additional Protocol I or in the other international humanitarian law treaties does it state that the unnecessary or wanton destruction of the environment will per se result in criminal sanction. However, the lack of an explicit treaty provision on the punishment of a breach of a principle is not a bar to criminal prosecution.[90] What is required is the clear and unequivocal recognition of the rules of warfare in international law and state practice indicating an intention to criminalise the provision.[91]

The laws of armed conflict criminalise several specific instances of unnecessary and wanton destruction, such as the extensive destruction and appropriation of property, not justified by military necessity and carried out unlawfully and wantonly.[92] Numerous international treaties contain prohibitions on damaging the environment.[93] Furthermore, there is no dispute that human beings rather than abstract entities make the decisions that result in breaches of these environmentally protective provisions.[94] In light of these considerations, the customary international law principle of necessity bears considerable potential for the prosecution of excessive environmental damage.

The principle of proportionality is a well-established doctrine underlying international humanitarian law. The proportionality principle demands that an operation against a legitimate military target, which is likely to result in harm to civilians or other protected values, be justified by the corresponding military advantage anticipated. Rule 43 clarifies that this protection extends to the environment. Disproportionate acts are criminalised in a number of provisions of international humanitarian law.[95]

88 *Hostages Case, (US* v. *List et al)*, XI Trials of War Criminals before the Nuremberg Military Tribunals under Control Council Law No.10, October 1946–April 1949, 759, 1253–54 (1950), cited in Schmitt, *supra* note 1, at 52.

89 *Prosecutor* v. *Dario Kordić & Mario Čerkez*, Judgement, Case No. IT-95–14/2-A, App.Ch., 17 December 2004, para. 686. It should be noted that the Appeals Chamber's statement was made in the context of a discussion of the commission of violent acts against people as reprisals for previous conduct.

90 Trials of War Criminals before the Nuremberg Military Tribunals under Control Council Law No. 10, Trial of Major War Criminals, Proceedings of the International Military Tribunal sitting at Nuremberg Germany, Part XXII, at 445, 467 (1950) ('Nuremberg Trial'), referred to in Tadic Jurisdiction Decision, *supra* note 28, para. 128.

91 Nuremberg Trial, *supra* note 90, at 445–47, 467.

92 Rome Statute, *supra* note 40, at Art. 8(2)(a)(iv).

93 See Section 3.2.4, *infra*.

94 Nuremberg Trial, *supra* note 90, at 447. Referred to by Appeals Chamber in Tadic Jurisdiction Decision, *supra* note 28, para. 128.

95 See, e.g., Rome Statute, *supra* note 40, at Art. 8(2)(b)(iv).

The proportionality test suffers from a lack of precision, partly because it requires an inherently fact-intensive evaluation. Nonetheless, in carrying out the proportionality assessment with regards to environmental damage, three general considerations should be borne in mind. First, armed conflict generally results in damage to the environment. Prohibitions against destruction of the environment were not supposed to apply to 'ordinary battlefield damage' as seen in France after the First World War.[96] Second, irreversible damage to the environment weighs heavily in favour of a finding of disproportionality. Acts such as the complete destruction of a forest, or causing the extinction of a species or subspecies of animal, cannot be undone. They are grave from the ecocentric perspective because they terminate the existence of the environmental entity and extinguish its intrinsic value for all time. They are grave from an anthropocentric perspective because they deny future generations the enjoyment of that environmental entity. Third, it will be relevant to the assessment whether other, less destructive means of achieving the necessary military objective were available. The need to minimise collateral damage is reflected in a number of provisions of international humanitarian law, including Article 57(2) and (3) of Additional Protocol I.[97] If other such means were available but not taken, this will weigh in favour of the attacks being disproportionate.[98] This approach is essentially an application of the precautionary principle, which has been established as customary international law in relation to military attacks resulting in environmental damage.[99]

The application of the principles of necessity and proportionality was considered by the committee examining NATO's actions in the FRY.[100] It noted that where the attack constituted a grave threat to the environment it would have to confer a very substantial military advantage to be considered legitimate.[101] The committee further observed that '[i]f there is a choice of weapons or methods of attack available, a commander should select those which are most likely to avoid, or at least minimize, incidental damage'.[102]

The underdeveloped nature of the proportionality principle renders any prosecution thereunder for environmental damage unlikely in the near future. However, as the scientific understanding of environmental damage progresses, the proportionality principle may well become a cornerstone mechanism for distinguishing acceptable from unacceptable environmental damage, just as this principle has been instrumental in the development of international humanitarian law relating to civilians and civilian objects.

96 See Section 3.1.1, *infra*.

97 1977 Additional Protocol Relating to the Protection of Victims of International Armed Conficts Art. 57 (2, 1125 UNTS 3) ('Additional Protocol I').

98 Schmitt, *supra* note 1, at 6; Schmitt, *supra* note 56, at 276, 313.

99 See ICRC Rules, *supra* note 26, at rule 43.

100 Final Report on NATO, *supra* note 68, at para. 15.

101 Final Report on NATO, *supra* note 68, at para. 20.

102 Final Report, *supra* note 68, at paras. 21, 24. The committee added that '[i]n doing so, however, he is entitled to take account of factors such as stocks of different weapons and likely future demands, the timeliness of attack and risks to his own forces'.

### 3.2. *Anthropocentric Prohibitions*

International humanitarian law is designed to alleviate human suffering. As well as protecting human values, many provisions of international humanitarian law provide incidental protection to the environment. Although these provisions are not primarily directed at the environmental harm per se, they present a viable alternative means of prosecuting the perpetration of environmental damage.

By no means is the breadth of protection offered by the anthropocentric provisions more limited than that offered by the ecocentric protections. In fact, it is more extensive in many cases, particularly in light of the stringent requirements of the ecocentric provisions.[103] For example, the following provisions could be used to prosecute the perpetrators of actions that cause incidental but serious harm to the environment.

#### 3.2.1. Rome Statute of the International Criminal Court

A number of war crimes within the jurisdiction of the ICC could apply to serious environmental damage where it was caused in conjunction with harm to civilians or civilian objects: Article 8(2)(a)(iv) (extensive destruction and appropriation of property, not justified by military necessity and carried out unlawfully and wantonly);[104] Article 8(2)(b)(ii) (intentionally directing attacks against civilian objects, that is, objects that are not military objectives); Articles 8(2)(b)(xiii), 8(2)(e)(xii)[105] (destroying or seizing the enemy's property unless such destruction or seizure be imperatively demanded by the necessities of war);[106] Article 8(2)(b)(xvii) (employing poison or poisoned weapons); Article 8(2)(b)(xviii) (employing asphyxiating, poisonous, or other gases and all analogous liquids, materials, or devices); Article 8(2)(b)(xxv) (intentionally using starvation of civilians as a method of warfare by depriving them of objects indispensable to their survival, including wilfully impeding relief supplies as provided for under the Geneva Conventions).[107]

It is also possible that the crime against humanity or other inhumane acts would cover serious environmental damage.[108] An example would be where the natural

[103] See Weinstein, *supra* note 5.

[104] See also ICTY Statute, *supra* note 86, at Art. 3(b) (Wanton destruction of cities, towns or villages, or devastation not justified by military necessity); 1949 Geneva Convention Relative to the Protection of Civilian Persons in Time of War Art. 53, 147, 75 UNTS 287; 1907 Convention Respecting the Laws and Customs of War on Land, Art. 23(g), 55, 36 Stat. 2277 ('Hague Conventions IV').

[105] This provision mirrors Article 8(2)(b)(xiii), but applies in non-international armed conflict.

[106] It is required that the property was protected from that destruction or seizure under the international law of armed conflict; ICC Elements of Crimes, *supra* note 51, at 44.

[107] See also Additional Protocol I, *supra* note 97, at art. 54; 1949 Protocol Additional to the Geneva Conventions of 12 August 1949, and Relating to the Protection of Victims of Non-International Armed Conflicts Art. 14 ('Additional Protocol II'), 1125 UNTS 609, which applies the prohibition to non-international armed conflict; Schmitt, *supra* note 56, at 301–02; Schwabach, *supra* note 29, at 25.

[108] Rome Statute, *supra* note 40, art. 7(1)(k); ICTY Statue, *supra* note 86, art. 5(i); 1994 Statute of the International Criminal Tribunal for Rwanda art. 3(i), 33 ILM 1598.

environment was of special significance to a people and the perpetrator knew that by destroying it he or she was causing that people great suffering.[109]

In addition to those direct provisions, a number of prohibitions could provide incidental regulation of environmental damage where that damage was inflicted as a means of causing suffering to human beings. In particular, destruction of the environment that was carried out as a means of deporting or forcibly transferring parts of the population would constitute a crime against humanity under Article 7(1)(d) of the Rome Statute, if it were carried out in a widespread or systematic manner. In cases where the environmental damage led to death, charges of murder and possibly extermination as crimes against humanity would also be feasible.

Additionally, the use of environmental destruction to cause serious harm to national, religious, racial, or ethnic groups of people (for example, through large-scale killing, severe mental or physical suffering, inflicting conditions of life on a group of people calculated to bring about its physical destruction in whole or in part, or imposing measures intended to prevent births within the group) could be charged as genocide if committed with the intent to destroy that group in whole or in part.[110] In this respect, the indictment of Omar Al-Bashir at the ICC has been instructive. The prosecution accused Al-Bashir of carrying out the genocide in Darfur using such methods as destroying 'food, wells and water pumping machines, shelter, crops and livestock, as well as any physical structures capable of sustaining life or commerce'.[111] Although the Trial Chamber rejected the prosecution's application for a warrant of arrest on genocide charges, it appeared to accept that Al-Bashir's genocidal intent was a reasonable inference based on the evidence.[112]

The prosecution of serious environmental damage that arises in connection with serious harm to human beings as crimes against humanity is advantageous for the prosecution of environmental damage as a war crime in at least one respect. Unlike war crimes, crimes against humanity are punishable under international criminal law irrespective of whether they occur in a state of armed conflict. This is a significant hurdle. By stepping outside this constraint, the potential to end the impunity of those damaging the environment is enhanced significantly.[113] However, it should also be borne in mind that crimes against humanity, in keeping with their name, are inherently anthropocentric. Consequently, the use of this category of crime can at best serve as a stepping-stone towards the prosecution of environmental damage per se under ecocentric prohibitions of international criminal law.

[109] See also Wattad, *supra* note 28, at 282.

[110] See Rome Statute, *supra* note 40, art. 6(a), (b), (c) and (d).

[111] Prosecution's Application under Article 58, ICC-02/05–151-US-Exp and ICC-02/05–151-US-Exp-Anxsl-89; Corrigendum ICC-02/05–151-US-Exp-Corr and Corrigendum ICC-02/05–151-US-Exp-Corr-Anxsl & 2. A public redacted version was filed on 12 September 2008, ICC-02/05–157-AnxA ('Prosecution Application'), para. 174.

[112] *Prosecutor* v. *Al Bashir*, Decision on the Prosecution's Application for a Warrant of Arrest against Omar Hassan Ahmad Al Bashir, ICC-02/05–01/09–3, Pre-T.Ch., 14 March 2009.

[113] See Weinstein, *supra* note 5, at 714.

### 3.2.2. Additional Protocol I to the Geneva Conventions

The prohibitions in Additional Protocol I that entail individual criminal responsibility overlap to a large degree with those set out in the Rome Statute. Nonetheless, several provisions merit particular mention due to their relevance to environmental damage.

Placed under the heading 'Civilian Objects', Article 55 prohibits the use of methods or means of warfare that are intended or may be expected to cause widespread, long-term, and severe damage to the natural environment, and thereby to prejudice the health or survival of the population. Its terms essentially mirror those of Article 35(3). Article 55 was specifically designed to be an anthropocentric provision that protected the environment, as shown by the additional requirement that the damage be expected to 'prejudice the health or survival of the population'.[114] Both were considered together by the committee examining the environmental impact of NATO's bombing campaign against the FRY in 1999.

Article 56 of Additional Protocol I prohibits attacking dams, dikes, and nuclear electrical power stations if the release of 'dangerous forces and consequent severe losses among the civilian population' might result. It also prohibits attacking any surrounding military objective that might result in the release of dangerous forces.[115] The fact that the dams, dikes, or power stations are military objectives does not remove this protection, unless they provide regular, significant, and direct support of military operations.[116]

The release of dangerous forces clearly has the potential to result in significant environmental damage. The disaster at Chernobyl in 1986 resulted in the release of large amounts of radioactive uranium and graphite into the atmosphere, rendering 70,000 square kilometres of cropland in Russia, Ukraine, and Belarus radioactive.[117] A military attack on a nuclear installation could easily lead to even greater damage. Despite concerns about the massive destruction potentially arising from such attacks, Article 56 remains controversial. For example, the United States has opposed its terms on the basis that they place too many constraints on military operations.[118] Because of concerns about the restrictions on military operations imposed by Article 56, it did not find its way into the Rome Statute.

### 3.2.3. Other Public International Law Treaties Prohibiting Means and Weapons of Warfare

Some international treaties contain prohibitions entailing individual criminal responsibility broader than those specifically listed in the statutes of the international

[114] Additional Protocol I, *supra* note 97, art. 55. Art. 55 is not applicable to warfare conducted at sea or in the air, unless the warfare affects civilians on land; see Schmitt, *supra* note 1, at 81.

[115] Additional Protocol I, *supra* note 97, art. 56(1).

[116] In the case of dams, they must also be used other than in their normal manner; *ibid.*, Art. 56(2).

[117] See Schofield, *supra* note 29, at 627.

[118] See Cohan, *supra* note 11, at 509.

criminal tribunals. The Chemical Weapons Convention of 1993, for example, prevents use or development of chemical weapons.[119] State parties are required to enact penal legislation to ensure that individuals within their jurisdiction who act in breach of those obligations are punished.[120] Similarly, under the 1997 Ottawa Treaty, 156 state parties agreed not to develop, use, or stockpile anti-personnel mines.[121] The convention entails criminal responsibility, because state parties are required to enact penal legislation to ensure that individuals within their jurisdiction who act in breach of those obligations are punished.[122]

Other treaties prohibiting certain means and weapons of warfare are less clear as to whether they entail individual criminal responsibility. For example, the United Nations Conventional Weapons Convention brings together a number of treaties containing prohibitions of certain uses of conventional weapons. Although the prohibitions are anthropocentric, they are relevant because they restrict or ban the use of weapons and means of warfare that typically result in significant environmental damage, such as the indiscriminate use of landmines, explosive remnants of war, and incendiary attacks.[123] The convention does not expressly require parties to implement penal legislation enforcing the prohibitions. Nonetheless, the provisions provide strong indications of the types of activities that may result in criminal sanctions in the future as international law applicable to environmental damage crystallises.

## 4. PROSECUTIONS FOR ENVIRONMENTAL DAMAGE

In the history of international criminal law, no individual has ever been convicted of environmental crimes.[124] However, several prosecutions for traditional war crimes have featured elements of environmental destruction. These cases provide useful guidance as to issues that are likely to arise in future prosecutions for environmental damage.

[119] 1993 Convention on the Prohibition of the Development, Production, Stockpiling and Use of Chemical Weapons and on their Destruction, 30 ILM 80 (1993) ('Chemical Weapons Convention'), Art. 1.

[120] *Ibid.*, at Art. 7.

[121] Convention on the Prohibition of the Use, Stockpiling, Production and Transfer of Anti-Personnel Mines and on their Destruction, 2056 UNTS 211, 36 ILM 1507 (1997) ('Landmines Convention'), Art. 1.

[122] *Ibid.*, at Art. 9.

[123] Convention on Prohibitions or Restrictions on the Use of Certain Conventional Weapons Which May be Deemed to be Excessively Injurious or to Have Indiscriminate Effects, 1342 UNTS 137 (1980) ('Conventional Weapons Convention'). The prohibition on incendiary attacks on forests is ecocentric in the subject it is protecting; Protocol III (Protocol on Prohibitions or Restrictions on the Use of Incendiary Weapons), Art. 2(4) ('It is prohibited to make forests or other kinds of plant cover the object of attack by incendiary weapons except when such natural elements are used to cover, conceal or camouflage combatants or other military objectives, or are themselves military objectives'); Schmitt, *supra* note 1, at 89.

[124] Weinstein, *supra* note 5, at 698.

### 4.1. *Second World War Cases*

A small number of cases arising from the Second World War concerned instances of serious environmental damage. As mentioned earlier, German General Lothar Rendulic was prosecuted before the International Military Tribunal at Nuremberg for scorched-earth tactics causing large-scale destruction of buildings and damage to the environment. In accordance with his orders, German troops burnt and destroyed villages and surrounding facilities in the Norwegian province of Finmark when retreating from the advancing Russian army. Rendulic was ultimately acquitted of the charge of wanton destruction of property on the basis of military necessity. Although the IMT did not accept that his decision to use scorched-earth tactics was reasonable, it accepted that he genuinely perceived it to be justified at the time.[125]

In other proceedings, nine German civilian officials in occupied Poland were charged with for their 'ruthless exploitation of Polish forestry', involving the 'wholesale cutting of Polish timber to an extent far in excess of what was necessary to preserve the timber resources of the country'. The committee of the United Nations War Crimes Commission found that a prima facie case of pillage under Article 53 of the Four Geneva Conventions was established and listed the German officials as accused war criminals.[126]

### 4.2. *International Tribunals*

Since Nuremberg, there have been no significant prosecutions under international criminal law for serious damage to the environment. Neither the ICTY nor the ICTR[127] has undertaken prosecutions for environmental war crimes. The ICTY would appear to have jurisdiction over breaches of Articles 35(3) and 55 of Additional Protocol I to the Geneva Conventions (AP I),[128] which prohibit causing widespread, long-term, and severe damage to the environment during international armed conflict. However, except for the report assessing the potential criminal responsibility of NATO for acts committed during the bombing campaign against FRY in 1999, there have been no prosecutions or investigations of environmental damage.

[125] *The Hostages Trial (Wilhelm List and Others)*, 8 *Law Reports of Trials of War Criminals* 66, 66–69 (1948); E. Yuzon, 'Deliberate Environmental Modification through the Use of Chemical and Biological Weapons: "Greening" the International Laws of Armed Conflict to Establish an Environmentally Protective Regime', 11 *American University Journal of International Law and Policy J* 793, 815, cited in Drumbl, *supra* note 11, at 134. Another German military officer, Alfred Jodl was also prosecuted in part for scorched-earth practices in the north of Norway; Trials of War Criminals before the Nuremberg Military Tribunals under Control Council Law No. 10, Part XXII, November 1945–October 1946, 568–71 (1948).

[126] History of the United Nations War Crimes Commission and the Development of the Laws of War 496 (Her Majesty's Stationary Office, 1948) (discussing Case No. 7150); cited in Schwabach, *supra* note 29, at 17.

[127] See Drumbl, *supra* note 11, at 145.

[128] See Final Report on NATO, *supra* note 68.

The Iraqi Special Tribunal has jurisdiction over crimes of serious environmental damage, but has not undertaken prosecutions for this provision.[129] The other major international tribunals would not appear to have direct jurisdiction over crimes of serious environmental damage and so have not undertaken prosecutions for these offences.[130]

After the Nuremberg Trials, the International Law Commission was tasked with creating a Draft Code of Crimes against the Peace and Security of Mankind. Article 26 of the text, which was adopted after a first reading, provided that '[a]n individual who wilfully causes or orders the causing of widespread, long-term and severe damage to the natural environment shall, on conviction thereof, be sentenced'.[131] A report provided to the ILC by one of its members, Christian Tomuschat, outlined progressive recommendations, including the incorporation of a *dolus eventualis mens rea* standard and a broad conception of the 'natural environment' for the proposed provision.[132] However, the ultimate text of the prohibition on harming the environment adopted in the Draft Code of Crimes against the Peace and Security of Mankind was considerably more restricted. It frames the crime as a war crime that is thus limited to times of armed conflict and phrases it in anthropocentric terms.[133]

## 4.3. *The International Criminal Court*

The International Criminal Court has jurisdiction over crimes of environmental destruction, particularly under Article 8(2)(b)(iv), but has not charged anyone under the relevant provision to date. However, the charges against Omar Al-Bashir are

[129] 2003 Statute of the Iraqi Special Tribunal art. 13(b)(5), 43 ILM 231 (2004) ('Intentionally launching an attack in the knowledge that such attack will cause widespread, long-term and severe damage to the natural environment which would be clearly excessive in relation to the concrete and direct overall military advantage anticipated'); Weinstein, *supra* note 5, at 705. As noted earlier, Hussein was not prosecuted for this environmental damage.

[130] See Statute of Special Court for Sierra Leone, *supra* note 86, art. 4 (limiting other war crimes to those enumerated); Law of the Establishment of Extraordinary Chambers in the Courts of Cambodia for the Prosecution of Crimes Committed during the Period of Democratic Kampuchea 2004 (only including grave breaches of the Geneva Conventions in its jurisdiction); 2007 Statute of the Special Tribunal for Lebanon art. 2, 46 ILM 999 (limiting crimes in the jurisdiction of the tribunal to terrorism and life and personal integrity).

[131] See ILC Draft Code of Crimes against Peace and Security of Mankind, 1991 YILC Vol. 2 (Part 2), at 107.

[132] See International Law Commission, Document ILC(XLVIII)/DC/CRD.3, Document on Crimes against the Environment, prepared by Mr. Christian Tomuschat, member of the Commission, 27 March 1996.

[133] See ILC Code of Crimes against the Peace and Security of Mankind, 1996 YILC, Vol. II, (Part Two), at 9 Art. 20(g): 'In the case of armed conflict, using methods or means of warfare not justified by military necessity with the intent to cause widespread, long-term and severe damage to the natural environment and thereby gravely prejudice the health or survival of the population and such damage occurs.'

founded upon the systematic pillaging of villages across a large area.[134] Such destruction is analogous to the widespread destruction discussed in the Second World War scorched-earth cases.[135]

## 5. UNENFORCEABLE PROVISIONS OR INSUFFICIENT ENFORCEMENT?

Serious environmental damage consistently accompanies armed conflicts. However, there have been very few prosecutions for environmental damage since the Second World War, and this trend does not appear to be changing. The discrepancy between the damage caused to the environment and the absence of individual accountability is a serious concern.

A number of commentators argue that the discrepancy arises from the incoherent nature of the legal provisions that address serious harm to the environment.[136] However, having surveyed the provisions and principles applicable to the prosecution of environmental damage, the problem emerges as one of a lack of application. The prohibitions relevant to environmental damage committed during armed conflict are plentiful, but often underdeveloped. In the absence of judicial consideration and application, the most important prohibitions or elements of prohibitions remain unclear in their ambit and contents. Article 8(2)(b)(iv) typifies this trend. Its key terms – widespread, long-term, and severe – have been interpreted in a variety of ways and remain subject to debate. Furthermore, the provision incorporates the proportionality test, which has not been clarified to any great extent in the international criminal law jurisprudence.

Despite its 30-year existence, Article 35(3) of Additional Protocol I has not been the subject of prosecutions in international tribunals and is thus also jurisprudentially underdeveloped. Similarly, the customary international law principles of necessity and proportionality suffer from a lack of judicial interpretation in relation to the environment. On this basis, the problem emerges as a lack of judicial application of the provisions and principles to specific factual scenarios, rather than the inherent incoherence of the prohibitions per se.

A whole raft of solutions to the problem of environmental damage were suggested in the wake of highly visible destruction wrought during the First Gulf War.[137] Of

[134] *Prosecutor* v. *Al Bashir*, Warrant of Arrest for Omar Hassan Ahmad Al Bashir, Case No. ICC-02/05–01-09, Pre-T.Ch. I, 4 March 2009, 5–7. See also the earlier discussion of the genocide charges that were laid against him but rejected by Pre-Trial Chamber I.

[135] Other ICC indictees facing charges of pillage and destruction of property include Germain 'Simba' Katanga and Mathieu Ngudjolo for crimes committed during the armed conflict in the Democratic Republic of Congo; Jean-Pierre Bemba Gombo for crimes committed in the Central African Republic; Ahmad Muhammad Harun and Ali Muhammad Ali Abd-Al-Rahman for crimes committed in Darfur, Sudan; Bahr Idriss Abu Garda for crimes committed in South Sudan; and Joseph Kony, Vincent Otti, Okot Odhiambo, and Dominic Ongwen for crimes committed in Uganda.

[136] See, *e.g.*, Schmitt, *supra* note 1, at 4, 95; Weinstein, *supra* note 5, at 698.

[137] Jensen, *supra* note 14, at 148.

these, the most promising is the stricter enforcement of existing standards of international criminal law. For enforcement to be effective, lawyers and military decision makers have a distinct need for enhanced scientific knowledge.[138] More assistance should be provided to these groups to raise their environmental awareness.[139] In this respect, the ICRC *Guidelines for Military Manuals* is an excellent resource that has already been distributed to military bodies throughout the world.

## 6. THE NEED TO PENALISE ENVIRONMENTAL DAMAGE IN PEACETIME

Despite the variety of provisions under which environmental harm could be prosecuted, such damage committed outside of armed conflict is not subject to any criminal sanction under international criminal law.[140] The preceding discussion culminates in the obvious question – should the prohibitions against environmental damage be extended to times of peace as well as times of war?

Serious and illegal harms to the environment are regularly committed during times of peace. For example, more than 600 tons of caustic soda and petroleum residues were dumped in open-air public waste sites in Abidjan, Ivory Coast, in August 2006. The choking fumes from the waste were reported to have caused nosebleeds, nausea, and vomiting. Casualties from the dumping of these chemicals were reported to include 16 dead, 75 hospitalised, and 100,000 seeking medical attention. The incident implicated European, Korean, and Russian companies, as well as a local company. Cleaning up the waste required the removal of more than 6,000 tons of the waste itself, as well as contaminated soil, water, and even concrete.[141]

The incident involved serious destruction of the environment. However, under current international criminal law, it would be extremely difficult to prosecute as it did not occur during an armed conflict. Where incidents like this occur as a result of organised and systematic activities, such as the transfer and dumping of dangerous chemicals, and where they have international implications – in this case due to the involvement of foreign companies and the removal of the waste to the Ivory Coast – international criminal prosecution is justified and necessary. The extension of international criminal law to encompass crimes committed outside of times of armed conflict would allow the prosecution and punishment of the responsible individual or individuals in international tribunals.

The need to prosecute environmental crimes outside of armed conflict is demonstrated by the threat of the following acts: reckless misconduct at nuclear power facilities;[142] testing biological weapons; intentional dumping of oil or chemical waste

[138] Schmitt, *supra* note 56, at 316.
[139] *Ibid.*, at 318.
[140] With the possible exception of the crime of humanity of causing great suffering.
[141] See O. Ibeanu, Report of the Special Rapporteur on the adverse effects of the movement and dumping of toxic and dangerous products and wastes on the enjoyment of human rights, UN Doc. A/HRC/12/26 (2009), para. 6; White, *supra* note 18, at 119.
[142] Schofield, *supra* note 29, at 622, 626–27.

at sea; trade in endangered species, hazardous wastes, or ozone-depleting substances; and intentional large-scale and illegal carbon emissions.[143]

More than 900 existing international treaties, applicable in times of war and peace, include environmental provisions, many of which criminalise breaches of their prohibitions.[144] This mass of international treaties and other instruments containing prohibitions against damaging the environment support the extension of environmental prohibitions to times of peace.[145] Furthermore, serious damage to the environment can itself lead to and perpetuate armed conflict. Large numbers of environmental refugees result from serious damage to the environment.[146] Conflicts can also be sparked or intensified by the plunder of natural resources.[147] Such secondary effects militate in favour of the application of environmental prohibitions whether or not they are committed during an armed conflict.

More profoundly, the environment is inherently a shared value with present and future generations of all countries. Intergenerational equity demands its protection. Deterring and punishing crimes against the environment are necessary not only to prevent wars from erupting and harm to human interests but also because such environmental devastation is wrong in and of itself. The destruction is reproachable irrespective of whether it occurs during armed conflict.

## 7. CONCLUSION

International criminal law is not a panacea for the problem of environmental damage but is an important tool in the fight to protect our natural surroundings from the ravages of human conflict and exploitation.[148] Environmental damage often affects multiple states or global commons, as in the case of oils spills, the emission of

[143] See Drumbl, *supra* note 11, at 325. There is an applicable convention that establishes the requirement to protect the ozone layer. This could be converted into criminal sanctions in state parties; Schmitt, *supra* note 1, at 49.

[144] See Jensen, *supra* note 14. See also Drumbl, *supra* note 11, at 139; Wattad, *supra* note 28, at 280; Schwabach, *supra* note 29, at 5, 13, 14–15. Byung-Sun Cho claims that the 'vast majority' of these treaties implicitly recognise the penal nature of the act by imposing duties to prohibit, prevent, prosecute or punish; Byung-Sun Cho, 'Emergence of an International Environmental Criminal Law?', (2001) 19 *UCLA Journal of Environmental Law and Policy* 11, at 17–18. But see Schmitt, *supra* note 1, at 50.

[145] Peacetime environmental law remains effective during times of armed conflict to the extent that it is compatible with international humanitarian law; L. D. Beck 'Le droit international humanitaire et l'avis consultatif de la Cour internationale de Justice sur la licéité de la menace ou de l'emploi d'armes nucléaires' (1997) 823 RICR 37, cited in Schmitt, *supra* note 1, at 32, 37.

[146] See Cohan, *supra* note 11, at 490.

[147] The UNSC has condemned the plunder of the natural resources during the ongoing armed conflict in the Democratic Republic of Congo and recognised that the illegal exploitation is fuelling the conflict; UN Doc. S/RES/1457 (2003); A. Lopez, 'Criminal Liability for Environmental Damage Occurring in Times of Non-International Armed Conflict: Rights and Remedies', (2007) 18 *Fordham Environmental Law Review* 231, at 238.

[148] Penal sanctions are necessary because civil sanctions have often proved insufficient to deter companies from polluting behaviour, see Schofield, *supra* note 29, at 639, 642.

harmful chemicals, and intentional deforestation. Moreover, responsibility for environmental destruction is often shielded or diluted by notions such as the corporate veil or functional immunity.[149] International criminal law presents a viable means of overriding such devices and holding accountable those responsible for serious environmental damage.[150] This branch of the law concerns itself with crimes that are of interest to the international community as a whole and seeks to prevent global problems from being ignored due to their enormity or complexity. Consequently, it is an appropriate mechanism to combat serious and illegal destruction of the environment.

Ecocentric provisions and principles of international criminal law provide a potential basis for prosecuting serious damage to the environment. However, these prohibitions are jurisprudentially underdeveloped. This chapter's survey indicates that several restrictions may hamper their application. Conversely, there is a large number and broad range of anthropocentric provisions of international law providing incidental protection to the environment. Many commentators maintain that these anthropocentric provisions may in fact be more effective in curbing environmental damage than their ecocentric counterparts.[151] The anthropocentric provisions certainly have the advantage of avoiding the restrictions of Article 8(2)(b)(iv), such as its limitation to international armed conflict and its requirement that the anticipated environmental damage be 'clearly excessive' to the military advantage sought. However, prosecution under these provisions alone is unsatisfying because it leaves unrecognised the full extent of the harm to the environment per se. International criminal law has an important declaratory function – it records the human race's moral opprobrium of crimes of concern to the international community. Accordingly, efforts to prosecute those responsible for serious environmental damage should not be eschewed. Instead, prosecutions under both ecocentric and anthropocentric provisions should be encouraged, particularly given that serious environmental damage is usually accompanied by humanitarian atrocities.

In the first case heard by the ICTY (*Tadic*, in 1995), the Appeals Chamber analysed the categories of crimes that fell within its jurisdiction. It noted that international law applicable to armed conflicts shifted during the twentieth century from a state–sovereignty-oriented approach to a human–being-oriented approach.[152] The latter approach is founded on the principle, *hominum causa omne jus constitutum est* (all law is created for the benefit of human beings).[153] Fifteen years later, civil society and

[149] See Jensen, *supra* note 14, at 152.

[150] See, *e.g.*, Rome Statute, *supra* note 40, Art. 27 (excluding head of state immunity or official capacity as a basis for avoiding liability).

[151] See, *e.g.*, Weinstein, *supra* note 5, at 698, 712 et seq.

[152] Tadic Jurisdiction Decision, *supra* note 28, at para. 97.

[153] *Ibid.* ('[a] State-sovereignty-oriented approach has been gradually supplanted by a human-being-oriented approach. Gradually the maxim of Roman law *hominum causa omne jus constitutum est* (all law is created for the benefit of human beings) has gained a firm foothold in the international community as well.')

commentators are calling for a further tectonic movement in the international legal landscape to enforce and expand the prohibitions against environmental damage. This development does not signify a shift in the law away from human interests. Rather, it represents an inclusive expansion of the conceptual foundations of international criminal law. The emerging principle would recognise human beings along with the environment per se as beneficiaries of international criminal law, rephrasing the principle as *natura et hominum causa omne jus constitutum sunt* (all law is created for the benefit of human beings and the natural environment). As noted in the analysis herein, the development presents a difficult but welcome challenge for jurists, academics, and those playing a role in the realisation of international criminal law.

# 6

# Violations of Social and Economic Rights and International Crimes

*Salim A. Nakhjavani*

## 1. INTRODUCTION

This chapter explores a number of conceptual challenges to the idea that the norms and institutions of international criminal law might directly address violations of socioeconomic rights by means of the attribution of individual criminal responsibility under international law for such violations.

It is trite to observe that socioeconomic rights will be acutely vulnerable, even unattainable, in the context of the mass violence that characterises all core international crimes.[1] Notable, in this regard, is that the Office of the High Commissioner for Human Rights has begun to assess how the promotion of socioeconomic rights should be built into post-conflict transition processes.[2] These transition processes may well include modes of post-conflict accountability that use the norms and institutions of international criminal law.

[1] The context of mass violence in which core international crimes occur will tend to satisfy the various legal thresholds that allow a state to derogate from all but a set of 'non-derogable' human rights. It is notable that certain family rights are the only socioeconomic rights expressly designated as non-derogable in times of 'war, public danger or other emergency', and only in one regional instrument, the *American Convention on Human Rights*, 22 November 1969, 1144 U.N.T.S. 123 (entered into force 18 July 1978), Arts. 17 and 27(2) [*ACHR*]. Of course, derogation from other socioeconomic rights may well fail to satisfy the applicable test of strict proportionality; see *ACHR*, Art. 27(1); *European Social Charter*, 529 U.N.T.S. 89 (entered into force 26 February 1965), as amended by the *European Social Charter (Revised)*, 3 May 1996, ETS 163 (entered into force Art. 1 July 1999), Art. F(1).

[2] See Office of the High Commissioner for Human Rights, 'The OHCHR Women's Human Rights and Gender Section (WRGUS) – Papers on Access to Justice Post-Conflict'; see especially the paper of Christine Chinkin, 'The Protection of Economic, Social and Cultural Rights Post-Conflict', available at www2.ohchr.org/english/issues/women/papers_access_to_justice.htm.

The views expressed in this article are the author's own and do not necessarily represent the views of the United Nations.

At first glance, enhanced protection of socioeconomic rights[3] seems a merely peripheral and contestable outcome of the prohibition and prosecution of core international crimes – *peripheral* to the relevant elements of crimes and legal requirements of modes of liability, and *contestable* in the claim that policy rationales for the attribution of individual criminal responsibility under international law mirror or complement policy rationales for protecting socioeconomic rights. In contrast to the protection of cultural heritage as a cultural right,[4] the legal interest in protecting socioeconomic rights cannot be characterised as a central concern underlying the prohibition of aggression or any particular subspecies of genocide, crimes against humanity, and war crimes – not, at least, without resort to overgeneralisation or contorted juridical gymnastics.

## 2. THE JUSTIFICATORY THEORY OF INTERNATIONAL CRIMINAL LAW REMAINS INSUFFICIENTLY MATURE TO ACCOUNT FOR THE DIRECT PROTECTION OF SOCIOECONOMIC RIGHTS

One might comment blithely that the entire discipline of international criminal law – embryonic at Nuremberg and steadily maturing in The Hague – remains undertheorised. This is no petty concern of abstractionist jurists, but a question that lies at the core of the moral foundations of the international legal order. As Philip Allott comments,

> To justify the imposition of a criminal sanction requires a theory which reconciles very many things, practical and moral and psychological. Criminal law is no better than the theory which justifies it. And a justificatory theory of the criminal law is no better than the theory which justifies the theory. In other words, the social repression of the form of evil which is socially identified as a crime is inseparable from the justification of the society which organises that repression. . . . As international society develops its own system of criminal justice, how will it find its justificatory theory, the theory which justifies its judgement of evil and the theory which justifies its power to judge, unless through the arbitrary imposition of a theory by those with exceptional international social power, or else by the fortuitous application of the theory of a national criminal justice system which chooses to act as the agent of international society?[5]

3 The 'socioeconomic' rights discussed here are tailored practically to the division of chapters in this volume, rather than seeking to artificially constrain or divide the norms of international human rights or to gloss over highly contested definitional terrain. For these purposes, 'socioeconomic' rights would include labour rights (including freedom of trade, occupation, or profession and rights to fair labour practices or just conditions of work, to form trade unions and employers' organisations, to bargain collectively, and to strike), and rights such as health and medical care, education, family life, an adequate standard of living (including food, land, water, and housing), social security, and partaking in the benefits of scientific progress, together with the right of a people to self-determination. This chapter does not seek to address environmental or cultural rights.

4 See Chapter 7.

5 P. Allott, *The Health of Nations: Society and Law beyond the State* (2002), at para. 2.67.

As described later, international law protects human rights, in large measure, through the instrumentality of the state as duty-bearer. Axiomatically, violations of human rights are conceived as aberrations from the international law norm. By comparison, core international crimes are committed in a context where, from a criminological perspective, the state itself has become criminogenic, in which the very norm *is* criminal.[6] Yet, even if the same conduct could 'only be committed with the means and mechanisms of a State and as part of a State policy',[7] it is individuals – 'men, not abstract entities'[8] – who are the sole object of criminal sanctions under international law, among whose primary subjects will include that very same state. Any proposal that individual criminal responsibility should attach for serious violations of socioeconomic rights *as such* must first encounter and overcome such theoretical deficiencies in the emerging international criminal justice system.

## 3. A ROBUST LEGAL FRAMEWORK TO DESCRIBE THE RELATIONSHIP BETWEEN RULES OF INTERNATIONAL CRIMINAL LAW AND INTERNATIONAL HUMAN RIGHTS REMAINS TO BE DEVELOPED

The legal theory that underpins the relationship between international human rights law and international criminal law has not, as yet, been wholly articulated or subject to careful analysis. There is a wealth of literature – buttressed by treaty law and the occasional judicial pronouncement – examining the relationship between human rights and one of the principal sources of international criminal law: international humanitarian law.[9] The rather tentative conclusion of a recent survey is that international criminal law and humanitarian law remain 'distinct categories, with their specific aims and fields of application', whose 'complementary application may guarantee the respect of the rule of law', especially in the 'grey areas' of military occupation, insurgency, and the 'war on terror'.[10]

By comparison, few have endeavoured to critically assess the nature of the interaction between human rights and international criminal law, to examine its

6 See, inter alia, P. Roberts and N. MacMillan, 'For Criminology in International Criminal Justice', (2003) 1 *Journal of International Criminal Justice* 315; A. Smeulers, 'What Transforms Ordinary People into Gross Human Rights Violators?', in S C. Poe and S. C. Carey (eds.), *Understanding Human Rights Violations: New Systematic Studies* (2004), 239.

7 Arrest Warrant of 11 April 2000 (*Democratic Republic of the Congo* v. *Belgium*) [2002] ICJ Rep. 3, dissenting opinion of Judge Van den Wyngaert at 162.

8 International Military Tribunal, Judgement, 1 October 1946, in *The Trial of the Major War Criminals: Proceedings of the International Military Tribunal Sitting at Nuremberg, Germany* (1946), Part 22 at 447.

9 See, inter alia, the useful survey by N. Quénivet, 'The History of the Relationship between International Humanitarian Law and Human Rights Law', in R. Arnold and N. Quénivet (eds.), *International Humanitarian Law and Human Rights Law* (2008), 1.

10 See R. Arnold, 'Conclusions', in R. Arnold and N. Quénivet (eds.), *International Humanitarian Law and Human Rights Law* (2008), 591 at 592.

characteristics, or to assess its implications.[11] Perhaps this is a consequence of the timing of evolution across these two fields of law. The period of rapid development of international humanitarian law (and the proscription of war crimes) began at the turn of the nineteenth century, with the adoption of the Hague Conventions. Some 50 years would pass before the Nuremberg trials and the adoption of the Genocide Convention[12] and almost a century before international criminal law experienced a similar burst in norm-creating, institution-shaping activity with the establishment of ad hoc, hybrid, and permanent international criminal tribunals. By comparison, important developments in international human rights law – particularly treaty law[13] – span the decades between the 1960s and 1980s, when the growth of international criminal law was largely stagnant.[14] Specific to the concerns of this chapter, Skogly characterises the historical development of crimes against humanity and socioeconomic rights as 'parallel but unconnected evolutions'.[15]

Nonetheless, one must note a potential and limited exception to the disconnected evolution of norms of international criminal law and socioeconomic rights over this time period. The 1976 Apartheid Convention describes apartheid as a crime against humanity attracting individual (and, interestingly, organisational and institutional) criminal responsibility.[16] The definition of the crime includes, as a material element, the commission of one of an enumerated list of 'inhumane acts' for a prohibited purpose: the establishment and maintenance of systematic oppression and domination of one racial group over another. In accordance with general principles of culpability in criminal law, this prohibited purpose would imply a distinctive mental element

[11] See, inter alia, S. I. Skogly, 'Crimes against Humanity – Revisited: Is There a Role for Economic and Social Rights?', (2001) 5(1) *International Journal of Human Rights* 58; D. Robinson, 'The Identity Crisis in International Criminal Law', (2008) 21 *Leiden Journal of International Law* 925 [*Robinson*]; G. Fletcher and J. D. Ohlin, 'Reclaiming Fundamental Principles in the Darfur Case', (2005) 3 *Journal of International Criminal Justice* 539; A. M. Danner and J. S. Martinez, 'Guilty Associations: Joint Criminal Enterprise, Command Responsibility and the Development of International Criminal Law', (2005) 93 *California Law Review* 75, at 81–89.

[12] *Convention on the Prevention and Punishment of the Crime of Genocide*, 78 U.N.T.S. 277 (entered into force 12 January 1951).

[13] Including, among other key texts. the adoption of the *International Covenant on Civil and Political Rights*, 999 U.N.T.S. 171 (entered into force 23 March 1976); the *International Covenant on Economic, Social and Cultural Rights*, 993 U.N.T.S. 3 (entered into force 3 January 1976); the *Optional Protocol to the International Covenant on Civil and Political Rights*, 999 U.N.T.S. 302 (entered into force 23 March 1976); and the *Convention against Torture and other Cruel, Inhuman or Degrading Treatment or Punishment*, 1465 U.N.T.S. 85 (entered into force 26 June 1987).

[14] See G. Werle, *Principles of International Criminal Law* (2005), 15; the author does refer to isolated examples of the national application of rules of international criminal law during and immediately following the Cold War period, including *Attorney General of the Government of Israel v. Adolf Eichmann*, (1968) 36 I.L.R. 5 (District Court of Jerusalem); (1968) 36 I.L.R. 277 (Supreme Court of Israel) [trial dating from 1961]; and *Féderation National des Déportées et Internés Resistants et Patriots et al. v. Barbie* (1995) 100 I.L.R. 331 (French Court of Cassation) [trial dating from 1984].

[15] Skogly, *supra* note 11, at 59.

[16] *Convention on the Suppression and Punishment of the Crime of Apartheid*, 1015 U.N.T.S. 243 (entered into force 18 July 1976), Arts. I and III.

of specific intent (*dolus specialis*) to establish or maintain the system of oppression as part of the definition of the crime. The list of inhumane acts includes violations of socioeconomic rights, described principally *as such*, rather than through the instrumentality of other protected interests of a civil or political character:

> For the purpose of the present Convention, the term 'the crime of apartheid' . . . shall apply to the following inhuman acts committed for the purpose of establishing and maintaining domination by one racial group of persons over any other racial group of persons and systematically oppressing them:
>
> . . .
>
> (c) any legislative measures and other measures calculated to prevent a racial group or groups from participation in the political, social, economic and cultural life of the country and the deliberate creation of conditions preventing the full development of such a group or groups, in particular by denying to members of a racial group or groups basic human rights and freedoms, including the right to work, the right to form recognized trade unions, the right to education, the right to leave and to return to their country, the right to a nationality, the right to freedom of movement and residence, the right to freedom of opinion and expression, and the right to freedom of peaceful assembly and association;
>
> (d) any measures, including legislative measures, designed to divide the population along racial lines by the creation of separate reserves and ghettos for the members of a racial group or groups, the prohibition of mixed marriages among members of various racial groups, the expropriation of landed property belonging to a racial group or groups or to members thereof;
>
> (e) exploitation of the labour of the members of a racial group or groups, in particular by submitting them to forced labour . . .[17]

Nonetheless, the intriguing example of the Apartheid Convention was not based on a robust conceptual inquiry into the relationship of socioeconomic rights and international criminal law as much on a rising tide of political opposition to the systems of racial segregation and discrimination prevalent in southern Africa at the time.[18] The redefinition of the crime in the 1998 Rome Statute removes all express reference to socioeconomic rights, restricting the 'inhumane acts' that may amount to the crime against humanity of apartheid to the enumerated list of crimes against humanity in the Rome Statute or acts similar in nature and gravity.[19]

The time is certainly ripe, as Robinson rightly observes, 'to foster a more sophisticated and principled discourse'[20] on the relationship of international criminal law to human rights generally and to socioeconomic rights specifically. As a starting point,

[17] *Ibid.* at Art. II (emphasis added).

[18] This is evident from the definition of the crime of apartheid in Art. II of the convention, which refers specifically to 'similar policies and practices . . . as practiced in southern Africa'.

[19] Rome Statute of the International Criminal Court, 2187 U.N.T.S. 90 (entered into force 1 July 2002), Art. 7(1)(j) and 7(2)(h), read with Elements of Crimes, Art. 7(1)(j).

[20] Robinson, *supra* note 12, at 963.

the literature is replete with assumptions and metaphors describing aspects of the relationship between international criminal law and human rights. It is useful to briefly survey the spectrum of ideas.

Addressing the Annual Meeting of the American Society of International Law in 1968, Professor Robert Woetzel – a vigorous, early proponent of a permanent international criminal court[21] – first suggested the fundamental parallelism of international criminal law and human rights, while also paving the way for the oft-repeated assertion that international criminal law is a specialised enforcement mechanism for particularly egregious violations of human rights:

> The protection of human rights may on occasion require the punishment of individuals and reparations from states. Most of the rights listed in the Universal Declaration of Human Rights are also protected by instruments of international criminal law such as the Charter and the Judgement of the International Military Tribunal (IMT) at Nuremberg. The Geneva Conventions of 1949 extend the universality principle[22] to war crimes and the kinds of grave breaches listed are related to the rights protected in various human rights covenants. It can be said, therefore, that international criminal law is the other side of the coin of human rights; it is also the sharp edge of the sword which establishes individual responsibility and punishes violators. . . . [I]n the protection of human rights, the punitive or corrective aspect plays as important a role as the reaffirmation of general principles of human rights. . . . [I]nstitutions such as the European Commission and European Court of Human Rights may be paralleled by penal jurisdictions, regional or international, dealing with such offences as crimes against humanity. . . .
>
> There is a relation between the protection of human rights violations which constitute offenses against international law and the preservation of peace in the international community. Crimes against humanity whether committed by governments against aliens or their own citizens often precede international conflict as in the case

[21] He was, at the time, professor of international law at Boston College and secretary-general of the International Criminal Law Commission. In 1989, together with Benjamin Ferencz, he helped draft the proposal to the General Assembly by President Arthur Robinson of Trinidad and Tobago that reintroduced the idea of a permanent international criminal court within the United Nations, a process that culminated in the 1998 Rome Diplomatic Conference that adopted the Rome Statute of the International Criminal Court, 17 June 1998, 2187 U.N.T.S. 90 (entered into force 1 July 2002) [*Rome Statute*]; see *International Criminal Responsibility of Individuals and Entities Engaged in Illicit Trafficking in Narcotic Drugs across National Frontiers and Other Transnational Criminal Activities: Establishment of an International Criminal Court with Jurisdiction over Such Crimes*, GA Res. 44/39, UN GAOR, 44th Sess., Supp. No. 49, UN Doc. A/RES/44/39, 311; see Letter dated 21 August 1989 from the Permanent Representative of Trinidad and Tobago to the Secretary-General, UN GAOR, 44th Sess., Annex 44, Agenda Item 152, UN Doc. A/44/195 (1989); see also M. Arsanjani, 'The Rome Statute of the International Criminal Court', (1999) 93(1) *American Journal of International Law* 22, note 1.

[22] That is, the principle of prescriptive universal jurisdiction; see GC I, Art. 49; GC II, Art. 50; GC III, Art. 129 and GC IV, Art. 146. See also the thorough analysis of R. O'Keefe, 'The Grave Breaches Regime and Universal Jurisdiction', (2009) 7 *Journal of International Criminal Justice* 811; and R. O'Keefe, 'Universal Jurisdiction: Clarifying the Basic Concept', (2004) 2 *Journal of International Criminal Justice* 735.

> of Nazi Germany. The preservation of international order requires a close watch on activities which constitute violations and which may, therefore, require sanctions. International criminal jurisdiction is part of the web of international organization culminating in world order.[23]

Contemporary scholarship largely takes up Woertzel's refrain that international criminal law complements human rights law, as an enforcement mechanism that punishes individuals for 'serious', 'severe', 'grave', 'massive', 'fundamental', or 'abusive and gross' violations of human rights or for violations of 'fundamental standards of humanity'.[24] The logic underlying this position is that all core international crimes will amount to human rights violations, although the converse does not hold.[25] Yet the logic also rests on the assumption that an unspecified spectrum of gravity connects human rights violations and international crimes. Other scholars posit a hierarchical relationship, treating international criminal law as a 'field of human rights law'.[26] Yet others, perhaps encouraged by the impetus of the Rome Conference, advocate a fusion of international criminal law and human rights law.[27] Finally, a specialist international criminal lawyer finds the discipline facing a philosophical disjunction with human rights law. On this view, international criminal law has a stark and urgent choice to make between serving the philosophical aims of its human rights and humanitarian law progenitors (i.e. securing justice for victims) or those of a liberal 'system of criminal justice' (i.e. principally, ensuring fair trials), because it has proven impossible to comply with both 'the strictures of criminal and non-criminal law'.[28]

## 4. HOW MIGHT INTERNATIONAL CRIMINAL LAW AND HUMAN RIGHTS COHERE?

These wide-ranging views share an unstated yet common objective – all seek coherence between international criminal law and human rights. Even Robinson's concerns – that assumptions and modes of legal argument in international criminal

[23] R. Woetzel, 'International Criminal Law and Human Rights: The Sharp Edge of the Sword', (1968) 62 *American Journal of International Law* 117, at 117–18.

[24] See, inter alia, Skogly, *supra* note 12; M. Drumbl, 'International Human Rights, International Humanitarian Law and Environmental Security: Can the International Criminal Court Bridge the Gaps', (2000) 6 ILSA *Journal of International and Comparative Law* 305, at 305–06; P. Finell, *Accountability under Human Rights Law and International Criminal Law for Atrocities against Minority Groups Committed by Non-State Actors*, Åbo Akademi Institute for Human Rights Working Paper (2002); M. Scheinin, *Background Paper to an International Expert Meeting on Fundamental Standards of Humanity* (Stockholm, 22–24 February 2000) [Unpublished].

[25] The converse assertion (that all human rights violations amount to core international crimes) is both a logical fallacy and legally unsound.

[26] W. Kaleck and M. Saage-Maaβ, 'Corporate Accountability for Human Rights Violations Amounting to International Crimes', (2010) 8 *Journal of International Criminal Justice* 699, at 700.

[27] P. Carter, 'International Criminal Law and Human Rights', in F. Butler (ed.), *Human Rights Protection: Methods and Effectiveness* (2002); C. Dias, 'Toward International Human Rights Crimes: An Asian Perspective on Human Rights and International Criminal Law', in D. Shelton (ed.), *International Crimes, Peace and Human Rights: The Role of the International Criminal Court* (2000).

[28] Robinson, *supra* note 12, at 932.

law are fettered by the intellectual inheritance of human rights and humanitarian law – would be allayed by the ideal of a genuinely coherent international legal system. But despite the sustained attention of legal theorists, the concept of coherence (especially in legal argument) has proven decidedly fuzzy. In a useful survey of arguments on coherence in legal theory, Bertea observes,

> While there is wide agreement among contemporary legal theorists on the characterization of coherence in the negative as lack of inconsistencies, it is still a question how coherence might be defined in positive terms. Coherence is generally held to be something more than logical consistency of propositions. But it is not entirely clear what this 'something more' amounts to. Thus, coherence is often described in figurative language as the equivalent of 'hanging together', 'making sense as a whole', 'cohesion', 'consonance' and 'speaking with one voice'. A coherent set might then be described as a 'tightly-knit unit'. Which makes coherence a 'kind of internal interconnectedness', a 'plausible connection' that is not lineal and asymmetrical but circular and symmetrical: the elements of a coherent structure are mutually supporting and reinforcing.[29]

Any discussion of coherence should be premised on a technical definition of the subject matter regulated by international criminal law and human rights law. On a classical, state-centred understanding of international law, international human rights law creates obligations owed *inter partes* or *erga omnes* between states to respect, protect, and fulfil certain minimum standards for the treatment of persons within their respective jurisdictions.[30] The state is indeed the duty-bearer, and the individual the rights-holder, but the duties are owed – as a matter of international law – to other states, and breach of those duties will engage its state responsibility, the international analogue of civil liability.[31] Although human rights treaty bodies and tribunals may well allow individuals to make claims directly against states for human rights violations, such institutions are themselves creatures of treaty law. When a state fails to adhere to the decisions of these institutions, the individual per se has no recourse under international law. The state's conduct may amount to a breach of an international obligation owed to other states and may attract state responsibility. By comparison, international criminal law refers to those offences under international law that, by their context (typically contextual elements of gravity and scale associated with mass violence), attract individual criminal responsibility under international law for individuals participating in those

[29] S. Bertea, 'The Arguments from Coherence: Analysis and Evaluation', (2005) 25(3) *Oxford Journal of Legal Studies* 369, at 371–72 [footnotes omitted].

[30] See, e.g. H. Steiner *et al.*, *International Human Rights in Context: Law, Politics, Morals* (2008), 185–90.

[31] In the course of the evolution of the International Law Commission's *Draft Articles on State Responsibility*, the distinction between international 'crimes' and international 'delicts' was found to be untenable; see J. Crawford, *The International Law Commission's Articles on State Responsibility: Introduction, Text and Commentary* (2002) 37 [Crawford].

offences (in addition to any state responsibility that may attach concerning the same facts).[32]

The underlying nature of the conduct prohibited by international human rights law and international criminal law appears to be largely comparable. The main differences between these two fields of international law would seem to consist in (i) the context of the prohibited conduct and (ii) the legal consequences of that conduct. So, for instance, a human rights treaty might oblige a state to prohibit a discriminatory act against an individual employee on the grounds of disability, failing which it would incur international responsibility towards other states party to that treaty. By comparison, the Rome Statute can be interpreted to prohibit persecutory acts of a given threshold of severity that discriminate against a group on the basis of disability, as part of a widespread or systematic attack against a civilian population – acts for which an individual may be held criminally responsible.[33] In this example, the nature of the conduct (wrongful discrimination on the basis of disability) is common.

In seeking coherence between these two fields of law, an initial observation, drawing from German and comparative criminal law, might suggest that the prohibitions enshrined in international criminal law and largely implicit in human rights law are both concerned with certain common 'legally-protected interests' or 'legal goods' (*Rechtsgüte*).[34] So, for instance, the German Federal Criminal Court has identified the protected interest of the prohibition of genocide as the 'social existence of the national, racial, religious or ethnic group being persecuted', suggesting that the individual victim is the object, not the subject of the protection.[35] Other scholars would include the protection of international peace as a *Rechtsgut* underlying the prohibition of genocide.[36] The ICTY has also weighed underlying 'legal values'

32 See International Law Commission, *Draft Articles on State Responsibility* in *Report of the International Law Commission on the Work of its Fifty-third Session*, UN GAOR, 56th Sess., Supp. No. 10, U.N. Doc. A/56/10 (2001) at 43, Article 58; Crawford, *ibid.*, at 312–313.

33 The Rome Statute does not expressly extend the discriminatory element of the crime of persecution to include grounds of disability under Article 7(1)(h), but this may be argued to be an analogous ground 'universally recognised as impermissible under international law', especially following the entry into force of Convention on the Protection and Promotion of the Rights and Dignity of Persons with Disabilities, G.A. Res. 61/106, Annex I, UN GAOR, 61st Sess., Supp. No. 49, at 65, UN Doc. A/61/49 (2006) (entered into force May 3, 2008). The crime of persecution is discussed in more detail later.

34 See K. Ambos, 'Toward a Universal System of Crime: Comments on George Fletcher's *Grammar of Criminal Law*', (2006) 28 *Cardozo Law Review* 2647 at 2655; H. Gropengießer, 'The Criminal Law of Genocide: The German Perspective', (2005) 5 *International Criminal Law Review* 329 at 333–35 [Gropengießer]; M. Dubber, 'The Promise of German Criminal Law: A Science of Crime and Punishment', (2005) 6(7) *German Law Journal* 1049. There is a vast literature on the comparative concepts of *Rechtsgut*, harm, and *bien protégé par la loi*, a review of which is beyond the scope of this chapter: see, e.g., R. Hefendehl, W. Wohlers, and A. von Hirsch (eds.), *Die Rechtsgutstheorie: Legitimationsbasis des Strafrechts oder dogmatisches Glasperlenspiel?* (2003).

35 BGHSt. 64, 91; see Gropengießer, *ibid.*, at note 26.

36 C. Kreß 's. 220a StGB' and 's. 6 VStGB' in W. Joecks and K. Miebach (eds.), *Münchener Kommentar zum Strafgesetzbuch* (2003).

(albeit without explicit recourse to the theory of *Rechtsgüte*), mainly in the context of the accumulation of charges and sentences.[37]

This proposition has intrinsic appeal both for its utility and its harmonising potential: if both international criminal law and international human rights law protect the same interests at a given level of abstraction, international lawyers would have at least some objective criterion by which to assess the proper limits of criminalisation under international law[38] versus the imposition of civil (i.e. state) responsibility for so-called ordinary human rights violations. Furthermore, this approach would direct judges to interpret and apply the law so as to optimise protection of the legal good at stake – although the practical impact of such an interpretative guideline is unlikely to exceed the generous scope of Article 21(3) of the Rome Statute.[39] Finally, the identification of underlying, shared legal interests builds an understanding of the conceptual unity of international criminal law and human rights that goes beyond the metaphor of the 'two sides of one coin' to an understanding that both seeks to uphold the oneness and wholeness of *humanity*, in its individual and collective dimensions. The following dictum of the ICTY Trial Chamber is illustrative:

> Crimes against humanity are serious acts of violence which harm human beings by striking at what is most essential to them: their life, liberty, physical welfare, health and/or dignity. They are inhumane acts which by their extent and gravity go beyond the limits tolerable to the international community, which must perforce demand their punishment. But crimes against humanity also transcend the individual because when the individual is assaulted, humanity comes under attack and is negated. It is therefore the concept of humanity as victim which essentially characterises crimes against humanity.[40]

But one can swiftly identify limitations to this cosmopolitan viewpoint. There is no neat, mathematical pairing between specific protections in human rights law and international criminal law. Even the extrapolation of 'ordinary' torture (as a human rights violation) to the crime against humanity of torture (as an international crime) is not simply a linear progression on a spectrum of severity, but requires the addition of distinctive legal elements, particularly contextual elements.[41] This gap is most striking in the case of socioeconomic rights.

37 See, e.g., *Prosecutor* v. *Zoran Kupreškić*, IT-95–16-T, Judgement (14 January 2000) (International Criminal Tribunal for the former Yugoslavia, Trial Chamber), Paras. 702, 709.

38 This is one of the main purposes of the *Rechtsgut* theory in German criminal law; see Gropengießer, *supra* note 35, at 334.

39 The implications of Art. 21(3) are discussed in more detail later.

40 *Prosecutor* v. *Dražan Erdemović*, IT-96–22-T, Sentencing Judgement (29 November 1996) (International Criminal Tribunal for the former Yugoslavia, Trial Chamber) at Paras. 27–28.

41 Namely the requirement that the act of torture forms part of a widespread or systematic attack directed against a civilian population, and that the perpetrator intends or knows that the act of torture will form part of this attack; see the Elements of Crimes document (subordinate to the Rome Statute), Art. 7.

As a first example, Skogly's 2001 study examines socioeconomic rights to food, health, and housing to identify how violations of these rights arising from the failure of the state to uphold its obligation to protect 'may represent crimes against humanity' and also, in some instances, genocide.[42] The following analytical table summarises her findings and illustrates how the scope of protection of socioeconomic rights through international criminal law does not disclose ready correlations or shared categorisations that might otherwise enhance human rights protections.

| Socioeconomic Rights Violation | Potential International Crime |
|---|---|
| Deliberately and intentionally blocking food aid in violations of the **right to food** [ICESCR, Art. 11] | Crime against humanity of other inhumane acts [Rome Statute, Art. 7(1)(k)] (but also potentially extermination, which is not mentioned) |
| *and* with intention to bring about physical destruction of a group | Genocide [Rome Statute, Art. 6] |
| Lack of health care used as a tool to destroy parts of the population (e.g. deliberate prevention of information about AIDS reaching a particular group in order to exterminate that group, in violation of the **right to health** [ICESCR, Art. 12] | Crime against humanity (presumably extermination) [Rome Statute, Art. 7(1)(b)] |
| Forced evictions in violation of the right to housing [ICESCR, Art. 11] | Crime against humanity of other inhumane acts [Rome Statute, Art. 7(1)(k)] (but also potentially forced transfer, which is not mentioned) |

As a second example, in describing the coercive mass movement of the Cambodian population from Phnom Penh in April 1975 after the takeover of the city by advancing Khmer Rouge forces, the co-investigating judges of the Extraordinary Chambers in the Court of Cambodia adopted the legal categorisation of the crime against humanity of 'other inhumane acts through forced transfer'.[43] The inhumane conditions associated with this forced transfer, based on the judicial investigation, included (i) the forced movement of the population from their places of residence without proper travel preparations; (ii) without sufficient water, food, or sanitation; (iii) without proper (or any) shelter; and (iv) without medical attention for vulnerable groups such as the sick and the elderly.[44] Despite the multiple violations of socioeconomic rights apparent on the facts, including violations of the right to food, health, and housing, the co-investigating judges chose not to use the flexibility of the crime against humanity of 'other inhumane acts' designation to categorise the

[42] Skogly, *supra* note 12, at 68–73.

[43] Case File 002/19-09-2007-ECCC-OCIJ, Closing Order (D427), 15 September 2010 at Paras. 1448–1469.

[44] *Ibid.*, at Para. 1436.

alleged criminal conduct in terms of violations of socioeconomic rights. Rather, they adopted the categorisation 'other inhumane acts though "attacks on *human dignity*"'.[45]

This second example may well demonstrate another missed opportunity to mainstream socioeconomic rights protection through the norms and institutions of international criminal justice. But more importantly, it demonstrates, as does the first example, how lawyers and judges cannot readily draw parallels between patent violations of socioeconomic rights and the legal categories of international criminal law.

## 5. COHERENCE IN PRACTICE: USING THE LENS OF COMPLEXITY THEORY

To propose a symmetry between international criminal law and international human rights law would be to engage in the very generalities and gymnastics we seek to avoid. Rather, it may prove more fruitful to use the lens of complexity theory to conceive of core international crimes and the suite of international human rights instruments, including those protecting socioeconomic rights, as co-evolving species within a complex adaptive system. In this approach, the 'fitness' of a particular legal rule within a given treaty-species influences the evolution of rules found in 'neighbouring' treaties, generating emergent effects rather than the linearly predictable triumph of one treaty over the rest.[46] Such an evolutionary model is better able to account for conceptual gaps in the protection of socioeconomic rights through international criminal law. Operating from within such a complex adaptive system, one can more readily accept the potential of international criminal law to evolve to more directly prohibit serious violations of socioeconomic rights. Reading one substantive crime (persecution as a crime against humanity) in light of one rule of interpretation (Article 21(3) of the Rome Statute) holds the greatest promise to catalyse such new legal approaches, which will most likely emerge in international jurisprudence in wholly unpredictable ways.

Article 7(1) of the Rome Statute provides that crimes against humanity include the following, when committed as part of a widespread or systematic attack directed against any civilian population, with knowledge of the attack:

> (h) Persecution against any identifiable group or collectivity on political, racial, national, ethnic, cultural, religious, gender . . . or other grounds that are universally recognized as impermissible under international law, in connection with any act referred to in this paragraph or any crime within the jurisdiction of the Court . . .

45 *Ibid.*, at Para. 1435 [emphasis added].

46 This argument is explored further in S. A. Nakhjavani, 'The Rough Edges of the Delicate Mosaic: Complexity Theory and the Early Jurisprudence of the International Criminal Court', in A. Smeulers (ed.), *Collective Violence and International Criminal Justice: An Interdisciplinary Approach* (2010), 236.

Article 7(2)(g) clarifies that '"[p]ersecution" means the intentional and severe deprivation of fundamental rights contrary to international law by reason of the identity of the group or collectivity'.

The Elements of Crimes document, a subordinate legal instrument adopted by the Assembly of States Parties to the Rome Statute to 'assist'[47] the judges in the interpretation of substantive crimes, provides the following nonbinding[48] but persuasive[49] guidance on the material, mental, and contextual elements of persecution:

1. The perpetrator severely deprived, contrary to international law, [21] one or more persons of fundamental rights.
2. The perpetrator targeted such person or persons by reason of the identity of a group or collectivity or targeted the group or collectivity as such.
3. Such targeting was based on political, racial, national, ethnic, cultural, religious, gender as defined in paragraph 3, or other grounds that are universally recognized as impermissible under international law.
4. The conduct was committed in connection with any act referred to in article 7, paragraph 1, of the Statute or any crime within the jurisdiction of the Court. [22]
5. The conduct was committed as part of a widespread or systematic attack directed against a civilian population.
6. The perpetrator knew that the conduct was part or intended the conduct to be part of a widespread or systematic attack directed against a civilian population.

[21] This requirement is without prejudice to paragraph 6 of the General Introduction to the Elements of Crimes.

[22] It is understood that no additional mental element is necessary for this element other that inherent in element 6.

The terms of the Rome Statute and Elements of Crimes leave no doubt that the 'fundamental rights' protected through the criminalisation of persecution can include socioeconomic rights. Although the term 'fundamental rights' was traditionally linked to those rights having peremptory status under international law,[50] the case law of the ICTY affirms that the crime of persecution extends to the full ambit of

47 Rome Statute, *supra* note 20, at Article 9(1).

48 See, e.g., K. Dörmann et al., *Elements of War Crimes under the Rome Statute of the International Criminal Court* (2002), 8.

49 In practice, the Chambers of the International Criminal Court have generally treated the Elements of Crimes document and the footnotes contained therein as persuasive, without the need for significant judicial scrutiny: see e.g. *Prosecutor* v. *Thomas Lubanga Dyilo*, ICC-01/04–01/06, Decision on the Confirmation of Charges (29 January 2007) at Paras. 205, 230, and 240 (International Criminal Court, Pre-Trial Chamber I).

50 A. Pellet, 'Applicable Law', in A. Cassese, P. Gaeta, and J. Jones (eds.), *The Rome Statute of the International Criminal Court: A Commentary* (2002), 1081; *Case Concerning the Barcelona Traction, Light and Power Company, Ltd.* (*Belgium* v. *Spain*) [1970] I.C.J. Rep. 3 at 32.

socioeconomic rights.[51] Nonetheless, the charging practice of the ICTY, ICTR, and ICC prosecutors on the crime of persecution seems to give only ancillary attention, if any, to violations of socioeconomic rights.[52]

Any co-evolutionary interaction between the first material element of the crime of persecution (i.e. the severe deprivation of fundamental rights contrary to international law) and the scope of a given socioeconomic right found in a human rights instrument would be mediated through the vehicle of Article 21(3) of the Rome Statute, which provides,

> The application and interpretation of law pursuant to this article must be consistent with internationally recognized human rights, and be without any adverse distinction founded on grounds such as gender . . . age, race, colour, language, religion or belief, political or other opinion, national, ethnic or social origin, wealth, birth or other status.

This article has wide-ranging implications, and the methodological rigour with which the Chambers of the International Criminal Court applies this provision of its statute warrants close attention in assessing the prospects of its deployment in argument or jurisprudence to buttress the better protection of socioeconomic rights. Article 21(3) is, first, a rule of interpretation to be applied together with the principles of interpretation enshrined in Articles 31–33 of the Vienna Convention on the Law of Treaties.[53] As the Pre-Trial Chamber observes,

> [T]he Chamber, in determining the contours of the statutory framework provided for in the Statute, the Rules and the Regulations, must, in addition to applying the general principle of interpretation set out in article 21(3) of the Statute, look at the general principles of interpretation as set out in article 31(1) of the Vienna Convention on the Law of Treaties, according to which 'a treaty shall be interpreted in good faith in accordance with the ordinary meaning to be given to the terms of the treaty in their context and in light of its object and purpose'.[54]

Article 21(3) establishes both a specific rule of interpretation for the Rome Statute and provides a particular instance of that rule: interpretation must be *consistent with internationally recognised human rights* and, as a particular instance of that

[51] See Kupreškić, *supra* note 38, at 610, 612, 614–15, noting, 'Persecution can also involve a variety of other discriminatory acts, involving attacks on political, social and economic rights' (at Para. 615).

[52] Notable exceptions are the 9 March 2001 Consolidated Indictment (Charge 7) and 7 March 2002 Amended Consolidated Indictment (Charge 3) issued against Momčilo Krajišnik and Biljana Plavsić by the Prosecutor of the ICTY; the first refers to the 'denial of fundamental rights . . . including the right to work, freedom of movement, the right to judicial process, and the right of equal access to public services including proper medical care', the second refers, inter alia, to failure to provide adequate shelter, food, water, and hygiene and the use of forced labour.

[53] 1155 U.N.T.S. 331 (entered into force: 27 January 1980).

[54] *Prosecutor* v. *Germain Katanga*, ICC-01/04–01/07, *Decision on the Joinder of the Cases against Germain KATANGA and Mathieu NGUDJOLO CHUI* (10 March 2008) (International Criminal Court, Pre-Trial Chamber) at 7.

same requirement, *without adverse discrimination* on enumerated and, arguably, analogous grounds.[55] Pellet argues that this interpretation rule creates 'a sort of international "super-legality"' for all internationally recognised human rights norms and not only such 'fundamental' rights as would be considered peremptory norms of international law.[56]

A review of the ICC's early jurisprudence suggests an expansive use of Article 21(3) as an interpretive tool. It is too early to draw firm conclusions, but it seems that Article 21(3), in common with most human rights instruments, is evolutive in character, allowing the court to draw on norms of international human rights as these evolve from time to time. The concept of the evolutive interpretation of treaties – whereby variable and changing concepts are interpreted in accordance with new conditions – has been suggested in a joint dissenting opinion of the European Court of Human Rights,[57] and finds support in the reasoning of the ICJ in the *Gabčikovo-Nagymaros* case.[58]

Nevertheless, it is all too easy to leap from using sources of international law beyond the Rome Statute as interpretative tools (as permitted by Article 21(3) of the Rome Statute) to the application of those sources directly to the facts, effectively sidestepping an incomplete interpretative process. A similar risk exists in recourse to Article 31(3(c) of the Vienna Convention, which permits reference to 'any relevant rules of international law applicable in the relations between the parties' as part of the assessment of context. Gardiner notes this problem in the approach of the majority of the ICJ in the *Oil Platforms* case, which had to consider whether U.S. action destroying Iranian oil platforms could be justified on the grounds of a treaty provision that permitted measures necessary to fulfil obligations for the maintenance or restoration of international peace and security:

> At the stage of considering the merits . . . the reasoning in the majority judgment took the general international law of self-defence as the starting point, making reference to article 31(3)(c) of the Vienna Convention in support of this approach.[59]

The separate opinion of Judge Higgins is apposite:

> The Court has, however, not interpreted [the treaty provision] by reference to the rules on treaty interpretation. It has rather invoked the concept of treaty interpretation to displace the applicable law. It has replaced the terms [of the treaty provision]

[55] The enumerated grounds in the statute are gender, age, race, colour, language, religion or belief, political or other opinion, national, ethnic, or social origin, wealth, birth, or other status. The use of the term 'such as' prior to this enumeration, as well as the words 'and other status', supports the argument that the list is not closed.

[56] Pellet, *supra* note 51, at 1081.

[57] *Feldbrugge* v. *Netherlands*, ECHR Case No. 8/1984/80/127 (Judgement of 23 April 1986); see R. Gardiner, *Treaty Interpretation* (2008), at 242–43.

[58] *Gabčikovo-Nagymaros Project (Hungary* v. *Slovakia)*, [1997] I.C.J. Rep. 7.

[59] Gardiner, *supra* note 58, at 279.

with those of international law on the use of force and all sight of the text of [the treaty provision] has been lost.[60]

Although international human rights law serves both as an interpretative tool and a normatively superior source of law, as discussed later, it will be important to keep interpretation and application conceptually – if not practically – distinct.

Article 21(3) enshrines a rule on applicable law that purports to give precedence to internationally recognised human rights over any other source of law in the application of law by the court.[61] Although Article 21(1)(b) recognises 'applicable treaties' and the 'established principles of the law of armed conflict' as a source of law that the court may apply,[62] the normative superiority of Article 21(3) would seem to privilege rules of international human rights law even over the treaty and customary rules of armed conflict. If, for instance, the elements of the war crime of causing widespread, long-term, and severe damage to the environment[63] were to evolve to better protect sustainable societies[64] – whether by the development of a new treaty or new customary norms – the court may find such an interpretation inconsistent with established human rights norms such as the rule *in dubio pro reo*. It is important to note, in this respect, that the Rome Statute explicitly provides that the rule *in dubio pro reo* applies to the definitions of crimes.[65] Nonetheless, the court has not, thus far, given credence to arguments advanced by the parties that would tend to extend the character of the rule *in dubio pro reo* to that of a general rule of interpretation or a presumption in favour of the accused in the application of law.[66]

However, the court has used Article 21(3) expansively, reading in a power to grant both permanent and conditional stays of proceedings – a power not provided in the Rome Statute or the International Criminal Court's Rules of Procedure and Evidence. In its judgement of 14 December 2006, addressing allegations that the appellant had been illegally detained and ill treated by the Congolese authorities, with the collusion of the prosecutor, the Appeals Chamber held that it follows from Article 21(3) that

60 *Oil Platforms (Islamic Republic of Iran* v. *United States of America)* (Preliminary Objections), [1996] I.C.J. Rep. 820, Para. 52.

61 See Pellet, *supra* note 35, at 1080; his view may be distinguished from Arsanjani, who suggests that Art. 21(3) only lays down a rule of interpretation; see Arsanjani, *supra* note 11.

62 Pellet argues that the usefulness of such customary norms will be limited by the requirement that their application must necessarily satisfy the principle of legality enshrined in Art. 23 of the Rome Statute; see Pellet, *supra* note 51, at 1072.

63 Rome Statute, *supra* note 20, at Art. 8.

64 For some proposals, see B.- S. Cho, 'Emergence of an International Environmental Criminal Law?' (2000) 19(11) *UCLA Journal of Environmental Law and Policy* 11; Drumbl, *supra* note 14.

65 Rome Statute, *supra* note 11, at Art. 22(2).

66 See, e.g., *Prosecutor* v. *Germain Katanga*, ICC-01/04–01/07 OA 3, *Judgement on the Appeal of Mr. Germain Katanga against the Decision of Pre-Trial Chamber I entitled, 'Decision on the Defence Request Concerning Languages*, 27 May 2008 (International Criminal Court, Appeals Chamber).

> [w]here fair trial becomes impossible because of breaches of the fundamental rights of the suspect or the accused by his/her accusers, it would be a contradiction in terms to put the person on trial. Justice could not be done. A fair trial is the only means to do justice. If no fair trial can be held, the object of the judicial process is frustrated and must be stopped.[67]

The final arbiter of the 'proper law' of the Rome Statute, its interpretation, and application, is the court itself.[68] For this reason, it is instructive to survey the interpretative methodology adopted in the court's early jurisprudence. It is unsurprising that these initial decisions – addressing such fundamental procedural matters as the right of victims to participate in proceedings and the scope of the prosecutorial duty of disclosure – have routinely attempted to apply the Vienna rules to the Rome Statute. Contrasting decisions from 2006 and 2008, one observes the initially perfunctory approach of the Pre-Trial Chamber maturing through the jurisprudence of the Appeals Chamber and reflecting the reality that 'the [Vienna] rules are not a step-by-step formula for producing an irrebuttable interpretation in every case'.[69] Rather, as the International Law Commission has observed, 'All the various elements, as they were present in any given case, would be thrown into the crucible, and their *interaction* would be given the legally relevant interpretation'.[70]

The Pre-Trial Chamber's 17 January 2006 *Decision for Participation in Proceedings of VPRS1–6* assesses whether, for the purposes of Article 68(3) of the Rome Statute, 'proceedings' can be said to exist when a situation within the jurisdiction of the court is being investigated by the Office of the Prosecutor, prior to the identification of a named suspect. Although the Pre-Trial Chamber does not invoke the Vienna Convention by name, the pedigree of its method is unmistakable: 'The Chamber will address the arguments as follows: first the terminological argument, second the contextual argument and third the "teleological argument."'[71] The Pre-Trial Chamber's 'teleological argument' begins by identifying the 'object and purpose'[72] of the victims' participation regime of the Rome Statute. It also refers to the 'ordinary

[67] *Prosecutor* v. *Thomas Lubanga Dyilo*, ICC-01/04–01/06–772, *Judgement on the Appeal of Mr. Thomas Lubanga Dyilo against the Decision on the Defence Challenge to the Jurisdiction of the Court pursuant to article 19(2)(a) of the Statute of 3 October 2006 (14 December 2006)* (International Criminal Court, Appeals Chamber), Para. 37.

[68] Indeed, absent an integrated, international constitutional order, international courts and tribunals are unfettered by the rule *nemo iudex in causa sua*. The suggestion that the Assembly of States Parties can amend the Rome Statute to address interpretative overreach or *lacunae* is impractical given the peculiarly onerous amending provisions of the Rome Statute; see Rome Statute, *supra* note 11, at Art. 121.

[69] Gardiner, *supra* note 58, at 9.

[70] [1966] *Yearbook of the ILC*, vol. II, 219–20, Para. 8 [emphasis added].

[71] *Situation in the Democratic Republic of Congo*, ICC-01/04, *Decision on the Applications for Participation in the Proceedings of VPRS1, VPRS2,VPRS3, VPRS4, VPRS5 and VPRS6*, 17 January 2006 (International Criminal Court, Pre-Trial Chamber), Para. 28. It is important to note that the substance of this decision has largely been vacated by subsequent judgements of the Appeals Chamber; what is of interest here is the interpretative method adopted.

[72] *Ibid.*, at Para. 50.

meaning' standard to define the term 'natural person' in a later part of its decision. It is perplexing, however, that in defining the key term 'proceedings', the Chamber does not inquire into its ordinary meaning at all, but rather dwells at length on the need for consistency with the equivalent term in the French version of the Rome Statute.[73] In effect, the Chamber hastens to apply Article 33 of the Vienna Convention without first exhausting Articles 31 and 32 as required.

Some six months later, the Appeals Chamber was called upon to determine whether the prosecutor had a legal basis to appeal the earlier decision through a purported 'extraordinary review', beyond the scope of rules on interlocutory appeals in the Rome Statute and Rules of Procedure and Evidence. Finding the request of the prosecutor procedurally unfounded, the Appeals Chamber makes a clear statement on the applicability of the Vienna rules to the Rome Statute:

> The interpretation of treaties, and the *Rome Statute* is no exception, is governed by the Vienna Convention on the Law of Treaties (23 May 1969), specifically the provisions of articles 31 and 32. The principal rule of interpretation is set out in article 31(1).... The Appeals Chamber shall not advert to the definition of 'good faith', save to mention that it is linked to what follows and that is the wording of the Statute. The rule governing the interpretation of a section of the law is its wording read in context and in light of its object and purpose. The context of a given legislative provision is defined by the particular sub-section of the law read as a whole in conjunction with the section of an enactment in its entirety. Its objects may be gathered from the chapter of the law in which the particular section is included and its purposes from the wider aims of the law as may be gathered from its preamble and general tenor of the treaty.[74]

The Appeals Chamber thus considers the textual, contextual, and teleological interpretation of provisions of the Rome Statute that allow for interlocutory appeals to assess whether a lacuna alleged by the prosecutor could be found to exist.[75] At this stage, the Chamber finds as an 'undisputed fact'[76] that the Rome Statute 'does not confer power or competence on the Appeals Chamber to review a decision not stating a subject for appeal'.[77]

The Chamber proceeds to confirm that its interpretation accords with internationally recognised human rights, citing Article 21(3) of the Rome Statute and surveying the provisions of international and regional human rights instruments[78] – though excluding any mention of the instrument most directly applicable to the situation before the Court, namely the African Charter on Human and Peoples

73 *Ibid.*, at Paras. 30–38.

74 *Prosecutor* v. *Thomas Lubanga Dyilo*, ICC-01/04–01/06–168, Judgment on the Prosecutor's Application for Extraordinary Review of Pre-Trial Chamber I's 31 March 2006 Decision Denying Leave to Appeal, 13 July 2006 (International Criminal Court, Appeals Chamber), Para. 33.

75 *Ibid.*, at Paras. 34–37.

76 *Ibid.*, at Para. 34.

77 *Ibid.*

78 *Ibid.*, at Para. 38 and note 43.

Rights.[79] By this point, the Chamber reaches an 'inexorable inference . . . that the Statute defines exhaustively the right to appeal against decisions of first-instance courts'.[80]

For good measure, the Chamber confirms its interpretation by referring to the preparatory works of the Rome Statute, particularly a specific reference to a decision of the drafters to exclude a provision designed to give effect to the broader right of appeal alleged by the prosecutor.[81] Although recourse to supplementary means of interpretation, such as preparatory works, is intended primarily to resolve absurdities emerging from the application of Article 31 of the Vienna Convention, that convention also allows for recourse to such means merely to confirm an interpretation arising from the application of Article 31. Referring to the practice of the International Court of Justice, Gardiner considers that

> in virtually all cases where there is an issue of treaty interpretation, it is the practice to look at the preparatory work, even if nothing comes of it . . . it probably boils down to doing justice to the parties and completing the interpretative exercise.[82]

More recent jurisprudence of the Appeals Chamber demonstrates the court's maturing approach, while grappling with the complex interplay of interpretation and application of the Vienna rules and the threefold character of Article 21 as a statement of sources of law, as a hierarchy of norms, and as an interpretative rule.

On 27 May 2008, the Appeals Chamber was called upon to interpret the meaning of the phrase, 'in a language which accused fully understands and speaks', in its review of a decision of a single judge of the Pre-Trial Chamber that the accused's competency in French met the standards of Article 67(1)(a) and (f) of the Rome Statute and that consequently, there was no requirement for the Registry to provide Lingala interpretation and translation services to the accused.[83]

The Appeal Chamber's narrow reason for remitting the appellant's request to the Pre-Trial Chamber was the application of an erroneous legal standard in the Chamber below – effectively due to use of an improper interpretative method.[84] The reasoning is also interesting in its finding that this particular standard in the Statute is higher than that prescribed by internationally recognised human rights norms.[85] The Appeals Chamber appears critical of the relative informality with which the single judge 'acknowledged' the jurisprudence of human rights courts and international criminal tribunals, and how the Chamber below went on to 'note' and was 'mindful'

79 21 ILM 58 (entered into force 21 October 1986).
80 *Supra* note 75, at Para. 39.
81 *Ibid.*, at Para. 40.
82 Gardiner, *supra* note 58.
83 *Supra* note 67.
84 *Ibid.*, at Para. 38.
85 *Ibid.*, at Para. 62.

of relevant cases of the European Court of Human Rights.[86] There is also concern with the depth of the single judge's analysis of the 'drafting history' of the Statute.[87]

The Appeals Chamber proceeds to interpret the key term 'in a language which the accused fully understands and speaks' using the Vienna rules. The maturity of the interpretative methodology is first evident in the Chamber's approach to alleged distinctions between the English and French versions of the text, which were central to the arguments of both the defence and prosecution. The Chamber considers only that the ordinary meaning of 'fully', both in English and French, provides for a standard that is 'very high', and it 'does not consider it necessary to enter further into any possible differences'.[88] There is no question of sidestepping Articles 31 and 32 of the Vienna Convention to engage in an Article 33 analysis.

The Chamber's consideration of international human rights standards draws upon regional instruments and the provisions of the statutes of the ad hoc tribunals. It makes no explicit reference to Article 21(3) at this stage. Given that these sources use the term 'understands and speaks' rather than 'fully understands and speaks', the Chamber finds them of limited assistance.[89] Were the Chamber mistakenly conflating the interpretative and normative uses of Article 21(3), one would have expected some reading down of the provisions of the statute at this stage. Instead, the Chamber completes the interpretative exercise, referring to Article 32 of the Vienna Convention and proceeding to assess the significance of preparatory works in great detail.[90]

## 6. CONCLUSION

This review of the interpretation and application of the Rome Statute in accordance with international human rights reveals a significant conceptual breeding ground for new approaches to the crime of persecution to emerge – approaches that might bring the protection of socioeconomic rights into the mainstream. To the extent that complexity theory provides a useful lens to analyse the potential for such evolution, it is axiomatic that developments will occur unexpectedly, even spasmodically, or as the product of seemingly insignificant events – the choices of one investigator in the field or the results of a literature search of one law clerk. But although predictions cannot be made, the field is open.

[86] *Ibid.*, at Para. 33.
[87] *Ibid.*, at Para, 36.
[88] *Ibid.*, at Para. 40.
[89] *Ibid.*, at Para. 48.
[90] *Ibid.*, at Paras. 50–56.

# 7

# Cultural Heritage and International Criminal Law

*Roger O'Keefe*

## 1. INTRODUCTION

The preamble to the 1954 Hague Convention for the Protection of Cultural Property in the Event of Armed Conflict,[1] concluded under the aegis of UNESCO, declares that 'damage to cultural property belonging to any people whatsoever means damage to the cultural heritage of all mankind'. Although the language is rhetorical rather than technical, the term 'heritage' and the reference to 'mankind' sound an unmistakable intergenerational fiduciary note,[2] a note with which a resolution of the first meeting of the High Contracting Parties to the Convention later chimed when it recalled 'that the purpose of the Convention . . . is to protect the cultural heritage of all peoples for future generations'.[3] Subsequent UNESCO instruments have developed this theme, with one declaration suggesting that 'present generations have the responsibility to . . . protect and safeguard the . . . tangible cultural heritage and to transmit this common heritage to future generations'.[4] Equally, it is now

[1] 249 UNTS 240.

[2] The rhetorical resonance is all the greater in the French text, in the light of Aubry and Rau's canonical elaboration of the legal concept of '*patrimoine*': see, e.g., C. Aubry and C. Rau, *Cours de droit civil français d'après la méthode de Zachariae* (1935–58), Vol. IX, paras 573–87.

[3] UNESCO Doc. CUA/120 (3 September 1962), para. 22.

[4] 1997 Declaration on the Responsibilities of the Present Generations towards Future Generations, UNESCO Doc. 29C/Res 44, Art. 7. See, similarly, 1972 Recommendation Concerning the Protection, at National Level, of the Cultural and Natural Heritage, UNESCO Doc. 17C/Res 30, preamble (fifth recital) ('every country in whose territory there are components of the cultural . . . heritage has an obligation to safeguard this part of mankind's heritage and to ensure that it is handed down to future generations'). See too 1976 Convention on the Protection of the Archeological, Historical and Artistic Heritage of the American Nations (Convention of San Salvador), OASTS No. 47, preamble (second recital) ('there is a basic obligation to transmit to coming generations the legacy of their cultural heritage') and 2005 Council of Europe Framework Convention on the Value of Cultural Heritage for Society, CETS No. 199 (not yet in force), Art. 2(b) (defining a 'heritage community' as 'people who value specific aspects of cultural heritage which they wish . . . to sustain and transmit to future generations').

recognised that the preservation and integration of the cultural heritage are essential elements of sustainable development. One UNESCO instrument, dating from as early as 1972, states,

> As the ultimate purpose of protecting, conserving and presenting the cultural... heritage is the development of man, Member States should, as far as possible, direct their work in this field in such a way that the cultural heritage... may no longer be regarded as a check on national development but as a determining factor in such development.[5]

It provides that '[t]he protection, conservation and effective presentation of the cultural... heritage should be considered as one of the essential aspects of regional development plans'.[6] A more recent Council of Europe framework convention emphasises 'the value and potential of cultural heritage wisely used as a resource for sustainable development'.[7]

International criminal law is one means of protecting the cultural heritage to enable it to play its role as an element in sustainable development and for transmission to future generations. The chief[8] juridical means by which it protects this

5 Recommendation Concerning the Protection, at National Level, of the Cultural and Natural Heritage, Art. 7.

6 *Ibid.*, Art. 8. See also *ibid.*, preamble (second recital).

7 Council of Europe Framework Convention on the Value of Cultural Heritage for Society, preamble (third recital). See also *ibid.*, Art. 1(d), in which the state parties agree to take the necessary steps to apply the provisions of the convention concerning the role of cultural heritage 'in the processes of sustainable development', and Art. 5, in which they undertake to promote cultural heritage protection 'as a central factor in... sustainable development'. Consider too, also under the auspices of the Council of Europe, Recommendation No. R (2003) 1 of the Committee of Ministers to member states on the promotion of tourism to foster the cultural heritage as a factor for sustainable development, the preamble to which affirms that the conservation of the cultural heritage, 'in its authenticity to be handed down to future generations', 'is part of the process of sustainable development'.

8 It is worth noting in passing that Art. 8 of the UNESCO-sponsored 1970 Convention on the Means of Prohibiting and Preventing the Illicit Import, Export and Transfer of Ownership of Cultural Property, 823 UNTS 231, obliges a state party to impose penalties or administrative sanctions, first, on any person responsible for importing cultural property stolen from a museum, religious or secular public monument, or similar institution in another state party and, second, on any person responsible for the exportation of cultural property from the state party's own territory without the appropriate export certificate. Art. 14 of the Convention on the Protection of the Archeological, Historical and Artistic Heritage of the American Nations provides that '[t]hose responsible for crimes against the integrity of cultural property or for crimes resulting from the illegal exportation or importation thereof are subject to extradition treaties, when appropriate'. Art. 2 of the 1998 International Convention for the Suppression of Terrorist Bombings, 2149 UNTS 284, provides for the offence of unlawfully and intentionally delivering, placing, discharging, or detonating an explosive or other lethal device in, into, or against a place of public use – defined in Art. 1(5) to include any cultural or historical place accessible or open to the public – with the intent to cause death or serious bodily injury, or to cause extensive destruction where such destruction results, or is likely to result, in major economic loss. In accordance with Art. 3, however, the convention does not apply (with the exception, 'as appropriate', of Arts. 10 to 15, on extradition, mutual legal assistance, and prevention) where the offence is committed within a single state, where the alleged offender and the victims are nationals of that state, where the alleged offender is found in the territory of that state, and where no other state has a basis under Arts. 6(1) or 6(2) of the convention to exercise jurisdiction. (This would mean that, if they occurred

heritage is by providing, in certain contexts, for individual criminal responsibility under the respective rubrics of war crimes and crimes against humanity for the intentional destruction or damage and the misappropriation of cultural property. (Although journalistic and speculative academic reference is frequently made to 'cultural genocide', the crime of genocide does not extend under positive international law to acts of hostility against and plunder of cultural property.) The present chapter offers a straightforward account of the relevant principles.

## 2. THE RELEVANT CRIMES

### 2.1. *War Crimes*

There is a range of both customary and treaty-based war crimes relevant to the protection of the cultural heritage in the event of armed conflict. Before examining each in turn, however, it is important to emphasise that, although the existence of an armed conflict (be it of an international or non-international character) is a necessary legal criterion for the commission of a war crime, it is not a sufficient one. To qualify as a war crime, the destruction of cultural property, in addition to occurring in time of armed conflict, must have some 'nexus' to that conflict, in the language of the Appeals Chamber of the International Criminal Tribunal for the Former Yugoslavia (ICTY).[9] That is, it must be 'closely related'[10] to the armed conflict, which means that the existence of the conflict must, at a minimum, play 'a substantial part in the perpetrator's ability to commit [the crime], his decision to commit it, the manner in which it was committed or the purpose for which it was committed'.[11] It is for this reason, for example, that the demolition of the Buddhas

today, the 1993 mafia car bombings in Italy – which in Florence destroyed the Torre dei Pulci, killing a family, and seriously damaged, inter alia, the Uffizi Gallery, and which in Rome devastated the twelfth-century portico of the Church of San Giorgio al Velabro and damaged both the Basilica of St John Lateran and the Lateran Palace – would not fall within the convention's scope of application.) In addition, Art. 19(2) of the convention excludes the activities of armed forces during armed conflicts. For its part, finally, the Council of Europe's 1985 European Convention on Offences Relating to Cultural Property, ETS No. 119, is not in force and may never be, not having a single state party to date.

9 *Prosecutor* v. *Akayesu*, Appeals Chamber Judgement, Case No. ICTR-96–4-A, 1 June 2001, para. 444; *Prosecutor* v *Rutaganda*, Appeals Chamber Judgement, Case No. ICTR-96–3-A, 26 May 2003, paras. 569–70; *Prosecutor* v. *Stakic*, Appeals Chamber Judgement, Case No. IT-97–24-A, 22 March 2006, para. 342.

10 *Prosecutor* v. *Tadic*, Appeals Chamber Decision on Defence Motion for Interlocutory Appeal on Jurisdiction, Case No. IT-94–1, 2 October 1995, para. 70; *Prosecutor* v. *Kunarac*, Appeals Chamber Judgement, Case No. IT-96–23 & IT-96–23/1-A, 12 June 2002, para. 55; *Rutaganda*, Appeals Chamber Judgement, paras. 569–70; *Stakic*, Appeals Chamber Judgement, para. 342.

11 *Kunarac*, Appeals Chamber Judgement, para. 58. The Chamber further states, 'What ultimately distinguishes a war crime from a purely domestic offence is that a war crime is shaped by or dependent upon the environment – the armed conflict – in which it is committed. . . . [I]f it can be established . . . that the perpetrator acted in furtherance of or under the guise of the armed conflict, it would be sufficient to conclude that his acts were closely related to the armed conflict.' This was

of Bamiyan did not constitute a war crime. Although sporadic non-international armed conflict continued in the far northeast of Afghanistan at the time of their destruction, the Buddhas were not destroyed in the course of fighting,[12] the Bamiyan Valley and the rest of the country being free of hostilities and securely under the Taliban government's control,[13] and their demolition, which was essentially an act of fundamentalist religious iconoclasm, was in no way facilitated or motivated by the conflict.

### 2.1.1. Customary International Law

2.1.1.1. BACKGROUND. The First World War witnessed many controversial acts of destruction of and grave damage to extremely significant cultural property in Belgium and France, including the international *causes célèbres* of the torching of the medieval university library in Leuven (Louvain) and the bombardment of the great gothic cathedral at Reims. In response, Sub-Commission III of the Commission on Responsibilities, established by the Preliminary Peace Conference of Paris in 1919, was mandated with investigating and making recommendations as to violations of the laws and customs of war committed by Germany and the Central Powers during the war. In its report,[14] the commission presented, inter alia, a draft list of war crimes that included the 'wanton destruction of religious, charitable, educational and historic buildings and monuments'. Political disagreement, however, thwarted trials before an inter-Allied criminal tribunal, and the Allied Powers sought instead the extradition from Germany of suspected war criminals for trial by national courts.[15] France entered 16 requests for persons suspected of offences of a cultural nature.[16] But extradition proved elusive as well.[17]

quoted and endorsed in *Rutaganda*, Appeals Chamber Judgement, paras. 569–70. See also *Stakic*, Appeals Chamber Judgement, para. 343.

12 Nor can there exist a legal state of belligerent occupation in non-international armed conflict.

13 Note, however, that the absence of hostilities at the time in the Bamiyan Valley does not in itself mean that no war crime could, as a matter of law, have been committed there. An act 'geographically remote from the actual fighting' can still be a war crime, provided that the impugned act was 'in furtherance of or under the guise of the armed conflict': *Kunarac*, Appeals Chamber Judgement, paras. 57–8; *Stakic*, Appeals Chamber Judgement, para. 342. For this reason, the January 1998 bombing by Tamil separatists of the Temple of the Tooth (Sri Dalada Maligawa or Temple of the Sacred Tooth Relic) in the World Heritage site of Kandy in Sri Lanka during that country's civil war could – if customary international law were held to be the same then as it is now – be considered a war crime.

14 Reproduced in United Nations War Crimes Commission, *History of the United Nations War Crimes Commission and the Development of the Laws of War* (1948), 33–34.

15 See J. Horne and A. Kramer, *German Atrocities 1914: A History of Denial* (2001), App. 4, 448–50.

16 See *ibid.*, 448.

17 As a result of an Allied-German compromise, trials of some suspected German war criminals took place in Leipzig, but to little avail, while some were tried in absentia in France and Belgium.

The loss of cultural heritage during the First World War soon paled in comparison with Nazi Germany's systematic devastation and plundering of the galleries, museums, libraries, and historic buildings and sites of Poland and the Soviet Union, along with its Europe-wide seizure of private Jewish-owned collections, during the Second World War. In the event, Article 6(b) of the charter of the International Military Tribunal at Nuremberg[18] vested it with jurisdiction over war crimes, including 'plunder of public or private property, wanton destruction of cities, towns or villages, or devastation not justified by military necessity'.[19] Those Nazis involved in organising the massive destruction and misappropriation of cultural property in and from the occupied territories were convicted, on these and many other counts, of war crimes.[20] Nor were lesser examples of crimes against cultural property ignored by the national war crimes tribunals established by the Allied powers after the war. The Permanent Military Tribunal set up under French jurisdiction at Metz found a German civilian – who had destroyed a monument in a French town commemorating the dead of the First World War and broken a statue of Joan of Arc – guilty of destroying public monuments, on the order of a German official, contrary to the laws and customs of war.[21]

Fifty years later, a hallmark of the savage wars that erupted in Croatia and Bosnia-Herzegovina during and after the dissolution of the former Socialist Federal Republic of Yugoslavia was the premeditated destruction of the cultural heritage of 'enemy' communities, in the form of attacks on the historic cities of Dalmatia and the laying waste of centuries-old mosques, mektebs, churches, monasteries, libraries, archives, and the like in Bosnia-Herzegovina and the Croatian Krajina. In response, the ICTY was granted competence in Article 3(d) of its statute[22] over the war crime of 'seizure

[18] Charter of the International Military Tribunal ('Nuremberg Charter'), annexed to the 1945 Agreement by the Government of the United Kingdom of Great Britain and Northern Ireland, the Government of the United States of America, the Provisional Government of the French Republic and the Government of the Union of Soviet Socialist Republics for the Prosecution and Punishment of the Major War Criminals of the European Axis, 82 UNTS 279.

[19] See also Control Council Law No. 10: Punishment of Persons Guilty of War Crimes, Crimes against Peace and against Humanity, 20 December 1945, 3 *Official Gazette Control Council for Germany* 50 (1946), Art. II(1)(b).

[20] See *Judgment of the International Military Tribunal for the Trial of German Major War Criminals*, 30 September and 1 October 1946 ('Nuremberg Judgment'), Misc. No. 12 (1946), Cmd 6964, reproduced (1947) 41 AJIL 172, especially 237–38, 287, and 330. Chief among the perpetrators was Alfred Rosenberg, head of the Einsatzstab Rosenberg, the special corps created by Hitler and mandated with the plunder of the public artworks and antiquities of Central and Eastern Europe, including the Soviet Union, and of private Jewish-owned collections across the continent. Others involved included Martin Bormann, Hermann Göring, and Joachim von Ribbentrop.

[21] See *Trial of Karl Lingenfelder*, 11 March 1947, 9 LRTWC 67 (1947).

[22] Statute of the International Criminal Tribunal for the former Yugoslavia, UN Doc. S/25704 (3 May 1993), Annex, as amended ('ICTY Statute'). See also, identically, Draft Code of Crimes against the Peace and Security of Mankind, *Report of the International Law Commission on the Work of Its Forty-Eighth Session, 6 May–26 July 1996* ('Draft Code of Crimes'), UN Doc. A/51/10, Chap. II D, Art. 20(e)(iv).

of, destruction or wilful damage done to institutions dedicated to religion, charity and education, the arts and sciences, historic monuments and works of art and science', a provision that has formed[23] and continues to form[24] the jurisdictional basis of numerous prosecutions before the tribunal.

The recent memory of the Yugoslav conflict and the example of the ICTY Statute inspired the drafters of the Rome Statute of the International Criminal Court to vest the court, in Articles 8(2)(b)(ix) and 8(2)(e)(iv), with jurisdiction over the war crime of '[i]ntentionally directing attacks against buildings dedicated to religion, education, art, science or charitable purposes [and] historic monuments', whether committed in international or non-international armed conflict.[25] Identical provisions were included in Regulation No. 2000/15 promulgated in 2000 by the United Nations Transitional Administration in East Timor (UNTAET), which established and empowered special panels within the district court in Dili for the prosecution of certain serious offences, including war crimes,[26] and in the Statute of the Iraqi

[23] See *Prosecutor* v. *Strugar*, Trial Chamber Judgement, Case No. IT-01–42-T, 31 January 2005 and *Prosecutor* v. *Jokic*, Trial Chamber Sentencing Judgement, Case No. IT-01–42/1-S, 18 March 2004 (guilty plea), both in respect of the bombardment of the World Heritage site of the Old Town of Dubrovnik on 6 December 1991. (The case of Vladimir Kovacevic, also indicted for his role in the attack, was transferred to the judicial authorities of the Republic of Serbia in late 2006.) See also, in relation to the destruction of Muslim and Roman Catholic cultural property across Bosnia-Herzegovina, *Prosecutor* v. *Blaskic*, Trial Chamber Judgement, Case No. IT-95–14-T, 3 March 2000, one count (regarding the destruction of religious property in Busovaca) being vacated in *Prosecutor* v. *Blaskic*, Appeals Chamber Judgement, Case No. IT-95–14-A, 29 July 2004, para. 533; *Prosecutor* v. *Kordic and Cerkez*, Trial Chamber Judgement, Case No. IT-95–14/2-T, 26 February 2001, one count (in relation to the mosque at Stari Vitez) being overturned in *Prosecutor* v. *Kordic and Cerkez*, Appeals Chamber Judgement, Case No. IT-95–14/2-A, 17 December 2004, para. 471; *Prosecutor* v. *Naletilic and Martinovic*, Trial Chamber Judgement, Case No. IT-98–34-T, 31 March 2003; *Prosecutor* v. *Brdanin*, Trial Chamber Judgement, Case No. IT-99–36-T, 1 September 2004; *Prosecutor* v. *Plavsic*, Trial Chamber Sentencing Judgement, Case No. IT-00–39&40/1-S, 27 February 2003 (guilty plea). (The case of Pasko Ljubicic, a commander of Bosnian Croat forces indicted for destruction of mosques, was transferred to the authorities of Bosnia-Herzegovina in mid-2006.) See too, in relation to destruction of and damage to Croat cultural property in Croatia, *Prosecutor* v. *Martic*, Trial Chamber Judgement, Case No. IT-95–11-T, 12 June 2007. In *Prosecutor* v. *Hadzihasanovic and Kubura*, Trial Chamber Judgement, Case No. IT-01–47-T, 15 March 2006; although the Trial Chamber found that foreign mujahedin had destroyed certain Serb cultural property in Bosnia-Herzegovina, it held that the first accused was not responsible for their actions.

[24] See *Prosecutor* v. *Prlic, Stojic, Praljak, Petkovic, Coric and Pusic*, Second Amended Indictment, Case No. IT-04–74-T, 11 June 2008, para. 229, as regards the destruction of historic and other Muslim cultural property in Bosnia-Herzegovina, among it much of the historic town of Mostar, including the Old Bridge (*Stari Most*) from which it takes its name; *Prosecutor* v. *Seselj*, Third Amended Indictment, Case No. IT-03–67-T, 7 December 2007, para. 34, for the destruction of mosques, Catholic churches, and a religious archive in Bosnia-Herzegovina.

[25] 1998 Rome Statute of the International Criminal Court, 2187 UNTS 90 ('Rome Statute'), Arts. 8(2)(b)(ix) (international) and 8(2)(e)(iv) (non-international).

[26] See UNTAET Regulation No. 2000/15 on the Establishment of Panels with Exclusive Jurisdiction over Serious Criminal Offences, UN Doc. UNTAET/REG/2000/15 (6 June 2000) ('UNTAET Reg. No. 2000/15'), §§ 6.1(b)(ix) (international) and 6.1(e)(iv) (non-international).

Special Tribunal promulgated by the Coalition Provisional Authority in Iraq,[27] in which the United States, a state not party to the ICC Statute, played the dominant role. For the United States' own part, it is worth noting that the Military Commissions Act,[28] as amended[29] and as applicable to 'any conflict subject to the laws of war',[30] recognises the war crime of 'attacking protected property',[31] which includes 'buildings dedicated to religion, education, art, science, or charitable purposes [and] historic monuments'.[32]

2.1.1.2. UNLAWFUL ATTACKS AGAINST CULTURAL PROPERTY. In terms of the specific offences recognised as customary war crimes, there is no doubt that customary international law embodies individual criminal responsibility for unlawfully directing attacks[33] against cultural property in the inclusive sense of the term,[34] whether in international or non-international armed conflict. This responsibility is distinct from that recognised for unlawfully directing attacks against a civilian object,[35] a species of

27 Statute of the Iraqi Special Tribunal, Coalition Provisional Authority Order No. 48, 10 December 2003, App. A, reproduced 43 ILM 231 (2004) ('IST Statute'), Art. 13(b)(10) (international) and Art. 13(d)(4) (non-international). Although the tribunal was replaced on 18 October 2005 by the Supreme Iraqi Criminal Tribunal (also known as the Iraqi High Tribunal), the latter was in substance a continuation of the former: see Law of the Supreme Iraqi Criminal Tribunal, Law No. (10) 2005, *Official Gazette of the Republic of Iraq*, No. 4006, 18 October 2005.

28 10 USC §§ 948a–950t.

29 See Military Commissions Act of 2009, Pub. L. No. 111–84 §§ 1801–7, 123 Stat. 2574.

30 10 USC § 950p(c), cross-referable to § 948a(9).

31 10 USC § 950t(4).

32 10 USC § 950p(a)(3).

33 The customary definition of the word 'attacks' is that reflected in Art. 49(1) of 1977 Protocol Additional to the Geneva Conventions of 12 August 1949, and Relating to the Protection of Victims of International Armed Conflicts, 1125 UNTS 3 ('1977 Additional Protocol I'), namely 'acts of violence against the adversary, whether in offence or defence'.

34 By this is meant all 'institutions dedicated to religion, charity and education, the arts and sciences, historic monuments and works of art and science', in the words of Art. 3(d) of the ICTY Statute, or, in the words of Arts 8(2)(b)(ix) and 8(2)(e)(iv) of the Rome Statute, all 'buildings dedicated to religion, education, art, science or charitable purposes [and] historic monuments'. It was incorrectly suggested in *Strugar*, Trial Chamber Judgement, para. 312, that the war crime recognised in ICTY Statute, Art. 3(d) applies only insofar as the cultural property in question constitutes 'the cultural or spiritual heritage of peoples', within the meaning of 1977 Additional Protocol I, Arts 53(a) and 16. But this was not followed in *Hadzihasanovic and Kubura*, Trial Chamber Judgement, paras. 60, 61, and 64 and *Kordic and Cerkez*, Appeals Chamber Judgement, paras. 89 and 92. Note that the term 'historic monuments' refers in this and similar contexts to immovable property, whether public or private, deserving of legal protection on its own historical, artistic, or architectural terms, rather than on account of its contents or purpose: see R. O'Keefe, *The Protection of Cultural Property in Armed Conflict* (2006), 27–28 and 102.

35 See, e.g., *Prosecutor* v. *Strugar*, IT-01-42-T, Appeals Chamber, Judgement, 17 July 2008, para. 277: 'The crime of destruction or wilful damage of cultural property under Article 3(d) of the Statute is *lex specialis* with respect to the offence of unlawful attacks on civilian objects.' The Appeals Chamber of the ICTY has held that individual criminal responsibility attaches under customary international law to attacks against civilian objects in both international and non-international armed conflict: see *Prosecutor* v. *Hadzihasanovic and Kubura*, Appeals Chamber Decision on Joint Defence Interlocutory Appeal of Trial Chamber Decision on Rule 98*bis* Motions for Acquittal, Case No. IT-01–47-AR73.3,

which cultural property *prima facie* constitutes,[36] even if the requisite material and mental elements of the two offences are, *mutatis mutandis*, the same.[37] In *Strugar*, a Trial Chamber of the ICTY found the accused guilty of the war crime of 'destruction or wilful damage done to institutions dedicated to religion, charity and education, the arts and sciences, historic monuments and works of art and science', within the meaning of Article 3(d) of the tribunal's statute, for his role in the bombardment of the Old Town of Dubrovnik on 6 December 1991. The Chamber stated that such conduct was a war crime regardless of whether the conflict was international or non-international,[38] a position also taken in a subsequent decision of the Appeals Chamber in *Hadzihasanovic*.[39] The accused in *Jokic* pleaded guilty to the same offence in respect of the same attack. It will be recalled too that Articles 8(2)(b)(ix) and 8(2)(e)(iv) of the Rome Statute give the court jurisdiction over the war crime, in international and non-international armed conflicts respectively, of '[i]ntentionally directing attacks against buildings dedicated to religion, art, science or charitable purposes [and] historic monuments'; that these provisions are reproduced verbatim in UNTAET Regulation No. 2000/15 and in the Statute of the Iraqi Special Tribunal; and that the U.S. Military Commissions Act recognises the war crime of 'attacking protected property', a term defined to include 'buildings dedicated to religion, education, art, science, or charitable purposes [and] historic monuments'.

As to the requisite material elements (*actus reus*) of the offence, customary international law presently accepts that attacks against cultural property are not unlawful

11 March 2005, para. 30. See also *Prosecutor* v. *Strugar, Jokic and others*, Appeals Chamber Decision on Interlocutory Appeal, Case No. IT-01-42-AR72, 22 November 2002, para. 10; *Kordic and Cerkez*, Appeals Chamber Judgement, para. 59. Civilian objects are defined negatively as those objects that are not military objectives. In turn, the customary definition of military objectives is reflected in Art. 52(2) of 1977 Additional Protocol I, viz 'objects which by their nature, location, purpose or use make an effective contribution to military action and whose total or partial destruction, capture or neutralization, in the circumstances ruling at the time, offers a definite military advantage': see, e.g., *Brdanin*, Trial Chamber Judgement, para. 596 n. 1509; *Western Front, Aerial Bombardment and Related Claims, Eritrea's Claims 1, 3, 5, 9–13, 14, 21, 25 & 26: Partial Award (Eritrea/Ethiopia)*, 19 December 2005, 135 ILR 565, 608, paras. 112–3; J. M. Henckaerts and L. Doswald-Beck, *Customary International Humanitarian Law* (2005), Vol. I, 29–32 (Rule 8). The definition is reproduced in, inter alia, 1999 Second Protocol to the 1954 Hague Convention for the Protection of Cultural Property in the Event of Armed Conflict ('1999 Second Hague Protocol'), 2253 UNTS 211, Art. 1(f). Note that the Rome Statute recognises the war crime of '[i]ntentionally directing attacks against civilian objects, that is, objects which are not military objectives', only when the attack takes place in international armed conflict: see Rome Statute, Art. 8(2)(b)(ii).

36 See, e.g., *Kordic and Cerkez*, Appeals Chamber Judgement, paras. 89 and 92; Henckaerts and Doswald-Beck, *Customary International Humanitarian Law*, Vol. I, 32–34 (Rule 9), especially 34, listing 'historic monuments, places of worship and cultural property' as *prima facie* civilian objects, 'provided, in the final analysis, they have not become military objectives'.

37 In neither case is the relevant property to be made the object of attack unless and for as long as it is a military objective, and in both cases the impugned attack must have been intentional: see later discussion.

38 *Strugar*, Trial Chamber Judgement, para. 230.

39 *Hadzihasanovic and Kubura*, Appeals Chamber Decision on Joint Defence Interlocutory Appeal, paras. 44–8.

if and for as long as such property is a military objective. This is reflected in Articles 8(2)(b)(ix) and 8(2)(e)(iv) of the Rome Statute ('provided they are not military objectives'), as reproduced word for word in UNTAET Regulation No. 2000/15[40] and in the Statute of the Iraqi Special Tribunal.[41] Similarly, the U.S. Military Commissions Act grants jurisdiction over the war crime of attacking, inter alia, buildings dedicated to religion, education, art, science, or charitable purposes and historic monuments 'only if and to the extent such property is not being used for military purposes or is not otherwise a military objective'.[42] A military objective is currently defined under customary international law as it is defined in Article 52(2) of 1977 Protocol I Additional to the 1949 Geneva Conventions ('1977 Additional Protocol I'), namely as an object 'which by [its] nature, location, purpose or use make[s] an effective contribution to military action and whose total or partial destruction, capture or neutralization, in the circumstances ruling at the time, offers a definite military advantage'.[43] The test is a modern refinement, in the specific context of attacks, of the classical rule whereby the destruction of enemy property (including cultural property) was justified if imperatively demanded by military necessity.[44]

The Trial Chamber in *Strugar*, however, stated that the only circumstance in which an intentional act of hostility against cultural property would not be criminal was when it was used for military purposes.[45] The view was reiterated by the

40 UNTAET Reg. No. 2000/15, §§ 6.1(b)(ix) and 6.1(e)(iv).

41 IST Statute, Arts 13(b)(10) and 13(d)(4).

42 10 USC § 950p(a)(3).

43 See, e.g., *Brdanin*, Trial Chamber Judgement, para. 596 n. 1509; *Western Front, Aerial Bombardment and Related Claims, Eritrea's Claims 1, 3, 5, 9–13, 14, 21, 25 & 26: Partial Award*, 608, paras. 112–3; Henckaerts and Doswald-Beck, *Customary International Humanitarian Law*, Vol. I, 29–32 (Rule 8). No definition of the term 'military objective' is included in the Rome Statute, UNTAET Reg. No. 2000/15, or the IST Statute. For its part, the U.S. Military Commissions Act defines the term to mean, in addition to combatants, 'those objects during hostilities which, by their nature, location, purpose, or use, effectively contribute to the war-fighting or war-sustaining capability of an opposing force and whose total or partial destruction, capture, or neutralization would constitute a definite military advantage to the attacker under the circumstances at the time of an attack': see 10 USC § 950p(a)(1). Although, in line with the United States' oft-stated position, this definition goes beyond the concept of an effective contribution to 'military action' to include an effective contribution to the 'war-sustaining capability' of the opponent, it is otherwise consonant with customary international law.

44 See, e.g., *Kordic and Cerkez*, Appeals Chamber Judgement, para. 54.

45 *Strugar*, Trial Chamber Judgement, paras. 310 and 312. The Trial Chamber relied on what it called 'the established jurisprudence of the Tribunal', which consisted of a strikingly bald and brief assertion in *Blaskic*, Trial Chamber Judgement, para. 185, as faithfully restated without serious analysis in *Kordic and Cerkez*, Trial Chamber Judgement, paras 361–62; *Naletilic and Martinovic*, Trial Chamber Judgement, paras. 603 and 605; and *Brdanin*, Trial Chamber Judgement, para. 598. Nor is the Trial Chamber's own reasoning convincing. First, it elides Art. 27 of the Regulations Concerning the Laws and Customs of War on Land ('Hague Rules'), annexed to the 1907 Convention Concerning the Laws and Customs of War on Land, UKTS No. 9 (1910), Cd 5030, and its proviso as to military use, with Arts. 4(1) and 4(2) of the 1954 Hague Convention, the latter referring more broadly to cases where imperative military necessity requires a waiver: see *Strugar*, Trial Chamber Judgement, para. 309. See also *ibid.*, para. 229. Second, and perhaps more to the point, it pays no attention to subsequent practice in the interpretation of Art. 27 of the Hague Rules, which seems to favour a construction

Trial Chamber in *Hadzihasanovic*,[46] which moreover expressly distinguished between the case law of the ICTY, which permitted attacks against cultural property when it was being used for military purposes, and the 'broader' protection afforded by the 1954 Hague Convention, under which an act of hostility against cultural property was permissible only where military necessity imperatively required it.[47] In short, according to these two Trial Chamber cases, attacks against cultural property gave rise to individual criminal responsibility under customary international law on grounds both more restrictive and more expansive than those posited earlier: the sole circumstance in which an attack against cultural property would not be a war crime was if, at the time of the attack, the property was being used for military purposes; if the property was being used for military purposes, an attack was ipso facto not a war crime.

The Appeals Chamber of the ICTY has not embraced the view of the Trial Chambers in *Strugar* and *Hadzihasanovic*. In *Strugar*, the Appeals Chamber characterised the Trial Chamber's conclusion on the facts as being that the attack on the Old Town of Dubrovnik was 'not justified by any military necessity'.[48] This implicit portrayal of use for military purposes as simply one instance giving potential rise to a situation of military necessity was also seen earlier in *Brdanin*, where the Appeals Chamber, '[t]urning to the question of whether [the cultural property] had not been used for military purposes', recalled 'that the Prosecution must establish that the destruction in question was not justified by military necessity'.[49] Moreover, it continued:

> Determining whether destruction occurred pursuant to military necessity involves a determination of what constitutes a military objective. Article 52 of Additional Protocol I contains a widely acknowledged definition of military objectives as being limited to 'those objects which by their nature, location, purpose or use make an effective contribution to military action and whose total or partial destruction, capture or neutralisation, in the circumstances ruling at the time, offers a definite military advantage'.[50]

whereby the provision prohibits only such bombardment of protected property as is not imperatively demanded by the necessities of war.

46 *Hadzihasanovic and Kubura*, Trial Chamber Judgement, paras. 58, 61, and 64.

47 *Ibid.*, para. 61.

48 *Strugar*, Appeals Chamber Judgement, para. 279.

49 *Prosecutor* v. *Brdanin*, Appeals Chamber Judgement, Case No. IT-99–36-A, 3 April 2007, para. 337.

50 *Ibid*, references omitted. See also, previously, *Brdanin*, Trial Chamber Judgement, para. 596, references omitted: '[Items of cultural property] may be attacked only when they become a military objective. Military objectives are limited to those objects which by their nature, location, purpose or use make an effective contribution to military action and whose total or partial destruction, capture or neutralisation, in the circumstances ruling at the time, offers a definite military advantage.' See too, again previously, *Kordic and Cerkez*, Appeals Chamber Judgement, para. 89, stating that 'the building or monument cannot be destroyed unless it has turned into a military object by offering the attacking side "a definite military advantage" at the time of the attack'. See also, subsequently, *Prosecutor* v. *Milutinovic, Sainovic, Ojdanic, Pavkovic, Lazarevic and Lukic*, Trial Chamber Judgement, Case No.

In other words, its use for military purposes is not the only way in which cultural property can be a military objective, and when it is so used, it may be attacked only if its 'total or partial destruction, capture or neutralisation, in the circumstances ruling at the time, offers a definite military advantage'.

In the overwhelming majority of cases, cultural property does not constitute a military objective, meaning that its intentional attack will generally constitute a war crime in both international and non-international armed conflict. But there are rare circumstances in which it may constitute a military objective. Historic fortresses, barracks, arsenals, and the like, might be said to make, by their nature, an effective contribution to military action, although when decommissioned they are better characterised as historic monuments and when still in service are better seen as contributing to military action by their use. Historic bridges, railways stations, docks, and other forms of civil infrastructure could conceivably, by their purpose (defined as 'the future intended use of an object'[51]), make an effective contribution to military action, even if today one might expect more modern transport links to bear most of the military burden. The location of cultural property – that is, its position on the battlefield in relation to the positions of the opposing parties – may also make an effective contribution to either's military action – for example by obstructing a line of sight or line of fire – although, in cases where a party has deliberately positioned itself so as to take advantage of this, the contribution to military action is better characterised as a function of the passive or de facto use of the property in question. In practice, then, of the four bases on which an object can be rendered a military objective, it is its use to make an effective contribution to military action that is the principal one on the basis of which an attack against cultural property may not be a war crime. In all cases, however, whatever the effective contribution that cultural property may make to military action, attacking it is lawful only if its total or partial destruction, capture, or neutralisation, in the circumstances ruling at the time, offers a definite military advantage. In 'extremely simple terms', any attack 'must be militarily necessary in order to reach a permissible operative goal',[52] meaning that there exists 'no feasible alternative for dealing with the situation'.[53]

As for whether destruction or damage is a necessary element of the war crime of attacking cultural property, the position under the ICTY Statute differs from

IT-05–87-T, 26 February 2009 (in relation to the destruction of Kosovar Albanian cultural monuments and religious sites), para. 208. With the acquittal of the accused Milutinovic, the last case is now listed as '*Sainovic* et al.'

51 *Western Front, Aerial Bombardment and Related Claims, Eritrea's Claims 1, 3, 5, 9–13, 14, 21, 25 & 26: Partial Award*, 611, para. 120, endorsing UK Ministry of Defence, *The Manual of the Law of Armed Conflict* (2004), 56, para. 5.4.4, in turn endorsing Y. Sandoz, C. Swinarski, and B. Zimmermann, *Commentary on the Additional Protocols of 8 June 1977 to the Geneva Conventions of 12 August 1949* (1987), 636, para. 2022 ('intended future use').

52 S. Oeter, 'Methods and Means of Combat', in D. Fleck (ed.), *The Handbook of International Humanitarian Law* (2008), 119, 180, para. 442, explanatory para. (6). See also *UK Manual*, 72, para. 5.26.3 n. 120.

53 *UK Manual*, 73, para. 5.26.8.

that under the Rome Statute. Article 3(d) of the former speaks of 'destruction or... damage' to cultural property, whereas Articles 8(2)(b)(ix) and 8(2)(e)(iv) of the latter – reproduced verbatim in UNTAET Regulation No. 2000/15 and in the Iraqi Special Tribunal Statute – refer to 'directing attacks against' such property.[54] Reason suggests that the ICC position is the better one, because the underlying rule of customary international humanitarian law prohibits directing attacks against cultural property.[55] For its part, when enumerating the elements of the war crime of 'attacking protected property', including cultural property, the U.S. Military Commissions Act includes no requirement of destruction or damage,[56] and this, in the final analysis, is the position under customary international law.

In terms of the requisite mental element (*mens rea*) of the offence, the attack in question must be committed with intent and knowledge,[57] the latter meaning 'awareness that a circumstance exists'.[58] That is, the accused must intentionally[59] (or, synonymously, wilfully[60]) direct an attack against the relevant object in the knowledge that it is cultural property[61] in the broad sense of the term. In *Strugar*,

[54] Nor do the respective Elements of Crimes require destruction or damage: see Elements of Crimes, ICC Doc. ICC-ASP/1/3 (Part II-B), Arts. 8(2)(b)(ix) and 8(2)(e)(iv). This accords with the International Committee of the Red Cross (ICRC)'s commentary to the reference in Art. 53(a) of 1977 Additional Protocol I to acts of hostility 'directed against' cultural property: see Sandoz et al., *Commentary*, 647, para. 2070.

[55] See, further, O'Keefe, *supra* note 35, at 318–26.

[56] 10 USC § 950p(a)(3). See also the elements of the crime specified in also U.S. Department of Defense, *Manual for Military Commissions (2007 Edition)* (2007), Part IV, para. 6(4)(b).

[57] Rome Statute, Art. 30(1). See also UNTAET Reg. No. 2000/15, § 18.1.

[58] Rome Statute, Art. 30(3). See also UNTAET Reg. No. 2000/15, § 18.3. Although the Trial Chamber in *Blaskic*, Trial Chamber Judgement, para. 185, posited the requirement that the object targeted 'may be clearly identified' as cultural property, this was probably no more than a clumsy way of demanding knowledge on the part of the accused that the object was, in fact, cultural property. The Trial Chamber's choice of words has not been reproduced in later cases, and the ICC's Elements of Crimes embody no explicit requirement that the institutions and historic monuments referred to in Arts. 8(2)(b)(ix) and 8(2)(e)(iv) of the Rome Statute may be clearly identified as such.

[59] Rome Statute, Arts 8(2)(b)(ix) and 8(2)(e)(iv); *Blaskic*, Trial Chamber Judgement, para. 185; *Kordic and Cerkez*, Trial Chamber Judgement, para. 361; *Naletilic and Martinovic*, Trial Chamber Judgement, para. 605; *Brdanin*, Trial Chamber Judgement, para. 599; *Strugar*, Trial Chamber Judgement, paras. 311–12; *Hadzihasanovic and Kubura*, Trial Chamber Judgement, paras. 57–58 and 64; *Martic*, Trial Chamber Judgement, paras. 96 and 99. See also UNTAET Reg. No. 2000/15, §§ 6.1(b)(ix) and 6.1(e)(iv); ITS Statute, Arts 13(b)(10) and 13(d)(4); 10 USC § 950t(4).

[60] *Strugar*, Appeals Chamber Judgement, para. 277. Somewhat curiously, Art. 3(d) of the ICTY Statute speaks of 'destruction or wilful damage' to cultural property, giving the impression that only damage need be intentional. The provision is modeled on Art. 56 of the Hague Rules, which, unlike Art. 3(d) of the ICTY Statute, is limited in application to belligerent occupation; Art. 56's drafters appeared to take the view that, whereas unintentional – and hence not culpable – damage to cultural property was conceivable in the absence of active hostilities, with the result that a requirement of intent needed to be expressly stipulated, the unintentional destruction (i.e. total razing) of such property was not. As seen earlier, the case law of the ICTY makes it clear that destruction of cultural property must also be intentional for the purposes of Art. 3(d) of the ICTY Statute.

[61] See *Strugar*, Trial Chamber Judgement, para. 329; *Strugar*, Appeals Chamber Judgement, para. 279.

the Appeals Chamber of the ICTY explained the requirement of intent as meaning 'either deliberately or through recklessness'.[62] It is unclear, however, whether recklessness would suffice under customary international law, especially given that the Rome Statute's definition of intent in relation to conduct is that the accused 'means to engage in the conduct'.[63] The accused's intent and knowledge can be inferred from relevant facts and circumstances.[64] In *Strugar*, the fact that copies of the distinctive emblem[65] of the 1954 Hague Convention 'were visible, from the JNA positions at Zarkovica and elsewhere, above the Old Town [of Dubrovnik] on 6 December 1991' was evidence going to the intent of the accused to destroy cultural property, 'as was the Old Town's status as a UNESCO World Heritage site'.[66]

2.1.1.3. UNLAWFUL INCIDENTAL DAMAGE TO CULTURAL PROPERTY. The implication from the ICTY Appeals Chamber judgements in *Blaskic*[67] and *Galic*[68] is that customary international law applicable in both international and non-international armed conflict recognises individual criminal responsibility for intentionally launching an attack in the knowledge that it will cause incidental damage to civilian objects, including cultural property, which is excessive in relation to the concrete and direct military advantage anticipated. No accused, however, has to date been prosecuted before the ICTY on this ground, just as none of the defendants at Nuremberg or Tokyo or before the post–Second World War national military tribunals were prosecuted for incidental damage to civilian objects. For its part, Article 8(2)(b)(iv) of the Rome Statute, as reproduced verbatim in UNTAET Regulation No. 2000/15[69] and in the statute of the Iraqi Special Tribunal,[70] vests the court with jurisdiction over the war crime of intentionally launching an attack during an international armed conflict in the knowledge that the attack will cause incidental damage to civilian objects 'which would be clearly excessive in relation to the concrete and direct overall military advantage anticipated'. But the Rome Statute, UNTAET Regulation No. 2000/15, and the statute of the Iraqi Special Tribunal do not recognise the

62 *Strugar*, Appeals Chamber Judgement, para. 277. See also *Brdanin*, Trial Chamber Judgement, para. 599, stating that the attack 'must have been either perpetrated intentionally, with the knowledge and will of the proscribed result or in reckless disregard of the substantial likelihood of the destruction or damage'; *Hadzihasanovic and Kubura*, Trial Chamber Judgement, para. 59; *Martic*, Trial Chamber Judgement, para. 96.

63 Rome Statute, Art. 30(2)(a). See also UNTAET Reg. No. 2000/15, § 18.2(a).

64 Elements of Crimes, general introduction, para. 3. See also *Prosecutor* v. *Tadic*, Trial Chamber Judgement, Case No. IT-94–1-T, 7 May 1997, para. 676.

65 See 1954 Hague Convention, Arts 6, 16 and 17. See also O'Keefe, *supra* note 35, at 116–18.

66 *Strugar*, Trial Chamber Judgment, para. 329. The Trial Chamber's conclusion, on the basis of this evidence, that the attack on the Old Town was deliberate was considered reasonable by the Appeal Chamber: see *Strugar*, Appeals Chamber Judgement, para. 279.

67 *Blaskic*, Appeals Chamber Judgement, para. 157.

68 *Prosecutor* v. *Galic*, Appeals Chamber Judgement, Case No. IT-98–29-A, 30 November 2006, paras. 190–92.

69 UNTAET Reg. No. 2000/15, § 6.1(b)(iv).

70 ITS Statute, Art. 13(b)(4).

equivalent conduct as a war crime if performed in non-international armed conflict, with the result that the customary position in this regard is unclear, especially given the absence to date of relevant prosecutions in other fora.

When it comes to determining whether the material conditions of the offence have been fulfilled, the test is one of proportionality,[71] even if the word is not used, and although the assessment called for is not an exact science, it must be made in good faith. As applied to cultural property, proportionality implicates qualitative as much as quantitative factors. The extent of incidental loss likely to be occasioned by damage to or destruction of such property is a question not just of square or cubic metres but also of the cultural value represented thereby. A textbook example of the application of the rule of proportionality came during the Gulf War in 1991, when Iraq positioned two fighter aircraft next to the world-renowned ancient Ziggurat of Ur. Coalition commanders decided not to attack the aircraft 'on the basis of respect for cultural property and the belief that positioning of the aircraft adjacent to Ur (without servicing equipment or a runway nearby) effectively had placed each out of action, thereby limiting the value of their destruction by Coalition air forces when weighed against the risk of damage to the temple'.[72]

The distinction between the standard of disproportionality laid down in the ICTY jurisprudence ('excessive') and that demanded by the Rome Statute ('clearly excessive') may not import a practical difference. The adverb 'clearly' was inserted in the latter so as to allay fears, especially on the part of the United States, that the ICC might hold an accused criminally responsible for a disproportionate attack resulting from no more than bona fide miscalculation or poor execution.[73] The insertion of 'clearly' goes as much to *mens rea* as to *actus reus*, being there to emphasise that criminal responsibility arises only in respect of consciously disproportionate attacks.

The Rome Statute and its imitators do not require that incidental damage to civilian objects, clearly disproportionate or otherwise, actually eventuates from the impugned attack. As far as the *actus reus* of the war crime goes, all that is necessary is that the attack 'was such that it would cause' clearly disproportionate incidental damage to civilian objects.[74] That said, it would be almost impossible to prove the requisite elements of the crime, both material and mental,[75] if such damage did not in fact materialise.

[71] See, e.g., *Galic*, Appeals Chamber Judgement, para. 190.

[72] U.S. Department of Defense, *Report to Congress on the Conduct of the Persian Gulf War, Appendix O: The Role of the Law of War*, 31 ILM 612 (1992), 626.

[73] The United States, which has long harboured strong reservations as to criminal responsibility for disproportionate attacks, does not include an equivalent war crime in its Military Commissions Act. Indeed, 10 USC § 950p(b) – applicable to the war crimes of, inter alia, intentionally attacking civilians, intentionally attacking civilian objects, and intentionally attacking protected property, including cultural property – provides that the intent required for these offences 'precludes [their] applicability . . . with regard to collateral damage or to death, damage, or injury incident to a lawful attack'.

[74] Elements of Crimes, Art. 8(2)(b)(iv), para. 2.

[75] See Elements of Crimes, Art. 8(2)(b)(iv), paras. 2 ('The attack was such that it would cause . . . ') and 3 ('The perpetrator knew that the attack would cause . . . ').

In terms of the requisite mental element of the crime, the attack in question (which is necessarily directed at a military objective) must, as the text of Article 8(2)(b)(iv) of the Rome Statute makes plain, be intentional and launched in the knowledge that it will, in the ordinary course of events,[76] cause clearly disproportionate incidental damage to civilian objects. It is not, strictly speaking, necessary that the accused know that the property likely to be damaged is cultural property. It is sufficient that he or she knows that it is a civilian object of some sort. But unawareness of the cultural character of the property makes a difference to the proportionality calculus: it is one thing to weigh the military advantage to be gained by an attack against the destruction of an architecturally and historically undistinguished multi-storey car park; it is quite another to weigh it against the flattening of a national museum of modern art.

2.1.1.4. UNLAWFUL ACTS OF HOSTILITY AGAINST CULTURAL PROPERTY OTHER THAN ATTACKS. Unlawful acts of hostility against cultural property other than attacks, such as its demolition by the planting of explosives or by bulldozers, jackhammers, or other wrecking equipment, also give rise to individual criminal responsibility under customary international law, regardless of whether the acts take place in international or non-international armed conflict and, in relation to international armed conflict, regardless of whether they occur during hostilities or belligerent occupation. In the international context, several of the major German war criminals tried at Nuremberg were convicted for their roles in the premeditated razing of cultural property in occupied territory. For the purposes of the ICTY, acts of hostility against cultural property other than attacks are dealt with, alongside attacks, under Article 3(d) of the tribunal's statute, which vests it with jurisdiction over the war crime of 'destruction or wilful damage done to institutions dedicated to religion, charity and education, the arts and sciences, historic monuments and works of art and science'; the accused in *Blaskic*, *Kordic*, *Naletilic*, and *Brdanin* were all convicted of such acts, whereas the accused in *Plavsic* pleaded guilty in respect of them and those in *Hadzihasanovic* were acquitted on this count. For its part, the Rome Statute treats acts of hostility against cultural property not amounting to attacks under the general rubric of the customary war crime of destroying (which is taken to encompass damaging) the enemy's property unless such destruction (or damage) is imperatively demanded by the necessities of war, which the statute recognises as being capable of commission in both international and non-international armed conflict.[77] The same goes for

[76] See Rome Statute, Art. 30(3). See also UNTAET Reg. No. 2000/15, § 18.3.

[77] Rome Statute, Arts. 8(2)(b)(xiii) (international) and 8(2)(e)(xii) (non-international). Common para. 3 of the Elements of Crimes for these offences requires that the property destroyed be 'protected from that destruction . . . under the international law of armed conflict'. Cultural property is protected from acts of hostility other than attacks by the customary international law of armed conflict in both international and non-international armed conflicts unless such acts are imperatively demanded by the necessities of war: see O'Keefe, *supra* note 35, at 331–34.

UNTAET Regulation No. 2000/15,[78] the statute of the Iraqi Special Tribunal,[79] and the U.S. Military Commissions Act.[80]

As regards the requisite material elements of the offence, destruction and damage of cultural property outside the context of an attack are not unlawful if and to the extent that, in the words of Articles 8(2)(b)(xiii) and 8(2)(e)(xii) of the Rome Statute, they are imperatively demanded by the necessities of war – in other words, as long and insofar as they are militarily necessary, which presupposes no feasible alternative for dealing with the situation. Demolitions may be necessary in some cases to impede the progress of enemy columns, to clear a line of fire, or to deny cover to enemy fighters, although their extent will need to be calibrated to the degree of the military necessity. In *Brdanin*, conversely, where the accused was held responsible for destroying mosques and churches with mines and other explosives, for tearing them down with heavy machinery, and for setting fire to them, there was 'nothing to suggest that their destruction provided any kind of advantage in weakening the military forces opposing the Bosnian Serbs, favoured the Bosnian Serb position, or was otherwise justified by military necessity'.[81] That is, the evidence did not indicate to the Appeals Chamber that the 'total or partial destruction [of the relevant cultural property] offered a definite military advantage to the Bosnian Serb forces'.[82]

As for *mens rea*, intent is again required,[83] as is knowledge.[84] For the purposes of the ICTY, the latter means knowledge that the destroyed or damaged property was an institution dedicated to religion, charity, and education or the arts and sciences, or a historic monument, or a work of art or science,[85] in the words of Article 3(d) of the ICTY Statute. For the purposes of the ROme Statute, it effectively means knowledge that the property was civilian in character.[86]

78 UNTAET Reg. No. 2000/15, §§ 6.1(b)(xiii) (international) and 6.1(e)(xii) (non-international).

79 IST Statute, Arts 13(b)(14) (international) and 13(d)(12) (non-international).

80 10 USC § 950t(16), which stipulates that the destruction of the relevant property be 'in violation of the law of war'. It will be recalled from the earlier discussion that the customary law of war prohibits acts of hostility against cultural property other than attacks, in both international and non-international armed conflict, unless such acts are imperatively demanded by the necessities of war.

81 *Brdanin*, Appeals Chamber Judgement, para. 342.

82 *Ibid*, para. 340.

83 See Rome Statute, Art. 30(1); *Blaskic*, Trial Chamber Judgement, para. 185; *Kordic and Cerkez*, Trial Chamber Judgement, para. 361; *Naletilic and Martinovic*, Trial Chamber Judgement, para. 605; *Brdanin*, Trial Chamber Judgement, para. 599; *Strugar*, Trial Chamber Judgement, paras. 311–12; *Hadzihasanovic and Kubura*, Trial Chamber Judgement, paras. 57–58 and 64; *Martic*, Trial Chamber Judgement, paras. 96 and 99. See also UNTAET Reg. No. 2000/15, § 18.1; 10 USC § 950t(16). Recall that it is unclear whether customary international law accords with the statement in *Strugar*, Appeals Chamber Judgement, para. 277, that intent encompasses both deliberate conduct and recklessness.

84 See Rome Statute, Art. 30(1); UNTAET Reg. No. 2000/15, § 18.1.

85 See *Strugar*, Trial Chamber Judgement, para. 329; *Strugar*, Appeals Chamber Judgement, para. 279.

86 It will be recalled that common para. 3 of the Elements of Crimes for the offences under Arts. 8(2)(b)(xiii) and 8(2)(e)(xii) requires that the property destroyed be 'protected from that destruction . . . under the international law of armed conflict'. Common para. 4 goes on to require that the perpetrator 'was aware of the factual circumstances that established the status of the property'.

2.1.1.5. UNLAWFUL APPROPRIATION OF CULTURAL PROPERTY. Customary international law recognises individual criminal responsibility for the unlawful plunder of public or private property, including cultural property, whether in international or non-international armed conflict, and, as regards international armed conflict, whether during hostilities or belligerent occupation.[87] Article 6(b) of the London Charter vested the International Military Tribunal (IMT) at Nuremberg with jurisdiction over the war crime of that name, viz 'plunder of public or private property'.[88] In the context of belligerent occupation, the IMT held the accused Rosenberg 'responsible for a system of organised plunder of both public and private property throughout the invaded countries of Europe'.[89] Article 3(e) of the ICTY Statute vests it with jurisdiction over the same war crime: it has held that the offence, which it has recognised as customary,[90] 'should be understood to embrace all forms of unlawful appropriation of property in armed conflict for which individual criminal responsibility attaches under international criminal law, including those acts traditionally described as "pillage"'.[91] In other words, the offence encompasses 'both widespread and systematised acts of dispossession and acquisition of property in violation of the rights of the owners and isolated acts of theft or plunder by individuals for their private gain'.[92] In addition to the offence in Article 3(e), Article 3(d) of the ICTY Statute grants it jurisdiction over the specific war crime of 'seizure of... institutions dedicated to religion, charity and education, the arts and sciences, historic monuments and works of art and science'. The relevant case law of the ICTY has proceeded on the basis that the war crimes referred to in Articles 3(d) and 3(e) of the statute apply to international and non-international armed conflict alike. For its part, the Rome Statute recognises, in both international and non-international armed conflict, the war crimes of seizing the enemy's property unless such seizure is imperatively demanded by the necessities of war[93] and of pillaging a town or place,

87 See *Kordic and Cerkez*, Appeals Chamber Judgement, para. 78.

88 See also Control Council Law No. 10, Art. II(1)(b).

89 Nuremberg Judgment, 287.

90 *Hadzihasanovic and Kubura*, Appeals Chamber Decision on Joint Defence Interlocutory Appeal, para. 37.

91 *Ibid.* See also *Blaskic*, Appeals Chamber Judgement, para. 147; *Kordic and Cerkez*, Appeals Chamber Judgement, paras. 77 and 79. Pillage refers to every-man-for-himself looting by the soldiery, with each keeping what he lays his hands on, as distinct from a military force's organised appropriation of property in the name of the state or at least of a superior. Stating the obvious, common para. 3 of the Elements of Crimes in respect of the crime of pillage under Arts. 8(2)(b)(xvi) and 8(2)(e)(v) of the Rome Statute requires that the appropriation 'was without the consent of the owner'.

92 *Kordic and Cerkez*, Trial Chamber Judgement, para. 352, quoted in *Hadzihasanovic and Kubura*, Trial Chamber Judgement, para. 49. See, similarly, *Prosecutor* v. *Delalic, Mucic, Delic and Landzo* ('*Celebici*'), Trial Chamber Judgement, Case No. IT-96–21-T, 16 November 1998, para. 590; *Prosecutor* v. *Jelisic*, Trial Chamber Judgement, Case No. IT-95-T-10, 14 December 1999, para. 48; *Blaskic*, Trial Chamber Judgement, para. 184; *Naletilic and Martinovic*, Trial Chamber Judgement, para. 612.

93 Rome Statute, Arts 8(2)(b)(xiii) (international) and 8(2)(e)(xii) (non-international). As with the destruction and damage of enemy property, common explanatory para. 3 of the Elements of Crimes for these offences requires that the property destroyed be 'protected from that... seizure under the international

even when taken by assault.[94] The same is the case[95] under UNTAET Regulation No. 2000/15[96] and the statute of the Iraqi Special Tribunal.[97]

As a formal matter, the appropriation of cultural property is not a war crime if it is imperatively demanded by the necessities of war.[98] In practice, it is impossible to envisage a legitimate military rationale for seizing cultural property.

The requisite *mens rea* of the respective offences is intent[99] and knowledge.[100]

### 2.1.2. Treaty Law

The 1954 Hague Convention for the Protection of Cultural Property in the Event of Armed Conflict ('1954 Hague Convention'),[101] 1977 Additional Protocol

law of armed conflict'. Cultural property is protected from seizure by the customary international law of armed conflict in both international and non-international armed conflicts unless such seizure is imperatively demanded by the necessities of war: see O'Keefe, *supra* note 35, at 336–38.

94 Rome Statute, Arts. 8(2)(b)(xvi) (international) and 8(2)(e)(v) (non-international).

95 Note, however, that the U.S. Military Commissions Act recognises only the war crime of pillage, namely 'in the absence of military necessity appropriat[ing] or seiz[ing] property for private or personal use, without the consent of a person with authority to permit such appropriation or seizure': 10 USC § 950t(5).

96 In respect of seizing the enemy's property, see UNTAET Reg. No. 2000/15, §§ 6.1(b)(xiii) (international) and 6.1(e)(xii) (non-international). In respect of pillage, see *ibid*, §§ 6.1(b)(xvi) (international) and 6.1(e)(v) (non-international).

97 In respect of seizing the enemy's property, see IST Statute, Arts. 13(b)(14) (international) and 13(d)(12) (non-international). In respect of pillage, see *ibid*, Arts. 13(b)(17) (international) and 13(d)(5) (non-international).

98 As regards Arts. 8(2)(b)(xiii) and 8(2)(e)(xii) of the Rome Statute, this is specified in the text. As regards pillage under Arts. 8(2)(b)(xvi) and 8(2)(e)(v), a common footnote to common explanatory para. 2 of the relevant Elements of Crimes states that 'appropriations justified by military necessity cannot constitute the crime of pillaging'.

99 Rome Statute, Art. 30(1); *Kordic and Cerkez*, Appeals Chamber Judgement, para. 84. See also UNTAET Reg. No. 2000/15, § 18.1. In the specific context of the crime of pillage under Arts. 8(2)(b)(xvi) and 8(2)(e)(v) of the Rome Statute, common explanatory para. 2 of the relevant Elements of Crimes requires that the perpetrator 'intended to deprive the owner of the property and to appropriate it for private or personal use'.

100 Rome Statute, Art. 30(1). See also UNTAET Reg. No. 2000/15, § 18.1. Recall that, for the purposes of Art. 3(d) of the ICTY, the latter means knowledge that the destroyed or damaged property was an institution dedicated to religion, charity and education, or the arts and sciences, or a historic monument, or a work of art or science, whereas for the purposes of the Rome Statute it effectively means knowledge that the property was civilian.

101 See note 1. The 1954 Hague Convention applies to a more selective range of cultural property than does customary international law. Whereas the latter serves to protect all historic monuments, works of art, and the like, the Hague Convention applies only to 'movable or immovable cultural property of great importance to the cultural heritage of every people' – that is, to cultural property of great importance to the national cultural heritage of each respective high contracting party, as determined by that party. In the practice of the parties, the total immovable cultural property to which the Hague Convention applies is generally in the order of tens of thousands of items in the territory of each party, whereas the few figures available for movable cultural property tentatively point to the contents of a hundred to a few hundred museums, art galleries, libraries, and archives per party. See O'Keefe, *supra* note 35, at 101–11 and R. O'Keefe, 'Protection of Cultural Property', in D. Fleck (ed.), *Handbook of International Humanitarian Law*, 433, 437–38, para. 901, explanatory paras. (2) and (3).

I,[102] and the 1999 Second Protocol to the 1954 Hague Convention ('1999 Second Hague Protocol')[103] each contains a provision or provisions on individual criminal responsibility for acts inimical to the protection of cultural property in armed conflict. None of these has yet served as a basis for prosecution in national or international proceedings, and perhaps none is likely ever to play a significant role.

Article 28 of the 1954 Hague Convention requires the High Contracting Parties

> to take, within the framework of their ordinary criminal jurisdiction, all necessary steps to prosecute and impose penal or disciplinary sanctions upon those persons, of whatever nationality, who commit or order to be committed a breach of the . . . Convention.[104]

It is unclear whether this provision is applicable only to international armed conflict or to non-international armed conflict as well.[105] War crimes within the meaning of Article 28 fall within the jurisdiction of the Extraordinary Chambers in the Courts of Cambodia,[106] mandated to try the remnants of the Khmer Rouge leadership, but no charges have to date been laid on this basis, and none is likely. For its part, Article 85(4)(d) of 1977 Additional Protocol I, applicable only to international armed conflict, defines as a grave breach of the protocol – with the various consequences that this entails[107] – the intentional[108] act of

> making the clearly-recognized historic monuments, works of art or places of worship which constitute the cultural or spiritual heritage of peoples and to which special protection has been given by special arrangement, for example, within the framework of a competent international organization, the object of attack, causing as a result extensive destruction thereof, where there is no evidence of the violation by the adverse Party of Article 53, sub-paragraph (b), and when such historic

[102] See note 33. The scope of cultural property covered by 1977 Additional Protocol I is essentially the same as that covered by the 1954 Hague Convention: see O'Keefe, O'Keefe, *supra* note 35, at 209–14 and O'Keefe, *supra* note 102, at 439–42, para. 901, explanatory paras (4) to (8).

[103] See note 35. The range of cultural property protected under the 1999 Second Hague Protocol is the same as that protected by the 1954 Hague Convention: see 1999 Second Hague Protocol, Art. 1(b).

[104] For a fuller discussion of the provision, see O'Keefe, *supra* note 35, at 188–92.

[105] See *ibid.*, 192. The UN's Group of Experts for Cambodia established pursuant to General Assembly Res. 52/135 suggested, not very helpfully, that breaches of the convention committed during non-international armed conflict 'perhaps' gave rise to individual criminal responsibility: UN Doc. A/53/850-S/1999/231 (16 March 1999), Annex, para. 76.

[106] See Cambodia's Law on the Establishment of Extraordinary Chambers in the Courts of Cambodia for the Prosecution of Crimes Committed during the Period of Democratic Kampuchea, as amended 27 October 2004, Doc. NS/RKM/1004/006 ('ECCC Law'), Art. 7, read in combination with the 2003 Agreement between the United Nations and the Royal Government of Cambodia Concerning the Prosecution under Cambodian Law of Crimes Committed during the Period of Democratic Kampuchea, 2239 UNTS 117, Art. 2.

[107] For a fuller discussion of the provision, see O'Keefe, *supra* note 35, at 224–28.

[108] The chapeau to Art. 85(4) requires that the relevant acts be committed wilfully.

monuments, works of art and places of worship are not located in the immediate proximity of military objectives.[109]

Finally, Article 15(1) of the 1999 Second Hague Protocol enumerates five war crimes, known collectively as serious violations of the protocol and capable of commission in international and non-international armed conflict alike, in respect of which Articles 15(2)–20 lay down a range of obligations on state parties.[110] The serious violations, which must all be committed with intent, comprise making cultural property under the Second Hague Protocol's regime of 'enhanced protection'[111] the object of attack; using cultural property under enhanced protection or its immediate surroundings in support of military action; extensive destruction or appropriation of cultural property protected under the 1954 Hague Convention and its Second Protocol; making cultural property protected under the convention and protocol the object of attack; and theft, pillage, or misappropriation of, or acts of vandalism directed against, cultural property protected under the convention.[112] Finally, Article 21, subparagraphs (a) and (b), respectively, of the 1999 Second Hague Protocol oblige state parties to adopt such legislative, administrative, or disciplinary measures as may be necessary to suppress any use of cultural property in violation of the convention or protocol and any illicit export, other removal or transfer of ownership of cultural property from occupied territory in violation of the convention or protocol. Article 21 would justify, although not require, legislative measures by a party to establish as criminal offences under its domestic law the violations referred to in subparagraphs (a) and (b). The obligation laid down in Article 21 of the protocol is declared to be without prejudice to Article 28 of the convention.

### 2.2. *Crimes against Humanity*

The IMT at Nuremberg held that the unlawful destruction and plunder of cultural property in the occupied territories of the East amounted not only to war crimes on a vast scale but also to crimes against humanity,[113] of which several of the German major war criminals, foremost among them plunderer-in-chief Alfred Rosenberg, were found guilty. Over half a century later, a Trial Chamber of the ICTY – quoting

[109] The requirement in the chapeau to Art. 85(4) that the acts enumerated be committed in violation of the Conventions or the Protocol means, in effect, that, for the purposes of Art. 85(4)(d), the attack in question must constitute a breach of Art. 53(a) of the Protocol, the provision that prohibits the commission of any act of hostility directed against the historic monuments, works of art, or places of worship that constitute the cultural or spiritual heritage of a people.

[110] For fuller details of the offences and the related obligations on States Parties, see O'Keefe, *supra* note 35, at 276–87.

[111] For the regime of enhanced protection, see 1999 Second Hague Protocol, Chap. 3. See also O'Keefe, *supra* note 35, at 263–74 and O'Keefe, *supra* note 102, at 456–61.

[112] 1999 Second Hague Protocol, Art. 15(1)(a) to (e), respectively. The chapeau to Art. 15(1) requires that the relevant acts be in violation of the Convention or Protocol.

[113] Nuremberg Judgment, 249.

from, inter alia, the Nuremberg judgement as it pertained to Rosenberg[114] and the International Law Commission (ILC)'s draft commentary to its Draft Code of Crimes against the Peace and Security of Mankind as provisionally adopted at its 43rd session[115] – held in *Blaskic* that the specific crime against humanity of 'persecutions on political, racial and religious grounds' recognised in Article 5(h) of the ICTY's Statute[116] 'encompasses not only bodily and mental harm and infringements upon individual freedom but also acts . . . such as those targeting property, so long as the victimised persons were specially selected on grounds linked to their belonging to a particular community'.[117] The Trial Chamber accepted the prosecution's contention that persecution could take the form of the discriminatory confiscation or destruction of symbolic buildings belonging to the Muslim population of Bosnia-Herzegovina.[118]

Various ICTY Trial Chambers have affirmed, first, that discriminatory destruction of or extensive[119] damage to cultural property can, as a matter of customary international law, amount to persecution as a crime against humanity.[120] The Appeals Chamber has effectively endorsed this position. In *Blaskic*, after quoting the Trial Chamber's finding that the discriminatory destruction of, inter alia, symbolic buildings could constitute persecution as a crime against humanity, the Appeals Chamber

[114] *Blaskic*, Trial Chamber Judgement, para. 228.

[115] *Ibid.*, para. 231. For the text of, and commentary to, the Draft Code of Crimes as provisionally adopted, see *Report of the International Law Commission on the Work of Its Forty-Third Session, 29 April–19 July 1991*, UN Doc. A/46/10, Chap. IV D. For the final text of the Draft Code of Crimes, see n. 22.

[116] See also Statute of the International Criminal Tribunal for Rwanda, SC Res 955 (1994), Annex, as amended ('ICTR Statute'), Art. 3(h). Although Art. 5(h) of the ICTY Statute refers conjunctively to persecution on 'political, racial and religious grounds', the tribunal has held that this should be read disjunctively, in accordance with customary international law, so that persecution on any one of these grounds suffices: *Tadic*, Trial Chamber Judgement, para. 713. See also Nuremberg Charter, Art. 6(c); Control Council Law No. 10, Art. II(1)(c); Rome Statute, Art. 7(1)(h); UNTAET Reg. No. 2000/15, § 5.1(h); Statute of the Special Court for Sierra Leone, UN Doc. S/2002/246, App. II, Annex, Art. 2(h); IST Statute, Art. 12(a)(8). Art. 5 of the ECCC Law refers to 'national, political, ethnical, racial or religious grounds' in the chapeau but to 'political, racial, and religious grounds' in the specific provision on persecutions.

[117] *Blaskic*, Trial Chamber Judgement, para. 233. See also, previously, *Tadic*, Trial Chamber Judgement, paras. 703–04, quoting the same passage from the ILC's provisionally adopted commentary on persecution.

[118] *Blaskic*, Trial Chamber Judgement, para. 227.

[119] *Milutinovic* et al., Trial Chamber Judgement, para. 207.

[120] See *Kordic and Cerkez*, Trial Chamber Judgement, para. 207; *Brdanin*, Trial Chamber Judgement, para. 1023; *Plavsic*, Trial Chamber Sentencing Judgement, para. 15; *Prosecutor* v. *Stakic*, Trial Chamber Judgement, Case No. IT-97–24-T, 31 July 2003, para. 768 (destruction of and wilful damage to Bosnian Muslim and Bosnian Croat religious property in Bosnia-Herzegovina); *Prosecutor* v. *Deronjic*, Trial Chamber Sentencing Judgement, Case No. IT-02–61-S, 30 March 2004, para. 122 (destruction of Bosnian Muslim religious property in Bosnia-Herzegovina); *Prosecutor* v. *Babic*, Trial Chamber Sentencing Judgement, Case No. IT-03–72-S, 29 June 2004, paras. 30–1 (destruction of and wilful damage to Croat and other non-Serb cultural institutions, historic monuments, and religious property in the Krajina region of Croatia); *Martic*, Trial Chamber Judgement, para. 119; *Prosecutor* v. *Krajisnik*, Trial Judgement Judgment, Case No. IT-00–39-T, 27 September 2006, paras. 782–83 (destruction of and wilful damage to Bosnian Muslim and Bosnian Croat religious property, historic monuments, and town centres in Bosnia-Herzegovina); *Milutinovic* et al., Trial Chamber Judgement, para. 205.

affirmed that 'the destruction of property, depending on the nature and extent of the destruction, may constitute a crime [against humanity] of persecutions of equal gravity to other crimes listed in Article 5 of the Statute'.[121] In short, as summarised by the Trial Chamber in *Milutinovic*, 'the Tribunal's jurisprudence specifically [recognizes] destruction of religious sites and cultural monuments as persecution, a crime against humanity',[122] when this destruction is impermissibly discriminatory. Nor is this jurisprudence contradicted as such by Article 7(1)(h) of the Rome Statute, as reproduced verbatim in Section 5(1)(h) of UNTAET Regulation No. 2000/15 and Article 12(a)(8) of the statute of the Iraqi Special Tribunal, which recognises as a crime against humanity '[p]ersecution against any identifiable group or collectivity . . . in connection with any [other crime against humanity] or any crime within the jurisdiction of the Court'.[123] Because the destruction of cultural property in either international or non-international armed conflict, with a sufficient nexus to that armed conflict and contrary to the laws of armed conflict, constitutes a war crime under Article 8 of the Rome Statute,[124] it can also, in and of itself, constitute a crime against humanity under Article 7(1)(h). If committed in time of peace, however, any destruction of cultural property must, to qualify as a crime against humanity, be accompanied by some other act amounting to a crime within the jurisdiction of the court. As for other requisite elements of the *actus reus* of persecution by means of discriminatory destruction of or damage to cultural property, the Trial Chamber stated in *Milutinovic* that the destruction or damage must have resulted from an act directed against the cultural property[125] and must not have been justified by military necessity[126] – the latter criterion implicating, in cases involving attacks, the question whether the property constituted a military objective.[127]

[121] *Blaskic*, Appeals Chamber Judgement, para. 149. See also *Kordic and Cerkez*, Appeals Chamber Judgement, para. 108.

[122] *Milutinovic* et al., Trial Chamber Judgement, para. 205. Many accused individuals are presently on trial for, inter alia, crimes against humanity of this sort: see *Seselj*, Third Amended Indictment, para. 17(j); *Prlic* et al., Second Amended Indictment, para. 229; *Prosecutor* v. *Dordevic*, Fourth Amended Indictment, Case No. IT-05–87/1-PT, 9 July 2008, para. 77(d); *Prosecutor* v. *Karadzic*, Prosecution's Marked-Up Indictment, Case No. IT-95–5/18-PT, 19 October 2009, para. 60(j); *Prosecutor* v. *Stanisic and Zupljanin*, Second Amended Consolidated Indictment, Case No. IT-08–91-PT, 23 November 2009, paras. 26(i) and 27(i).

[123] 'Persecution' is defined in Rome Statute, Art. 7(2)(g) to mean 'the intentional and severe deprivation of fundamental rights contrary to international law by reason of the identity of the group or collectivity'. See also, identically, UNTAET Reg. No. 2000/15, § 5.2(f); IST Statute, Art. 12(b)(6).

[124] In relation to attacks, see Rome Statute, Arts. 8(2)(b)(ix) and 8(2)(e)(iv). In relation to other forms of destruction, see *ibid.*, Arts. 8(2)(b)(xiii) and 8(2)(e)(xii).

[125] *Milutinovic* et al., Trial Chamber Judgement, para. 209. The situation may, at least theoretically, be different under the Rome Statute, given that intentionally launching an attack during international armed conflict in the knowledge that the attack will cause disproportionate incidental damage to cultural property is a war crime under Art. 8(2)(b)(iv) of the Rome Statute, with the result that the same act, provided it satisfies the other elements of the offence, may also constitute the crime against humanity of persecution.

[126] *Milutinovic* et al., Trial Chamber Judgement, para. 208.

[127] *Ibid.*

Several ICTY Trial Chambers have similarly held that the plunder of public or private property, if discriminatory, can amount to the crime against humanity of persecution,[128] a ruling that would encompass the plunder of cultural property. In *Blaskic*, in contrast, the Appeals Chamber, although not referring specifically to cultural property, thought that 'there may be some doubt . . . as to whether acts of plunder, in and of themselves, may rise to the level of gravity required for crimes against humanity'.[129] It did acknowledge, however, that Article 7(1)(h) of the Rome Statute was more expansive in this regard.[130] In the subsequent Trial Chamber judgement in *Krajisnik*, the Trial Chamber, referring to the Nuremberg judgment and to the case law of the U.S. Military Tribunal at Nuremberg, concluded that 'an act of appropriation or plunder that has a severe impact on the victim, carried out on discriminatory grounds, and for which the general elements of crimes against humanity are fulfilled, constitutes the crime of persecution'.[131] It is relevant in this regard that in *Strugar*, in relation to the destruction of cultural property, the Trial Chamber stated not only that 'the victim of the offence at issue is to be understood broadly as a "people", rather than any particular individual' but also that the consequences of the offence for this victim (viz. that people) could be said to be grave.[132] As for Article 7(1)(h) of the Rome Statute, because the seizure of the enemy's or other adversary's property in either international or non-international armed conflict, with a sufficient nexus to that conflict and not imperatively demanded by the necessities of war, constitutes a war crime under Article 8 of the Rome Statute,[133] and because the same goes for pillaging,[134] these same acts can, in and of themselves, represent crimes against humanity. Misappropriation of property (including cultural property) in time of peace, on the other hand, will constitute a crime against humanity only if it accompanies other crimes within the ICC's jurisdiction. In the final analysis, nonetheless, it is sufficiently clear that the discriminatory plunder of cultural property is capable of constituting under customary international law the crime against humanity of persecution.

As for the grounds of discrimination deemed impermissible in the context of the crime of persecution, although Article 5(h) of the ICTY Statute restricts itself to political, racial, and religious traits, customary international law probably accords with the more expansive approach taken by Article 7(1)(h) of the Rome Statute,

[128] *Tadic*, Trial Chamber Judgement, para. 704; *Kordic and Cerkez*, Trial Chamber Judgement, para. 205; *Naletilic and Martinovic*, Trial Chamber Judgement, para. 698. See also *Plavsic*, Trial Chamber Sentencing Judgement, para. 15.

[129] *Blaskic*, Appeals Chamber Judgement, para. 148.

[130] *Ibid.*, para. 148, n. 310.

[131] *Krajisnik*, Trial Chamber Judgement, para. 711.

[132] *Strugar*, Trial Chamber Judgement, para. 232.

[133] See Rome Statute, Arts. 8(2)(b)(xiii) and 8(2)(e)(xii).

[134] See *ibid.*, Arts. 8(2)(b)(xvi) and 8(2)(e)(v), the latter being cited in *Blaskic*, Appeals Chamber Judgement, para. 148 n. 310.

which refers to persecution 'on political, racial, national, ethnic, cultural, religious, gender . . . or other grounds that are universally recognized as impermissible under international law'.

Turning to the generic material elements of crimes against humanity, the cardinal feature of such crimes is that they are directed against a civilian population (meaning any civilian population, not just the civilian population of occupied territory).[135] In addition, they must be committed 'as part of a widespread or systematic attack' on that civilian population.[136] In *Kunarac*, the Appeals Chamber of the ICTY made it clear that 'only the attack, not the individual acts of the accused, must be widespread or systematic', so that 'all other conditions being met, a single or relatively limited number of acts on his or her part would qualify as a crime against humanity, unless those acts may be said to be isolated or random'.[137] This is the case even in relation to the crime against humanity of persecution, including, it would seem, persecution comprising at least the destruction of cultural property – with the accused in *Deronjic* pleading guilty to, and being duly sentenced in respect of, the crime against humanity of persecution in relation to, inter alia, the destruction of a single mosque.[138] The Appeals Chamber in *Kunarac* also rejected the condition posited by earlier Trial Chambers that crimes against humanity must be committed in pursuance of some sort of policy.[139] It is unclear, however, whether this decision accords with custom, and it is not the position under the Rome Statute.[140]

As a general rule, a state of armed conflict is not a legal precondition to the commission of a crime against humanity.[141] That is, a crime against humanity can be committed in time of peace. It is *a fortiori* immaterial whether a crime

[135] See Nuremberg Charter, Art. 6(c); Control Council Law No. 10, Art. II(1)(c); ICTY Statute, Art. 5; ICTR Statute, Art. 3; ICC Statute, Art. 7(1); UNTAET Reg. No. 2000/15, § 5.1; IST Statute, Art. 12(a); ECCC Law, Art. 5.

[136] *Report of the Secretary-General pursuant to paragraph 2 of Security Council resolution 808 (1993)*, UN Doc. S/25704 (3 May 1993), para. 48; ICTR Statute, Art. 3; Draft Code of Crimes, Art. 18 ('committed in a systematic manner or on a large scale'); Rome Statute, Art. 7(1); UNTAET Reg. No. 2000/15, § 5.1; IST Statute, Art. 12(a); ECCC Law, Art. 5.

[137] *Prosecutor* v. *Kunarac, Kovac and Vukovic*, Appeals Chamber Judgement, Case No. IT-96–23 & IT-96–23/1-A, 12 June 2002, para. 96.

[138] See *Deronjic*, Trial Chamber Sentencing Judgement, disposition.

[139] *Ibid.*, para. 98. See also *Prosecutor* v. *Semanza*, Appeals Chamber Judgement, Case No. ICTR-97–20-A, 20 May 2005, para 274.

[140] See the definition of the expression 'attack directed against any civilian population' in Rome Statute, Art. 7(2)(a) ('pursuant to or in furtherance of a State or organizational policy to commit such attack'). See also IST Statute, Art. 12(b)(1).

[141] *Tadic*, Trial Chamber Judgement, para. 713; ICTR Statute, Art. 3; Draft Code of Crimes, Art. 18 and para. (6) of commentary thereto; Rome Statute, Art. 7(1); UNTAET Reg. No. 2000/15, § 5.1; IST Statute, Art. 12; ECCC Law, Art. 5. Although Art. 5 of the ICTY Statute makes the existence of an armed conflict (international or non-international) a condition of a crime against humanity for the purposes of the tribunal's jurisdiction, it was recognised by the drafters that customary international law was not so restrictive: *Report of the Secretary-General pursuant to paragraph 2 of Security Council resolution 808 (1993)*, para. 47.

against humanity is indeed committed in armed conflict, whether the conflict is international or non-international, and whether the crime against humanity has a nexus to it. But in the specific context of persecution as per Article 7(1)(h) of the Rome Statute, the existence or otherwise of an armed conflict does, in fact, as seen earlier, have a bearing on whether the destruction and plunder of cultural property amount to crimes against humanity.

The requisite *mens rea* for a crime against humanity is intent to commit the underlying offence combined with knowledge of the widespread and systematic attack on the civilian population.[142] The latter means that the perpetrator 'knew that the conduct was part of or intended the conduct to be part of a widespread or systematic attack against a civilian population'.[143] To satisfy the additional requisite intent of the specific offence of persecution, the accused must have acted with the intent to discriminate on one of the specified grounds.[144] As for persecution specifically in the form of the discriminatory destruction of cultural property, the accused must have intended to destroy or extensively damage the property or have acted in reckless disregard of the likelihood of such destruction or damage.[145]

### 2.3. *Genocide*

In UN General Assembly Resolution 96 (I) of 11 December 1946, the member states of the United Nations affirmed that genocide was a crime under general international law.[146] This affirmation was confirmed in Article I of the 1948 Convention on the Prevention and Punishment of the Crime of Genocide ('Genocide Convention'),[147] which specifies that genocide is a crime under international law 'whether committed in time of peace or in time of war'.[148] Article II of the Genocide Convention defines the international crime of genocide as

[142] *Kunarac*, Appeals Chamber Judgement, para. 102. See also Rome Statute, Arts. 7(1) and 30(1); UNTAET Reg. No. 2000/15, §§ 5.1 and 18.1; IST Statute, Art. 12(a).

[143] Elements of Crimes, Art. 7(1)(a), para. 3. But this 'should not be interpreted as requiring proof that the perpetrator had knowledge of all the characteristics of the attack or the precise details of the plan or policy of the State or organization': *ibid.*, Art. 7, Introduction, para. 2. 'In the case of an emerging widespread or systematic attack against a civilian population, the intent clause . . . indicates that this mental element is satisfied if the perpetrator intended to further such an attack': *ibid.* See, similarly, *Kunarac*, Appeals Chamber Judgement, para. 102.

[144] *Prosecutor* v. *Tadic*, Appeals Chamber Judgement, Case No. IT-94-1-A, 15 July 1999, para. 305.

[145] *Milutinovic* et al., Trial Chamber Judgement, paras. 206 and 210.

[146] The word 'affirmed' is rhetorical, because the genocidal acts of Nazi Germany were prosecuted after the Second World War by both the IMT and the U.S. Military Tribunals at Nuremberg as a species of crime against humanity, not as the crime of genocide as such. Moreover, only those genocidal acts committed after the outbreak of the war were prosecuted.

[147] 78 UNTS 277.

[148] *A fortiori*, it is immaterial whether the commission of genocide in wartime is in international or non-international armed conflict.

any of the following acts committed with intent to destroy, in whole or in part, a national, ethnical [*sic*], racial or religious group, as such:

(a) Killing members of the group;
(b) Causing serious bodily or mental harm to members of the group;
(c) Deliberately inflicting on the group conditions of life calculated to bring about its physical destruction in whole or in part;
(d) Imposing measures intended to prevent births within the group;
(e) Forcibly transferring children of the group to another group.

Draft versions of the Genocide Convention had encompassed the concept of 'cultural genocide'. This concept referred, in the earliest draft, to '[s]ystematic destruction of historical or religious monuments or their diversion to alien uses' and 'destruction or dispers[al] of documents and objects of historical, artistic, or religious value and of objects used in religious worship'.[149] A later version spoke of '[d]estroying . . . libraries, museums, schools, historical monuments, places of worship and other cultural institutions and objects of the group' with the intent to destroy the culture of that group.[150] But the concept of cultural genocide was rejected by the Sixth Committee of the General Assembly,[151] which prepared the final text of the Genocide Convention as eventually adopted in plenary.

In *Reservations to the Convention on Genocide*, the International Court of Justice (ICJ) stated that the principles of the Genocide Convention 'are principles which are recognized by civilized nations as binding on States, even without any conventional obligation',[152] a statement that applied as much to the definition of the crime as to the obligations arising for states. The definition laid down in Article II of the Genocide Convention was subsequently reproduced verbatim in Article 4(2) of the ICTY Statute, the UN secretary-general having taken the view that the convention's definition of genocide accorded with customary international law,[153] and in Article 2(2) of the statute of the International Criminal Tribunal for Rwanda (ICTR). It

[149] Draft Convention for the Prevention and Punishment of Genocide, UN Doc. E/447 (26 June 1947), Part I, Art. I(II)(3)(e).

[150] Draft Convention on the Prevention and Punishment of the Crime of Genocide, UN Doc. E/794 (24 May 1948), Annex, Art. III(2).

[151] Many delegates to the Sixth Committee opposed, in the words of the South African representative, 'any attempt to destroy the cultural heritage of a group or to prevent a group from making its specific contribution to the cultural heritage of mankind': *United Nations. Official Records of the Third Session of the General Assembly, Part I. Sixth Committee, Summary Records of Meetings 21 September–10 December 1948*, 202. But they equally thought that a convention on genocide was not the place to express this opposition. In the event, the motion to remove the reference to cultural genocide was carried 25:16:4, with 13 delegations absent during the vote.

[152] *Reservations to the Convention on the Prevention and Punishment on the Crime of Genocide, Advisory Opinion*, ICJ Reports 1951, 15, 23. See also *Armed Activities on the Territory of the Congo (New Application: 2002) (Democratic Republic of the Congo v Rwanda), Jurisdiction and Admissibility*, ICJ Reports 2006, 6, 31, para. 64.

[153] *Report of the Secretary-General pursuant to paragraph 2 of Security Council resolution 808 (1993)*, para. 45, citing *Reservations to the Convention on the Prevention and Punishment on the Crime of Genocide*, 23.

was again restated unamended in Article 17 of the Draft Code of Crimes against the Peace and Security of Mankind, as finally adopted by the ILC in 1996. Paragraph 12 of the commentary to Article 17 of the Draft Code explicitly dismisses the concept of 'cultural genocide':

> As clearly shown by the preparatory work for the Convention, the destruction in question is the material destruction of a group either by physical or by biological means, not the destruction of the national, linguistic, religious, cultural or other identity of a particular group. The national or religious element and the racial or ethnic element are not taken into consideration in the definition of the word 'destruction', which must be taken only in its material sense, its physical or biological sense. It is true that the 1947 draft Convention prepared by the Secretary-General and the 1948 draft prepared by the *Ad Hoc* Committee on Genocide contained provisions on 'cultural genocide' covering any deliberate act committed with the intent to destroy the language, religion or culture of a group, such as prohibiting the use of the language of the group in daily intercourse or in schools or the printing and circulation of publications in the language of the group or destroying or preventing the use of libraries, museums, schools, historical monuments, places of worship or other cultural institutions and objects of the group. However, the text of the Convention, as prepared by the Sixth Committee and adopted by the General Assembly, did not include the concept of 'cultural genocide' contained in the two drafts and simply listed acts which come within the category of 'physical' or 'biological' genocide. The first three subparagraphs of the present article list acts of 'physical genocide', while the last two list acts of 'biological genocide'.[154]

Three years later, Article 6 of the Rome Statute reproduced word for word the definition of genocide used in Article II of the Genocide Convention.[155] Never at any point during the proceedings of the Ad Hoc Committee on the Establishment of an International Criminal Court, the Preparatory Committee on the Establishment of an International Criminal Court, or the United Nations Diplomatic Conference of Plenipotentiaries on the Establishment of an International Criminal Court was it proposed to widen the definition of genocide to embrace the concept of 'cultural genocide'.

The idea of cultural genocide was explicitly rejected once more by a Trial Chamber of the ICTY in *Krstic*. Recalling the drafting of the Genocide Convention and the view of the ILC, the tribunal concluded that 'customary international law limits the definition of genocide to those acts seeking the physical or biological destruction of all or part of the group', with the consequence that 'an enterprise attacking only the cultural or sociological characteristics of a human group in order to annihilate these elements which give to that group its own identity distinct from the rest of

[154] *Report of the International Law Commission on the Work of Its Forty-Eighth Session*, 90–1, references omitted.

[155] See also UNTAET Reg. No. 2000/15, § 4; IST Statute, Art. 11; ECCC Law, Art. 4.

the community would not fall under the definition of genocide'.[156] But the Trial Chamber added a rider:

> The Trial Chamber however points out that where there is physical or biological destruction there are often simultaneous attacks on the cultural and religious property and symbols of the targeted group as well, attacks which may legitimately be considered as evidence of an intent to physically destroy the group. In this case, the Trial Chamber will thus take into account as evidence of intent to destroy the group the deliberate destruction of mosques and houses belonging to members of the group.[157]

The Appeals Chamber subsequently affirmed that the conventional definition of genocide represented customary international law[158] and that the Trial Chamber had 'correctly identified the governing legal principle'.[159] In his partial dissenting opinion, Judge Shahabuddeen, accepting that the notion of 'cultural genocide' fell outside the *actus reus* of genocide as defined by customary international law, nonetheless emphasised what the Trial Chamber had suggested in its rider, namely that '[t]he destruction of culture may serve evidentially to confirm an intent, to be gathered from other circumstances, to destroy the group as such'.[160] In *Krstić* itself, 'the razing of the principal mosque confirm[ed] an intent to destroy the Srebrenica part of the Bosnian Muslim group'.[161]

The rejection of cultural genocide as an international legal concept was wholeheartedly endorsed by the ICJ in *Application of the Genocide Convention*:

> [I]n the Court's view, the destruction of historical, cultural and religious heritage cannot be considered to constitute the deliberate infliction of conditions of life calculated to bring about the physical destruction of the group. Although such destruction may be highly significant inasmuch as it is directed to the elimination of all traces of the cultural or religious presence of a group, and contrary to other legal norms, it does not fall within the categories of acts of genocide set out in Article II of the Convention. In this regard, the Court observes that, during its consideration of the draft text of the Convention, the Sixth Committee of the General Assembly decided not to include cultural genocide in the list of punishable acts. Moreover, the ILC subsequently confirmed this approach. . . . Furthermore, the ICTY took a similar view in the *Krstic* case, finding that even in customary law, 'despite recent developments', the definition of acts of genocide is limited to those seeking the physical or biological destruction of a group (*Krstic*, IT-98–33-T, Trial Chamber Judgment, 2 August 2001, para. 580). The Court concludes that the destruction of

[156] *Prosecutor* v. *Krstic*, Trial Chamber Judgdment, Case No. IT-98–33-T, 2 August 2001, para. 580.
[157] *Ibid.*
[158] *Prosecutor* v. *Krstic*, Appeals Chamber Judgement, Case No. IT-98–33-A, 19 April 2004, para. 25.
[159] *Ibid.*, para. 26.
[160] *Ibid.*, partial diss. op. Shahabuddeen, para. 53.
[161] *Ibid.*

historical, religious and cultural heritage cannot be considered to be a genocidal act within the meaning of Article II of the Genocide Convention.[162]

However, the ICJ added the following:

At the same time, [the Court] also endorses the observation made in the *Krstic* case that 'where there is physical or biological destruction there are often simultaneous attacks on the cultural and religious property and symbols of the targeted group as well, attacks which may legitimately be considered as evidence of an intent to physically destroy the group' (ibid.).[163]

In the light of the ICJ's statements, these principles seem set in stone.

## 3. SENTENCING

When it comes to sentencing in respect of war crimes and crimes against humanity against cultural property, the ICTY Trial Chamber in *Strugar*, relating to the attack on the Old Town of Dubrovnik, noted – citing Article 1(a) of the 1954 Hague Convention – 'that such property is, by definition, of "great importance to the cultural heritage of [a] people"', with the consequence that 'the victim of the offence at issue is to be understood broadly as a "people", rather than any particular individual'.[164] Moreover, the Trial Chamber continued, the consequences of the offence for this victim could be said to be grave.[165] Similarly, in *Krajisnik*, relating to the destruction of religious and other cultural property in Bosnia-Herzegovina (including the Alidza mosque in Foca, dating from 1550, and the Arnaudija mosque in Banja Luka, built in 1594), the Trial Chamber held that sentencing in respect of such crimes may take into account the social consequences of the destruction of the relevant religious and cultural monuments for the targeted community.[166] Nor is it only the local or national community whose interests may be acknowledged. In the Sentencing Judgement in *Jokic*, also relating to the attack on Dubrovnik, the Trial Chamber referred to the war crime of destroying or wilfully damaging historic monuments and works of art as 'a violation of values especially protected by the international community',[167] and it stated that any sentence in the case before it had to acknowledge that the attack on the Old Town of Dubrovnik was an attack 'against the cultural heritage of humankind'.[168] The presence of the Old Town on the World

[162] *Application of the Convention on the Prevention and Punishment of the Crime of Genocide (Bosnia and Herzegovina* v *Serbia and Montenegro), Merits*, ICJ Reports 2007, 4, 124, para. 344.
[163] *Ibid.*
[164] *Strugar*, Trial Chamber Judgement, para. 232, references omitted.
[165] *Ibid.*
[166] *Krajisnik*, Trial Chamber Judgement, para. 1148. The first mosque referred to is also known as the Aladza mosque, the Coloured Mosque, and the Mosque of Hasan Nazir.
[167] *Jokic*, Trial Chamber Sentencing Judgement, para. 46.
[168] *Ibid.*, para. 51. Recall, in this regard, the preamble (second recital) to the 1954 Hague Convention, which expresses the conviction of the high contracting parties that 'damage to cultural property

Heritage List[169] appeared to add to the gravity of the offence in both *Strugar* and *Jokic*,[170] with the Trial Chamber in *Jokic* drawing attention to the statement in the preamble to the World Heritage Convention that 'deterioration or disappearance of any item of the cultural . . . heritage constitutes a harmful impoverishment of the heritage of all the nations of the world'.[171] The latter Trial Chamber further observed, more prosaically, that 'since it is a serious violation of international humanitarian law to attack civilian buildings, it is a crime of even greater seriousness to direct an attack on an especially protected site, such as the Old Town, constituted of civilian buildings'.[172] For its part, the Trial Chamber in the Sentencing Judgement in *Plavsic*, a case involving much the same cultural property as *Krajisnik*, went beyond textual indicators and abstract considerations to take into account the historical and architectural significance of the specific cultural property destroyed:

> Some of these monuments . . . dated from the Middle Ages. They were, quite obviously, culturally, historically and regionally significant sites. As one example, the Prosecution referred to the wanton destruction of the Alidza mosque in Foca, which had been in existence since the year 1550. According to the witness, this mosque was a 'pearl amongst the cultural heritage in this part of Europe'.[173]

For these and other reasons, the tribunal concluded that the accused was guilty of 'a crime of the utmost gravity'.[174] Additionally, the Trial Chamber in *Jokic* considered relevant to the sentence to be imposed for the criminal destruction or damage of cultural property the fact that '[r]estoration of buildings of this kind, when possible, can never return the buildings to their state prior to the attack because a certain amount of original, historically authentic, material will have been destroyed, thus affecting the inherent value of the buildings'.[175] Finally, and more mundanely, the extent of the damage weighed against the accused in both *Jokic* and *Strugar*.[176]

belonging to any people whatsoever means damage to the cultural heritage of all mankind, since each people makes its contribution to the culture of the world'.

169 See 1972 Convention Concerning the Protection of the World Cultural and Natural Heritage ('World Heritage Convention'), 1037 UNTS 151, Art. 11(2).

170 See *Strugar*, Trial Chamber Judgement, para. 461; *Jokic*, Trial Chamber Sentencing Judgement, paras. 49 and 66–67.

171 *Jokic*, Trial Chamber Sentencing Judgement, para. 49, emphasis omitted. This preambular statement extends to all elements of the cultural heritage, not just (as the Trial Chamber seems to suggest) to those inscribed on the World Heritage List. That said, the latter are defined, in accordance with Art. 1 of the World Heritage Convention, to be 'of outstanding universal value from the point of view of history, art or science', with the consequence that their destruction ought to weigh particularly heavily in the balance. Consider also the cultural property protected under the regime of 'enhanced protection' laid down in Chap. 3 of the 1999 Second Hague Protocol, which is defined in Art. 10(a) of the protocol as 'cultural heritage of the greatest importance for humanity'.

172 *Jokic*, Trial Chamber Sentencing Judgement, para. 53.

173 *Plavsic*, Trial Chamber Sentencing Judgement, para. 44, references omitted.

174 *Ibid.*, para. 52.

175 *Jokic*, Trial Chamber Sentencing Judgement, para. 52.

176 *Ibid.*, para. 53; *Strugar*, Trial Chamber Judgement, para. 461.

## 4. CONCLUSION

When, in 1877, William Morris – a proponent of sustainable development *avant la lettre* – founded the Society for the Protection of Ancient Buildings, he saw such sites as belonging 'partly to all generations of mankind who are to follow us'.[177] This vision of intergenerational trusteeship is supported today by, inter alia, international criminal law, in accordance with which a variety of war crimes and crimes against humanity serve to punish those individuals who wilfully destroy or damage or wilfully plunder elements of the cultural heritage. Although such punishment after the event cannot restore the cultural property in question to its previous condition, it can serve publicly and emphatically to reaffirm, for the present and for posterity, 'values especially protected by the international community'.[178]

[177] Quoted in N. Boulting, 'The Law's Delays: Conservationist Legislation in the British Isles', in *The Future of the Past. Attitudes to Conservation 1174–1974* (1976), 9, 16.

[178] *Jokic*, Trial Chamber Sentencing Judgement, para. 46.

# 8

# The Crime of Aggression and Threats to the Future

*Alexandra R. Harrington*

## 1. INTRODUCTION

Typically, the legal community views in a negative light a statute or other legal instrument – international or domestic – that features undefined terms; this reaction tends to be stronger when the particular statute or instrument involved is of a criminal nature. An example of this reaction can be found in the many critiques of the Rome Statute's inclusion of the 'crime of aggression' within the International Criminal Court (ICC)'s prosecutorial jurisdiction without providing a definition of this crime in the statute. Well over a decade after the Rome Statute was signed – despite the dedicated work of panels established through the Rome Statute to address the appropriate definition of a 'crime of aggression' sufficient to convey jurisdiction in the ICC[1] – the crime of aggression was only defined as a matter of international law in 2010. Unlike its cousins – war crimes, crimes against humanity, and genocide – it was impossible for the most heinous crimes of the past decade to be considered as crimes of aggression at international law due to this void in definition. Indeed, although a definition of the crime of aggression was finally agreed upon at the 2010 Kampala Conference of the Parties, due to the non-retroactivity principles that are an essential underpinning of international law, those who committed crimes that would fall under the definition of the crime of aggression over the past decade are not able to be tried through this vehicle.

This chapter examines the newly created crime of aggression to determine whether its definition can include environmental and socioeconomic harms that rise to the level of legal and societal seriousness that requires the ICC to exercise jurisdiction over them. Section 2 of this chapter discusses the relation between the Rome Statute and the creation of the crime of aggression in international law. This section necessarily provides a brief description of the other crimes set out in the Rome

[1] See *infra* Part 2.

Statute – war crimes, crimes against humanity, and genocide. Section 3 discusses environmental and socioeconomic crimes that would rise to the level of seriousness necessary for inclusion under the Rome Statute as crimes of aggression. Section 4 of this chapter analyses the possible inclusion of the crimes set out in Section 3 as crimes of aggression under the Rome Statute. To understand the potential place of the prosecution of such crimes in the international arena, Section 4 also reviews other suggested methods of criminalising and prosecuting these crimes, for example through the creation of the specific crimes of 'ecocide' and 'geocide' and through the creation of tribunals solely authorised to hear cases of environmental crimes. Section 5 discusses the issue of 'disappearing states' as an example of environmental and socioeconomic harms that are currently a problem to the domestic and international community and that will pose an ever greater threat to future generations. This section concludes that, although climate change has been attributed to the actions of the global community, the effects of climate change on disappearing states would not result in a crime of aggression for several reasons, not the least of which being a lack of intent and knowledge. Ultimately, Section 6 of this chapter concludes that there is a place for some environmental crimes and their attendant socioeconomic harms within the definition of the crime of aggression for the purposes of conveying ICC jurisdiction, provided that these acts meet certain levels of seriousness and harm.

## 2. THE ICC STATUTE AND THE CRIME OF AGGRESSION

### 2.1. *History*

As several scholars have noted, the concept of aggression as being wrongful has existed for centuries within the international political and legal community.[2] However, for most of this time the concept was not concretely available as a legal charge. There was no legal ramification to the accusation of aggression; rather, the only ramification that existed was in terms of state practice and international relations, where acts of aggression could be punished in a nonlegal method and forum.[3] This trend continued for centuries, and even the ravages of the First World War and its aftermath were not enough to create a consensus among members of the international community that acts of aggression were indeed worthy of recognition as crimes.[4]

[2] See, e.g., M. Wattad, 'The Rome Statute & Captain Planet: What Lies Between "Crimes against Humanity" and the "Natural Environment?"', (2009) 19 Fordham Envt'l L. Rev. 265, 270.

[3] J. Boeving, 'Note: Aggression, International Law, and the ICC: An Argument for the Withdrawal of Aggression from the Rome Statute', (2005) 43 Colum. J. Transnat'l L. 557, 561–62.

[4] *Ibid.*, at 561–63.

The first prosecutions for crimes akin to the crime of aggression occurred at the end of the Second World War in both the Nuremburg and Tokyo trials.[5] As a matter of law, the concept of 'crimes against peace', used at both of these tribunals, was very similar to the concept of the crime of aggression.[6] However, the definition of 'crimes against peace' was not particularly detailed or nuanced, leading to mixed results for prosecutors using the statute.[7]

After Nuremburg, there were several attempts to define a 'crime of aggression', but none resulted in international consensus.[8] Perhaps the most concrete attempt at establishing a definition of a crime of aggression was offered by United Nations General Assembly Resolution 3314 in 1974.[9]

The International Criminal Court (ICC) was established in 1998.[10] The official agreement through which the ICC was established, the Rome Statute, created four crimes for which prosecutions could occur at the ICC level: (1) war crimes, (2) crimes against humanity, (3) genocide, and (4) crimes of aggression.[11] In 1998 the Rome Statute provided the first three of these crimes with explicit definitions,[12] and one crime – war crimes – would arguably encompass certain acts of environmental degradation and damage when conducted during the course of a military campaign and without the excuse of military necessity.[13]

Although relatively clear definitions were provided for war crimes, crimes against humanity, and genocide, the issue of defining crimes of aggression for the purposes of ICC jurisdiction and potential prosecution proved to be an exceedingly contentious one.[14] After much debate, the parties to the Rome Statute ultimately decided that the appropriate course of action would be to leave the term undefined in the original text of the Rome Statute.[15] Instead, the parties agreed to make provisions for the establishment and support of a committee to address the issue of its definition and to set a minimum amount of time during which the definition of crimes of aggression should be debated.[16] This was ultimately how crimes of aggression were placed

5 See Y. Kim, 'The Preconditions to the Exercise of the Jurisdiction of the International Criminal Court: With Focus on Article 12 of the Rome Statute', (1999) 8 MSU DCL J. Int'l L. 47, 50–51; Wattad, *supra* note 2, at 273–75; T. Meron, 'Defining Aggression for the International Criminal Court', (2001) 25 Suffolk Transnat'l L Rev. 1, 5–6.

6 Kim, *supra* note 5, at 50–51; *see also* Wattad, *supra* note 2, at 270.

7 See Charter of the International Military Tribunal, Art. 6, available at http://avalon.law.yale.edu/imt/imtconst.asp (last visited Dec. 27, 2009); see also Boeving, *supra* note 3, at 569–70.

8 See Kim, *supra* note 5, at 51.

9 Meron, *supra* note 5, at 6.

10 1998 Rome Statute of the International Criminal Court.

11 *Ibid.*, at Art. 5.

12 *Ibid.*, at Arts. 6–8.

13 *Ibid.*, at Art. 8.

14 See *infra* Part II (B); Meron, *supra* note 5, at 1–3.

15 See Kim, *supra* note 5, at 51–54 (discussing the internal debate process and the ultimate compromise that was made regarding the definition and operability of the crime of aggression in order to allow the remainder of the Rome Statute to move forward); Meron, *supra* note 5, at 1–3.

16 Meron, *supra* note 5 at 1–3.

within the parameters of the Rome Statute, but doing so made it impossible to prosecute anyone for crimes of aggression under the original Rome Statute text.[17] This impasse was only breached after the 2010 Kampala Conference of the Parties to the Rome Statute, during which the requisite number of states agreed to a definition of the crime of aggression.[18]

### 2.2. *Discussions at the ICC Special Working Group on the Crime of Aggression*

Prior to the Rome Statute and the creation of the Special Working Group on the Crime of Aggression ('Working Group'), the UNGA Resolution 3314 that sought to define aggression is notable for its discussion of the relationship between the crime of aggression and environmental/socioeconomic harms. The resolution contemplates the use of dangerous materials as part of warfare and aggression and specifically references this use – and the attendant dangers – as a reason for the necessity of defining and seeking to prevent aggression.[19] The resolution is also quite broad in its application to interstate and intrastate acts of aggression, '[r]eaffirming the duty of States not to use armed force to deprive peoples of their right to self-determination, freedom and independence, or to disrupt territorial Integrity'.[20] In terms of interstate conflicts, there is an express provision that 'bombardment' or other weapons-based attacks would constitute an act of aggression.[21] Resolution 3314 is clear that, although it provides a list of qualifying acts of aggression, the list is not exhaustive and that the Security Council retains the ability to add other acts to the definition of aggression.[22] Much of these terms and considerations have been mirrored in the debates and suggestions of the Working Group.

The negotiations of the Working Group became entrenched in a cleavage between state parties that viewed ICC jurisdiction over the crime of aggression as appropriate and state parties that believed the appropriate venue for the determination of whether aggression was committed was the UN Security Council.[23] The latter school of thought based its assertions on the idea that, pursuant to the terms of the United Nations Charter itself, the appropriate body for making determinations regarding aggression is the UN Security Council.[24]

[17] Rome Statute of the International Criminal Court, at Art. 5.
[18] *Ibid.*, at Art. 8 *bis*.
[19] 1974 United Nations General Assembly Resolution 3314 (XXIX), Preamble.
[20] *Ibid.*
[21] *Ibid.*, at Art. 3(b).
[22] *Ibid.*, at Art. 4.
[23] Meron, *supra* note 5, at 2; Boeving, *supra* note 3, at 575–80.
[24] However, the initial proposals for the inclusion of the crime of aggression in the Rome Statute explicitly stated that the proposal was being made in conjunction with the powers of the UN Security Council. See: C. K. Hall, Current Development: The Third and Fourth Sessions of the UN

Despite this cleavage, discussions regarding the definition of the crime of aggression continued within the Working Group, focusing on several key areas of debate. These areas centred around the distinction between individual and state responsibility for crimes of aggression and superior-orders-based responsibility,[25] whether this distinction should solely be used for the purposes of mitigating or enhancing guilt or whether it should be considered when determining whether jurisdiction in fact exists for the ICC, and, at a fundamental and basic level, what types of acts would be encompassed within the definition of a crime of aggression. There was also a consistent debate regarding the need for a general or specific definition of the crime of aggression.[26] These arguments tended to include a debate regarding the place of Resolution 3314 within the definition of a crime of aggression for the purposes of ICC jurisdiction.[27]

An increasingly important question within the debates between Working Group member states was whether nonstate actors – particularly those linked to terrorism – could be subject to ICC jurisdiction through the definition of a crime of aggression.[28] In 2007, the Working Group was faced with the question of whether the crime to be punished should be an 'act of aggression' or an 'armed attack'.[29] It was made clear that the use of the term 'act of aggression' could include an 'armed attack' within its own definition, whereas the converse was not true.[30] In the end, the majority of the Working Group decided to use the 'act of aggression' terminology, thus leading to a more open definition of the crime of aggression.[31] Extensive debates also occurred in 2007 over the issue of scale of harms and actions necessary for an event or series of events to qualify as an act of aggression.[32] By 2008, the Working Group established that a high threshold must be met before prosecution for a crime of aggression could occur, specifically intending to weed out cases in which the gravity of acts committed does not clearly rise to the level needed to fall within the concept of aggression as

Preparatory Committee on the Establishment of an International Criminal Court, (1998) 92 AJIL 124, 132.

25 See Report of the CICC Team on the Crime of Aggression, Informal Inter-Sessional Meeting of the Special Working Group on the Crime of Aggression, held at the Liechtenstein Institute on Self-Determination, Woodrow Wilson School, at Princeton University, New Jersey, United States, from 13 to 15 June 2005 [CICC Team 2005]; Report of the CICC Team on Aggression, Informal Inter-Sessional Meeting of the Special Working Group on the Crime of Aggression, held at the Liechtenstein Institute on Self-Determination, Woodrow Wilson School, at Princeton University, New Jersey, United States, from 11 to 14 June 2007 [CICC Team 2007].

26 J. Bertram-Nothnagel, Report of the CICC Team on Aggression, Assembly of States Parties to the Rome Statute of the International Criminal Court Third Session, The Hague, 6–10 September 2004; CICC Team 2005, *ibid.*

27 *Ibid.*

28 Bertram-Nothnagel, *supra* note 26.

29 CICC Team 2007, *supra* note 25.

30 *Ibid.*

31 *Ibid.*

32 *Ibid.*

a crime under international law.[33] Throughout the debates, there was concern that the crime of aggression be framed in a manner that makes it applicable solely in the future and not as an ex post facto offense. There was also considerable debate over whether the definition of the crime of aggression should include an open-ended list of acts that would qualify for ICC jurisdiction or whether there should be a closed list of qualifying acts.[34]

Various definitions for the 'crime of aggression' were proposed by the Working Group throughout its history. For example, in 2005, the Working Group proposed that the basis for the crime of aggression be that 'a person commits a "crime of aggression" when, being in a position to exercise control over or to direct the political or military action of a State, that person participates actively in an act of aggression'.[35] At the same time, the Working Group proposed to limit the applicability of the crime of aggression 'only [to] persons who are in a position effectively to exercise control over or to direct the political or military action of a State',[36] and it proposed to define the crime of aggression as 'engaging a State, when being in a position effectively to exercise control over or to direct the political or military action of that State'.[37]

The 2008 draft of the crime of aggression statute reads as follows:

1. For the purpose of this Statute, 'crime of aggression' means the planning, preparation, initiation or execution, by a person in a position effectively to exercise control over or to direct the political or military action of a State, of an act of aggression which, by its character, gravity and scale, constitutes a manifest violation of the Charter of the United Nations.
2. For the purpose of paragraph 1, 'act of aggression' means the use of armed force by a State against the sovereignty, territorial integrity or political independence of another State, or in any other manner inconsistent with the Charter of the United Nations.

Any of the following acts, regardless of a declaration of war, shall, in accordance with United Nations General Assembly resolution 3314 (XXIX) of 14

December 1974, qualify as an act of aggression:

(a) The invasion or attack by the armed forces of a State of the territory of Another State, or any military occupation, however temporary, resulting from such invasion or attack, or any annexation by the use of force of the territory of another State or part thereof;

33 Coalition for the International Criminal Court, The ICC and the Crime of Aggression: Resumed Sixth Session 2008.

34 CICC Team 2007, *supra* note 25.

35 CICC Team 2005, *supra* note 25.

36 *Ibid.*

37 *Ibid.*

(b) Bombardment by the armed forces of a State against the territory of another State or the use of any weapons by a State against the territory of another State;
(c) The blockade of the ports or coasts of a State by the armed forces of another State;
(d) An attack by the armed forces of a State on the land, sea or air forces, or marine and air fleets of another State;
(e) The use of armed forces of one State which are within the territory of another State with the agreement of the receiving State, in contravention of the conditions provided for in the agreement or any extension of their presence in such territory beyond the termination of the agreement;
(f) The action of a State in allowing its territory, which it has placed at the disposal of another State, to be used by that other State for perpetrating an act of aggression against a third State;
(g) The sending by or on behalf of a State of armed bands, groups, irregulars or mercenaries, which carry out acts of armed force against another State of such gravity as to amount to the acts listed above, or its substantial involvement therein.[38]

In June 2009, the Working Group again convened to discuss the issues related to defining the crime of aggression.[39] Attempts were made to define elements of the crime of aggression, as well as how states would subject themselves to jurisdiction for this crime, because it had not been defined for the signatory states when the ICC was created.[40] However, there was no discussion of extending the crime beyond its originally conceived of areas of jurisdiction, thereby leaving the inclusion of environmental and socioeconomic harms outside the realm of the crime of aggression.

The Rome Statute itself contains provisions regarding criminal penalties for those convicted of a crime over which it has jurisdiction[41] and also makes limited provisions for financial payments to victims through an established Trust Fund.[42] Thus, the penalties involved in a conviction by the ICC for any of the crimes over which it has jurisdiction are not a function of the definition of the crime itself. However, the long fight over the definition of the crime of aggression was finally ended in 2010 in Kampala, when the Conference of the Parties agreed to the following definition:

1) For the purpose of this Statute, 'crime of aggression' means the planning, preparation, initiation or execution, by a person in a position effectively to exercise control over or to direct the political or military action of a State, of an act

38 Report of the Special Working Group on the Crime of Aggression Annex II, ICC-ASP/6/20/Add.1 (2008).

39 Informal Inter-Sessional Meeting on the Crime of Aggression, hosted by the Liechtenstein Institute on Self-Determination, Woodrow Wilson School, at the Princeton Club, New York, from 8 to 10 June 2009, ICC-ASP/8/INF.2.

40 *Ibid.*

41 1998 Rome Statute of the International Criminal Court Arts. 77–78.

42 *Ibid.*, at Art. 79.

of aggression which, by its character, gravity and scale, constitutes a manifest violation of the Charter of the United Nations.

2) For the purpose of paragraph 1, 'act of aggression' means the use of armed force by a State against the sovereignty, territorial integrity or political independence of another State, or in any other manner inconsistent with the Charter of the United Nations. Any of the following acts, regardless of a declaration of war, shall, in accordance with United Nations General Assembly resolution 3314 (XXIX) of 14 December 1974, qualify as an act of aggression:
   (a) The invasion or attack by the armed forces of a State of the territory of another State, or any military occupation, however temporary, resulting from such invasion or attack, or any annexation by the use of force of the territory of another State or part thereof;
   (b) Bombardment by the armed forces of a State against the territory of another State or the use of any weapons by a State against the territory of another State;
   (c) The blockade of the ports or coasts of a State by the armed forces of another State;
   (d) An attack by the armed forces of a State on the land, sea or air forces, or marine and air fleets of another State;
   (e) The use of armed forces of one State which are within the territory of another State with the agreement of the receiving State, in contravention of the conditions provided for in the
   (f) agreement or any extension of their presence in such territory beyond the termination of the agreement;
   (g) The action of a State in allowing its territory, which it has placed at the disposal of another State, to be used by that other State for perpetrating an act of aggression against a third State;
   (h) The sending by or on behalf of a State of armed bands, groups, irregulars or mercenaries, which carry out acts of armed force against another State of such gravity as to amount to the acts listed above, or its substantial involvement therein.

### 3. ENVIRONMENTAL CRIMES AND SOCIOECONOMIC DAMAGES

By its history and definition, the ICC is intended to exert its jurisdiction to punish those who have committed atrocities, particularly during conflict, be it internal or international conflict. Indeed, the Rome Statute criminalises the most heinous acts committed in the course of modern-day conflicts. However, with the exception of Article 8(2)(b)(iv), there is no explicit provision for the punishment of those who cause severe harm to the environment or to the socioeconomic potentials of peoples living in areas affected by conflict.[43]

[43] See Chapter 5 by Matthew Gillett on environmental damage and other international crimes.

Environmental crimes have become a part of domestic jurisprudence throughout the global community as the importance of environmental integrity and preservation has gained in prominence. Indeed, many constitutions contain provisions that make the environmental and natural resources of the state the property of its people, vesting them with rights to these resources.[44] Thus, in many states there are ample venues in which to bring a claim against a corporate entity or a governmental actor for violations of environmental protection laws. However, as with many forms of law, including criminal law, merely having a forum in which one is authorised to bring claims – particularly against state and quasi-state actors – is not indicative of the incidences of use or successful prosecution within this particular apparatus. Currently, there is no international forum with jurisdiction over the adjudication of major environmental crimes or over the socioeconomic impacts that stem from them.

What are examples of environmental and socioeconomic acts that, arguably, rise to the level of international crimes sufficient to warrant prosecution at the ICC level as crimes of aggression?[45] Although the definition of the crime of aggression is quite new, several key and established international agreements and statements provide a general platform on which to elaborate acts that could rise to the level of harm and gravity necessary to be classified as a crime of aggression for the purposes of ICC jurisdiction.

One of the first statements of the international community in regards to environmental protection and sustainability was the 1972 Stockholm Declaration, which set out a number of principles to guide states and citizens in their conduct towards each other and the environment.[46] Although these principles are nonbinding, they have come to form the backbone of international environmental law and of environmental protections at the international and domestic level. For the purposes of this chapter, Principle 6 of the Stockholm Declaration is particularly relevant.[47] It states that '[t]he discharge of toxic substances or of other substances and the release of heat, in such quantities or concentrations as to exceed the capacity of the environment to render them harmless, must be halted in order to ensure that serious or irreversible damage is not inflicted upon ecosystems'.[48]

44 See, e.g., Brazil Const. Arts. 23, 24; Cambodian Const. Arts. 58, 59; Chile Const. Art. 8, 19; Colombia Const. Art. 226; Cuba Const. Art. 11; Ecuador Const. Arts. 86–91; Indonesian Const. Ch. XIV Art. 33; Lao Const. Ch. II. Art. 17; Malaysia Const. Pt. VI Ch. 4; Myanmar Const. Arts. 8, 13; Paraguay Const. Art. 8; Thai Const. Ch. V § 78; Vietnam Const. Ch. II Art. 17.

45 For a discussion on the need to restrict prosecutions at the ICC level to only the gravest of crimes in order to preserve the integrity of the ICC mechanism as a legitimate tool of the international legal order and community, *see* Meron, *supra* note 5.

46 1972 Declaration of the United Nations Conference on the Human Environment, available at www.unep.org/Documents.Multilingual/Default.asp?DocumentID=97&ArticleID=1503 (last visited 27 December 2009).

47 *Ibid.*, at Art. 6.

48 *Ibid.*

Nearly 20 years after the Stockholm Declaration, the international community agreed to the Rio Declaration, which set out a further refined set of principles.[49] Key among these principles is Principle 24, which states that '[w]arfare is inherently destructive of sustainable development. States shall therefore respect international law providing protection for the environment in times of armed conflict'.[50] The overarching premise of the Rio Declaration is that its provisions and protections place people and humanity at the highest level of concern.[51]

International agreements and policy statements in the environmental and sustainability realm, such as the Stockholm Declaration and the Rio Declaration, establish that there is a sovereign right over natural resources and that part of this right implies the duty to preserve and protect these resources. This conception reflects the international norm of sovereignty over natural resources and the attendant responsibilities that are enshrined in such seminal instruments of international law as the International Convention on Civil and Political Rights (ICCPR)[52] and the International Covenant on Economic, Social and Cultural Rights (ICESCR).[53] The ICCPR is emphatic in its provision that '[i]n no case may a people be deprived of its own means of subsistence'.[54] This language is mirrored in the ICESCR.[55]

Environmental crimes do more than simply damage or destroy the particular environmental area concerned. Indeed, it is often the case that the intent involved in an environmental crime is not in fact to harm the environment itself, but rather to harm or destroy a people or way of life as a result of the environmental damage attendant in the crime. In this instance, the damages to the environment also result in socioeconomic damages and harms to the targeted peoples – or even innocent bystanders – such that this damage becomes part of the crime itself. The idea of extending international criminal liability for the socioeconomic outcomes of environmental crimes, although perhaps novel in articulation, has a strong foundation in the earlier referenced environmental and sustainable development agreements; it finds particularly strong support from the ICCPR and the ICESCR's statements regarding the rights to life and economic and cultural practices as norms of international law.

49 1992 Rio Declaration on the Environment and Development, *available at* www.unep.org/Documents.Multilingual/Default.asp?DocumentID=78&ArticleID=1163 (last visited 27 December 2009).

50 *Ibid.*, at Principle 24.

51 See generally: *ibid.*

52 See 1966 International Convention on Civil and Political Rights, at Art. 1 [ICCPR].

53 See 1966 International Covenant on Economic, and the Social and Cultural Rights, at Art. 1 [ICESCR].

54 ICCPR, *supra* note 53, at Art. 1.

55 ICESCR, *supra* note 54, at Art. 1.

## 4. POTENTIAL EXTENSION OF THE ROME STATUTE TO INCLUDE ENVIRONMENTAL CRIMES

### 4.1. *Theories of Environmental Crimes*

Some scholars have argued that the inclusion of environmental crimes under the Rome Statute would necessitate the creation of an additional crime over which the ICC would have jurisdiction, rather than simply including environmental crimes within the definition of the crime of aggression.[56] One suggestion includes the creation of a specific 'environmental crime' category of jurisdiction for the ICC, which would include the following:

> the intentional or reckless commission by an individual or individuals, regardless of the status of the act under any applicable domestic regulation, of any of the following acts: (a) directly causing large scale or serious pollution of the: 1) sea; 2) atmosphere; 3) [other relevant sites/mediums of pollution]; or (b) conducting an activity, the widespread harmful effects of which should have been contemplated by a reasonably prudent individual; or (c) breaching an obligation within the established framework of international law, the observance of which is recognized as essential for the protection of the environment; or (d) aiding or abetting any of the above acts.[57]

Several problems have been identified with this definition and with including environmental crimes within the Rome Statute, including obtaining proof and victimhood/establishment of harms.[58] In addition to these problems, the creation of an 'environmental crime' as a separate crime under the jurisdiction of the ICC would face practical problems such as the requirement that the ICC Statute itself be amended to include the crime. When one recalls that the ICC signatory states did not establish a binding definition for the crime of aggression for more than a decade after the creation of the ICC – despite the fact that the crime of aggression was a crime contemplated at the outset of the ICC – the likelihood of prompt success for the creation and implementation of environmental crimes as a separate category seems rather dim.

It has also been suggested that environmental crimes might include the proposed crime of 'ecocide'[59] or 'geocide', with proponents of this view attempting to draw parallels between destructive acts towards the environment and those against the

[56] R. McLaughlin, 'Improving Compliance: Making Non-State International Actors Responsible for Environmental Crimes', (2000) 11 Colo. J. Int'l Envt'l L. & Pol'y 377.

[57] *Ibid.*, at 395–96.

[58] *Ibid.*, at 396–98.

[59] M. A. Drumbl, 'Waging War against the World: The Need to Move from War Crimes to Environmental Crimes', (1998) 22 Fordham Int'l L.J. 122, 142–43; A Lopez, 'Criminal Liability for Environmental Damage Occurring in Times of Non-International Armed Conflict: Rights and Remedies', (2007) 18 Fordham Envt'l. L. Rev. 231, 266. For a detailed discussion of the potential framing of 'ecocide' as

qualifying groups for genocide.[60] Those framing these concepts of environmental crime often argue that they can be used to prosecute actions beyond purely military actions in relationship to the environment and might be extended to a variety of public and even private actors.[61] Indeed, many who advocate for the creation of either ecocide or geocide principally argue that the best place to try such crimes is through an apparatus created in a separate and environment-oriented treaty.[62]

Although there is certainly a point to the argument that environmental crimes are different from other crimes currently incorporated in the Rome Statute and merit their own criminal category, this argument seems to overlook the fact that many environmental crimes do fall within the newly adopted definition of the crime of aggression per se. For example, the action of a state invading and laying waste to or contaminating some portion of the territory of another state would arguably fall within the definition of the crime of aggression.

There are, however, many questions with regard to the ability of the international community to extend the Rome Statute to cover environmental crimes that are not the direct result of warfare and/or military actions.[63] Within the context of creating a new category of international environmental crime as a crime of aggression, it has been suggested that the scope of potential defendants could be extended to include corporate and other similar actors engaged in peacetime activities as well as wartime activities.[64] Scholars have noted that, under the Rome Statute, there is a 'delinkage' of crimes against humanity and the existence of a war in and of itself, provided that there is a calculated attack on a civilian population[65] that rises to the levels intended by the drafters.[66] Thus, there is precedent for delinking crimes under the Rome Statute from an explicit wartime situation.

This is one of a host of issues that arise in the discussion of extending the crime of aggression to cover environmental crimes and also, at a more basic level, in the discussion of defining and shaping the crime of aggression under the Rome Statute.

an international delict outside the strict ICC context, see M. A. Gray, 'The International Crime of Ecocide', (1996) 26 Cal. W. Int'l L.J. 215.

60 M. A. Drumbl, 'International Human Rights, International Humanitarian Law, and Environmental Security: Can the International Criminal Court Bridge the Gaps?', (2000) 6 ILSA J Int'l & Comp. L. 305, at 324–25. For a detailed discussion on the proposed legal framework for geocide, see L. Berat, 'Right to a Healthy Environment', (1993) 11 B.U. Int'l L.J. 328.

61 *Ibid.*

62 See, e.g., *ibid.*

63 *See* Drumbl, 'Waging War against the World,' *supra* note 59 at 134–35.

64 McLaughlin, *supra* note 57, at 377.

65 See Rome Statute of the International Criminal Court Art. 7 (2)(a) (affirming that an armed attack is not equivalent to a military attack for the purposes of the Rome Statute).

66 D. M. Koenig, 'The International Criminal Court: Comparing and Contrasting the Views of a Canadian and an American Member of Their Delegations to the International Criminal Court Plenipotentiary (Rome) Conference', (1999) 8 MSU-DCL Int'l L. 15; G. W. Mugwanya, 'Expunging the Ghost of Impunity for Severe and Gross Violations of Human Rights and the Commission of Delicti Jus Gentium: A Case for the Domestication of International Criminal Law and the Establishment of a Strong Permanent International Criminal Court', (1999) 8 MSU-DCL Int'l L. 701, 732.

Additionally, the issue of *mens rea* has been raised in the context of including environmental crimes as crimes of aggression under the Rome Statute – or indeed when including them under any section of the Rome Statute – due to the generally accepted concept that the element of recklessness would be crucial to obtaining a conviction under the standards of the ICC in particular and in international law generally.[67] In a general attempt to evaluate the applicability of the Rome Statute to environmental crimes, it has also been argued that the *mens rea* element of the current Rome Statute could be too lenient for environmental crimes.[68] In the military context, the issue of superior orders functioning as a defense to environmental crimes has also been raised.[69]

Some have suggested that, to include environmental crimes within the ambit of the Rome Statute, it would be necessary to change the concept of the 'victim' under the ICC's jurisdiction from people affected by the criminalised acts to the environment itself.[70] This would constitute a particularly controversial break with the currently accepted concept of the victim under the crime of aggression definitions.[71] Others do not see the need for such a drastic shift in the conception of victimhood. This viewpoint conceives of the victim as the people(s) who are harmed as a result of the environmental crime, for example the Kuwaitis who suffered environmental damage when the retreating Iraqi forces set fire to Kuwaiti oil wells during the First Gulf War.[72] This concept of victimhood is more akin to that used throughout and embodied by the Rome Statute and the ICC per se.

In terms of compensation, it has been suggested that, at least in the context of an environmental crime within the ICC's jurisdiction, the ICC could adopt a similar scheme to the 'polluter pays' principle.[73] However, the difficulty in crafting appropriate penalties and forms of restitution for environmental crimes under the current provisions of the Rome Statute has been highlighted as a reason to question whether environmental crimes should in fact be prosecuted under the auspices of the ICC itself.[74]

### 4.2. *Connections between Environmental and Socioeconomic Harms and Aggression*

When thinking about the extension of the crime of aggression to environmental and socioeconomic crimes, it is important to go beyond abstract discussions to fully

67 McLaughlin, *supra* note 57, at 392–93.

68 *Ibid.*, at 401–04.

69 *Ibid.*

70 Drumbl, 'Waging War against the World,' *supra* note 59, at 129–30.

71 For a discussion of victims and victimhood under the Rome Statute, and potentially for the purposes of the crime of aggression, *see* Boeving, *supra* note 3, at 583–88.

72 See Gray, *supra* note 60, at 217.

73 McLaughlin, *supra* note 58, at 399–400; Gray, *supra* note 60 at 218.

74 Drumbl, 'Can the International Criminal Court Bridge the Gaps', *supra* note 60, at 328.

explore the ramifications of this potential extension. What are specific, historical examples of environmental and socioeconomic consequences that stemmed from aggressive acts? There are many well-known cases, going back as far as Carthage.[75] However, it is helpful to consider several modern examples that demonstrate the fusion between environmental and socioeconomic harms and aggression in light of the technological components of aggression and warfare that have come to the forefront of conflict from the First World War to the present.

As mentioned earlier in the discussion of victimhood, at the end of the First Gulf War – itself found to be an act of aggression by the Security Council – Iraqi forces set fire to a number of Kuwaiti oil wells before retreating from the territorial boundaries of the Kuwaiti state.[76] For the purposes of this chapter, there are several important aspects to this act. The act of setting fire to oil wells was, at least in part, intended to ruin the wells in the short and long term, causing devastation to the economic stability of Kuwait, because the state depended on oil revenues for state funding.[77] Thus, the oil well fires resulted in inherent, intended socioeconomic harm to Kuwait and the Kuwaiti people. The length of time necessary to extinguish the fires and the amount of oil wasted while the fires burned are further evidence of this harm.[78] In addition, there was the environmental damage that resulted from prolonged oil well fires, which resulted in the constant emissions of toxic substances into the air in and around the oil well locations.[79] Indeed, one of the iconic images from the First Gulf War is the menacing plume of smoke rising from an oil well during live news broadcasts.

Aggressive acts involving environmental and socioeconomic harms are not limited to the international context. In fact, some brutal examples of these harms have occurred in the intrastate context. For example, natural resource exploitation has become a key issue in recent African civil wars, such as that in the Democratic Republic of the Congo; there the exploitation of diamond mines and the timber industry for conflict-related reasons has resulted in the removal of natural resources in a way that causes environmental damage through poor mining practices and the destruction of forests, as well as socioeconomic harms in the form of depriving the local population of the ability to harvest and use these resources.[80] This is one area in which the proposed definitions of crimes of aggression, without amplification, would fail to address a significant form of environmental and socioeconomic aggression, because these acts are committed within the state.

75 See E. F. J. Yuzon, 'Deliberate Environmental Modification through the Use of Chemical and Biological Weapons: "Greening" the International Laws of Armed Conflict to Establish an Environmentally Protective Regime', (1996) 11 Am. U. J. Int'l L. & Pol'y 793, 795.

76 See *ibid.*, at 793–95.

77 *Ibid.*

78 *Ibid.*

79 *Ibid.*

80 See Lopez, *supra* note 60, at 238.

At a fundamental level, environmental and socioeconomic harms such as those discussed earlier are violations of *jus in bello*. In the example of the First Gulf War, the actions of the Iraqi state in invading Kuwait were deemed by the Security Council to be acts of aggression, and thus violations of *jus ad bellum*; however, it is not this violation or form of aggression that would make the environmental and socioeconomic harms inflicted upon Kuwait crimes of aggression. Rather, it is the violation of accepted norms of state conduct in warfare itself and the rights established as a matter of international law that would qualify environmental and socioeconomic harms as acts of aggression. However, in evaluating the applicability of crimes of aggression to environmental and socioeconomic harms, it is limiting to simply restrict the concept to harms caused during interstate warfare; this has been demonstrated in the earlier example from the Democratic Republic of the Congo.

## 5. THE LIMITS OF AGGRESSION AND ENVIRONMENTAL AND SOCIOECONOMIC HARMS

The newly created definition of the crime of aggression fails to take into account interstate or intrastate acts and subsequent environmental and socioeconomic harms. Additionally, the definition does not contemplate the wider series of harms that have been argued to stem from nonmilitary actions that cause damage to the environment and, subsequently, to socioeconomic standing in an affected area.

One example of an environmental issue that has been argued to be the result of criminal conduct and that demonstrates the limits of the crime of aggression in the non-international military context is the example of 'disappearing states'. More precisely, this term refers to states such as the Maldives, which are faced with complete or partial submersion (or in some cases desertification) as the result of rising sea levels (or droughts) that have been scientifically attributed to climate change.[81] Thus the environmental threats to these states generally stem from a conglomeration of influences on the sea level and not from one identifiable act by any particular actor.

Taking the case of the Maldives as an example, how might the crime of aggression be used in the context of disappearing states? As noted earlier, the new definition of the crime of aggression would be inapplicable to a disappearing state because of the lack of military involvement in the actions giving rise to the harms affecting the disappearing state, as well as the indeterminate actors involved in causing the environmental and associated socioeconomic damage. This is not to say, however, that environmental and socioeconomic harms in disappearing states could never be classified as crimes of aggression under the new definition if the harms were the

[81] See, e.g., R. Rayfuse, 'W(h)ither Tulvalu? International Law and Disappearing States', available at http://papers.ssrn.com/sol3/papers.cfm?abstract_id=1412028.

result of bombardment, the use of chemical weapons to render the soil infertile, or the use of mercenaries for the perpetuation of environmental harms.

Yet, even if the definition of the crime of aggression were to be expanded to include environmental and socioeconomic harms and to move beyond force-based requirements, the phenomenon of disappearing states would not fall within its ambit for several reasons. The most obvious reason would of course be that disappearing states would seek recourse against states for acts that would necessarily be ex post facto, and thus invalid under the terms of the ICC Statute and generally accepted tenets of international law. Beyond this initial hurdle is the issue of intent and knowledge. Climate change, especially conditions leading to rising sea levels, cannot be tied to one act or even to one actor. Nor can it be attributed to the malevolent actions of any combination of actors – indeed, as the global society slowly learns more about the toxic effects of pollution and the like, the lack of knowledge or intent to cause harm is reiterated.

In the context of future crimes, even if the crime of aggression would be fashioned to take into account environmental and socioeconomic harms, this would be of limited application to future disappearing states, because the threshold of the intent/knowledge element would be quite high. Additionally, because much of the underlying causes of disappearing states have been attributed to industrial developments, it would be difficult for the crime of aggression to be made applicable even if extended to intrastate conflicts.

## 6. CONCLUSIONS

The relationship between environmental crimes and harms and the well-being of humanity cannot be denied. Damage to the environment, be it the result of natural phenomena or human activities, accidental or intentional, has devastating consequences that endure far beyond the initial act of humans or nature. This is particularly the case in times of conflict, where, throughout history, damage to and destruction of the environment have been used as a part of the weaponry of war.

Domestic law has increasingly incorporated environmental crimes within its orbit in criminal and constitutional laws. These are important developments for the recognition of the impact of environmental crimes on the present and also on the future. However, much as the international community has come to realise that there are situations in which international or intranational actions of states/state actors can merit prosecution at the international level, the potential use of international criminal law to punish and prevent environmental crimes has also become a more popular argument.

Environmental crimes are envisioned in the Rome Statute as part of the definition of war crimes. This indeed validates the idea that environmental crimes can rise to the level of gravity necessary to trigger the jurisdiction of the ICC. And yet, it is possible that simply allowing environmental crimes to exist as part of war crimes can deny the ways outlined earlier in which environmental crimes are used as part of the campaigns of atrocity that the ICC seeks to punish and deter. In this context, the crime of aggression could be used to punish environmental crimes that are part of a wrongful act of aggression committed by state or other responsible actors. Indeed, punishing environmental crimes as part of the crime of aggression would be a powerful statement and method to protect future generations by ensuring that the international community deters the use of aggressive acts that would make life in a particular area (or areas) dangerous or impossible due to environmental conditions and challenges.

Certainly there are challenges to including environmental crime within the definition of crimes of aggression under the Rome Statute. This chapter has discussed many of these difficulties to highlight the need for serious discussion and debate on how to include environmental crimes within the definition of crimes of aggression without altering the focus of the ICC or using too narrow a scope for criminalising environmental crimes. These difficulties should not, however, be regarded as fatal to the possibility of incorporating environmental crimes into crimes of aggression under the Rome Statute. In fact, they frequently parallel the difficulties and debates that the Working Group has encountered in trying to draft and create a consensus surrounding the very definition of the crime of aggression for the purposes of the ICC and the Rome Statute.

Socioeconomic damages that result from environmental crimes are, in many ways, parallel to the already accepted concepts of harms that are criminalised under the Rome Statute and that have been suggested for inclusion in the crime of aggression definition. Indeed, it is not difficult to conceive of socioeconomic damages from environmental crimes that would qualify as crimes of aggression – or even war crimes – as being an inherent part of the Rome Statute if the concept of socioeconomic damages is examined at the level of societal impact rather than glossed over as a merely economic, as opposed to humanitarian, concern.

Thus, it is entirely plausible and in keeping with the goals of the Rome Statute to argue that future large-scale environmental and associated socioeconomic harms be classified as the result of crimes of aggression under the auspices of the Rome Statute in order to confer justiciability at the ICC level.

PART III

# Sustainable Development and the Mechanisms of International Criminal Justice

# 9

# Intergenerational Equity and Rights and International Criminal Law

*Jarrod Hepburn*

## 1. INTRODUCTION

This chapter introduces the concepts of intergenerational equity and rights in international law and examines the extent to which they are legally protected through current international criminal law.

Although thoughts of the obligations owed by the present generation to the future have occupied philosophers at least since Kant in 1785,[1] it is generally considered that John Rawls's 1971 work, *A Theory of Justice*, provided the first systematic study of the question.[2] Following this, questions of justice for future generations began to take on international prominence at the 1972 Stockholm Conference on the Human Environment. During the 1980s, other philosophers such as Brian Barry, Derek Parfit, and Ernest Partridge developed Rawls's ideas and added critiques of their own.[3] Around ten years later, Edith Brown Weiss highlighted early connections of the concept of intergenerational equity with international legal discourse,[4] and since 2001, increasingly regular references to generational justice in the global media have propelled the concept into public consciousness.[5]

[1] Kant was troubled that later generations should receive the benefits of the progress made by earlier generations, without contributing anything to it. See J. Rawls, *A Theory of Justice* (1971) 254.

[2] *Ibid.*, at Section 44. This work applied Rawls's concept of the 'veil of ignorance' to the intergenerational problem. Rawls's just savings principle suggests that the rate at which present resources are conserved for the benefit of the future should be the rate that would be chosen by a hypothetical generation of people behind the veil of ignorance – knowing that they are *one* generation on the temporal spectrum, but not knowing which one.

[3] B. Barry, 'Justice between Generations' in P. M. S. Hacker and J. Raz (eds.), *Law, Morality and Society: Essays in Honour of H.L.A. Hart* (1977); D. Parfit, 'Future Generations: Further Problems', (1982) 11 Phil. & Pub. Aff. 113; E. Partridge (ed.), *Responsibilities to Future Generations: Environmental Ethics* (1981).

[4] E. Brown Weiss, *In Fairness to Future Generations: International Law, Common Patrimony, and Intergenerational Equity* (1989).

[5] J. Tremmel, 'Introduction', in J. Tremmel (ed.), *Handbook of Intergenerational Justice* (2006), at 1.

The author acknowledges the assistance of Ashfaq Khalfan with an earlier version of this chapter.

Of course, law is no stranger to intertemporal questions. All human interactions occur over time, and so the legal rules governing them necessarily include references to time. Contractual offers must precede acceptance; causes must precede their effects; parents must precede their children.[6] Although the time scales considered by these rules are mostly quite short when compared with a human lifespan, some laws address longer term issues. Roman law, for instance, is considered to be the origin of the public trust doctrine applicable in some countries, which views the natural heritage of the Earth to be held on trust for the benefit of all (present) people, with an implied eye towards preservation for future generations.[7] Indeed, as this chapter discusses, the concepts of intergenerational equity and rights have found most resonance in law in an environmental context. However, there are connections in other areas of law as well. Human rights law, for instance, has been linked to intergenerational equity in addressing climate change – which is not only an environmental problem but touches also on the human rights to health, economic necessities, and subsistence.[8] Economic laws and guidelines in some countries also mandate the use of particular discount rates (economic tools used to place present values on long-term projects imposing costs or benefits far in the future).[9] Furthermore, as discussed in Section 6, international criminal law displays some key aspects of intergenerational equity.

This chapter thus opens with a discussion of the definition and scope of intergenerational equity and an outline of philosophical debates on the notion of intergenerational rights. Sections 3, 4, and 5 examine references to intergenerational equity in treaties, international courts, and international soft law instruments, respectively, cutting across many areas of international law. Section 6 highlights the connections between obligations owed to future generations and legal obligations in the area of international criminal justice owed in the present. The chapter concludes with some observations on the role of international law in protecting the rights and interests of future generations.

## 2. CONCEPTS OF INTERGENERATIONAL EQUITY AND RIGHTS

One prominent definition of the concept of intergenerational equity, in the International Law Association's 2002 New Delhi Principles, is 'the right of future generations

[6] R. Epstein, 'Past and Future: The Temporal Dimension in the Law of Property', (1986) 64 Wash. U. L. Q. 667.

[7] T. Brady, '"But Most of It Belongs to Those Yet to be Born": The Public Trust Doctrine, NEPA, and the Stewardship Ethic', (1990) 17 B.C. Envtl Aff. L. Rev. 621 at 624–25.

[8] S. Caney, 'Human Rights, Climate Change, and Discounting', (2008) 17 Envtl Politics 536.

[9] C. Hepburn, Use of Discount Rates in the Estimation of the Costs of Inaction with Respect to Selected Environmental Concerns, OECD Working Party on National Environmental Policies, Doc. No. ENV/EPOC/WPNEP(2006)13/FINAL (2007).

to enjoy a fair level of the common patrimony'.[10] It has also been defined as 'that principle of ordering of the community of mankind which will make it possible for every generation, by virtue of its own effort and responsibility, to secure a proportionate share in the common good of the human species'.[11] Over recent decades, it has been widely accepted that, for the first time in the history of humankind, human activity has the potential to irreversibly alter the world on a massive scale. This concern has emerged in the context of our obligations to future generations in particular; as noted in the Brundtland Report of the World Commission on Environment and Development:

> Many present efforts to guard and maintain human progress, to meet human needs, and to realize human ambitions are simply unsustainable – in both the rich and poor nations. They draw too heavily, too quickly, on already overdrawn environmental resource accounts to be affordable far into the future without bankrupting those accounts. . . . We act as we do because we can get away with it: future generations do not vote, they have no political or financial power; they cannot challenge our decisions. But the results of the present profligacy are rapidly closing the options for future generations.[12]

Intergenerational equity is conceptually connected to sustainable development. At the root of sustainable development is the belief that the resources of the earth belong to all generations. From this belief it follows that the present generation has no right to intervene irreversibly and exhaustively in human relations with the natural world so as to deprive future generations of environmental, social, and economic opportunities of well-being. No country, continent, or generation has an exclusive right to the natural resources of the earth. These resources have been handed over from past generations, and consequently, the present generation has an obligation to transmit them in good and even enhanced conditions to posterity.[13] The concept of intergenerational equity, as employed in current international instruments, calls for states to 'ensure a just allocation in the utilisation of resources between past, present and future generations'. It requires attaining a balance between meeting the consumptive demands of existing societies and ensuring that adequate resources are available to accommodate the needs of future generations.[14]

It is important, however, to consider intergenerational equity in a more holistic fashion, beyond its historic home of environmental issues and the sustainable use of

[10] International Law Association, 2002 New Delhi Declaration on Principles of International Law Relating to Sustainable Development, ILA Resolution 3/2002 in ILA, Report of the Seventieth Conference, New Delhi (London: ILA, 2002), Principle 2, available at www.ila-hq.org.

[11] E. Agius, 'Obligations of Justice towards Future Generations: A Revolution on Social and Legal Thought', in E. Agius, (ed.), *Future Generations and International Law* (1998), 10.

[12] World Commission on Environment and Development, *Our Common Future* (1987), 13.

[13] *Ibid.*

[14] See O. Schachter, *Sharing the World's Resources* (1977), at 11–12. See also Brown Weiss, *supra* note 4 and T. M. Franck, *Fairness in International Law and Institutions* (1995).

natural resources. Fairness across generations requires consideration of *all* the ways in which present action can cause harm in the long-term future. This includes not only present actions that cause the depletion of natural resources but also extends to other actions such as the destruction of the cultural and human-made heritage; damage to political, social, and economic institutions; and the impoverishment of human life and health in both tangible and intangible ways.[15] Nuclear warfare, for instance, would violate principles of intergenerational justice not only for the long-lasting environmental damage that it would cause but also for the adverse effects on human health and global human relations that would undoubtedly persist long after the warfare ceased.[16] Most obviously, the existence of any future generations at all would be jeopardised by the widespread deaths caused by nuclear weapons. International legal prohibitions against genocide and racial discrimination similarly engage the non-environmental aspects of intergenerational equity, because they are arguably aimed just as much at preserving the existence and societal participation of future generations as of present generations.[17] Moreover, intergenerational justice might also call for positive actions today that *improve* the long-term future, such as medical advances or the resolution of longstanding international, ethnic, or religious disputes.

Philosophers have questioned the use of the term 'rights' in an intergenerational context. A common objection in this vein is that rights can only attach to entities that already exist. On this view, it simply makes no sense to speak of the rights of future generations, because it is impossible for them to claim or exercise those rights.[18] (As Beckerman points out, this is not necessarily to deny any *obligations* owed by the present to the future; it is simply to say that these obligations do not flow from any *rights*.[19]). One way posited to counter this objection is simply to speak in the future tense, asserting that future generations *will* have rights and thus are worthy of consideration today.[20] There are also many categories of humans who cannot claim rights directly, such as children, the mentally impaired, seriously ill or infirm adults, and perhaps even foetuses; yet we are generally comfortable attaching rights to these humans. Some would further argue that animals and plants have rights, naturally without claiming any possibility of direct exercise of those rights.[21] There may be a

15 B. Frischmann, 'Some Thoughts on Shortsightedness and Intergenerational Equity', (2005) 36 Loyola U. Chi. L.J. 457, at 463.

16 Cf. *Advisory Opinion on the Legality of the Use by a State of Nuclear Weapons in Armed Conflict*, Advisory Opinion, [1996] ICJ Rep. 226, at 452–61 (Weeramantry J.).

17 E. Brown Weiss, 'Our Rights and Obligations to Future Generations for the Environment', (1990) 84 AJIL 198, at 203. For further discussion of genocide in this context, see Section 6.

18 See, e.g., W. Beckerman, 'The Impossibility of a Theory of Intergenerational Justice', in J. Tremmel (ed.), *Handbook of Intergenerational Justice* (2006), 54.

19 *Ibid.*, at 58.

20 J Tremmel, 'Establishing Intergenerational Justice in National Constitutions', in J. Tremmel (ed.), *Handbook of Intergenerational Justice* (2006), 200.

21 *Ibid.*, at 201.

distinction, however, between attaching rights to currently existing things (such as foetuses or plants) and attaching rights to things that do not (yet) exist.

Others have even argued, adopting the tenets of chaos theory, that any action done ostensibly out of an obligation towards future generations will subtly affect the composition of those future generations, thus inevitably denying some of those members their very existence.[22] One response to this view is that it relies on an individualistic notion of rights, suggesting that rights cannot exist until particular individuals are attached to them and can exercise them. Intergenerational rights can instead be thought of as group rights, enforceable by a guardian regardless of the exact numbers or composition of the group.[23] Even if chaos theory is correct in suggesting that present actions will have consequences that change which particular humans are brought into existence, it does not change the character of future generations' rights, because they belong to the future generations as a group and not to any identifiable future humans.[24] Beckerman highlights a problem with this response, however, in that future humans are unable to play any role in appointing the guardian necessary to claim these group rights, nor can future humans influence the kinds of policies for which the guardian will advocate.[25] Indeed, it may well be impossible for any present guardian to formulate appropriate policy suggestions given the inherent unknowability of the future and the actual needs of future generations.

No attempt is made here to resolve these debates over the nature of intergenerational equity and rights. For present purposes, it is enough to acknowledge the existence of debate and to demonstrate in the remainder of this chapter how this uncertainty on occasion affects the extent to which intergenerational equity can be recognised in international law.

## 3. INTERGENERATIONAL EQUITY AND RIGHTS IN TREATIES

The principle of intergenerational equity most often finds expression as a concern for both 'present and future generations' in environmental treaties and texts. It is difficult to point to a concrete application of the principle, however, and it is seen most often as a guiding or preambular concept in international law. Given the philosophical disagreement outlined earlier, it is not surprising that treaty language employing the principle usually prefers the language of 'interests' or 'benefits' accruing to future generations rather than 'rights'. The obligations that can be linked to the principle are largely related to conservation and the efficient utilisation of natural resources.

22 Parfit calls this situation the 'Non-Identity Problem': any action that 'damages' future humans also prevents those humans from ever existing, because the actions taken will cause different humans to be born. See D. Parfit, *Reasons and Persons* (1984), ch. 16.

23 Tremmel, *supra* note 20, at 191–98, discusses various countries that have appointed institutional guardians of future generations' rights.

24 Brown Weiss, *supra* note 17, at 204–06.

25 Beckerman, *supra* note 18, at 60.

One non-environmental and highly significant treaty in which the concept appears is the *UN Charter*, which in the preamble aims 'to save succeeding generations from the scourge of war'. Another such treaty is the *International Covenant on Economic, Social and Cultural Rights* (ICESCR).[26] The UN Committee on Economic, Social and Cultural Rights' interpretation of several ICESCR rights raises several concrete intergenerational equity considerations. For example, according to *General Comment No. 15*, the right to water must be realised for both 'present and future generations'. This means, for example, increasing the efficiency of water use by end-users, assessing the impacts of actions that may impinge on water availability, reducing and eliminating water contamination, or even simply monitoring water reserves.[27] Similarly, the right to food requires that food be made accessible for both present and future generations.[28] It restricts states from engaging in agricultural or food production activities that adequately feed the present generation but undermine the ability of future generations to feed themselves.

The ICESCR's provisions on the right to education do not explicitly mention future generations. However, it can easily be seen that measures taken to fulfil the right to education for present generations will directly contribute to its availability for future generations, because future people will require educated present people to serve as teachers, preservers, and disseminators of knowledge. The right to education recognised in Article 13 of ICESCR thus plays an important role in achieving intergenerational equity by giving younger members of the present generation the tools and knowledge necessary to implement policies that protect their own (future) children's rights. *General Comment No. 13* acknowledges this in describing education as an 'empowerment right' and an 'indispensable means of realising other human rights'.

Most other treaty references to intergenerational equity come from the domain of international environmental law.[29] As one prominent example, Article 3 of the *United Nations Framework Convention on Climate Change* states that '[p]arties should protect the climate system for the benefit of present and future generations of humankind, on the basis of equity and in accordance with their common but differentiated responsibilities'.[30] More specifically, the *International Convention for the Regulation of Whaling* notes the 'interest of the nations of the world in safeguarding for future generations the great natural resources represented by the whale stocks'.[31] The 1992 *Convention on the Protection and Use of Transboundary Watercourses and International Lakes* states that 'water resources shall be managed so that the needs

26 1966 International Covenant on Economic, Social and Cultural Rights, 993 UNTS 3.

27 CESCR, *General Comment 12*, *supra* note, at paras. 11 and 28.

28 CESCR, *General Comment 15*, *supra* note, at para. 7.

29 C. Redgwell, *Intergenerational Trusts and Environmental Protection* (1999), 122, cites other preambular references to future generations in binding environmental conventions not mentioned here.

30 1992 United Nations Framework Convention on Climate Change, 1771 UNTS 107, Art. 3(1).

31 1946 International Convention for the Regulation of Whaling, 161 UNTS. 72, preamble.

of the present generation are met without compromising the ability of future generations to meet their needs'.[32] Under the *World Heritage Convention*, the state has the duty to ensure the transmission to future generations of cultural and natural heritage.[33]

Several international and regional environmental agreements refer to a responsibility to future generations in their preambles. The *Biodiversity Convention* expresses states' determination to 'conserve and suitably use biological diversity for the benefit of present and future generations', while recognising that 'economic and social development and poverty eradication are the first and overriding priorities of developing countries'.[34] Article 2 of the convention defines the 'sustainable use' of components of biological diversity in a way that 'maintain[s] its potential to meet the needs and aspirations of present and future generations'. One of the purposes of the *African Convention on the Conservation of Nature and Natural Resources*, according to its preamble, is 'the conservation, utilization and development of [natural resources] by establishing and maintaining their rational utilization for the present and future welfare of mankind'.[35] The *Convention on International Trade in Endangered Species of Wild Fauna and Flora*, in its preamble, recognises that wild flora and fauna must be protected 'for this and the generations to come'.[36] The prologue of the *Desertification Convention* declares the state parties' determination 'to take appropriate action in combating desertification and mitigating the effects of drought for the benefit of present and future generations'.[37] In the preamble of the *Seed Treaty*, states express their 'aware[ness] of their responsibility to past and future generations to conserve the World's diversity of plant genetic resources for food and agriculture'.[38] The general provisions of the treaty establish a system aimed at the conservation and use of plant genetic resources for food and agriculture for present and future generations.

The eight parties to the *Jeddah Convention* aim to protect the marine environment of the Red Sea and Gulf of Aden 'for the benefit of all concerned, including future generations'.[39] Article 1 of the Jeddah Convention further defines 'conservation' as allowing 'optimum benefit for the present generation while maintaining the potential of [the Red Sea] environment to satisfy the needs and aspirations of future generations'. The *Convention on Conservation of Nature in the South Pacific* also

32 1992 Convention on the Protection and Use of Transboundary Watercourses and International Lakes, 31 I.L.M. 1312, Art. 2, para. 6(c).

33 1972 Convention Concerning the Protection of World Cultural Property and Natural Heritage, 1037 UNTS 151, Art. 4.

34 1992 United Nations Convention on Biological Diversity, 1760 UNTS 79.

35 1968 African Convention on the Conservation of Nature and Natural Resources, 1001 UNTS 3.

36 1973 Convention on International Trade in Endangered Species of Wild Fauna and Flora, 993 UNTS 243.

37 1994 United Nations Convention to Combat Desertification in Countries Experiencing Serious Drought and/or Desertification, Particularly in Africa, 1954 UNTS 3.

38 2001 International Treaty on Plant Genetic Resources for Food and Agriculture.

39 1985 Regional Convention for the Conservation of the Red Sea and Gulf of Aden Environment.

aims for resource management 'for the benefit of present and future generations'.[40] The European states that are party to the *Bonn Convention* are 'aware that each generation of man holds the resources of the earth for future generations and has an obligation to ensure that this legacy is conserved'.[41] Under the *Nairobi Convention*, the Eastern African state parties are 'conscious of their responsibility to preserve their natural heritage for the benefit and enjoyment of present and future generations'.[42] The ASEAN nations recognise the 'importance of natural resources for present and future generations' in the *ASEAN Agreement on the Conservation of Nature and Natural Resources*.[43] The three parties to the *North American Agreement on Environmental Cooperation* adopt the objective of 'foster[ing] the protection and improvement of the environment in the territories of the parties for the well-being of present and future generations'.[44]

Outside the environmental context, another notable reference occurs in the preamble of the Charter of Fundamental Rights of the European Union.[45] The charter guarantees certain rights under the six headings of dignity, freedom, equality, solidarity, citizens' rights, and justice. The preamble notes that enjoyment of these rights 'entails responsibilities and duties with regard to other persons, to the human community and to future generations'.

One problem arising in all these formulations of intergenerational equity is that, even where the language is mandatory and non-preambular, they do not detail exactly how states should act, in the present, to take future generations sufficiently into account. There is little guidance on how the interests of future generations might differ from those of present generations and little acknowledgement of extrinsic factors, such as the possibility of technological advancement reducing future generations' need for resources at the same degree as current humans. This lack of detail reflects the difficulties expressed by some philosophers with the utility of institutional guardians of future generations' rights, outlined in Section 2.

## 4. INTERGENERATIONAL EQUITY AND RIGHTS IN INTERNATIONAL COURTS

Outside of treaty law and other multilateral instruments, the International Court of Justice (ICJ) has addressed intergenerational aspects of state activities in at least one court case – albeit in a separate opinion. In the *Maritime Delimitation in the*

40 1976 Convention on Conservation of Nature in the South Pacific, preamble.

41 1979 Convention on the Conservation of Migratory Species of Wild Animals, 19 I.L.M. 15 (1980).

42 1985 Convention for the Protection, Management and Development of the Marine and Coastal Environment of the Eastern African Region, IELMT 985:46, preamble.

43 ASEAN Agreement on the Conservation of Nature and Natural Resources, (1985) 15 Envt'l Pol'y & L. 64, 68, preamble (treaty not yet in force).

44 32 ILM 1480 (1993).

45 The EU Charter of Fundamental Rights became legally binding on 1 December 2009, following the ratification of the Lisbon Treaty by EU member states.

*Area between Greenland and Jan Mayen (Denmark* v. *Norway)*,[46] in his extensive separate opinion on the issue of 'equity', Judge Weeramantry discussed a historical and cultural framework for intergenerational equity in global legal traditions. He subsequently insisted on the recognition of equity as an international legal principle in his dissents in *Nuclear Tests (New Zealand* v. *France)*[47] and *Advisory Opinion on the Legality of the Threat or Use of Nuclear Weapons (Nuclear Weapons Advisory Opinion)*.[48]

In *Denmark* v. *Norway*, Judge Weeramantry referred to intergenerational equity and specifically to 'the concept of wise stewardship [of natural resources] . . . and their conservation for the benefit of future generations'.[49] These statements were included in his separate concurring opinion as dicta and were not decisive in the court's decision regarding delimitation of a maritime boundary. In his dissenting opinion in *Nuclear Tests 1995*, Judge Weeramantry stated,

> The case before the court raises, as no case before the court has done, the principle of intergenerational equity – an important and rapidly developing principle of contemporary environmental law. . . . The court has not thus far had occasion to make any pronouncement on this rapidly developing field . . . [The case] raises in pointed form the possibility of damage to generations yet unborn.[50]

The court in *Nuclear Tests 1995* rendered its decision on other grounds before it had the opportunity to address the normative status of intergenerational equity. In *Nuclear Weapons Advisory Opinion*, in which the ICJ was asked to hold whether the threat or use of nuclear weapons by a state was unlawful per se under international law, Judge Weeramantry found that

> [a]t any level of discourse, it would be safe to pronounce that no one generation is entitled, for whatever purpose, to inflict such damage on succeeding generations. . . . This Court, as the principal judicial organ of the United Nations, empowered to state and apply international law . . . must, in its jurisprudence, pay due recognition to the rights of future generations. . . . The rights of future generations have passed the stage when they were merely an embryonic right struggling for recognition. They have woven themselves into international law through major treaties, through juristic opinion and through general principles of law recognized by civilized nations.[51]

46 See *Case Concerning Maritime Delimitation in the Area between Greenland and Jan Mayen (Denmark* v. *Norway)*, 1993 ICJ Rep. 38 (separate opinion of Judge Weeramantry) at 211–79 [*Denmark* v. *Norway*].

47 *Case Concerning Nuclear Tests (New Zealand and Australia v. France)* (1974) ICJ Rep. 457 (dissenting opinion by Judge Weeramantry) at 341–42.

48 *Advisory Opinion on the Legality of the Use by a State of Nuclear Weapons in Armed Conflict*, Advisory Opinion, [1996] ICJ Rep. 226 at 888.

49 *Denmark* v. *Norway*, *supra* note 46 (separate opinion of Judge Weeramantry) 274.

50 *Nuclear Tests*, *supra* note 47 (dissenting opinion by Judge Weeramantry), at 341–42.

51 Nuclear Weapons, *supra* note 48, at 888.

In the majority opinion, the ICJ determined that it could not hold that, based on existing international law, use of nuclear weapons would be unlawful in all circumstances. Although it did not address the legal status of intergenerational equity, the court did acknowledge the catastrophic implications for future generations due to environmental harm from nuclear weapons.[52]

In a brief reference in the *Gabcikovo-Nagymaros* case, the ICJ considered that traditional rules of international law must be read in light of the contemporary development of new environmental norms and standards that are inspired partly by concerns for intergenerational equity.[53] The court ordered the parties to conduct good faith negotiations in relation to aspects of the project, looking afresh at its effects on the environment. More recently, Uruguay has argued before the ICJ that its pulp mill on the River Uruguay is being administered in accordance with both the principles of sustainable development and the needs of future generations.[54]

The judicial institutions of international economic law have been less keen to draw on intergenerational equity as a concept to inform their decisions. The Appellate Body of the World Trade Organisation, for instance, has made very limited reference to intergenerational equity. In the *Shrimp/Turtle* case, in the context of locating the 'objectives of WTO Members with respect to the relationship between trade and the environment', the Appellate Body acknowledged Principle 3 of the Rio Declaration.[55] As noted later, this principle employs the concept of intergenerational equity to balance the developmental and environmental needs of present and future generations. Beyond this reference, the concept does not feature in WTO jurisprudence. Similarly, tribunals constituted under international investment agreements have not as yet adopted intergenerational equity as a guiding principle in any awards.

## 5. INTERGENERATIONAL EQUITY AND RIGHTS IN SOFT LAW

There is much soft law embodying the principle of intergenerational equity, again largely in an environmental context.[56] It formed part of the New International Economic Order via the 1974 Charter of Economic Rights and Duties of States, which provides, 'The protection, preservation and enhancement of the environment

[52] *Ibid.*, at 821.

[53] Case Concerning the Gabcikovo-Nagymaros Project (*Hungary* v. *Slovakia*), (1997) ICJ Rep 7, para. 140.

[54] Oral argument of 22 September 2009 in *Case Concerning Pulp Mills on the River Uruguay (Argentina* v. *Uruguay)*, available at www.icj-cij.org/docket/files/135/15447.pdf, at 47–48.

[55] *United States – Import Prohibition of Certain Shrimp and Shrimp Products*, WT/DS58/AB/R, 6 November 1998, para. 154 and note 147.

[56] In addition to those nonbinding instruments discussed here, see also C. Redgwell, *Intergenerational Trusts and Environmental Protection* (1999) 119, for others.

for the present and future generations is the responsibility of all States. All States shall endeavour to establish their own environmental and developmental policies in conformity with such responsibilities'.[57]

Humankind's 'solemn responsibility to protect and improve the environment for present and future generations' is declared in Principle 1 of the *Stockholm Declaration* of 1972.[58] Principle 5 further requires that humankind must 'guard against the danger of [the] future exhaustion' of the non-renewable resources of the earth, ensuring that the benefits of these resources are shared by all humans. Principle 3 of the *Rio Declaration*, coming out of the 1992 UN Conference on Environment and Development (UNCED), provides that 'the right to development must be fulfilled so as to equitably meet developmental and environmental needs of present and future generations'. Article 11 of the *Vienna Declaration* of the World Conference on Human Rights uses very similar language.[59] UNCED also produced a set of *Principles for a Global Consensus on the Management, Conservation and Sustainable Development of All Types of Forest*, including the principle that '[f]orest resources and forest lands should be sustainably managed to meet the social, economic, ecological, cultural and spiritual needs of present and future generations'.[60] The *Copenhagen Declaration*, which accompanied the *Programme of Action of the World Summit for Social Development*, declares that states are to fulfil their 'responsibility for present and future generations by ensuring equity among generations'.[61] In addition, UN General Assembly Resolution 35/8, of 30 October 1980, proclaimed 'the historical responsibility of States for the preservation of nature for present and future generations'.[62] Similarly, Resolution 43/53 was concerned with the 'protection of the global climate for present and future generations'.[63] This phrase has since headed a series of further General Assembly resolutions, such as Resolution 60/197 of 22 December 2005 and 61/201 of 20 December 2006.

Principle 4 of the *Draft Principles on Human Rights and the Environment* by the UN Sub-Commission on Prevention of Discrimination and Protection of Minorities recognises a right to an environment 'adequate to meet equitably the needs

57 14 ILM 251 (1975), Art. 30. G.A. Res. 3281 (xxix), UN GAOR 29 th Sess, Supp No 31 (12 Dec 1974) 50.

58 Declaration of the United Nations Conference on the Human Environment, (1972), UN Doc. A/CONF.48/14/Rev.1 (1973), reprinted in 11 ILM 1416 (1972).

59 Vienna Declaration and Programme of Action of the World Conference on Human Rights, (1993), UN Doc. A/CONF.157/23.

60 Non-Legally Binding Authoritative Statement of Principles for a Global Consensus on the Management, Conservation and Sustainable Development of All Types of Forest, August 14, 1992, UN Doc. A/CONF.151/26 (Vol. III), Principle 2(b).

61 World Summit for Social Development Programme of Action, UN Doc. A/CONF.166/9 (1995), Part B, Art. 26(b).

62 Historical Responsibility of States for the Preservation of Nature for Present and Future Generations, G.A. Res. 35/8, UN GAOR, 1980.

63 Protection of Global Climate for Present and Future Generations of Mankind, G.A. Res. 43/53, UN GAOR, 1988.

of present generations . . . that does not impair the rights of future generations to meet equitably their needs'.[64] This is one of the few formulations in an (albeit non-binding) international legal instrument to explicitly employ the language of 'rights' of future generations. In 1994, for instance, UNESCO considered a draft *Universal Declaration of Human Rights for Future Generations*, but the rights language was found to be too controversial for its adoption.[65] An amended version, called the *Declaration on the Responsibilities of the Present Generation Towards Future Generations*, was eventually adopted in 1997. Its preamble asserts the necessity of promoting 'inter-generational solidarity for the perpetuation of humankind'. The declaration sets out a broadly worded statement entrusting the present generation with the responsibility of 'ensuring that the needs and interests of future generations are fully safeguarded'.[66] Environmental issues are covered in two articles that note each generation's temporary inhabitation of the Earth and remind present generations of their responsibility to avoid irreversibly damaging the planet. Interestingly, the declaration moves beyond environmental issues into matters such as the human genome and biodiversity, cultural diversity, peace, and development. The preservation of the human genome is connected in Article 6 to respect for human dignity, and scientific and technological progress is subordinated to the preservation of humans and other species. Present generations are called on to identify, protect, and safeguard cultural heritage and to transmit it to future generations. Looking ahead to the discussion of international criminal law in Section 6 of this chapter, it should be highlighted that Article 9, paragraph 1 of the declaration encourages present generations to 'learn to live together in peace', whereas paragraph 2 provides that present generations should avoid exposing future generations to the harmful consequences of armed conflicts. The development of present generations, through 'a fair and prudent use of available resources for the purpose of combating poverty', is seen as a tool for ensuring the development of future generations. The declaration also recognises the role of education in fostering intergenerational equity when directed to teaching 'peace, justice, understanding, tolerance and equality for the benefit of present and future generations'.

The Food and Agriculture Organisation Council recently adopted Voluntary Guidelines aiming to 'provide practical guidance to countries in their

64 This is a draft text attached as Ann. I, to the Review of Further Developments in Fields with which the Sub-Commission has been concerned, Human Rights and the Environment: Final Report prepared by Mrs. Fatma Zohra Ksentini, Special Rapporteur, UN Doc. E/CN. 4/Sub.2/1994/9 (1994), Principle 4. This body, now known as the UN Sub-Commission on the Promotion and Protection of Human Rights, comprises 26 experts elected by the UN Commission on Human Rights (which is composed of 53 elected tates).

65 The Responsibilities of the Present Generations towards Future Generations: Preliminary Draft Declaration, (1995), UN Doc. 28 C/INF.20.

66 Art. 1.

implementation of... the right to adequate food'.[67] The guidelines suggest wide-ranging measures, including encouraging corporate social responsibility, development of small-scale local markets, strengthening domestic law to grant access by women heads of households to poverty reduction programmes, promoting agricultural research, establishing food safety programmes, and education on balanced diets.[68] Guideline 8E also encourages states to 'consider specific national policies, legal instruments, and supporting mechanisms... to ensure the possibility for increased, sustainable food production for present and future generations', invoking intergenerational equity obligations.

A nonbinding attempt at codification of the principle of intergenerational equity was undertaken by the Experts Group on Environmental Law of the World Conference on Environment and Development (WCED).[69] Linking to the Stockholm Declaration that also arose from the WCED, Article 2 of the Experts Group's codification would require states to 'ensure that the environment and natural resources are conserved and used for the benefit of present and future generations'. This basic obligation is coloured in by the other 20 articles in the codification. Another attempt to set out a scheme of implementation for the principle is represented by the Goa Guidelines on Intergenerational Equity.[70] These comprise seven principles:

1) representation by states not only of present but also future generations;
2) designation of ombudsmen or commissioners for protecting the interests of future generations;
3) monitoring systems for cultural and natural resources;
4) conservation assessments giving particular attention to long-term consequences;
5) measures to ensure use of renewable resources and ecological systems on a sustainable basis;
6) commitment to scientific and technical research to advance the purposes set out above; and
7) programmes of education and learning at all social levels and age groups especially the young generations.[71]

67 Food and Agriculture Organisation, *Voluntary Guidelines to Support the Progressive Realization of the Right to Adequate Food in the Context of National Food Security*, adopted by the 127th Session of the FAO Council, November 2004, para. 6 of Section I.

68 *Ibid.*, Guidelines 4, 7, 8, 9, and 11.

69 Ann. 1: Summary of Proposed Legal Principles for Environmental Protection and Sustainable Development Adopted by the WCED Experts Group on Environmental Law, World Commission on Environment and Development, *Our Common Future* (1987).

70 See Brown Weiss, *supra* note 14, at App. A.

71 *Ibid.*, at 294.

## 6. INTERGENERATIONAL EQUITY IN INTERNATIONAL CRIMINAL LAW

The discussion so far has focused first on establishing some basic concepts of intergenerational equity and reviewing some problems with these concepts, and then on identifying the adoption of these concepts in various areas and kinds of international law. This section turns to examine one area of international law more closely, namely international criminal law (ICL).

International criminal law is here understood, following Cassese, as a body of international rules designed to proscribe certain categories of conduct (most relevantly including genocide, war crimes, and crimes against humanity), together with the international institutional mechanisms for prosecuting individuals who engage in such conduct.[72] The focus here is on the constitutive instruments and jurisprudence of the International Criminal Tribunal for the former Yugoslavia (ICTY), the International Criminal Tribunal for Rwanda (ICTR), and the International Criminal Court (ICC).

Intergenerational equity is arguably at the heart of the international criminal justice system. The preamble of the Rome Statute, the foundational instrument of the ICC, recognises that the court, with 'jurisdiction over the more serious crimes of concern to the international community as a whole', has been established 'for the sake of present and future generations'. This recognition is reflected in the objectives of ICL, which extend beyond those commonly recognised in domestic criminal law systems, such as retribution and deterrence. ICL purports to pursue a range of wider goals: the development of a historical record of a conflict, support for peace and reconciliation of fractured societies, prevention of international crimes not only through deterrence but also through public memorialisation, capacity building in domestic judicial systems, and a sense of closure for victims.[73]

ICL's objective in recording history has been described as aiming to 'set down a permanent record of the crimes that will stand the test of time.'[74] International criminal tribunals have explicitly adopted this goal in at least some cases. The ICTY's judgment in *Krstic* displays a clear intention to record and memorialise the Srebrenica massacre and to discourage future denial of the crimes. The reports of the Nuremberg International Military Tribunals have played a similar role in combating denial. The judgements of the ICTR suggest its goal of labelling the events in Rwanda precisely as genocide – not some lesser crime – and preserving a public memory of this characterisation. Other judgements generally include much

[72] A. Cassese, *International Criminal Law* (2003), at 3.

[73] R. Cryer et al., *An Introduction to International Criminal Law and Procedure* (2010), at 22; M.C. Bassiouni, 'International Criminal Justice in Historical Perspective: The Tension between States' Interests and the Pursuit of International Justice', in A. Cassese (ed.), *The Oxford Companion to International Criminal Justice* (2009), at 140. For arguments that this multiplicity of goals creates practical and logical problems for ICL, see M. Damaska, 'Problematic Features of International Criminal Procedure', in Cassese, *ibid.* at 175.

[74] Cryer, *ibid.* at 31. See generally R. A. Wilson, *Writing History in International Criminal Trials* (2011).

detail on the background of the crimes in question and the social circumstances surrounding them.

Admittedly, there are certain problems inherent in the idea that a court of law, issuing a single, static judgment created under particular legalistic processes, should serve as the sole authoritative locus of history on a set of events.[75] However, these efforts to preserve history by international criminal tribunals serve important functions for the future generations of people both inside and outside the societies affected by the crimes. For those in the society most directly affected, ICL can help create a narrative that will be drawn on in postconflict reconstruction to provide for a more stable future.[76] For those on the outside, ICL records significant lessons to be learned by later generations, preserving the darker corners of the past for the ultimate benefit of the future. Some have suggested, for instance, that the lack of public recognition of the Armenian genocide in the early 20th century paved the way for Hitler to proceed with his policies against the Jews, similarly confident that no public repercussions would result.[77]

As noted, postconflict reconstruction and reconciliation are themselves further expressed goals of ICL. It is said that there can be no peace without justice; ICL thus aims to provide a sense of justice such that those victimised, or their families and descendants, can begin to reconcile themselves to live alongside perpetrators and *their* descendants.[78] Only with reconciliation, it is suggested, can come a return to or a new commitment to democracy and pluralism, a gradual demise of ethnic and religious hatred, and the return of refugees.[79] ICL reflects this goal in several ways. The preamble of the ICC Statute recognises that international crimes 'threaten the peace, security and well-being of the world'. In the *Nikolic* case, the ICTY acknowledged that it aimed to 'contribute to the restoration and maintenance of peace through criminal proceedings'.[80] Similarly, in *Plavsic*, the ICTY noted that 'the acknowledgment and full disclosure of serious crimes are very important when establishing the truth in relation to such crimes. This, together with acceptance of responsibility for the committed wrongs, will promote reconciliation.'[81] This goal of reconciliation has clear links to the future, because in many cases where a present generation is so fractured, it will only be future generations that will enjoy most fully the dividends of the peace and reconciliation that ICL aims to bring about.

Certainly, the objective of deterrence has one eye to the future, because it premises criminal responsibility on the desire to avoid further commission of crimes by others.

75 For instance, there is a risk of distortion of history to suit the political purposes of the trial. See Cryer, *supra* note 73, at 32 and sources there cited.

76 M. Osiel, *Mass Atrocity, Collective Memory and the Law* (1997).

77 A. Cassese, 'Reflections on International Criminal Justice', (1998) 61 Modern L. Rev. 1, at 2.

78 *Ibid*, at 6.

79 *Ibid.*, at 9.

80 *Momir Nikolic* ICTY T. Ch. I 2.12.2003 para. 60.

81 *Plavsic* ICTY T. Ch. III 27.2.2003 para. 80.

Paragraph 5 of the preamble to the ICC Statute demonstrates some acceptance that deterrence does play a role in international criminal law in its acknowledgement of the parties' determination to 'put an end to impunity for the perpetrators of these crimes and thus to contribute to the prevention of such crimes'. However, the international criminal justice system has been unwilling to give deterrence too much prominence as an underpinning rationale.[82] The Appeals Chamber of the ICTY in *Nikolic*, for instance, has expressed the hope that the ICTY and other international courts 'are bringing about the development of a culture of *respect* for the rule of law and not simply the *fear* of the consequences of breaking the law'.[83] In the ICTY's view, the accused persons brought before it should not be viewed merely as instruments used to send a message to society and to achieve the goal of the establishment of the rule of law. In any case, the presently limited and sporadic nature of international criminal justice may well restrict its ability to play a real deterrent role.[84]

A further objective of ICL, similar to deterrence in its attempt to affect a wider audience than the accused alone, is that of education and communication. On this view, part of the goal of ICL is to engage with the accused, together with the victims and with wider society, in an attempt to help them understand the gravity of the wrong done and to reaffirm the norm violated within the community in question.[85] This educative approach to the punishment of international crimes serves the interests not only of current societies but also of future generations, who may benefit from any present reduction in the large-scale criminal conduct prohibited by international law.

In conjunction with these forward-looking general aims of ICL, specific crimes prohibited within the substance of ICL serve to protect future generations in important ways. For instance, one class of war crimes outlawed under the Rome Statute consists of crimes against the enemy or civilians using prohibited methods of warfare, including 'intentionally launching an attack in the knowledge that such attack will cause . . . widespread, long-term and severe damage to the natural environment'.[86] No case has yet arisen in which this crime has been alleged; indeed, the requirement that damage be 'widespread, long-term and severe' may limit the cases in which this crime can be proved.[87] However, this requirement also

[82] See the Appeal Chamber in the *Tadic* sentencing appeal: deterrence 'must not be accorded undue prominence in the overall assessment of the sentences to be imposed on persons convicted by the International Tribunal'. *Tadic* ICTY A.Ch. 26.1.2000 para. 48.

[83] *Momir Nikolic* ICTY T. Ch. I 2.12.2003 paras. 89–90.

[84] Bassiouni, *supra* note 73, at 140; P. Akhavam, 'Beyond Impunity: Can International Criminal Justice Prevent Future Atrocities' (2001) 95 AJIL 7.

[85] Cryer, *supra* note 73, at 29.

[86] Art. 8(2)(b)(iv), ICC Statute.

[87] S. Jodoin, 'Crimes against Future Generations: Implementing Intergenerational Justice through International Criminal Law', (2010) 10 Intergen. Just. Rev. 10, at 11.

demonstrates that the crime takes intergenerational equity as its premise, aiming to prevent methods of warfare that cause effects persisting long after the conflict itself has ended and that reach not only to present disputants but also to future generations.

The international crime of genocide seems the clearest example of intergenerational equity at work within the substance of ICL. Genocide revolves around acts committed 'with intent to destroy, in whole or in part, a national, ethnical, racial or religious group'.[88] Obviously, the wholesale (or even partial) destruction of a community has significant ramifications for the future generations of that community. In addition, the definition of genocide goes beyond blatant killing of populations to include acts such as 'causing serious bodily or mental harm to members of the group' and 'deliberately inflicting on the group conditions of life calculated to bring about its physical destruction in whole or in part'.[89] As discussed at various points earlier in this chapter, the ability of future generations to provide for themselves is dependent on the situation and actions of present generations.[90] Thus, acts that place significant portions of communities under physical or mental hardship, on a scale large enough to constitute genocide for the purposes of ICL, are highly likely to have an impact upon the future generations of those communities, even if the acts do not destroy the communities outright. From this perspective, intergenerational equity is at the heart of prosecutions for genocide within the ICL regime.

Another major class of crime falling within the purview of ICL is crimes against humanity. As defined in the Rome Statute, this class includes a range of acts (such as murder, extermination, enslavement, torture, rape, and persecution) 'committed as part of a widespread or systematic attack directed against any civilian population'.[91] Similarly to the case of genocide, the 'widespread or systematic' nature of a crime against humanity infuses an intergenerational element. Activity on a scale large enough to amount to a crime against humanity will almost inevitably have effects on the self-image and psyche of the (surviving) members of the victimised community. Without public recognition and condemnation of the crimes, and the processes of justice that ICL seeks to bring, these effects on the victimised community may well fester and be transmitted to future generations. These future generations then remain cursed by their history and the unfinished business of the crimes committed against their ancestors. In declaring such acts as international crimes and in providing for mechanisms to prosecute those who perpetrate them, ICL manifests its concern for intergenerational equity.

88 Art. 6, ICC Statute.
89 Art. 6(b) and (c), ICC Statute.
90 See also Brown Weiss, *supra* note 17, at 201.
91 Art. 7, ICC Statute.

## 7. CONCLUSION

Some countries make explicit or implicit references to intergenerational rights and equity in their constitutions.[92] These references typically come in three forms: references in the preamble to responsibility for future generations, environmental and ecological provisions in the main constitutional text requiring the prudent use and preservation of natural resources, and financial provisions in the main text limiting public borrowing or requiring balanced budgets. Although these constitutional provisions are expressed in vague terms and are difficult to enforce directly, they serve at least as obligations of guidance for the legislative and executive branches of government.[93] However, many of the problems that are most closely engaged by intergenerational equity (such as climate change, war, or poverty) are essentially global problems that call for global solutions.[94] Domestic constitutional provisions may help rein in profligacy specific to certain jurisdictions and are certainly commendable in encouraging long-term policy thinking, but ultimately an international (or internationally co-ordinated) legal approach will be necessary to meet the full philosophical stringencies of the concept.

Indeed, many international legal materials dealing with sustainable development already adopt intergenerational equity as an integral feature, particularly in international laws dealing with environmental protection, resource utilisation, and socioeconomic development. This chapter demonstrates that international criminal law can be added to this list, with many of its objectives and substantive elements tied to concern for future generations. Although in the international forum as in the domestic, the application of intergenerational equity is difficult to define in terms of scope, the objective behind the term is clear. Regular references to the interests and needs of 'present and future generations' in contemporary international legal instruments dealing with sustainable development, as well as both explicit and implicit references within international criminal law, suggest that the international community has come to recognise both the use of natural resources and the resolution of large-scale conflicts in an intertemporal context.

There are few formulations of the concept that adopt the language of 'rights' of future generations. Most texts and judgements refer instead to future generations' interests or needs or, in the case of international criminal law, place obligations upon present generations (without necessarily acknowledging any corresponding right on behalf of future generations) to act or to refrain from acting in particular ways to preserve the benefit of the Earth and its human communities for the future. The language of rights may, nevertheless, remain relevant to intergenerational equity.

92 J. Tremmel, 'Establishing Intergenerational Justice in National Constitutions' in J. Tremmel (ed.), *Handbook of Intergenerational Justice* (2006).

93 *Ibid.*, at 204.

94 E. Brown Weiss, *Environmental Change and International Law: New Challenges and Dimensions* (1992), at 398.

For instance, fulfilment of certain socioeconomic rights attaching to disadvantaged segments of the present generation will have a large beneficial impact on future generations.

Regardless of the specific concept or language drawn on to underpin the notion of intergenerational equity, however, it is clear that manifestations of the notion can be located in international law beyond its original home of environmental protection and sustainable development, in the relatively new regime of international criminal law. ICL is a means of dealing with the crimes of the past, with a view to the future.

# 10

# Corporate Liability and Complicity in International Crimes

*Ken Roberts*

## 1. INTRODUCTION

Corporations have long been involved in natural resource extraction and other business activities in conflict-affected countries and so-called weak governance zones.[1] This involvement often brings them into contact with local political and military authorities, rebel groups, other businesses, and powerful warlords. Some of these groups and individuals and those associated with them, including corporations, have in turn been accused of serious human rights abuses and other violations of international law. Increasingly, international lawmakers are beginning to focus on the various roles played by corporations and their officers in such crimes and the possibilities for holding them liable for their actions. Indeed, NGOs, commentators, and some authorities have been tracking such cases for years with a view to ensuring that redress is secured for victims and that the alleged abuses remain in the public eye.[2]

[1] Organisation for Economic Co-operation and Development (OECD), 'OECD Risk Awareness Tool for Multinational Enterprises in Weak Governance Zones' (2006). See also OECD, 'OECD Guidelines for Multinational Enterprises: Text, Commentary and Clarifications' (2001); and International Committee of the Red Cross, 'Business and International Humanitarian Law: An Introduction to the Rights and Obligations of Business Enterprises under International Humanitarian Law' (2006) Geneva.

[2] For examples, see Corporate Legal Accountability Portal of Business and Human Rights Resource Centre (www.business-humanrights.org/LegalPortal/Home); Red Flags (www.redflags.info); the *Anvil Mining/Kilwa Case* reviewed by Rights and Accountability in Development (http://raid-uk.org/index.php); and the use of Caterpillar bulldozers for possible human rights violations in Occupied Palestinian Territories, Human Rights Watch (see, e.g., www.hrw.org/en/news/2004/11/21/israel-caterpillar-should-suspend-bulldozer-sales). See also I. Khan, 'Understanding Corporate Complicity: Extending the Notion Beyond Existing Laws', AI Index: POL 34/0001/2006; ESCR-NET Corporate Accountability Working Group Joint NGO Submission, 'Consultation on Human Rights and the Extractive Industry' (2005) Geneva.

The views expressed herein are those of the author alone and do not necessarily reflect the views of the International Tribunal or the United Nations in general. The author would like to thank Norman Farrell, Reinhold Gallmetzer, and Gabriël Oosthuizen for their comments on an earlier draft of this chapter, and Klair O'Brien for her research assistance. The law described in this chapter is current as of May 2010.

They work to ensure that these issues do not disappear from our view or simply fail to ever garner such attention.

### 1.1. *Business in Countries of Conflict*

In 2003, the Prosecutor of the International Criminal Court (ICC), Luis Moreno Ocampo, gave notice to businesses operating in the eastern Democratic Republic of Congo (DRC) in particular, when he reported to the Assembly of State Parties of the ICC that,

> [a]ccording to information received, crimes reportedly committed in Ituri appear to be directly linked to the control of resource extraction sites. Those who direct mining operations, sell diamonds or gold extracted in these conditions, launder the dirty money or provide weapons could also be authors of the crimes, even if they are based in other countries.[3]

Corporate officers are now expressly considered to be legitimate targets for investigation by the ICC for crimes under its jurisdiction. Following an incident in the town of Kilwa, DRC, in October 2004, a criminal trial began in which three employees of the respected multinational corporation, Anvil Mining, faced war crimes charges.[4] This trial emphasised for businesses the reputational and other risks they face when operating in conflict-affected areas.

Various types of business activities, ranging from the financial to private security industries, are currently facing international scrutiny for potential violations of international law. However, business activities related to natural resource extraction are receiving the most attention, partly because of an increasingly documented connection between natural resources and armed conflict, culminating in violations of international law. Internal armed conflict in resource-rich countries is a major cause of human rights violations around the world.[5] For example, the participation of corporations in the 'blood diamond' trade came to international attention in the late 1990s and early 2000s. This trade helped finance civil wars in Angola, Sierra Leone, the DRC, and Liberia – wars that were characterised by widespread rape,

[3] L. M. Ocampo, 'Second Assembly of States Parties to the Rome Statute of the ICC: Report of the Prosecutor of the ICC 4' (2003).

[4] In the course of countering a local rebellion near the mine, DRC troops were alleged to have massacred about 30 civilians. The allegations against three Anvil Mining employees included that they made the company's plane available to fly the troops to the area, made the company's jeeps available to transport the troops to the massacre site and to bury the victims in a mass grave, and gave the troops food during the operation. In addition to the proceedings in the DRC, criminal and civil initiatives have arisen in three other jurisdictions as a result of this incident. See http://raid-uk.org/work/anvil_dikulushi.htm.

[5] A. Ganesan and A. Vines, 'Engine of War: Resources, Greed and the Predatory State', (2004) *Human Rights Watch World Report* (www.hrw.org/legacy/wr2k4/14.htm#_Toc58744963).

amputations, and the use of child soldiers.[6] Gold mining companies have provided financial and logistical support to rebel groups known for committing human rights atrocities in the DRC's Ituri region. Dutch businessman Guus van Kouwenhoven obtained timber rights in exchange for providing weapons to Charles Taylor, then president of Liberia.[7] Charles Taylor is currently on trial for crimes against humanity before the Special Court for Sierra Leone (SCSL).

The UN has recognised the need to monitor the activities of corporations where those corporations are implicated in serious violations of international law. For example, in June 2000, the Security Council requested that the UN Secretary-General establish an expert panel on the illegal exploitation of natural resources and other forms of wealth of the DRC. The Report of the Panel of Experts concluded that 'illegal exploitation of the mineral and forest resources of the Democratic Republic of the Congo is taking place at an alarming rate. Two phases can be distinguished: mass-scale looting and the systematic and systemic exploitation of natural resources.'[8] The panel established that 'top army commanders and business men on the one hand, and government structures on the other, have been the engines of this systematic and systemic exploitation'.[9] The panel found further that

> [t]he role of the private sector in the exploitation of natural resources and the continuation of the war has been vital. A number of companies have been involved and have fuelled the war directly, trading arms for natural resources. Others have facilitated access to financial resources, which are used to purchase weapons. Companies trading minerals, which the panel considered to be 'the engine of the conflict in the Democratic Republic of Congo' have prepared the field for illegal mining activities in the country.[10]

The mandate of the Panel of Experts was subsequently renewed with further reports drawing similar conclusions.[11] The conclusions of the Panel of Experts were

6 W. C. Wanless, 'Corporate Liability for International Crimes under Canada's Crimes against Humanity and War Crimes Act', (2009) 7 JICJ, at 204. Wanless refers to the Amnesty International news release, 'Blood Diamonds Are Still a Reality' (www.amnesty.org/en/news-and-updates/feature-stories/blood-diamonds-are-still-reality-20070123), stating that an estimated 3.7 million people died in the conflicts fuelled by blood diamonds.

7 Wanless, *supra* note 6, at 204.

8 Report of the Panel of Experts on the Illegal Exploitation of Natural Resources and Other Forms of Wealth in the Democratic Republic of Congo, UN Doc. S/2001/357 (2001), para. 4.

9 *Ibid.*, para. 6.

10 *Ibid.*, para. 215. The panel further concluded at para. 184 that the increase in revenues of the Rwandan army from coltan sales was facilitated by two key factors: '(a) the passive role of some private companies such as Sabena and SDV for the transport of coltan, Citibank for the financial transaction as the corresponding bank of BCDI. . . . (b) The rush to profit of some foreign companies that were ready to do business regardless of elements of unlawfulness and irregularities . . . '

11 See, e.g. Report of the Panel of Experts on the Illegal Exploitation of Natural Resources and Other Forms of Wealth in the Democratic Republic of Congo, UN Doc. S/2002/1146 (2002), para. 156: 'Restrictive measures nevertheless need to be taken vis-à-vis the role of companies and individuals involved in arms supply and resource plundering. The international and multinational dimension of these illegal activities is very important.'

eventually endorsed by the UN Security Council in Resolution 1856 (2008), in which all states, especially those in the Great Lakes region, were urged to 'take appropriate steps to end the illicit trade in natural resources, including if necessary through judicial means'.[12]

## 2. A FRAMEWORK FOR ACCOUNTABILITY

Against this background, we are seeing an increasing number of calls for corporations as well as corporate officers to be held to account. This chapter focuses on one aspect of the issue: the potential for corporate accountability under international criminal law. In this regard, it is necessary to distinguish between corporate entities as such (legal persons) and corporate officers (natural persons). To date, international criminal courts only have jurisdiction over natural persons.[13] Indeed, at the Rome conference on the establishment of the ICC, the possibility of including corporate liability within the jurisdiction of that court was expressly raised by France and effectively rejected when the proposal was withdrawn.[14] Although there have been calls for the provision of corporate criminal liability in the future,[15] the jurisdiction of international courts currently remains limited to the criminal liability of individuals.

Accordingly, this chapter focuses on the individual criminal liability of corporate officers for three categories of international crimes: crimes against humanity, war crimes, and genocide.[16] It reviews the basis for such liability as found in international criminal law applicable at international and hybrid criminal courts.

The term 'corporate officers' is used loosely to refer to employees as well as other close associates, including long-standing contractors, of large, often multinational, corporations. This chapter briefly examines modes of liability that have been or may be used in the future to link corporate officers to the international crimes in which they are most likely to be implicated. It is common for such officers to incur liability for indirect forms of involvement in criminal activity, rather than as direct

See also, para. 175: '[B]y contributing to the revenues of the elite networks, directly or indirectly, those companies and individuals contribute to the ongoing conflict and to human rights abuses.'

[12] UN Doc. S/RES/1856 (2008), para. 21.

[13] See, e.g., Rome Statute of the ICC, UN Doc. A/CONF. 183/9 (1998); 2187 UNTS 90, Arti. 25(1): 'The Court shall have jurisdiction over natural persons pursuant to this Statute.' Neither the ad hoc tribunals (ICTY and ICTR) nor the hybrid tribunals set up to try international crimes (SCSL, ECCC) provide jurisdiction over legal persons.

[14] Wanless, *supra* note 6, at 201–02.

[15] See, e.g., 'Corporate Complicity & Legal Accountability: Report of the International Commission of Jurists Expert Legal Panel on Corporate Complicity in International Crimes', (2008) ICJ, vol. 2 ('ICJ Report'), at 56. None of the proposed amendments to the Rome Statute considered at the review conference of the ICC in 2010 concerned an expansion of jurisdiction to cover legal persons.

[16] The ability to hold a natural person to account for certain behaviour under international criminal law will necessarily depend on whether such behaviour is criminalised. Although it is undoubtedly arguable that there are certain lacunae in the current framework of international crimes, for example with respect to environmental crimes, this chapter does not address this question and takes as its departure point crimes currently existing under international criminal law.

perpetrators.[17] This working assumption guides the selection of relevant modes of liability examined later.

## 3. LIABILITY FOR CORPORATE OFFICERS UNDER INTERNATIONAL LAW

The possibility of holding corporate officers liable as accomplices in some form has been clear since the Second World War. The Nuremberg and related national military tribunals in Germany represented the first international judicial efforts to both try and convict individual businessmen. The Nuremberg Judgement expressly recognised the importance of corporations in the conflict by referring to the 'organizations of German business as instruments of economic mobilization for war'.[18] Individual trials conducted subsequently by military tribunals involved businessmen who were found to have, on behalf of their employers, participated (usually in an accomplice role) in a number of crimes, including forced labour, plunder and the exploitation of property in occupied territories, and the violation of laws and customs of war by providing poison gas for use in the concentration camps.[19] These cases stood for the principle that civilians who assist in violations of international law are themselves also liable. Interestingly, the language of some of the Second World War cases tended to reference the actions of the corporate entities before proceeding to find individual liability, as if individuals were being tried as proxies for the corporations themselves.[20]

[17] This of course does not exclude the possibility that a corporate officer or someone engaged by a corporation (for example, an employee of a contracted private military or security company) may personally physically commit a violation of international law, such as murder or rape. However, insofar as the physical perpetrator of any crime may expect to be prosecuted, this falls outside the scope of consideration of this chapter.

[18] See ICJ Report, *supra* note 15, at 14.

[19] In *USA* v. *Krupp et al.*, U.S. Military Tribunal at Nuremberg (1948) TWC, vol. 9, 1327–484 ('*Krupp Case*'), Krupp and ten directors of the eponymous German industrial conglomerate were convicted of, inter alia, war crimes for spoliation and plunder of public and private property in occupied territory, and war crimes and crimes against humanity for employing prisoners of war, foreign civilians, and concentration camp inmates in arms factories under inhumane conditions. In *Re Röchling et al.*, General Tribunal of the Military Government of the French Zone of Occupation in Germany (GT), 30 June 1948; Superior Military Government Court of the French Occupation Zone in Germany (SMC), 25 January 1949, Hermann Röchling of Röchling Enterprises was convicted of, inter alia, plunder and spoliation of factories and machineries in the Alsace Lorraine, deportation and forced labour. In *UK* v. *Tesch et al.* (1947) 1 L.R.T.W.C. 93 (British. Military Court) ('*Zyklon B Case*'), at 93–101, two defendants were convicted for the war crime of supplying poison gas used for the extermination of allied nationals interned in concentration camps, knowing that the gas was to be so used. In *USA* v. *Flick et al.*, U.S. Military Tribunal at Nuremberg (1947) TWC, vol. VI, 1187–223 ('*Flick Case*'), Flick and two other leading officials of his industrial enterprise were convicted of the unlawful seizure and exploitation of property in occupied France. In *Krauch et al.* (IG-Farben) U.S. Military Tribunal at Nuremberg (1948); TWC, vol. 8, 1081–210, 12 defendants were convicted of plunder and/or slave labour charges.

[20] Wanless, *supra* note 6, at 217.

Today, the ad hoc UN international criminal tribunals for the former Yugoslavia (ICTY) and Rwanda (ICTR), the hybrid SCSL, and the Extraordinary Chambers in the Courts of Cambodia (ECCC), as well as the permanent ICC, all have jurisdiction over various modes of liability that would allow (where other jurisdictional requirements are met) the prosecution of corporate officers for international crimes. Indeed, although the ICTY has focused on military and political leaders, a number of cases prosecuted at the ICTR have involved businessmen.[21] The modes of liability found in these jurisdictions and examined in greater detail in this chapter are as follows:

1. aiding and abetting;
2. joint criminal enterprise/co-perpetration; and
3. superior responsibility.

Before considering each of these in turn, the chapter addresses a few general concerns that are inevitably relevant when assessing the criminal accountability of corporate officers.[22]

The first general issue relates to crimes committed at a geographically distant location. Remoteness might not be an issue in all crimes involving corporate officers, but it is in many, especially for claims against senior executives and managers. The concern over how to attribute such crimes to corporate officers based far away in the same country or in another country has featured in a number of the trials at the ad hoc and hybrid courts. The best examples are the trials of Slobodan Milosevic at the ICTY and Charles Taylor at the SCSL, in which both men were charged with crimes in countries that they did not govern at the time the crimes were committed.[23]

The second general issue concerns the *mens rea*, or mental element, of the crime. More specifically, where it can be demonstrated that acts carried out by a corporate officer on behalf of the corporation ultimately contribute to or assist in the commission of a crime, the corporate officer's intentions or knowledge must meet a certain threshold before giving rise to criminal accountability. This chapter considers the *mens rea* of the corporate officer with respect to each of the modes of liability examined later.

[21] For example, Michel Bagaragaza was the director general of OCIR/Thé, the government office that controlled the tea industry in Rwanda. He was convicted of complicity in genocide for activities including the authorisation of vehicles and fuel from two tea factories being used to transport members of the *Interahamwe* for attacks, the provision of weapons to attackers, allowing weapons to be concealed at the tea factories, and allowing personnel from the factories to participate in the attacks: ICTR *Bagaragaza*, T. Ch., 5 November 2009.

[22] For analysis of some of the general issues set out here, see also N. Farrell, 'Attributing Criminal Liability to Corporate Actors: Some Lessons from the International Tribunals', for publication in JICJ (draft on file with the author).

[23] For information on the charges against Milosevic and Taylor, as well as other case-related information, see, respectively, the ICTY website (www.icty.org/cases/party/738/4) and the SCSL website (www.sc-sl.org/CASES/ProsecutorvsCharlesTaylor/tabid/107/Default.aspx).

A third issue, related to the first issue but beyond the scope of this chapter, concerns the practical realities of prosecuting international crimes and their relevance to prosecuting corporate actors at international courts: the difficulty of securing arrests, the size and nature of the cases, decision on what charges to proceed with, access to relevant evidence to link the high-ranking accused individual to the crimes on the ground, co-operation of a state that perceives its national interests as being common with the interests of an accused, and witness vulnerability, especially where witnesses live in the foreign country in which the crimes have been committed.

A fourth issue is the ability to prosecute corporate officers who may be shielded by their corporate structures. Corporations are often designed to protect business activities from tax, legal, and other liabilities in the host and other countries. Corporate officers are often shielded by corporate veils that make pinpointing individual liability difficult. The influential role of big businesses in global and national affairs may also mean a reluctance to prosecute them.

## 4. THE RELEVANT MODES OF LIABILITY

### 4.1. *Aiding and Abetting*

Perhaps the most obviously relevant form of liability is aiding and abetting, which has been generally described as a form of assistance provided to a principal perpetrator, with knowledge.[24]

Aiding and abetting is criminalised under the statutes of both the ad hoc tribunals (ICTY Article 7(1); ICTR Article 6(1)) and the hybrid courts (SCSL Statute Article 6(1); ECCC Article 29).[25] In addition, Article 25(3)(c) of the Rome Statute prohibits and condemns a person who, for the purpose of facilitating a crime within the jurisdiction of the ICC, 'aids, abets or otherwise assists in the commission or its attempted commission of a crime, including providing the means for its commission'.

The Appeals Chambers of the ICTY and ICTR have held that the *actus reus* of this mode of liability consists of acts directed to assist, encourage, or lend moral support to the perpetration of a specific crime and having a substantial effect upon the perpetration of the crime.[26] These acts may occur before, during, or after the act of the principal offender, who need not even be aware of the accomplice's contribution.[27] Although there is no *sine qua non* requirement, the jurisprudence requires that these actions must have a demonstrable 'substantial effect' on the

[24] See ICJ Report, *supra* note 15, at 17.

[25] ECCC Article 29 is titled 'Law on the Establishment of the Extraordinary Chambers in the Courts of Cambodia for the prosecution of crimes committed during the period of Democratic Kampuchea, 27 October 2004'.

[26] See *Prosecutor* v. *Blagojevic & Jokic*, Case No.: IT-02–60 A.Ch., 9 May 2007, para. 127 (*Blagojevic & Jokic*); *Prosecutor* v. *Ntagerura et al.*, Case No.: ICTR-99–46 A.Ch., 7 July 2006, para. 370 (*Ntagerura et al.*).

[27] See *Blagojevic & Jokic, supra*; *Ntagerura et al., ibid.*, para. 372. The acts of the principal offender that the accused is alleged to have aided and abetted must be established: *Prosecutor* v. *Kupreskic et al.*,

commission of the crime.[28] The substantial effect is to be demonstrated in any given case on the basis of a fact-based inquiry.[29] The requirement that the assistance in question be substantial does not exist in the Rome Statute, but it has been suggested that the same interpretation would be followed at the ICC.[30]

Clearly, the *actus reus* of aiding and abetting as defined before the ad hoc tribunals could encompass actions undertaken in the pursuit of business. Indeed, an International Commission of Jurists Panel of Experts (ICJ Panel of Experts) found numerous examples of acts of aiding and abetting in existing international jurisprudence to be relevant to contemporary private sector activities[31]:

- the provision of goods and services used in the commission of crimes;[32]
- the provision of information that leads to the commission of crimes;[33]
- the provision of personnel to commit crimes;[34]
- the provision of logistical assistance to commit crimes;[35]
- the procurement and use of products or resources (including labour) in the knowledge that the supply of these resources involves the commission of crimes;[36] and
- the provision of banking facilities so that the proceeds of crimes can be deposited.[37]

Beyond positive acts, it is important to note that an omission or a failure to act may also amount to substantial assistance that constitutes aiding or abetting if the omission/failure to act has a decisive effect on the crime, regardless of whether the accused was present at the scene of the crime.[38] Omissions may lead to liability where a legal duty to act exists.[39]

IT-95–16 A.Ch., 23 October 2001, para. 254. See also *Prosecutor* v. *Tadic*, Case No.: IT-94–1 A.Ch., 15 July 1999, para. 229.

28 *Blagojevic & Jokic*, *supra* note 26, para. 187.

29 *Ibid*., para. 134.

30 See ICJ Report, *supra* note 15, at 18, referring to Kai Ambos, in O. Triffterer (ed.), *Commentary on the Rome Statute* (1999) Art. 25, lines 15–18.

31 The Expert Legal Panel on Corporate Complicity in International Crimes was comprised of eight expert jurists asked in 2006 by the International Commission of Jurists to explore when companies and their officials could be held legally accountable under criminal and/or civil law when they are complicit in gross human rights abuses and to provide guidance as to the kind of situations prudent companies should avoid ICJ Report, *supra* note 15, at 19.

32 See, e.g., *Blagojevic & Jokic*, *supra* note 26, para. 134.

33 See, e.g., *Zyklon B Case*, 93–102; *Public Prosecutor* v. *Van Anraat*, LJN: BA4676, District Court, The Hague, 23 December 2005.

34 See, e.g., *Blagojevic & Jokic*, *supra* note 26, paras. 130–35.

35 *Prosecutor* v. *Brđanin*, Case No.: IT-99–36, T.Ch., 1 September 2004, paras. 571–83, 533; *Prosecutor* v. *Brđanin*, Case No.: IT-99–36 A.Ch., 3 April 2007, paras. 305–06.

36 See, e.g., *Farben Case*, at 1187; *Krupp Case*, at 1399; *Flick Case*, *supra* note 19, at 1202.

37 See, e.g., Trial of the Major War Criminals before the International Military Tribunal, Nuremberg, 14 November 1945–1 October 1946, vol. 1, at 305–6.

38 *Prosecutor* v. *Blaskic*, Case No.: IT-95–14 A.Ch., 29 July 2004 (*Blaskic*), para. 47.

39 *Prosecutor* v. *Brdanin & Talic*, Case No.: IT-99–36 A.Ch., 3 April 2007 (*Tadić* Appeal), para. 274; *Blaskic*, *supra*, paras. 47 and 663.

A failure to act when present during the commission of a crime can attract liability where it is demonstrated that the failure had a significant legitimising or encouraging effect on the principal perpetrator.[40] This was the case in the ICTR conviction of the commune mayor Akayesu for aiding and abetting sexual violence. Akayesu was found to have tacitly shown approval by allowing the violence to take place in the official commune office.[41] An individual may also be held liable even if located far from the actual crime scene if that person becomes aware of the crime and does nothing to stop it or mitigate it, despite having the power and (at least implicitly) the obligation to do so. For example, a military commander was held liable after he became aware that prisoners were being mistreated by soldiers on a recurring basis over a period of time, yet allowed the mistreatment to continue.[42] In another case, a government official in charge of medical facilities who deliberately denied adequate medical care to prisoners in detention facilities was deemed to have lent substantial assistance to their confinement under inhumane conditions.[43]

The ICJ Panel of Experts has suggested, while acknowledging that the idea is untested in court, that there could be situations in which a company official exercises such influence, weight, and authority over the principal perpetrators of a crime that they could take his or her silent presence as approval and even moral encouragement. Accordingly, if a company official has the power to prevent, stop, or mitigate the crime being committed and does not do so, that official could be guilty of aiding and abetting.[44] By the same token, if remotely located corporate officials become aware of repeated criminal behaviour over which they could have some influence and yet fail to take action, they could be guilty of aiding and abetting.

Perhaps most importantly for corporate officers, a single act or omission may be sufficient to attract criminal liability under international law:

> For example, in order to be criminally liable for aiding and abetting a crime against humanity . . . a company representative need not have participated in the entire plan or attack. It is sufficient if the company representative assists *one act* that takes place in the context of the widespread or systematic attack, or takes a calculated risk that the act being assisted may not be part of such an attack. So if a company offers trucks, the use of airstrips, fuel, helicopters, shelters or buildings or provides services that substantially assist the principal perpetrator to carry out *one act* such as killing, unlawful destruction of houses, rape or other acts of torture, and this act forms part of a widespread or systematic attack, there may be a basis for criminal liability.[45]

40 *Prosecutor* v. *Krnojelac*, Case No.: IT-97–25 T.Ch., 15 March 2002 (*Krnojelac*), para. 89.

41 *Prosecutor* v. *Akayesu*, Case No.: ICTR-96–4 T.Ch., 2 September 1998 (*Akayesu*), paras. 691–4.

42 *Prosecutor* v. *Aleksovski*, Case No.: IT-95–14/1 A.Ch, 24 March 2000 (*Aleksovski*), paras. 169 and 172.

43 *Prosecutor* v. *Simic et al.*, Case No.: IT-95–9 A.Ch., 28 November 2006 (*Simic*), para 134.

44 ICJ Panel of Experts, 20.

45 *Ibid.*, 12.

Of course, an act or omission on its own is insufficient to incur liability for aiding and abetting – the individual must also have the required *mens rea*. ICTY jurisprudence clearly requires knowledge that the acts performed assist the commission of the specific crime of the principal perpetrator.[46] It is not necessary to know which crime was intended by the principal perpetrator; rather it is sufficient that one is aware of one or more crimes that might occur and intends to facilitate the crime that eventually occurred.[47] Although an aider and abettor need not share the intent of the principal perpetrator, he or she must be aware of the essential elements of the crime that is ultimately committed, including the principal offender's state of mind and specific intent (where the crime in question is a specific intent crime such as genocide or persecution).[48] The knowledge required for aiding and abetting need not be explicitly expressed by the defendant, but can be inferred from all relevant circumstances on the basis of direct or circumstantial evidence.[49]

It is unclear whether the ICC standard for aiding and abetting, set out in Article 25(3)(c), will be interpreted differently because of the additional phrase requiring that a person act 'for the purpose of facilitating' the crime.[50] This extra requirement is not found in the jurisprudence of the ad hoc tribunals. Arguably, this phrase could be interpreted as requiring the aider and abettor to share the intent of the principal perpetrator of the crime, which would significantly raise the threshold of difficulty for establishing the requisite *mens rea*. Alternatively, the phrase could be interpreted as requiring an intention to assist in the crime, which is different from sharing the intent of the principal perpetrator, in addition to the knowledge requirement as it existed before the ad hoc tribunals.[51] The development of the ICC's jurisprudence on this point will certainly influence the extent to which this mode of liability can be applied in the context of corporate actors.

Understanding the ICTY jurisprudence's definition of the relevant *mens rea* (knowledge that the acts performed assist the commission of the specific crime of the principal perpetrator) is important insofar as it would act as a bar to certain arguments that might be anticipated from corporate officers. For example, where a corporate officer is aware that the equipment sold by his or her company is to be used for one of a number of crimes, uncertainty as to the exact crime intended

46 *Blagojevic & Jokic*, *supra* note 26, at para. 127.

47 *Blaskic*, *supra* note 38, at para. 50.

48 *Simic*, *supra* note 43, at para. 86; *Aleksovski*, *supra* note 42, at para. 162.

49 *Prosecutor* v. *Limaj*, Case No.: IT-03–66 T.Ch, 30 November 2005, para. 518; *Prosecutor* v. *Galic*, Case No.: IT-98–29 T.Ch., 5 December 2003, para. 172.

50 Art. 25(3)(c) states:

> In accordance with this Statute, a person shall be criminally responsible and liable for punishment for a crime within the jurisdiction of the Court if that person ... (c) For the purpose of facilitating the commission of such a crime, aids, abets or otherwise assists in its commission or its attempted commission, including providing the means for its commission.

See also ICJ Report, *supra* note 15, at 22.

51 Farrell, *supra* note 22.

would be irrelevant. Further, the fact that the principal intention was simply to carry out business is insufficient to avoid liability where it is demonstrable that the corporate officer had prior knowledge that the equipment sold would be used to commit crimes.[52]

There are many sources from which the requisite knowledge for aiding and abetting can be inferred, including the following: information readily available to the corporate officer at the time the assistance was provided, specific information provided to corporate officers (e.g. by NGOs and governments) that their company's products or services are being used to commit crimes, the existence of widespread knowledge that crimes are being committed using a company's goods or services, the context of the particular business transaction, and the past behaviour of the principal perpetrator and the duration and nature of his or her business relationship with the corporate officer.[53] Companies may want to examine their own activities carefully for such potential liability.

Clearly, aiding and abetting could therefore be part of a framework for holding corporate officers accountable for violations of international criminal law. The ICJ Expert Panel has taken the view that 'a company official who knows that his acts will facilitate, encourage or provide moral support for the commission of a crime and nonetheless proceeds, will be in grave danger of being held criminally accountable for aiding and abetting'.[54]

### 4.2. *Collective Criminal Action: Joint Criminal Enterprise/Co-Perpetration*

A second form of liability applicable to the actions of corporate officers is known variably as joint criminal enterprise (JCE) or co-perpetration. Although these two concepts are not identical, they both criminalise collective action that furthers a common illegal purpose.

JCE is relied upon greatly in the jurisprudence of the ad hoc tribunals and, in particular, the ICTY.[55] JCE has proven particularly useful in attaching accountability to political and military leaders for crimes committed on a large scale that are physically perpetrated by others. Although not expressly set out in the statutes of the ICTY and ICTR, JCE arises in the jurisprudence as a subsection of the concept of 'committing', found in Articles 7(1) and 6(1) of the respective statutes.

[52] ICJ Report, *supra* note 15, at 20–21.

[53] *Ibid.*, at 23–4.

[54] *Ibid.*, at 22.

[55] JCE was first set out by the ICTY Appeals Chamber in the *Tadić* Appeal, in which it was referred to as common purpose liability. After *Tadić*, JCE became the favoured nomenclature for this mode of liability as it was applied increasingly in cases involving senior military and political leaders. JCE has also been relied upon by the SCSL and the East Timor Special Panels for Serious Crimes. The Investigating Judges at the ECCC have also indicated that JCE may be used with respect to international crimes within the jurisdiction of that court.

There are three categories of JCE. In the first or 'basic' category, a plurality of persons acts pursuant to a common purpose and shares the intent to commit a crime. Each participant contributes in some way to the commission of the crime, and all share the same intent. The contribution need not be a *sine qua non* of the intended crime, but must assist or contribute to the execution of the common plan.[56] In ICTY cases, this category of JCE has commonly related to crimes associated with ethnic cleansing such as deportation, forcible transfer, and persecution; it has been used to link both military personnel and civilians to crimes.[57]

The second category of JCE, also known as 'systemic', is characterised by an organised system of ill treatment, the awareness of that system, and the active participation in enforcing that system. The accused must have personal knowledge of the system and intend to further its criminal purpose. This category has been most associated with crimes committed in the context of detention camps.[58]

The third or 'extended' category of JCE encompasses crimes derived from the basic JCE category, namely the natural and foreseeable consequences of the common-purpose crimes committed by other participants. For example, where the agreed common purpose is persecution and deportation, the jurisprudence of the ICTY has demonstrated that it is often the case that crimes such as murder and rape can take place as a natural and foreseeable consequence. Liability attaches where the crime is foreseeable and the perpetrator willingly took the risk.

At the ICC, Article 25(3)(d) creates liability where a person intentionally contributes to the commission of a crime by a group of people acting with a common purpose, either intending to further the crime or criminal purpose or knowing that the group intends to commit the crime. Although there is no reference here to JCE, commentators have suggested that this article embodies the first two categories of JCE, as interpreted at the ICTY, but not the extended category, which encompasses crimes that are the natural and foreseeable consequence of the common purpose.[59] The *Lubanga* pre-trial chamber at the ICC observed that Article 23(3)(d) is 'closely akin' to the concept of JCE, although the chamber characterised the article as a form of residual accessory liability rather than

56 *Tadić* Appeal, *supra* note 39, para 204.

57 See, e.g., *Prosecutor* v. *Krajisnik* & Plavsic, Case No.: IT-00–39&40, T.Ch., 27 September 2006, in which Krajisnik was convicted at trial of participation in a JCE the purpose of which was to ethnically recompose the territories targeted by the Bosnian-Serb leadership by drastically reducing the proportion of Bosnian Muslims and Bosnian Croats through expulsion, encompassing the crimes of deportation and forcible transfer.

58 See e.g. *Krnojelac, supra* note 40, concerning the warden of the KP Dom detention center in Foča; and *Prosecutor* v. *Kvočka et al.*, Case No.: IT-98–30 T.Ch., 2 November 2001, concerning a number of guards and one regular visitor to camps established in Omarska and Trnopolje villages and at the Keraterm factory in Prijedor.

59 R. C. Thompson, A. Ramasastry, and M. B. Taylor, 'Translating *UNOCAL*: The Expanding Web of Liability for Business Entities Implicated in International Crimes', (2009) 40 Geo. Wash. Int'l L. Rev 28.

a form of co-perpetration, the distinction being the element of control over the crime.[60]

In considering the applicability of a basic JCE category to corporate officers or leaders, it is important to note that the contribution of an individual participant need not be criminal in and of itself. Therefore, acts that might otherwise be considered legitimate business activities can also establish this liability, as demonstrated in the following example:

> [A] corporation and governmental authorities in an area engage in a common objective to forcibly remove local peoples from places where they have the lawful right to reside in order to facilitate the extraction of oil. The corporation engages in discussions with government leaders about how to remove these people from areas where the oil company intends to operate. The corporation provide the means and equipment necessary to carry out the unlawful displacement operations. Depending on the specific facts, an argument could be made that the corporate leaders and the leaders of the government forces share the common purpose to forcibly transfer the local population. The provision of means necessary to carry out the forcible displacement is a significant contribution to the execution of this criminal objective. Assuming the requisite elements for crimes against humanity or war crimes are evident, the conduct of these corporate and government leaders could be captured by this mode of liability.[61]

As noted by the author of this example, the difficulty in applying this mode of liability is obtaining the requisite proof that the various participants had a common criminal purpose and that they shared an underlying intent to commit the crimes to give effect to said criminal purpose. In practice, proving this shared intent on the part of the corporate officers or leaders would be much more difficult than proving the knowledge required for liability for aiding and abetting.[62]

Common purpose as defined under Article 25(3)(d) of the Rome Statute may provide a better reflection of the reality of the way in which business is conducted.[63] Under Article 25(3)(d)(i), if groups such as militia, government, or rebel leaders act with the purpose of committing a crime – for example, acting to create a buffer zones for resource extraction – and the corporate officer contributes to the commission of that crime with the aim of furthering that activity, liability could result (similar to the second category of JCE at the ad hoc tribunals). Using the same example, Article 25(3)(d)(ii) provides that even in the event the corporate officer does not intend to further the criminal activity but merely acts in the knowledge of the group's intent, he or she may be liable (in a manner more akin to aiding and abetting, for which

60 *Prosecutor* v. *Dyilo*, Decision on the Confirmation of Charges, Case No.: ICC-01/04–01/06, 29 January 2007 (*Dyilo*), paras. 337–38.

61 Farrell, *supra* note 22.

62 *Ibid.*, note 22.

63 *Ibid.*, note 22.

the *mens rea* element is not intent but knowledge that one's acts assist the principal perpetrator).

The Rome Statute also provides for another mode of liability for collective criminal action under Article 25(3)(a). This article refers to joint commission, pursuant to which liability attaches to an individual who commits a crime 'jointly with another or through another'. Committing an act jointly with another is interpreted as co-perpetration,[64] whereas committing an act through another is interpreted as perpetration-by-means.[65] However, co-perpetration is defined much more strictly than JCE under ICTY jurisprudence: one must prove that the co-perpetrators knowingly and intentionally provided essential contributions to a common plan that involves a criminal element. The essential role assigned to co-perpetrators requires that they be able to exercise functional control over the crime, such that they can frustrate the commission of the crime by not performing the role assigned to them.[66] It would accordingly be even more difficult to demonstrate joint commission with respect to corporate activities and, as such, although it remains part of the possible framework for accountability, it is less likely to be relied upon than aiding and abetting or even JCE.

### 4.3. *Superior Responsibility*

A third form of liability that may apply to corporate officers and leaders is superior/command responsibility.[67] This form of liability is found in the statutes of the ICTY (Article 7(3)), ICTR (Article 6(3)), SCSL (Article 6(3)), ECCC (Article 29), and ICC (Article 28). Although historically more often applied to military leaders, the liability of civilian superiors is also well established in international criminal law.[68]

It is important to note that superiors are not charged with the crime committed by their subordinate. Rather, superiors are charged with the failure to carry out their duty as superiors to prevent or punish the criminal conduct of their subordinates or others under their control.[69] Superiors maintain such a duty even where the criminal conduct of the subordinate would be for aiding and abetting a crime.[70]

Under the jurisprudence of the ad hoc tribunals there are three fundamental elements of this mode of liability.[71] First, a superior–subordinate relationship must

64 *Dyilo, supra* note 60, para. 322.

65 *Prosecutor v. Katanga & Chui*, Decision on the Confirmation of Charges, Case No.: ICC-01/04–01/07–717, 30 September 2008 ('*Katanga & Chui*'), para. 489ff.

66 *Dyilo, supra* note 60, para. 341; *Katanga & Chui, supra*, para. 525.

67 For a comprehensive view of this subject, see G. Mettraux, *The Law of Command Responsibility* (2009).

68 See, e.g., *Prosecutor* v. *Delalic et al.*, Case No.: IT-96–21 A.Ch., 20 February 2001 (*Delalic* Appeal), para. 195; *Prosecutor* v. *Musema*, Case No.: ICTR-96–13 T.Ch., 27 January 2000 (*Musema*), para. 148.

69 *Prosecutor* v. *Krnojelac*, Case No.: IT-97–25 A.Ch., 17 February 2003, para. 171.

70 *Prosecutor* v. *Oric*, Case No.: IT-03–68 T.Ch., 30 June 2006, paras. 301–5.

71 *Prosecutor* v. *Delalic et al.*, Case No.: IT-96–21 T.Ch., 16 November 1998 (*Delalic* Trial), para. 346; *Delalic* Appeal, *supra* note 68, paras. 189–98, 225–6, 238–9, 256, and 263.

exist. This relationship involves an effective exercise of power or control in either a de jure or de facto position of authority.

Second, the accused superior must know or have reason to know that the crime would occur, was occurring, or previously occurred. Thus, either actual or constructive knowledge is sufficient to establish the requisite *mens rea*. Direct or circumstantial evidence may be used to prove that the superior had actual knowledge.[72] To establish constructive knowledge, a superior must have received information that provided him or her with notice of the risk that offences would occur.[73] In this respect, wilful blindness by a superior may meet the threshold for requisite knowledge.[74] Proving a superior's negligence in failing to obtain relevant information may also be sufficient to demonstrate requisite knowledge where the negligence is so serious as to be tantamount to acquiescence or malicious intent.[75]

Third, the accused superior must fail to take necessary and reasonable measures to prevent the crime or punish the perpetrator thereof. The measures that a superior is required to take are limited to those within the scope of his or her power. A superior's scope of power is not limited to formal power, but a superior is not required to perform the impossible.[76] It is clear that civilian superiors are subject to different considerations than are military superiors in this regard, as clarified by the ICTY Appeals Chamber:

> [T]he concept of effective control for civilian superiors is different in that a civilian superior's sanctioning power must be interpreted broadly. It cannot be expected that civilian superiors will have disciplinary power over their subordinates equivalent to that of military superiors in an analogous command position. For a finding that civilian superiors have effective control over their subordinates, it suffices that civilian superiors, through their position in the hierarchy, have the duty to report whenever crimes are committed, and that, in light of their position, the likelihood that those reports will trigger an investigation or initiate disciplinary or criminal measures is extant. In situations of armed conflict, it is often the case that civilian superiors assume more power than that with which they are officially vested. In such circumstances, *de facto* authority may exist alongside, and may turn out to be more significant than, *de jure* authority. The capacity to sign orders will be indicative of some authority; it is necessary to look to the substance of the documents signed and whether there is evidence of them being acted upon.[77]

72 *Prosecutor* v. *Blaskic*, Case No.: IT-95–14 T.Ch., 3 March 2000 (*Blaskic* Trial), para. 308; *Prosecutor* v. *Aleksovski*, Case No.: IT-95–14/1 T.Ch, 25 June 1999 (*Aleksovski* Trial), para. 80; *Krnojelac* Trial, *supra* note 41, para. 94.

73 *Delalic* Appeal, *supra*, paras. 223 and 241.

74 *Ibid.*, para. 226.

75 *Akayesu*, *supra* note 41, 2 September 1998, paras. 479 and 489.

76 *Delalic* Trial, *supra* note 68, para. 395.

77 *Brđanin* Appeal, *supra* note 35, para. 281. See also *Musema*, *supra* note 68, para. 135: The 'superior's actual or formal power of control over his subordinates remains a determining factor in charging civilians with superior responsibility'.

The Rome Statute reinforces the idea that civilian superiors can be held criminally responsible, expressly distinguishing between military commanders (or persons effectively acting as a military commander) in Article 28(a) and other situations in Article 28(b), which states as follows:

> With respect to superior and subordinate relationships not described in paragraph (a), a superior shall be criminally responsible for crimes within the jurisdiction of the Court committed by subordinates under his or her effective authority and control, as a result of his or her failure to exercise control properly over such subordinates, where;
>
> (i) The superior either knew, or consciously disregarded information which clearly indicated, that the subordinates were committing or about to commit such crimes;
> (ii) The crimes concerned activities that were within the effective responsibility and control of the superior; and
> (iii) The superior failed to take all necessary and reasonable measures within his or her power to prevent or repress their commission or to submit the matter to the competent authorities for investigation and prosecution.

One notable difference in the treatment of military and civilian superiors in the Rome Statute is that, although military superiors may be liable where they 'should have known' that the forces over whom they have effective control were committing or about to commit a crime, civilian superiors may be held liable where they 'consciously disregarded information which clearly indicated' that subordinates were committing or about to commit a crime. The express choice of different wording in the two provisions seems to indicate an intention to create a higher threshold for civilian liability as superiors. However, even if the ICC Chambers interpret these provisions as imposing a higher threshold of civilian liability, the fact remains that civilians are to be held accountable for their actions as superiors.

Another difference between military and civilian superiors, as seen in the jurisprudence of the ad hoc tribunals, likely relates to the requisite proof of effective responsibility and control. For corporate leaders, in particular, the essential requirement is to establish a demonstrable duty to prevent and punish arising from their superior position. It will be possible to establish this duty if a corporate leader can be defined as a civilian superior, as analysed in the jurisprudence of the ad hoc tribunals.[78] Once this duty is established, a demonstrable breach thereof will lead to a finding of criminal responsibility.

In summary, although trials before international courts have focused on the liability of military leaders, examples of civilian leaders being tried and convicted for superior responsibility also exist in jurisprudence ranging from post–Second World

[78] *Brđanin* Appeal, *supra* note 35, para. 281; *Musema, supra* note 68, para. 135.

War military tribunals to the ICTR.[79] The doctrine of superior responsibility therefore may allow for findings of criminal responsibility to extend to corporate leaders where a subordinate corporate official is held responsible for a crime under international law. The possibility for the extended application of this doctrine may be of particular concern to companies that operate in conflict zones conducting private security functions, or to mining or resource companies that employ their own security personnel.[80]

## 5. OTHER ISSUES RELATED TO LIABILITY AT THE INTERNATIONAL LEVEL

A number of other issues affect the effectiveness of legal action at the international level. Although this chapter cannot give sufficient consideration to them all, it is important to briefly note a few such issues that merit further exploration. First, any case concerning corporate officer liability under international criminal law will inevitably involve the invocation of one or more defences by the accused. The defences most likely to be relevant in a business context are those of self-defence and duress.[81] Another issue that requires consideration before pursuing legal action is the selection of an appropriate forum that has the jurisdiction to hear international trials of corporate officers. Existing international fora have very specific and limited jurisdictions, including both geographic and temporal limitations. The ad hoc and hybrid tribunals are all slated to complete their activities within the next few years.

79 Post–Second World War, in the *Flick Case*, *supra* note 19, an official of the Flick industrial enterprise procured forced labour to meet increased production quota of freight cars; Flick knew and approved of these steps; the UN War Crimes Commission observed that the U.S. Military Tribunal found Flick accountable as a superior with a duty to prevent. See also the ICJ Panel of Experts, at 35. See also *Musema*, *supra* note 68, para. 880: The Trial Chamber found respecting Musema, a tea factory manager,

> it has been established beyond reasonable doubt that Musema exercised *de jure* authority over employees of the Gisovu Tea Factory while they were on Tea Factory premises and while they were engaged in their professional duties as employees of the Tea Factory, even if those duties were performed outside factory premises. The Chamber notes that Musema exercised legal and financial control over these employees, particularly through his power to appoint and remove these employees from their positions at the Tea Factory. The Chamber notes that Musema was in a position, by virtue of these powers, to take reasonable measures, such as removing, or threatening to remove, an individual from his or her position at the Tea Factory if he or she was identified as a perpetrator of crimes punishable under the Statute. The Chamber also finds that, by virtue of these powers, Musema was in a position to take reasonable measures to attempt to prevent or punish the use of Tea Factory vehicles, uniforms or other Tea Factory property in the commission of such crimes. The Chamber finds that Musema exercised *de jure* power and *de facto* control over Tea Factory employees and the resources of the Tea Factory.

80 ICJ Report, *supra* note 15, at 34.

81 *Ibid.*, at 44–8 for an overview of defences that might be expected to be advanced under international criminal law, including both those that would likely be recognised as valid (self-defence, insanity, duress/necessity) and numerous other arguments that do not constitute a proper defence.

Future prosecutions will therefore likely have to fit themselves within the jurisdiction of the ICC or a new forum will have to be created. As discussed earlier, the ICC Prosecutor has already announced that he will be investigating the possibility of trying corporate criminals.[82]

## 6. ALTERNATIVES TO INTERNATIONAL CRIMINAL PROSECUTION

Although existing international criminal law provides much of the necessary framework for the prosecution of crimes committed by civilian business people, two other possible approaches should also be considered.

First, criminal prosecutions at national levels are on the increase, with more countries incorporating international criminal legislation into their domestic laws.[83] Although many states have made such changes pursuant to the entering into force of the Rome Statute in July 2002, national obligations were created much earlier under the Genocide Convention, the 1949 Geneva Conventions, and 1977 Additional Protocols.[84] A number of countries already have specialised war crimes units.[85] Given the multinational character of many relevant corporations and their business activities, more than one country may have jurisdiction over a corporate crime that is connected to multiple locations. In some instances, the ICC may have concurrent jurisdiction. However, national investigators and prosecutors may

[82] *Supra* note 3. In 2003, Luis Moreno Ocampo, ICC Prosecutor, announced that the ICCwould consider investigating 'the financial aspects of the alleged atrocities' in the DRC as crucial to prevent future crimes and prosecute crimes already committed: 'Press Release of the Prosecutor', PIDS.009.2003-EN (2003):

> Various reports have pointed to links between the activities of some African, European and middle Eastern companies and the atrocities taking place in the Democratic Republic of Congo. . . . Their activities allegedly include gold mining, the illegal exploitation of oil, and the arms trade. There is general concern that the atrocities allegedly committed in the country may be fuelled by the exploitation of natural resources there and the arms trade, which are enabled through the international banking system. Although the specific findings of these reports have not been confirmed, the Prosecutor believes that investigation of the financial aspects of the alleged atrocities will be crucial to prevent future crimes and for the prosecution of crimes already committed.

[83] G. Oosthuizen, 'Another Regulatory Avenue: Criminal Liability of Business People for International Crimes', presentation at *Business and Fundamental Rights: The State Duty to Protect dnd Domestic Legal Reform* of the South African Institute for Advanced Constitutional, Public, Human Rights and International Law, Johannesburg, 3 November 2008 (on file with the author). Oosthuizen references past, current and possible prosecutions and related civil suits in the Netherlands, the DRC, Canada, Australia, and South Africa since the 1990s. See also G. Oosthuizen, 'Potential Individual Criminal Liability of Business People for Crimes against Humanity, War Crimes and Genocide under International Law', presentation at annual conference of British Institute of International and Comparative Law, London, 5 June 2009 (on file with the author).

[84] Wanless, *supra* note 6, at 203.

[85] R. Gallmetzer, 'Prosecuting Persons Doing Business with Armed Groups in Conflict Areas – The Strategy of the OTP and the OTP's Law Enforcement Network', for publication in JICJ (draft on file with the author).

face difficulties gathering evidence outside their borders, including gaining access to conflict zones generally and surmounting the legal and diplomatic hurdles of conducting investigations in other states.[86] In some cases, countries may not have a complete understanding of international criminal law, especially where it has only recently been incorporated into national criminal law.[87]

As a result, the ICC is likely to be most useful when playing a supporting role to prosecutions of corporate criminals at national levels. Such a role is contemplated within the mandate of the ICC where, pursuant to Article 93(10) of the Rome Statute, it may 'cooperate with and provide assistance to a State party conducting an investigation into or trial in respect of conduct which constitutes a crime within the jurisdiction of the Court or which constitutes a serious crime under national law of the requesting state'.

Such co-operation would respect the principle of complementarity, pursuant to which the ICC is not meant to replace domestic criminal jurisdictions regarding the investigation and prosecution of international crimes. Rather, the ICC is supposed to intervene if and when domestic jurisdictions are unwilling or unable to carry out the investigation and prosecution.[88] Co-operation would also maximise the effect of the ICC by engaging domestic resources.[89] Indeed, it has been suggested that the ICC's engagement with national courts in war crimes prosecutions may be its most enduring effect on the implementation of international criminal law.[90] The means by which to facilitate such assistance remain to be determined, but the development of a network of national law enforcement agencies and other partner organisations by the ICC appears to have already borne success, with a number of arrests by national authorities.[91]

In one well-known example of domestic criminal prosecution for international crimes, Frans van Anraat, a Dutch businessman, was charged in December 2004 by The Hague District Court as an accomplice to genocide and war crimes committed by Saddam Hussein.[92] Van Anraat brokered the delivery of thousands of tons of thiodiglycol (TDG), a substance used in the creation of mustard gas, to the Saddam regime. TDG was subsequently used in the Iraqi chemical weapons programme,

[86] *Supra* note 86.

[87] ICJ Report, *supra* note 15, at 9.

[88] A. Cassese (ed.), *The Oxford Companion to International Criminal Justice* (2009), 346–47.

[89] The experience of the ad hoc tribunals is informative in this regard. Each tribunal, although equipped to deal with only a limited number of cases themselves, was able to provide information to domestic authorities relating to many hundreds of potential suspects: ICTY (2009) *ICTY Manual on Developed Practices*, UNICRI Publisher, Turin, Italy, at 167.

[90] J. Iontcheva, 'Nationalizing International Criminal Law', *18th Conference of the International Society for the Reform of Criminal Law*, 8–12 August 2004, at 33.

[91] See R. Gallmetzer, supra note 83, regarding the Law Enforcement Network. Gallmetzer refers to the recent arrest by the German police authorities of Ignace Murwanashyaka, a leader of the FDLR rebel group operating in the Kivu provinces, and his aide Straton Musoni, for allegedly belonging to a terrorist organisation and for having committed crimes against humanity in the Eastern DRC.

[92] ICJ Report, *supra* note 15, at 9–10.

including against Iraq's Kurdish population. Van Anraat was acquitted of complicity to commit genocide due to insufficient evidence to prove that he knew of the regime's genocidal intent towards the Kurds. However, he was convicted as an accomplice to war crimes of inhuman treatment and causing death or severe bodily harm to others by the use of chemical weapons: it was proved that van Anraat knew he was exporting the substance to Iraq, was aware that it could be used for producing poison gas, and was aware that it could be used for chemical attacks (noting that Iraq had done so during the Iran-Iraq war). The Hague District Court found that van Anraat had acted consciously and had made an essential contribution to the chemical warfare program of Iraq, which facilitated mustard gas attacks against civilians. Van Anraat was sentenced at trial to 15 years' imprisonment. His conviction for war crimes was upheld on appeal and his sentence increased to 17 years.

Notably, a number of developed nations already have legislation that provides for the criminal prosecutions of legal persons (and therefore corporate entities). Such prosecutions, as addressed earlier, are outside the jurisdiction of the ICC and other existing international fora. The results of a survey of 16 domestic jurisdictions (all developed nations) – examining whether there are mechanisms in existing domestic criminal processes for holding business entities accountable for involvement in certain grave breaches of international law – indicate that 'it is the prevailing practice to apply criminal liability to legal persons among 11 of the [16] countries surveyed'.[93] The potential liability attaching to a business entity or legal person varies from one jurisdiction to another.

Where countries do not provide for criminal corporate liability domestically, civil corporate liability may be an option. In addition to the fact that it may be the only way to seek redress directly from a corporate entity, civil actions in some jurisdictions may lead to more accountability and contribute to changing corporate practices as a result of the civil damages awards, including asset seizures and forfeitures and fines levied against both individual corporate officers and corporations. Particularly relevant in common law systems, the civil process allows victims and their representatives to set the judicial process in motion and to obtain material compensation generally and for their pain and suffering specifically. Finally, the threshold of proof in civil matters (namely, the balance of probabilities) is lower than that in criminal cases (namely, proof beyond a reasonable doubt).[94]

The number of lawsuits brought concerning 'corporate complicity' in international crimes has been rising in recent years, particularly in the United States under the Alien Tort Claims Act (ATCA), an eigthteenth-century statute that has been

93 Notably Australia, Canada, France, India, Japan, the Netherlands, Norway, South Africa, the UK, and the US. See A. Ramasastry and R. C. Thompson, 'Commerce, Crime and Conflict: Legal Remedies for Private Sector Liability for Grave Breaches of International Law' (2006) Fafo-report 536, at 13 (http://www.fafo.no/pub/rapp/536/536.pdf).

94 E. Mongelard, 'Corporate Civil Liability for Violations of International Humanitarian Law', 88(863) *International Review of the Red Cross* (2006) 666–67. Mongelard refers to preponderance of evidence rather than balance of probabilities.

revived by human rights lawyers to bring civil lawsuits in U.S. courts on behalf of foreign human rights victims against their abusers.[95] Litigation against a corporation, Unocal Corp., is particularly significant – being both the first instance in which the ATCA was used to pursue a corporate entity for human rights damages[96] and, in 2002, the first ruling to confirm that a corporation may be held liable under the ATCA for its complicity in a violation of international criminal law occurring outside the United States.[97] The claim was eventually dismissed by the federal United States Court of Appeals for the Second Circuit, but has paved the way for future litigation. In 2009, another high-profile U.S, lawsuit was decided in the Court of Appeals against Talisman Energy Inc. This matter related to the actions of Talisman, a Canadian oil company, accused of aiding and abetting genocide in the Sudan. The matter referenced international criminal law jurisprudence in a domestic court concerning the issue of liability of corporations in situations of conflict where crimes are committed.[98] The Court of Appeals affirmed the lower court's dismissal of the lawsuit. In April 2010, the plaintiffs filed a petition for certiorari with the Supreme Court, asking the court to hear the case on appeal.[99]

## 7. CONCLUSION

In the past, corporations may have been able to operate with virtual impunity in carrying out their business activities in remote corners of the world. We are now seeing increasing pleas for accountability of corporations and corporate officers where their actions are linked to gross abuses of human rights. Where such abuses amount to violations of international criminal law, a framework exists at the international level to ensure criminal accountability – although liability is limited to natural persons. Within this framework there are a few existing modes of liability that are most likely to be applicable to corporate officers and their leaders. These modes include JCE,

95 Ramasastry and Thompson, *supra* note 93, at 21.

96 In 2002, the U.S. Court of Appeals for the Ninth Circuit held that Unocal could be potentially found liable under the ACTA for aiding and abetting the Burmese military in forced labour, murder, and rape: *Doe I.* v. *Unocal*, 395 F.3d932 (9th Cir. 2002). The case was later ordered to be reheard, and eventually a settlement was reached in December 2004 between Unocal Corp. and Burmese plaintiffs.

97 See decisions by a California federal district court (*Doe 1* v. *Unocal Corp*, 110 F. Supp. 2d 1294 (C.D. Cal. 2000)) and a panel of the Ninth Circuit (*Doe I.* v. *Unocal*, 395 F.3d932 (9th Cir. 2002)). See Thompson, Ramasastry, and Taylor, *supra* note 59, at 1–2.

98 U.S. Court of Appeals for the Second Circuit, October 2, 2009, *The Presbyterian Church of Sudan* v. *Talisman Energy, Inc.* In this regard, see Farrell, *supra* note 22, who argues that the Court of Appeals erred in its interpretation of the requisite *mens rea* for aiding and abetting under international criminal law.

99 Business & Human Rights Resource Centre (www.business-humanrights.org/Categories/Lawlawsuits/Lawsuitsregulatoryaction/LawsuitsSelectedcases/TalismanlawsuitreSudan?sort_on=sortable_title&batch_size=10&batch_start=6), accessed 1 May 2010.

co-perpetratorship, superior responsibility, and, arguably the most obviously applicable mode of liability, aiding and abetting – the mode requiring the lowest *mens rea* threshold and thus the most likely to be successful.

As the ICC Prosecutor has now expressly put corporate officers within his sights, it may just be a matter of time before the international criminal law framework is put to the test as a means of enforcing accountability in this area. When that time comes, prosecutions will necessarily be limited to crimes falling within the jurisdiction of the ICC. Regardless, there is sufficient scope for liability within the ICC as it now stands to give prudent corporate officers and leaders ample reason to think twice before engaging in business activities in the knowledge that their actions will or may contribute to crimes under international law.

# 11

# The Contribution of International Criminal Justice to Sustainable Peace and Development

*Fannie Lafontaine and Alain-Guy Tachou-Sipowo*

## 1. INTRODUCTION

The interaction between and compatibility of peace and security, on the one hand, and justice on the other, are at the heart of a raging debate that plays out in most if not all postconflict settings, as well as in situations of ongoing violence and human rights abuses. Yet, the idea that individual criminal accountability for the gravest international crimes is an essential component of postconflict recovery is now firmly embedded in both practice and rhetoric at the international level. This chapter provides an overview and critically assesses some of the actual and potential contributions of international criminal justice to sustainable peace and development.

Criminal accountability is part of an array of measures that can be adopted in a postconflict environment to address past violations while contributing to a peaceful present and building a sustainable future: '[T]he idea that a durable peace requires countries to address past violence is now widely held and promoted by influential leaders and institutions under the broad heading of "transitional justice."'[1] Crucial discussions are taking place regarding the relevance, meaning, and scope of transitional justice, concerning both its justifiability as a legal discipline and its complex interaction with other aspects of post-conflict peace building, such as development programmes and rule of law reforms.[2] This chapter has a more modest

[1] B. A. Leebaw, 'The Irreconcilable Goals of Transitional Justice', (2008) 30 *Human Rights Quarterly* 95, at 95. See definition of transitional justice in Report of the Secretary-General, The Rule of Law and Transitional Justice in Conflict and Post-Conflict Societies, UN Doc. S/2004/616, 23 August 2004, at para. 8.

[2] See e.g., C. Bell, 'Transitional Justice, Interdisciplinarity and the State of the 'Field' or 'Non-Field', (2009) 3 *International Journal of Transitional Justice* 5; L. J. Laplante, 'Transitional Justice and Peace Building: Diagnosing and Addressing the Socioeconomic Roots of Violence through a Human Rights Framework', (2008) 2 *International Journal of Transitional Justice* 331; R. Duthie, 'Toward a Development-sensitive Approach to Transitional Justice', (2008) 3 *International Journal of*

The research for this chapter is, save a few exceptions, up to date as of March 2010.

aim. Its focus is on the specific contributions of *criminal* accountability measures in conflict and postconflict environments.

This chapter presupposes that the adoption of some criminal law measures to deal with international crimes cannot be ignored in peace-building processes (though they may, arguably, be delayed). It further acknowledges that criminal prosecutions are mandated by international treaty law for some international crimes[3] and arguably by international customary law for others.[4] It thus assumes, without romanticising the transformative potential of such trials, that criminal justice for international crimes has a role to play in postconflict recovery and indeed in ongoing conflict situations. Hence, the discussion is more oriented toward identifying and critically assessing some actual and potential contributions of criminal accountability measures rather than questioning whether they are justified at all.

Despite its deliberate focus on criminal accountability, this chapter is based on the premise that only holistic strategies devised on a case-by-case basis after consultation with national constituencies, including the groups most affected by conflict, can hope to balance 'a variety of goals, including the pursuit of accountability, truth and reparation, the preservation of peace and the building of democracy and the rule of law'.[5] Insistence on criminal trials without due regard to complementary and alternative (legal and nonlegal) mechanisms can indeed jeopardise

*Transitional Justice* 292; P. de Greiff and R. Duthie (eds.), *Transitional Justice and Development: Making Connections* (2009); Z. Miller, 'Effects of Invisibility: In Search of the "Economic" in Transitional Justice', (2008) 2 *International Journal of Transitional Justice* 266.

3 1948 Convention on the Prevention and Punishment of the Crime of Genocide, 78 UNTS 277, Article IV-VI; 1949 Convention (I) for the Amelioration of the Condition of the Wounded and Sick in Armed Forces in the Field, 75 UNTS 31 (1950), Art. 49; 1949 Convention (II) for the Amelioration of the Condition of Wounded, Sick and Shipwrecked Members of Armed Forces at Sea, 75 UNTS 85 (1950), Art. 50; 1949 Convention (III) relative to the Treatment of Prisoners of War, 75 UNTS 135(1950), Art. 129; 1949 Convention (IV) relative to the Protection of Civilian Persons in Time of War, 75 UNTS 287 (1950), Art. 146; 1977 Protocol Additional to the Geneva Conventions of 12 August 1949, and relating to the Protection of Victims of International Armed Conflicts (Protocol I), 1125 UNTS 3 (1979), Arts. 85–87; 1973 International Convention on the Suppression and Punishment of the Crime of Apartheid, 1015 UNTS 243 (1976), Art. IV. Note that, as an exception, at Art. V, the exercise of jurisdiction is phrased in permissive terms ('may'); 2006 New York International Convention for the Protection of All Persons from Enforced Disappearance (not yet into force), Doc.A/61/48, Arts. 4–11; 1984 New York Convention against Torture and Other Cruel, Inhuman or Degrading Treatment or Punishment, 1465 UNTS 85 (1987), Arts. 4–7. Jurisprudence interpreting various regional and international human rights treaties has also increasingly recognised the duty to prosecute those responsible for human rights violations: see, e.g., review in A. Seibert-Fohr, 'Reconstruction through Accountability', (2005) 9 *Max Planck Yearbook of United Nations Law* 555.

4 See review of argument in, e.g., R. Cryer et al., *An Introduction to International Criminal Law and Procedure* (2007), 31–33 and 58–61.

5 Secretary-General Report on the Rule of Law and Transitional Justice, *supra* note 1, at para. 25. On national consultations, see Office of the High Commissioner for Human Rights (OHCHR), *Rule-of-Law Tools for Post-Conflict States: National Consultations on Transitional Justice* (HR/PUB/09/2), 2009.

the quest for truth, justice, and reconciliation. Complementarity is necessary not only with other, noncriminal transitional justice mechanisms but also, for instance, with judicial and political measures aimed at recognising state responsibility for the crimes committed.[6] The various transitional justice approaches in turn need to be implemented in co-ordination with overlapping initiatives such as security sector and rule of law reforms, as well as human-rights-based development programming.[7]

In this light, and following broadly the United Nations' approach to the rule of law,[8] albeit with nuances, this chapter first addresses the role of international criminal justice (ICJ) in promoting and building the rule of law at the international level, maintaining international peace and security, and building an international normative public order. To be legitimate and worthwhile, these contributions at a more global level must have an impact on reinforcing similar values and norms in the domestic systems of states emerging from conflict.[9] The chapter thus turns in Section 3 to the more concrete contribution of international criminal justice to the rule of law at the national level. This section focuses on ICJ's impact on local domestic legal systems and the role that truth-telling and reparations to victims within a criminal law context may play in promoting national reconciliation and sustainable peace.

[6] See, S. Mohamed, 'A Neglected Option: The Contributions of State Responsibility for Genocide to Transitional Justice', (2009) 80 *University of Colorado Law Review* 327.

[7] J. E. Stromseth, 'Pursuing Accountability for Atrocities after Conflict: What Impact on Building the Rule of Law?', (2006–2007) 38 *Georgetown Journal of International Law* 251, at 256; Office of the High Commissioner for Human Rights, 'Frequently Asked Questions on a Human Rights-Based Approach to Development Cooperation', UN Doc. HR/PUB/06/8 (2006). See also the interesting proposal of an emergency form of postconflict justice that would work alongside other justice initiatives such as international criminal proceedings: L. Otis and E. H. Reiter, 'Front-Line Justice', (2006) 46 *Virginia Journal of International Law* 677.

[8] Resolution adopted by the General Assembly, "The Rule of Law at the National and International Levels", UN Doc. A/RES/62/70 (2008); Guidance Note of the Secretary-General, UN Approach to Rule of Law Assistance, April 2008; 2005 World Summit Outcome Document, U.N. Doc. A/RES/60/1 (16 September 2005), para. 134. We do acknowledge that the rule of law is an evasive and criticised concept: see, e.g., S. Cherterman, 'An International Rule of Law?' (2008) 56 *American Journal of Comparative Law* 331; B. Rajagopal, 'Invoking the Rule of Law in Post-Conflict Setting: A Critical Examination', (2008) 49 *William and Mary Review* 1345; D. Kairys, 'Searching for the Rule of Law', (2003) 36 *Suffolk University Law Review* 307. It is outside the scope of this chapter to enter into these issues. We take the UN definition as a reference so that the rule of law also encompasses an ideal of justice and values of impartiality and accountability reflected in international human rights law: Secretary-General Report on the Rule of Law and Transitional Justice, *supra* note 1, at para. 6; see also J. Rose, 'The Rule of Law in the Western World: An Overview', (2004) 35 *Journal of Social Philosophy* 461.

[9] We indeed see the two levels of contribution (i.e. to the rule of law at both international and national levels) as mutually reinforcing and overlapping in certain regards. See, also, A. Nollkaemper, 'The Internationalized Rule of Law', (2009) 1 *Hague Journal on the Rule of Law* 74.

## 2. PROMOTING AND BUILDING THE RULE OF LAW AT THE INTERNATIONAL LEVEL

### 2.1. *Criminal Accountability to Restore International Peace and Security*

Although international criminal justice has historically been interwoven with armed conflicts,[10] it is only with the establishment of the United Nations international criminal tribunals in the 1990s that the conviction that criminal accountability was necessary for the restoration and maintenance of peace and security was explicitly expressed.[11] Massive human rights violations, including those occurring within a state's borders, were considered threats to international peace and security, and establishing individual accountability for such violations was seen as a measure to restore or maintain them. Practice shows a steady trend within the international community of requests being made to the UN Security Council to refer situations of massive human rights violations to criminal mechanisms.[12]

#### 2.1.1. Action with Respect to a Threat or Breach of International Peace and Security

Initially harshly criticised as not falling within the measures contemplated by Article 41 of the UN Charter,[13] the creation of criminal justice mechanisms by the Security Council to address situations threatening international peace and security has been

[10] A.- G. Tachou-Sipowo, 'Peace and Security in Central Africa: The Role of International Justice', in C. Ayangafac (ed.), *Political Economy of Regionalisation in Central Africa* (2008), 79, at 79.

[11] Security Council, 'Tribunal (former Yugoslavia)' (ICTY), UN Doc. S/RES/827 (1993), 6th para. of the preamble; Security Council, 'establishment of an International Tribunal and adoption of the Statute of the Tribunal' (ICTR), UN Doc. S/RES/955 (1994), 7th para. of the preamble. As regards the Special Court of Sierra Leone (SCSL), see Security Council, 'Situation in Sierra Leone', UN Doc. S/RES/1315 (2000), 7th para. of the preamble; for the International Criminal Court (ICC), see 1998 Rome Statute of the International Criminal Court, 2187 UNTS 3, 3rd and 5th paras. of the preamble, and Art. 13 (b). Similar links between peace and justice can be found as regards the establishment of the Panels in Timor-Leste: Security Council, 'Situation in East Timor' UN Doc. S/RES/1272 (1999), 25 October 1999, preamble and para. 1; The Khmers Rouge Trials in Cambodia: General Assembly, 'Khmer Rouge Trials', UN Doc. A/RES/57/228 B, 22 May 2003, preamble and the Special Tribunal for Lebanon: Security Council, 'Situation in the Middle East' UN Doc. S/RES/1757 (2007) 30 May 2007, preamble.

[12] See for instance Human Rights Council, 'Report of the United Nations Fact Finding Mission on the Gaza Conflict', UN Doc. A/HRC/12/48, 15 September 2009, para. 1766. Political considerations here admittedly play a determinant role; Secretary-General, 'Letter dated 18 December 2009 from the Secretary-General addressed to the President of the Security Council (Guinea – Report of the International Commission of Inquiry)', UN Doc. S/2009/693, 18 December 2009 para. 263§b.

[13] Art. 41 of the 1945 Charter of the United Nations provides that '[t]he Security Council may decide what measures not involving the use of armed force are to be employed to give effect to its decisions, and it may call upon the Members of the United Nations to apply such measures. These may include complete or partial interruption of economic relations and of rail, sea, air, postal, telegraphic, radio, and other means of communication, and the severance of diplomatic relations.'

legitimised over the years[14] and has received ultimate consecration in the International Criminal Court (ICC) Statute. Indeed, the Security Council is among the trigger mechanisms of the ICC's machinery. This triggering power is restricted to an action taken 'under Chapter VII of the Charter of the United Nations'.[15] This action presupposes that the Security Council is of the view that a situation of massive human rights violations is constitutive of a threat or breach to international peace and security. As noted earlier, numerous Security Council actions, particularly since the 1990s, confirm that the political body conceives massive violations of human rights, including those that threaten regional stability and those occurring within a state's borders, as sufficient to trigger Chapter VII powers.[16]

Based on this power granted to it in the Rome Statute, the Security Council has thus far referred two situations of gross human rights abuses for investigation and prosecution to the Prosecutor of the ICC, one from Sudan regarding the conflict in Darfur[17] and another concerning Libya.[18] Similarly to the International Criminal Tribunal for the Former Yugoslavia (ICTY), which operated for some time in the context of the raging conflict in the former Yugoslavia, the ICC's involvement in Sudan, Uganda, the Democratic Republic of Congo (DRC), Côte d'Ivoire, the Central African Republic, and Kenya is taking place in the midst of ongoing armed conflicts or violent social tensions. Its potential preventive and deterrent effect, which cannot be measured with accuracy, accounts at the very least for a growing awareness amongst warring stakeholders of the readiness of criminal liability mechanisms to investigate their misconduct.[19] The ICC's watchful eye can also act as a threat to actual and potential perpetrators of international crimes, as it has done in Colombia.

14 *Prosecutor* v. *Tadić*, Decision on the Defence Motion for interlocutory Appeal on Jurisdiction, ICTY Case No. IT-95-1-A, App. Ch. 2 October 1995, para. 40.

15 1998 Rome Statute of the International Criminal Court, Art. 13(b).

16 Interventions of the Council in Somalia (1992), Rwanda (1993), Albania (1997), Timor-Leste (1999), Sierra Leone (2000), Congo and Liberia (2003) Haiti (2004), for instance, were based on such findings. See S. Chesterman, *Just War or Just Peace? Humanitarian Intervention and International Law* (2001), 112; A. Viotti, 'In Search of Symbiosis: the Security Council in the Humanitarian Domain', (2007) 89 *International Review of the Red Cross* 131, at 145. See also Security Council, 'Protection of Civilians in Armed Conflicts', UN Doc. S/RES/1674 (2006), 28 April 2006, para. 26.

17 Security Council, UN Doc. S/RES/1593 (2005), 31 March 2005, para. 1. In doing so, the Council followed the recommendation of the International Commission of Inquiry on Darfur: 'Letter dated 31 January 2005 from the Secretary-General addressed to the President of the Security Council (Report of the International Commission of Inquiry on Darfur to the Secretary-General – Pursuant to Security Council Res. 1564 (2004) of 18 September 2004)', UN Doc. S/2005/60, 1 February 2005.

18 Security Council, UN Doc. S/RES/1970 (2011), 26th February 2011, para. 4 (referring the situation in the Libyan Arab Jamahiriya since 15 February 2011 to the Prosecutor of the ICC).

19 The International Crisis Group reported, for instance, that in the aftermath of the indictment of LRA's warlords, the ICC's implication 'raised stakes for Khartoum as it could fall within the ICC's criminal investigation in Uganda for supporting the LRA'; see also Human Rights Watch, 'Selling Justice Short: Why Accountability Matters for Peace', New York, July 2009, at 54.

Despite their potential capacity as a deterrent, it is acknowledged that justice initiatives may in certain circumstances need to yield temporarily to short-term peace objectives.[20] Article 16 of the Rome Statute[21] recognises both this potential necessity and the overarching role of the Security Council in that regard. The provision, which allows deferral by resolution adopted under Chapter VII, is indeed premised on the rationale that prosecution, which can sometimes be considered a redress to a threat to peace and security, may at other times constitute a possible impediment to its restoration. To explicitly declare that justice is at odds (even temporarily so) with peace is a very delicate statement to make. It is hoped and expected that the Security Council will use this power with great circumspection and only in exceptional circumstances.[22]

One should also be cautious about having excess confidence in international criminal justice as an instrument of peace, absent strong political sponsorship – namely, the backing of an organ such as the Security Council. As Bassiouni rightly put it, 'threats to peace and security are essentially political judgments'.[23] Even when the Security Council has found that criminal prosecutions are a desirable measure for the restoration of peace and security in a given situation, its lack of effective support of enforcement of subsequent measures adopted within the criminal justice system seriously undermines the credibility of the international legal order: 'Impunity through non-enforcement of international arrest warrants that have been backed

[20] M. P. Scharf, 'From the eXiles Files: An Essay on Trading Peace for Justice', (2006) *Washington and Lee Law Review* 339, at 342.

[21] According to Art. 16, 'No investigation or prosecution may be commenced or proceeded with under this Statute for a period of 12 months after the Security Council, in a resolution adopted under Chapter VII of the Charter of the United Nations, has requested the Court to that effect; that request may be renewed by the Council under the same conditions'. The application of this provision has been requested by the African Union (AU) in the situation in Sudan; see Peace and Security Council of the African Union, *Communiqué of the 142nd Meeting of the Peace and Security Council*, Doc PSC/MIN/Comm (CXLII), 21st July 2008 at para. 11 (following decision of Prosecutor Ocampo to request an arrest warrant against the president of Sudan, Omar Al Bashir). See also Assembly of Head of States and Government of the African Union, Sixteenth Ordinary session, 30–31 January 2011, Addis-Ababa, Ethiopia, *Decision on the Implementation of the Decisions of the International Criminal Court*, Doc EXCL/639(XVIII), para 6 (calling African states not to co-operate with ICC with respect to the situation in Kenya following 2007–08 postelectoral violence and ICC's indictment of six high-ranking officials).

[22] L. Condorelli and S. Villalpando, 'Referral and Deferral by the Security Council', in A. Cassese et al., *The Rome Statute of the International Criminal Court: A Commentary* (2002), 571, at 646–47; R. Cryer, 'The Security Council, Article 16 and Darfur' (2008) *Oxford Transitional Justice Research Working Paper Series*, available at www.csls.ox.ac.uk/documents/CryerFi.pdf.

[23] C. Bassiouni, 'International Crimes: "Jus Cogens" and "Obligatio Erga Omnes"', (1996) 59 *Law and Contemporary Problems* 69. This explains the Council's lack of action as regards Syria despite human rights violations likely amounting to crimes under the jurisdiction of the ICC: See Human Rights Council, *Report of the Independent International Commission of Inquiry on the Syrian Arab Republic*, Seventeenth special session, UN Doc A/HRC/S-17/2/Add.1, 23 November 2011 (recommending that Syria ratify the Rome Statute and establish a mechanism to investigate the abuses).

with Chapter VII authority cannot be permitted without fundamentally undermining the credibility of the notion of an international rule of law.'[24] For example, this lack of follow-up in the situation of Darfur gravely undermines the credibility of both the ICC and the Security Council and weakens the international legal order.

In any event, to understand how international criminal justice has the potential to restore international peace, it is necessary to look at how it can contribute to the marginalisation of those who bear the greatest responsibility for gross human rights abuses.

### 2.1.2. Disempowerment and Marginalisation of Those Responsible for International Crimes

Disempowerment and marginalisation can be linked to the adoption, by international criminal tribunals, of a prosecutorial strategy that aims at targeting those who bear the greatest responsibility. At the ICTR and ICTY, the policy of targeting leaders has been crafted as part of the completion strategy.[25] These tribunals were the first international courts after Nuremberg to try a head of government and a head of state.[26] A high-profile approach to perpetrators of international crimes may be fruitful in that

> [b]y arresting the architects of the genocide, the ICTR deprived the perpetrators of their main leaders. The overarching feeling among survivors is that without such arrests, the former political and military leaders involved in the genocide would have continued to destabilize Rwanda, eliminate witnesses and aggravate the moral suffering of survivors.[27]

The policy of targeting the 'big fish' also applies at the ICC according to the Office of the Prosecutor's *Prosecutorial Strategy*.[28] The most recent Prosecutorial Strategy report defines those who bear the greatest responsibility as 'those situated at the highest echelons of responsibility, including those who ordered, financed, or otherwise organised the alleged crimes'.[29] The mandates of hybrid courts such as the Special Court for Sierra Leone and the Extraordinary Chambers in the Courts of Cambodia are also explicitly limited to the prosecution of those

[24] C. Reiger, 'Fulfilling the Justice Promise: Guiding Principles for Resolving the Ongoing Responsibilities of International Tribunals', 8 October 2009, at 2, www.ictj.org/static/Prosecutions/Arria_Presentation091008.pdf. For instance, the arrest warrants issued by the Pre-Trial Chamber of the ICC in the situation of Darfur against state officials and affiliated nonstate armed groups are, at the date of writing, yet to be executed.

[25] Security Council, Res. 1503(2003); E. Mose, 'Main Achievements of the ICTR', (2005) 3 *Journal of International Criminal Justice* 920, at 932.

[26] *Ibid.*, at 935.

[27] F.-X. Nsanzuwera, 'The ICTR Contribution to National Reconciliation', (2005) 3 *Journal of International Criminal Justice* 944, at 948.

[28] ICC, Office of the Prosecutor, 'Report on Prosecutorial Strategy 2006–2009', 16 September 2006, at 5.

[29] ICC, Office of the Prosecutor, 'Report on Prosecutorial Strategy 2009–2012', 1 February 2010, para. 19.

'who bear the greatest responsibility for serious violations of international humanitarian law'.[30]

Targeting abusive leaders may sometimes facilitate peace talks and contribute to stability.[31] The inquisitive eye of the international community into the wrongdoings of warlords, especially through the lens of criminal prosecution, can weaken their most radical positions in the peace talks. Although, as in Uganda, blackmail may be used by threatening to not conclude the peace agreement, it seems clear that international indictments can discredit the legitimacy of some of the criminal negotiators' requests. International indictments can also prevent the escalation of war or at the very least diminish the capacity of a group to commit violations, and they can act as a deterrent to others involved. The Rome Statute recognises that the issuance of an arrest warrant can be based on the necessity 'to prevent the person from continuing with the commission of that crime or a related crime which is within the jurisdiction of the Court and which arises out of the same circumstances'.[32] The Prosecutorial Strategy goes so far as to state that 'the announcement of an investigation' and 'the mere monitoring of a situation could deter future crimes from being committed'.[33] Although because of immunities or non-co-operation by states, indictments of major perpetrators may stay unanswered for some time, the fact that abusive leaders are in the line of sight of international criminal justice places them, if not in the dock, at least on trial by the international community.[34] Finally,

30 Statute for the Special Court for Sierra Leone, 2178 UNTS 138, Art. 1; see also, Law on the Establishment of the Extraordinary Chambers in the Courts of Cambodia for the Prosecution of Crimes Committed during the Period of Democratic Kampuchea (2001) (Cambodia), as amended by NS/RKM/1004/006 (Oct. 27, 2004), Art. 1.

31 Human Rights Watch, *supra* note 19, at 4 (arguing that the indictment of Radovan Karadzić marginalised him and prevented him from taking part in the peace talks, which led to the success of the Dayton negotiations in ending the Bosnian war. Similarly the unsealing of the indictment of Taylor on the eve of the Lomé peace talks helped move the negotiations forwards). See, also, A. D'Amato, 'Peace vs. Accountability in Bosnia', (1994) 88 *American Journal of International Law* 500, at 503; A. A. Rosen, 'D'Amato's Equilibrium: Game Theory and a Re-Evaluation of the Duty to Prosecute under International Law', (2004) 37(1) *New York University Journal of International Law and Politics* 79, at 111; see Scharf, *supra* note 20, at 375.

32 ICC Statute, Art. 58(1)(b)(iii).

33 ICC, Office of the Prosecutor, *supra* note 28 at 6.

34 For instance, since his indictment in 2008 by the ICC, President Al-Bashir of Sudan is theoretically restricted from travelling at least to the 121 states parties to the Rome Statute. Recent decisions at the ICC confirm this highly controversial position: *The Prosecutor* v. *Omar Hassan Ahmad Al Bashir, Decision Pursuant to Article 87(7) of the Rome Statute on the Failure by the Republic of Malawi to Comply with the Cooperation Requests Issued by the Court with Respect to the Arrest and Surrender of Omar Hassan Ahmad Al Bashir*, ICC-02/05–01/09–139, 12 December 2011; *The Prosecutor* v. *Omar Hassan Ahmad Al Bashir, Decision Pursuant to Article 87(7) of the Rome Statute on the Refusal of the Republic of Chad to Comply with the Cooperation Requests Issued by the Court with Respect to the Arrest and Surrender of Omar Hassan Ahmad Al Bashir*, ICC-02/05–01/09–140, 13 December 2011. See D. Akande, 'The Legal Nature of Security Council Referrals to the ICC and Its Impact on Al Bashir Immunities', (2009) 7 *Journal of International Criminal Justice* 333 and debate on the EJIL: Talk! Blog, *ICC Issues Detailed Decision on Bashir's Immunity (... At long Last...) But Gets the Law Wrong*, available at www.ejiltalk.org/icc-issues-detailed-decision-on-bashir's-immunity-at-long-last-but-gets-the-law-wrong.

peace processes that include accountability mechanisms for international crimes, while disempowering and marginalising those who bear the greatest responsibility, empower victims by taking into account their interests in justice and by amplifying and legitimising their voices in a struggle for power from which they are typically excluded.

### 2.2. *The Normative and Jurisprudential Contribution of International Criminal Justice*

The potential of international criminal justice to contribute to sustainable peace and development is also grounded in the development of a permanent and functional international normative legal order. This contribution to a credible international rule of law is appraised here in two ways: as regards normative and jurisprudential developments in international criminal law and as regards the general trend toward limiting exceptions to the principle of accountability for international crimes.

#### 2.2.1. Developing International Criminal and Humanitarian Law

International criminal statutes and courts have brought greater clarity to the definitions of international crimes and to the modes of participation to such crimes. The impressive amount of jurisprudence emanating from these courts and the vibrant academic literature that has accompanied it certainly have made an immense contribution to the international legal framework. What follows is a brief overview of the most significant developments as regards crimes and modes of liability, which have been so determinant in the evolution of international law that they are now almost considered trite.

Starting with the crime of genocide, it is through the two first genocide judgements in *Akayesu*[35] and *Kambanda*[36] that the ICTR gave unprecedented 'vitality and relevance' to the 1948 Genocide Convention.[37] Before these judgements, the customary nature of genocide could only be deduced from an ICJ advisory opinion of 1951 that stated that 'the principles underlying the Convention are principles which are recognized by civilized nations'.[38] The ICTR went beyond the fact that Rwanda was party to the Genocide Convention since 1975 and declared that genocide is 'undeniably considered part of customary international law'.[39]

35 *Prosecutor* v. *Akayesu*, Judgement, Case No. ICTR-96–4-T, T. Ch. I, 2 September 1998.

36 *Prosecutor* v. *Kambanda*, Judgement and sentence, case No. ICTR-97–23-S, T. Ch., 4 September 1998.

37 1948 New York Convention on the Prevention and Punishment of the Crime of Genocide, 78 UNTS 277; P. Akhavan, 'The Crime of Genocide in the ICTR Jurisprudence', (2005) 4 *Journal of International Criminal Justice* 989, at 990; See Mose, *supra* note 25, at 934.

38 International Court of Justice, Reservations to the Convention on the Prevention and Punishment of the Crime of Genocide, Advisory Opinion, 28 May 1951, [1951] ICJ Rep. 15, at 23.

39 *Prosecutor* v. *Akayesu*, *supra* note 35, at 495.

The legal and societal impact of this decision is monumental. Legally, it strengthens the bases of genocide,[40] and socially, by recognising that genocide occurred in Rwanda in 1994, 'the ICTR rendered human dignity back to the survivors of the genocide, who had been robbed of it by the perpetrators'.[41] Remarkably, by developing a subjective theory in order to classify the Tutsi as a protected group, the ICTR avoided making blunt assumptions of objective ethnicity and hence unwillingly reinforcing the social construction of the difference between Tutsi and Hutu.[42]

The *Akayesu* judgment is also groundbreaking for its affirmation of rape as constitutive of international crimes.[43] As with other crimes of sexual violence, rape is now considered an underlying crime of all core crimes by international courts and can also be constitutive of torture or persecution.[44] The Rome Statute codified this statement of international customary law and lists numerous acts of sexual violence within its definitions of crimes against humanity and war crimes.[45] The contours of the definitions of sexual crimes also continue to evolve. For instance, the Special Court for Sierra Leone (SCSL) Appeals Chamber ruled that forced marriage is distinct from sexual slavery and can be charged as 'other inhumane acts'.[46]

40 See Akhavan, *supra* note 37.

41 See Nsanzuwera, *supra* note 27, at 946.

42 The approach taken in *Akayesu*, *supra* note 35, was criticised as constituting a significant departure from the 1948 Convention. See Akhavan, *supra* note 37, at 1001; see also G. Verdirame, 'The Genocide Definition in the Jurisprudence of the *Ad Hoc Tribunals*', (2000) 49 *International and Comparative Law Quarterly* 578, at 592 (arguing that the Chamber in *Akayesu* resorted to an incomparable interpretation of the Genocide Convention). Since *Akayesu*, the ICTR 'is of the view that a subjective definition alone is not enough to determine victim groups'. Thus identification of a group must also take 'into account both the relevant evidence proffered and the political, social and cultural context': *Prosecutor* v. *Rutanganda*, Judgement , Case No. ICTR-96–3, T.Ch. 6 December 1999, paras. 56–57 and 373; See also *Prosecutor* v. *Musema*, Judgement, Case No. ICTR-96–13-A, T.Ch., 27 January 2000, para. 161; *Prosecutor* v. *Kumuhanda*, Judgement, Case No. ICTR-95–51A-T, T.Ch., 22 January 2004, para. 630; See also, *Proecutor* v. *Krstic*, Judgement, Case No. IT-98–33-T, T.Ch., 2 August 2001, para. 557; *Prosecutor* v. *Bagilishema*, Judgement, Case No. ICTR-95–1A-T, T.Ch. I, 7 June 2001, para. 65. For discussion, see R. Young, 'How Do We Know Them When We See Them? The Subjective Evolution in the Identification of Victim Groups for the Purpose of Genocide', (2010) 10(1) *International Criminal Law Review* 1, at 12.

43 Mose, *supra* note 25, at 935; K. D. Askin, 'Gender Crimes Jurisprudence in the ICTR: Positive Developments', (2005) 4 *Journal of International Criminal Justice* 1007, at 1011.

44 Askin, *supra* note 43 at 1014; See *Prosecutor* v. *Semanza*, Judgement and Sentence, Case No. ICTR-97–20-T, T.Ch. III, 15 May 2003; *Prosecutor* v. *Gacumbitsi*, Judgement, Case No. ICTR-01–64-T, T.Ch. III, 17 June 2004, para. 215; *Prosecutor* v. *Nahimana et al.*, Judgement and Sentence, Case No. ICTR-99–52-T, T.Ch., 3 December 2003. The test of equal gravity has helped enlarge the scope of acts falling under the crime of persecution: *Prosecutor* v. *Karadzic*, Decision on Six Preliminary Motions Challenging Jurisdiction, Case No. IT-95–5/18-PT, T.Ch., 28 April 2009, para. 43.

45 Rome Statute, Arts. 7(1)(g), 8(b) (xxii) and 8(e) (vi). The *Elements of Crimes of the International Criminal Court*, ICC-ASP OR, ICC-ASP/1/3, (2002) 108, also confirm that it can be constitutive of genocide, Art. 6(b), note 3.

46 *Prosecutor* v. *Brima, Kamara and Kanu*, Judgement, Appeals Chamber, 22 February 2008, para. 186. On 'forcible transfer' as 'other inhumane acts', see *Prosecutor* v. *Brdanin*, Judgement, case No. IT-99–36-T, Trial Chamber, 3 April 2007, at para. 544.

One of the most significant developments in international criminal law has occurred with respect to crimes against humanity. These crimes have grown out of their link with armed conflicts, and their definition has been progressively refined (regarding the attack requirement, for instance) and expanded (a broad list of sexual crimes and enforced disappearance, for instance). They cover a wide range of conduct committed in both peacetime and war that would not necessarily qualify as genocide or war crimes. Despite the current absence of a specific treaty concerning crimes against humanity, they now form a central part of the international criminal legal order.

As regards war crimes, the ad hoc tribunals and the ICC Statute have made numerous important contributions, only some of which are highlighted here. The ICTY was the first international body to interpret and apply the grave breaches regime enshrined in the Geneva Conventions.[47] It concluded that they were limited to situations where the armed conflict qualified as international.[48] However, the ICTY provided in subsequent case law for a broad interpretation of international armed conflict, acknowledging, for instance, that an internal armed conflict may become international with the intervention of a third state or if one of the participants acts on behalf of that other state.[49] With respect to the latter point, the tribunal departed from the ICJ's 'effective control' test, adopting a less stringent threshold of 'overall control'.[50] The practical effect of the overall control test is significant, because it broadens the scope of the grave breaches regime.[51] The tribunal also construed a theory of nexus between the armed conflict and the punishable offences that is flexible and allows for a significant reach of the war crimes' definition.[52] Perhaps the most significant and well-known contribution of the ad hoc tribunals to the legal regime applicable to war crimes is its extension in essence to internal armed conflicts.[53] This development has been codified generally in the Rome Statute, which sets forth the most detailed listing thus far of underlying offences constitutive of war crimes committed in internal armed conflicts.[54]

47 K, Roberts, 'The Contribution of the ICTY to the Grave Breaches Regime', (2009) 7 *Journal of International Criminal Justice* 743, at 744.

48 *Prosecutor* v. *Tadić, supra* note 14, para. 80.

49 *Prosecutor* v. *Tadić*, Judgement, Case No. IT-94–1-A, App.Ch., 15 July 1999, para. 84.

50 *Ibid.*, para. 137.

51 See, Roberts, *supra* note 47, at 749.

52 *Prosecutor* v. *Kunarac et al.*, Judgement, Case No. IT-96–23, App.Ch., 12 June 2002, para. 58–60.

53 Secretary-General, 'Report of the Secretary-General Pursuant to Paragraph 5 of Security Council Resolution 955', UN Doc. S/1995/134, 13 February 1995, para. 12. See *Prosecutor* v. *Tadić, supra* note 14, para. 134; *Prosecutor* v. *Delalic*, Judgement, Case No. IT-96–21,T.Ch., 16 November 1998, para. 308; L. Moir, 'Grave Breaches and Internal Armed Conflicts', (2009) 7 *Journal of International Criminal Justice* 763, at 764; D. Plattner, 'The Penal Repression of Violations of International Humanitarian Law Applicable in Non-International Armed Conflicts', (1990) 30(278) *International Review of the Red Cross* 409, at 414.

54 Art. 8(2)(c) and (e) of the ICC Statute.

In addition to the definitions of crimes, modes of individual criminal liability deserve consideration. Because international crimes are collective in nature, the concern of the tribunals has therefore been to find a way to deal with individual criminal responsibility in a context where there is a plurality of perpetrators, some of whom may not have physically committed the crime.[55] The doctrines of superior responsibility and joint criminal enterprise were developed to cope with what has been labelled 'system criminality'.[56] Though they have been criticised[57], the doctrines have been the basis for a great number of convictions before all international criminal tribunals[58] and have contributed, along with the vibrant literature that they have stimulated, to building a better understanding of how criminal law may capture collective and massive criminality. The ICC Statute has a detailed provision on superior liability, answering some of the earlier critiques; although it rejects the idea of joint criminal enterprise to instead extend principal liability to 'co-perpetration' and 'perpetration through another person'[59], the attempt to reflect the collectivisation of criminality in the individual modes of liability is no less present.[60]

These legal developments – now well known, criticised, commented upon, reiterated in numerous cases, and almost trite – confirm the point made here: international criminal justice has contributed and will undeniably continue to contribute to the development of the international legal order.

### 2.2.1. Limiting Exceptions to Accountability: Immunities, Statutes of Limitations, and Amnesties

The role of international criminal justice in building an international rule of law is also concerned with the availability of exceptions that may dangerously narrow its (ideally) universal scope. International criminal law has contributed to weakening the legal basis for amnesties for gross human rights violations, it has opened a breach in the long-standing legal regime concerning immunities, and it has severely limited the application of statutes of limitations.

55 H. G. Van der Wilt, 'The Continuous Quest for Proper Modes of Criminal Responsibility', (2009) 7(2) *Journal of International Criminal Justice* 307, at 307–08.

56 *Ibid.*

57 See, among many others, J. D. Ohlin, 'Three Conceptual Problems with the Doctrine of Joint Criminal Enterprise', (2005) 5(1) *Journal of International Criminal Justice* 69, at 69–90.

58 G. Boas, J. L. Bischoff, and N. L. Reid, *Forms of Responsibility in International Criminal Law*, Vol. 1 (2007) at 9.

59 Art. 25(3)(a) of the Rome Statute. See also Art. 25(3)(d); *Prosecutor* v. *Lubanga*, Decision on the Confirmation of Charges, Case No. ICC-01/04–01/06), Pre-trial Ch. I, 29 January 2009, paras. 327–367; *Prosecutor* v. *Germain Katanga and Mathieu Ngudjolo Chui*, Decision on the Confirmation of Charges, Case No. ICC-01/04–01/07, Pre-trial Ch. I, 30 September 2008, paras. 477–518.

60 Van der Wilt, *supra* note 55.

With respect to immunities, all international tribunals since Nuremberg have rejected that immunities may bar prosecutions of senior state officials,[61] and this rejection has probably led to the development of a rule of customary law in this regard.[62] The growing understanding that official capacity should not in all circumstances shield perpetrators of international crimes from prosecution finds application also before national courts – if not for incumbent heads of states, at least with respect to functional immunities.[63] This is a significant tribute to the rule of law: no one is above the law when the 'most serious crimes of concern to the international community'[64] are involved. As for statutes of limitations, international law is quite affirmative that they cannot be applied to the crimes of genocide, crimes against humanity, and war crimes.[65]

The question of whether amnesties for international crimes are permitted or illegal according to international law continues to spur passionate debates. The issue is at the heart of the alleged dichotomy between peace and justice. It is not the place to fully discuss this highly contentious issue, but it is apposite to mention that the development of international criminal law has led to a growing understanding that amnesties are either illegal (i.e. contrary to states' obligations under certain treaties or under international customary law) or at least counterproductive in postconflict situations, 'even when adopted in the hope of advancing national reconciliation rather than with the cynical aim of shielding depredations behind a fortress of impunity'.[66]

61 See respectively Arts. 6 and 7 of the Tokyo and Nuremberg Charters and the ensuing Principle III of the Principles of International Law Recognized in the Charter of the Nuremberg Tribunal and in the Judgement of the Tribunal, 1950 (in Report of the International Law Commission covering its Second Session, 5 June – 29 July 1950, Document A/1316); see also Art. 7(2) of the ICTY Statute, Art. 6(2) of the ICTR Statute, Art. 27 of the Rome Statute (but see also Art. 98 of the Statute). For hybrid courts, see Art. 6(2) of the SCSL, but it is controversial as to whether a third-country official can claim for immunities: SCSL, *Prosecutor* v. *Charles Taylor*, Decision on Immunity from Jurisdiction, Case No. SCSL-2003–01-I, App.Ch., 31 May 2004. On this decision, see, S. M. H. Nouwen, 'The Special Court for Sierra Leone and the Immunity of Taylor: The Arrest Warrant Case Continued', (2005) 18 *Leiden Journal of International Law* 645–69.

62 International Court of Justice, Case concerning the arrest warrant of 11 April 2000 (*Democratic Republic of the Congo* v. *Belgium*) ('Arrest Warrant case'), Judgement, 14 February 2002, para. 61. It is debated as to whether this rule is part of customary international law, but it is likely the case: see Paola Gaeta, 'Does President Al Bashir Enjoy Immunity from Arrest?', (2009) 7 *Journal of International Criminal Justice* 315.

63 See House of Lords, *Regina* v. *Bartle and the Commissioner of Police for the Metropolis and Others Ex Parte Pinochet*, 24 March 1999; *Arrest Warrant case*, *supra* note 62, para. 61 and separate opinion of Higgins et al., para. 85.

64 Rome Statute, 4th preambular paragraph.

65 Rome Statute, Art. 29; Convention on the Non-Applicability of Statutory Limitations to War Crimes and Crimes against Humanity 1968, Annexed to GA Res. 2391 (XXIII), 26 November 1968; See also European Convention on the Non-Applicability of Statutory Limitations to War Crimes and Crimes against Humanity (1974) (not in force); F. Lafontaine, 'No Amnesty or Statute of Limitation for Enforced Disappearances: The Sandoval Case before the Supreme Court of Chile', (2005) 3 *Journal of International Criminal Justice* 469, at 480.

66 See Office of the High Commissioner for Human Rights (OHCHR), *Rule-of-Law Tools for Post-Conflict States: Amnesties* (HR/PUB/09/1). See also A. Brannigan and N. A. Jones, 'Genocide and the

The general trend within the international community is indeed in favour of prosecution.[67] The United Nations' policy is to oppose amnesties for war crimes and for gross violations of human rights, even in the context of peace negotiations.[68] The Rome Statute is silent with respect to amnesties, and scholars are divided as to how to interpret this silence. For some commentators, it implicitly allows for deferrals to alternative justice mechanisms that comprise amnesties,[69] whereas for others, the establishment of the ICC is proof that the international community has 'decided that justice, in the form of prosecution, must take priority over peace and national reconciliation'.[70] The debate also highlights the tension between principle and practice.

Indeed, *international* criminal justice mechanisms cannot realistically hope to judge all those responsible for international crimes. In fact, in certain situations, *criminal* mechanisms, be they national or international or both acting in complementarity, will not be able to deal with the massive numbers of alleged perpetrators while respecting fundamental due process rights. In other cases, the pursuit of peace and national reconciliation may call for a sequencing of efforts to these ends, while keeping justice as the ultimate objective. As we discussed earlier, we agree with the growing consensus that views justice as broader than criminal justice and as inclusive of alternative mechanisms such as truth commissions and reparations programmes. This understanding comes with an acknowledgement that justice mechanisms may need to be sequenced to achieve shorter term peace objectives. Such sequencing may mean that criminal justice is delayed in favour of alternative justice mechanisms or that different accountability mechanisms are applied to different

Legal Process in Rwanda: From Genocide Amnesty to the New Rule of Law', (2009) 19 *International Criminal Justice Review* 192, arguing that the amnesty law that existed prior to 1994 in Rwanda had a role in creating a culture of impunity that led to the genocide. The jurisprudence of the Inter-American Court for Human Rights is probably the most affirmative as regards the incompatibility of amnesties with its human rights instrument: see, e.g., *Velasquez Rodriguez case*, Judgement of 29 July 1988, Inter-Am Ct HR (Ser. C) No. 4 (1988) (quoted at para. 49), and *Barrios-Altos Case (Chumbipuma Aguirre et al.* v. *Peru)*, Judgement of 14 March 2001, Inter-Am Ct HR (Ser C) No. 75 (2001) (quoted at paras. 84–86).

67 L. M. Keller, 'Achieving Peace with Justice: The International Criminal Court and Ugandan Alternative Justice Mechanisms', (2008) 23 *Connecticut Journal of International Law* 209, at 229.

68 See e.g., Report of the Secretary-General, *The Rule of Law and Transitional Justice in Conflict and Post-Conflict Societies*, UN Doc. S/2004/616, 23 August 2004, paras. 40, 64; OHCHR, *Rule-of-Law Tools for Post-Conflict States: Amnesties, supra* note 66. The policy is quite recent. It is worth recalling that a peace accord negotiated in 1994 under the auspices of the United States and the United Nations gave amnesties to military leaders in Haiti despite their brutal atrocities records. See M. P. Scharf, 'Swapping Amnesty for Peace: Was there a Duty to Prosecute International Crimes in Haiti?', (1996) 31 *Texas International Law Journal* 1, at 2.

69 Keller, *supra* note 67, at 237; T. H. Clark, 'The Prosecutor of the International Criminal Court, Amnesties, and the 'Interests of Justice': Striking a Delicate Balance', (2005) 4 *Washington University Global Studies Law Review* 389, at 414; J. Gavron, 'Amnesties in Light of Developments in International Law and the Establishment of the International Criminal Court', (2002) 51 *International Law and Comparative Law Quarterly* 91, at 108.

70 J. Dugard, 'Possible Conflicts of Jurisdiction with Truth Commissions', in A. Cassese et al. (eds.), *The Rome Statute of the International Criminal Court: A Commentary* (2002), 693, at 702. At 700, he argues that amnesties could be a mitigating factor for sentencing purposes.

perpetrators according to levels of responsibility, for instance. The Rwandan Gacaca or the Sierra Leonean Truth and Reconciliation Commission operating alongside the international/ised courts are examples in point, although the interaction between these mechanisms inevitably creates a different set of concerns. The powers of the Security Council under Article 16 of the Rome Statute are recognition of such possible sequencing necessity. The Security Council can also choose to promote alternative mechanisms as part of its collective security strategies to deal with a particular threat to the peace.[71] Crucial in this practical understanding of justice in postconflict settings, however, is that 'sequencing should not be used as a pretext for delay or as basis for abandoning a commitment to criminal accountability'.[72]

Alternative mechanisms that are not criminal in nature may not satisfy the ICC complementarity (Article 17) or *ne bis in idem* principles (Article 20).[73] However, it is recognised that these forms of justice can be considered within the discretion of the prosecutor not to open an investigation or continue with prosecution if it would not be 'in the interests of justice' to do so.[74] In this regard, though a policy paper of the Office of the Prosecutor is quite affirmative as to the necessity of criminal prosecutions in postbuilding contexts, it 'fully endorses the complementary role that can be played by domestic prosecutions, truth seeking, reparations programs, institutional reform and traditional justice mechanisms in the pursuit of a broader justice'.[75] It also recognises the role of the Security Council pursuant to Article 16. International criminal justice evolves in an increasingly sophisticated way, insisting on accountability as a necessary ingredient of a sustainable peace – thus rejecting

[71] See, e.g., para. 5 of Security Council resolution 1593(2005) referring the situation in Darfur to the ICC. This approach, which tends to reconcile peace and justice, has gained an important support in the literature: Carsten Stahn, 'Complementarity, Amnesties and Alternative Forms of Justice: Some Interpretive Guidelines for the International Criminal Court', (2005) 3 JICJ 695, at 708–09; R. J. Goldstone and N. Fritz, '"In the Interests of Justice" and Independent Referral: The ICC Prosecutor's Unprecedented Powers', (2000) 13 *Leiden Journal of International Law* 655, at 660; M. P. Scharf, 'The Amnesty Exception to the Jurisdiction of the International Criminal Court', (1999) 32 *Cornell International Law Journal* 507, at 508.

[72] International Center for Transitional Justice, 'Peace and Justice: A Talk by Paul van Zyl', 25 September 2009, www.ictj.org/en/news/features/3098.html.

[73] Nevertheless, many are of the view that the ICC should defer to noncriminal mechanisms of justice provided that they satisfy a threshold requirement of necessity and legitimacy and that they further the goals of international criminal justice, namely retribution, reparation, deterrence, and expressivism: see Keller, *supra* note 67, at 261; Scharf, *supra* note 20, at 349.

[74] 1998 Rome Statute of the International Criminal Court, Article 53(1)(c) and 53(2) c). See Keller, *supra* note 67, at 346, citing also Dugard, *supra* note 70, at 702; M. A. Drumbl, Atrocity, *Punishment, And International Law* (2007), 142–43; D. Majzub, 'Peace or Justice? Amnesties and the International Criminal Court', (2002) 3 *Melbourne Journal of International Law* 247, at 247; D. Robinson, 'Serving the Interests of Justice: Amnesties, Truth Commissions and International Criminal Court', (2003) 14 *European Journal of International Law* 483, at 486; Van de Wyngaert and T. Onega, 'Ne bis in idem including amnesty', in A. Cassese et al. (eds.), *The Rome Statute of the International Criminal Court: A Commentary* (2002), 705, at 727.

[75] ICC, Office of the Prosecutor, Policy Paper on Interests of Justice, September 2007, at 4, 8.

most amnesties as a matter of principle – while recognising that alternative justice proceedings may act as a necessary complement.

The impact that international criminal justice has on strengthening the rule of law at the international level is an important contribution to sustainable peace and development in various postconflict settings. However, its effective impact on the rule of law at the national level may be its biggest challenge in this regard, an issue to which we now turn.

## 3. PROMOTING AND BUILDING THE RULE OF LAW AT THE NATIONAL LEVEL

### 3.1. *Impact on Domestic Legal Systems*

It is generally understood that 'long-term and sustainable solutions to impunity should aim mostly at building domestic capacity to try [international] crimes'.[76] The need to internationalise accountability initiatives to address past human rights violations is often due to a lack of institutional capacity or political will at the local level, a situation that effective 'legacy' efforts can contribute in reversing.[77]

This section looks at two important contributions – normative and institutional – that international criminal justice can make to domestic legal systems, provided there is due emphasis on participation, ownership, and outreach to local communities,[78] which among other things must succeed in managing expectations. Leaving a lasting impact on domestic systems is arguably the primary challenge facing international criminal justice in order for it to credibly claim a positive contribution to sustainable peace and security.[79]

#### 3.1.1. Entrenching a Rule of Law Culture and Domestic Implementation of International Criminal Law

The rule of law as we understand it must be built on the faith and confidence of people in a given society that rules and legal enforcement institutions are meant to

[76] OHCHR, *Rule-of-Law Tools for Post-Conflict States: Prosecution Initiatives*, UN Doc. HR/PUB/06/4 (2006) at 1. See also, Secretary-General Report on the Rule of Law and Transitional Justice, *supra* note 1, at para. 34; K. McCourt, 'Judicial Defenders: Their Role in Postgenocide Justice and Sustained Legal Development', (2009) 3 *International Journal of Transitional Justice* 272, at 272–73.

[77] See, e.g., C. Reiger, '*Where to from Here for International Tribunals? Considering Legacy and Residual Issue*', September 2009, ICTJ Briefing Paper http://www.ictj.org/static/Publications/bp_reiger_hybrid_courts_rev4.pdf.

[78] Secretary-General Report on the Rule of Law and Transitional Justice, *supra* note 1, paras. 15, 17, 64(h).

[79] J. Stromseth, 'Justice on the Ground: Can International Criminal Courts Strengthen Domestic Rule of Law in Post-Conflict Societies?' (2009) 1 *Hague Journal on the Rule of Law* 87, at 88.

protect them and not harm them.[80] International criminal justice has an 'educational' role aimed at 'conveying the message that rules of international humanitarian law have to be obeyed under all circumstances'.[81] Indeed, it can 'convey to citizens a *disapproval of violations* . . . [which] can help draw the distinction between conduct that is condoned and conduct that is condemned by the State, which contributes to the public's trust in State institutions'.[82]

The lack of international and national political courage to address impunity can have dire consequences on people's confidence in national institutions, jeopardising fragile transitions to democracy. Afghanistan, Nepal, and Sri Lanka are all cases in point, among many others, in which victims' demands for criminal accountability (and other measures such as vetting) were constantly ignored, electoral candidates committed serious human rights violations, and true peace continues to be far from sight.[83]

Furthermore, in many states, even after formal peace agreements have been signed or after elections have been held, structural violence and inequalities often continue. The incapacity or unwillingness to address past violations typically also translates into a lack of attention to ongoing abuses, further undermining confidence in national institutions. International involvement, including in criminal matters, can serve to counter-balance the risks that local or community-based initiatives replicate the 'exclusionary or sexist practices and unequal power or hierarchical relationships'[84] that were present in the period marked by conflict or violence that they aim to leave behind. International criminal justice can thus play a central role in building trust in the law and in the legal enforcement institutions after periods of chaos and violence.

International criminal justice initiatives also have the potential to stimulate domestic legal reforms. The focus here is on the implementation of international criminal law norms, rather than on the broader legal changes necessary in transitional periods to ensure general compliance with international human rights standards, better

[80] See J. Stromseth, D. Wippman, and R. Brooks, *Can Might Make Rights?: Building the Rule of Law after Military Interventions* (2006), at 310 and following.

[81] *Prosecutor* v. *Kordić and Čerkez*, Judgement, Case No. IT-95–14/2-A, ICTY App. Ch., 17 December 2004, para. 1080.

[82] OHCHR, *Rule-of-Law Tools for Post-Conflict States: Prosecution Initiatives*, *supra* note 76, at 4 (emphasis in the original).

[83] See, e.g., International Crisis Group, *Afghanistan: The Need for International Resolve, Crisis Group Asia* Report N° 145, 6 February 2008; Human Rights Watch, 'Selling Justice Short', *supra* note 19 (also discusses the DRC and Bosnia and Hervegozina); Stromseth, *supra* note 7 at 315 and following. In early 2010, the 'National Stability and Reconciliation' Bill was made public. It would grant amnesty to all parties from prosecution for serious violations of human rights, including war crimes and crimes against humanity committed, in the past 30 years: www.amnesty.org/news-and-updates/news/afghanistan-must-not-grant-impunity-war-criminals-20100209%20; for Sri Lanka, see, e.g., International Crisis Group, *Sri Lanka: A Bitter Peace*, Asia Briefing N° 99, 11 January 2010; for Nepal, see, International Crisis Group, *Nepal: Peace and Justice*, Asia Report N° 184, 14 January 2010.

[84] P. MacAuliffe, review of K. McEvoy and L. McGregor (eds.), *Transitional Justice from Below: Grassroots Activism and the Struggle for Change*, (2010) 10 *Human Rights Law Review* 199, at 203.

access to justice, judges' independence and impartiality, and so on. The strengthening of the normative framework is an essential first step for effective domestic prosecutions of past, current, and future international crimes. It is also an important component of any transition to a rule of law founded upon respect for universal standards from either an inexistent rule of law or from one that facilitated or justified abuses and discrimination.

Internationalised (hybrid) tribunals often have a deep impact on national law, particularly where they are built within a particular domestic system, as in Cambodia and Bosnia and Herzegovina and, to a different extent, in UN-administered territories such as East Timor and Kosovo. In such cases, states internalise fundamental rules of international criminal law and criminalise the core international offences in national law. The Special Court for Sierra Leone has had a tangible impact in the country through a successful outreach programme and effective capacity-building initiatives, as we discuss later, but it has failed to stimulate legal reforms that would have allowed domestic prosecutions of crimes against humanity and war crimes. In fact, public frustration with the Special Court was often linked to the fact that only those 'bearing the greatest responsibility' were prosecuted, with no mechanism, apart for the noncriminal Truth and Reconciliation Commission, for the prosecution of lower level perpetrators.[85] Sierra Leone has not yet enacted legislation implementing its obligations as a party to the ICC Statute.

Despite a low-profile and inefficient capacity-building strategy, at least in their early stages, the ad hoc tribunals did stimulate legal reforms at the domestic level. The very creation of the tribunals by the Security Council put emphasis on legal accountability for international crimes, spurring general interest in prosecutions in states the world over based on various heads of jurisdiction, including territorial jurisdiction. Rwanda modified its legislation in 1996 to implement its obligations under the *Convention on the Prevention and Repression of the Crime of Genocide* and underwent significant legal reforms aimed at ensuring consistency with international standards and strengthening domestic capacity in regards to the crime of genocide.[86] It conducted hundreds of trials in domestic courts and in the Gacaca jurisdictions, with mixed results, but in an attempt to overcome the past with the aid of criminal or semi-criminal accountability mechanisms. Bosnia and Herzegovina, Croatia, and Serbia also all eventually adopted laws criminalising crimes against

[85] Stromseth, *supra* note 7 at 302.

[86] Organic Law N° 08/96 of August 30 1996, on the Organization of Prosecutions for Offences constituting the Crime of Genocide or Crimes against Humanity committed since October 1, 1990. Since then other relevant laws were adopted (e.g. Law N° 33 BIS/2003 Repressing the Crime of Genocide, Crimes against Humanity and War Crimes; Law N° 09/2007 of 16/02/2007 On the Attributions, Organisation and Functioning of the National Commission for the Fight against Genocide; and the controversial Law N° 18/2008 of 23 July 2008 Relating to the Punishment of the Crime of Genocide Ideology). See the detailed account of parts of the legislative reforms in A. Brannigan and N. A. Jones, 'Genocide and the Legal Process in Rwanda: From Genocide Amnesty to the New Rule of Law', (2009) 19 *International Criminal Justice Review* 192.

humanity and war crimes and granting jurisdiction to national courts.[87] Special chambers were created in 2003 to facilitate this process. Interestingly, most of the work in this regard, particularly in Bosnia and Herzegovina and Croatia, was done concurrently with action taken to implement these states' obligations under the ICC Statute. The completion strategy of the ICTY and the coming into force of the ICC Statute might have worked as two powerful sources for legal reform at the domestic level.

The ICC complementarity scheme indeed works as a strong incentive for legal reforms, not only to fulfil states' co-operation obligations but also to ensure criminalisation of the offences contained in the Rome Statute and to establish jurisdiction of domestic courts over these crimes. The criminalisation in domestic legal systems of genocide and crimes against humanity is, in and of itself, a significant contribution of the ICC to the rule of law at the national level. Statistics are not easy to glean, but of the current 121 state parties, 40 states have enacted some form of implementing legislation.[88] The Assembly of States Parties promotes universal ratification of the ICC Statute and encourages criminalisation of the core crimes and the establishment of jurisdiction over them by national courts.[89] The Office of the Prosecutor has adopted a policy of 'positive' complementarity, referred to later, which can potentially stimulate domestic action against impunity for international crimes. Many observers argue that the impact of the complementarity principle on domestic legal systems – particularly if promoted 'proactively' by the court's organs – is the ICC's most promising contribution to the fight against impunity and to lasting peace and security.[90]

### 3.1.2. Capacity Building in the Administration of Justice

The internationalisation of criminal measures in postconflict settings may serve as a formidable opportunity to invest in the (re)building of local capacity in the administration of justice. In addition to the legal reforms discussed earlier, it can contribute to the reinforcement of local civil society, the development of

87 These laws are available notably through the ICC Legal Tools database, under national implementing legislation: www.legal-tools.org/en/go-to-database. See also ICTY website on outreach and capacity building, www.icty.org/sections/Outreach/CapacityBuilding, which also links to the websites of national courts.

88 *Ibid*, (Note that not all countries listed in the ICC Legal Tools under National Implementing Legislation are states parties). The adoption of implementing legislation in March 2010 in Uganda is particularly significant considering the court's involvement in the country.

89 ICC, Strengthening the International Criminal Court and the Assembly of States Parties, Resolution ICC-ASP/8/Res.3, 26 November 2009, paras. 3–4.

90 See e.g. W.W. Burke-White, 'Proactive Complementarity: The International Criminal Court and National Courts in the Rome System of Justice', (2008) 49 *Harvard International Law Journal* 53; M. S. Ellis, 'International Justice and the Rule of Law: Strengthening the ICC through Domestic Prosecutions', (2009) 1 *Hague Journal on the Rule of Law* 79.

professional staff working in the justice system, the building of physical infrastructure, and so on.[91] The serious criminality that often has to be addressed in transitional periods puts enormous pressure on fragile legal systems, where most defendants will, or should, face justice.[92] In Rwanda, for instance, the precarious state of the judiciary was compounded by the adoption of a policy of maximal accountability by the government, which pressured the legal system to the point of implosion.[93]

The impact of international criminal justice on national legal systems can come not only from the direct involvement of the institutions themselves but also through the blossoming transnational networks of nongovernmental institutions, United Nations actors, diplomatic missions in the field, notably the major donor states, and humanitarian and development agencies. The resurgence of international criminal justice in the 1990s led to the emergence of a 'global compact' in which different actors promote the international norms and contribute to local reforms that take account of these norms. Collectively, they can have a noticeable impact in different local settings. For instance, despite the *current* lack of involvement of an international or internationalised tribunal, significant capacity-building efforts by numerous actors led to important initiatives with respect to accountability in Guatemala, Nepal, Liberia. and Burundi, for instance.

It was not until their completion strategy had to be crafted that the ICTY and ICTR really saw national capacity building as being a central part of their mandate.[94] As a result, these tribunals' impact could be summarised as 'too little too late'.[95] The outreach programme of the ICTY effectively began in 1999 and was limited essentially to redressing negative domestic perceptions of its work.[96] The ICTY has stepped up its outreach efforts in the course of its completion strategy and legacy is very much at the core of current preoccupations before closure.[97]

91 This form of legacy, essentially relevant to nonpermanent institutions, is not further discussed herein. This impact, if carefully planned, can be significant. For instance, in November 2009, the Special Court for Sierra Leone handed over its detention facility, which meets international standards, to the Sierra Leone Prison Service.

92 OHCHR, *Rule-of-Law Tools for Post-Conflict States: The Legacy of Hybrid Courts* (HR/PUB/08/2), at 1.

93 Amnesty International, *Rwanda: Gacaca, a Question of Justice* (AI Index AFR 47/007/2002).

94 UN Doc. S/RES/1503 (2003), inter alia, '*Noting* that the strengthening of national judicial systems is crucially important to the rule of law in general and to the implementation of the ICTY and ICTR Completion Strategies in particular'. See also statement of 23 July 2002 made by the President of the Security Council, UN Doc. S/PRST/2002/21.

95 See, generally, Stromseth, *supra* note 7 at 279.

96 See. J. N. Clark, 'International War Crimes Tribunals and the Challenge of Outreach', (2009) 9 *International Criminal Law Review* 99, at 104. For an insightful study on victims' perceptions on ICTY trials, see, R. Hodić, 'Living the Legacy of Mass Atrocities: Victims' Perspectives on War Crimes Trials', (2010) *Journal of International Criminal Justice*, doi:10.1093/jicj/mqq008. For an early critical appraisal of the impact of the ICTY on local legal systems, see, D. Tolbert, 'The International Criminal Tribunal for the Former Yugoslavia: Unforeseen Successes and Foreseeable Shortcomings', (2002) 26 *Fletcher Forum of World Affairs* 7.

97 See the detailed outreach section on ICTY's website: www.icty.org/sid/7.

Despite these shortcomings, the most important contribution to capacity building is probably the establishment of a Section for War Crimes within the State Court and the State Prosecutor's Office of Bosnia and Herzegovina, inaugurated in 2005.[98]

The ICTR has worked in a different environment. Indeed, Rwanda made extensive use of its national courts and of the Gacaca to solve the accountability puzzle. There has been tension created by the fact that extensive resources were devoted to an international jurisdiction at the expense of investments in local systems. Some observers have discarded the outreach programme as 'ineffective' or as having failed to properly inform the Rwandans about the work of the tribunal.[99] Others have opined that the failure of the prosecutor to bring charges against members of the Rwandan Patriotic Front who had been implicated in war crimes jeopardises the tribunal's long-term legacy.[100] The outreach efforts have quickened their pace in the recent years, and legacy is also a vivid concern for the ICTR as it winds down its activities.[101] However, the general failure to effectively contribute to domestic capacity building has led to difficult issues in the phasing-out period. The most striking example is the initial refusal by the ICTR Appeals Chamber to transfer cases to Rwanda because of ongoing concerns with the domestic justice system, despite the country's institution of reforms, such as abolition of the death penalty, to alleviate some of these concerns. The capacity-building efforts of the completion strategy are partly aimed at ensuring that Rwanda can take over the cases, though the president continued to call on other states with jurisdiction to do so.[102] Cases began to be transferred to Rwanda by the ICTR at the end of 2011, though not without practical difficulties.[103]

98 For an account of the completion of the first Srebrenica trial in this court, see A. Strippoli, 'National Courts and Genocide: The *Kravica* Case at the Court of Bosnia and Herzegovina', (2009) *Journal of International Criminal Justice* 577.

99 V. Peskin, 'Courting Rwanda: The Promises and Pitfalls of the ICTR Outreach Programme', (2005) 3(4) *Journal of International Criminal Justice* 950. See R. Byrne, 'Promises of Peace and Reconciliation: Previewing the Legacy of the International Criminal Tribunal for Rwanda' (2006) 14 *European Review* 485, at 495, which highlights surveys that show that the overall perception of the tribunal is more positive than negative, but that '[t]he real verdict on the legacy of the ICTR, however, may rest with the evolving views of the other 50% of Rwandans surveyed who were unable to respond to the proposition because they were either "uncertain" or "not informed"'.

100 Human Rights Watch, 'ICTR Rwanda Tribunal Creates Rich Legal Precedent', Press Release, 15 January 2010. See, on this perception of victors' justice, Byrne, *supra* note 99 at 495.

101 See, e.g., *Report on the Completion Strategy of the International Criminal Tribunal for Rwanda*, UN Doc. S/2009/587, 12 November 2009.

102 See, e.g., Address to the United Nations Security Council, Sixth-monthly report on the completion strategy, Justice Dennis Byron, President ICTR, 3 December 2009.

103 See, e.g., *Uwikindi* v. *The Prosecutor, Decision of Uwikindi's Appeal against the Referral of His Case to Rwanda and Related Motions*, ICTR Case No. ICTR-01–75-AR11bis, 16 December 2011. The practical difficulties were linked, inter alia, to the negotiations with the African Commission on Human and People's Rights (ACHPR), which was tasked by the ICTR to monitor prison conditions and trial procedures.

The nonpermanent nature of all international and internationalised tribunals to date, except the ICC, leads to complex residual issues once their work is completed. The manner in which these institutions close will be determinant for their impact to be positive and long-lasting in the affected societies that should be the main beneficiaries of such expensive international involvement.[104]

The internationalised or hybrid mechanisms, though based on diverse models, were quickly seen as particularly promising with respect to capacity building and now work consciously towards this objective.[105] Internationalised courts may indeed have marked a certain shift in the way international involvement has been conceived in postconflict environments: deterrence, both specific and general, and retribution, still at the core of all criminal institutions, have gradually made room for other objectives, amongst which capacity building at the national level is most prominent.[106] Despite justified criticism, the belated capacity-building efforts of the ad hoc tribunals are entirely consonant with this trend.

Although it may be too early to evaluate the lasting impact of more recent hybrid courts, the tribunals in Kosovo, East Timor, and Sierra Leone show mixed results.[107] In Kosovo, for instance, international judges were said to have brought the appearance of impartiality to local trials, but often lacked the much hoped-for expertise in international law and practical experience of fair criminal trials.[108] The SCSL faced serious financial challenges, but there seems to be broad agreement that it became an important player in the larger reconstruction process. It was mostly perceived as legitimate, primarily because of an effective outreach programme, and it 'strengthened public awareness of the importance of accountability and contributed to domestic capacity-building'.[109] Nevertheless, many observers evaluate that its impact in terms

[104] Secretary-General, Report of the Secretary-General on the administrative and budgetary aspects of the options for possible locations for the archives of the International Criminal Tribunal for the Former Yugoslavia and the International Criminal Tribunal for Rwanda and the seat of the residual mechanism(s) for the Tribunals, UN Doc. S/2009/258, 21 May 2009; C. Reiger, *supra* note 77.

[105] OHCHR, *Rule-of-Law Tools for Post-Conflict States: The Legacy of Hybrid Courts*, *supra* note 92, at 7. The now explicit mission of Sierra Leone Special Court's outreach program is to educate Sierra Leoneans on the rule of law and operations of the court: www.sc-sl.org/ABOUT/CourtOrganization/TheRegistry/OutreachandPublicAffairs/tabid/83/Default.aspx.

[106] V. Hussain, 'Sustaining Judicial Rescues: The Role of Outreach and Capacity-Building Efforts in War Crimes Tribunals, (2004–2005)], 45 *Virginia Journal of International Law* 547, at 559, referring to 'changing models of accountability'.

[107] C. P. R. Romano, A. Nollkaemper, and J. K. Kleffner (eds.), *Internationalized Criminal Courts: Sierra Leone, East Timor, Kosovo, and Cambodia* (2004); see also Stromseth, *supra* note 7, at 280–311.

[108] See, e.g., E. A. Baylis, 'Reassessing the Role of International Criminal Law: Rebuilding National Courts through Transnational Networks', (2009) 50 *Boston College Law Review* 1, at 19; J. Cerone and C. Baldwin, 'Explaining and Evaluating UNMIK Court System', in C. P. R. Romano, A. Nollkaemper, and J. K. Kleffner (eds.), *Internationalized Criminal Courts: Sierra Leone, East Timor, Kosovo, and Cambodia* (2004), 41, at 51–56.

[109] Stromseth, *supra* note 7, e.g. at 320.

of capacity building did not fully meet expectations, which were perhaps set too high in the first place.[110]

The ICC potentially continues the jurisdictional shift of international criminal law from international to domestic courts, increasing the need to invest in building capacities of national legal systems. The positive complementarity approach of the Office of the Prosecutor involves encouragement for national proceedings, positive interaction with domestic actors, and 'acting as a catalyst with development organizations and donors' conferences to promote support for relevant accountability efforts'.[111] The limited resources of the ICC to build local know-how as regards prosecutions and trials for international crimes indeed suggests that this daunting challenge will need to be tackled in conjunction with other actors involved in postconflict peace building.[112] The specific needs of war crimes trials may call for the creation, as some have suggested, of a supranational body that would aim specifically at providing 'technical and unbiased assistance to domestic war crimes courts'.[113] Clearly, lack of co-ordination and potential mêlées for a place under the sun should not happen at the expense of coherence and national involvement, thus threatening the attainment of the ultimate objective pursued by all.

Finally, efforts should be made to avoid the potentially damaging 'reverse legacy' effect – international or internationalised institutions competing with and diverting resources from national institutions, draining domestic capacity, or contributing to negative perceptions of the domestic legal system.[114] These arguments were made by Sierra Leoneans regarding the Special Court[115] and equally apply to international jurisdictions. The tension between the ICTR and local Rwandan initiatives, discussed earlier, is an example of this competition. There should thus be explicit efforts to narrow the gap between investments in prosecuting a limited number of serious crimes in the immediate aftermath of conflict through a hybrid court and the

110 R. Kerr and J. Lincoln, *The Special Court for Sierra Leone: Outreach, Legacy and Impact*, Final Report, February 2008, War Crimes Research Group (WCRG), Kings College London; International Crisis Group, *The Special Court for Sierra Leone: Promises and Pitfalls of a 'New Model'*, Africa Briefing No. 16, 4 August 2003; S. Horowitz, 'Sierra Leone: Interaction between International and National Responses to Mass Atrocities', DOMAC/3, December 2009, http://www.domac.is/media/domac/DOMAC3-SH-2009.pdf.

111 ICC, *Prosecutorial Strategy 2009–2012*, 1 February 2010, para. 17; see also Art. 93 (10) of the Rome Statute.

112 See the extensive review of current practice and challenges in A. Chehtman and R. Mackenzie, 'Capacity Development in International Criminal Justice: A Mapping Exercise of Existing Practice', Domac Project, September 2009.

113 M. S. Ellis, 'International Justice and the Rule of Law: Strengthening the ICC through Domestic Prosecutions', (2009) 1 *Hague Journal on the Rule of Law* 79, at 81.

114 OHCHR, *Rule-of-law Tools for Post-Conflict States: The Legacy of Hybrid Courts, supra* note 92, at 15; see Stromseth, *supra* note 7, at 266, which provides examples of this potential tension from Rwanda, Sierra Leone, and East Timor.

115 C. C. Jallow and V. O. Nmehielle, 'The Legacy of the Special Court for Sierra Leone', (2006) 30 *Fletcher Forum of World Affairs* 107, at 109.

frequent lack of investment in the local justice system in the postconflict context'.[116] However, narrowing the gap does not mean investing less in international(ised) mechanisms, but rather that '*more attention and resources* should be afforded to post-conflict domestic justice systems as a whole'.[117]

### 3.2. *Restorative Justice: Truth-telling and Reparations as Ingredients of National Reconciliation*

Criminal justice is retributive and repressive, but it can also be distributive and restorative, aiming at addressing more directly the needs of victims and the inequalities at the source of the crimes it adjudicates. The following discussion sees how this trend may contribute to sustainable peace and development. It fully recognises, however, that a blind focus on criminal law may overshadow a range of other initiatives, from internationally supported ones to community-based ones that can better address political or economic inequalities often lying at the root of conflict and violence.[118]

#### 3.2.1. Truth-Telling and Building an Historical Record

The role of international criminal proceedings in acting as a cathartic forum for victims in postconflict settings and as collector of an impartial historical record is fairly controversial.[119] Criminal proceedings have as a principal objective the determination of individual liability. Particularly where founded on an adversarial model, they cannot realistically hope to build a complete factual record of en entire conflict or years of abuse, and the ad hoc tribunals have been criticised for attempting to do so.[120] However, as the ICC Prosecutor's Office notes, 'While the Office's mandate does not include production of comprehensive historical records for a given conflict, incidents are selected to provide a sample that is reflective of the gravest incidents and the main types of victimization'.[121]

[116] OHCHR, *Rule-of-law Tools for Post-Conflict States: The Legacy of Hybrid Courts*, *supra* note 92, at 41.

[117] *Ibid.*, at 15.

[118] R. Mani, *Beyond Retribution: Seeking Justice in the Shadows of War* (2002). For an enlightening perspective on how cultural practices and local needs and ideas of justice can be better taken into account in transitional periods, see K. McEvoy and L. McGregor (eds.), *Transitional Justice from Below: Grassroots Activism and the Struggle for Change* (2008). International crimes should also be interpreted to take better account of serious violations of economic, social, and cultural rights: see Chapter 6 in this book.

[119] J. Alvarez, 'Rush to Closure: Lessons from the Tadić Judgment', (1998) 96 *Michigan Law Review* 2031; M. Osiel, *Mass Atrocity, Collective Memory and the Law* (2007); M. Minow, *Between Vengeance and Forgiveness* (1998).

[120] See e.g. *Prosecutor* v. *Tadić*, Case No. IT-94-1-T, ICTY T.Ch., 7 May 1997; *Prosecutor* v. *Akayesu*, *supra* note 35; for critiques, see e.g., Alvarez, *supra* note 119; see also J. Alvarez, 'Lessons from the Akayesu Judgment' (1998–1999)', 5 *ILSA Journal of International and Comparative Law* 359.

[121] ICC, *Prosecutorial Strategy 2009–2012*, 1 February 2010, para. 20.

Furthermore, despite its focus on individual liability and the abhorrence of criminal law of collective guilt,[122] international criminal justice is concerned primarily with collective criminality.[123] Crimes also have a contextual constitutive element that will force an analysis that goes beyond individual conduct (for example, a systematic or generalised attack against a civilian population for crimes against humanity or an armed conflict for war crimes). The factual nexus of a case thus provides important information about the broader context that fosters specific crimes. The records that criminal trials generate thus have an important 'secondary value for memory, education and research'.[124] As the report of the Sierra Leone Truth and Reconciliation underlines, 'the struggle for control over the national or "collective" memory lies at the heart of post-conflict or post-authoritarian accountability policies'.[125]

Criminal processes can also contribute to establishing an historical record of facts that will be fairly labelled in accordance with international law.[126] They can contribute, ideally alongside other truth-telling mechanisms, to preventing revisionism or official silencing of past crimes. Stimulated by the setting up at long last of the Extraordinary Chambers in the Courts of Cambodia (ECCCC), Cambodian schools' curriculum began to include in 2009 educational material about crimes committed during the Khmer Rouge period, more than 30 years after the events.[127] The ECCC also develop projects related to its 'historical legacy', for instance, by digitally making widely available to the public, during and beyond its operation, all trial-related materials such as decisions, filings, trial transcripts, and videos of the court proceedings.[128]

Furthermore, '[t]he goal of using such trials to preserve an accurate collective memory is also based on the model of closure. It is said that war crimes trials

[122] On collective responsibility, see M. Futamura, 'Individual and Collective Guilt: Post-War Japan and the Tokyo War Crimes Tribunal', (2006) 14 *European Review* 471; M. Drumbl, 'Collective Violence and Individual Punishment: The Criminality of Mass Atrocity', (2004) 99 *Northwestern University Law Review* 539.

[123] M. Drumbl, *Atrocity, Punishment, and International Law* (2007), see particularly chapter 2.

[124] Secretary-General, *supra* note 104, which 'contains a study on best practices for the effective implementation of the right to truth, in particular practices relating to archives and records concerning gross violations of human rights'.

[125] *Witness to Truth: Report of the Sierra Leone Truth and Reconciliation Commission*, Appendix Four, by A. Christodulou, at 1.

[126] See Osiel, *supra* note 119; *Prosecutor* v. *Krstić*, Judgement, Case No. IT-98–33, ICTY App. Ch., 19 April 2004, para. 37: 'Where these [stringent genocide] requirements are satisfied, however, the law must not shy away from referring to the crime committed by its proper name.' See Nsanzuwera, *supra* note 27, at 945.

[127] Documentation Center of Cambodia, Genocide Education Project, *The Teaching of A History of Democratic Kampuchea (1975–1979)*, Interim Report, October 2009, available online with other resources concerning the project: www.dccam.org/Projects/Genocide/Genocide_Education.htm, referring to genocide education as a Cambodian form of truth and reconciliation commission.

[128] ECCC, 'ECCC Enters into Agreement for the Creation of a 'Virtual Tribunal', Press Release, 17 February 2010.

permit entire societies to "draw . . . a clear line between past and future, allowing the beginning of a healing process."'[129] If not achieving closure, which is said to be too ambitious an agenda for criminal trials, such trials can promote debates about the history of a conflict or specific cases through the lens of the law, lessening the chances of blank assertions of guilt from both sides.[130] However, postconflict criminal trials can hope to fulfil this promise only if they look at both sides of the conflict. The failure to do so by the ICTR has arguably led to tensions in Rwanda.[131]

Truth-telling, even if only partially achieved in criminal proceedings, can also contribute to providing a sense of justice for victims, whose voices may otherwise be silenced in the political power struggles that take place in transitional periods. International human rights law provides for a right to the truth for victims of human rights violations.[132] Clearly, '[j]udicial criminal proceedings, with a broad legal standing in the judicial process for any wronged party and to any person or non-governmental organization having a legitimate interest therein, are essential to ensuring the right to the truth'.[133]

Victims have increasingly been given a more prominent role in international criminal proceedings. The ICC has various provisions regarding victims' participation based on these principles contained in international instruments regarding victims' rights[134]: '[P]ositive engagement with victims can have a significant effect on how victims experience and perceive justice and, as such, contribute to their healing process,' and the 'ICC has not only a punitive but also a restorative function. It reflects growing international consensus that participation and reparations play an important role in achieving justice for victims.'[135] Participation in criminal proceedings is not without difficulties, however, particularly where it clashes with the rights of the accused.[136] It also of course needs to be complementary to participation in other forums – truth commissions, commissions of inquiry, national criminal

[129] Alvarez, *supra* note 119, at 2034, citing N. Roth-Arriaza, 'Introduction', in N. Roth-Arriaza (ed.), *Impunity and Human Rights in International Law and Practice* (1995) 3, at 7–8.

[130] Alvarez, *supra* note 119, at 2084–85.

[131] Human Rights Watch, 'Rwanda: End Attacks on Opposition Parties', Press Release, 10 February 2010: '[An opposition figure] has been widely condemned in official and quasi-official media and described as a "negationist" of the genocide for stating publicly that crimes committed against Hutu citizens by the RPF and the Rwandan army should be investigated and those responsible brought to justice.'

[132] United Nations, Updated Set of principles for the protection and promotion of human rights through action to combat impunity, UN Doc. E/CN.4/2005/102/Add.1, 8 February 2005; see further references cited in Report of the Office of the United Nations High Commissioner for Human Rights, *Study on the Right to the Truth*, UN Doc. E/CN.4/2006/91, 8 February 2006.

[133] Report of the OHCHR, *Study on the Right to the Truth*, *supra* note 132, para. 61.

[134] ICC, Report of the Court on the strategy in relation to victims, UN Doc. ICC-ASP/8/45, 10 November 2009, para. 6. The Office of the Prosecutor has also prepared a Policy Paper on Victims' Participation, April 2010, available at www.icc-cpi.int/NR/rdonlyres/BC21BFDF-88CD-426B-BAC3-D0981E4ABE02/281751/PolicyPaperonVictimsParticipationApril2010.pdf.

[135] *Ibid*., paras. 2–3.

[136] See S. Zappalà, 'The Rights of Victims v. the Rights of the Accused', (2010) 8 *Journal of International Criminal Justice* 137.

tribunals, and national human rights institutions, – so that victims can obtain satisfaction and the factual record is as truthful and comprehensive as possible.[137] The ECCC and the Special Tribunal for Lebanon also allow for victims' participation in court proceedings.[138] This confirms the trend of recognising victims not only as potential witnesses and sources of information but also as active actors in the criminal process who are granted specific rights.[139]

### 3.2.2. Reparations to Victims

International law provides that human rights violations give rise to a right to obtain reparation, which can take various forms: restitution, compensation, rehabilitation, satisfaction, and guarantees of nonrepetition.[140] However, reparations for victims were not given a prominent status in the ad hoc international criminal tribunals' statutes, which were heavily based on the common-law model. The ICTY and ICTR Statutes provide for restitution of property acquired though criminal conduct once a finding of guilt has been made, but the victims have no direct standing in claiming restitution.[141] The individual victim can also claim compensation through the national courts or other competent bodies, once the accused has been convicted and the judgement has been transmitted to the national authorities.[142] However, these provisions have had little if no impact for victims involved in proceedings before the tribunals.[143]

137 *Ibid.*, para. 15.

138 See, e.g. Rule 23 to 23 *quinquies* of the Internal Rules of the ECCC; Rules 86–87 STL RPE; Explanatory Memorandum by the Tribunal's President, 10 June 2009, para. 14; for a comment, see J. de Hemptinne, 'Challenges Raised by Victims' Participation in the Proceedings of the Special Tribunal for Lebanon', (2010) 8 *Journal of International Criminal Justice* 165.

139 There are a growing number of jurisprudential interpretations of the criteria necessary to qualify as a victim under Art. 68(3) of the ICC Statute, including the notion of harm suffered by the victim and the link with the alleged crime. See, e.g., Situation in DRC – Case Lubanga, Judgement on the appeals of The Prosecutor and The Defence against Trial Chamber I's Decision on Victims' Participation of 18 January 2008, Case No. ICC-01/04–01/06–1432, 11 July 2008.

140 See, e.g., Universal Declaration of Human Rights, UN Doc A/810 at 71 (1948), Art. 8; 1966 International Covenant on Civil and Political Rights, 999 UNTS 171, Art. 2(3); 1984 Convention against Torture and Other Cruel, Inhuman or Degrading Treatment or Punishment, 1465 UNTS 85, Art. 14; Basic Principles and Guidelines on the Right to a Remedy and Reparation for Victims of Gross Violations of International Human Rights Law and Serious Violations of International Humanitarian Law, UN Doc. A/RES/60/147 (2005).

141 Art. 24(3) of the ICTY Statute and 23(3) of the ICTR Statute; Rules 98*ter*(B) and 105 of the ICTY Rules of Procedure and Evidence (RPE); Rules 88(b) and 105 RPE ICTR.

142 Rule 106 ICTY and ICTR RPE.

143 See, e.g., A-M De Brouwer, *Supranational Criminal Prosecution of Sexual Violence: The ICC and the Practice of the ICTY and the ICTR* (2005), at 394 and following; W. A. Schabas, *The UN International Criminal Tribunals: The former Yugoslavia, Rwanda and Sierra Leone* (2007), at 149 and following; S. Malstrom, 'Restitution of Property and Compensation to Victims', in R. May et al. (eds), *Essays on ICTY Procedure and Evidence in Honour of Gabrielle Kirk McDonald* (2001), 376; M. Husejnovic and E. Mackic, 'Victims Miss Out on Right to Compensation', Balkan Investigative Reporting Network, Justice Report, 4 March 2009 on compensation at ICTY and before the Bosnian War Crimes Chamber

The ICC Statute, in a significant development, affirms the right of victims to reparations with respect to crimes within its jurisdiction (Article 75). It also establishes a trust fund for victims (Article 79), which holds much promise in terms of its potential direct impact on victims.[144] Reparations in the ICC regime, which can be individual or collective,[145] are defined as including restitution, compensation, and rehabilitation (art. 75(1)). The issue of whether the ICC can issue reparations that are less financial or material in character, but more symbolic, is unclear.[146] However, these forms of reparation – such as commemorative shrines, memorials, and public apologies – may in certain circumstances prove essential to victims as a form of satisfaction.[147]

The trend to ensure that international criminal proceedings in the wake of atrocities take into consideration victims' reparations can also be seen in recently established internationalised settings. The ECCC has the power to issue 'collective and moral reparations'.[148] The Special Tribunal for Lebanon's Statute does not afford victims a right to claim compensation before the internationalised body, but the tribunal 'may identify victims who have suffered harm as a result of the commission of crimes by an accused convicted by the Tribunal' and transmit this information to the relevant domestic authorities. The victim 'may bring an action in a national court or other competent body to obtain compensation'.[149] This legislative choice tracks closely the far from convincing system established by the ICTY and ICTR Statutes that we discussed earlier. It remains to be seen whether the participation rights of victims before the STL and the tradition of Lebanese courts regarding civil parties will change the effective outcome.

Whether they rely exclusively on national jurisdictions or they provide for their own internal reparations schemes, international or internationalised criminal jurisdictions need to strongly rely on co-operation by states to ensure effective reparation

(see Art. 112 of the Criminal Code of Bosnia and Herzegovina). In Rwanda, the compensation orders have not been implemented: International Crisis Group, *International Criminal Tribunal for Rwanda: Justice Delayed*, 7 June 2001, Africa Report No. 30.

144 See Regs. of the Trust Fund for Victims, ICC-ASP/4/Res.3; the first concrete initiative for victims by the Fund was taken before the first trial at the ICC had started: Notification of the Board of the Trust Fund for Victims in accordance with Reg. 50 of the Regs. of the Trust Fund for Victims with Confidential Annex, Case No. ICC-01/04–439, January 24, 2008; see also T. Dannenbaum, 'The International Criminal Court, Article 79, and Transitional Justice: The Case for an Independent Trust Fund for Victims', (2010) *Wisconsin International Law Journal* 28.

145 International Criminal Court, Rules of Procedure and Evidence, U.N. Doc. PCNICC/2000/1/Add.1 (2000), Rules 97–98.

146 F. Mégret, 'The International Criminal Court and the Failure to Mention Symbolic Reparations', (2009) *International Review of Victimology* 127; S. A. Khan, *Rights of the Victims: Reparation by International Criminal Court* (2007), 33.

147 F. Mégret, 'Of Shrines, Memorials and Museums: Using the International Criminal Court's Victim Reparation and Assistance Regime to Promote Transitional Justice', (2010) 16 *Buffalo Human Rights Law Review* 17.

148 Rule 23 (1) (b) and 23 *quinquies* of the Internal Rules of the ECCC.

149 Statute of the Special Tribunal for Lebanon, UN.Doc. S/RES/1757 (2007), Art. 25.

to victims. In this spirit, states' obligations to co-operate with the ICC for the enforcement of orders for victim's reparations, whether monetary or nonmonetary, should be duly reflected in national implementing legislation.[150] An interesting consequence of the ICC Statute is the creation of reparation mechanisms in domestic legal systems, including in countries where victims normally have minimal involvement in criminal proceedings. For instance, Canada has created a 'Crimes against Humanity Fund' as part of its national implementing legislation.[151] If such initiatives do not involuntarily act 'at cross-purposes to the ICC Trust Fund for Victims',[152] they can be crucial tools for victims in national proceedings for ICC crimes and a positive indirect consequence of the complementarity principle.

Clearly, reparations at the ICC cannot hope to fulfil all the needs for reparation in postconflict societies, where hundreds or thousands of victims will have a rightful claim for reparations. They should indeed be seen as complementary to other reparation mechanisms. The regime put in place by the ICC 'represents a step towards entrenching the coherence of justice and reparations',[153] but obviously it does and should not replace broader reparations initiatives. The postconflict transitional justice strategy on reparations must be 'externally coherent' or have 'external integrity'[154] (i.e. connecting all the mechanisms so as to achieve the fundamental goal of contributing to a durable peace and reconciliation).

## 4. CONCLUSION

The seeming contradiction between peace and justice will always occur where the voices of the victims – those who make the demands for justice – are silenced or drowned out by the louder voices of those who have the most to fear from accountability. International criminal justice has begun to offer a counterbalance to this traditional dominance of brute force and power over humanity and justice. It is slowly becoming engrained in both the discourse and practice of post-conflict reconstruction. Young scholars from all over the world engage in civil society and in undergraduate and graduate studies related to human rights, international humanitarian law, and international criminal law. The human rights

150 See, e.g., Art. 9.2 of the Canadian *Mutual Legal Assistance in Criminal Matters Act*, (1985, c. 30 (4th Supp.)); *Report of the Commonwealth Expert Group on Implementing Legislation for the Rome Statute of the International Criminal Court*, Marlborough House, London 7–9 July 2004, paras. 132–34 and Clause 42. Complex issues may arise in the eventuality of competing claims for assets: see C. Ferstman, 'The Reparation Regime of the International Criminal Court: Practical Considerations', (2002) 15 *Leiden Journal of International Law* 667, at 683.

151 Canada's *Crimes against Humanity and War Crimes Act*, (2000, c. 24), art. 30 (not yet operational).

152 Ferstman, *supra* note 150, at 686.

153 OHCHR, Rule-of-Law Tools for Post-Conflict States: Reparations Programmes, UN Doc. HR/PUB/08/1, at 34.

154 *Ibid*, at 33, citing P. d. Greiff, 'Addressing the Past: Reparations for Gross Human Rights Abuses', in A. Hurwitz and R. Huang (eds.), *Civil War and the Rule of Law: Security, Development, Human Rights* (2007).

and accountability culture is slowly but surely influencing generations of lawyers, political scientists, politicians, and civil society actors in a trend that will, we believe and hope, have lasting effects on how peace and security are theorised and understood in practice. The rapid development of this global accountability consciousness has not yet reached the point where its tangible effects are indisputable in each and every postconflict society. However, the lessons learned in the process, and the sophisticated standards that have been developed, form a solid bedrock of principles upon which this generation can rely to build a better understanding of postconflict sustainable peace and development – an understanding that future generations, both intuitively and knowingly, should not fundamentally question.

# 12

# Reparations for Victims and Sustainable Development

*Pubudu Sachithanandan*

## 1. INTRODUCTION

Providing reparations for victims of violations of international criminal law is a challenging exercise, subject to severe budgetary, social, political, and other constraints. It is vital that reparations are not envisioned in a legalistic vacuum, but as an exercise that takes place within the framework of sustainable development. This chapter provides a brief description of the types of reparations provided to victims of international crimes and the mechanisms set up to make reparations. It then discusses the challenges faced by these mechanisms, explores the policy innovations designed to address such challenges, and considers how reparations could be used to promote sustainable development.

## 2. TYPES OF REPARATIONS

International human rights law and, increasingly, international criminal law, offer a legal basis for reparations to victims of crimes against humanity, war crimes, and genocide. There is also a growing tendency in criminal law to take the procedural rights of victims into account.[1]

There are various types of reparations, some symbolic (e.g. a public apology), some monetary, and some that are process-related (e.g. providing rehabilitation or counselling). The *Basic Principles and Guidelines on the Right to a Remedy and Reparation for Victims of Gross Violations of International Human Rights Law and Serious Violations of International Humanitarian Law*, adopted by the United Nations

[1] T. van Boven, 'The Right to Compensation and Related Remedies for Racial Discrimination', 2001 *Human Rights Development Yearbook* 428, at 429.

The opinions expressed in this chapter are those of the author and do not necessarily reflect the views of my former, current or future employers. The author is indebted to Mariana Ticolaz, Gwawr Thomas, and Sashini Jayawardane for their assistance in preparing this chapter.

General Assembly in 2005, recognise that victims of mass abuses have a right to 'adequate, effective and prompt reparation for harm suffered'.[2] The *Basic Principles* identify the following forms of reparation: restitution, compensation, rehabilitation, satisfaction, and guarantees of nonrepetition.[3] As the following overview evinces, the concept of reparations is broad and may contain a wide variety of measures.

According to the *Basic Principles*, restitution should, whenever possible, restore the victim to the original situation that existed before the gross violations of international human rights law or serious violations of international humanitarian law occurred. Restitution includes the restoration of liberty; enjoyment of human rights, identity, family life, and citizenship; return to one's place of residence; restoration of employment; and the return of property.[4]

Compensation is to be provided for any economically assessable damage, as appropriate and proportional to the gravity of the violation and the circumstances of each case that results from gross violations of international human rights law and serious violations of international humanitarian law. These violations include (i) physical or mental harm; (ii) lost opportunities, including employment, education, and social benefits; (iii) material damages and loss of earnings, including loss of earning potential; (iv) moral damage; and (v) costs required for legal or expert assistance, medicine and medical services, and psychological and social services.[5]

Rehabilitation includes medical and psychological care, as well as legal and social services.[6] It may also secure future treatment and services, in addition to any care already identified as needed.

Satisfaction refers to the type of redress that is not aimed at specific harm or loss, but to the general collective harm. Usually satisfaction attempts to remedy non-economic losses. It includes various remedial activities such as measures aimed at the cessation of the continuing activities; verification of facts and full and public disclosure of the truth to the extent that such disclosure does not cause further harm or threaten the safety and interests of the victim, the victim's relatives, witnesses, or persons who have intervened to assist the victim or prevent the occurrence of

[2] Basic Principles and Guidelines on the Right to a Remedy and Reparation for Victims of Gross Violations of International Human Rights Law and Serious Violations of International Humanitarian Law, UN Doc. A/RES/60/147 (2005). See, also, The United Nations Declaration of Basic Principles of Justice for Victims of Crimes and Abuse of Power, UN Doc. A/RES/40/34 (1985).

[3] M. Bassiouni, Final Report of the Special Rapporteur on the Civil and Political Rights, Including the Question of: Independence of the Judiciary, Administration of Justice, Impunity, UN Doc. E/CN.4/2000/62 (2000).

[4] Basic Principles, *supra* note 3; Final Report of the Special Rapporteur, *supra* note 4, at para. 19.

[5] *Ibid.*, para 20; See also Truth and Reconciliation Commission of South Africa Report, Vol. V, Ch. V, para. 26; see also Overview of the Sierra Leone Truth and Reconciliation Commission Report, paras. 47–48, available at www.leonenet.net/overviewtrcsl.pdf (last visited Jan. 24, 2010); Final Report of the Commission for Reception, Truth and Reconciliation in East Timor, part 11, para. 12.2.

[6] Final Report of the Special Rapporteur, *supra* note 4, at para. 21; see also *ibid.*, Truth and Reconciliation Commission of South Africa Report, at paras. 30–31; see also *ibid.*, Sierra Leone Truth and Reconciliation Commission Report, at paras. 47–48; see also *ibid.*, Final Report of the Commission for Reception, Truth and Reconciliation in East Timor, at part 11, para. 12.2.

further violations; public apology, including acknowledgement of the facts and acceptance of responsibility; judicial and administrative sanctions against persons liable for the violations; commemoration and tributes to the victims; and inclusion of an accurate account of the violation that occurred in international human rights law and international humanitarian law training and in educational material at all levels.[7] It also may include searching for the whereabouts of the disappeared, the identities of the children abducted, and the bodies of those killed, as well as providing assistance in recovery, identification, and reburial of the bodies in accordance with the expressed or presumed wished of the victims or other cultural practices of the families and communities. Satisfaction may also encompass declarations that may be an official declaration or a judicial decision restoring the dignity, reputation, and rights of the victim and of persons closely connected with the victim.

Finally, guarantees of nonrepetition are measures that can be taken to prevent a relapse into conflict[8] (see the discussion of such measures in the section on the relationship between reparations and development).

## 3. MECHANISMS

Reparations for violations of international criminal law are provided by a range of institutional mechanisms, including truth and reconciliation commissions, courts, administrative departments, voluntary funds, and traditional bodies. A few examples are described briefly in this section. The challenges faced by these mechanisms and policy innovations designed to address such challenges are explored in later sections.

### 3.1. *Truth Commissions*

Many countries that experienced human rights atrocities established investigatory commissions, often referred to as truth and reconciliation commissions (TRCs). Such institutions generally focus on the past and do not concentrate on any specific event, 'but attempt to paint the overall picture of certain human rights abuses, or violations of international humanitarian law, over a period of time'.[9] They exist temporarily 'for a pre-defined period of time, ceasing to exist with the submission of a report with its findings'.[10]

7 Final Report of the Special Rapporteur, *supra* note 4; see also Truth and Reconciliation Commission of South Africa Report, *supra* note 6, para. 27–29; see also Sierra Leone Truth and Reconciliation Commission Report, *supra* note 6, paras. 47–48; Final Report of the Commission for Reception, Truth and Reconciliation in East Timor, at part 11, para 12.2.

8 Final Report of the Special Rapporteur, *supra* note 4; see also Truth and Reconciliation Commission of South Africa Report, *supra* note 6, para. 32; see also Final Report of the Commission for Reception, Truth and Reconciliation in East Timor, *supra* note 6, part 11, para 12.2.

9 P. Hayner, 'Fifteen Truth Commissions – 1974 to 1994: A Comparative Study', (1994) 16 Hum. Rts. Q. 604.

10 *Ibid.*

These commissions are a relatively recent form of accountability. Truth commissions have been established in Argentina, Chile, El Salvador, Guatemala, Liberia, Peru, Sierra Leone, South Africa, and East Timor. They have addressed abuses of previous governments, but many also investigated violations committed by rebel groups (e.g. Guatemala and South Africa). TRCs can impose moral condemnation and prepare the ground for other sanctions, but do not usually function like a criminal trial. However, they can also make specific recommendations for reform.[11] Many truth commissions had the provision of reparations as a core part of their mandate and made recommendations regarding their provision. For example, in South Africa, the Truth and Reconciliation Commission established in 1995 had, as one of its objectives, 'affording victims an opportunity to relate the violations they suffered; the taking of measures aimed at the granting of reparation to, and the rehabilitation and the restoration of the human and civil dignity of, victims of violations of human rights'.[12] The Committee on Reparations was an important part of the work of the commission.[13]

Sierra Leone's Truth Commission was inaugurated in July 2002 in accordance with the Lome Peace Agreement. Its main purposes were 'to investigate and report on the causes, nature and extent of the violations and abuses' and 'to work to help restore the human dignity of victims and promote reconciliation by providing an opportunity for victims'.[14] The Lome Peace Agreement also provided that the TRC 'shall, among other things, recommend measures to be taken for the rehabilitation of victims of human rights violations'.[15]

The truth commission set up in 1990 in Chile was required to (i) establish as complete a picture as possible of the crimes, as well as their antecedents and circumstances; (ii) gather evidence that may make it possible to identify the victims and determine their fate or whereabouts; (iii) recommend measures of reparation and reinstatement; and (iv) recommend legal and administrative measures that should be adopted to prevent actions such as those mentioned in this chapter from being committed.[16]

In East Timor the Commission for Reception, Truth, and Reconciliation was established in 2002 and concluded its work in 2005. The regulation setting up the commission provides that 'the act of reconciliation may include: (a) community

[11] *Ibid.*, at 609.

[12] Act 95–34, Promotion of National Unity and Reconciliation Act 1995 (July 26, 1995).

[13] C. J. Colvin, *Overview of the Reparations Program in South Africa in the Handbook of Reparations*, (2006), 176.

[14] The Truth and Reconciliation Commission Act (2000), Supplement to the Sierra Leone Gazette Vol. CXXXI, No. 9, Feb. 10, 2000, Part III, para. 6(2)(a) and para. 6(2)(b).

[15] Peace Agreement between the Government of Sierra Leone and the Revolutionary United Front of Sierra Leone, (July 7, 1999), Art. 26 .

[16] Ministry of Justice, National Commission for Truth and Reconciliation, Supreme Decree No. 355, Creation of the Commission on Truth and Reconciliation (April 25, 1990), Santiago, Chile,

service; (b) reparation; (c) public apology; and/or (d) other act of contrition'.[17] The commission recommended in its final report that the government implement a programme of reparations for the most vulnerable victims of human rights violations, create memorials to commemorate the victims, and conduct further inquiry into mass graves and the fate of the disappeared.[18]

### 3.2. *UN Voluntary Fund*

In 1982, the General Assembly created the United Nations Voluntary Fund for Victims of Torture. This fund receives voluntary contributions and distributes them to treatment centres and other organisations to assist victims of torture and their relatives. It also funds projects for training health care professionals in treating victims of torture.[19] The types of supported assistance include psychological, medical, social, legal, and financial assistance.

### 3.3. *International/Ad Hoc and Mixed Courts*

Although reparations did not receive much attention during the establishment of international/ad hoc and mixed courts in the past, the mandates of newer bodies such as the International Criminal Court (ICC) and the Extraordinary Chambers in the Courts of Cambodia (ECCC) expressly incorporate the provision of reparations to victims.

#### 3.3.1. The International Criminal Court

The ICC is required to establish principles relating to reparations, including restitution, compensation, and rehabilitation.[20] Victims can make requests for reparations,[21] as well as participate in proceedings.[22] The court can make an order directly against a convicted person specifying appropriate reparations to, or in respect of, victims. It may award reparations on an individualised basis or – where

[17] Regulation No. 2001/10 on the Establishment of a Commission for Reception, Truth and Reconciliation in East Timor, UNTAET/REG/2001/10 (2001), sec. 27.

[18] Final Report of the Commission for Reception, Truth and Reconciliation in East Timor, *supra* note 4, part 11, para 12.1.

[19] "UN Support to Victims of Torture", available at www.un.org/events/torture/fund.htm (last visited Jan. 24, 2010).

[20] Rome Statute of the International Criminal Court, Art. 75(1). Text of the Rome Statute circulated as document A/CONF.183/9 of 17 July 1998 and corrected by process-verbaux of Nov. 10, 1998, July 12, 1999, Nov. 30, 1999, May 8, 2000, January 17, 2001 and January 16, 2002. The Statute entered into force on July 1, 2002.

[21] Rules of Procedure and Evidence of the International Criminal Court, rule 94. Adopted by the Assembly of States Parties, September 3–10, 2002, ICC-ASP/1/3.

[22] Rome Statute, *supra* note 21, Art. 68(3).

appropriate – on a collective basis, or both.[23] The ICC is in the early stages of developing its jurisprudence on reparations.

3.3.1.1. TRUST FUND FOR VICTIMS. The Statute of the ICC also provides for a trust fund for the benefit of victims and families of victims[24] that can receive voluntary contributions and to which money/other property collected via fines/forfeiture can be transferred. During the negotiations for establishing the International Criminal Court, the Trust Fund for Victims was considered an appropriate body to administer collective awards[25] (see the later section on collective reparations). As a result, where the number of victims and the scope, forms, and modalities of reparations make a collective award more appropriate, the court can now order that an award for reparations against a convicted person be made through the Trust Fund.[26] It can also be used for individual reparations; the court can order that an award for reparations against a convicted person be deposited with the Trust Fund when, at the time of making the order, it is impossible or impracticable to make individual awards directly to each victim. The award for reparations so deposited in the Trust Fund is to be separated from its other resources and must be forwarded to each victim as soon as possible.[27]

As of November 2009, the Trust Fund for Victims had raised 4.5 million Euros in voluntary contributions,[28] of which approximately 2.3 million has been allocated for activities in the Democratic Republic of the Congo (DRC) and northern Uganda. Another 600,000 Euros has been earmarked for activities in the Central African Republic, which the Trust Fund began supporting in 2010. It also maintains a reserve of 1 million Euros to complement any potential orders for reparations by the court.[29]

By late 2009, the Trust Fund had 34 approved projects pursuant to its mandate to provide general, non-court-ordered assistance to victims of crimes under the ICC's jurisdiction in northern Uganda and the DRC. In these two states, the relevant crimes include enlistment and conscription of child soldiers, sexual enslavement, rape, murder, pillage, destruction of property, and attacks directed against a civilian population. As of 2012, 31 projects are active and three projects have been competed.[30]

[23] Rules of Procedure and Evidence of the International Criminal Court, *supra* note 22, rule 97.

[24] Rome Statute, *supra* note 21, art. 79. See further Procedure for the nomination and election of judges of the International Criminal Court, Res. ICC-ASP/I/Res.6, ASP, (2002).

[25] P. Lewis and H. Friman, 'Reparations to Victims', in R. Lee (ed.), *The International Criminal Court, Elements of Crimes and Rules of Procedure* (2001), 487.

[26] Rules of Procedure and Evidence of the International Criminal Court, *supra* note 22, rule 98(3).

[27] *Ibid.*, at rule 98(2).

[28] Statement by Ambassador Altangerel, Assembly of State Parties, Trust Fund for Victims 2 (Nov. 2009), available at www.icc-cpi.int/iccdocs/asp_docs/ASP8/Statements/ICC-ASP-ASP8-statements-TFV-ENG.pdf.

[29] *Ibid.*

[30] The Trust Fund for Victims, "Projects," available at http://www.trustfundforvictims.org/projects.

3.3.1.2. APPOINTMENT OF EXPERTS. At the request of victims or their legal representatives, or at the request of the convicted person, or on its own motion, the ICC can appoint appropriate experts to assist it in determining the scope and extent of any damage, loss, and injury to or in respect of victims. Importantly, the experts can also be used *to suggest various options concerning the appropriate types and modalities of reparations*. The court is required to invite, as appropriate, victims or their legal representatives, the convicted person, as well as interested persons and states, to make observations on the reports of the experts.[31] This appointment of experts may prove to be a useful provision for ensuring that any collective reparations ordered are the appropriate types, have the appropriate modalities, and contribute to sustainable development.

### 3.3.2. The Extraordinary Chambers in the Courts of Cambodia

The ECCC is the first internationalised (i.e. with a combination of international and national personnel) tribunal with a specific reparations mandate. Reparations can be sought by victims who participate in the proceedings as civil parties, although Rule 23(11) of the ECCC allows victims to seek only 'collective and moral reparations'.[32] Awards can include 'an order to publish the judgement in any appropriate news or other media at the convicted person's expense; an order to fund any nonprofit activity or service intended for the benefit of victims; or other appropriate or comparable forms of reparation'.[33] These reparations are to be borne by the convicted person.[34]

### 3.3.3. Ad Hoc Tribunals

Unlike the ICC and the ECCC, the International Criminal Tribunals for Rwanda and the Former Yugoslavia are not authorised to make orders for reparations and have not generated significant practice in this area. However, the statutes of both ad hoc tribunals provide the following: 'In addition to imprisonment, the Trial Chambers may order the return of any property and proceeds acquired by criminal conduct, including by means of duress, to their rightful owners.'[35] In both tribunals the Registrar is required to transmit to the competent authorities of the states concerned the judgement finding the accused guilty of a crime that has caused injury to a victim. Pursuant to the relevant national legislation, a victim or persons claiming

31 Rules of Procedure and Evidence of the International Criminal Court, *supra* note 22, rule 97(2).

32 C. Sperfeldt, 'Reparations for Victims of the Khmer Rouge' 4, Oxford Transitional Justice Research Working Paper Series, May 2009, available at www.csls.ox.ac.uk/documents/SperfeldtFinal.pdf.

33 *Ibid.*

34 *Ibid.*

35 International Criminal Tribunal for Rwanda Statute, Arts. 23(3) and 24(3).

through the victim may bring an action in a national court or other competent body to obtain compensation.[36]

### 3.4. *Overlapping Mechanisms*

In certain jurisdictions, several mechanisms can function simultaneously. This was the case, for example, in Sierra Leone[37] and East Timor[38] where criminal tribunals and truth commissions operated simultaneously. This may also be the case with future situations investigated by the International Criminal Court. It is important in such situations to ensure (to the extent possible, without prejudice to the independence of the relevant institutions) that reparations orders do not contradict or overlap with each other.

### 3.5. *National Courts and Traditional Conflict Resolution Mechanisms*

National courts and traditional conflict resolution mechanisms have been used in several postconflict contexts as a means of providing reparations to victims of war crimes, crimes against humanity, and genocide. Rwanda is a useful example in this context, because it highlights several of the challenges that arise when dealing with mass victimisation in the context of limited resources.

Rwanda enacted the 1996 Organic Law to deal with persons suspected of participating in the Rwandan genocide. Although the approach was focused on individual criminal responsibility, the government also utilised a 'civil parties' system through which victims could become party to a criminal trial and claim reparations; the state was required to compensate the victims. Due to the heavy caseload, Rwanda also used a traditional conflict resolution process named Gacaca, in which the focus was not punishment, but the 're-establishment of social order'. More than 11,000 local Gacaca tribunals were established via the Gacaca Law adopted in 2001. Although no compensation was available under this system, a new law adopted in 2004 provided for tribunals to award compensation for material damages. Other types of victimisation (e.g. loss of family members, physical or psychological harm) were to

[36] Rules of Evidence and Procedure, International Criminal tribunal for Rwanda, rule 106, UN Doc. ITR/3/Rev.17 (2008); Rules of Evidence and Procedure International Criminal Tribunal for the Former Yugoslavia, rule 106, UN Doc. IT/32/Rev. 43 (2009).

[37] W. Schabas, 'The Relationship between Truth Commissions and International Courts: The Case of Sierra Leone', (2003) 25 *Human Rights Quarterly* 4, at 1035; International Center for Transitional Justice, *Exploring the Relationship between the Special Court and the Truth and Reconciliation Commission*, New York (June 2002); W. Schabas and S. Darcy (eds.), *Truth Commissions and Courts: The Tensions between Criminal Justice and the Search for Truth* (2004), 50; *Prosecutor* v. *Norman*, No. SCSL-2003–08oPT, Decision on the Request by the Truth and Reconciliation Commission of Sierra Leone to Conduct a Public Hearing with Samuel Hinga Norman, 29 October 2003, para. 33.

[38] M. Hirst and H. Varney, JUSTICE ABANDONED? An Assessment of the Serious Crimes Process in East Timor 12–13, *International Center for Transitional Justice*, June 2005, available at www.ictj.org/images/content/1/2/121.pdf.

be handled by the Indemnification Fund (FIND). The only mechanism for reparations that existed prior to FIND was the *Fonds d'Assistance aux Rescapés du Génocide* (FARG), intended to benefit only limited categories of victims.[39]

Civil redress for victims of human rights abuses is available within the legal systems of most countries. The U.S. Alien Tort Claims Act (ATCA) is an interesting example. It provides that '[t]he district courts shall have original jurisdiction of any civil action by an alien for a tort only, committed in violation of the law of nations or a treaty of the United States'.[40] ATCA provides federal courts with jurisdiction if three conditions are fulfilled: (i) the plaintiff is an alien; (ii) the defendant is responsible for a tort; and (iii) the tort violates the law of nations or a treaty to which the United States is party.[41] Notable among the ATCA cases is the *Kadic* v. *Karadzic* judgement[42] that culminated in an award of $745 million. (Although this judgement is a significant precedent, it is unlikely that the plaintiffs will receive the sum awarded.)

## 4. THE RELATIONSHIP BETWEEN REPARATIONS AND DEVELOPMENT

It is vital that state authorities bear in mind that any reparations program is a small part of what should be a broad postconflict reconstruction process.[43] The chances for a civil war to occur tend to be higher in post-civil-war societies than in societies with no such prior experience.[44] One reason is that survivors of atrocities are often denied access to employment, education, housing, medical care, and the like; such inequalities tend to provide a basis for a future conflict.[45] Repeated relapses into conflict may also spread to neighbouring countries, leading to regional destabilisation.[46]

Accordingly, reparations programs should be designed so that co-ordination and synchronicity exist between the reparations program and other postconflict development. Reparations become pointless if postconflict development fails and there is a relapse into conflict. Thus, states must take steps to ensure that the atrocities of the past are not repeated. Postconflict development must ensure effective civilian control of military and security forces and that all civilian and military proceedings abide by international standards of due process, fairness, and impartiality. Programmes

39 H. Rombourts, 'Women and Reparations in Rwanda: A Long Path to Travel', in R. Rubio-Marin (ed.), *What Happened to the Women? Gender and Reparations for Human Rights Violations* (2006).

40 28 U.S.C. para. 1350 (1994).

41 S. Ratner and J. S. Abrams, *Accountability for Human Rights Atrocities in International Law: Beyond Nuremberg Legacy* (2001), at 241.

42 *Kadic* v. *Karadzic*, 74 F.3d 377 (2d. Cir. 1996).

43 L. Magarrell, International Center for Transitional Justice, Reparations in Theory and Practice 3, available at www.ictj.org/static/Reparations/0710.Reparations.pdf.

44 K. Brouneus, 'Reconciliation and Development', in K. Ambos and J. Large (eds.), *Building a Future on Peace and Justice: Studies on Transitional Justice, Peace and Development* (2009), 212.

45 *Ibid.*

46 *Ibid.*

must strengthen the independence of the judiciary and review and reform laws that contribute to or allow gross violations of international human rights law and serious violations of international humanitarian law.[47] Strengthening protection of key service personnel in the legal, medical, and health care professions; the media and other related professions; and human rights defenders is just as important as providing, on a priority and continued basis, human rights and international humanitarian law education to all sectors of society, as well as training for law enforcement officials and military and security forces. This training and reforms should include promoting codes of conduct. To ensure nonrepetition, it is imperative that public servants – including law enforcement, correctional, media, medical, psychological, social services, and military personnel – and economic enterprises observe codes of conduct and ethical norms, in particular international standards. Mechanisms that monitor, prevent, and resolve social conflict must also be promoted and established within the postconflict framework.

In addition to being co-ordinated and compatible with other sustainable postconflict development, reparations programmes *themselves* must promote sustainable development. It is crucial that they incorporate and reflect various aspects of sustainable development, including empowerment, co-operation, equity, sustainability, and security.[48] The relationship between reparations and sustainable development is explored in the following sections on financing reparations, setting the parameters of victimhood, choosing among collective/individual/mixed reparations, accountability, reparations and gender, and implementation.

### 4.1. *Financing Reparations*

States emerging from conflicts are often poor and find it difficult to muster the funding to provide monetary or other material reparations. Even if a TRC or other mechanism makes recommendations regarding reparations, it may be difficult to implement the reparations in the context of extreme poverty, corruption, and dysfunctional state institutions. Indeed, even if implemented, such reparations will not necessarily reduce poverty and corruption nor optimise the functioning of state institutions.[49] Therefore, where resources are limited, it may be more realistic to focus on community-oriented (i.e. collective) reparations[50] (see the later section on collective reparations).

Regardless of the resources available, it is vital that victims perceive that they are not forgotten and that whatever resources are available are being put to optimum

47 Basic Principles, *supra* note 3, at para. 23.

48 C. O. Lerche III, Truth Commissions and National Reconciliation: Some Reflections on Theory and Practice, Peace and Conflict Studies, 2000, at 13–14, available at pcs/journalsPDF/V7N1.pdf#page=2, listing the UNDP's '5 aspects of Sustainable Development'.

49 B. Dougherty, 'Searching for Answers: Sierra Leone's Truth & Reconciliation Commission', (2004) 8 *African Studies Quarterly* 1, available at www.africa.ufl.edu/asq/v8/v8i1a3.htm#_edn36#_edn36.

50 P. Hayner, *Unspeakable Truth: Facing the Challenge of Truth Commissions* (2001), at 182.

use on their behalf. The absence of this perception will not only increase the suffering of the victims but also have a detrimental impact on other reconciliation and accountability initiatives. For example, many of the approximately 1000 amputees who survived the conflict in Sierra Leone felt ignored, with attention and funds perceived as being directed towards other priorities.[51] On one occasion, several members of this group of victims warned that they would withhold their co-operation with the TRC unless their demands were met.[52]

Innovative efforts must be used to finance reparations. These efforts could include tracing and recovering the assets stolen by previous regimes and other parties to the conflict, as well as requesting cancellations of foreign debt in exchange for focusing certain budgetary allocations on development projects that relate to reparations.[53] However, it is crucial that the funding for reparations is provided at least partly from the country's ordinary budget. Funding that relies on temporary funds based on voluntary contributions has been less successful in the past. Reparations projects can also be linked to micro-finance mechanisms, given the success of such mechanisms in postconflict states.[54]

Micro-finance institutions (MFIs) could be useful institutions for linking reparations with sustainable development in several ways. First, micro-financing is a mechanism that can be used for the safekeeping of reparation payments. It could strengthen the self-financing capacity of the victims who receive reparations payments. Second, MFIs could offer credit for investments and working capital for victims to become micro-entrepreneurs and may attract external finance for the same ventures. Third, victims who receive reparations may have the opportunity to build MFIs, thus mobilising their 'self-help capacity' both as shareholder-owners and borrowers. This would be 'especially useful in states or regions where functional institutions are scarce.'[55]

When local capacity is deficient and the local political environment unfavourable, it is also vital that the international community commit sufficient resources and political pressure to ensure the provision of reparations.[56]

### 4.2. *Which Victim, Which Reparations?*

Many difficult decisions have to be made about which persons or which category of persons can be recognised as a victim and thus be eligible to receive reparations. It is important when crafting reparation initiatives, especially in light of the limited resources available, that victims who have the greatest needs are prioritised. Factors

51 B. Dougherty, *supra* note 50.

52 *Ibid.*

53 Magarrell, *supra* note 44, at 14.

54 *Ibid.*

55 H. D. Seibel and A. Armstrong, 'Reparations and Micro-Finance Schemes', in P. de Grieff (ed.), *The Handbook of Reparations* (2006), 678.

56 Hirst and Varney, *supra* note 39, at 31.

to be considered in this context include the health, age, gender, and other characteristics that have an impact upon the ability of victims to recover from harm. These priorities may evolve over time. Decisions on which victims take priority should be made in a transparent and fair manner, and the decision-making process must be understood by all stakeholders.[57] When prioritising, it is useful to note that appropriately targeted reparations can be a powerful tool to empower women. The lessons learned from the field of micro-credit – where focusing loans on women has proved very successful[58] – could prove useful in targeting collective reparations.

Linked to this issue of prioritisation is the question of what types of reparations should be provided and how such decisions should be made. It is important to ensure that the types of reparations provided match the needs of the victims. For example, for some victims in Argentina, the creation of a new legal status of 'forcibly disappeared' proved more important than financial reparations. This status is considered the legal equivalent of death for purposes of civil matters and allows families to process wills, close the victim's bank account, and distribute his or her estate, yet it stops short of declaring the person dead. The legislation creating this status holds open the possibility of the reappearance of the person – a measure adopted at the insistence of surviving family members. The law allowing families to obtain a 'certificate of forced disappearance' came to be known as the 'law on historical sincerity'. Argentina was the first state to create this new status.[59]

### 4.3. *Collective versus Individual Reparations*

Choices also have to be made about whether reparations are provided to categories/groups of persons (collective reparations) or to specific individuals (individual reparations).

#### 4.3.1. Collective Reparations

Several challenges arise when providing collective reparations; they are blunter instruments by nature and often do not highlight the specific, individual nature of the suffering of individual victims.[60] They raise questions such as whether a victim who spent a week in the prison should receive the same amount of reparations as one who spent a year in prison.[61]

Systems of collective reparations can be abused for nepotistic or political purposes. They can also overlap with development initiatives in a way that makes them less

57 Magarrell, *supra* note 44, at 9.

58 See presentation by Muhammad Yunus at the Google campus, New York City, NY on 10 January 2008 regarding the Grameen Bank at www.youtube.com/watch?v=E-W6yoHzFWk.

59 Hayner, *supra* note 51, at 177.

60 Magarrell, *supra* note 44, at 6.

61 Hayner, *supra* note 51.

useful in highlighting the violations to which victims have been subjected, thereby diluting the political importance of reparations. The *sole* provision of generalised development is not the same as reparations because it does not distinguish persons who have suffered harm.[62]

Programs of collective reparations have been successful where they take the form of services provided to categories of victims, such as counselling/rehabilitation/ educational assistance (e.g. the provision of mental health services to victims in Chile).[63] These services must be calibrated realistically to the resources available.

Proper management of collective reparations programmes is crucial for their success. In Rwanda, the FARG funded education, health, and credit-provision programmes. The management of the credit programme has been criticised – many recipients reportedly spent the funds without repaying them.[64]

The impact of the reparations programme in Chile was limited by the fact that it did not cover the survivors of illegal imprisonment or torture, who formed the majority of victims in the country. In addition, just as the truth commission could not investigate individual cases of torture or include survivors of torture in its list of victims, the reparation program gave almost no assistance to these persons except free access to a state medical programme. This programme has been little used by torture survivors and has received mixed reviews about its quality.[65] The only recourse for these victims is referral to nongovernmental organisations that try to assist them.[66]

On occasion, the provision of services on an ongoing basis can be more useful than the provision of funds. For example, sometimes survivors who received monetary reparations described ongoing suffering, due to lack of access to medical care.[67]

The International Criminal Court's reparation regime also features some service delivery components. Its Trust Fund estimates that approximately 39,000 victims benefit directly from Trust Fund-supported services, including counselling, community reconciliation workshops, education grants, reconstructive surgery, and start-up grants for income-generating activities. An additional 187,000 family and other community members are also estimated to be benefiting from these services.[68]

During the negotiations of the Rules of the International Criminal Court, the delegates recognised that the Trust Fund 'may not be in the best position to distribute monies or organise, for example, the building of a school or hospital'. Hence, the delegates thought it appropriate to allow the Trust Fund to 'call on intergovernmental, international or national organisations approved by the Trust Fund to carry out tasks

62 Magarrell, *supra* note 44, at 6.
63 *Ibid.*, at 12.
64 'Women and Reparations in Rwanda', *supra* note 40, at 228.
65 Hayner, *supra* note 51, at 174.
66 *Ibid.*
67 Brouneus, *supra* note 45, at 213.
68 Statement by Ambassador Altangerel, *supra* note 29, at 3.

on its behalf'.[69] However, this reliance on external agencies was a controversial topic. Many negotiators opined that such involvement could not be practicable without the involvement and co-operation of the relevant state with the court. Some delegations were concerned about the 'implied infringement of sovereignty if it was suggested that these organisations could simply intervene in the internal affairs of a country'.

This recognition of the need to rely on external agencies, as well as the related concerns about the role of the relevant state, are both reflected in Rule 98[70] Sub-rule 4: they provide that the court may order that an award for reparations be made through the Trust Fund to an intergovernmental, international, or national organisation approved by the Trust Fund, following consultations with interested States and the Trust Fund.[71]

### 4.3.2. Individual Reparations

Individual reparations usually involve the identification of specific victims and an individualised assessment of the nature and extent of their victimisation. This is usually done through a judicial or quasi-judicial process. The provision of reparations to individual victims of war crimes, crimes against humanity, and genocide has been carried out with varying degrees of success. In the context of sustainable development, it is important to bear in mind the limitations and possible consequences of providing individual reparations.

4.3.2.1. DEALING WITH MASS VICTIMISATION. The type of process that is required for individual reparations (i.e. tribunals or similar bodies that inquire into individual circumstances) may have difficulty handling the sheer scale of victimisation, because large-scale conflicts often result in thousands of victims.[72] For example, despite approximately 1.7 million deaths during the Khmer Rouge regime, as of May 2009, the ECCC's Victims Unit received only approximately 3,500 applications for participation by victims.[73]

The procedural complexities of judicial and quasi-judicial bodies may limit access and slow the reparations process.[74] For example, claims for reparation in some fora may hinge on whether the alleged perpetrator is still alive. Following a recent amendment, Rule 23(13) of the ECCC stipulates that the 'civil action against a charged person shall end on the death of that person'.[75] Moreover, where truth commissions has the responsibility to establish the list of beneficiaries, as in South Africa and Chile, they have to individually corroborate each victim statement, which

[69] Lewis and Friman, *supra* note 25, 487.
[70] *Ibid.*
[71] Rules of Procedure and Evidence of the International Criminal Court, *supra* note 22, rule 98(4).
[72] Magarrell, *supra* note 44, at 3.
[73] Sperfeldt, *supra* note 33, at 4.
[74] van Boven, *supra* note 1, at 428, 429.
[75] Sperfeldt, *supra* note 33, at 6.

is time consuming and distracts the commission from broader investigations into patterns of crimes and responsibility.[76] (Given the time and personnel involved in corroborating the claims and enabling reparations programs to be open to those who do not testify to the truth commission, it may be best that reparations programs are implemented by a body other than a truth commission.[77])

4.3.2.2. RE-TRAUMATISATION. Re-traumatisation of victims (especially victims of torture or sexual crimes who may have to relive their experiences in public) may result from investigative procedures used in dealing with mass victimisation.[78] Many courts have tried to minimise such impact by using special procedures. For example, at the International Criminal Court, any chamber can, taking into account the views of the victim or witness, order special measures to facilitate the testimony of a traumatised victim or witness or a victim of sexual violence.[79]

In addition, making standardised payments to individuals may have a disruptive effect on communities. For example, in Chile, payment of individual reparations to members of indigenous communities that had a strong collective ethos reportedly had an adverse impact on the harmony within the communities.[80] In South Africa, some of those who did not receive Urgent Interim Reparations, because they were not considered urgent cases, reportedly threatened to use violence.[81] Reparations to individuals may increase their vulnerability in environments where there is a weak security infrastructure (e.g. the interim reparations process in South Africa).

It may also be that different victims have access to different types of fora, leading to inequalities in access. For example, some victims may have access to regional human rights courts and others may not, so that individual-focused reparations may result in inequities. Although there may be no short-term solution to such inequities, it is important that victims be given as much choice as possible about which programme they wish to access. This way, it is possible to ensure that the system of reparations becomes less of a blunt instrument.[82]

It is vital that the provision of reparations remains fair and nondiscriminatory. Any (real or perceived) lack of even-handedness may negatively affect the legitimacy of the programme. For example, in Rwandan national courts, the amount of financial reparations reportedly differed from one award to another (within the same jurisdiction, for the same crimes). This discrepancy has been criticised.[83]

76 Hayner, *supra* note 51, at 182.
77 *Ibid.*, 182–83.
78 Magarrell, *supra* note 44, at 12.
79 Rules of Procedure and Evidence of the International Criminal Court, *supra* note 22, rule 88(1).
80 Magarrell, *supra* note 44, at 6.
81 P. de Grieff, 'Overview of the Reparations Program in South Africa,' in *The Handbook of Reparations* (2006), 189.
82 Magarrell, *supra* note 44.
83 Rombourts, *supra* note 40.

### 4.3.3. Combined Approaches

It is often useful to provide a combination package of individual and collective reparations. For example, in East Timor the truth commission recommended a programme that 'combined individual benefits with a form of delivery designed to promote collective healing'. In addition, war widows and persons subject to sexual violence were given scholarship grants for their children. They obtained these benefits in regional service centres where they were given support/training/health services.[84]

The Statute and Rules of the International Criminal Court also take a 'combined' approach to reparations. Although there was little explicit discussion of reparations within the framework of sustainable development during the negotiations at Rome, the discussions surrounding Rule 97 of the Rules of Procedure and Evidence of the Court, and the issue of whether collective reparations should be permissible, indicate the fault-lines that existed at the time. Some delegations 'saw Reparations as a method for victims to enforce their civil claims through the court'.[85] For other delegations, reparations 'were another form of sanction imposed by the Court . . . and were not a means of satisfying civil debts'.[86] Alternatively reparations were viewed as 'very much a matter of trying to address the needs of victims and for this reason victims should have a say in how any resources were used'.[87] For example, if the court identified a certain sum to be awarded as reparations to X village, the villagers should have input into whether each family should be awarded a specific share or whether resources should be used collectively to benefit the entire village (e.g. to build a school).[88]

As a compromise between these views, Rule 97 of the Rules of Procedure and Evidence now provides for reparations on an individual basis, collective basis, or a combination of both.

### 4.4. *Accountability*

The requirement of accountability is recognised in some form in most legal systems, as well as in international law. Redress is the primary obligation of the perpetrators or those liable for them.[89] If it is not possible to identify the perpetrator or he or she is unable to pay, other mechanisms must be in place whereby the collective takes responsibility for meeting the victim's claim.[90] When the state or its representatives

84 Magarrell, *supra* note 44, at 6.
85 Lewis and Friman, *supra* note 25, at 486.
86 *Ibid.*
87 *Ibid.*
88 *Ibid.*
89 S. Gloppen, 'On the Role of Reparations in Transitional Justice Theory', 2001 *Human Rights Development Yearbook* 385, at 389.
90 *Ibid.*

violate citizens' rights, the state is obliged to provide appropriate redress.[91] For example, in East Timor, the truth commission placed reparations in a human rights context that included 'three essential components which cannot be substituted for each other: truth, justice, and reparations'.[92]

Reparations tend to be more effective when combined with complementary mechanisms for accountability. In fact, when reparations projects are not accompanied by measures for accountability, they can be counterproductive.[93] Accountability is particularly important when designing programmes of *collective* reparations. Such programmes may move the focus away from the accountability of any actor. Although this shift in focus makes such programs popular with some postconflict governments, the lack of accountability has a negative impact on reestablishing the rule of law and may increase the chance of the country relapsing into conflict.

Choices have to be made about *who* should be held accountable. In Sierra Leone, as part of the demobilisation, disarmament, and reintegration process, approximately 7,000 children were reintegrated into their communities. Many in Sierra Leone saw the child combatants as victims and welcomed the decision of the Special Court for Sierra Leone not to prosecute child soldiers.[94]

When examining the accountability of various actors in a given situation, it is important not to ignore the potential responsibility of nonstate actors such as corporations. The reconciliation process in South Africa, for example, has been criticised for not effectively examining such responsibility.[95]

### 4.5. *Reparations and Gender*

Women often bear a greater burden during times of war.[96] When establishing a reparations program that is intended to contribute positively to sustainable development, it is necessary to consider the specific needs of women and include women in all processes that deliver redress for the past.[97] The cultural and political context (and power relations within it) must be well understood and dealt with in the design and implementation of the program.[98]

Some women victims live under two or more sets of laws: the statutory regime of the nation-state and relevant customary regime(s). The coexistence of these legal

91 *Ibid.*

92 Final Report of the Commission for Reception, Truth and Reconciliation in East Timor, *supra* note 7, at part 11, para 12.2.

93 Magarrell, *supra* note 44, at 3. See also Brouneus, *supra* note 45, at 207.

94 Dougherty, *supra* note 50.

95 C. J. Colvin, 'Overview of the Reparations Program in South Africa,' in P. de Greiff (ed.), *The Handbook of Reparations* (2006), 205.

96 N. Valji, 'Gender Justice and Reconciliation', in K. Ambos and J. Large (eds.), *Building a Future on Peace and Justice: Studies on Transitional Justice, Peace and development* (2009), 218.

97 *Ibid*, at 224.

98 *Ibid*, at 230.

regimes can affect women's access to legal and administrative remedies or result in other kinds of discrimination; for example, in cases where a woman must obtain her husband's consent to approach the legal system[99] or where a girl of marriageable age is exchanged as 'compensation' for a crime.[100] Traditional practices can, however, also play a positive role in the process of social reintegration of the victims and combatants. It is necessary to focus and build on such positive elements.[101]

Reparation policies have sometimes failed to consider gendered hierarchies within family units. In South Africa reparations were once-off payments of approximately USD$4,000. Despite the fact that most of the beneficiaries were African women, the policy reportedly did not take into consideration the lack of access to bank accounts and the fact that money was often deposited into the bank accounts of men, to which women may have had limited access.[102]

Adequate support must be given for women who seek redress. Mechanisms should also be established for those who cannot come forward to seek redress. Broader structural changes can also form part of the reparations programme. For example, the Truth Commission of Sierra Leone recommended that political parties/government reserve 30 per cent of government posts for women.[103] In East Timor, the TRC report paid special attention to women as victims of the conflict and recommended that at least 50 per cent of programme resources be directed to female beneficiaries.[104]

Gender budgeting tools offer advantages for reparations programs – in particular, programmes that are created to deliver long-term social services, such as trust funds for pension payments, scholarships for the children of victims of sexual violence, and the provision of social security for victims. Gender budgeting tools could enable policy makers to track the transitional governments' expenses priorities to ensure that victims will continue to receive reparation if it is paid out in instalments.[105]

It is important to note, additionally, that gender-based violence is not limited to women victims. Its use against male victims may also need to be addressed in innovative ways.[106]

The International Criminal Court's Trust Fund for Victims considers its assistance to victims of sexual and other forms of gender-based violence 'a key step towards ending impunity for human rights abusers and establishing durable peace and reconciliation in conflict settings'.[107] The Trust Fund has stated publicly that achieving

[99] C. Duggan and A. Abusharaf, 'Reparations of Sexual Violence in Democratic Transitions: The Search for Gender Justice', in P. de Greiff (ed.), *The Handbook of Reparations* (2006), 632.

[100] Valji, *supra* note 97, at 234.

[101] *Ibid.*

[102] *Ibid.*, at 232.

[103] *Ibid.*, at 231.

[104] Final Report of the Commission for Reception, Truth and Reconciliation in East Timor, *supra* note 7, at part 11, para 12.6.

[105] Duggan and Abusharaf, *supra* note 100, at 643.

[106] Valji, *supra* note 97, at 230.

[107] Statement by Ambassador Altangerel, *supra note* 29, at 3, 4.

its mission of addressing the harm resulting from crimes under the jurisdiction of the International Criminal Court necessitates both mainstreaming a gender-based perspective across all programming (including reparations) and targeting crimes of sexual violence.[108] Pursuant to this, the Board of Directors of the Trust Fund initiated a filing with the ICC to launch support for victims of sexual violence in the Central Africa Republic.[109]

### 4.6. *Implementation*

Even if the finances are available, it is sometimes difficult to muster the political will necessary for implementation within states emerging from conflict. Victims' groups do not usually have the type of lobbying power necessary,[110] and they may not, for example, be considered an actor that requires priority treatment (i.e. unlike former combatant groups, they may be seen as less of a threat for making the state relapse into conflict).

Campaigners for reparations must use litigation, advocacy, and other available options to speed up the reparations process. For example, the reparations law for families of the disappeared in Argentina was reportedly not implemented until 1994, ten years after the Truth Commission completed its work.[111] The reparations program was prompted in part by some cases brought before the Inter-American Commission of Human Rights by political prisoners who requested compensation for their time in jail.[112]

It is also crucial that the entities charged with recommending and/or implementing reparations have the power and capacity to take and implement decisions. If such responsibility is given to nonfunctional or toothless bodies, the reparations process will be undermined.[113]

It may be useful to consider innovative ways of implementing the reparations decisions/recommendations of international courts and other entities at the national level. For example in Colombia, if the Inter-American Court or Commission finds that Colombia violated the American Convention on Human Rights by adopting a judicial decision that 'unfairly exonerates a perpetrator of serious human rights violations', the relevant decision can be reconsidered at the national level.[114] This provision is invaluable to victims seeking redress at the national and subnational levels.

[108] *Ibid.*, at 4.
[109] *Ibid.*
[110] Magarrell, *supra* note 45, at 14.
[111] Hayner, *supra* note 51, at 175–76.
[112] *Ibid.*, at 176. The cases brought before the Inter-American Commission and the friendly settlement with the government are contained in the Annual Report of the Inter-American Commission of Human Rights, 1992–93, OEA/Ser.L/V/II.83, doc.14, Corr. I, March 12, 1993, 35–40.
[113] Magarrell, *supra* note 45, at 12.
[114] Transcript of the conference "Reparations in the Inter-American System: A Comparative Approach", March 6, 2007 at American University Washington College of Law, 56 Am. U. L. Rev. 1375, at 1396.

Many of the recommendations of truth commissions require legislative action or even constitutional reform, whereas others require only the initiative of the president to make administrative changes. It is clear that the implementation of the truth commissions' recommendation remains the weakest aspect of the process. After the commission closes, the list of recommendations remains at the discretion of the government and usually receives little attention.[115] One way to improve this process is the legislation for the Truth Commission in Sierra Leone that calls for the creation of a follow-up committee to track the implementation of its recommendations and requires the governments to make quarterly reports on the progress made.[116]

It is important that reparations programs take into consideration the cultural/historical and political context in which they are delivered.[117] Consider, for example, the customary law regimes discussed in the section on reparations and gender.

It is vital that the victims who are to benefit from reparations programs participate in designing, implementing, and monitoring the program. Ensuring victim participation can be a challenge, given the differences amongst victim groups, their lack of resources and organisation, and the security risks they may often face.[118]

It is also important to manage the expectations of victims. Without a realistic understanding of the limits of what can be achieved, reparations projects can become unpopular and unsustainable.

## 5. CONCLUSION

An intelligent effort to provide reparations should begin with recognising the challenges related to financing, setting the parameters of victimhood, choosing between collective/individual/mixed reparations, and addressing issues of accountability, gender, and implementation. It should then innovate to make the best use of the limited resources available. As observed at the beginning of this chapter, it is vital that reparations are not envisioned in a legalistic vacuum, but as an exercise that integrates the various aspects of sustainable development, including empowerment, co-operation, equity, sustainability, and security.

[115] Hayner, *supra* note 51, at 169.
[116] *Ibid.*
[117] Magarrell, *supra* note 45, at 15.
[118] *Ibid.*, at 9.

PART IV

# Making International Criminal Justice More Sustainable

# 13

# Sustainable Development, Conflicts, and International Crimes

*Charles Séguin*

## 1. INTRODUCTION

The concept of sustainable development is founded on a long-term perspective that seeks to ensure that human activities undertaken in the present do not impair the interests of future generations. In this way, the pursuit of sustainable development can contribute to the prevention of harmful and deleterious human conduct in the long term.

In this chapter, I consider how the pursuit of sustainable development could help alleviate three factors associated with the prevalence of international crimes: economic inequality and underdevelopment, resource scarcity, and natural resource predation. I argue that the implementation of all the facets of sustainable development will contribute to the reduction of these factors in the long run and hence will decrease occurrences of international crime. The short-run picture, although somewhat positive, is not as promising, which might explain why the concept of sustainable development has not been implemented more widely yet.

The point, of course, is not that economic inequality and underdevelopment, resource scarcity, and natural resource predation actually lead to the commission of international crimes, but rather that they contribute to the emergence of contexts where the commission of international crimes is more likely. After all, international crimes may be committed for a number of reasons and motives, both individual and collective.[1] The underlying premise of this chapter is that certain economic and environmental factors may explain why individuals or groups may decide to turn to armed violence and international criminality in a given context. I argue therefore that, by addressing the challenges posed by economic inequality and underdevelopment, resource scarcity, and natural resource predation, the pursuit of

[1] See O. S. Liwerant, 'Mass Murder. Criminological Perspectives', (2007) 5 *Journal of International Criminal Justice* 917.

sustainable development has the potential to play a role in preventing the emergence of contexts conducive to the commission of international crimes.

To this end, this chapter evaluates how several key principles of sustainable development affect those aforementioned factors and how their implementation may prevent future occurrences of international crimes. I discuss six of the seven principles of sustainable development identified in the ILA 2002 New Delhi Declaration of Principles of International Law Relating to Sustainable Development, namely:

- the duty of states to ensure the sustainable use of natural resources;
- the principle of equity and the eradication of poverty;
- the principle of common but differentiated responsibilities;
- the principle of the precautionary approach to human health, natural resources, and ecosystems;
- the principle of public participation and access to information and justice; and
- the principle of good governance.[2]

I briefly introduce the key elements of each of these principles before discussing their potential to influence economic inequality and underdevelopment, resource scarcity, and natural resource predation. I conclude by relating the principles to each other and providing a perspective on the opportunities and challenges that lie ahead in the implementation of sustainable development and its potential to reduce the prevalence of international crime.

## 2. THE DUTY OF STATES TO ENSURE THE SUSTAINABLE USE OF NATURAL RESOURCES

By providing that states have the duty to ensure the sustainable use of their natural resources this principle has significant potential to reduce the prevalence of international crimes, primarily by tackling the challenges posed by resource scarcity and natural resource predation.

Resource scarcity has often been associated with armed violence and conflict.[3] One obvious example of how scarcity can lead to violence relates to water. Consider a river flowing across two countries. If the upstream country affects the quality of the

[2] I do not discuss the principle of integration and interrelationship, in particular in relation to human rights and social, economic, and environmental objectives. This principle formalises the complexities associated with sustainable development, highlighting the multidimensionality of sustainable development and the need for all levels of governance to be involved in its implementation. To that extent, it does not directly affect the causes of crime and conflict. Nonetheless, it is critical to the realisation of sustainable development, which cannot be achieved only in terms of certain dimensions and not others. Indeed, when sustainable development acts on the causes of crime and conflict from several directions at once, this improves the potential for reducing the occurrences of those two problems.

[3] See, e.g., L. Ohlsson, *Environment, Scarcity and Conflict: A Study of Malthusian Concerns* (1999); T. Homer-Dixon, *Environment, Scarcity, and Violence* (1999); M. Klare, *Resource Wars: The New Landscape of Global Conflict* (2002).

river in the downstream country, either by way of pollution or excessive derivation, the downstream country might be tempted to take control of the entire watershed and thus engage in conflict with its neighbour. If the upstream country makes sure not to unduly affect the quality and flow of the water, the downstream country has one less cause for quarrel. Although it has never been the sole cause of a full-scale war, with a notable exception in antiquity, access to water has been a source of tension between countries. It has also been a source of conflict at the subnational level. A prime example is the interethnic conflicts that have affected the Darfur region of Sudan. In that case, climate change has been identified as a culprit for the increased scarcity of several resources, including water, which has exacerbated the tensions between farmers and herders.[4]

Natural resource predation is also identified as a factor contributing to conflicts and international crimes in situations in which a society fails to manage them properly. The interests of armed groups that benefit from violent economic activity are thus a key factor in understanding a number of conflicts today. Because primary commodity exports are the principal source of lootable resources, the looting of natural resource rents is the primary objective of such groups.[5] This has led Collier and Hoeffler to conclude that an important cause of conflicts is the opportunity for primary commodity predation.[6] Notable examples of such resources and their role in recent conflicts include timber in Cambodia, drugs in Colombia, and diamonds in Angola and Sierra Leone.

The principle of the sustainable use of natural resources is composed of three elements, each of which is relevant when dealing with resource scarcity and natural resource predation. The first element specifies that all states have 'the responsibility to ensure that activities within their jurisdiction or control do not cause significant damage to the environment of other States or of areas beyond the limits of national jurisdiction'. States behaving along these lines would thus reduce the potential for resource scarcity and natural resource predation. Returning to the example of water, bilateral agreements often govern shared water bodies or watersheds. A classic case is the International Joint Commission, which is in charge of managing the lake and river systems along the US–Canada border.

The second element of this principle pertains to the internal duties of states in managing their own natural resources. In addition to taking into account the needs of future generations in their use of natural capital, states are mandated to protect their environment.

Environmental protection naturally reduces the likelihood of resource scarcity, which in turn reduces the potential for conflict. Environmental degradation can lead to increased poverty and population migration. In many cases, these factors

4 UNEP, Sudan: Post-Conflict Environmental Assessment, DEP/0816/GE (2007).

5 P. Collier, 'Rebellion as a Quasi-Criminal Activity', (2000) 44 *Journal of Conflict Resolution* 840.

6 P. Collier and A. Hoeffler, Greed and Grievance in Civil War, World Bank Policy Research Paper, no 2355 (2000), at 26.

have contributed to the emergence of conflicts.[7] The impact of taking into account the need of future generations is somewhat more ambiguous. In the long run, making sure that today's resource consumption is sustainable reduces the potential for exhaustion. Many conflicts that could have arisen because of increased resource scarcity would therefore be prevented.

Numerous developing countries have been exploiting their natural resources at an unsustainable pace in an attempt to catch up with the living standards of developed countries. Switching to a sustainable resource extraction path, although having the potential to avert conflicts in the long run, could be very painful during the transition. Indeed, moving from an unsustainable rate of resource use to a sustainable one almost certainly implies a temporary reduction in the living standards of part of the population as the economy restructures itself. This transition will lead to a short-term increase in inequality, where those people most dependent on natural resource industries will be hardest hit. It is also possible that underdevelopment will linger for longer than it would have otherwise. Inequality and underdevelopment have been established as contributing factors to crime and conflicts. Hence, for countries now developing by running down their natural capital, sustainable development may lead to a short-term increase in crime and conflicts.

To understand how big of a hurdle this transition is to the spread of sustainable development, one has only to look at the developing countries that are deemed to have unsustainable economies. Indeed, countries that base their development on an unsustainable use of their resources could be reluctant to undergo a potentially difficult transition towards sustainability. Measuring this sort of transition is, however, easier said than done, because there is no universally accepted indicator of sustainable development.

Green net national product (GNNP) is one way to measure the sustainability of an economy. Using this method, the standard measure of gross national product (GNP) is adjusted for capital depreciation to derive the net national product; it is then further adjusted for environmental elements, such as natural resource depletion and pollution, to arrive at the GNNP. Whereas GNP is a relatively available measure, GNNP has proven difficult to calculate and has only been computed for a handful of countries. Despite the fact that we have little data about GNNP, we can use a measure that is more widely computed and related to it: genuine savings. Also called net investment, it focuses only on the change in all forms of capital of an economy. That means it accounts for changes both in human-made capital, such as machinery, and in natural capital – oil reserves, forests, fish stocks, and the like. Whereas investment into productive assets contributes positively to genuine savings, human-made capital depreciation and natural resource extraction decrease genuine savings. Positive genuine savings would indicate a sustainable economy, whereas negative genuine savings would suggest the contrary.

[7] See Section 5 of this chapter for some examples.

The World Bank compiles data on genuine savings for more than 100 countries. The most recent data, for 2006, indicate that 32 countries had negative genuine savings for that year (see the following table). Most countries with negative genuine savings (i.e. unsustainable economies) are developing countries. Convincing such countries to make their economies more sustainable could be very difficult, because of the likelihood of temporary cutbacks in their standards of living.

| Country Name | Genuine Savings* |
|---|---|
| Angola | −37.63 |
| Azerbaijan | −39.71 |
| Bolivia | −24.16 |
| Burundi | −10.95 |
| Cameroon | −6.25 |
| Chad | −46.63 |
| Chile | −12.08 |
| Comoros | −0.58 |
| Congo, Dem. Rep. | −6.34 |
| Cote d'Ivoire | −2.96 |
| Ecuador | −11.78 |
| Egypt, Arab Rep. | −10.17 |
| Estonia | −20.87 |
| Ethiopia | −1.71 |
| Georgia | −2.24 |
| Guinea | −9.67 |
| Iran, Islamic Rep. | −23.23 |
| Kazakhstan | −33.21 |
| Kyrgyz Republic | −2.29 |
| Lebanon | −15.38 |
| Mauritania | −6.96 |
| Mozambique | −13.77 |
| Nigeria | −29.57 |
| Peru | −3.36 |
| Romania | −1.19 |
| Russian Federation | −13.81 |
| South Africa | −0.27 |
| Sudan | −16.16 |
| Syrian Arab Republic | −23.96 |
| Uzbekistan | −64.83 |
| Venezuela, RB | −9.49 |
| Zambia | −14.44 |

* As a percentage of gross national investment.

The third element of this first principle pertains to the protection of the environment. This element is closely related to the sustainable management of natural resources. Although natural resources are part of the environment and often offer benefits other than through their exploitation, the natural environment also comprises commercially unexploitable elements that are nonetheless important to the well-being of local and worldwide populations. Fresh air is a prime example of such a noncommercially exploitable resource that is tremendously important and requires protection.

Even excluding exploitable natural resources, the protection of the environment poses a particular challenge to some developing countries. Using the fresh air example, even though one cannot harvest it for sale, it can still be used as a pollution sink. One country might derive a competitive advantage over others by having looser environmental regulations and hence allowing for more air pollution. Especially in the case of pollutants that accumulate in the environment over long periods of time, countries that benefit from nonrestrictive environmental regulation could suffer a temporary setback in the economic activity generated by polluting industry if they enforced more stringent regulations.

To the extent that protecting the environment can lead to a temporary slump in the economic activity of some developing countries, as measured by GNP, reluctance to engage in serious environmental protection, similar to that related to the sustainable management of natural resources, can be expected from part of the international community.

The effects of marginal environmental degradation on crime and conflict are similar to those of unsustainable resource extraction. Indeed, although resource extraction provides direct monetary benefits, the environment provides amenities to populations that are also valuable, despite being nonmonetary. However, when extreme environmental events occur, the consequences on crime and conflict can be quite dramatic. These events are very closely related to the precautionary principle, and are discussed in the section pertaining to that principle.

Overall, when states ensure that they are using their natural resources sustainably, they provide an environment conducive to the reduction of crime and conflict. In the long run, resource sustainability reduces the prospect for resource scarcity and helps avoid underdevelopment and natural resource predation, which are both important factors contributing to international crimes. However, short-run adverse impacts may occur in situations in which unsustainable resource use has allowed a population to gain a temporary improvement in their living conditions.

## 3. THE PRINCIPLE OF EQUITY AND THE ERADICATION OF POVERTY

The principle of equity refers both to intragenerational and intergenerational equity. Intragenerational equity refers to the right of all people within the current generation to fair access to their share of the Earth's natural resources. Intergenerational equity extends that concept across generations.

To the extent that the fairness implied by intragenerational equity reduces economic inequalities, we can expect it to reduce the potential for crime and conflicts. The practical definition of equity, however, could take many forms, and there is no guarantee that it will actually reduce economic inequalities. Indeed, although equity relates to fairness, different concepts of what is fair might or might not lead to equality. For example, if what is deemed equitable is equality of opportunities, it might not translate into equality of conditions; hence some economic inequalities could remain.

The inclusion of poverty eradication in this principle makes its implementation much more likely to reduce some of the causes of crime and conflict. Although crime in general is broader than international crime and conflict per se, there are important links between the two. Indeed, factors that are conducive to crime and conflicts could in general also contribute to international crime.

Income inequality has long been associated with crime rates. Looking at the impact of several economic factors on crime, Fajnzylber et al. use panel data on 45 countries for the period 1970–1994 and find that income inequality raises crime rates.[8] They also find that crime rates appear to vary inversely with the business cycle, which suggests that economic growth contributes to moderating crime rates. Although this and other economic studies relate to the prevalence of ordinary crime, there is every reason to think that inequality is also a factor contributing to international criminality.

To begin with, Murshed points out that underdevelopment can be both a contributing factor and a consequence of conflicts.[9] Underdeveloped societies often have weak institutions that fail to channel the social pressures brought about by low standards of living and distributional conflict. In addition, the extreme poverty often associated with underdevelopment provides a pool of more readily available combatants, facilitating the outbreak of conflicts. Kniss argues, however, that macro-level studies that try to link measures of inequality at the state level with the prevalence of conflict have yielded widely contradictory results, ranging from a positive relationship between inequality and occurrences of conflicts to the opposite conclusion.[10] Alternatively, Kniss identifies several studies indicating that horizontal inequalities within countries are likely to be important causes of conflicts. Horizontal inequalities refer to inequalities across different groups of a population, as opposed to vertical inequalities, which are inequalities between individuals regardless of the group that they belong to. How those groups are defined depends on the perception of the local population as to which group they identify themselves with along ethnic, religious, linguistic, or even geographic lines. When inequalities are within defined groups (vertical), members are more likely to accept them because they feel that they have the opportunity to overcome them or that those inequalities are due to personal abilities. On the contrary, when inequalities are horizontal, group members are less likely to accept them because they do not perceive opportunities to improve their situation or because the inequalities appear arbitrary. When inequalities are not

8 P. Fajnzylber, D. Lederman & N. Loayza, 'What causes violent crime?' (2002) 46 *European Economic Review* 1323.

9 S,M. Murshed, 'Conflict, Civil War and Underdevelopment: An Introduction' (2002) 9(4) *Journal of Peace Research* 387.

10 M. Kniss, 'Intertwined Inequities: Micro-Level Economic Determinants of Civil Conflict', Center for International and Security Studies at Maryland, November 2009.

well accepted, disadvantaged groups are more likely to organise protest movements, which can lead to conflict.

Moreover, much of the literature on the emergence of armed rebellions, the onset of civil wars, and the appeal and rise of terrorism has identified economic grievance, including inequality, as an important factor in the motivation of individuals and groups resorting to armed violence.[11] Walter thus explains that the enlistment of ordinary citizens in rebel armies depends on two conditions:

> The first and most important is a situation of individual hardship or severe dissatisfaction with one's current situation. The second is the absence of any nonviolent means for change. Violence must be perceived as the only available tool for the average citizen to improve his or her situation.[12]

Like civil war, mass violence may be something that appeals to individuals in contexts characterised by hopelessness and squalor. It is not surprising therefore that recent instances of mass violence have by and large emerged in impoverished parts of the world such as Cambodia, Rwanda, Sierra Leone, and Indonesia.

Although even developed countries have not been able to eradicate poverty within their borders, it is still much less prevalent there than in developing countries. As the following figure shows, the relationship between some measure of poverty (here the percentage of the population of a country living on less than $2 a day) and per capita GDP is a highly nonlinear one. From that figure, we can see that poverty rates are very negatively correlated with per capita GDP at low levels of per capita GDP, and only slightly correlated at higher per capita GDP levels. This negative correlation implies that, as per capita GDP increases from very low levels, poverty initially falls sharply. However, that decrease in poverty becomes much less apparent, if not invisible, when a country reaches a certain level of per capita economic activity.

**Relationship between poverty and GDP**

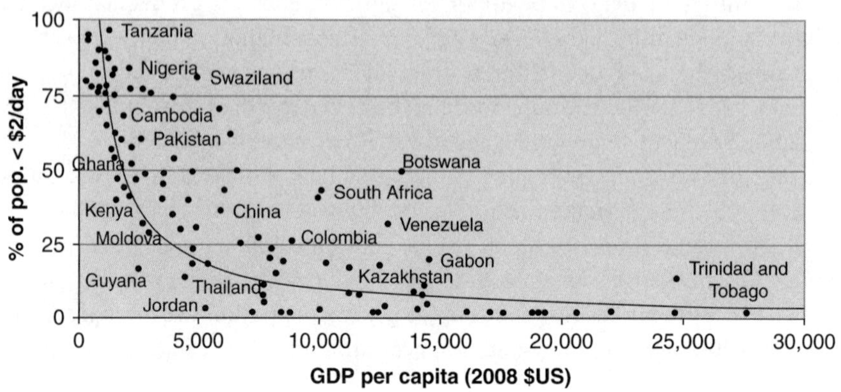


[11] See generally K. Ballentine and J. Sherman (eds.), *Political Economy of Armed Conflict: Beyond Greed and Grievance* (2003).

[12] B. Walter, 'Does Conflict Beget Conflict? Explaining Recurring Civil War', (2004) 41 *Journal of Peace Research* 371, at 374.

Clearly the greatest amount of work that remains to be done to eradicate poverty will take place in countries where large parts of the population face underdevelopment. Indeed, the correlation between GDP per capita and poverty indicates that poverty reduction, not even eradication, should be accompanied by a diminution in underdevelopment. Although poverty is more of an individual condition, underdevelopment qualifies the situation of a group, potentially a country. Because underdevelopment is one of the prime causes of crime and conflict, this principle of tackling poverty will certainly foster a reduction in crime and conflicts.

As with poverty eradication, the implementation of intergenerational equity is likely to have a bigger impact than the implementation of intragenerational equity on the causes of crime and conflict. By guaranteeing future generations a fair portion of our common patrimony, we reduce the potential for future resource scarcity and limit conflicts that could have stemmed from that scarcity.

## 4. THE PRINCIPLE OF COMMON BUT DIFFERENTIATED RESPONSIBILITIES

Through the concept of common responsibilities, this principle fosters international co-operation in facing the challenges posed by sustainable development. This notion is particularly relevant to the management of natural resources. The geographical distribution of natural resources rarely follows the boundaries of states, and their exploitation is part of a web of integrated markets that reach far beyond the point of extraction.

The mismatch between the location of resources and the borders of countries has been the source of many conflicts. Even if they are not the sole source of conflicts, natural resources have played a significant role in many conflicts. For example, conflicts in Angola and Sierra Leone have been fuelled by diamond smuggling. Before its invasion of Kuwait in 1990, Iraq had been accusing its neighbour of stealing oil by slant drilling near the border.

Because of its necessity to human life and agriculture, water has been the source of many conflicts. Indeed, because watersheds rarely follow national borders, there is plenty of cause for transboundary water conflicts. In that regard, Wolf et al. develop an interesting framework to measure the intensity of conflicts over water basins. Using indicators that they have found to be positively correlated with occurrences of water disputes, the authors identify four basins that currently suffer from conflicts or are subject to active negotiations: the Aral Sea, the Jordan River, the Nile, and the Tigris and Euphrates basins.[13]

Common responsibilities, assumed through international cooperation, have been able to alleviate some of the conflicts stemming from natural resources. In the case of diamonds, governments, industry, and civil society, representing 75 countries,

[13] A.T. Wolf, S.B. Yoffe and M. Giordano 'International waters: identifying basins at risk' (2003) 5 Water Policy 29.

joined together in the Kimberley Process to create a certification scheme guaranteeing the traceability of conflict-free diamonds. In 2006, three years after the launch of the process, an independent review assessed that 'Kimberley controls have reduced enormously the market for illicit diamonds'.[14] Delli Priscoli and Wolf also present an extensive review of water conflict resolution. In general, water conflicts are prevented or resolved through interstate negotiations or formal multistate agreements.[15]

Natural resources can also lead to conflicts at the national or subnational level. Within states, there is the potential for a greater diversity of agents to be involved in a conflict. Different agents often rely on natural resources for competing uses, which in turn creates potential for conflict. A classic example is that of a lake surrounded by both farmers and recreational users. Farmers benefit from the lake as a sink for their agricultural runoff, whereas recreational users benefit when practicing their recreational activities in water of good quality. Whereas farmers would prefer to use a lot of fertilisers regardless of their impact on the quality of the lake, recreational users would rather that farms be shut down to keep the lake as pristine as possible. By establishing the common responsibility of both types of agents, it is possible to foster the resolution of the apparent conflict. In addition, asserting the 'polluter pays' principle highlights a clear and simple mechanism through which some conflicts can be avoided or resolved.

As for the differentiated aspect of the responsibilities, this principle can help alleviate the particular burden that falls on developing countries. However, it can also undermine the attainment of sustainable development at the national level.

Developing countries face two particular challenges to achieving sustainable development. The first, as mentioned earlier, is related to the fact that these countries tend to be overly represented in the group of those that are not sustainably managing their resources. The second is that many environmental problems associated with unsustainable economies, such as climate change, are likely to disproportionately affect developing countries. By specifying that responsibilities are common but differentiated, this principle ensures that developing countries' particular situation will be taken into account and that developed countries will assist them in facing those challenges.

Such assistance is not a form of charity: it is both necessary for an efficient achievement of global sustainable development and equitable insofar as developed countries have often contributed more to some of the environmental problems from which developing countries disproportionately suffer. Take, for example, the case of climate change. Whereas the current concentrations of greenhouse gases in the atmosphere are mainly due to the historical levels of emissions of developed

[14] Global Witness, 'An Independent Commissioned Review Evaluating the Effectiveness of the Kimberley Process', 2006, available at http://www.globalwitness.org/media_library_get.php/272/1277890630/GW%20Commissioned%20Report%20on%20KP.pdf, at 4.

[15] J. Delli Priscoli and A.T. Wolf, Managing and Transforming Water Conflicts.

countries, the impact of the change in climate will most adversely affect developing countries. Beyond reasoning on the grounds of equity, to have any hope of addressing the emissions of greenhouse gases, developed countries must take advantage of their technological and financial means to help developing countries avoid a development path that would be just as carbon intensive as their own.

In dealing with global pollutants such as greenhouse gases, differentiation may, however, create some conflicts. Indeed, given that those pollutants are global, co-ordination among nations is required to ensure sustainable development. Because differentiated responsibilities imply that different countries will have to engage in different levels of effort to reach the common goal, some countries might feel unfairly burdened by the pollution control requirements. A developed country could push for a developing one to do more, given its current contribution to the problem, whereas the developing country could argue that it is already doing too much, given its economic disadvantage and its low historical and per capita contribution. Conflicts could arise over the appropriate level of pollution control or over the implementation the pollution control process itself, which would reduce the prospects for sustainable development.

## 5. THE PRINCIPLE OF THE PRECAUTIONARY APPROACH TO HUMAN HEALTH, NATURAL RESOURCES, AND ECOSYSTEMS

By definition, sustainable development has to be conceived of in the very long term. Over such a long horizon, there will always be a great deal of uncertainty: uncertainty about how technology will evolve, uncertainty about population growth, uncertainty about the impact of long-term environmental problems, and the like. The precautionary principle states that, in such situations of uncertainty, decisions are to be taken with particular emphasis on potential negative impacts even if their likelihood of occurrence seems low.

The precautionary principle, applied to human health, natural resources, and ecosystems, reduces the likelihood of extreme or even irreversible events in all of these three domains. Examples include the spread of new diseases, the extinction of wildlife, and abrupt changes in climate. Such extreme events have the potential to create many conflict situations.

The case for environmental extreme events is particularly well fleshed out by Thomas F. Homer-Dixon.[16] As previously mentioned, he proposes that environmental change will greatly affect poorer countries and identifies four consequences of environmental change that could lead to conflict: reduced agricultural production, economic decline, population displacement, and disruption of regular and legitimised social relations. Those factors, in turn, could lead to different types

16 T. Homer-Dixon, 'On the Threshold: Environmental Changes As Causes of Acute Conflict,' (1991) 16(2) *International Security* 76–116.

of conflicts: interstate conflicts and disputes concerning scarce resources, ethnic tensions and clashes, and civil unrest and the emergence of insurgencies'.

Several examples of the causal elements described by Homer-Dixon have indeed led to conflicts. Many countries suffer from fragile food security and are thus vulnerable to food-related civil strife. Although food commodity prices experienced spectacular growth between 2006 and 2008, several countries, including Morocco, Mexico, Egypt, Ethiopia, and the Philippines, experienced food-related social unrest. Examples of environmentally induced population displacement include storms and droughts in Bangladesh, which have caused 12 to 17 million people to move to neighbouring India since the 1950s, and dust storms in the US Great Plains that have forced about 2.5 million people to relocate. In Bangladesh, significant conflicts erupted between locals and migrants, whereas the US example of relocation is believed to have led to increased criminality in California.

However, the precautionary principle also has drawbacks. It often involves stopping or preventing projects that may be partially beneficial. For example, a polluting industry might be forced to shut down under the precautionary principle because it leads to a low probability risk of serious health and environmental damage. Nevertheless, that industry was employing people and producing output, benefits that would be lost under the precautionary principle.

This problem relates very closely to the argument linked to the sustainable use of natural resources. Some countries, especially developing ones, might not be able to afford to adopt the precautionary principle, at least not in the short term. For these countries, applying the precautionary principle could lead to a temporary increase in inequality and underdevelopment, which are causative factors of crime and conflicts.

## 6. THE PRINCIPLE OF PUBLIC PARTICIPATION AND ACCESS TO INFORMATION AND JUSTICE

Public participation fosters good governance, which moderates the elements conducive to crime and conflict. How good governance helps alleviate crime and conflicts is discussed in the next section. The critical element of crime and conflict reduction within this principle is access to justice, which has both direct and indirect effects on crime and conflict.

The indirect effect of public participation is the impact that access to justice has on poverty. As the United Nations Development Programme points out, 'access to justice is also closely linked to poverty reduction since being poor and marginalized means being deprived of choices, opportunities, access to basic resources and a voice in decision-making'.[17] As previously argued, poverty reduction is critical to

[17] UNDP, 'Access to Justice. A Practice Note', 2004, available at: http://siteresources.worldbank.org/INTLAWJUSTINST/Resources/ACCESSTOJUSTICEUNDPPRACTICENOTE.pdf at 3.

easing underdevelopment, which is one of the primary factors leading to crime and conflicts.

The direct effect of public participation is the impact that access to justice has on crime and conflicts. For example, people may be dissuaded from committing crimes if they know that their victims will be able to use the justice system. Moreover, victims seeking justice may be less likely to resort to criminality if they can gain access to the formal justice system. A programme aimed at increasing access to justice in Nicaragua has proven very effective in reducing crime and conflicts. Since 2002, the introduction of judicial facilitators in rural Nicaragua has led to significant decreases in several crime and conflict indicators. For example, it was found that the number of denunciations in courts and police stations decreased by approximately 24–53 percent after the introduction of the programme.

## 7. THE PRINCIPLE OF GOOD GOVERNANCE

As defined by the New Delhi Declaration, good governance includes four main aspects: democracy, corruption reduction, respect of the rule of law and human rights, and implementation of public procurement approaches according to WTO rules.[18] As such, good governance can contribute in many ways to the reduction of occurrences of crime and conflict. By promoting economic growth, good governance helps reduce underdevelopment, one of the causes of crime and conflict.

Several studies and organisations underline the impact of good governance. The World Bank has contributed to several studies linking good governance to improved economic growth. Huther and Shah develop a measure of good governance and find a positive correlation between good governance and economic growth, as well as evidence suggesting that governance leads to growth and not the other way around.[19] A more recent report by World Bank economists studying Eastern European and Central Asian countries also reports a positive relationship between good governance and economic growth.[20] A report commissioned by the United Nations Centre for Human Settlements and the International Centre for the Prevention of Crime highlights the complex interactions between good governance and police duties in urban environments. Its authors conclude that good governance can aid police forces in reducing crime in urban settings, whereas the police as an organisation can help institutions improve governance. In that case, good governance and police forces can reinforce each other to help reduce crime in urban areas.[21]

18 ILA New Delhi Declaration of Principles of International Law Relating to Sustainable Development, *supra* note 2, at 215.

19 J. Huther, and A. Shah, Applying a Simple Measure of Good Governance to the Debate on Financial Decentralization, World Bank Policy Research Working Papers WPS1894 (1998).

20 C. Gray, T. Lane, and A. Varoudakis, Fiscal Policy and Economic Growth Lessons for Eastern Europe and Central Asia, World Bank Report (2007).

21 M. Chalom, L. Léonard, and C. Vézina, Urban Safety and Good Governance: The Role of the Police, Habitat and ICPC Report HS/625/01E (2001), at 56.

The effect of good governance appears to be significant on both crime and conflict. A sophisticated empirical study by Neumayer finds that good governance and good economic policy are important determinants of lower homicide rates across countries.[22] With regard to conflict, Nathan provides an interesting analysis of militarisation in Africa.[23] Arguing that militarisation arises mainly from security vacuums within states, he advocates that improved security cannot be reached by disarmament alone and that good governance is an essential prerequisite to successful disarmament initiatives. Without good governance, the power vacuum will remain, and any attempt at disarmament is bound to fail because of either a takeover by another militarised group or rearmament by a failed government acting to prevent its own demise.

Good governance also has an indirect effect on the reduction of crime and conflict. By making the public administration more effective, it improves the prospects for achieving the other principles of sustainable development. Indeed, sustainable development is a very complex and challenging endeavour for public administrations. To achieve it, we will need the best from our national governments.

## 8. CONCLUSION

Other chapters in this book have considered how international criminal justice might play a role in enabling states to avoid conduct that hampers the pursuit of sustainable development and harms the rights of future generations. In this chapter, I have examined the relationship between sustainable development and the international criminal law regime from the opposite perspective – by considering how implementing the principles of sustainable development influences the prevalence of international crimes. By reducing or eliminating critical contributing factors, such as economic inequality and underdevelopment, resource scarcity, and natural resource predation, laws and policies implementing key principles of sustainable development promise to reduce occurrences of international crimes.

The principles examined fall into two broad categories, those that affect the factors contributing to the prevalence of crime and conflict directly and those that affect these factors indirectly by reinforcing the effect of other principles.

The first four principles fall in the first category. The principle of the sustainable use of natural resources has the potential to reduce underdevelopment, resource scarcity, and natural resource predation. The principle of equity and the eradication of poverty obviously tackles underdevelopment and economic inequality. The principle of common but differentiated responsibilities contributes to diffusing situations in which natural resource predation could otherwise prevail. Finally, the

[22] E. Neumayer, 'Good Policy Can Lower Violent Crime: Evidence from a Cross-National Panel of Homicide Rates, 1980–97', (2003) 40 *Journal of Peace Research* 619.

[23] L. Nathan, 'Good Governance, Security and Disarmament in Africa', (1998) 3 *African Journal of Political Science* 69.

precautionary principle would reduce the likelihood of crime and conflict arising from resource scarcity and predation.

The second category comprises the last two principles.[24] The principle of public participation and access to information and justice can lead to a decrease in underdevelopment, as well as directly reducing crime levels. The principle of good governance affects crime and conflict by reducing underdevelopment and improving the prospects of achieving the other principles of sustainable development.

Although laws and policies for sustainable development show promise for the reduction of international crimes and armed conflicts, there are several hurdles that could derail the achievement of that objective. In addition to the sheer complexity of implementing a sustainable development agenda, I identify two types of challenges that might prevent the implementation of sustainable development or at least impede its ability to reduce crime and conflict.

The first is the difficulty of transitioning from an unsustainable to a sustainable form of development. The transition, far from occurring instantaneously, might take many years and probably several decades. Because many of the benefits of sustainable development occur over long periods of time, the short-run costs for certain societies might be larger than the benefits. Whether because of individual short-sightedness, lack of consideration for future generations, or simply the pursuit of short term political goals, there are plenty of possible impediments that could prevent the adoption of sustainable development. I have highlighted how the sustainable management of natural resources and the precautionary principle might lead to a short-term exacerbation of economic inequalities and underdevelopment. Nevertheless, the long-term effect of these two elements of sustainable development should be to diminish the prevalence of crime and conflicts.

The second hurdle to the widespread adoption of sustainable development is the necessity of co-operation among states to obtain some of its benefits. Indeed, many of the principles of sustainable development deal with global public goods or public bads (such as greenhouse gases) and transnational common access resources (such as fisheries). These common access resources suffer from the usual problem of free-riding, where some can benefit from the initiatives of others without incurring the costs of taking those initiatives themselves. To avoid such free-riding, countries must devise mechanisms to encourage more effective co-operation. The larger the numbers of countries involved, the harder the negotiations to devise these co-operation mechanisms. For agreements on the global commons to be effective, however, they must include the greatest number of concerned parties. This apparent contradiction is one of the main challenges in advocating sustainable development.

24 Although not discussed in any length here, the principle of integration has the indirect effect of ensuring that no principles are less forcefully applied, especially to the detriment of other principles.

Despite its potential for reducing international crime, not all countries have moved or plan to move in the direction of more sustainable development. This situation is in part due to the complexity of and potential for short-term challenges when implementing sustainable development, as well as the failure of countries to effectively co-ordinate their efforts.

As this book attests, there is undoubted enthusiasm for adopting an approach of judicial accountability and deterrence to prevent international crimes. I have argued in this chapter, however, that the implementation of the principles of sustainable development may also be an effective means of preventing international crimes. Given that it is unlikely that we will ever completely eliminate problems such as income equality, there is little hope that the pursuit of sustainable development will ever completely obviate the need for an international criminal law regime. Nonetheless, there is no doubt that we should seek international justice capable not only of providing individual accountability for international crimes but also of supporting the turn to sustainable development.

# 14

# Transitional Justice and Peace Building for the Future

## *Diagnosing and Addressing the Socioeconomic Roots of Violence through a Human Rights and Intergenerational Framework*

*Lisa J. Laplante*

We don't inherit the earth from our ancestors; we borrow it from our children.
– David Bower

### 1. INTRODUCTION

In the immediate aftermath of conflicts and political violence, the theory of transitional justice aims for sustainable peace by seeking to establish the rule of law, democracy, and a culture of rights.[1] To reach these goals, it employs a full range of judicial and nonjudicial mechanisms designed to address legacies of mass atrocities.[2] Typically, the checklist of such remedies includes prosecuting perpetrators of human rights violations, revealing the truth about past crimes, providing victims/survivors with reparations, and reforming governmental institutions.[3] In this way, transitional justice holds the dual purpose of being forward- and backward-looking: its activities seek to clarify, expose, and come to terms with repressive, violent, and abusive pasts, as well as promote peace and democracy in the future.[4]

1 R. G. Teitel, *Transitional Justice* (2002); M. Minow, *Between Vengeance and Forgiveness: Facing History after Genocide and Mass Violence* (1998).

2 N. J. Kritz, 'The Dilemmas of Transitional Justice', in N. J. Kritz (ed.), *Transitional Justice: How Emerging Democracies Reckon with Former Regimes* (1995), vol. I.

3 L. Bickford, 'Transitional Justice', in D. Shelton (ed.), *The Encyclopedia of Genocide and Crimes against Humanity* (2004).

4 P. van Zyl, 'Promoting Transitional Justice in Post-Conflict Societies', in A. Bryden and H. Hänggi (eds.), *Security Governance in Post-Conflict Peacebuilding* (2005).

This chapter is a revised version of an article originally published in the *International Journal of Transitional Justice* (IJTJ). The author thanks the Institute for Advanced Study at Princeton University, where she worked on preliminary drafts of this chapter while a member at the School of Social Science, as well as the United States Institute for Peace for supporting the study that led to some observations shared in this chapter. All opinions and any errors are those of the author alone. The author thanks the anonymous reviewers of the IJTJ for their thoughtful comments and suggestions and the editors of the IJTJ for the permission to partially reprint her earlier article.

Until now, the concept of justice underpinning these activities has related exclusively to accountability and redress for violations of civil and political rights.[5] Yet, what about redress for historical inequality and violations of economic, social, and cultural rights that often predate, run concurrently with, or follow episodes of political violence? A narrow focus on restoring political order and the rule of law often overlooks the underlying and long-term issues relating to development and socioeconomic rights. Yet, it is precisely attention to these latter conditions that directly influences whether or not a state will ensure and protect the rights and interests of future generations – especially in terms of preventing future cycles of violence. I would argue that, even with trials and reparations, if economic and social inequalities go unaddressed and the grievances of the poor and marginalised go unheard, we are left with only uncertain guarantees of nonrepetition. It is like treating the symptoms while leaving the underlying illness to fester. To continue with the analogy, this lingering disease continues to jeopardise the rights of future generations.

Indeed, this effect can already be seen. In countries such as Chile, Peru, South Africa, and Guatemala, we are witnessing rising incidences of violent street protest and riots. Significantly, this violence often arises out of the same types of socioeconomic grievances that caused earlier periods of political violence and human rights violations in these same countries – situations later studied by their national truth commissions (TCs). New cycles of violence and repression in countries lauded for their transitional justice projects push us to ask whether these types of projects could do more to ensure achievement of the goals of postconflict recovery: reconciliation and a sustainable peace capable of securing the rights of future generations.[6] With that question in mind, I explore how transitional justice mechanisms such as TCs can better contribute to longer term processes of political and economic transformation.[7]

This discussion builds on the notion that the aim of prevention motivates the constantly evolving transitional justice movement, as reflected in the frequently invoked motto *nunca más* (never again), originally the title of Argentina's TC report. Prevention also embodies the principle of 'nonrepetition' – the foundation of international human rights law.[8] I argue that the overarching aim of prevention rests on the basic

[5] N. R. Arriaza and J. Mariezcurren (eds.), *Transitional Justice in the Twenty-first Century: Beyond Truth versus Justice* (2006).

[6] I use the term 'postconflict' more broadly than war so as to include situations in which the state uses repressive measures against dissidents and opponents, such as occurred in the 'dirty wars' of Latin America. For a discussion on sustainable peace and reconciliation as aims of transitional justice, see B. A. Leebaw, 'The Irreconcilable Goals of Transitional Justice', (2008) 30(1) *Human Rights Quarterly* 95.

[7] As explained by Juan Méndez, president of the International Center for Transitional Justice, transitional justice has become 'a sort of term of art to describe how we help societies leave behind a legacy of massive and systematic human rights violations and start on the path to a more humane dispensation of rights and a more democratic society.' J. Méndez, 'Lou Henkin, Transitional Justice, and the Prevention of Genocide', (2007) 38(3) *Columbia Human Rights Law Review* 479.

[8] L. J. Laplante, 'Bringing Effective Remedies Home: The Inter-American Human Rights System, Reparations, and the Duty of Prevention', (2004) 22(3) *Netherlands Quarterly of Human Rights* 347.

premise that postconflict recovery entails a holistic approach that should include economic, political, and social structural reform. This approach potentially can be spearheaded by transitional mechanisms such as TCs, but ultimately requires long-term political will, vision, and commitment. This broader approach grounds the notion of prevention in the principle of intergenerational equity that encompasses civil and political rights as much as it does economic, social, and cultural rights.

With this in mind, we need to explore how transitional justice can expand its concept of justice to address what anthropologist and physician Paul Farmer terms 'structural violence', referring to the entrenched socioeconomic conditions that cause poverty, exclusion, and inequality.[9] In this sense, the concept of social justice folds into the general definition of transitional justice.[10] If attended to properly, social justice in the present can contribute to achieving intergenerational justice and equity in the future. To accomplish this end, I propose that TCs expand their mandates to analyse violations not only of civil and political rights but also of economic, social, and cultural rights. They could include any findings of violations of all of these fundamental rights in their final reports and recommendations for how a state should redress them.[11]

This mandate expansion would serve several purposes. First, it would allow TCs to treat the root causes of political violence as more than just 'historical context' for the study of civil and political violations, framing them in terms of state obligations that were not fulfilled and thus require redress. Second, this approach would increase attention to the oft-forgotten tasks of institutional reform and development in transitional justice processes. Third, it would help bridge parallel but rarely intersecting postrecovery initiatives, making reform efforts more efficient and cohesive. Fourth, it would help strengthen growing recognition of economic, social, and cultural rights, as well as the right to development, and thus provide local actors with a platform to legitimise their own lobbying efforts for socioeconomic reform. With regard to the last purpose, the rights-based approach would allow grievances to be channeled through democratic mechanisms, not rejected as disruptive and subversive and thus made susceptible to repression.

Before discussing my proposal, I offer a brief historical overview of TCs within postconflict recovery schemes to suggest the significance, possible challenges, and necessity of this proposed expansion in transitional justice work. I also discuss the present-day consequences of not viewing socioeconomic conditions as state failure to ensure minimum living conditions. States leave the structural reasons for violence in place through more-of-the-same development policy, encouraging economic growth without adopting redistributive policies to assure human development. In this way, old grievances become new ones, sparking renewed conflict.

9 P. Farmer, *Pathologies of Power: Health, Human Rights, and the New War on the Poor* (2003).

10 Commonly accepted notions of justice already include retributive and corrective justice (criminal trials), historical justice (truth gathering), and restorative and reparative justice (reparations).

11 For a fuller discussion of the goals of TCs, including reconciliation, see Minow, *supra* note 1.

Innovations in development theories are helping shift traditional approaches to postconflict recovery. In this chapter I discuss how this trend has recently begun to influence the UN's peace-building operations through what I call a 'development–security nexus' approach. I then explore ways to build a bridge between the UN's work and that of transitional justice, because they both relate to postconflict recovery. Although the UN recently highlighted the link between its own peace-building work and transitional justice, it did so in terms of criminal trials and reparation. I argue that this link could be strengthened by examining how TCs could promote the development–security nexus. I conclude by offering some concrete suggestions of what this might look like in practice. Throughout the chapter, I integrate observations from my own ethnographic work on Peru's transitional justice experience since 2002, as well as comparative experiences from other countries that also opted for a TC. Ultimately, I propose that TCs can set political agendas for future social justice reforms aimed at true conflict prevention in the interests of both present and future generations.

## 2. DEEPER TRUTHS: TCS DELVING INTO THE CAUSES OF VIOLENT CONFLICT

As official investigatory bodies, TCs hold the potential to ask not only what happened during periods of political violence and armed conflict but also why the violence occurred at all. The 'why' question opens the possibility of addressing, and ultimately redressing, the broader socioeconomic root causes of conflict that, if ignored, hold the potential to spark new cycles of violence. At their inception, however, TCs tended to interpret their mandates more narrowly, often limiting their study only to crimes that constitute violations of civil and political human rights and overlooking, avoiding, or otherwise ignoring the socioeconomic causes of conflict.[12]

For instance, the TC reports of Argentina (1984), Chile (1991), and El Salvador (1993) present brief procedural explanations of political polarisation, such as repressive state apparatuses, corrupt judiciaries, faulty rule of law, and other institutional type weaknesses, which contributed to the continuation of violence. These commissions failed to delve into the underlying structural causes of the conflict, particularly political clashes over socioeconomic ideologies. Yet, the 'dirty wars' of all these countries consisted of authoritarian repression and state terror aimed at suppressing oppositional voices that spoke about what dissidents perceived to be socioeconomic inequalities.[13] Anthropologist Richard Wilson speculates that the Cold War made impossible any inquiry into the grievances that motivated the insurgent movements of these countries, given the high political price of appearing too sympathetic to

[12] L. J. Laplante, 'On the Indivisibility of Rights: Truth Commissions, Reparations, and the Right to Development', (2007) 10 *Yale Human Rights and Development Law Journal* 142.

[13] S. Borzutzky, 'The Politics of Impunity: The Cold War, State Terror, Trauma, Trials and Reparations in Argentina and Chile', (2007) 42(1) *Latin American Research Review* 167.

their communist causes.[14] The restraint exercised by both Argentina's National Commission on the Disappearance of Persons and Chile's National Commission on Truth and Reconciliation (CNVR) arose out of a fear of justifying or condoning the violence.[15]

Undoubtedly influenced by a changing geopolitical context, later TCs showed less self-restraint. The TCs of Guatemala and Peru, for example, explored historical context as a cause of the wars in their countries even if they did not frame their analysis in terms of violations of economic and social rights. For instance, the 1999 final report of Guatemala's Commission on Historical Clarification (CEH) analyses the systemic causes of state violence, including economic exploitation, racism, and political exclusion. It includes the country's health, education, literacy, and nutritional indicators to show the extreme social inequality that has made the country among the most unjust in the world despite an abundance of national wealth. It also examines how these inequalities and consequent social conflict dated back hundreds of years to the Spanish colonial culture that subordinated the Mayan population. Structural inequality resulted in ongoing cycles of violence, often sparked by popular masses protesting for change, which provoked state repression. In this way, historian Greg Grandin contends, 'political violence was thus a direct expression of structural violence'.[16]

Similarly, the Peruvian Truth and Reconciliation Commission (PTRC) offered a fairly in-depth analysis of the socioeconomic causes of its internal armed conflict between state armed forces and the Maoist insurgent group, *Sendero Luminoso* (Shining Path or SL). Although showing more caution in directly critiquing the 'established economic order', the PTRC nevertheless describes how SL recruited marginalised discontents for its bloody campaign with utopian promises of communism, thereby justifying violent revolution in the minds of the poor and excluded, who lived in rural communities historically abandoned and ignored by the state.[17] Significantly, SL failed to infiltrate communities with more state presence, which were provided a minimum standard of living in terms of health, education, and security.[18]

Although the PTRC report avoids saying that poverty caused the conflict, it speaks of an 'evident relation' between poverty and social exclusion and political violence

14 R. A. Wilson, 'Is the Legalization of Human Rights Really the Problem? Genocide in the Guatemalan Historical Clarification Commission', in S. Meckled-Garcia and B. Çali (eds.), *The Legalisation of Human Rights Multidisciplinary Approaches* (2005).

15 G. Grandin, 'The Instruction of Great Catastrophe: Truth Commissions, National History, and State Formation in Argentina, Chile, and Guatemala', (2005) 110(1) *American Historical Review* 56.

16 *Ibid.*, at 66.

17 Final Report of the Truth and Reconciliation Commission (Lima: Truth and Reconciliation Commission of Peru, 2003) [hereinafter 'Peru TRC Report'], vol. 3.

18 *Hatun Willakuy: Version Abreviada del Informe Final de la Comisión de la Verdad y Reconciliación* (Lima: Truth and Reconciliation Commission of Peru, 2004).

that 'ignited' and then became the backdrop of the war.[19] Its statistical findings indicate that 75 per cent of the estimated 70,000 killed came from the poorest regions of the country, being mostly indigenous farmers with minimal education and a native tongue other than Spanish. Thus, those most affected by conflict are often the same as those suffering dire poverty and inequality.

The TCs of Peru and Guatemala provide evidence to support a now recognised phenomenon: poverty and exclusion can trigger armed conflict and political violence. Farmer writes,

> Rights violations are . . . symptoms of deeper pathologies of power and are linked intimately to the social conditions that so often determine who will suffer abuse and who will be shielded from harm.[20]

Thus, the decontextualised approach, such as that taken by the TCs of Chile and Argentina, ends up presenting a diagnosis of human rights violations 'abstracted' from 'the dynamics of social power and conflict'.[21] The more recent approach taken by the Guatemalan and Peruvian TCs provides compelling empirical evidence, based on raw data from thousands of testimonies, of a causal connection between violence and structural inequalities.

The latter approach informs current debates arising from a growing body of academic literature on the causes of violence, including the contention that violence flows from persistent socioeconomic inequalities, coupled with a lack of effective channels for redress.[22] Social scientists argue that 'conflict entrepreneurs' and 'spoilers' tap into the frustration of populations whose historic socioeconomic grievances largely have been ignored by the state.[23] As former UN Secretary-General Kofi Annan wrote in 2001,

> The proximate cause of conflict may be an outbreak of public disorder or a protest over a particular incident, but the root cause may be, for example, socio-economic inequities and inequalities, systematic ethnic discrimination, denial of human rights, disputes over political participation or long-standing grievances over land and other resource allocation.[24]

[19] *Ibid.*, 22, 337.

[20] Farmer, *supra* note 9, at 7.

[21] Grandin, *supra* note 15, at 54.

[22] See, for example, Cynthia J. Arnson and I. William Zartman (eds.), *Rethinking the Economics of War: The Intersection of Need, Creed, and Greed* (2005). For an overview of theories on why individuals choose to join insurgency movements, see N. Sambanis, 'Poverty and the Organization of Political Violence', (2004) *Brookings Trade Forum*, 165.

[23] Paul Collier and Anke Hoeffler argue that the profit motive explains most armed rebellion, thus provoking the greed versus grievance debate. P. Collier and A. Hoeffler, 'Greed and Grievance in Civil War', (2004) 56(4) *Oxford Economic Paper* 563. Others argue that 'spoilers' and 'conflict entrepreneurs' manipulate the perception (real or not) of 'elite capture' to provoke disempowered groups to violence. M. Darrow and A. Tomas, 'Power, Capture, and Conflict: A Call for Human Rights Accountability in Development Cooperation', (2005) 27 *Human Rights Quarterly* 2.

[24] Prevention of Armed Conflict: Report of the Secretary-General, U.N. Doc. A/55/985–S/2001/574 (7 June 2001), para. 7.

Thus, even if it is still debated whether poverty constitutes a direct cause of political violence, the consensus seems to be that poverty is at least a contributing factor to conflict and 'a symptom of the decline of a state's capacity to protect and provide for its citizens'.[25]

### 2.1. *More of the Same: Economic Growth Policy in Postconflict Nation Building*

Even when TCs reveal how conflict often arises from underlying socioeconomic inequalities, their findings frequently fail to affect the direction of economic policy or institutional reform in a way that will help protect the right to security of future generations. On the contrary, their countries more often than not follow the precepts of the so-called Washington Consensus, adopted by international lending institutions such as the World Bank, which promotes the idea that macroeconomic growth alleviates poverty and thus social inequalities.[26] With their heavy reliance on international lenders, developing nations often have implemented the neoliberal policies upon which loans are conditioned with the hope of creating the conditions for lasting peace. Thus, until recently, the dominant economic development model has meant that conflict recovery schemes have focused on military intervention to keep the peace, humanitarian relief to address immediate socioeconomic needs, and macroeconomic stabilisation that at most might include rule-of-law institutional reforms.[27] Only 'radical' economists have tended to discuss class-based conflicts and to call for more state intervention, as well as alternative models of development.[28]

For example, at the end of apartheid in South Africa, the black majority political party, the African National Congress, followed the global trend and implemented free-market reforms as part of its recovery strategy.[29] These policies sought to address the consequences of prolonged political violence arising from structural inequalities based on discriminatory economic policies – a situation exposed, however minimally, during sectorial hearings of the country's Truth and Reconciliation Commission.[30] Yet, the results of this policy made victims of apartheid into victims of

[25] J. Mendelson Forman, 'Achieving Socioeconomic Well-Being in Postconflict Settings' (2002) 25(4) *Washington Quarterly* 126.

[26] J. Williamson, 'What Washington Means by Policy Reform', in J. Williamson (ed.), *Latin American Readjustment: How Much Has Happened* (1989); Daniel D. Bradlow and Claudio Grossman, 'Limited Mandates and Intertwined Problems: A New Challenge for the World Bank and the IMF', (1995) 17(3) *Human Rights Quarterly* 411; UN Development Programme, *Evaluation of UNDP Assistance to Conflict-Affected Countries* (2006).

[27] *Ibid.*

[28] J. P. Blair, *Local Economic Development: Analysis and Practice* (1995).

[29] J. Saul, 'Cry for the Beloved Country: The Post-Apartheid Denouement' (2001) 52(8) *Monthly Review* 1.

[30] Mahmood Mamdani argues that the South African Truth and Reconciliation Commission's mandate narrowly focused on individual acts of political violence instead of viewing apartheid as 'the crime itself.' M. Mamdani, 'Reconciliation without Justice' (1996) 46 *Southern African Review of Books* 3.

neoliberalism. South Africa's experience is not confined to its geographical boundaries. Across the globe, macroeconomic reforms are failing to eliminate poverty and inequalities while enriching capital owners. With their emphasis on the decreased role of the state and minimal economic regulation, neoliberal policies lack redistributive or protective mechanisms that ensure the well-being of poor citizens. A shrinking fiscal base reduces public expenditure, which weakens public institutions and services.[31] More-of-the-same economic development policy has meant that the social justice issues of yesterday linger in most post-TC countries.

Worse, globalisation appears to have deepened poverty, inequality, and social injustice in these and other countries. Yale law professor Amy Chua warns that free markets and the accumulation of wealth by a rich minority create ethnic hatred and genocidal violence throughout the developing world.[32] Governments fail to sustain popular backing when unable to disperse prosperity.[33] Social and economic polarisation looms like dynamite. It is a sobering realisation that this reality ultimately may undermine the work of TCs to set countries on a course of sustainable peace and reconciliation.

### 2.2. *Continued Grievances: Violent Protest in Postconflict Settings*

Indeed, a quick survey of post-TC countries provides evidence of rising social conflict due to the socioeconomic inequalities exacerbated by globalisation – thus throwing salt on the wound of the same unfair conditions that troubled past generations. The Centre for the Study of Violence and Reconciliation in South Africa recently documented case studies of 'urban, poor communities that have experienced, and continue to experience, conflict with the state over basic socio-economic struggles'.[34] Sociologist Javier Auyero has shown that riots in Argentina over the past decade have been a response to economic structural adjustments.[35] UN development workers have found that the urban street gang violence in El Salvador that often provokes state repression arises from the same underlying socioeconomic inequalities that fuelled that country's war.[36]

Peru falls in line with this trend. On the heels of the PTRC final report, published in 2003, popular protest began steadily to increase. In fact, just a year later, the *Defensoría del Pueblo* (the Peruvian ombudsman) formed the Unit on Social Conflict, whose monthly reports have shown a steady increase in conflicts between

[31] UNDP, *supra* note 26.

[32] A. Chua, *World on Fire: How Exporting Free Market Democracy Breeds Ethnic Hatred and Global Instability* (2004).

[33] A. F. Lowenthal, 'Latin America at the Century's Turn', in L. Diamond and M. F. Plattner (eds.), *The Global Divergence of Democracies* (2001), 307, 312–26.

[34] D. McKinley and A. Veriava, *Arresting Dissent: State Repression and Post-Apartheid Social Movements* (2005), 2.

[35] J. Auyero, 'Glocal Riots', (2001) 16(1) *International Sociology* 33.

[36] N. Hertvik, 'El Salvador: Effecting Change from Within', (2002) 39(3) *UN Chronicle* 75.

the state and communities.[37] Protesters have included teachers, laborers, rural villagers, farmers, university students, and health professionals, each with his or her own exhaustive narrative of how frustrated attempts to seek redress from the state led to, as a last resort, street marches or blockades.[38] The protesters' complaints vary, but all relate to socioeconomic grievances, such as environmental pollution caused by extractive industries, poor labor conditions, unfair trade competition, and the lack of basic necessities like health and education in rural villages and urban ghettos.

When Alan García became president of Peru in 2006, he began calling these protesters 'terrorists', and soon the press began to cover more cases of violent, sometimes fatal, clashes with the police.[39] After a year in office, García issued a new draconian law that, in effect, shields the police and the military from prosecution for lethal force used in the course of 'fulfilling their duty' in suppressing street protests.[40] This decision was made despite ongoing criminal trials for human rights violations committed during Peru's 20-year internal armed conflict (1980–2000) between the state's armed forces and insurgent groups.

From the capital of Lima, elites view the country's violence as irrational and as a regression to terrorism. They rarely discuss how it may be a continuation of past violence. In this way, Peruvians may be examples of the maxim that 'a society is condemned to repeat its mistakes if it does not learn the lessons of the past'.[41] Certainly after hundreds of years, Peru's poor are still marginalised, lacking the most basic social services and necessities despite a booming national economy. This situation spans generations, adding to the growing discontent and anti-neoliberal sentiment that threads through Peruvian protests, as local people feel deprived of the shared benefits of the neoliberal reforms instituted by former President Alberto Fujimori (1990–2000).

The 2006 presidential elections in Peru provided the clearest barometer of this national crisis. In the first round, the nationalist candidate, Ollanta Humala, won 80 per cent of the vote in the poorest regions of the country, where Peru's conflict hit hardest and where much of the violence reported by the *Defensoría* occurred. The act of voting for Humala took on symbolic purchase against the country's neoliberal reforms, which had managed to pull the nation from the World Bank's poorest nations list but also failed to reduce the economic gap between classes. Thus, the election served as a wake-up call, and the local press covered what became known as Peru's '*bomba de tiempo*' (time bomb). Newly elected President García accused

37 'Defensoría del Pueblo registró en Setiembre 76 conflictos sociales en el país,' *La República*, 7 October 2007.

38 See the award-winning documentary, *Tambogrande: Mangos, Murder, Mining*, directed by Stephanie Boyd and Ernesto Cabellos (Lima: Guarango Film and Video, 2007).

39 M. E. Castillo, 'Un muerto y nueve heridos en las protestas de Andahuaylas', *La República*, 17 July 2007.

40 'Seguridad ante el crimen', *El Peruano*, 24 August 2007.

41 M. P. Scharf and P. R. Williams, 'The Functions of Justice and Anti-Justice in the Peace-building Process' (2003) 35(2) *Case Western Reserve Journal of International Law* 174.

the outgoing president, Alejandro Toledo, of forgetting 70 per cent of the country, thus '*sembrando minas*' (laying mines) for future conflict. Amid this controversy, very little public space was devoted to the PTRC's analysis of the underlying socioeconomic causes of the war. The commission's findings still have not been widely disseminated and discussed because of the society's resilient fear of terrorism. García, himself implicated in human rights violations during his first term in office (1985–1990), continues to tap into this societal fear. Even when protesters assemble peacefully with legitimate claims, he accuses them of belonging to 'anti-development' factions (read terrorists). He encourages a new intolerance for public dissent and an unwillingness to open democratic channels for resolving socioeconomic claims.

In view of this national crisis, Peru's Congress requested that the *Defensoría* conduct a special study on the extractive industry, which generates significant community clashes with the state.[42] The resulting report offers general observations about the renewed cycle of violence, as well as decisive insight into the complex causes of the rising social conflict – discussing the people's high level of distrust of the government's will to protect fundamental socioeconomic rights (to health, to housing, to employment), as well as feelings of historical exclusion that build resentment towards third-party foreigners, whom many Peruvians perceive as having become unjustly wealthy on their ancestral lands.[43] Inadequate distribution of benefits means disappointed expectations for sustainable development. The report concludes that the accumulation of unattended frustration leads to the escalation of violence.

It is perplexing that the alarming trend of increasing violence over socioeconomic conditions occurs even in a country whose truth commission's final report discusses the root causes of political violence. Why does this compelling information have minimal influence on national economic policy choices and the government's response to the grievances of poor citizens? I argue that the PTRC's analysis did not evoke the type of persuasive compulsion that comes from declaring that state actions are giving rise to human rights violations. The consequences of the two different approaches are subtle: presenting socioeconomic root causes of conflict as historical context leaves policy change to the discretion of political leaders, whereas presenting them as rights violations makes redress and reform a political imperative.[44] Countries transitioning to democracy worry about their legitimacy in the international community and react to accusations of human rights violations, even if just to avoid

[42] L. J. Laplante and S. A. Spears, 'Out of the Conflict Zone: The Case for Community Consent Processes in the Extractive Sector', (2008) 11 *Yale Human Rights and Development Law Journal* 59.

[43] Defensoría del Pueblo, *Los Conflictos Socioambientales por Actividades Extractivas en el Peru* (April 2007), 4. Translation by author.

[44] Even if treaties that establish state obligations in regards to economic, social, and cultural rights concede that the state must 'progressively' fulfill these obligations, this doctrine nevertheless clearly establishes that states must make a steady and good faith effort to work towards the obligations.

international scrutiny.[45] In addition, the PTRC missed an opportunity to educate the public that the underlying grievances of the insurgency existed because of violations of basic rights, thus going beyond pure political ideology. Still pending is a national conversation about why hundreds of Peruvians were willing to take up arms to change an economic system that had failed to improve their families' and their own socioeconomic situation.[46]

If TCs present the socioeconomic roots of violence in terms of human rights violations, they could better set the tone of postconflict recovery. I in no way wish to suggest that the onus for a sea change in national policy and large-scale structural reform rests on TCs alone. Instead, I take a more modest approach, suggesting that TCs can help initiate a longer term reform process by creating the possibility for viewing underlying socioeconomic conditions not as unchangeable facts of life but as consequences of conscious policy decisions that fail to protect fundamental rights.[47]

Certainly, the Peruvians' current rejection of neoliberal policies is occurring in a changed geopolitical context, one no longer informed by the superpower ideologies that made questioning the dominant economic policy suspect or subversive. Yet, in Peru, contemporary demands for social justice do resemble those made just over a decade ago, when calls for social justice and socialist reforms prompted vicious reprisal and 'dirty wars' in Latin America. In the absence of a critical national dialogue on how these conditions constitute violations of basic human rights, political leaders still may manipulate popular opinion to reject the grievances of the poor, marginalising them as terrorists and even criminalising their protest. To protect against this tendency, TC reports and recommendations that include the economic, social, and cultural rights framework could serve as important tools for local actors. Demands for social justice would be perceived as legitimate, sensible, and humane calls on a state to fulfill its international obligations and carry forward a reform agenda. National grassroots movements, meanwhile, would contribute to a global effort to contest the dominant neoliberal development model. This symbiotic national–international relationship promises to cause a major shift in our global thinking on development.

45 Elsewhere I discuss Peru's clear concern about international opinion. L. J. Laplante, 'Entwined Paths to Justice: The Inter-American Human Rights System and the Peruvian Truth Commission', in M.-B. Dembour and T. Kelly (eds.), *Paths to International Justice: Social and Cultural Perspectives* (2007).

46 I do not propose that the ends justify the violent means used by the illegally armed groups, nor that those responsible for crimes of terrorism should not be held criminally accountable. Rather, I suggest that even if condemning the violence, it is only wise to begin examining the underlying motivation for terrorist tactics if we hope to prevent their recurrence in the future. See L. Richardson, *What Terrorists Want: Understanding the Enemy, Containing the Threat* (2005).

47 I take a measured approach similar to that of Margaret Popkin and Naomi Roht-Arriaza, who argue, 'The truth commission model has become so well known that it runs the danger of being perceived as something of a panacea rather than as one of a panoply of measures needed to undertake the complex process of coming to terms with the past'. M. Popkin and N. Roht-Arriaza, 'Truth as Justice: Investigatory Commissions in Latin America' (1995) 20(1) *Law and Social Inquiry* 80.

## 3. THE SECURITY–DEVELOPMENT NEXUS IN UN PEACE-BUILDING OPERATIONS

This growing international movement recently has begun to influence postconflict recovery and reconstruction schemes in which transitional justice mechanisms generally apply. Most notably, the UN began to contemplate the role of development theory in its 'peace-building' activities, whose origins lie in the end of the Cold War. Initially, the UN exercised the same self-restraint as early TCs, perhaps because of the proximity of the Cold War. In the 1990s it rarely addressed the socioeconomic causes of conflict – an angle that would take a decade to gain general institutional support.[48]

In 2000, the so-called Brahimi Report recommended moving away from a model of pure military intervention for UN peace-keeping operations toward an integrated approach that recognises that peace is more than just the absence of war.[49] Significantly, the report promotes a 'conflict prevention lens' as the 'less costly option' because it treats the causes and not just the symptoms of war.[50] The report signifies a turning point in the mainstreaming of the concept of prevention in peace-building operations, as noted in recent UN Security Council resolutions that create a shared goal with transitional justice.[51]

With the new millennium, UN Secretary-General Annan began to issue decisive reports that further clarified the link between development and security. Just months before 9/11, Annan posed what in retrospect appears an ominous question: 'Why is conflict prevention still so seldom practiced, and why do we so often fail when there is a clear potential for a preventive strategy to succeed?'[52] Indeed, after the tragic events of 9/11, interest in conflict prevention and development increased, especially as weak or collapsed states came to be viewed as sanctuaries for leaders of terrorist groups who could 'exploit [these] dysfunctional environment[s]'.[53]

Annan voiced concern about renewed violence in countries with peace agreements, noting that within five years roughly half of all countries that emerge from war lapse into violence. He pointed to 'a gaping hole in the United Nations institutional machinery', which allows a system to exist that fails to help countries make the transition from war to lasting peace.[54] Ultimately, he proposed moving away from

48 In 1992, former UN Secretary-General Boutros Boutros-Ghali spoke of how 'cooperative work to deal with underlying economic, social, cultural and humanitarian problems can place an achieved peace on a durable foundation. Preventive diplomacy is to avoid a crisis; post-conflict peace-building is to prevent a recurrence.' B. Boutros-Ghali, *An Agenda for Peace: Preventive Diplomacy and Related Matters*, UN Doc. A/47/277–S/24111 (1992), para. 57.

49 *Report of the Panel on United Nations Peace Operations*, UN Doc. A/55/305–S/2000/809 (2000).

50 *Ibid.*, at paras. 29–30.

51 For instance, the Security Council affirms that 'development, peace and security and human rights are interlinked and mutually reinforcing'. UN Security Council Resolution 1674 (2006).

52 *Prevention of Armed Conflict*.

53 John J. Hamre and Gordon R. Sullivan, 'Toward Postconflict Reconstruction' (2002) 25 *Washington Quarterly* 4, 85.

54 See *supra* note 26, at para. 114.

the reactive mentalities and practices adopted during the Cold War and toward a 'culture of prevention' that requires 'the deep-rooted socio-economic, cultural, environmental, institutional and other structural causes that often underlie the immediate political symptoms of conflicts' to be addressed. This approach incorporates short- and long-term methods that encompass political, diplomatic, humanitarian, human rights, developmental, institutional, and other measures taken by the international community in co-operation with local actors. In this way, he argued, 'conflict prevention and sustainable and equitable development are mutually reinforcing activities'.[55]

In 2003, Annan convened the High-level Panel on Threats, Challenges and Change, tasked with examining the major threats and challenges the world faces in the broad field of peace and security, including economic and social issues insofar as they relate to peace and security, and making recommendations for the elements of a collective response.[56] The resulting report, *A More Secure World: Our Shared Responsibility*, bolstered the evolving security–development agenda.[57] Soon after, in 2005, the UN created the Peacebuilding Commission to help ensure the sustainability of peace once attained, melding postconflict reconstruction and conflict prevention.

As the UN strove to link security with development in traditional peace-keeping operations, a parallel stream of actions promoted alternative development models that opened the door to asking this question: '*What kind* of development is best in war-torn societies?'[58] The concept of 'human security' has redefined security to mean more than protecting against external military risks. It includes 'safety from such chronic threats as hunger, disease and repression, and protection from sudden and hurtful disruptions in the patterns of daily lives'.[59]

This expansive view of development can be seen in Annan's *In Larger Freedom* report, published in anticipation of a summit of world leaders in 2005 to review progress made since the UN Millennium Declaration. The report articulates a progressive vision of development as 'freedom from want, freedom from fear and freedom to live in dignity'. Here, Annan establishes a now well-recognised triad:

> In an increasingly interconnected world, progress in the areas of development, security and human rights must go hand in hand. There will be no development

[55] *Ibid.*, para. 11.

[56] Significantly, Annan began to lay a novel legal foundation that makes prevention an international obligation of the 'state duty to protect' (now referred to as the 'responsibility to protect' doctrine), as grounded in the UN Charter. *Ibid.*, para. 17. Although he refers to collective action for civil and political human rights violations, I would argue that the same doctrine someday could apply to violations of socioeconomic human rights that result in grave and fatal harm to a population.

[57] *A More Secure World: Our Shared Responsibility: Report of the Secretary-General's High-Level Panel on Threats, Challenges and Change* (2004).

[58] D. Moore, 'Levelling the Playing Fields and Embedding Illusions: "Post-Conflict" Discourse and Neo-liberal "Development" in War-torn Africa' (2000) 27(83) *Review of African Political Economy* 17.

[59] UNDP, *New Dimensions of Human Security: Human Development Report* (1994), at 23.

> without security and no security without development. And both development and security also depend on respect for human rights and the rule of law.[60]

This definition of development aims for all people to have

> the freedom to choose the kind of lives they would like to live, the access to the resources that would make those choices meaningful and the security to ensure that they can be enjoyed in peace.[61]

This approach echoes the pivotal work of Amartya Sen and his idea of a 'capability approach', which refers to 'the capabilities to realize certain freedoms that are themselves fundamentally valuable for minimal human dignity'.[62] Sen's work, which has greatly influenced the UN's *Human Development Report*, reinforces the idea that states have a positive duty to assure core minimum standards for all citizens. It also recognises the indivisibility of all rights, as reflected in the preamble of the International Covenant on Economic, Social and Cultural Rights (ICESCR):

> The ideal of free human beings enjoying civil and political freedom and freedom from fear and want can only be achieved if conditions are created whereby everyone may enjoy his economic, social and cultural rights, as well as his civil and political rights.

The indivisibility principle makes it difficult, and perhaps futile, to scrutinise conflict situations without looking at the spectrum of rights violations – a perspective that supports my proposal that TCs expand their mandates. In this way, the human-rights-based approach to development recognises asymmetries of power and the phenomenon of 'elite capture' (the economic benefits of growth going to the few), as well as that

> the distribution of assets and capabilities does not occur by accident, but is the product of conscious policy choices and political and social struggle. The quest for equitable redistribution of overall gains is a political as well as legal imperative.[63]

Street protesters recognise that inequitable socioeconomic policy arises from human design; that is why they demand that their governments embrace new models of sustainable development.

The new emphasis on development in conflict recovery situations reflects a critical time in history in which a sea change in development theory is already underway. Specifically, the neoliberal model no longer enjoys unconditional deference. We stand on the brink of a tipping point, after which a more humane approach to development may finally enjoy global acceptance. This momentum began because of a combination of factors.

60 *In Larger Freedom: Towards Development, Security and Human Rights for All: Report of the Secretary-General*, UN Doc. A/59/2005 (2005), Ann., para. 2.

61 *Ibid.*, Ann., para. 17.

62 A. Sen, *Inequality Reexamined* (1992), 109. See also A. Sen, *Development as Freedom* (2001).

63 Darrow and Tomas, *supra* note 23, at 474.

First, a cadre of eminent economists, including Joseph Stiglitz, a former senior vice president and chief economist of the World Bank, began to criticise 'free market fundamentalists'.[64] Even John Williamson, the creator of the Washington Consensus, began to concede that the model had flaws.[65] Second, a growing global grassroots anti-neoliberal movement began contesting the assertions made by international institutions and governments that free markets would improve the well-being of all people, thereby de-radicalising the idea that capitalism should be critiqued.[66] Third, the 'right to development' movement grew, especially as it was integrated into a larger human rights network that sought to increase recognition of economic, social, and cultural rights, which the Cold War climate had relegated to 'second-generation' status.[67] The rights-based approach offers an alternative legal framework and counter-ideology to hegemonic economic models, especially in that it converts development into a social justice issue.[68] The new understanding is that, even if economic growth is necessary, it is not sufficient to reduce poverty and inequalities, and thus to prevent conflicts.[69] Rather, something more needs to happen, such as well-planned and executed redistributive policies that ensure that a state meets the basic needs of all its citizens.[70] In essence, this approach assures sustainable development that meets the needs of present generations while contemplating those of future generations.

## 4. MERGING THE FIELDS OF CONFLICT RECOVERY AND CONFLICT PREVENTION

With the confluence of fields in postconflict recovery, there has been a still modest flurry of recent commentary that discusses how transitional justice supports the UN's peace-building operations. Indeed, the former executive secretary of the South

[64] See J. E. Stiglitz, *Globalization and Its Discontents* (2003).

[65] J. Williamson, 'Did the Washington Consensus Fail?' (Outline of speech at the Center for Strategic and International Studies, Washington, DC, 6 November 2002).

[66] Specifically, in the Cold War, challenges to capitalism were viewed in terms of ideology, as opposed to factual policy discussions on effective approaches to development. See J. Seoane and E. Taddei, 'From Seattle to Porto Alegre: The Anti-Neoliberal Globalization Movement', (2002) 50(1) *Current Sociology* 99.

[67] For further discussion, see, P. Uvin, *Human Rights and Development* (2005); A. Sengupta, 'On the Theory and Practice of the Right to Development', (2002) 24(4) *Human Rights Quarterly* 837; A. R. Chapman, 'A "Violations Approach' for Monitoring the International Covenant on Economic, Social and Cultural Rights', (1996) 18(1) *Human Rights Quarterly* 23; K. Roth, 'Defending Economic, Social and Cultural Rights: Practical Issues Faced by an International Human Rights Organization', (2004) 26(4) *Human Rights Quarterly* 63.

[68] R. E. Mazur, 'Realization or Deprivation of the Right to Development under Globalization? Debt, Structural Adjustment, and Poverty Reduction Programs', (2004) 60(1) *GeoJournal* 61.

[69] S. Minushkin, 'Financial Globalization, Democracy, and Economic Reform in Latin America', (2004) 46(2) *Latin American Politics and Society* 151.

[70] The UN Millennium Development Goals have set benchmarks for reducing poverty and inequalities by 2015, noting that 'every step taken towards reducing poverty and achieving broad-based economic growth is a step toward conflict prevention'. See official website, www.un.org/millenniumgoals/.

African Truth and Reconciliation Commission, Paul van Zyl, observes, 'It is somewhat surprising that so little analysis has been devoted to the intersection between transitional justice and post-conflict peacebuilding.'[71] This lack of co-ordination began to change in 2004 when Annan published his report on transitional justice, which constituted a watershed moment in terms of international recognition of the field.[72] In *In Larger Freedom*, Annan refers to the 2004 report in pointing out the general lack of co-ordination and planning amongst the various approaches to post-conflict recovery, which results in 'often piecemeal, slow and ill-suited' activities for the ultimate goal of sustainable peace.[73] This opinion echoes an earlier call for co-ordination in which he explains,

> All these tasks – humanitarian, military, political, social, and economic – are interconnected, and the people engaged in them need to work closely together. We cannot expect lasting success in any of them unless we pursue all of them at once as part of a single coherent strategy.[74]

Academics and practitioners are making similar calls for co-ordination.[75] Along these lines, van Zyl poses various research questions on how transitional justice may contribute to postconflict peace building, viewing the two fields as complementary.[76] As may be expected, these calls implicitly take as their starting point the premise that transitional justice contributes to the peace-building paradigm by addressing and redressing grievances that arise from violations of civil and political rights. As an alternative, I propose ways in which transitional justice mechanisms such as TCs can contribute to general postconflict recovery efforts as they relate to the socioeconomic roots of conflict. Where relevant, I also suggest how the new development–security nexus discourse may support national transitional justice experiences. Space does not allow me to unpack fully each of the themes that emerge, but I present a preliminary discussion with the hope of inspiring further inquiry and research.

### 4.1. *Diagnosing the Problem*

TCs offer a preliminary diagnostic tool of the socioeconomic conditions before, during, and after conflict that can set reform agendas for longer term conflict-recovery

71 Van Zyl, *supra* note 4.

72 Report of the Secretary-General on the Rule of Law and Transitional Justice in Conflict and Post-conflict Societies, UN Doc. S/2004/616 (2004).

73 See *supra* note 60, at para. 137.

74 UN Secretary-General Kofi Annan, speech to the UN General Assembly, New York (February 2002).

75 For example, John Hamre, president of the Center for Strategic and International Studies at the Massachusetts Institute of Technology, and Gordon Sullivan, U.S. army general. See Hamre and Sullivan, *supra* note 53; Gerhard Thallinger argues that even if the UN Peacebuilding Commission does not explicitly refer to transitional justice in its provisions, the fields have the common purpose of sustainable peace. G. Thallinger, 'The UN Peacebuilding Commission and Transitional Justice', (2007) 8(7) *German Law Journal* 681.

76 Van Zyl, *supra* note 4.

efforts. Van Zyl points out that 'development of a post-conflict peacebuilding strategy must be based on a rigorous examination of the causes, nature and effect of the prior conflict'.[77] As in Guatemala and Peru, TCs, in addition to presenting individual cases of human rights violations, can explain the structural and institutional causes of these abuses. Ultimately, these grievances point to the failure of states to provide a minimum standard of living for all citizens, which could be presented as a violation of economic, social, and cultural rights.

The recent experience of East Timor's Commission for Reception, Truth and Reconciliation (CAVR) provides an exceptional example of this legalistic diagnostic approach. CAVR operated for three years as an independent statutory body investigating the political conflict of 1974–2005. Its mandate included study of 'the context, causes, antecedents, motives and perspectives which led to the violations'.[78] Yet, it went beyond looking at civil and political rights abuses to analyse these conditions within a framework of economic and social rights violations. In its report, CAVR recognises the brutal violation of civil and political rights, but also notes that 'the impact of the conditions in which [the population] lived, while often less remarked on, was equally damaging and possibly more long-lasting'.[79] It refers to numerous international treaties, including the ICESCR and the Fourth Geneva Convention's obligation that an occupying power protect civilians' social and economic circumstances. The report summarises the types of violations that rested on the discriminatory fashion of failing to 'meet the basic needs of the population for food, shelter and essential medicines' and caused 'their economic and social situations to deteriorate'.[80] CAVR has found that Indonesia failed to raise the well-being of the East Timorese people and instead prioritised private interests. Thus, despite significant overall macroeconomic growth, the country now lags 'well behind that of even the poorest Indonesian provinces'.[81]

The report discusses the problematic outcomes of free-market policy choices, finding that 'the discriminatory use of resources served to create new divisions and to entrench existing ones'.[82] It specifically refers to the freedom approach, which now figures as part of the development–security nexus discourse, citing the 'freedom from fear and want' phrase in the preamble of the ICESCR.[83] In this vein, it cautions that the 'long-lasting impacts' of the economic and social conditions that 'in many cases, continue to this day' are 'impediments to reconciliation and need to be addressed

77 *Ibid.*, at 213.

78 Regulation 2001/10 on the Establishment of a Commission for Reception, Truth and Reconciliation in East Timor, sec. 2(2).

79 *Chega!* Final Report of the Commission for Reception, Truth and Reconciliation in East Timor (Dili: Commission for Reception, Truth and Reconciliation in East Timor, 2005), at para. 1.

80 *Ibid.*, at paras. 131–35.

81 *Ibid.*, at para. 8.

82 *Ibid.*, at para. 135

83 *Ibid.*, at para. 14.

within that context'.[84] It will be important to follow how this report influences local politics and whether it serves as a platform for national protesters seeking to address socioeconomic grievances.

### 4.2. *Promoting Macro-Reconciliation Processes That Include Social Justice*

With a broader diagnostic approach, TCs set the stage for national reconciliation projects to take on macro-level dimensions. Although prominently stated as an aim of TCs and the subject of extensive academic writing, the concept of reconciliation in postconflict settings has yet to be fully defined or understood.[85] Often it conjures up images of South Africa's experience of 'spiritual reconciliation', which encouraged victims to forgive perpetrators.[86] Yet, the hope for victims to reconcile with perpetrators has been viewed as 'wishful thinking' when economic inequities between the two remain steady.[87] Susan Dwyer contends that reconciliation in the wake of atrocity requires 'the credibility that can be established only by implementation of social and economic programs that concretely address the substantive injustices' of the past. She goes on to ask,

> How much reconciliation can be achieved if in post-apartheid South Africa, for example, whites admit that their economic, social, and political status was based on a morally bankrupt system, but then refuse to accept sharply redistributive taxation?[88]

In this way, the path to reconciliation would include mending (or creating) the social-economic-political conditions that bolster the foundational social contract needed for stable peace.

Alternatively, the Peruvian TRC sought to promote a model of 'political reconciliation' that includes efforts to reintegrate the formerly marginalised – the majority of victims/survivors – as equal citizen to contribute to 'democratic consolidation, the return of faith in the future and to lay the foundation of a new social pact'.[89] Unlike individualised and interpersonal micro versions of reconciliation, this approach seeks

[84] *Ibid.*, at para. 135.

[85] J. Sarkin and E. Daly, 'Too Many Questions, Too Few Answers: Reconciliation in Transitional Societies', (2004) 35(3) *Columbia Human Rights Law Review* 661.

[86] D. Tutu, *No Future without Forgiveness* (1999). For a critical analysis of this perspective, see, R. A. Wilson, *The Politics of Truth and Reconciliation in South Africa: Legitimizing the Post-Apartheid State* (2001); H. van der Merwe, 'National and Community Reconciliation: Competing Agendas in the South African Truth and Reconciliation Commission', in N. Biggar (ed.), *Burying the Past: Making Peace and Doing Justice after Civil Conflict* (2001).

[87] S. Wilson, 'The Myth of Restorative Justice: Truth, Reconciliation and the Ethics of Amnesty', (2001) 17(4) *South African Journal on Human Rights* 531.

[88] S. Dwyer, 'Reconciliation for Realists', (1999) 13 *Ethics and International Affairs* 95.

[89] Peru TRC Report, vol. 9, at 29.

wider societal and political change processes.[90] This macro-reconciliation approach acknowledges the need for addressing the type of endemic inequality that motivates the development–security discourse. Robert Orr writes,

> Enabling disenfranchised groups to begin to play a role in determining the country's direction and mobilizing them to defend a new peaceful order not only facilitates democratic development but also provides the means to progressively squeeze armed combatants, warlords, and other spoilers out of the picture.[91]

This approach directs reform efforts to go beyond just revamping institutional structures such as the judiciary and law enforcement agencies to including more fundamental questions on economic and social policy. As explained by Stiglitz,

> We recognize today that there is a 'social contract' that binds citizens together, and with their government. When government policies abrogate that social contract, citizens may not honor their 'contracts' with each other, or with the government. Maintaining that social contract is particularly important, and difficult, in the midst of the social upheavals that so frequently accompany the development transformation.[92]

The term 'contract' no longer serves as pure metaphor in a rights framework, however. Here, TCs contribute to the notion of 'broken social contracts' by spelling out how socioeconomic conditions may violate rights. These types of recommendations sketch a roadmap for more profound transformation by informing future political and legal decisions made in postconflict settings. This approach contemplates a form of social justice that would have long-term effects because it would protect and advance the rights of future generations.

Of course, these recommendations do not guarantee action on the part of the government. For example, the Guatemalan CEH elaborated policy recommendations that included a progressive tax system and increased state spending on human necessities, in addition to other unfulfilled political, legal, and economic reforms that could be found in the peace accords but remained dormant. Similarly, the Peruvian TRC realised that reconciliation involves 'concrete solutions for profound problems' that arise at every level of development: the ethnic and racial, social, economic, juridical, educational, sanitary, security, and communication, amongst others.[93] The failure of these countries to implement the TC recommendations no

[90] Harvard anthropologist Kimberly Theidon uses the term 'micro reconciliation' to describe how local communities in Peru reintegrate former combatants into communities. K. Theidon, 'Justice in Transition: The Micropolitics of Reconciliation in Postwar Peru', (2006) 50(3) *Journal of Conflict Resolution* 433.

[91] R. Orr, 'Governing When Chaos Rules: Enhancing Governance and Participation', (2002) 25(4) *Washington Quarterly* 145.

[92] Stiglitz, *supra* note 64, at 78.

[93] Peru TRC Report, vol. 9, at 31.

doubt has various explanations, with the lack of political will being among the top few. Ultimately, the success of prevention depends on the

> extent to which local authorities are willing and able to take difficult but necessary political and economic decisions and to participate in the establishment of processes and mechanisms to manage internal disputes and pre-empt violence or the reemergence of conflict.[94]

I contend that had the TCs made these recommendations as part of a rights-based analysis, they would have given national groups a powerful lobbying tool to challenge the government's inaction or resistance.[95] For example, in Peru, victims/survivors and sympathetic civil servants rely on the authority of the Peruvian TRC to support and legitimise their demands that the state fully implement the recommended reparations plan, *Plan Integral de Reparaciones*, which frames their arguments in terms of rights. Meanwhile, those who advocate structural change would enjoy more protection from persecution because they no longer could be viewed as subversive or 'terrorist' when they call on the state to take a more proactive role in 'regulating the distribution of power and resources and the peaceful settlement of grievances'.[96] Human rights language supports victims/survivors who frame their demands for development as social justice.[97]

Presentation of the socioeconomic roots of conflict in terms of rights helps expand the notion of justice within the transitional justice paradigm, making social justice a legitimate priority in postconflict recovery. The responsibility is put back on states as a matter of state obligation and of citizens' rights to address the original socioeconomic injustices suffered by most victims/survivors of political violence. Development is no longer subject to discretion or a gesture of charity. Instead of voluntary international humanitarian relief, postconflict reconstruction would entail national governments creating comprehensive and sustainable approaches to development. Postconflict recovery work would be decentralised, with greater likelihood of ensuring lasting peace.

### 4.3. *Restorative Justice as Reparations and Development*

TCs could issue recommendations for development. They thus would help overcome the great difficulty of separating the causes of victimisation when violations of human rights arise from both historically unjust social and economic conditions and grave political violence. The Peruvian TRC's comprehensive diagnosis of the psychosocial, sociopolitical, and socioeconomic harms caused by the conflict reveals

94 Peace Operations Report, at para. 27.
95 R. Ashby Wilson, 'Justice and Retribution in Postconflict Settings', (2003) 15(1) *Public Culture* 187.
96 Darrow and Tomas, *supra* note 23, at 490.
97 *Ibid.*

that Peru's war left widespread personal and material loss, which only worsened already dismal socioeconomic conditions.[98]

While interviewing victims/survivors, the Peruvian TRC found that they requested redress for their current needs, which arose from inequitable social and economic conditions and not necessarily the war. They demanded equal access to education, attention to health for their whole family, and opportunities for micro-businesses, among other practical solutions to concerns of everyday survival.[99] They expressed the same long-standing grievances that the TRC blamed for sparking the insurgency.[100] These are the conditions that they wanted fixed to improve their well-being – a precondition for the new social pact envisioned by the commission.

The TRC struggled to distinguish the 'damage' and 'harm' caused by the war from that caused by historical conditions. Its PIR is geared specifically to responding to civil and political rights violations, yet it implicitly moves towards repairing all rights violations because it aims to help victims/survivors 'recuperate mental and physical health, reconstruct social support networks and strengthen their capacities for personal and social development'. It aims for the 'autonomous development of the victims to reconstruct their individual and collective life plan ('proyecto de vida') that was cut off by the conflict'.

Yet, as the Peruvian government attempts to implement collective reparations, controversy has emerged because victims/survivors complain that the state is merely fulfilling its preexisting obligation to guarantee economic and social rights and development. Perhaps if TCs diagnose a state's failure to provide core minimum socioeconomic conditions as rights violations, then subsequent development would be perceived (and would be presented) as fulfilling these social justice claims. Thus, the tensions arising from the reparation versus development debate would be alleviated, because the government would seek to redress the full spectrum of rights violations and thus serve the overriding justice component promoted by transitional justice. Moreover, reparations would be designed to have an impact upon long-term economic and social conditions of a country, and thus ultimately benefit future generations. For example, if a village receives a new school or potable water as part of its reparations this will necessarily go towards improving the lives of its children, many of whom will be descendants of the conflict's victims.

### 4.4. *Instituting Participatory Mechanisms: Empowering Victims to Become Citizens*

By promoting and strengthening participatory mechanisms, TCs help address conditions of historical exclusion that contribute to political marginalisation. This

98 *Hatun Willakuy*, *supra* note 18.

99 For a more expanded version of this discussion, see Laplante, *supra* note 12.

100 *Ibid.*

approach supports alternative development theories that require beneficiaries to participate in matters that directly affect their well-being. Certainly, the right to participation underscores development theory.[101] For example, the World Bank's *Empowerment and Poverty Reduction: A Sourcebook* now calls for 'the expansion of assets and capabilities of poor people to participate in, negotiate with, influence, control, and hold accountable institutions that affect their lives'.[102] In its *Voices of the Poor*, the World Bank underscores the importance of participation, finding that poor citizens think that their lack of well-being relates to the psychological experience of lacking voice, power, and independence more than to the anxiety of meeting their basic material needs.[103]

This distinction could explain why violence erupts in some poor communities and not in others. Poverty coupled with social and political exclusion exacerbates frustration, which may turn into violence, especially in undemocratic, overcentralised, and authoritarian governments that let the grievances of the politically excluded go unheard and unaddressed.[104] Yet, Darrow and Tomas clarify that 'participation, to be considered effective, must ultimately be characterized by a genuine capacity to influence economic and political agendas'.[105]

TCs could jumpstart an empowerment process by offering the first official opportunity to institute inclusive democratic dialogues through their testimony-taking process. Here, official spaces open 'for previously marginalized or silenced populations to share their stories', which contributes to their empowerment.[106] In addition, TCs could make recommendations for strengthening democratic participatory mechanisms, including some type of commission to advocate for the rights of future generations.[107]

[101] Development is a comprehensive process that requires 'active, free and *meaningful* participation'. Declaration on the Right to Development, UN Doc. A/RES/41/128 (4 December 1986).

[102] D. Narayan (ed.), *Empowerment and Poverty Reduction: A Sourcebook* (2002), at 14.

[103] D. Narayan, *Voices of the Poor: Can Anyone Hear Us?* (2000). For a discussion on this text, see S. Moller Okin, 'Poverty, Well-Being, and Gender: What Counts, Who's Heard?' (2003) 31 *Philosophy & Public Affairs* 280, at 306–10.

[104] M. Ndulo, 'The Democratization Process and Structural Adjustment in Africa', (2003) 10(1) *Indiana Journal of Global Legal Studies* 315.

[105] Darrow and Tomas, *supra* note 23, at 507.

[106] Leebaw, *supra* note 6, at 112. See also M. Barnett, 'Building a Republican Peace: Stabilizing States after War', (2006) 30(4) *International Security* 87; V. Sanford, *Buried Secrets: Truth and Human Rights in Guatemala* (2003); R. Sieder, 'War, Peace, and Memory Politics in Central America', in A. Barahona De Brito, C. Gonzalez Enriquez, and P. Aguilar (eds.), *The Politics of Memory: Transitional Justice in Democratizing Societies* (2001).

[107] The topics of empowerment and participation have been written on extensively across disciplines, a summary of which goes beyond this chapter. I present the writings here as integrated components of human rights theory, the field on which I ground my own research. See, for example, L. J. Laplante and M. Rivera, 'The Peruvian Truth Commission's Mental Health Reparations: Empowering Survivors of Political Violence to Impact the Public Health Policy', (2006) 9(2) *Health and Human Rights* 136; L. J. Laplante, 'The Process of the Peruvian Truth Commission's Historical Memory Project: Empowering Truth Tellers to Confront Truth Deniers', (2007) 6 *Journal of Human Rights* 433.

Broad-based participation utilises local knowledge to ensure the most efficient allocation of resources, while 'maximizing ownership and sustainability of development processes and outcomes'.[108] The Peruvian TRC spearheaded this inclusive approach by convening victims/survivors to participate in the development of the PIR and recommending that they be included in its implementation.

Along these lines, Stiglitz has noted that participation not only resolves disputes of competing interests but also assures greater acceptance of reforms and a sense of ownership.[109] Similarly, the UN Development Programme includes participation in its definition of good governance, explaining that it 'encompasses the mechanisms, processes, and institutions through which citizens and groups articulate their interests, exercise their legal rights, meet their obligations, and resolve their differences'.[110] TCs could recommend that a state create democratic channels for the voices of poor citizens, which could lead to corrective redistributive measures that address the inequalities produced by free-market reforms in postconflict recovery settings.

In the end, participatory mechanisms strengthen the aim of prevention. As Muna Ndulo succinctly puts it,

> One cannot successfully lead an insurgency against a government that is democratic, strong and effective and meets the basic social and economic needs of its people. It stands to reason that recruitment to the cause of the insurgency will be nearly impossible when people are happy and believe that warfare is not the only way to draw attention to their grievance or to create change.[111]

Spoilers are neutralised by 'solutions that mitigate tensions at the mass level'.[112]

## 5. CONCLUSION

As a relatively new field, transitional justice continues to grow as it responds to the complexity and nuances of postconflict recovery. Given its growing influence, the field must see how it may expand to better promote the important goals of sustainable peace and conflict resolution. In her analysis of the evolution of transitional justice, Ruti Teitel confirms that TCs have tended to adopt a historical view of justice, 'rather than a broader structural reform project'. She comments that transitional responses have 'tended to miss the broader dimensions associated with the bipolar power

[108] D. L. Hafner and E. B. L. King, 'Beyond Traditional Notions of Transitional Justice: How Trials, Truth Commissions, and Other Tools for Accountability Can and Should Work Together' (2007) 30(1) *Boston College International and Comparative Law Review* 94; Darrow and Tomas, *supra* note 23, at 506.

[109] J. Stiglitz, *Towards a New Paradigm for Development: Strategies, Policies, and Processes* (1998).

[110] United Nations Development Programme, Governance for Sustainable Human Development: A UNDP Policy Document (1997), at chapter 1.

[111] Ndulo, *supra* note 104, at 325.

[112] J. Snyder and L. Vinjamuri, 'Trials and Errors: Principles and Pragmatism in Strategies of International Justice', (2003) 28(3) *International Security* 5; see also S. J. Kaufman, *Modern Hatreds: The Symbolic Politics of Ethnic War* (2001).

relations of the last decades, as well as with economic and political globalization'. She continues,

> Contemporary transitional justice is being renegotiated at the same time as debates are being waged on globalization-related economic reforms. The coincidence of these developments makes the increase in the disparities associated with the free market economy readily apparent, even as there has been an increasing resort to transitional justice discourse. Whatever reform transitional justice-seeking implies, it is limited and determinate, and couches the economic question in terms of human restitution for known past losses. Post-Cold War transitional justice has, in large part, displaced broader reform projects, and appears to represent a move away from progressive politics.[113]

Her observation compels us to look at how transitional justice mechanisms may begin to better accommodate socioeconomic issues so as to meet more effectively the challenges of preventing new cycles of violence and protecting the rights of future generations. Certainly, the UN has helped create new momentum for the idea that the most sensible, rational, and efficient policy embraces development that is lasting and sustainable.

These types of radical shifts in national socioeconomic policies may occur only in a tipping-point-like fashion. The changes are most likely to occur through the sustained and co-ordinated development of the various streams of national and international contestation discussed earlier. Every effort to challenge the predominant economic model counts, including the work of TCs. TCs can help raise awareness and influence policy to ameliorate the harsh consequences of neoliberalism by reinforcing the principle that a state must provide minimum care for all its citizens. In the end, the goal of conflict prevention – assuring the mental and physical well-being and integrity of thousands of people – motivates this approach. Ultimately, assuring sustainable development offers the surest means of protecting the rights of future generations and ensuring that they do not suffer the same tragic fate of their predecessors. Even if difficult, the vision of transforming vicious circles of violence into 'virtuous circles' of peace is the root of the idealism that motivates our work.[114]

[113] R. G. Teitel, 'Theoretical and International Frameworks: Transitional Justice in a New Era', (2003) 26(4) *Fordham International Law Journal* 900.

[114] Darrow and Tomas, *supra* note 23, at 476.

# 15

# Protecting the Majority of Humanity

## *Towards an Integrated Approach to Crimes against Present and Future Generations*

*Riane Eisler*

### 1. INTRODUCTION

The last half-century has seen an expansion of the purview of international criminal law from war crimes to crimes against humanity, as most recently codified in the Rome Statute, which lists a number of human rights violations as crimes against humanity whether they are committed in war or peace.[1] This has been a development of major importance, incorporating into international criminal law core principles, such as the right to life, not to be tortured, to liberty, and to security of the person, that are laid down in international human rights declarations and conventions.[2]

Activities that destroy our natural life-support systems infringe on the human right to life and security, and thus can be considered crimes against humanity. But to change policies and behaviours that fail to respect these and other human rights, we need an integrated approach that takes into account what is considered normal and acceptable in all spheres of life, both public and private, and in all relations, from intimate to international.

### 1.1. *The Invisible Majority*

Until recently, human rights theory and action have focused primarily on the public sphere from which the majority of humanity – women and children – were traditionally barred. However, if we are serious about a more just, peaceful, and sustainable future, we have to recognise that our first, and most lasting, lessons about human

[1] Rome Statute of the International Criminal Court, 17 July 1998.

[2] See, e.g., A. Cassese, *International Criminal Law* (2003), chapter 4.

The author thanks Margaret Frimoth, PhD candidate, 2011, California Institute for Integral Studies, San Francisco, California, for her assistance in researching and compiling the notes for this chapter.

relations are learned not in the public but in the private sphere. This is where people learn to respect the rights of others – or where they learn to view human rights violations as normal.

An effective approach to protecting the human rights of present and future generations must include the private sphere of family and other intimate relations.[3] This is essential not only because widespread, chronic, and abhorrent violations of the human rights of women and of children are a global pandemic but also because psychology and neuroscience show that what children observe and/or experience in the family affects their adult beliefs, behaviours, and political attitudes – even the neural structures of their developing brains.[4]

To be sure, not all people raised in households where women and children are subjected to abuse, discrimination, and oppression accept human rights violations in the public sphere. But studies, going back decades to the classic *The Authoritarian Personality*, document how individuals who participate in and/or acquiesce to authoritarianism, violence, and scapegoating in the state or tribe tend to be individuals from families where authoritarianism, violence, and scapegoating were the norm.[5]

Yet many people still see family and other relations in the private sphere as separate or, at best, less important than political and economic relations in the public sphere. In reality, these two spheres are integrally interconnected, as is shown in this chapter and is briefly illustrated by the following findings:

- Although poverty and hunger are still discussed in generalities, the majority of the world's poor and the poorest of the poor are women and children.[6]
- Study after study, including for example the annual Arab Human Development Reports, document that economic development hinges on gender equality.[7]
- Studies indicate that armed conflicts are less likely where there is gender equity.[8]

3 Examples of publications urging the expansion of human rights theory and action to include women and children are R. Eisler, 'Human Rights: Toward an Integrated Theory for Action', (1987) 9(3) *Human Rights Quarterly*; R. Eisler, 'Human Rights: The Unfinished Struggle', (1983) 6(4) *International Journal of Women's Studies*; and R. Eisler, 'Human Rights and Violence: Integrating the Private and Public Spheres', in L. Kurtz and J. Turpin (eds.), *The Web of Violence* (1996), 161.

4 See, e.g., D. Niehoff, *The Biology of Violence* (1999); National Research Council, *From Neurons to Neighborhoods* (2000); B.D. Perry, 'Aggression and Violence: The Neurobiology of Experience', retrieved from http://teacher.scholastic.com/professional/bruceperry/aggression_violence.htm.

5 T. W. Adorno et al., *The Authoritarian Personality* (1964).

6 See, e.g., M. Buvinic, 'Women in Poverty: A New Global Underclass', (1997) *Foreign Policy*; *UNDP Human Development Report* (1995); R. Eisler, *The Real Wealth of Nations* (2008).

7 The annual *Arab Human Development Reports* cite three obstacles to progress in the region: the knowledge deficit, the gender deficit, and the freedom deficit. Studies such as R. Eisler, D. Loye, and K. Norgaard, *Women, Men, and the Global Quality of Life* (1995), show that the three are interconnected.

8 See, e.g., M. Caprioli, 'Gendered Conflict', (2000) 37(1) *Journal of Peace Research* 51–68.

- Research from both psychology and neuroscience shows that childhood experiences are key to human capacity development.[9]
- Research indicates that children who witness or experience violence in their families are more likely to accept and perpetuate violence in other relations.[10]

### 1.2. *Opposition to an Integrated Approach*

Just as some people argue there must be no interference in the internal affairs of states, it is sometimes argued that what happens inside a family should be free from outside interference. But the same grounds for the rejection by international law of 'non-interference' regarding the conduct of states are applicable to the rejection of 'non-interference' regarding human rights violations in families.[11]

A related argument invokes the right to privacy. But privacy is not the same as immunising family decisions – *or, more specifically, the decisions of those who wield power in a family* – from public scrutiny and regulation. In short, *the protection of personal rights is not synonymous with non-interference with actions within the family – and there often is a direct conflict between the two.*

Perhaps the most frequent ground for opposing challenges to widespread and systemic human rights violations in family and other intimate relations is that what we are dealing with is largely a matter of customary law deeply embedded in traditions. By challenging these traditions, it is argued, we are eradicating traditional cultures. Again, this is a fallacious argument. To help eradicate human rights violations is *not* the same as eradicating traditional cultures.

A related objection is that people from the West have no right to point to cultural traditions as crimes against present and future generations if these traditions are found in the global South. This cultural relativism relies on a patronising double standard that would give less human rights protection those who happen to be in the global South. Further, crimes against women and children are also still a major problem in the global North and are also still justified on traditional/moral grounds in some Western subcultures.

To build a world where human rights and human dignity have any meaning, we must support social justice movements in all areas of the world. Indeed, the emerging international doctrine of 'responsibility to protect' (R2P) recognises that

9 See, e.g., B.D. Perry, 'Brain Structure and Function II: Special Topics Informing Work with Maltreated Children' (2000). Retrieved from www.childtrauma.org/ctamaterials/brain_II.asp; Niehoff, *supra* note 4; NRC, *supra* note 4.

10 *Ibid.*

11 See, e.g., H. Charlesworth, C. Chinkin, and S. Wright, 'Feminist Approaches to International Law', (1991) 85 AJIL 613R.; R. Eisler, 'Human Rights: Toward an Integrated Theory for Action', (1987) 9(3) *Human Rights Quarterly*.

we have the responsibility to 'interfere' wherever systemic and egregious human rights violations are involved.[12]

### 1.3. *Proposed Actions: Making the Invisible Visible*

The Rome Statute (especially Article 7 on crimes against humanity), the principle of responsibility to protect (R2P), and a growing number of UN conventions, covenants, and declarations[13] offer a springboard for applying emerging international law principles to widespread, abhorrent, and systemic violations of the human rights of women and children that a state condones when it fails to prohibit them or establish adequate protection against these practices. The principle of R2P is particularly important, because it strengthens the interpretation of the crimes against humanity section of the Rome Statute to hold those officially or unofficially acting for governments responsible for practices that are well-known, widespread, large-scale abuses against civilian populations that cause great suffering or serious injury to physical or mental health, but are not included in a state's laws, or if there are laws, they are not enforced.[14]

Of course, we cannot expect the international community to immediately support what is proposed here. Nonetheless, concrete proposals for expanding the purview of international law are an important step towards making visible crimes that have basically been invisible.[15]

To this end, this chapter proposes the following measures:

1. Expand the interpretation of relevant sections of the Rome Statute, particularly sections of Article 7 (crimes against humanity), to include as crimes against both present and future generations egregious, widespread, and systemic practices that cause women and children great suffering or serious injury

[12] The responsibility to protect (R2P) is a new international security and human rights norm. After the first report on R2P by UN Secretary General Ban Ki-moon released on 12 January 2009, the first resolution on the Responsibility to Protect (A/RES/63/308) was adopted by the General Assembly on 14 September 2009. Retrieved from www.responsibilitytoprotect.org/.

[13] See, e.g., United Nations, Treaty Series, vol. 1249. *Convention on the Elimination of All Forms of Discrimination against Women*, 18 December 1979, UN General Assembly resolution 44/25. *Convention on the Rights of the Child*, 20 November 1989, UN General Assembly A/RES/48/104. 85th plenary meeting. *Declaration on the Elimination of Violence against Women*. 20 December 1993. Retrieved from www.un.org/womenwatch/daw/cedaw/cedaw.htm, www2.ohchr.org/english/law/pdf/crc.pdf, www.unicef.org/crc/, and www.un.org/documents/ga/res/48/a48r104.htm.

[14] See, e.g., Cassese, *supra* note 2, at 93.

[15] For example, U.S. Secretary of State Hillary Clinton has repeatedly emphasised her intention to make women's human rights a global priority; a bill introduced in both the House and Senate, the 'International Violence against Women Act of 2010' (HR 4594 IH; S.2982), is designed not only to implement policies to reduce violence against girls and women worldwide but also to direct the U.S. secretary of state to establish an Office for Global Women's Issues headed by an Ambassador-at-Large for Global Women's Issues, which shall coordinate and advise on activities, policies, programmes, and funding relating to gender integration and empowerment of women internationally. Retrieved from http://thomas.loc.gov/cgi-bin/query/F?c111:4:./temp/~c111FBvBLY and http://thomas.loc.gov/cgi-in/query/D?c111:3:./temp/~c111FBvBLY.

to physical or mental health but are not punishable under a state's laws or, if there are laws, they are not enforced.

2. Where necessary, amend the Rome Statute to include gender and childhood under the description of protected groups.

The sections that follow describe widespread, abhorrent, and systemic crimes against women and children that are still not outlawed and/or adequately prosecuted. They offer statistics and examples, show the individual and social damage they cause to both present and future generations, and propose legal remedies using the Rome Statute.

The crimes are divided into two sections: crimes against the female half of humanity and crimes against children of both genders. These sections overlap because girls are in both categories. But because many crimes are committed against children because they happen to be born female, I have included these crimes against female children under the section of crimes against the female half of humanity.

## 2. CRIMES AGAINST THE FEMALE HALF OF HUMANITY

### 2.1. *Selective Female Infanticide and Denial to Girl Children of Food and Health Care*

Selective female infanticide has long been condoned by cultural tradition. Today, the murder of female babies is still a culturally accepted practice in parts of Asia, the Middle East, and Africa. For instance, although in China the government has condemned these murders, especially after the one-child policy led to an epidemic of female infanticide, female babies are still often murdered with impunity in rural areas, and abortions of female fetuses have been replacing infanticide in many Chinese areas.[16] The Indian government too has taken a stand against female infanticide, but again, particularly at the local level it is still not prosecuted. In other parts of Southeast Asia there is even less governmental effort to protect female babies.

Closely related is the widespread practice of parents denying girl children food and health care that is found in parts of Asia, as well as other world regions, including Latin America. For example, in her autobiography Rigoberta Menchu wrote (with no condemnation) that boys are by custom breastfed longer than girls in her indigenous community.[17]

Obviously, children who are malnourished and denied adequate health care fail to develop their full physical and mental capacities. But it is also well known that children of malnourished women are often born with poor health and below-par

[16] 'The Worldwide War on Baby Girls', *The Economist*, 4 March 2010. Retrieved from www.economist.com/research/articlesBySubject/displaystory.cfm?subjectid=348951&story_id=15636231.

[17] R. Menchú, E. Burgos-Debray, and A. Wright, *I, Rogoberta Menchu: An Indian Woman in Guatemala* (1987).

brain development, affecting their potential for optimal development. This in turn affects children's and later adults' abilities to adapt to new conditions, tolerance of frustration, and propensity to use violence – which in their turn impede solutions to chronic hunger, poverty, and armed conflict.[18]

Also associated with increases in armed conflicts is the male surplus, resulting from selective infanticide of girl babies and selective female abortions because of the preference for sons. Studies show extremely skewed sex ratios in China, India, Bangladesh, Pakistan, Korea, Taiwan, and other parts of Asia. According to economist Amartya Sen, in 2001 there were more than 100 million missing women in the world due to son preference.[19] As Theresa Hesketh and Zhu Wei Xing write, 'The large cohorts of 'surplus' males now reaching adulthood are predominantly of low socioeconomic class, and concerns have been expressed that their lack of marriageability, and consequent marginalization in society, may lead to antisocial behaviour and violence, threatening societal stability and security.'[20] Historical analyses also verify this link between male surplus and armed conflicts.[21]

In addition, cross-cultural studies show a strong correlation between rigid male dominance (which includes a strong preference for sons), authoritarian control in both the family and the state or tribe, and a high degree of inbuilt, institutionalised, even idealised violence not only in intimate relations but also in tribal, national, intertribal, and international relations.[22]

### 2.1.1. Legal Remedies

Although greater attention has been given to violence against girls and women in recent decades and some progress has been made to reduce it, that progress has been much too slow. For example, the 2010 *Asia-Pacific Human Development Report* states that '[f]ew countries have adopted or implemented laws prohibiting violence against women, despite widespread evidence of discrimination and assault. Nearly half of the countries in South Asia, and more than 60 percent of those in

[18] For more on the economic effects of gender discrimination, see *Real Wealth*, *supra* note 6.

[19] A. Sen, 'Missing Women – Revisited', (2003) BMJ. See also S. Klasen and C. Wink, 'A Turning-Point in Gender Bias in Mortality? An Update on the Number of Missing Women', (2000) *Population and Development Review* 285–312. Sen noted that compared with the normal ratio of about 95 girls being born per 100 boys (which is what we observe in Europe and North America), Singapore and Taiwan have 92, South Korea 88, and China a mere 86 girls born per 100 boys.

[20] T. Hesketh and Z. W. Xing, 'Abnormal Sex Ratios in Human Populations: Causes and Consequences', (2006) *Proceedings of the National Academy of Sciences*. They write that measures to reduce sex selection must include strict enforcement of existing legislation, the ensuring of equal rights for women, and public awareness campaigns about the dangers of gender imbalance.

[21] See, e.g., B. Griffith, *The Gardens of their Dreams: Desertification and Culture in World History* (2001), 184–85.

[22] See, e.g., P. Sanday, *Female Power and Male Dominance* (1981); S. Coltrane, 'Father-Child Relationships and the Status of Women: A Cross-Cultural Study', (1988) *American Journal of Sociology* 93; R. Eisler, *The Chalice and The Blade* (1987); *Real Wealth*, *supra* note 6. I want to emphasise that when we speak of statistically significant correlations, this does not mean invariable correlations; it means central tendencies.

the Pacific, have no laws against domestic violence.'[23] This highlights the need for international intervention, including through recourse to the following sections of the Rome Statute: Article 7, Crimes against Humanity, especially Article 7(a) – Murder; Article 7(b) – Extermination; Article 7(h) – Persecution; and Article 7(k) – Other inhumane acts.

The Rome Statute specifically includes 'the most serious crimes of concern to the international community as a whole' – which the murder of babies and the systemic and socially/legally condoned starvation and denial of health care to children should be. The section on crimes against humanity covers murder, extermination, persecution, and other inhumane acts 'when committed as part of a widespread and systemic attack directed against any civilian population, with knowledge of the attack' and when widespread, systemic, and widely known. According to Section 7(b), extermination includes 'the intentional infliction of conditions of life, *inter alia* the deprivation of access to food and medicine, calculated to bring about the destruction of part of a population.' Persecution, in Section 7(h) means 'the intentional and severe deprivation of fundamental rights contrary to international law by reason of the identity of the group or collectivity' (and includes gender), and 7(k) covers 'other inhumane acts of a similar character intentionally causing great suffering, or serious injury to body or to mental or physical health'.

According to the Rome Statute, an 'attack' is 'a course of conduct involving the multiple commission of acts referred to in paragraph 1 against any civilian population, pursuant to or in furtherance of a State or organizational policy to commit such an act'. This clause should be interpreted to include a state's failure to protect against murder, extermination, persecution, and other inhumane acts, because of the emerging norm of a responsibility to protect civilian populations from mass atrocities.

As Antonio Cassese notes, characterising an action as an attack means that it is part of a widespread or systematic practice that is either part of a governmental policy or is tolerated, condoned, or acquiesced to by a government or de facto authority. He further states that crimes against humanity may be committed by individuals acting in a private capacity, provided that governmental authorities approve of, condone, or fail to prohibit and punish such private actions.[24] Hence, tolerance or acquiescence by a government to official acts or widespread acts by individuals should be sufficient to be included in the crimes against humanity clause of the Rome Stature.[25]

Moreover, Section 7(h) (Persecution) lists gender under the categories of protected groups. Although other sections of Article 7 do not specifically list gender, they should also protect against gender-based crimes, because not including such widespread and systemic crimes would be contrary to many United Nations declarations, covenants, and conventions, as well as the most basic human rights principles. Already in the 2003 edition of his comprehensive work on international

[23] 2010 *Asia-Pacific Human Development Report*, available at www2.undprcc.lk/ext/pvr.

[24] Cassese, *supra* note 2, at 65.

[25] A. Cassese, *International Criminal Law* (2003), 125.

criminal law, Cassese criticised the language of Section 7(1) as being too restrictive, writing: 'Would it not be sufficient for the practice to be accepted, or tolerated, or acquiesced in by the State or organisation, for those offenses to constitute crimes against humanity? Clearly, this requirement goes beyond what is required under international customary law and unduly restricts the notion under discussion.'[26]

In the longer term, efforts should therefore be made to amend Article 6 (Genocide) of the Rome Statute to list gender and childhood in addition to 'national, ethnical, racial, or religious group' so as to protect girl babies and children under the provisions *of* Article 6(a) – Killing members of the group, 6(b) – Causing serious bodily or mental harm to members of the group, and 6(c) – Deliberately inflicting on the group conditions of life calculated to bring about its physical destruction in whole or in part.

### 2.2. *The Sex Trade and Sexual Slavery*

These two closely related crimes affect millions of girls and women every year. UNICEF reported that approximately 30 million children lost their childhood through sexual exploitation over the past 30 years,[27] and two million children are subjected to prostitution in the global commercial sex trade annually.[28]

The vast majority of these children are girls, some as young as five years old. An example is Srey, who was sold to a brothel in Phnom Penh by her parents when she was five. Although she was rescued at the age of six, she will probably never recover from her traumas – first the betrayal of her parents and then being forced to have sex with hundreds of men, some of whom specifically asked for very young girls under the mistaken belief that this would protect them from AIDS. In fact, one of these men infected Srey with HIV, as have been countless other children and women trapped in the multimillion dollar sex industry in Phnom Penh.[29]

Cambodia is only one of the many countries where sexual slavery and sex trafficking are a normal part of life and business. Russia, Ukraine, Albania, Bulgaria, Lithuania, Romania, China, Thailand, and Nigeria are major countries of origin of trafficking victims.[30] And many of these victims are children.[31]

Sex trafficking and sexual slavery obviously have devastating consequences for its victims, who are often chained, caged, beaten, and threatened with death. In addition, children and women in the commercial sex industry are often drugged,

[26] Cassese, *supra* note 2 at 65.

[27] 'Commercial Sexual Exploitation Position Statement', (2004) UNICEF UK.

[28] U.S. State Department, 'Trafficking in Persons 2009 Report', downloaded from www.state.gov/g/tip/rls/tiprpt/2009/123126.htm.

[29] D. Rivers, 'Girl, 6, Embodies Cambodia's Sex Industry', *CNN*, 26 January 2007. Retrieved from www.cnn.com/2007/WORLD/asiapcf/01/23/sex.workers/index.html.

[30] United Nations Office on Drugs and Crime, *Trafficking in Persons: Global Patterns* (2004).

[31] U.S. Department of State, *Country Reports on Human Rights Practices – 2005* (2006).

causing addiction and dependency; they suffer unwanted pregnancy, malnutrition, social ostracism, and, in many cases, AIDS and, like Srey, early death.[32]

The governmental complicity in sex trafficking perpetuates traditions of corruption that corrode the entire social fabric. In addition, by not prosecuting the perpetrators of these crimes – not only the sex industrialists and traffickers, colluding officials, pimps, and madams but also the patrons (as is being done in Sweden, where the 'johns' and not the prostitutes are arrested) – states that do not forcefully act to punish these crimes and even collude in them perpetuate not only the brutalisation and dehumanisation of women and children but also a cultural desensitisation to human suffering, which inevitably spills over into other social relations.

#### 2.2.1. Legal Remedies

Article 7 of the Rome Statute could be used to hold governments accountable, especially through Section 7(g), which specifically lists these acts: rape, sexual slavery, enforced prostitution, forced pregnancy, enforced sterilisation, or any other form of sexual violence of comparable gravity. Other relevant sections are 7(c) Enslavement, 7(d) Deportation or forcible transfer of population, and 7(e) Imprisonment or other severe deprivation of physical liberty in violation of fundamental rules of international law.

### 2.3. *Female Genital Mutilation/Cutting (FGM/C)*

This crime is one of the most horrible forms of torture imaginable, yet it is perpetrated on millions of children. The World Health Organization reports that in Africa three million girls are at risk for FGM annually, and 92 million girls aged ten and older have undergone FGM in that continent alone.[33] In Egypt more than 90 per cent of women are genitally mutilated. FGM/C is widespread in other countries in the Middle East and Asia and is exported by immigrants to North America, Europe, and Australia.[34] FGM/C practices vary from region to region, from the excising of the clitoris to also cutting out the labia and sewing the vagina together so it must be cut open for intercourse and again for childbirth.

Even though at last genital mutilation is gaining international attention and some progress has been made in eliminating this practice, untold numbers of children still die from these barbaric mutilations. For the 140 million women and girls worldwide

[32] Rivers, *supra* note 29. For a moving account of the horrors, and courage, of girls and women sold into the sex trade, see N. Kristof and S. WuDunn, *Half the Sky* (2009).

[33] World Health Organization, *Fact Sheet: Female Genital Mutilation* (2010) [WHO]. Retrieved from www.who.int/mediacentre/factsheets/fs241/en/.

[34] UNIFEM, Donors Working Group, 'Platform for Action towards the Abandonment of Female Genital Mutilation/Cutting (FGM/C)', (2008). Retrieved from www.unifem.org/attachments/products/Platform_for_Action_FGM-C_English.pdf.

living with its consequences,[35] life is often a nightmare of daily torture due to the psychological traumas and medical complications resulting from FGM/C. Because in many cases urine and menstrual blood cannot drain properly, they experience infections, abscesses, and cysts. Intercourse is not only *not* pleasurable, but painful, and childbirth is often an ordeal.

Women who have themselves been subjected to FGM/C are often so desensitised to the pain it causes that they even perform these inhumane procedures on their own daughters and the daughters of their neighbors. Of course, they are pressured to do so by their traditions, which define women as sexual objects and breeders for men. But to so betray the trust of helpless children from generation to generation requires a psychological numbing that is characteristically associated with trauma.

Indeed, neuroscientists have found that severe trauma affects the brain itself, especially the amygdala and hippocampus (regions involved in emotions) and the prefrontal cortex (involved in reasoning and planning).[36] It is not far-fetched therefore to argue that culturally enshrined traumas affect those subjected to them in their roles as parents and community members, and thus as transmitters of mental maps about relationships based on domination and submission.

As the Egyptian physician Nawal El Saadawi notes, genital mutilation is an instrument for desensitising women not only to the pain of those of their gender but also to the realities of their oppression: 'False consciousness makes women obedient instruments of their own oppression and transmitters of this false consciousness to future generations of children.'[37] In short, cultural traditions that justify and perpetuate traumas such as FGM/C serve an integral function in maintaining oppressive and unjust social systems from generation to generation.

#### 2.3.1. Legal Remedies

Rome Statute's Article 7, Crimes against humanity, especially Section 7(f) – Torture can be used.

### 2.4. *Domestic Violence: From Murder in the Name of Honor and Bride Burning to Acid Throwing and Battery*

In its 'Fact Sheet on Domestic Violence as Torture', Amnesty International points out that this global pandemic not only takes the lives of millions of girls and women

35 WHO, *supra* note 33.

36 See, e.g., J. D. Bremner, 'Effects of Traumatic Stress on Brain Structure and Function', (2003) 6(2) *Journal of Traumatic Dissociation* 51–68; B. Van der Kolk, 'Developmental Trauma Disorder', (2005) 35(5) *Psychiatric Annals* 401–08.

37 N. El Sadawi, 'War against Women, Women against War – Waging War on the Mind', Speech at the World Social Forum, 2004. Retrieved from http://womensspace.wordpress.com/2007/02/07/nawal-al-saadawi-war-against-women-women-against-war-waging-war-on-the-mind/.

but also criminally torments them.[38] An estimated 40 to 70 per cent of homicides of women are perpetrated by intimate partners.[39] According to UNIFEM, the United Nations Development Fund for Women, as many of six of every ten women experience physical and/or sexual violence in their lifetime. A WHO study of 24,000 women in ten countries found that the prevalence of physical and/or sexual violence by a partner varied from 15 per cent in urban Japan to 71 per cent in rural Ethiopia, with most areas in the 30–60 per cent range.[40] A World Bank report estimated that violence against women was as serious a cause of death and incapacity among women of reproductive age as cancer and a greater cause of ill health than traffic accidents and malaria combined.[41]

Yet despite numerous UN declarations, conventions, and covenants,[42] to this day even murder in the name of honor is not classified as a crime in many regions of the Middle East, Africa, and Asia. Nor are dowry-motivated crimes such as the infamous bride burnings, which are still frequent in India, prosecuted with the same zeal as other kinds of murder. Neither is disfiguring a girl by throwing acid in her face for spurning a suitor, or other 'customary' violence, such as beating a woman to 'chastise' her for not obeying her husband. All these crimes are still culturally accepted, often by the women themselves.

In addition to the perpetuation of traumas, with all the adverse human and social consequences that follow, the economic costs of this violence are huge. For instance, a 2003 report from the US Centers for Disease Control and Prevention estimated that the cost of intimate partner violence in the United States alone exceeds US$5.8 billion per year: $4.1 billion in health care services, and nearly $1.8 billion in productivity losses due to absenteeism.[43]

Those economic costs do not include the cost of lost human potential resulting from the brutalisation of girls and women. Then there are the enormous costs to our world when children observe this violence. They internalise a model of our species in which difference, beginning with the most fundamental difference between female

38 Amnesty International, *End Domestic Violence. End Torture. A Fact Sheet on Domestic Violence as Torture* (2005). Retrieved from www.amnestyusa.org/women/pdf/DV_as_Torture_Fact_Sheet.pdf.

39 World Health Organization, 'Intimate Partner Violence' (2002). Retrieved from www.who.int/violence_injury_prevention/violence/world_report/factsheets/en/ipvfacts.pdf.

40 C. García-Moreno et al., *WHO Multi-Country Study on Women's Health and Domestic Violence against Women* (2005), xii, xiv. Retrieved from www.who.int/gender/violence/who_multicountry_study/Introduction-Chapter1-Chapter2.pdf; also available: www.saynotoviolence.org.

41 L. Heise, *Violence against Women: The Hidden Health Burden*, Discussion Paper 255, World Bank (1994).

42 See, e.g., the United Nations Declaration on the Elimination of Violence against Women (1993). It states that 'States should exercise due diligence to prevent, investigate, and in accordance with national legislation, punish acts of violence against women, whether those acts are perpetrated by the State or private persons'. It sets forth ways in which governments should act to prevent violence and to protect and defend women's rights. These measures form the standard of 'due diligence' that states are obligated to live up to.

43 UNIFEM website, 'Violence against Women' (2007). Retrieved from: www.unifem.org/gender_issues/violence_against_women.

and male, is automatically equated with dominating or being dominated, They also learn that it is permissible, even moral, to use force to impose one's will on others.

### 2.4.1. Legal Remedies

Legal remedies include recourse to Rome Statute, Article 7a – Murder; 7(e) Imprisonment; 7(g), Rape, sexual slavery, etc. 7(c) Enslavement, 7k – Inhumane acts; as well as amendments to Article 6b – Causing Serious bodily or mental harm to members of a group to include gender.

## 2.5. *Rape*

There is growing attention to preventing rapes worldwide. Yet according to the United Nations Population Fund (UNFPA), one in five women worldwide will become a victim of rape or attempted rape in her lifetime.[44] A huge proportion of victims are raped by people in their families or circle of acquaintances; for example, according to the US Department of Justice, approximately 28 per cent of victims are raped by husbands or boyfriends, 35 per cent by acquaintances, and 5 per cent by other relatives.[45] The number of women and girls raped during civil and other wars is also huge.[46] And the millions of girls and children kidnapped or sold into the sex trade or forced into child marriage are raped not just once, but over and over again.

Rape is still used in Afghanistan, Pakistan, and other regions of Southeast Asia, the Middle East, and Latin America to avenge real or imagined intertribal, intercaste, or intergang insults. Statistics understate the real frequency of rape because in most regions rapes are not reported since the 'dishonor' of rape falls on a woman or girl, rather than on her rapist, and the victims are often cast out by their families or even killed by family members.

Although rapes occur in all nations, all socioeconomic groups, and virtually all circumstances, refugees or populations displaced by natural disasters are especially vulnerable. For example, rape was a significant problem in Haiti even before the 2010 earthquake, but in the tent cities where hundreds of thousands huddled after the quake, with no lighting or security, sexual assaults became rampant. Not only women but also children as young as two were victimised by rapists. Yet, according to aid workers, these crimes went mostly unreported because of shame, social stigma, and fear of reprisals from attackers.[47]

44 UNFPA, *State of World Population 2005. The Promise of Equality: Gender Equity, Reproductive Health and the Millennium Development Goals* (2005), at 65.

45 Violence against Women, Bureau of Justice Statistics, U.S. Dept. of Justice, 1994. Retrieved from www.paralumun.com/issuesrapestats.htm.

46 Geneva Centre for the Democratic Control of Armed Forces, *Women in an Insecure World: Violence against Women – Facts, Figures and Analysis* (2005).

47 'Haiti Post-Quake Rapes Rise', *Women's ENews*, 20 March 2010. Retrieved from: www.womensenews.org/story/cheers-and-jeers/100319/us-under-scrutiny-haiti-post-quake-rapes-rise.

Beyond the terrible human suffering are the social costs of rape as a crime against humanity: from the transmission of traumas, to the desensitisation of men to suffering when rape is culturally condoned, to the enormous economic costs, to the fact that as long girls and women are not protected by states from rape we can predict that future generation will continue to bear this pain and cost.

#### 2.5.1. Legal Remedies

Mass rape is already included in the Rome Statute in the context of armed conflicts. But because rape occurs so frequently yet goes unpunished, it should also be included under the purview of Article 7f – Torture and Article 7k – inhumane acts. When gender is added to Article 6, rape falls under 6b – Causing Serious bodily or mental harm to members of a group.

### 2.6. *Denial of Access to Maternal Health Care and Family Planning*

The UN Population Fund, International Planned Parenthood, and many other organisations have been working diligently to ensure that women have adequate access to maternal care and family planning services. Yet every minute a woman still dies as a result of problems related to pregnancy, unsafe abortions, and childbirth, the vast majority in Asia and sub-Saharan Africa.[48] Many of them became pregnant because they were denied access to family planning.

Those who survive complications related to childbirth – approximately 10 million women each year – are often left with horrible health problems due to inadequate delivery care.[49] Similarly, often women do not have access to maternal care because they are not permitted to be treated by a male doctor and there are no female physicians.

Most critically, despite unconscionably high maternal death rates and unwanted pregnancies, governments around the world still fail to make family planning and maternal health care a priority. This is true even in rich nations such as the United States, where maternal mortality rates have more than doubled since the 1980s and are now higher than in 40 other countries.[50]

As Lee Jong-wook, former director-general of WHO, noted, 'Mothers, the newborn, and children represent the well-being of a society and its potential for the future. Their health needs cannot be left unmet without harming the whole of

[48] World Health Organization, 'Why Do So Many Women Still Die in Pregnancy or Childbirth?' Retrieved from www.who.int/features/qa/12/en/index.html.

[49] J. Calder, 'Fertility Control Essential for All Women', (2008) *The Argus Blog*. Retrieved from http://jeancalder.wordpress.com/2008/05/24/fistula.

[50] Amnesty International, *Deadly Delivery: The Maternal Health Care Crisis in the USA* (2010). Retrieved from www.amnestyusa.org/dignity/pdf/DeadlyDelivery.pdf.

society.'[51] Indeed, when states fail to make family planning and maternal health care a priority, they are committing crimes against both present and future generations, failing to meet their Responsibility to Protect (R2P).[52]

#### 2.6.1. Legal Remedies

Rome Statute Article 7 – Crimes against Humanity: especially Section 7(k) – Inhumane acts; amend Article 6 to include gender: Article 6b – Causing Serious bodily or mental harm to members of a group.

### 2.7. *Gender-Based Discrimination: From Denial of Education to Girls to Economic, Political, and Judicial Discrimination Against Women and Denial to Them of Freedom of Movement*

Stimulated by UN Conferences on Women from 1975 to 1995 and grassroots groups worldwide, systemic discrimination against girls and women has finally begun to receive scholarly, legal, and public notice, and some progress has been made to reduce it. Yet even in the United States, where women have made substantial cultural and legal gains, the earning gap between women and men is still large. In fact, it is much larger than generally believed.[53] A study by the Institute for Women's Policy Research found that over the span of women's work lives, the average working woman earned only $273,592 over her lifetime, largely due to her caregiving responsibilities, whereas the average man earned $722,693 (in 1999 dollars). So the real gender earning gap is 62 per cent – more than double the 20–23 per cent officially reported.[54]

Women's situation is even more dismal when it comes to property ownership. In many regions women are, by tribal law and/or tradition, denied the right to own land.[55] As Helen Clark, administrator of the United Nations Development Programme, noted, although agricultural jobs account for more than 40 per cent of women's jobs in East Asia and 65 per cent in South Asia, women control only 7 per cent of farms.[56]

51 World Health Organization, *World Health Report 2005: Make Every Mother and Child Count* (2005), xi.

52 For more information on the responsibility to project (R2P), see www.responsibilitytoprotect.org.

53 According to the 2009 Gender Pay Gap Report, the gap was 79.9 per cent on the average. Retrieved from www.docstoc.com/docs/5681750/The-Gender-Pay-Gap-Report-April-2009/.

54 S. J. Rose and H. I. Hartmann, 'Still a Man's Labor Market: The Long-Term Earnings Gap' (2004), Institute for Women's Policy Research.

55 B. Agarwal, *A Field of One's Own: Gender and Land Rights in South Asia* (1994).

56 H. Clark, Speech at the 2010 Asia-Pacific Human Development Report Launch, 8 March 2010, New Delhi, India. Retrieved from: http://content.undp.org/go/newsroom/2010/march/helen-clark-remarks-at-the-2010-asia-pacific-human-development-report-launch.en.

As for education, although some nations have reached educational parity, in others, girls are systematically denied access to school. For instance, almost half the adult women in South Asia are illiterate, and the situation is not much better in many parts of sub-Saharan Africa.[57]

These crimes against girls and women are related to other forms of gender-based discrimination, such as women's dismally low representation in political office and blatant judicial discrimination. For example, in Muslim fundamentalist areas that impose the Sharia (Islamic law), the testimony of two women is required to counter that of one man, and women must produce witnesses to being raped, a virtual impossibility.

The denial of freedom of movement to women has resulted in higher mortality. For example, during a 2007 flood in Bangladesh 71 of every 1,000 women were killed – as compared to 15 men per 1,000.[58] A major cause of this radically disproportionate casualty rate was that women were not permitted to leave their homes without a male family member, and because this social norm was so embedded in their minds, they stayed – and drowned.

Studies in Africa, Latin America, and other world regions show that children do better where mothers have greater access to and control over household resources. This is because on average women spend a much larger percentage of their resources on food and other necessities for children than do fathers – in male-dominated cultures men are often socialised to first spend on themselves.[59] Many other studies also show that gender inequality is a major barrier to justice, economic development, and social stability. For instance, a Center for Partnership Studies report based on statistical data from 89 nations found that in significant respects the status of women can be a better predictor of a nation's general quality of life than its GDP.[60]

### 2.7.1. Legal Remedies

Legal remedies include recourse to Rome Statute, Article 7 – Crimes against Humanity and amendments to Article 6 to include gender.

57 2010 Asia-Pacific Human Development Report: 'Power, Voice and Rights: A Turning Point for Gender Equality in Asia and the Pacific.' Retrieved from http://content.undp.org/go/newsroom/2010/march/asiapacific-has-one-of-the-worlds-worst-gender-gaps.en.

58 United Nations Environment Programme (UNEP), 'Mainstreaming Gender in Environmental Assessment and Early Warning' (2005). Retrieved from: www.unep.org/dewa/products/publications/2005/mainstreaming_gender.pdf.

59 See, e.g., J. Bruce and C. B. Lloyd, 'Finding the Ties that Bind: Beyond Headship and Household', in L. Haddad, J. Hoddinott, and H. Alderman (eds.), *Intrahousehold Resource Allocation in Developing Countries: Methods, Models, and Policy* (1997); D. Thomas, 'Intra-Household Resource Allocation', (1990) 25(4) *Journal of Human Resources*; *Real Wealth*, *supra* note 6, at chapter 6.

60 R. Eisler, D. Loye, and K. Norgaard, *Women, Men, and the Global Quality of Life* (1995).

## 3. CRIMES AGAINST CHILDREN OF BOTH GENDERS

Although some crimes against children were addressed in the preceding section, I now turn to additional crimes against children that should be included under the purview of the Rome Statute: 'the most serious crimes of concern to the international community as a whole,' especially under section 7k: 'inhumane acts . . . intentionally causing great suffering, or serious injury to body or to mental or physical health'.

### 3.1. *Violence against Children in Their Homes*

Although in recent years a number of nations have passed laws against physical discipline of children, in most cultures, violence against children is still considered an acceptable, even moral, form of discipline, and corporal punishment within the family is not defined as an act of violence to a child, even though it would be criminal if used against an adult.[61] Thus, 84 per cent of adults queried in a 2005 study agreed 'that it is sometimes necessary to discipline a child with a good hard spanking'.[62]

Some of this violence is extremely severe, involving not only physical blows (on many areas of the body, not only on the buttocks), kicking, shaking, throwing, scratching, pinching, and biting but also burning, whipping, scalding, suffocating, and beatings with belts, bats, sticks, metal rods, and other instruments. In other words, children are subjected to acts that in other circumstances would be classified as torture.

Children from violent families are frequently diagnosed with posttraumatic stress, anxiety disorders, depression, and feelings of hopelessness. To cope, some find relief in drugs, alcohol and tobacco abuse, self-injurious behaviours, risky or extreme behaviours, violent behaviours, sexual promiscuity, and desire to have their own children in the hope of receiving love. Chronic health and dietary problems are frequent, as are learning difficulties; in many cases they experience life-long problems in personal, work, and other relations.

In addition to these devastating individual and social effects, because their home is the first educational venue for children, their experiences establish clear delineations about power imbalances and gender role expectations. Without appropriate intervention, violence against children adds to the possibility that they will inflict violence towards children in future generations.[63]

61 Committee on the Rights of the Child (2006). General Comment No. 8. *The Right of the Child to Protection from Corporal Punishment and Other Cruel or Degrading Forms of Punishment* (Articles 19, 28(2) and 37, inter alia), CRC/C/GC/8, at Para. 11.

62 B.A. Lehman, 'Making a Case against Spanking', *The Washington Post*, 23 March 1989. Cited in M. A. Straus and A. K. Mathur, 'Social Change and Trends in Approval of Corporal Punishment by Parents from 1968 to 1994', in D. Frehsee et al. (eds.), *Violence against Children* (1996), 91–105. See also J. E. Durrant, 'Corporal Punishment: Prevalence, Predictors and Implications for Child Behaviour and Development', in S. N. Hart (ed.), *Eliminating Corporal Punishment* (2005).

63 UNICEF, *World Report on Violence against Children* (2006), 48. Retrieved from www.unicef.org/violencestudy/3.%20World%20Report%20on%20Violence%20against%20Children.pdf.

### 3.1.1. Legal Remedies

In 1979, Sweden became the first country to outlaw slapping and spanking.[64] Since then, other countries have addressed this issue: Finland (1983), Norway (1987), Austria (1989), Cyprus (1994), Italy (1996), Denmark (1997), Latvia (1998), Croatia (1999), Bulgaria (2000), Germany (2000), Israel (2000), Iceland (2003), Ukraine (2004), Romania (2004), Hungary (2005), Greece (2007), Netherlands (2007), and New Zealand (2007).[65] In 2006, the report of the independent expert for the United Nations study on violence against children recommended that 'States should build community confidence in the justice system by bringing all perpetrators of violence against children to justice and ensure that they are held accountable through appropriate criminal, civil, administrative and professional proceedings and sanctions'.[66] It is now up to international law to begin to hold accountable states that still condone violence against children in homes. Once again, the Rome Statute can be used to this end: Article 7(a) – Murder; Article 7(k) – inhumane acts; Amend 6b – Causing Serious bodily or mental harm to members of a group to include childhood.

### 3.2. *Violence against Children in Schools*

Even though some progress has also been made to reduce violence in schools, corporal punishment in schools is still legal in 90 countries, and 350 million students around the world face violence in their schools each year.[67] The report 'Learn without Fear,' identified 33 types of violence, including beatings, hitting children on the head, and 'penciling' (putting a pencil between two fingers and tightly squeezing the fingers). It also found that this violence has lasting impacts on children's well being and is a major contributor to high student dropout rates.[68]

In India, two out of every three students are victims of physical abuse at school. Not surprisingly, a 2007 UNICEF statistical review found that of every ten children

[64] Prior to the enactment of the anti-spanking laws, opinion polls from 1965 revealed that 53% of the Swedish people considered physical punishment indispensable. An anti-spanking campaign during the 1970s resulted in a shift to 30% of the population believing that physical punishment was indispensable. By 1994, survey results show that a majority (89%) of Swedes were opposed to every form of physical punishment. Resent research (2000) indicates that the percentage of the population opposing all forms of physical punishment has risen to 92%, and among today's generations of parents and the generation to come, there is a greater abhorrence of physical punishment. Save the Children, Sweden, 'The First Anti-Spanking Law in the World: Historical Background to the Swedish Legislation' (2001). Retrieved from www.wallsofsilence.com.

[65] Project No Spank, 'Countries where spanking is prohibited by law in the home, at school, everywhere!' Retrieved from www.nospank.net/totalban.htm.

[66] P. S. Pinheiro, Report of the Independent Expert for the United Nations Study on Violence against Children, 29 August 2006, UN Doc. A/61/299, at para. 109.

[67] 'Millions Face School Violence across Asia', Australia Broadcasting Corporation (ABC), 8 October 2008 available at www.abc.net.au/ra/programguide/stories/200810/s2385881.htm.

[68] Plan International, 'Leanr without Fear' available at http://plan-international.org/learnwithoutfear/files/learn-without-fear-global-campaign-report-english.

who begin primary school in India, four drop out by the time they reach the fifth grade. In the United States, paddling –hitting a child's buttocks with a wooden instrument – is still legal in 21 states, and, according to the Office for Civil Rights at the US Department of Education, is used frequently in rural areas of 13 Southern states, including Texas.[69]

Violence is painful both physically and psychologically. It also promotes violence and bullying by children against one another, impedes learning, and leads many to drop out of school.[70] As Randeep Kaur noted, 'the impact of years of caning, slapping and humiliation can extend far beyond school days. . . . [I]t actually leads to an intergenerational cycle of violence, you know, that I was hit so its ok for me to hit my kids and then the children will go about hitting their children.'[71]

### 3.2.1. Legal Remedies

Legal remedies include the use of article 7k (Crimes against Humanity, other inhumane acts) and an amendment to Article 6 – Causing Serious bodily or mental harm to members of a group that includes childhood.

### 3.3. *Child Marriage and Forced Marriage*

Despite efforts to outlaw it, child marriage is common in many parts of the world. And although marriages arranged by children's parents sometimes also involve boys, it is again girls who are the vast majority of those who suffer. More than 51 million girls under 18 in the developing world are forced to marry, sometimes to men more than twice their age. One in seven girls is given in marriage before the age of 15. More than 100 million girls will be child brides during the next ten years if current practices continue.[72]

The practice is most common in sub-Saharan Africa and southern Asia, but is also found in other parts of Asia, the Middle East, North Africa, and Latin America. In Ethiopia and parts of West Africa, girls are married as young as age seven.[73]

The consequences for these child brides are brutal. They are often victims of beatings and other violence by their husbands and family; for example, India has

[69] 'Corporal Punishment in Public Schools', *CNN.com/US*, 20 August 2008. Retrieved from www.cnn.com/2008/US/08/20/corporal.punishment/#cnnSTCOther1.

[70] Arun Kumar Rath, quoted in C. S. Kasturi, 'Spare the Rod, Keep Child in School', *The Telegraph*, Calcutta, 4 February 2008. Retrieved from www.telegraphindia.com/1080204/jsp/nation/story_8860681.jsp.

[71] Randeep Kaur interview, in 'Millions Face School Violence across Asia', Australia Broadcasting Corporation (ABC), 8 October 2008. Retrieved from www.abc.net.au/ra/programguide/stories/200810/s2385881.htm.

[72] UNFPA, State of the World Population 2005, Child Marriage Fact Sheet Retrieved from www.unfpa.org/swp/2005/presskit/factsheets/facts_child_marriage.htm.

[73] *Ibid.*

the highest levels of domestic violence among women married before the age of 18.[74] Some die from injuries due to too early forced intercourse, and many die from becoming pregnant too young. Survivors also face enormous health risks, including obstructed labour leading to fistulas. In Nigeria alone, up to 800,000 women suffer from fistulas, and many are thrown out by their husbands and families to die on the streets.[75] Yet child marriage is still justified on moral grounds. As a man who married a 14-year old girl when he was 80 asserted, 'It is to preserve the purity of our girls'.[76]

For the most part, the world is still indifferent to the cruel lives and deaths of the millions of children forced into marriage and sexual relations with men often twice or even four times their age. Because these girls are deprived not only of their childhoods but also of their education, there is enormous economic damage from lost human potential, which perpetuates poverty, illiteracy, and other impediments to economic development. There are other important cultural consequences, such as acceptance by people of brutality as moral.

#### 3.3.1. Legal Remedies

Legal remedies include the use of Rome Statute, especially Article 7(c) – Imprisonment; Article 7(g) – Forced pregnancy, Article K –Other Inhumane Acts, as well as amendments to Article 6 to include gender and childhood.

### 3.4. *Child Sexual Abuse*

Once a taboo subject, sexual abuse of children is now widely documented. UNICEF estimates that globally 'five to ten percent of girls and up to five percent of boys suffer penetrative sexual abuse over the course of their childhood'.[77] Other data indicate a higher percentage; for example, in one study, 7–36 per cent of adult women and 3–29 per cent of adult men reported being sexually victimised in their homes during their childhood.[78] The WHO estimated that 150 million girls and 73 million boys under the age of 18 experienced forced sexual intercourse or another form of sexual violence during 2002.[79]

74 *Ibid.*

75 R. Navai, 'Broken Lives: Nigeria's Child Brides Who End up on the Streets', *The Times*, 28 November 2008. Retrieved from www.timesonline.co.uk/tol/news/world/africa/article5248224.ece.

76 Quoted in *ibid.*

77 UNICEF, *Celebrating 20 Years of the Convention on the Rights of the Child* (2009), at 25 [*Celebrating*].

78 United Nations, Promotion and Protections of the Rights of Children, UN Doc A/61/150 (2006), at 13 [Promotion at Protections].

79 United Nations, *Global Estimates of Health Consequences due to Violence against Children* (2006). World Health Organization, *Comparative Quantification of Health Risks: Global and Regional Burden of Disease Attributable to Selected Major Risk Factors, Volume 2* (2004), at 1851–1940, and using data of the Population Division of the United Nations Department of Economic and Social Affairs for population under 18 years.

Although much of the statistical data focuses on sexual abuse within the family, reports of victimisation within educational and workplace settings and care facilities are increasing.[80] For example, as noted earlier, since 2000, as many as 1.2 million children have been trafficked annually and used for sexual exploitation.[81] According to Interpol, pornography also victimises many children.[82] And the high incidence of sexual abuse by Catholic priests, whom the Catholic Church transferred from parish to parish where their sexual abuses continued, is still another piece of the mounting evidence that not only our laws but even many of our religious institutions have failed miserably in protecting children.[83]

The injuries and psychological damage from sexual abuse often haunt children throughout their lives.[84] It has been found to disrupt not only normal childhood development but also normal brain functioning.[85] In addition, there is still a social stigma associated with this egregious form of child abuse, with the veil of secrecy and silence that surrounds it ensuring that survivors must endure their pain and sense of betrayal and violation alone.

Sexual abuse also does enormous damage to society at large, from the spread of sexually transmitted diseases and teen pregnancies[86] to the lost human potential that results from the use and abuse of children who are unable to protect themselves.

#### 3.4.1. Legal Remedies

Legal remedies include the use of Article 7(c) – Imprisonment; Article 7(g) – Forced pregnancy, Article K –Other Inhumane Acts. Another avenue to better protect children is to add childhood to Article 6b – Causing Serious bodily or mental harm to members of a group.

### 3.5. *Child Labour*

According to the International Programme on the Elimination of Child Labour (IPEC), worldwide millions of children are still coerced, bonded, or forced to work in inhuman and dangerous conditions.[87] The International Labour Organisation

80 Promotion and Protections, *supra* note 77, at 15–18.

81 *Celebrating, supra* note 76 at 25.

82 V. Jones and E. Skogrand, Save the Children Europe Group, *Position Paper Regarding Online Images of Sexual Abuse and Other Internet-Related Sexual Exploitation of Children* (2005). Retrieved from www.childoscope.net/2009/httpdocs/publications/2db2aa03d8bf3530d93306f887dbce92.pdf.

83 For a report on the discussion on whether the Pope can be prosecuted by the International Criminal Court under the Rome Statute's Crimes against Humanity provision, see P. Dodds, 'British Could Challenge Pope's Immunity', *Associated Press*, 5 April 2010.

84 WHO, *supra* note 78, at chapter 23.

85 Perry, *supra* note 9.

86 WHO, *supra* note 78, at Chapter 23.

87 International Programme on the Elimination of Child Labour (IPEC), *About Child Labor: Defining Child Labor*. Retrieved from www.ilo.org/ipec/facts/lang–en/index.htm.

(ILO) reported that in 2004, 218 million children between the ages of 5 and 17 were involved in child labour, of whom 126 million were in hazardous work.[88] In many poorer world regions, children are expected to work long hours by their parents. Children working in farms are often exposed to pesticides, herbicides, and other hazardous chemicals without adequate protective or safety gear.[89] Many children have to work in a country other than their own, isolated by the work and language barriers so they are at the mercy of their employers' demands, anytime day or night.[90] Children are also often placed in combat-related roles, setting explosive devices or being trained as suicide bombers. Some are also forced to be sex slaves.[91] When children are deprived of freedom and education, indeed deprived of their childhood, this limits not only their ability to develop their potentials but also the human capacities of our societies and our world.[92]

### 3.5.1. Legal Remedies

The principle legal remedy would be the expansive interpretation of Rome Statute, Article 7 of Crimes against Humanity.

## 4. CONCLUSION

Historically, international criminal law has developed by incorporating concepts of human rights law. This has been the case with the Rome Statute, especially Article 7, Crimes against Humanity, which, as Antonio Cassese notes, 'incorporates or overlaps with concepts of human rights law (the right to life, not to be tortured, to liberty and security of the person, etc.) laid down in provisions of international human rights instruments'. These instruments include the Universal Declaration of Human Rights and subsequent covenants, declarations, and conventions that, as Cassese writes, are 'intended to protect the human person'.[93]

Following this precedent, the integrated approach outlined in this chapter proposes that the next step for international criminal law is to incorporate concepts of human rights law laid down in human rights instruments specifically designed to protect the majority of humanity, including the Convention on the Elimination of All Forms of Discrimination against Women, the Convention on the Rights of the

88 International Labour Office, *The End of Child Labour: Within Reach* (2006), as cited in Promotion and Protections, *supra* note 77, at 10.

89 U.S. Dept. of Labor, *2008 Findings on the Worst Forms of Child Labor* (2009). Retrieved from www.dol.gov/ilab/programs/ocft/PDF/2008OCFTreport.pdf.

90 *Ibid.*

91 *Ibid.*

92 UNICEF, *Child Protection from Violence, Exploitation and Abuse: Child Labor* (2006). Retrieved from www.unicef.org/protection/index_childlabour.html.

93 Cassese, *supra* note 2, at 64–65.

Child, and the Declaration on the Elimination of Violence against Women.[94] These instruments, developed with the goals of binding states to protect the women and children in their jurisdictions, apply to human rights violations in both the public and private spheres; they require that states enact laws to this end and enforce these laws.

1. A first step to enforce these goals through international criminal law is to protect women and children from the widespread, egregious, systemic crimes against them by using existing provisions of Article 7 (Crimes against Humanity) of the Rome Statute.
2. A second step is expanding the purview of Article 6 (Genocide) to include 'gender' and 'childhood' under the categories protected from 'killing', 'serious bodily or mental harm', 'infliction of conditions of life calculated to bring about its physical destruction in whole or in part', and 'imposing measures intended to prevent births within the group'.

These proposals are in line not only with the principle of responsibility to protect (R2P) but with the most elementary principles of ethics and morality. They are foundational to the protection of human rights in both the private and public spheres – from protection from violence to protection from the destruction of our natural environment.

A central principle of international criminal law is that when a state fails to protect people from widespread, large-scale abuses that cause great suffering or serious injury to physical or mental health through its policies and laws or through the failure to enforce its laws, it is complicit in these abuses. Indeed, we are all complicit if we avert our eyes from the widespread, systemic, and atrocious crimes against women and children that continue unabated and unprosecuted in our world. It is generally recognised that failure to report a crime is itself a crime. For their sake – and for the sake of us all – we cannot continue to fail the most vulnerable among us.

[94] United Nations, Treaty Series, vol. 1249. Convention on the Elimination of All Forms of Discrimination against Women. 18 December 1979. New York; UN General Assembly resolution 44/25. Convention on the Rights of the Child, 20 November 1989. New York; UN General Assembly A/RES/48/104. 85th plenary meeting. Declaration on the Elimination of Violence against Women. 20 December 1993. Retrieved from www.un.org/womenwatch/daw/cedaw/cedaw.htm, www2.ohchr.org/english/law/pdf/crc.pdf, www.unicef.org/crc/, and www.un.org/documents/ga/res/48/a48r104.htm.

# 16

# The Responsibility to Prevent

## *Early Warning Systems to Protect Future Generations*

*Maja Göpel*

### 1. INTRODUCTION

In our international order, states are duty-bearers towards individuals and communities endowed with inalienable rights and have the obligation to secure these rights now and over time.[1] This means that it is the duty of states to prevent serious violations not only of civil and political rights but also of economic, social, cultural, and environmental rights that fuel cases of international crimes. Sustainable development in the World Commission on Environment and Development's original definition clearly encompasses this human rights angle, especially with respect to the lives of future generations: 'Sustainable development is development that meets the needs of the present without compromising the ability of future generations to meet their own needs.'[2]

If states fail to meet the universally agreed goal of sustainable development, future generations are liable to be victims of living conditions below agreed human rights standards. As resource-connected cases of today show, this outcome will make it much more likely that individuals will commit crimes as defined under current

[1] Here, some may voice the argument that today's generation should not dictate to tomorrow's generations what they will consider to be appropriate rights and entitlements. My position is that all law is continuously evolving and the moral baseline should therefore be to secure equal expression and participation in this development, thus maintaining rights until they are changed in circumstances of open participation.

[2] World Commission on Environment and Development, *Our Common Future*, 1987, Chapter 2, Para. 1. Available at www.un-documents.net/ocf-02.htm.

The idea of discussing an early warning system to prevent the violation of social, economic, environmental, and cultural rights to such a degree that they should be classified as crimes against future generations first came up in the deliberations of the Future Justice Commission of the World Future Council (for its mission and members, see www.worldfuturecouncil.org/futurejustice_commission.html). The responsibility for this elaboration of the idea, the selection of cases, and their interpretation with the principled standard, however, solely lies with this author. Alice Vincent and Christiane Bossé were of tremendous support in research and editing, as was Sébastien Jodoin for his overall feedback and coordination.

international law. Thus, from the perspective of preventing international crimes in the future and fostering sustainable development, it would be helpful to identify an early warning system for situations that already have an unsustainable imprint and risk escalation. The primary instrument of states through which to live up to their duty to protect rights and prevent crimes is the issuance of good policies, rules and laws, and a code of conduct to protect all members of the populace now and subsequently. In line with the preventive intent of criminal law, good policy making for sustainable development therefore involves the avoidance of systemic conditions that make it more likely that individuals will violate human rights and commit crimes.

What an early warning system that would alert policy makers to close such loopholes could look like is the topic of this chapter. Given that many unsustainable developments and human rights violations today involve foreign actors, the question arises as to how the international community of states could support each other, rather than standing by while others are exploited in transnational operations.

The proposal discussed here refers to the internationally agreed doctrine of 'responsibility to protect' (R2P), an attempt by the international community to prevent genocide and other crimes of mass atrocity. The R2P doctrine, while accepting that states have the primary responsibility for the protection of their own population, recognises that there is an ethical and institutional responsibility vested in the wider international community to ensure that this duty is fulfilled. If a state fails or is unwilling to protect its citizens from genocide, war crimes, ethnic cleansing, and crimes against humanity, the international community has a duty to act. Prevention is the most important dimension of the responsibility to protect as reflected in the 2005 World Summit's conclusions, which first recognised the R2P doctrine:

> 138. Each individual State has the responsibility to protect its population from genocide, war crimes, ethnic cleansing and crimes against humanity. This responsibility entails the *prevention of such crimes, including their incitement*, through appropriate and necessary means. *We accept that responsibility* and will act in accordance with it. *The international community should*, as appropriate, *encourage and help States to exercise this responsibility* and support the United Nations in establishing an *early warning capability*.
>
> 139. The international community, through the United Nations, also has the *responsibility to use appropriate diplomatic, humanitarian and other peaceful means, in accordance with Chapter VI and VIII of the Charter*, to help to protect populations from genocide, war crimes, ethnic cleansing and crimes against humanity. . . . We also intend to commit ourselves, as necessary and appropriate, to *helping States build capacity to protect* their populations from genocide, war crimes, ethnic cleansing and crimes against humanity and to assisting those which are under stress *before crises and conflicts break out*.[3]

[3] UN General Assembly, World Summit Outcome 2005, UN Doc. A/RES/60/1 (2005), at Paras. 138–39. Available at www.un.org/summit2005/documents.html. As emphasised in G. Evans, *The Responsibility to Protect: Ending Mass Atrocity Crimes Once and For All* (2002), 79–80.

Although prevention is at its core of its wording, the 2005 World Summit Outcome Document does not specify its scope. This chapter argues that R2P may well include the protection of economic, social, cultural, and environmental rights as a means to prevent international crimes, including those foreseeable in the future if basic conditions for life with dignity are destroyed.

Regulatory measures are important preventive means that arise well before forceful interventions might be needed to protect a given population at a point of escalation. What is established here is a *responsibility to legislate*; creating, changing, or abolishing laws should become obligatory if unchecked development initiatives or business conduct is likely to contribute to the emergence of conditions under which the commission of international crimes is more likely. In reference to Chapter 17 of this book, one may also argue that the anticipated long-term consequences of a failure to prevent may in themselves qualify as international crimes: crimes against future generations.

This chapter is therefore structured as follows. First, it argues how the R2P doctrine could be expanded to include regulatory intervention for social, cultural, environmental, and economic rights, drawing on case law where a human rights court (the European Court of Human Rights) has established such a state duty and responsibility.

Second, it discusses experiences with early warning systems and introduces a policy warning methodology based on the International Law Association's seven principles for sustainable development law (New Delhi Declaration of 2002). With this approach, a systematic analysis of how certain laws and policies lead to environmental and social disruptions and collapse can allow for the tracking of the evolution of an unsustainable development pattern into an international crime. It could make preventive action possible and help avoid full-blown crises. Reference to one historical example, the Group Areas Act of 1950 in South Africa, illustrates the connection between worst policies and the long-term consequential violation of social, cultural, and economic rights.

Third, a potential example of a currently upheld worst policy – small arms trading – is discussed in relation to its expected long-term criminal consequences. This example also shows that in our globalised world, the drivers of unsustainable and exploitative development often cut across national borders. It supports the necessity for multinational responsibility and expands analytical attention from existing laws to cases of regulatory omission: despite the documented consequences, no binding legislative action has been undertaken.

At present, there exists no systematic early warning scrutiny for unsustainable development, so policy makers must rely on technical experts and scientific calculations. These methods are sometimes able to anticipate the nature of an ecocide, industrial disaster, structural exclusion from economic well-being, or the perpetrated relations of conflict, but frequently cannot. To systematically develop R2P to include prevention, the concluding part of this chapter argues that a Special Rapporteur or

Working Group for Sustainable Development or Future Generations at the UN Human Rights Council may be a viable solution for this task.

## 2. THE RESPONSIBILITY TO PROTECT PRINCIPLE THROUGH LEGISLATION

Under international law, when states sign and ratify a treaty, they agree to become duty-bearers with respect to the goals and rights inscribed therein. Thus, they also commit to refraining from interfering or curtailing these rights and to protecting individuals against human rights abuses by state authorities and nonstate actors. To fulfil the goals of the treaty, states must take active steps to reach the agreed goals and to enable citizens to enjoy their rights.[4]

From this perspective, a failure to anticipate and prevent deadly and disruptive collapses of ecosystems and livelihoods translates into the failure of a state to live up to its duties to secure the rights of its people.[5] It imbues a responsibility to do better and to be held accountable for legislative responsibility.

Initial debates on the justiciability of economic, social, and cultural rights (ESCR) under international law have shown a reluctance to address these issues in courts. In particular, poorer countries have been concerned about accusations of ESCR violations because of bad policies or insufficient anticipation of detrimental developments.[6] This is a likely reason why ESCR violations are primarily dealt with in complaints procedures or political negotiations, but rarely in the courts.

Yet, with respect to young people and future generations, the continued destruction of our ecosystems and the social fabric of communities is implicitly connected to international crimes. The 1997 United Nations Educational, Scientific and Cultural Organization (UNESCO) Declaration on the Responsibilities of the Present Generations towards Future Generations, for example, clearly outlines these connections and establishes a direct responsibility for current generations to prevent such transgressions. Its chapeau paragraph contains powerful language:

> Conscious that, at this point in history, the very existence of humankind and its environment are threatened,
>
> Stressing that full respect for human rights and ideals of democracy constitute an essential basis for the protection of the needs and interests of future generations,

4 E. Aba and M. Hammer, 'Yes We Can? Options and Barriers to Broadening the Concept of Responsibility to Protect to Include Cases of Social, Economic and Cultural Rights Abuse', Briefing Paper 116, One World Trust (2009), at 6. Available at www.oneworldtrust.org/index.php?option=com_docman&task=doc_download&gid=302&Itemid=55.

5 M. J. Dennis and D. P. Stewart, 'Justiciability of Economic, Social and Cultural Rights: Should There Be an International Complaints Mechanism to Adjudicate the Rights to Food, Water, Housing and Health?', (2004) *American Journal of International Law* 462, at 492.

6 *Ibid.*

> Asserting the necessity for establishing new, equitable and global links of partnership and intra-generational solidarity, and for promoting intergenerational solidarity for the perpetuation of humankind, . . .
>
> Convinced that there is a moral obligation to formulate behavioural guidelines for present generations within a broad, future-oriented perspective.[7]

The articles of the UNESCO Declaration cover environmental issues as much as the preservation of peace. Given the transnational quality of most of the issues raised in the articles, the responsibility to *prevent* these conditions from evolving into serious human rights violations amounting to international crimes should implicate all governmental institutions at different governance levels. The primary duty of governments to intervene in the prevention of such violations is of a legislative character, structuring the relationships between humans and their environment in a sustainable manner, so that sources of conflict and ecological disaster are mitigated.

Interesting case law related to this argument can be found with the European Court of Human Rights (ECHR), in cases involving a state's duty to regulate private actors so they do not violate individual rights. For example, in the case of *Hatton and Others* v. *The United Kingdom*, the court asserted that 'State responsibility arises from the failure to regulate private industry properly'.[8] Although the court has reiterated the fundamentally subsidiary role of the European Convention on Human Rights, it has also positively established the responsibility to regulate on several occasions. In one case in which nine people died in an accident, the Chamber

> emphasised that the protection of the right to life, as required by Article 2 of the Convention, could be relied on in connection with the operation of waste-collection sites, on account of the potential risks inherent in that activity. It accordingly held that the positive obligation on States to take appropriate steps to safeguard the lives of those within their jurisdiction, for the purposes of Article 2, applied in the instant case.[9]

The Chamber ruled that

> *the positive obligation to take all appropriate steps to safeguard life for the purposes of Article 2 (see paragraph 71 above) entails above all a primary duty on the State to put in place a legislative and administrative framework designed to provide effective deterrence against threats to the right to life. . . .* [I]n addition, special emphasis must

7 UNESCO (1997), Declaration on the Responsibilities of the Present Generations Towards Future Generations. Available at http://portal.unesco.org/en/ev.php-URL_ID=13178&URL_DO=DO_TOPIC&URL_SECTION=201.html.

8 See *Hatton and Others* v. *The United Kingdom*, no 36022/97, Decision of 8 July 2003, at Para. 98. Available at http://cmiskp.echr.coe.int/tkp197/view.asp?action=html&documentId=835996&portal=hbkm&source=externalbydocnumber&table=F69A27FD8FB86142BF01C1166DEA398649.

9 See *Öneryildiz* v. *Turkey*, no 48939/99, Decision of 30 November 2004, Para. 65. Available at http://cmiskp.echr.coe.int/tkp197/view.asp?action=html&documentId=708579&portal=hbkm&source=externalbydocnumber&table=F69A27FD8FB86142BF01C1166DEA398649.

> be placed on regulations geared to the special features of the activity in question, particularly with regard to the level of the potential risk to human lives. They must govern the licensing, setting up, operation, security and supervision of the activity and must make it compulsory for all those concerned to take practical measures to ensure the effective protection of citizens whose lives might be endangered by the inherent risks.[10]

In several cases, Article 8 of the European Convention on Human Rights protecting the individual's right to respect for his or her private and family life, home, and correspondence was interpreted to also cover environmental issues where an individual is directly and seriously affected by noise or other pollution.[11]

In the original 2001 Report of the International Commission on Intervention and State Sovereignty (ICISS), which set forth the doctrine of R2P, environmental destruction is also included as a case justifying intervention, described as 'overwhelming natural or environmental catastrophes, where the state concerned is either unwilling or unable to cope, or call for assistance and significant loss of life is occurring or threatened'.[12] Returning to the focus on the prevention of, rather than protection during, a full-blown crisis, a global responsibility to prevent human rights violations and environmental catastrophes through appropriate legislation seems justifiable. If a state fails or is unwilling to stop activities likely to result in widespread human rights violations or the commission of international crimes in the mid or long term, the international community has a duty to act to prevent such unsustainable developments.

An important point to facilitate the widespread acceptance of this interpretation will be to emphasise that the responsibility to legislate and enact need not necessarily lie with the country within which the unsustainable activities occur; the globalisation of production chains and relationships and increasing interdependence in the last decades make bi- or even multinational involvement in unsustainable activities very likely. Rather than blaming one single country, the identification of worst policies or of the absence of sufficient policies in one country could lead to a call for legislative responsibility in countries whose individual or corporate citizens take advantage of this regulatory gap. A global early warning system conducted by an independent third party would be a prerequisite for such collaboration.

10 *Ibid.*, at paras. 89 & 90 (emphasis added).

11 See, for example *Tatar* v. *Rumania*, no 67021/01, Decision of 27 January 2009, at paras. 87 & 88. Available at http://cmiskp.echr.coe.int/tkp197/view.asp?action=html&documentId=846165&portal=hbkm&source=externalbydocnumber&table=F69A27FD8FB86142BF01C1166DEA398649, with reference to *Budayeva* v. *Russia*, no 15339/02, 21166/02, 20058/02, 11673/02, and 15343/02, §§ 129–132, 20 March 2008, at para. 88.

12 International Commission on Intervention and State Sovereignty, *The Responsibility to Protect: Report of the International Commission on Intervention and State Sovereignty* (2001), at 33, available at www.iciss.ca/pdf/Commission-Report.pdf.

## 3. EXPERIENCES WITH EARLY WARNING SYSTEMS

The first step in the prevention of international crimes is identifying the situations that may lead to their commission. In the 1970s and 1980s, the first conflict early warning approaches were designed as a means of protecting and preserving life. After the Cold War, they made a significant appearance on the political agenda, but the mechanisms proved insufficient to prevent genocide in Rwanda in 1994 or to turn around the conflict in the Balkans. There were some success stories, however, such as the prevention of an ethnic conflict in Macedonia in the 1990s by the deployment of a UN peacekeeping force; the role of the UN Special Adviser on the Prevention of Genocide in putting pressure on the authorities of Côte d'Ivoire to end radio broadcasts inciting ethnic hatred in the middle of an intensifying conflict; and the preventive diplomacy that has occurred in Burundi since 2002.[13] Furthermore, in the wake of the Rwandan genocide, the Steering Committee of the Joint Evaluation of Emergency Assistance to Rwanda concluded that 'pieces of information were available that, if put together and analyzed, would have permitted policy makers to draw the conclusion that both political assassinations and genocide may occur'.[14] This finding led to a number of institutional initiatives from international organisations and academics to compare, elaborate, and develop early warning systems.[15] The focus of prevention was, however, narrowed from conflicts more broadly to mass atrocities. Most of the existing early warning systems therefore focus on discrimination, ethnic tension, and racial hatred.

The current body of research on early warning can be divided into two branches: qualitative and quantitative analysis. Qualitative analysis relies mainly on area specialists who research the underlying causes of the conflict, whereas quantitative analysis relies primarily on statistical observation of quantifiable factors designed via a theory of conflict.

To bridge the gap between identifying typical risks and pinpointing the likely onset of a crisis, several quantitative genocide scholars have worked on the reform of preventive early warning systems to include wider civil and political rights violations.[16] Barbara Harff and Helen Fein, for example, have found that six factors enhance the likelihood of genocide: prior genocide in the same polity, autocracy, ethnic minority rule, political upheaval during war or revolution, exclusionary ideology, and closure

13 See P. Akhavan, 'Preventing Genocide: Measuring Success By What Does Not Happen', (2011) 22 *Criminal Law Forum* 23–31.

14 D. Nyheim, *Preventing Violence, War and State Collapse: The Future of Conflict Early Warning and Response* (2009), 27.

15 Including the Forum on Early Warning and Early Response (FEWER), the West Africa Network for Peacebuilding (WANEP), the Network for Ethnological Monitoring and Early Warning (EAWARN), and Early Analysis of Tensions and Fact-finding (FAST).

16 See B. Harff, 'Risk Assessment and Early Warning of Genocide: Some Guidelines for the Office of the Special Adviser to the UN Secretary-General on the Prevention of Genocide', Working Paper for the Office of the Special Adviser to the UN Secretary-General on the Prevention of Genocide (2006).

of borders to international trade.[17] Others such as Gregory H. Stanton have devised a developmental model of the stages of genocide. The eight stages of genocide are classification ('us vs. them'), symbolisation, dehumanisation, organisation (the formation of hate groups), polarisation, preparation (the identification, expropriation, rounding up, and transportation of victims), extermination, and denial. Stanton's model is designed so that policy makers can recognise early warning signs and implement specific countermeasures to prevent genocide.[18]

David Nyheim, a peace-building strategist, puts even more emphasis on qualitative data gathered from precarious regions. In a meta-study for the OECD, he points out that a successful approach to conflict early warning is distinct from intelligence-based analysis that focuses on the protection of state interests. The model of a successful early warning system 'sought multi-stakeholder solutions, was gender-sensitive, used open source information and aimed at protecting human lives and creating sustainable peace based on locally owned solutions'.[19] However, this engaging qualitative approach has been overshadowed by changes in perceptions of international threats after the terrorist attacks of 2001.

Nevertheless, several of the findings of Nyheim's meta-study can inform the discussion of this proposed principled approach to worst policy identification. Overall, Nyheim found that a good early warning system provides

> a crisis prediction capacity that enables proactive decision making; a stronger basis for evidence-based decision making on countries affected by crisis; improved programming through systematic country reviews and expert analysis; a priority-setting contribution through watch-list type products; a starting point for developing a shared problem definition for crisis-affected countries that sets the stage for more coherent responses; and an ideas pool for responses and sometimes the forum to meet fellow responders and plan joint response strategies.[20]

From the point of view of future generations and sustainable development it is also vital to include broader economic, social, and environmental conditions into the set of early warning criteria, because they provide background conditions for the commission of international crimes in the mid to long term.

## 4. IDENTIFYING WORST POLICIES FOR FUTURE GENERATIONS

Experience with early warning systems has shown that it is possible to identify laws and policies enacted by governments that make it easier to commit the crime of

[17] B. Harff, 'No Lessons Learned from the Holocaust? Assessing Risks of Genocide and Political Mass Murder since 1955' (2003) 97(1) *American Political Science Review* 573; H. Fein, 'Accounting for Genocide after 1945: Theories and Some Findings' (1993) 1(1) *International Journal on Group Rights* 7906.

[18] G. Stanton, (2004) 'Could the Rwandan Genocide Have Been Prevented?', (2004), 6(2) *Journal of Genocide Research*, 211–28, at 212–17.

[19] Nyheim, *supra* note 14, at 14.

[20] *Ibid.*, at 16.

genocide[21] and, conceivably, crimes against humanity. From the point of view of sustainable development, such 'worst policies', both in intent and effect, threaten the livelihoods, health, and even the very survival of future generations. The reliable detection of such laws and policies would therefore help identify where the established rules of conduct and the systemic conditions of individual activities fail to deter or, in some cases, even encourage human rights violations or the commission of international crimes. What kind of criteria or principles might be used to select the worst examples of laws and policies or to detect the absence of 'good' policies? And how can the identification of such laws and policies help *prevent* the escalation of unsustainable developments into full-blown crises?

The most important precondition for such an early warning system is the establishment of an independent, reliable, and legitimate universal standard with which to evaluate the laws and policies in question. In the last three decades, several important international processes have been undertaken to develop principles of international law on sustainable development. These include the 1972 *Stockholm Declaration*,[22] the 1987 Brundtland Commission's *Report of the Legal Experts Group on Principles of International Law for the Protection of the Environment and Sustainable Development*,[23] the 1992 *Rio Declaration* and *Agenda 21*[24] of the United Nations Conference on Environment and Development, the 2002 *Johannesburg Plan of Implementation*[25] of the World Summit on Sustainable Development, and the 2002 *New Delhi Declaration* of the International Law Association.[26]

21 Harff, *supra* note 16. See also B Harff, 'No Lessons Learned from the Holocaust? Assessing Risks of Genocide and Political Mass Murder since 1955' (2003) 97 *American Political Science Review* 57, at 73.

22 UN Conference on the Human Environment, Stockholm Declaration, UN Doc. A/Conf 48/14/Rev.1 (1972). For discussion, see, e.g., G. D. Meyers & S. C. Muller, 'The Ethical Implications, Political Ramifications and Practical Limitations of Adopting Sustainable Development as National and International Policy', (1996) 4 *Buffalo Environmental Law Journal* 1; and A. Geisinger, 'Sustainable Development and the Domination of Nature: Spreading the Seed of the Western Ideology of Nature', (1999) 27 *British Columbia Environmental Affairs L Rev* 43.

23 Brundtland Commission, Our Common Future: Report of the World Commission on Environment and Development, UN Doc. A/42/427 (1987).

24 UN Conference on Environment and Development, Rio Declaration on Environment and Development (Annex 2), UN Doc. A/CONF.151/26 (Vol I), (1992); UN Conference on Environment and Development, Agenda 21 (Annex 2), UN Doc. A/CONF.151/26 (Vol I) (1992).

25 The official documents from the World Summit for Sustainable Development (WSSD) are available at WSSD Documents www.un.org/jsummit/html/documents/summit_docs.html, accessed 1 January 2008; see also World Summit on Sustainable Development, Johannesburg Declaration on Sustainable Development and Johannesburg Plan of Implementation, UN Doc. A/CONF.199/L20 (2002).

26 See International Law Association, 'New Delhi Declaration of Principles of International Law Relating to Sustainable Development', (2002) 2 *International Environmental Agreements* 209; N. Schrijver and F. Weiss, 'Editorial Introduction', (2002) 2 *International Environmental Agreements* 105. See also International Law Association, *Report of the Expert Group on Identification of Principles of International Law for Sustainable Development* (1995); International Law Association, *Report of the Sixty-Second Conference* (1987), 409–87.

The New Delhi Declaration was the result of a decade of consultation and study. It summarises seven criteria for policy making for sustainability. Mirroring these positive principles, a draft questionnaire to identify policies that are detrimental to the interests of future generations can be derived as follows:[27]

**Delhi Principle 1: The duty of countries to ensure sustainable use of natural resources**

***Worst Policy Criterion 1: Promote the unsustainable use of natural resources***

1.1 Does the law/policy promote the unsustainable exploitation of the Earth's scarce resources?
1.2 Does it contribute to the destruction of the global commons (e.g. climate change, extinction of species, collapse of world fish stocks)?
1.3 Does it threaten to destroy natural areas, artifacts, and traditional knowledge, including those that are the common heritage of humankind?

**Delhi Principle 2: The principle of equity and the eradication of poverty**

***Worst Policy Criterion 2: Exacerbate inequity and poverty***

2.1 Does the law/policy threaten to contribute to poverty or exacerbate human rights challenges?
2.2 Does it increase inequality between generations by including provisions that prevent actors from taking into account the needs and aspirations of future generations?
2.3 Does it increase inequality within present generations of life by compromising social justice and equity for all peoples, promoting gender discrimination, violating the rights of indigenous peoples and local communities, increasing poverty, and harming other species?

**Delhi Principle 3: The principle of the precautionary approach to human health, natural resources, and ecosystems**

***Worst Policy Criterion 3: Make precautionary approaches to human health, natural resources, and ecosystems more difficult to achieve***

3.1 Does the law/policy discourage prevention and precaution in the face of scientific uncertainty about the threat of serious or irreversible harm?
3.2 Does it place the burden of proof for demonstrating that a project or activity is unsafe, or that risks are unreasonable, on those who will be impacted by the venture?
3.3 Where there is insufficient scientific evidence, does it take the right to set acceptable levels of risk or threat away from those most affected by a project?

[27] This definition of the standard is reproduced from an informal legal research paper on the identification of worst policies for future generations that the Centre for International Sustainable Development Law produced for the World Future Council in 2008. It is available upon request.

**Delhi Principle 4: The principle of public participation and access to information and justice**

***Worst Policy Criterion 4: Prevent public participation and access to information and justice***

4.1 Does the law/policy prevent or create obstacles to public consultation and genuine engagement, in either its design or its implementation?
4.2 Does it decrease transparency and access to information for concerned citizens, local communities, and others who might be affected?
4.3 Does it block avenues for appeal and redress for citizens, communities, and others?

**Delhi Principle 5: The principle of good governance**

***Worst Policy Criterion 5: Encourage bad governance in practice and increase human insecurity***

5.1 Does the law/policy weaken or displace institutions that ensure transparent, prompt, effective, and fair implementation of sustainable development laws and policies?
5.2 Does it promote the violent resolution of conflicts or increase the likelihood that human beings will live in fear and want?
5.3 Does the law/policy include provisions that might contribute to corruption, bribery, or unethical conduct or promote the abuse of rights or the misimplementation of sustainable development laws and policies?

**Delhi Principle 6: The principle of integration and interrelationship, in particular in relation to human rights and social, economic, and environmental objectives**

***Worst Policy Criterion 6: Promote the fragmentation and exploitation of social or ecological systems, ignoring legitimate human rights and social, economic, and environmental objectives***

6.1 Does the law/policy encourage the separation and fragmentation of social justice and environmental protection concerns from economic development plans and projects?
6.2 Does it separate development decision making from environmental and social impact, making identification, mitigation, modification, and cancellation of such decisions, if warranted, more difficult?
6.3 Does it threaten to damage societies or the environment?

**Delhi Principle 7: The principle of common but differentiated obligations**

***Worst Policy Criterion 7: Violate the principle of common but differentiated obligations***

7.1 Does the law/policy ignore or exacerbate historical and other inequalities, including recognition of who has benefitted from past activities and policies, when imposing obligations? Does it block avenues to redress such inequalities?

7.2 Does the law/policy disregard the society or region's present level of technology, scientific knowledge, and human/financial resources? Does it ignore or promote disrespect for the society's cultural values and traditions?
7.3 Does it place inappropriate burdens on vulnerable groups or impose costs on those least equipped to bear them?

Although not a 'check-list', answering these questions can clarify one overarching question: What are the actions, practices, and policies whose adoption or maintenance could radically destroy the prospects of sustainability on our planet and therefore compromise the integrity of future generations? These 'principled questions' are not exhaustive, nor will all of them apply to every law or policy. However, the continued and systematic collection of available data on these questions will support several of the characteristics of effective early warning systems that Nyheim defined. It can systematically strengthen evidence-based decision making and region or country-level reviews; include growing numbers of experts; and generate a watch-list of common shortcomings in regulation and a shared problem definition for affected countries, as well as a strategic exchange of ideas for responses through regulatory intervention, including joint intervention. The last point seems particularly relevant, because an absence of tighter controls on industry conduct or the presence of low production and reliability standards is often and perversely beneficial in the competition over foreign direct investments.

By enabling the increased scrutiny, this questionnaire also helps detect loopholes or insufficient accountability in existing legislation that can facilitate human rights violations and possibly consequent international crimes. In this way, it can enable 'worst' policies and laws to be recognised and changed while acknowledging regional, cultural, and technological diversity. Such an assessment also draws attention to surrounding legislation and policy contexts that may contribute to the problem. In addition, a reiterated application of the questionnaire will continuously improve the awareness, capacity, and engagement of groups and stakeholders living in precarious regions. This approach meets several of the principles for good practice of prevention mechanisms identified by Nyheim: understanding the problem and basing analysis on evidence on the ground; ensuring that responses are diverse, flexible, and sustainable; investing time in planning and strategy; being conflict-sensitive; not pushing technical solutions for political problems; balancing the speed of intervention; and ensuring ownership and coordination. The discursive and participatory methodology also promotes more consensus-based decision making – one of the recommendations for improving existing early warning mechanisms.[28]

This early warning system would provide guidance on the responsibility to legislate for economic, social, and environmental rights as defined in international law and

[28] *Ibid.*, at 16.

policy. With it comes the prevention of severe damages to the long-term health, safety, and means of survival of future generations.

### 4.1. *Tracking Effects of Former Worst Policies: Apartheid Laws*

There are many cases of worst policies in the past that illustrate the consequences of bad governance of societies and the environment. The treatment of Aboriginal peoples in Australia and the South African apartheid, for example, were both characterised by systemic discrimination against an entire ethnic or racial group from the highest echelons of political power. The extermination (in the case of Australia) or repression (in the case of South Africa) of one group by another was inscribed in intent and effect. Although these violations of human rights were based on discrimination amongst those living at that time, the resulting damage heavily affected the opportunities of future generations for a dignified life. These policies resulted in the loss or erosion of culture, the exploitation of natural resources, the suffocation of human capacity and personal development potential, community segregation, and racism. Gross inequality in all aspects of socioeconomic development and perpetuated relationships of discrimination, mistrust, and hostility prevail even today, although apartheid policies were abolished almost a generation ago. Such long-term impacts are living examples of how pervasively intergenerational the effects of bad governance can be on societies.

The apartheid regime in South Africa[29] presents an example of worst governance in which society was divided racially and an entire cultural, legal, and economic infrastructure was built to ensure the systematic suppression of the development of the black population. Interracial marriages or relations were illegal, and forced relocation into homelands was part of the segregation process. The unacceptability of such policies is manifested in the definition of Crimes of Apartheid in the Rome Statutes of the International Criminal Court.[30] Applying the standard of worst policy identification to policies that have later been recognised to facilitate an international crime allows for an assessment of the validity of its criteria.

The Group Areas Act of 1950 (Act No. 41 of 1950)[31] was an act of parliament designed to geographically separate racial groups. It excluded non-Whites from living in the most developed areas and forcibly removed them to 'homelands'. Overall, the effect of the law was that whites lived in areas with better employment opportunities and transport links and superior access to schooling, health, and information.

29 Due to the word limits of this chapter, the Australian case is not discussed, but the analysis is available upon request from the author.

30 UN General Assembly, Rome Statute of the International Criminal Court, UN Doc. A/CONF.183/9 (1998) at Article 7 (j). The original statute can be found at www.icc-cpi.int/NR/rdonlyres/EA9AEFF7–5752-4F84-BE940A655EB30E16/0/Rome_Statute_English.pdf.

31 The Group Areas Act of 1950 (Act No. 41 of 1950) was adopted by the government on the 27 April 1950. The original text can be found at www.disa.ukzn.ac.za/index.php?option=com_displaydc&recordID=leg19500707.028.020.041.

The most powerful economic restriction on black people was the prohibition of private ownership of immovable property. They were banned from ownership of any property or business in the 'white areas', which made up 87% of the country, and were severely restricted from property ownership even in the 'black areas'.[32] Thus, the Group Areas Act made the primary institutional contribution to the systematic suppression of development of the black population and particularly satisfied worst policy criterion number two – the exacerbation of inequity and poverty. It also promoted the fragmentation of the social system (worst policy criterion number six) by physically dividing South African society, and breeding distrust, animosity, and racism by intentionally entrenching social and physical distance between black and white people. The 'homelands' where black South Africans were forcibly relocated comprised only 13 per cent of South Africa's surface area, while hosting three-quarters of the population. This led to severe environmental degradation (worst policy criterion number one), especially because the prohibition of private property by the Group Areas Act meant that the land could seldom be rationally used and cultivated. As a consequence, human and physical degradation escalated, translating into worst policy criteria numbers three and six.[33]

This policy of racial geographical exclusion was accompanied by rules against free movement, employment, or access to justice (worst policy criterion number four). As a result, black people had little opportunity to progress in life, and their discriminatory treatment as inferior human beings caused severe psychological damage and low morale. The extreme levels of inequity, crime, and socioeconomic disadvantages still continue today, hampering the equitable living conditions of young people, the future generations of the 1970s. Estimations of the annual per capita personal income by race group between 1917–2005 show that in 1917, black South Africans were earning 9.1 per cent of what white South Africans were earning. This relative distribution dropped to as low as 6.8 per cent in 1970, and in 2008 black citizens were still earning an average of only 13 per cent of what white people earned.[34] These numbers prove that the legacy of apartheid is strongly persistent even today.

### 4.2. *Identifying Current Worst Policies: Small Arms Trading*

This section discusses one example of a current policy that seems to allow for severe long-term damage of living conditions, makes human rights violations more likely, and creates background conditions more conducive to the commission of genocide, war crimes, ethnic cleansing, and crimes against humanity. This is the small arms trade (particularly the small arms trade in conflict zones), which is made possible by

[32] A. Hirsch, *The Season of Hope* (2005). Online version, of 'Chapter 3: The Economic Legacy of Apartheid' accessible at www.idrc.ca/en/ev-91102–201-1-DO_TOPIC.html.

[33] *Ibid.*

[34] M. Leibbrandt, S. van der Berg, and H. Bhorat, 'Introduction', in H. Bhorat et al. (eds.), *Fighting Poverty: Labour Markets and Inequality in South Africa* (2001), 1, at 1–20.

the failure to ban certain activities. The UN General Assembly has recognised that the 'absence of common international standards for the import, export and transfer of conventional arms is one of the contributory factors to conflict, the displacement of people, crime and terrorism'.[35]

Taking a broader view that includes social, economic, and cultural rights, armed violence – not only when used in mass conflict but also in single criminal acts – has a significant impact upon human security and related development potentials. Each year, 740,000 children, women, and men die as a result of armed violence. The majority of these deaths – approximately 490,000 – are not related to an official conflict; most of them occur in low-income countries, and the vast majority are undertaken with small arms and light weapons.[36] In 2002, the United Nations Security Council first raised the issue of the destabilising accumulation of illicit small arms and light weapons as 'a major concern of the international community, posing a complex challenge that involves security, humanitarian and development dimensions'.[37] The *Report of the Secretary-General on Small Arms* outlined how the end of the Cold War had led to a decline in control over these weapons in many parts of the world and pointed to the significant increase in their circulation in the form of legal and illegal cross-border transfers involving state and commercial agents. It observed that movement from stages of underdevelopment to instability to fragility to crisis to conflict and to war had become more fluid. The connection between the uncontrolled spread of small arms and light weapons (SALW) in the world and the destabilisation of communities and degradation of resources, especially in poorer countries, was the primary concern discussed. The report called for the international community to take responsibility for better monitoring and control of the spread of SALW, programmatic action towards the resolution of conflicts and disarmament, and thorough investigation into the connection between armed violence and the development of societies.[38]

Research by the Geneva Declaration, signed by 90 states and supported by the UNDP, estimated the loss of economic productivity due to armed violence to be about US$95 billion per year in 2008 and predicted it could reach up to US$163 billion annually worldwide.[39] Yet, the indirect corrosive effects for society and the economy of heightened distrust, perceived insecurity, and psychological distress reach far beyond these quantified estimations: forced displacement; loss of social capital, schools, and clinics; destroyed markets and impeded investment in reconstruction

35 *Towards an Arms Trade Treaty: Establishing Common International Standards for the Import, Export and Transfer of Conventional Arms*, UN General Assembly Resolution A/63/240 (2008).

36 See leaflet of The Geneva Declaration (2008), supported by UNDP and 90 states, www.genevadeclaration.org/fileadmin/docs/Geneva-Declaration-Leaflet.pdf.

37 UN Security Council, Report of the Secretary-General on Small Arms, UN Doc. S/2002/1053 (2002), at 1.

38 UN Security Council, Report of the Secretary-General on Small Arms, UN Doc. S/2008/258 (2008), at 1.

39 *Ibid.*

and reconciliation; loss of trust in public institutions; facilitated corruption; and a climate of impunity are conditions that make human security difficult to achieve. The Geneva Declaration issued a background paper in 2008 that highlighted the relationship between armed violence and the Millennium Development Goals on poverty eradication, health, education, gender equality, sustainability, and development partnerships, outlining the detrimental effects of armed violence on agreed targets of the global community.[40]

Thus, it is unsurprising that in identifying the worst policies responsible for detrimental living conditions, the 'excessive accumulation and universal availability' of SALW has been at the center of discussions for amelioration in the UN Security Council. The earlier mentioned report found that these weapons 'aggravate conflicts by increasing lethality and duration of violence and by increasing the sense of insecurity which leads to a greater demand for weapons'.[41] The Security Council was also very clear in its demand for action: 'Ensuring that small arms in private ownership do not enter illicit circuits where their use may contribute to instability and to exacerbating poverty must be part of the equation for every Government.'[42] The Security Council report identified regulatory shortcomings in the production, registration, and distribution of SALW, pointing to the increasing fragmentation and commercialisation of trading patterns that would make it difficult to differentiate between trading – which is regulated to a certain extent – and brokering. Eighty per cent of states have not enacted specific laws or regulations within their systems of arms export control regarding brokering, and there exist plenty of loopholes that make it difficult to define whether such distributive activities are covered by other laws.[43]

For example, in 2003 the United States transferred arms to 18 of the 25 countries involved in active conflicts at that time. Twenty of those 25 countries – 80 per cent – were either undemocratic regimes or governments with a record of major human rights abuses.[44] Of the top ten arms-exporting countries worldwide in 2006, seven are EU Member States, and the value of EU arms exports amounts to approximately 360 billion Euros (about US$480 billion) annually. In contrast, the Millennium Campaign of the United Nations estimates the amount necessary to reach all Millennium Development Goals in 2015 to be US$189 billion.[45] EU member states have said that they plan to give the existing Code of Conduct on Arms Exports (CoC) a legally binding status, but this has not yet happened.

40 Geneva Declaration Secretariat, *Armed Violence Prevention and Reduction. A Challenge for Achieving the Millennium Development Goals* (2008), 18.

41 *Small Arms*, Report of the General Secretary to the Security Council, S/2008/258, at 2.

42 *Ibid.*

43 *Ibid.*, at 5.

44 F. Berrigan and W. D. Hartung, *U.S. Weapons at War 2005: Promoting Freedom or Fuelling Conflict?* (2005). Available at www.worldpolicy.org/projects/arms/reports/wawjune2005.html.

45 *Investing in Development: A Practical Plan to Achieve the Millennium Development Goals*, Overview Report, 2005, Millennium Project, at 57.

These examples clearly show that the responsibility to regulate for prevention often does not lie within one country. Here, the EU – and similarly the United States – would be identified as breaching their duties, or R2P, in the broader sense: they are implicated in the indirect exacerbation of poverty and inequity (worst policy criterion 2), undermine the precautionary principle (criterion 3), lack transparency and efforts to provide sufficient information (criterion 4), lack good governance in terms of policy coherence or implementation (criterion 5), and ignore the effects of profit making on human rights, human security, and social equity (criterion 6). In terms of shared but common obligations (criterion 7), states with greater governing capacity should control their citizens' or companies' business affairs so that they do not undermine goals of conflict resolution, peace building, and development in other countries. Consequently, arms trading on the part of the EU or the United States with a country to which they are also paying development assistance for disarmament projects[46] is a worst policy that not only facilitates human rights violations today but is also likely to aggravate the deterioration of living conditions in the mid to long term. Legislative responsibility to prevent the escalation of these unsustainable trends lies with the global community, so that the heightened chance for future generations to become subject to international crimes is not ignored.

## 5. SUMMARY AND OUTLOOK ON INSTITUTIONALISATION

At present, the global community has no detailed map of which actions work to prevent ecocide or international crimes in the long term that are caused by the systemic violation of social, economic, and cultural rights. Yet, the overall discourse on R2P should include just such a map, especially if the international community seeks to live up to its multifarious commitments to sustainability and intergenerational justice. This kind of mapping is new territory for the global community that should be embraced in collaboration and exchange.

Recent global failures to anticipate the deadly and disruptive collapse of ecosystems and livelihoods demonstrate the need to do better. There is a need to develop a model to identify the circumstances in which certain laws and policies encourage the exploitation of natural resources to a degree that risks survival in the long term; where the financing of severely risky genetic or chemical testing is hampering the long-term health of entire communities; where overzealous investment in hazardous technologies and weapon markets blocks the cultivation of peaceful relationships over long time frames or escalates conflict into armed violence; or where cultural discrimination destroys the social fabric required for human security and quality of life. Such early warning models help narrow the time frame between the

[46] For the EU this does hold true; see *Policy Coherence for Development: A Practical Guide*, 2007, EU Coherence Project, at 33 a.

identification of high-risk scenarios and escalation to full-blown crisis, and they make participatory preventive action possible.

Although there will rarely be one single law, policy, or other factor that clearly stands out as the ultimate trigger of international crimes, using the principled assessment described in this chapter will lead to the identification of a number of combinations of laws, policies, and other factors. The example of the arms trade indicates the need to search widely for the drivers of such dangerous developments. Tracking identified factors over time will ultimately yield the type of early warning that will be extremely useful for responsible governance in the long term.

This chapter does not claim to propose an easy solution; early warning systems are not free from challenges and obstacles. Firstly, they can be extremely complex, requiring data that are neither available nor easily interpreted. Obtaining data from official sources poses problems, because those with the data may be accused by potential culprits as being "pawns" of certain governments. The means to conduct and interpret complex statistical analysis may also be lacking. Secondly, one must exercise caution in calling for immediate actions to halt escalation to international crimes because at present, we do not know exactly what types of action will work in different countries and cultures nor which actions will balance intragenerational justice and intergenerational justice best and which specific phases of an economic policy-making process provide the most promising point of intervention. What may work perfectly well in one context may be a recipe for disaster or completely irrelevant in another, and it may be hard to identify policy options that meet the approval of policy makers with short-term attention spans and cost concerns. Furthermore, leaders in democratic nations seldom act without the stimulus of public pressure, so early warnings must get through to the media and groups that can organise campaigns for action calling for regulatory responsibility. An objective and interactive methodology like the principled assessment described in this chapter could be turned into a well-communicated and user-friendly model. Serving as a benchmark, it would increase transparency, coherence, and trust in the monitoring efforts of multiple stakeholders. In addition, the results of assessments would have to be documented carefully and frequently evaluated. Thirdly, an early warning is only *as good as the action that accompanies it*. Yet, especially for poorer countries, it can be challenging in the extreme to initiate rapid and effective interventions. Therefore, this proposal uses a questionnaire that connects early warning with the R2P doctrine and international engagement for responsible governance. Designed as a learning process, the questionnaire could involve all states as equal partners. The R2P doctrine in this context would be a truly global effort to protect the succeeding generations on our planet.

Future generations cannot defend their own rights. In the case of impending genocide, the natural first addressees of early warnings are members of the victim groups, so that they can prepare to flee or defend themselves. In the case of future generations, these warnings need to be addressed to the institutions responsible for the well-being of their citizens now and in the future – our public institutions.

The establishment of a trusted institution executing the analyses, issuing the recommendations, and potentially even overseeing the regulatory responses and policy implementation will be a necessary next step to explore. Its legitimacy will be crucial, because the first goal is to increase public information and pressure for regulatory action, rather than deciding on a mandate of (military) intervention, as in the case of genocide. One possibility could be to establish a new Special Rapporteur on the Rights of Future Generations, or a Working Group on the Rights of Future Generations under the Special Procedures of the UN Human Rights Council. Special procedure mandates usually call on mandate holders to examine, monitor, advise, and publicly report on human rights situations in specific countries or territories, known as country mandates, or on major phenomena of human rights violations worldwide, known as thematic mandates.[47] Issuing early warnings on worst policies for future generations would be a thematic mandate and would include many of the typical activities of special procedures, such as response to individual complaints, studies on the most pressing issues, the provision of advice on technical and legal cooperation at the country level and between countries, and engagement in general promotional activities. In addition, this special procedure may require a strong educational mandate on integrated policy assessment and direct engagement with local group members, who would be important informants in identifying cases with the potential to escalate. UN Human Rights Special Rapporteurs have an excellent reputation and are known for their ability to bring issues forward and give them legitimacy in the eyes of the world. Such a Special Rapporteur – or even a UN Human Rights Council Working Group with five leading members from major regions of the world – may be seen as sufficiently independent from lobbying groups and national interests that its recommendations could be regarded as reflecting supranational moral standards. Investigating the potential impacts of existing and planned policies should go hand in hand with the issuance of recommendations on how to improve the identified regulation and of its communication strategy, which should be geared at building coalitions between the states concerned with jointly preventing international crimes.

47 For a detailed description of the mandates and procedures, see the manual provided by the Human Rights Council. Available at www2.ohchr.org/english/bodies/chr/special/docs/Manual_August_2008.doc.

# 17

# Conclusion

## *Protecting the Rights of Future Generations through Existing and New International Criminal Law*

*Sébastien Jodoin*

### 1. INTRODUCTION

The international community's ongoing failure to address the urgent challenges and injustices associated with massive violations of economic, social, and cultural rights; extreme poverty; unsustainable use of natural resources; and widespread environmental degradation requires the development of a new approach to fulfilling the demands of intergenerational justice.

In this chapter, I discuss one such novel approach: the potential for protecting the rights of future generations through international criminal law. My basic premise is that intergenerational justice requires not only the adoption of best practices and policies but also the prevention and repression of deleterious and morally blameworthy human behaviour. Although I agree with Gerry Simpson's concerns that a focus on individual responsibility can be reductive and unproductive,[1] I take the position that an exclusive focus on structural causes in the development and environmental fields is equally unhelpful, obscuring the reality that serious human rights violations and severe environmental degradation often result from intentional human conduct. As such, I argue that certain acts or conduct that have severe impacts on the long-term health, safety, and means of survival of present and future generations are of such scale and gravity that they should be prosecuted under international criminal law. To ensure consistency with existing international criminal law, I focus on acts or conduct that amount to serious violations of existing international law (regarding economic, social, and cultural rights or the environment). I agree therefore with many of the arguments put forward by Frédéric Mégret in this book and elsewhere[2] in favour of using international criminal law as a means of implementing international environmental law.

[1] See Chapter 3 in this book and more generally, chapter 3 in G. Simpson, *Law, War & Crime* (2007).

[2] See Chapter 4 in this book and F. Mégret, "The Problem of an International Criminal Law of the Environment" (2010) 36(2) *Columbia Journal of Environmental Law* 195.

Other chapters in this book have explored the links between different components of sustainable development and the specific elements of international crimes (see Part II). In this concluding chapter, I focus more generally on the protection of the rights of future generations through international criminal law. I first review the potential for using existing international crimes to protect the rights of future generations. I then focus on the creation of a new category of international crime, crimes against future generations, which would prohibit acts and conduct that have severe impacts on the long-term health, safety, and means of survival of human groups and collectivities. I conclude by discussing the advantages and prospects of implementing intergenerational justice through international criminal law.

## 2. EXISTING INTERNATIONAL CRIMES AND THE RIGHTS OF FUTURE GENERATIONS

In many ways, most international crimes have long-term consequences for affected persons or populations. In this section, I examine the potential for using international criminal law to protect the rights of future generations by focussing on how serious violations of economic, social, and cultural rights and severe environmental harm could be prosecuted making use of the three existing core crimes included in the Rome Statute: war crimes, crimes against humanity, and genocide.[3]

### 2.1. *War Crimes*

War crimes are serious violations of international law applicable in situations of armed conflict. There are of course many such violations that could infringe upon the rights of future generations. Indeed, international humanitarian law limits the means and methods of warfare of the parties to those that are necessary to achieve a military victory.[4] As a general rule, actions amounting to violations of the rights of future generations could be prosecuted as war crimes if they involved serious violations of the norms of international humanitarian law, such as the principle of distinction, which protects civilians and civilian objects from attack,[5] and the principle of proportionality, which prohibits attacks that would have disproportionate effects on civilians or civilian objects in relation to the anticipated concrete and direct military advantage.[6]

[3] Although the crime of aggression is also included in the Rome Statute, its elements have not been defined and it is not yet in force.

[4] See S. Oeter, 'Methods and Means of Combat,' in D. Fleck (ed.), *The Handbook of Humanitarian Law in Armed Conflicts* (1999), 105, at 401–06.

[5] See, e.g., Protocol Additional to the Geneva Convention of 12 August 1949 and Relating to the Protection of Victims of Internal Armed Conflict, 1125 UNTS. 3, (1977), Arts. 51–52.

[6] See *ibid.*, Arts. 51(5)(b), 57(2)(a)(iii) and 57(2)(b). See also, *Prosecutor* v. *Galic*, Trial Judgement, Case No. IT-98–29-T, T.Ch. I, 5 December 2003, para. 58 (and sources cited therein) and *Prosecutor* v. *Galic*, Appeal Judgement, Case No. IT-98–29-T, A. Ch., 30 November 2006, paras. 191–92.

Any number of the numerous provisions relating to war crimes in the Rome Statute could thus be used to protect the rights of future generations. The most relevant of these provisions include the following: torture or inhuman treatment, including biological experiments (Article 8(2)(a)(ii)); wilfully causing great suffering or serious injury to body or health (Article 8(2)(a)(iii)); extensive destruction or appropriation of property, not justified by military necessity and carried out unlawfully and wantonly (Article 8(2)(a)(iv)); intentionally directing attacks against civilian objects, that is, objects that are not military objectives (Article 8(2)(b)(ii)); intentionally launching an attack in the knowledge that such an attack will cause incidental loss of life or injury to civilians or damage to civilian objects or widespread, long-term, and severe damage to the natural environment that would be clearly excessive in relation to the concrete and direct overall military advantage anticipated (Article 8(2)(b)(iv)); subjecting persons who are in the power of an adverse party to physical mutilation or to medical or scientific experiments of any kind that are neither justified by the medical, dental, or hospital treatment of the person concerned nor carried out in his or her interest and that cause death to or seriously endanger the health of such persons (Article 8(2)(b)(x)); employing weapons, projectiles, and material and methods of warfare that are of a nature to cause superfluous injury or unnecessary suffering or that are inherently discriminatory in violation of the international law of armed conflict, provided that such weapons, projectiles, or material and methods of warfare are the subject of a comprehensive prohibition (Article 8(2)(b)(xx)); and intentionally using starvation of civilians as a method of warfare by depriving them of objects indispensable to their survival (Article 8(2)(b)(xxv)).

Any number of these provisions in the Rome Statute could thus be used to prosecute conduct violating the rights of future generations. One particular type of war crime is particularly relevant for the purposes of protecting the rights of future generations: the war crime of '[i]ntentionally launching an attack in the knowledge that such attack will cause . . . widespread, long-term and severe damage to the natural environment which would be clearly excessive in relation to the concrete and direct overall military advantage anticipated'.[7] This crime is extensively discussed by Matthew Gillett in Chapter 5, and I do not reiterate his detailed analysis here. Instead let me point out that, although this war crime could conceivably be used to prosecute one type of conduct that violates the rights of future generations (military acts that cause widespread, long-term, and severe damage to the natural environment), like all war crimes, it could only be prosecuted if it was committed in connection with an armed conflict and as such it does not apply in peacetime.

Indeed, the scope of application of war crimes is closely connected to the scope of application of international humanitarian law, which applies to armed conflicts and as such does not apply to situations of violence that go below a certain threshold. The first condition for the application of war crimes is the existence of an armed

7 Additional Protocol I, *supra* note 4, Art. 8(2)(b)(iv).

conflict, which was defined by the International Criminal Tribunal for the former Yugoslavia Appeals Chamber in the *Tadic* case as 'a resort to armed force between States or protracted armed violence between governmental authorities and organized armed groups or between such groups within a State'.[8] The second condition for the application of war crimes is that there be a nexus between the alleged crime and the armed conflict.[9] These two conditions are reflected in the provisions on war crimes included in the Rome Statute. The Rome Statute provides that war crimes listed in subparagraphs (a) and (b) of Article 8(2) apply to international armed conflicts only and that the war crimes listed in paragraphs (c) and (d) of Article 8(2) apply 'to armed conflicts not of an international character' and not 'to situations of internal disturbances and tensions, such as riots, isolated and sporadic acts of violence or other acts of a similar nature'. The ICC Elements of Crimes further provide that it is necessary that '[t]he conduct took place *in the context of* and was *associated with*'[10] the armed conflict. In addition to these two conditions, the ICC Elements of Crimes also provide that it is necessary that '[t]he perpetrator was aware of factual circumstances that established the existence of *an armed conflict*'.[11]

### 2.2. *Crimes against Humanity*

Article 7 of the Rome Statute defines crimes against humanity as a series of prohibited acts, such as murder, extermination, or torture, 'committed as part of a widespread or systematic attack directed against any civilian population'. There are two prohibited acts in particular that could be used to prosecute acts or conduct that might also violate the rights of future generations: persecution (Article 7(1)(h)) and other inhumane acts (Article 7(1)(k)).

The Rome Statute defines the offence of persecution 'as the intentional and severe deprivation of fundamental rights contrary to international law by reason of the identity of the group or collectivity.'[12] The Rome Statute defines 'other inhumane acts' as including any act that is of 'a similar character [to other crimes against humanity] intentionally causing great suffering, or serious injury to body or to mental or physical health'. As such, whether a given act falls within the category of other inhumane acts is a question to be assessed on a case-by-case basis.[13] The

[8] *Prosecutor* v. *Tadic*, Decision on the Defence Motion for Interlocutory Appeal on Jurisdiction, Case no. IT-94–1, A. Ch., 2 October 1995, para. 70.

[9] *Prosecutor* v. *Kunarac*, Appeal Judgement, Case No. IT-96–23 & IT-96–23/1-A, A. Ch., 12 June 2002, paras. 58–9 See also *Prosecutor* v. *Rutaganda*, Appeal Judgement, Case No. ICTR-96-3-A, A. Ch., 26 May 2003, paras. 569–70.

[10] See Report of the Preparatory Commission for the International Criminal Court, Addendum: Finalized Draft Text of the Elements of Crimes, UN Doc. PCNICC/2000/INF/3/Add.2 (2000), Art. 8(2) (emphasis added).

[11] See ICC Elements of Crimes, *supra* note 9 (emphasis added).

[12] See Rome Statute, *supra* note 1, Art. 7(2)(g).

[13] *Prosecutor* v. *Kordic and Cerkez*, Trial Judgement, IT-95–14/2, T. Ch. III, 26 February 2001, paras. 271–72.

elements of the act that should be 'comparable' to enumerated acts are severity, character, infliction of mental or physical harm in fact, intent to cause harm, and a nexus between act and harm.[14]

Using these two crimes to prosecute violations of the rights of future generations would require interpreting the elements of these crimes to cover violations of economic, social, and cultural rights. There is limited case law that supports such an expansive approach to the interpretation of these crimes. With respect to persecution, the *Kupreskic* Trial Chamber has held that 'the comprehensive destruction of homes and property' constitutes 'a destruction of the livelihood of a certain population' and thus 'may constitute a gross or blatant denial of fundamental human rights, and, if committed on discriminatory grounds, it may constitute persecution'.[15] Most interpretations of the scope of persecution and other inhumane acts, however, have in practice been largely limited to violations of civil and political rights that cause severe mental or physical harm.

Ultimately, the greatest impediment to prosecuting conduct harming the rights of future generations is the chapeau requirement of crimes against humanity that requires that they be 'committed as part of a widespread or systematic attack directed against any civilian population'.[16] The requirement of an attack against any civilian population encompasses any mistreatment of the civilian population of the same gravity as crimes against humanity.[17] The term 'attack' refers to 'a course of conduct involving the multiple commission of acts' amounting to crimes against humanity.[18] The attack against any civilian population must moreover either be widespread or systematic in nature. The Rome Statute also introduces a policy element to the attack requirement: the acts must be committed 'in furtherance of a State or organizational policy'.[19] As such, the Rome Statute requires for an offence to be considered a crime against humanity that a state or organisation, whether by its actions or exceptionally by its deliberate failure to take action, actively promote or encourage an attack against a civilian population.[20]

### 2.3. *Genocide*

Article 2 of the United Nations Convention on the Prevention and Punishment of the Crime of Genocide[21] defines genocide as a number of acts, such as killing or the

14 *Prosecutor* v. *Kayishema*, Trial Judgement, ICTR-95–1, T. Ch. I, 21 May 1999, paras. 148–51.

15 *Prosecutor* v. *Kupreskic et al.*, Trial Judgement, IT-95–16-T, T. Ch. II, 14 January 2000, para. 631.

16 In addition to the chapeau requirement, the Rome Statute requires with respect to persecution that it be committed in connection with another international crime and that it be committed with specific discriminatory intent.

17 *Prosecutor* v. *Kunarac*, *supra* note 8, para. 86.

18 See Rome Statute, *supra* note 1, Art. 7(2)(a).

19 *Ibid.*

20 ICC Elements of Crimes, *supra* note 9, Art. 7(3).

21 1948 Convention on the Prevention and Punishment of the Crime of Genocide, 78 UNTS 277, (1948), Art. 2.

forcible transfer of children, 'committed with intent to destroy, in whole or in part, a national, ethnical, racial or religious group, as such'. Three of the underlying acts amounting to genocide could be used to prosecute conduct harming the rights of future generations: causing serious bodily or mental harm to members of the group (Rome Statute, Article 2(b)); deliberately inflicting on the group conditions of life calculated to bring about its physical destruction in whole or in part (Rome Statute, Article 2(c)); and imposing measures intended to prevent births within the group (Rome Statute, Article 2(b)).

In order to use these crimes for the purposes of protecting the rights of future generations, it would be necessary, as it was for the case for crimes against humanity, to expand their scope to encompass violations of social, economic, and cultural rights. The quintessential examples of acts causing serious bodily or mental harm are 'torture, rape, and non-fatal physical violence that causes disfigurement or serious injury to the external or internal organs' and 'the infliction of strong fear or terror, intimidation or threat'.[22] Likewise, the ICC Elements of Crimes provide that these acts 'include, but are not necessarily restricted to, acts of torture, rape, sexual violence or inhuman or degrading treatment'.[23] With respect to the deliberate infliction of conditions of life calculated to bring about a group's physical destruction, an ICTR Trial Chamber held that it includes 'circumstances which will lead to a slow death, for example, lack of proper housing, clothing, hygiene and medical care or excessive work or physical exertion', as well as 'rape, the starving of a group of people, reducing required medical services below a minimum, and withholding sufficient living accommodations for a reasonable period'.[24] The ICC Elements of Crimes largely reiterate the ICTR's definition, providing that conditions of life 'may include, but is not necessarily restricted to, deliberate deprivation of resources indispensable for survival, such as food or medical services, or systematic expulsion from homes'.[25] Finally, the offence of imposing measures intended to prevent births within the group has been defined as including sexual mutilation, sterilisation, forced birth control, the separation of the sexes, the prohibition of marriages, and rape.[26] Again, the possibilities of interpreting the material element of these crimes in a manner that would cover the types of human rights violations of concern to the rights of future generations are limited.

In any case, even if these crimes of genocide could be interpreted to cover acts that violate the rights of future generations, the chapeau requirement of genocide would remain a serious barrier to its use for this purpose, requiring proof of 'the intent to destroy, in whole or in part, a national, ethnical, racial or religious group'. Moreover, the definition of a group is limited to one of the enumerated grounds of

[22] *Prosecutor* v. *Seromba*, Appeal Judgement, ICTR-2001–66-A, A. Ch., 12 March 2008, para. 46.
[23] ICC Elements of Crimes, *supra* note 9, Art. 6(b), fn. 3.
[24] *Prosecutor* v. *Kayishema*, *supra* note 13, paras. 115–16.
[25] ICC Elements of Crimes, *supra* note 9, Art. 6(c), fn. 4.
[26] *Prosecutor* v. *Akayesu*, Appeal Judgement, ICTR-96–4-T, A. Ch., 1 June 2001, paras. 507–08.

nationality, ethnicity, race, or religion and does not encompass groups defined on other grounds.

### 2.4. *Conclusion*

This analysis demonstrates that it might indeed be possible to use existing international criminal law to prosecute conduct involving violations of the rights of future generations. Most notably, the war crime of an attack that causes widespread, long-term, and severe damage to the natural environment is of direct relevance to the rights of future generations. However, because this crime could only be used to prosecute acts that had been committed in connection with an armed conflict, it does not cover damage caused to the environment in peacetime. Using crimes against humanity and genocide would require certain innovations in the application of these crimes to cover the types of human rights violations and environmental harm that are of most concern to the rights of future generations. That said, the greatest impediments to the use of these two crimes are their chapeau requirements that essentially restrict their application to situations involving mass violence or gross violations of civil and political rights. In sum, although many international crimes have indirect consequences on the rights and interests of affected future generations, it cannot be said that existing international criminal law is currently well placed to directly and clearly protect intergenerational rights.

## 3. CRIMES AGAINST FUTURE GENERATIONS

### 3.1. *The Concept of Crimes against Future Generations*

Given the limitations of existing international criminal law, I was commissioned in 2007 through a project established by the World Future Council[27] and involving the collaboration of the Centre for International Sustainable Development Law[28] to develop a new international crime to protect the rights and interests of future generations. Through three years of research as well as workshops and consultations

27 The World Future Council brings the interests of future generations to the centre of policy making. Its 50 eminent members from around the globe have already successfully promoted change. The Council addresses challenges to our common future and provides decision makers with effective policy solutions. In-depth research underpins advocacy work for international agreements, regional policy frameworks, and national lawmaking, thus producing practical and tangible results. See The World Future Council, online: www.worldfuturecouncil.org.

28 The Centre for International Sustainable Development Law (CISDL) is an independent research centre that aims to promote sustainable societies and the protection of ecosystems by advancing the understanding, development, and implementation of international sustainable development law. Through legal research, teaching, conferences, and capacity building, the centre contributes to ongoing policy processes and initiatives on the intersections of international law in the environment, human rights, human health, trade, and development. See CISDL, online: www.cisdl.org.

held with leading international judges and lawyers,[29] this collaboration yielded the concept and definition of crime against future generations that is presented below.[30]

The definition of crimes against future generations reads as follows:[31]

1. Crimes against future generations means any of the following acts within any sphere of human activity, such as political, military, economic, cultural, or scientific activities, when committed with knowledge of the substantial likelihood of their severe consequences on the long-term health, safety, or means of survival of any identifiable group or collectivity:
   (a) Forcing members of any identifiable group or collectivity to work or live in conditions that seriously endanger their health or safety, including forced labour, enforced prostitution and human trafficking;
   (b) Unlawfully appropriating or acquiring the public or private resources and property of members of any identifiable group or collectivity, including the large scale embezzlement, misappropriation or other diversion of such resources or property by a public official;
   (c) Deliberately depriving members of any identifiable group or collectivity of objects indispensable to their survival, including by impeding access to water and food sources, destroying water and food sources, or contaminating water and food sources by harmful organisms or pollution;
   (d) Forcefully evicting members of any identifiable group or collectivity in a widespread or systematic manner;

29 Meetings were held in Santa Barbara, The Hague, London, Arusha, Montréal, Bali, Kampala, and Ottawa. The members and advisers of the WFC Commission on Future Justice who actively fostered work on crimes against future generations included Hon. Christopher J. Weeramantry, Bianca Jagger, Prof. Marie-Claire Cordonier Segger, Hon. Arthur Robinson, Dr. Scilla Elworthy, Dr. Rama Mani, Count Hans von Sponeck, Dr. Ernst Ulrich von Weizsäcker, Dr. Hans Peter Dürr, David Krieger, Prof. Stephen Marglin, Jakob von Uexküll, Herbert Girardet, Alexandra Wandel, Neshan Gunaskera, Miguel Mendonca, and Milo Wagner. Many individuals assisted in this work and were generous with their time, advice, and expertise. They most notably include Hon. Fausto Pocar, former president, Appeals Chambers of the International Criminal Tribunal for the former Yugoslavia (ICTY) and the International Criminal Tribunal for Rwanda (ICTR); Hon. Abdul G. Koroma, judge, International Court of Justice (ICJ); Hon. Mohamed Shahabuddeen, former judge, Appeals Chambers of the ICTY and ICTR, former judge, ICJ; Hon. Erik Møse, former president, ICTR; Hon. Catherine Marchi-Uhel, judge, Extraordinary Chambers in the Courts of Cambodia (ECCC); Mr. Ken Roberts, deputy registrar, ICTY; Mr. Matthew Gillett, legal officer, Office of the Prosecutor, ICTY; Mr. Chris Gosnell, defence counsel before the ICTY; and, Pubudu Sachithanandan, associate trial attorney, Office of the Prosecutor, International Criminal Court (ICC). This chapter does not represent the views or positions of the above individuals or the organisations with which they are affiliated.

30 For a complete analysis and commentary, see S. Jodoin and Y. Saito, 'Crimes against Future Generations: Harnessing the Potential of Individual Criminal Accountability for Global Sustainability', 2012 7(2) *McGill Journal of Sustainable Development Law & Policy* 115–55.

31 It is important to note that the initiative of developing crimes against future generations sought to produce a definition that would be consistent with the language and principles of the Rome Statute. The analysis below does not therefore discuss issues relating to standards of proof, defences, and modes of liability because these are all governed by existing provisions in the Rome Statute.

(e) Imposing measures that seriously endanger the health of the members of any identifiable group or collectivity, including by impeding access to health services, facilities and treatments, withholding or misrepresenting information essential for the prevention or treatment of illness or disability, or subjecting them to medical or scientific experiments of any kind which are neither justified by their medical treatment, nor carried out in their interest;
(f) Preventing members of any identifiable group or collectivity from enjoying their culture, professing and practicing their religion, using their language, preserving their cultural practices and traditions, and maintaining their basic social and cultural institutions;
(g) Preventing members of any identifiable group or collectivity from accessing primary, secondary, technical, vocational and higher education;
(h) Causing widespread, long-term and severe damage to the natural environment, including by destroying an entire species or ecosystem;
(i) Unlawfully polluting air, water or soil by releasing substances or organisms that seriously endanger the health, safety or means of survival of members of any identifiable group or collectivity;
(j) Other acts of a similar character gravely imperilling the health, safety, or means of survival of members of any identifiable group or collectivity.

2. The expression 'any identifiable group or collectivity' means any civilian group or collectivity defined on the basis of geographic, political, racial, national, ethnic, cultural, religious or gender grounds or other grounds that are universally recognized as impermissible under international law.

As the definition makes clear, crimes against future generations would not be future crimes nor crimes committed in the future. They would apply instead to acts or conduct undertaken in the present that have serious consequences in the present and that are substantially likely to have serious consequences in the future. Moreover, just as crimes against humanity are not directly committed against all of humanity, crimes against future generations would not be directly committed against future generations either. Rather, they would penalise conduct that is of such gravity that it can be characterised as injuring the rights of future generations belonging to an affected group or collectivity.

As are other international crimes, crimes against future generations are comprised of two parts: (i) an introductory chapeau paragraph that serves to elevate certain prohibited acts to the status of an international crime and (ii) a list of prohibited acts. The establishment of a crime against future generations would thus require the commission of one of the prohibited acts listed at subparagraphs 1(a) to (j) of the definition with knowledge of 'the substantial likelihood of their severe consequences on the long-term health, safety, or means of survival of any identifiable group or collectivity'. It is important to emphasise, however, that this requirement does not imply that the prohibited act must affect each and every member of the identifiable group or collectivity in question, but only that it must be committed against the members of the identifiable group or collectivity and be of such magnitude or scale that it is substantially likely to have the prohibited consequences on this identifiable group or collectivity in the long term.

In the context of crimes against future generations, this requirement is a knowledge requirement, as it is for war crimes and crimes against humanity. To avoid difficulties in proving that certain activities were undertaken with the intent to cause long-term harm to an identifiable group or collectivity, this requirement is not a special intent requirement, as it is for genocide. The knowledge requirement in the chapeau of the crime would be met if it were shown that a perpetrator knew of the substantial likelihood of the prohibited consequences listed in the chapeau or if he or she knowingly took the risk that these prohibited consequences would occur in the ordinary course of events.[32] Moreover, knowledge could be inferred from the relevant facts and circumstances of a given case,[33] such as, inter alia, the perpetrator's statements and actions, functions and responsibilities, knowledge or awareness of other facts and circumstances, the circumstances in which the acts or consequences occurred, the links between the perpetrator and the acts and consequences, the scope, gravity, and nature of the acts or consequences, and the degree to which these are common knowledge. The language of 'substantial likelihood' is drawn from the customary international law standard for the *mens rea* element in ordering as a mode of liability. It requires that the perpetrator knew that his or her acts would be substantially likely to have the prohibited consequences listed in the chapeau element; the perpetrator need not know therefore that his or her acts or conduct is likely be the *only* cause or the *sine qua non* cause of the prohibited consequences.[34]

Crimes against future generations have a fairly broad scope of application. The chapeau paragraph explains that they are intended to cover a wide range of acts or conduct and can be committed in peacetime and in wartime. In addition, the second paragraph adopts a broad definition of 'any identifiable group or collectivity'. This definition, drawing on a similar expression included in Article 7(1)(h) of the Rome Statute, means that crimes against future generations would apply to a wide variety of discrete or specific human populations defined on the basis of shared geographic, political, racial, national, ethnic, cultural, religious, gender, or other grounds.

### 3.2. *Acts Prohibited as Crimes against Future Generations*

The following table sets out the purpose and sources for the prohibited acts listed in subparagraphs 1(a) to 1(j) of the definition of crimes against future generations. It shows that crimes against future generations would penalise conduct that is already prohibited as a violation of international human rights law or other international

32 See Rome Statute, *supra* note 1, Art. 30(3) and *Prosecutor* v. *Kunarac*, *supra* note 8, para. 102.

33 See ICC Elements of Crimes, *supra* note 9, para. 3.

34 *Prosecutor* v. *Blaskic*, IT-95–14-A, Appeal Judgement, 29 July 2004, para. 42.

conventions, such as the International Covenant on Economic, Social and Cultural Rights (ICESCR) and the International Covenant on Civil and Political Rights (ICCPR),[35] or would extend the scope of application of conduct that is already prohibited as a crime against humanity and or a war crime.

| Subparagraph | Purpose | Interpretive Sources |
|---|---|---|
| 1(a) | Penalises serious violations of the rights to liberty and security of the person and to freedom of residence and movement, ICCPR, Articles 9 and 12, and the rights to work of one's choosing and to work in safe and healthy conditions, ICESCR, Articles 6(1) and 7(1). | Draws on the crimes of forced labour and human trafficking found in the crime against humanity of enslavement, Rome Statute, Article 7(1)(c), and the crime against humanity of enforced prostitution, Rome Statute, Article 7(1)(g). |
| 1(b) | Penalises grave violations of the customary international law principle of permanent sovereignty over resources, which provides that the citizens of a state should benefit from the exploitation of resources and the resulting national development.[36] | Extends a similar war crime of pillaging to the context of peacetime, Rome Statute, Article 8(2)(b)(xvi), and is also based on the crime of corruption as set out in Article 17 of the UN Convention against Corruption.[37] |
| 1(c) | Penalises serious violations of the right to life, referring in particular to the rights to food and water, ICESCR, Article 11. | Extends a similar war crime to the context of peacetime, Rome Statute, Article 8(2)(v)(xxv), and draws upon the underlying act of genocide, Rome Statute, Article 6(c). |
| 1(d) | Penalises one of the most serious violations of the right to housing, ICESCR, Article. 11(1). | Draws on the general comment of the UN Committee on the ICESCR relating to the right to housing (General Comment no. 7). |
| 1(e) | Penalises one of the most serious violations of the right to health, ICESCR, Article 12. | Draws on the general comment of the UN Committee on the ICESCR relating to the right to health, General Comment no. 12, and extends a similarly worded war crime to the peacetime context, Rome Statute, Article 8(2)(b)(x). |

[35] The later references are to the 1966 International Covenant on Economic, Social and Cultural Rights (ICESCR), 993 UNTS 3 or the 1966 International Covenant on Civil and Political Rights (ICCPR), 999 UNTS 171.

[36] N. Schrijver, *Permanent Sovereignty over Natural Resources: Balancing Rights and Duties* (1997), 390–92.

[37] 2003 UN Convention against Corruption, 2349 UNTS 41.

| Subparagraph | Purpose | Interpretive Sources |
|---|---|---|
| 1(f) | Penalises serious violations of the right to culture, ICCPR, Article 27, and ICESCR, Article 15. | Draws on the previous drafts of the Genocide Convention that included the crime of cultural genocide.[38] |
| 1(g) | Penalises one of the most serious violations of the right to education, ICESCR, Article 13. | Draws on the general comment of the UN Committee on the ICESCR relating to the right to education, General Comment no. 13. |
| 1(h) | Penalises serious violations of the customary international law duty to prevent grave environmental harm and damages.[39] | Based on a similarly worded war crime, Rome Statute, Article 8(2)(b)(iv). |
| 1(i) | Penalises serious violations of the right to life, particularly the rights to health, housing, food, and water, ICESCR, Articles 11 and 12. | Draws on the general comments of the UN Committee on the ICESCR relating to the rights to health, housing, food, and water, General Comments no. 12, 14, and 15. |
| 1(j) | Penalises serious violations of the rights protected by other subparagraphs. | Draws on a similar catch-all provision for crimes against humanity, Rome Statute, Article 7(1)(k). |

## 4. CONCLUSION

Although there is some potential for using international criminal law to prosecute conduct having severe consequences for the rights of future generations, the limitations of the definitions of existing international crimes make this option of limited utility. This is why the creation of crimes against future generations may be required to explicitly and clearly protect the interests of future generations in international law.

I envisage two main pathways for creating crimes against future generations in international law. The first, more ambitious pathway would involve amending the Rome Statute to include crimes against future generations within the jurisdiction of the International Criminal Court. This would have the principal advantage of inserting crimes against future generations into an existing system and institutional machinery that enjoy broad support from a majority of states hailing from all regions of the world. After the adoption and ratification of an amendment of the Rome

38 Report of the Ad Hoc Committee on Genocide, 5 April–10 May 1948 (Official Records of the Economic and Social Council, Third Year, Seventh Session, Supplement No. 5 (E/794), Art. HI.

39 See Stockholm Declaration on the Human Environment, UN Doc. A/C. 48/14 (1972), 11 ILM 1461 (1972), principle 21. See also 1991 Draft Code of Crimes against Peace and Mankind, 1991 YILC, Vol. II (Part Two), at 107.

Statute, state parties would be given the primary responsibility of investigating and trying the perpetrators of crimes against future generations within their jurisdiction. The International Criminal Court could take jurisdiction over a case involving such crimes in two restricted cases: if a state party with a special interest in the matter takes no action, or if state party action is taken but reflects an unwillingness or genuinely inability to carry out a meaningful, timely, and effective investigation or prosecution.[40]

There are obvious limitations to this approach, perhaps the most important of which is that the International Criminal Court remains a comparatively fragile institution.[41] A number of major states have not become state parties, including the United States, China, India, and Russia.[42] Meanwhile, numerous African states have criticised the ICC for what they see as its Western bias towards the prosecution of crimes on the African continent.[43] Even its most enthusiastic supporters would acknowledge that the ICC's performance in terms of the efficiency of investigations and trials has been underwhelming.[44] It may ultimately prove counterproductive to provide a fledging and under-resourced institution like the ICC the mandate to prosecute a whole new category of international crimes, especially when it is already struggling to provide justice for existing international crimes.[45] To be sure, the issue of institutional overload and capacity is one that must be addressed if the creation of crimes against future generations is going to make a difference to the victims of the serious violations of international law that it seeks to address. Accordingly, whether or not the ICC forms a suitable institutional vehicle for addressing conduct similar to crimes against future generations, there is little doubt that an amendment to the Rome Statute along the lines presented in this chapter is not a reasonable option at the present time.

The second, more feasible pathway would entail the adoption of a stand-alone international convention that would require state parties to exercise jurisdiction over

40 Rome Statute, Art 17(1).

41 Another limitation relates to the complications occasioned by the Rome Statute's amendment provisions. These complications were exposed when the Assembly of State Parties adopted an amendment to include the crime of aggression within the jurisdiction of the ICC at a review conference held in Kampala in June 2010. See Jennifer Trahan, 'The Rome Statute's Amendment on the Crime of Aggression: Negotiations at the Kampala Review Conference', (2011) 11 *International Criminal Law Review* 49. One particular challenge is that any amendment to add crimes against future generations within the jurisdiction of the Rome Statute would only apply to those states that have ratified or accepted the amendment, whether through Art. 121(5) of the statute or the combined effect of Arts. 121(4) and (6): see Rome Statute, *supra* note 26, at art 121.

42 R. Cryer et al., *An Introduction to International Criminal Law and Procedure* (2007), 139–48.

43 Victor Peskin, 'Caution and Confrontation in the International Criminal Court's Pursuit of Accountability in Uganda and Sudan,' (2009) 31 *Human Rights Quarterly* 655, at 677.

44 IBA/ICC Monitoring and Outreach Programme, Enhancing Efficiency and Effectiveness of ICC Proceedings: A Work In Progress: An International Bar Association Human Rights Institute Report (2011), online: International Bar Association, www.ibanet.org.

45 Amnesty International, *International Criminal Court: Concerns at the 9th Assembly of State Parties (6 to 10 December 2010)* (2010) 9–11, online: Amnesty International www.amnesty.org.

crimes against future generations. This follows the model employed for crimes of international concern, such as the theft of nuclear materials, terrorist bombings, or torture.[46] A convention on crimes against future generations could commit states to enacting or amending crimes in their national legislation, investigating and prosecuting cases falling within their jurisdiction, and co-operating with other states in investigations and prosecutions. The ultimate utility of such a convention would depend on whether it provided states with the authority to investigate and prosecute crimes committed in other countries through extraterritorial forms of jurisdiction such as active and passive personal jurisdiction.[47]

A stand-alone convention would avoid the controversial charge of potentially weakening the Rome Statute system. It also presents a less intrusive and less costly means of creating crimes against future generations, by forsaking a complementary international mechanism for prosecuting crimes against future generations. As a result, the idea of a stand-alone convention on crimes against future generations is likely to attract greater support from the states and mainstream human rights constituencies that may want to protect the ICC from agenda overload as well as from those states that may be concerned about the sovereignty and costs implications of adding to the ICC's jurisdiction. Without a doubt, a stand-alone convention is a much more realistic pathway for creating crimes against generations than an amendment to the Rome Statute.

The question that remains, with either pathway, is whether the concept of crimes against future generations could ever generate enough support among states to become binding international law. There are reasons to be optimistic that the creation of crimes against future generations in international law is a reasonable possibility in the long term.

Although the concept of crimes against future generations presented in this chapter certainly seeks to move international law forward, it does so in the spirit of attaching the appropriate penal consequences to behaviour that the international community has already recognised as being reprehensible. The concept of crimes against future generations builds upon international law by seeking to extend the scope of application of existing international crimes from wartime to peacetime or to establish criminal liability for existing prohibitions in international law. Moreover,

[46] See, e.g., *Convention on the Physical Protection of Nuclear Material*, 3 March 1980, 2149 UNTS 256, 18 ILM 1419 (entered into force 8 February 1987); *International Convention for the Suppression of Terrorist Bombings*, 15 December 1997, 2149 UNTS 256, 37 ILM 249 (entered into force 23 May 2001); *Convention against Torture and Other Cruel, Inhuman or Degrading Treatment or Punishment*, 10 December 1984, 1465 UNTS 85, 23 ILM 1027 (1984) as modified by 24 ILM 535 (1985) (entered into force 26 June 1987).

[47] Active personality jurisdiction provides states with jurisdiction over crimes committed by their nationals. Passive personality jurisdiction provides states with jurisdiction over crimes committed against their nationals. Active personality jurisdiction provides states with jurisdiction over crimes committed by their nationals. Passive personality jurisdiction provides states with jurisdiction over crimes committed against their nationals.

the wording of many of the specific crimes against future generations presented earlier is based on the definition of existing international crimes as expressed in the Rome Statute or customary international criminal law, as well as on language derived from international treaties or the general comments of the UN Committee on Economic, Social, and Cultural Rights. In other words, the concept of crimes against future generations is about the *criminalisation* of existing violations of international law, as opposed to the creation of new substantive standards of international law. Accordingly, the creation of crimes against future generations would amount to an exercise in the codification of serious violations of international law deserving the status of international crimes.

It is important to note that crimes against future generations can be distinguished from other potential candidates for the status of international crimes, such as drug trafficking or terrorism. In Rome, a majority of states opposed the inclusion of the latter crimes for three principal reasons: the different character of these crimes, the danger of overloading the ICC with less important crimes, and the existence of effective systems of international co-operation in repressing these crimes.[48] Unlike these crimes, crimes against future generations are of a similar character to other international crimes in that they are violations of customary or treaty norms that are intended to protect values considered important by the international community,[49] and existing mechanisms for sanctioning violations of economic, social, and cultural rights and serious environmental harm are clearly inadequate.

To be sure, the principal objections put forth by states against the enforcement of economic, social, and cultural rights are that they are vague, subject to progressive realisation, and nonjusticiable because they impose positive obligations (to adopt certain conduct) rather than negative obligations (to refrain from certain conduct).[50] However, evidence shows that the adjudication of economic, social, and cultural rights in jurisdictions around the world has been widespread.[51] The UNCESR has concluded that state obligations to secure a minimum core of obligations for each right cannot be excused by a lack of resources.[52] The concept of crimes against future generations thus avoids the principal objections against the enforcement of economic, social, and cultural rights by specifically focusing on criminalising the deliberate denials of the minimum essential levels of economic, social, and cultural

48 See H. Von Hebel & D. Robinson, 'Crimes within the Jurisdiction of the Court,' in R. S Lee (ed.), *The International Criminal Court: Elements of Crimes and Rules of Procedure and Evidence* (2001), 79, at 81 and 86.

49 A. Cassese, *International Criminal Law* (2008), 23.

50 See the discussion of these objections in International Commission of Jurists, *Courts and the Legal Enforcement of Economic, Social and Cultural Rights: Comparative Experiences of Justiciability*, Geneva, International Commission of Jurists (2008) at 99–105, online: United Nations Refugee Agency, www.unhcr.org ([t]he ICJ concludes that the idea that economic, social, and cultural rights are not fit for judicial adjudication is seriously misguided).

51 *Ibid.*, at 99.

52 *Committee on Economic, Social and Cultural Rights*, Maastricht Guidelines on Violations of Economic, Social and Cultural Rights, *UNESCOR, 24th Sess, UN Doc E/C.12/2000/13*, (2000) 16.

rights. As such, the definition of crimes against future generations provides a clear 'negative' approach to these rights appropriate for judicial adjudication.

In the end, the promise of a concept such as crimes against future generations lies in its potential to demonstrate that serious breaches of international law, including violations of economic, social, and cultural rights and severe environmental harm, are morally wrong and deserving of condemnation in the strongest possible terms. The idea of using international criminal law for the implementation of intergenerational justice is therefore as much about punishing and deterring morally wrong conduct as it is about strengthening taboos regarding morally opprobrious behaviour. As has been argued throughout this book, scholars, advocates, and policy makers concerned with sustainable development may want to increasingly consider the role that criminal accountability could play in deterring, punishing, and condemning reprehensible conduct harmful to future generations.

# Index